T0353986

YOU CAN NEVER SATISFY A WOMAN

ROBERT GONZALEZ

authorHOUSE®

AuthorHouse™
1663 Liberty Drive
Bloomington, IN 47403
www.authorhouse.com
Phone: 833-262-8899

Published by AuthorHouse   09/13/2021

ISBN: 978-1-6655-3778-0 (sc)
ISBN: 978-1-6655-3779-7 (hc)
ISBN: 978-1-6655-3777-3 (e)

Library of Congress Control Number: 2021918791

Print information available on the last page.

Chapter 1

This is a story that is being told to the world. You Can Never Satisfy A Woman. What I mean is a woman has many mood swings, personalities, thoughts and her life. There are broken down into different multiple categories some good, bad or indifferent. When we as couple get into an argument/fight whether verbal or physical do we think what causes situation and how do we resolve it. Do we know how to compromise and conclude? We know that a compromise will give each person a chance to say what's on their mind in a civil way and try to resolve the issue. Not every woman or man will do that because of the heat of the moment. Woman if you are not afraid you will stand up for yourself and feel like they are right. There is no changing of the mind with a woman who feel she is always right and never wrong, most of the time until she must calm down first on most problems then come back to apologize after the matter making an excuse to get away with a charm or secret weapon of a strategy. A woman can be wrong if they jump to conclusions about what a man has to say. Listening is the key. Now when a man is doing everything to keep the relationship/marriage going why is it the woman is ridiculing him about the pass. He is given you the world with everything you want and respecting you. Women when we keep bad thoughts in mind that a man is doing wrong all the time where is the good in him. Our thoughts, moods and personality are what gets women into situation that we have yet resolved from our pass. Women do you agree, do you think before you react because you have in your mind that the man is no good if he did something in the pass and you did not forgive him with as well adding the forget as a testimony praying and doing no it's your way or no way!! You say forgive but actions speak and show differently. In a woman's the word FORGET is used as a weapon and a tool not to move forward when she think it is just only because she goes to church, prays, forgives, a good mother, wife, help mate, friend but the thing that is missing is not letting the thoughts go! The FORGET can be silent treatment, bitterness, drama that is silence and open, pain, a seed that she plants in and never water or the man has put in and she uses the BUT never to remove it. See there is things that can trigger off a memory off something that happen from the past we all know if the man is doing the same thing repeatedly that's not right remove him out your life and I agree leave his ass but we he have change for the better and you have told him, and you have not change and added in doing your part really and point of view it's deeper than I think it's serious and especially reliant. You must change because that's still your husband. CHANGE IS CHANGE does it matter what or when or how you get out of it is A BIG CHANGE OF HEART. You Can Never Satisfy A Woman because they expect many things from men. Women looks for love, affection, understanding, communication, happiness, joy and trust. They look for things. There are most women that looks for the ring and the marriage. Those are the main things a woman wants and still not getting enough of it. There are some women that live off materialistic things, but to be satisfied is what I mention firsts and most women feel they are not getting enough. Women have been hurt by a man and loses trust in them. There are different types of women who is never satisfied because there in a relationship that have the twist and turn, and the man or woman is not doing what she wants them to do. (DEPENDING ON THE WOMAN MATTER OR SITUATION!!) A woman/woman can say I want a great life with you especially when she needs a person to have her back, uplift them, be there when they need them and show some action. You as woman can give 100% of their mind, body, spirit but will you give that back? Most women consider that as no, because you do not either want to or do not know how to. There are women who keep secrets because they do not wish to tell the story of their past life. They feel it's too painful or bitter to speak about it or they want to bury it forever. A secret can be what happen to you when you were younger or an adult or something she been taking through and took others through. A secret can be held in for so long within you that you will not tell it. As a woman/women you know your boundaries to speak or not to speak depending on the situation or matter as well with reverse psychology. A secret can be something was told to you in confidences good or bad spirits, and it is to remain with you forever and ever. A woman can hold many secrets about herself or others depending on who, what or where.

I appreciate who I am for that special woman I care about and her children that's my stepchildren. When she says stop saying my children not your children these will always be my children. She will always be my wife. See if she would have appreciated the little things I did she would have seen how much I was going out of my way for her. She saw shit only and a fuck up. My mother always said when you're always pointing your finger at someone like your perfect and have no flaws for fingers are pointed right back at you. Every human being needs to be respected even though you can't make no one respect you or do anything, but you want to stay in that way be mad at yourself don't take it out on the other person who's trying to move on and you're not holding their hand, you're not letting go you have to let go. Please give your husband/man space to express himself and forgiveness without making demands on him, getting over on him, provoking him, pushing him away by bringing up he cheated but, but, but can run out just like you tell him your just too stubborn to receive and accept! You would not want this done to you and only thing would come up is BECAUSE YOU WAS NOT THE ONE THAT CHEATED in so many words. The woman will say the man is still on the past when it is all in her mind, emotions, heart, body gestures, soul, and spirit it really gets to the thoughts. The man will say you still is holding on to the past then she would say what would you say is any different from what I did. See right there your confused how you are going to be right about getting back at the man also being rude with a selfish behavior. You are always right in your mind until you say enough is enough on letting the man a go to start over fresh with a new life saying you had to get you right to get from around that man when at times you cause bad things on yourself as well and did not want to know or believe it! Everything the woman say is not always right and stating from lots of them it will be said we did not say that at that time being this why at times it goes back and forth. Can you accept your man needs even though you don't like them sometimes watch out now, we did do that, but most men are no good and they messed that up I can agree on that for they actions, sins and flaws and what about yours? As the same things you want for yourselves when your right or wrong as I hear from a lot of women your emotional women are different. Cleopatra did not know she was being so angry, mean, bitter, selfish, and forcing revenge putting Jeffrey down all times she was essentially emasculating Jeffrey by taking away her love away from him not showing no actions not seeing his. She knew she was wrong when she was to herself thinking because telling me did not mean anything when she come on her own up to me most of the times because she is dealing with her inner self was not easy so she will be by herself knowing and holding the secrets in afraid to let them out thinking negative always that he will hurt her again! It was not easy for me or her, but she had to be the one to put a stop to the way she was handling that because the way she thought she was doing it was the best, right, good way at all times when she was emotionally killing her soul quietly! I was feeling lower than shit itself as well as my ability to provide as a man because it did not mean anything to her it was not enough, I felt like I was not doing my job. I felt defeated and retreated into a corner with my back up against the wall she would not let me do what I wanted to do because I did wrong in the past, but don't keep treating me like I'm that same person she did not bond with me fairly nor connect with me right it was only on her time in her mood when she felt like when and where it was time to. Now some women will say then why you still were there putting up with that or what you have done so bad to make her be this woman or why you did not leave did you pray? Love is wonderful and when you love someone you will stick and stay through good and bad times, and you just can't walk away like that if you think I'm lying why don't you ask the woman/women/wives we don't need an encyclopedia right ladies? I'm expressing this from my heart do I know too many women? Cleopatra did not support Jeffrey when he tried, she will say out loud and mean, I DID! Where the action in and with love showing with expression, I was full of shit every time. She did it in every way that she could feel like a failure. There was no empowering me. How are you going to bring the best out in your husband/man when all you see in him is a fuck up and coming back and forth to apologize. She wanted and did blame me for everything for the painful past all on me. A lot of times she wanted me to be this then that from me not seeing mines she made me feel. I was feeling lower than shit as to well as my ability to provide. I felt like I wasn't doing my job. I felt defeated and retreats. She wouldn't let me do what

I wanted to do, because did wrong in the past, but don't keep treating me like I'm that same person from the past. She did not bond with me fairly, she did not connect with me right, she did not even support me. When I tried, she will say loud and mean, I did! Where was those actions she did it in the way that I was a failure, there was no empowering me? How are you going to bring the best in your man when all you see him as is a fucked up, coming back and forth to apologize? She wanted and blamed me for everything for that painful past all on me. A lot of times she wanted me to be this and that wanting me. What she wanted me to be rather accepting me as I am and encouraging me to become myself. She can sense everything. No, she can't on most things. She is a strong woman. I gave her that credit, but I couldn't sense nothing off her. She did not do what I did. I am considered green shit incredible Hulk, controlling fuck up, she's wonder woman always with the A+. Never falls with the star. This was not motivating me. This was pushing me down with pigs. Women let me tell you something to learn it's crippling and defeating. She got flash backs only just her. As woman you should sit down and ask your man at times what it is you will like dear? What it is I am doing wrong? Because you pressure him to do this and that, make more money, be more this, more that, you want this. You want all these things that is great, but what you really need to sit your ass there. You need to ask yourself is if you're trying to get him to be that way. It would be good for you 80% and less for him or want him to be that way only for you, because he owes you everything in the world. Don't see the good in him only what she wanted to see. Now I learned about the silent woman from being married I needed to worry, because at times Jeffrey was about Cleopatra he already lost she just told him in so many ways and words with feelings and attitude. A woman silence is her loudest cry, Jeffrey knows this, because Cleopatra use to ignore him all the time. She was over thinking and tired of waiting, falling apart, crying inside when she loved him. She loved hard one minute she loved me the next minute, then she hated me. She couldn't live with me or without me I'm only me one man there will not be no man that she ever gets with in the future like him. When Cleopatra was silent and Jeffrey could feel her cry she said to herself he done so many things that hurt me, but inside she was crying to herself and out loud.

When I was away, and I could see it standing in front of her. She will say when did I work it out finally you hurt me again. She really didn't until her apologizes. She never showed it she just kept saying it. Her actions were showing force and hatred. She was to bitter for words this is the silent woman. When she took me back and was telling me sitting right there in front of my face, I shouldn't never take you back. It was her telling me I don't want to be married to you ever again in love with you, I can't stand you and I didn't forgive you. I can't stand you. I didn't forgive. When she kept sitting down talking with me. We weren't supposed to give up on one another it was not all about her. Cleopatra had a heart that was bleeding with blood was everything and all my fault. I said most of it yes, but not everything. Some women silence can be loud, some can silently depend what mood she's in. Then some women will say you act like you know me. Like Jeffrey never told Cleopatra she wasn't shit, that didn't mean he didn't mess up in a lot of ways. I like this saying that Robert Mugabe quotes you cannot give a woman everything and satisfy her it goes like this. thing and satisfy it off her it goes like this. You cannot give a woman everything she needs. If God himself gave them eyebrows they shared it and draw their own. God gave them nails, they cut it if and fixed their own. God gave them hair, they cut it off and fixed their own. He gave them breast; they repackage it to what they want. God still gave them buttocks they arrange it to the size they want. If they are not satisfied with the things God gave them. Who are you to think that you can please them? My brother doesn't kill yourself. I did more than satisfying I was a strong man to accept somebody else children and stepped up to the plate and they been other man left on the damn table, so I be damn If I let anyone put me down. No matter it was winter, spring, summer, and fall. Jeffrey made Cleopatra feel special. She holds on to unforgiveness with her daughter being Scorpio stinging me with anger of poison expecting me to die and I was not alive to her. I am not going to lie Jeffrey did Cleopatra wrong, because he didn't love himself. I was raped, so many times. I wanted love I was looking for it and I felt it, but I wasn't showed it, so the sex was to make me feel worse, because that's all I knew. I understood it felt good, it felt bad, it felt uncomfortable, it felt like evil spirits and good spirits. It was confusing can you women understand me? Now you will say I'm making an excuse to hurt women continually over and over again and not manning up to my wrongs I agree, so what you have to say about this to your women sides is it any different are they any different? Will they say they prostitute, because they been rape, so much their lesbians, because they been beat, so much is that an excuse to keep hurting men? You will say it's not right. She is a woman you got to understand where she is coming from and been through you can't feel pain. Pain is pain. Hurt is hurt. Everyone goes through it. A woman doesn't want to only make love that's not the first thing on her mind. Jeffrey read that experience with Cleopatra he was a man to understand and learn that it was tough for him to do. I thought with my dick. What I mean is I was affectionate with making love. I was soft, had playful intention and cheering her up. The more I showed that the more she fucked my brains out. Yes, I'm a man I said it she put it on me I'm whipped it was good. This is another secret man hide. They feel weak that if they don't tell the woman. How good she pleased him she will be taking over the bedroom and everything in the relationship, not true! Both should be honest, upfront and don't play mind games or sex games. Now Cleopatra initiate intimacy it was more than a need, but then she pulled away, because she couldn't keep her promise of forgiveness. A woman says she wants her man to pray with her because God love. He is the spiritual leader, but ladies and to Cleopatra. How can I be a spiritual leader? She didn't ever give me a chance, encourage me, and put me down? Well women will say you can't make her, so is she not breaking up a home and tearing it down? No! Everything is on the man it falls all on him, because he's the head I know God sees everything. When I wanted to make love, she rejected me selfishly. When she wanted to make love while cursing me out or not, I still made love to her, because unresponsiveness means rejection. A husband that gives his life to the Lord, have changed and build his home back up it don't have to be about money hell no be thankful, faithful, fruitful, joyful, positive, because let me tell you something wives if your husband does not feel and see connection or paying attention and focused on him you will push him away. Then when he goes away as the queen bitter strong woman, I don't need to run him down. What he did to me. Hmmm he got some nerve. He did this to me first he will be back. I got this you're not with no marriage you're with the servant in garden with Adam and Eve punching him in the face. Women don't realize sometimes punishing your husband with silence is punishment enough and bad communication. You all know what I am talking about, so don't go there with what are saying, shut up, stay quiet, we under control, you can't tell me when to talk, No! I'm saying hurt people therefore me and Cleopatra went back and forth. She was so smart to where she was dumb blaming me for everything in our marriage. She couldn't set me free for forgiving me for what I had done to her, so she didn't forgive herself. Cleopatra thought she was the only one always feels sad. She couldn't change me or anything. She was the only one determined. She felt like she was the teacher to change my only bad thoughts. I have sat back, seen and knew that you can learn something new every day with a woman. Today a lot of men don't know how to approach certain women, because these days there is a new generation and old generation. Which do you choose? A lot of women feel the thug men are safer. When they want money, the women feel the richer man gives them things they want in life then being with a poor man with a 9 to 5 job. They want a fool that is rich instead of a faithful man that's poor that is trying. He can show he's trying we got this together. A boy and a real man are two different people just like a girl and a woman. Jeffrey found out Cleopatra perspective. Every woman has one! Cleopatra had needs and concerns. She was with me and wanted a comfortable, healthy relationship, her time, meaning feelings and communication. Cleopatra also in her ways a black woman that loved me and made me slap Monday, beat me up with making love on Tuesday, put me in her hospital, physically, spiritually, mentally, financially on Wednesday call me up on Thursday to let me know on Friday and Saturday she will be burying me and dig me up to take me to church on Sunday. I love the story about Abraham and Pharaoh they both wanted Sarah. Pharaoh wanted Sarah because she was beautiful and sexy. God went to Pharaoh and let him know don't touch her because I will kill you. Pharaoh did not touch her because he knew God was nothing to play with. What God put together no man can separate or come between what was put together by God. A woman is serious about her feelings that is why I had to improve my behavior for Cleopatra. It was showing her how

much as a man I was being for the Lord, a her man and father for the family and relationship, but she was to blind to see that it was good and bad, sorry then not back and forth. What she didn't know and see that she forgot I was a human being to. She can't expect me to be perfect in her mind like she said you can't tell me what I'm thinking, but she can tell me quick in her mind as a woman it's just like that leave like that! I'm a man I couldn't help her with every problem! Communication and understanding for both sides not the woman most or all women mostly including Cleopatra know, feel, and say falsely accusing, provoking your man or husband can't push him away. Women if you like this is not just words this is actions towards the person that loves you and you love back. Women don't know that bullying and controlling your man, because the man is doing right, he is not being believed, drained out and can't fight back with love with no true story or faith, because your bitter. Your man like I was under scrutiny, security, he is let down, helplessness and overwhelming right. Cleopatra or women please understand where this man is coming from. Women do you have a family member or anyone who have not forgiving you and it hurts? A lot of family is like this today they can't come together, because there is no real let go let God and forgiveness. Now I feel you men the family will gang up on you and attack. When the other side does wrong, they are looking in the mirror with good things to make it look good. I got this I got that I'm doing it better than you. It's not about that it's about God's love and coming together. Now Cleopatra would say you don't need to talk about coming together. Yes! I sinned I did wrong I repented. What have I got out of that? A slap on the back in the face an eye for an eye, but I say to her she can say whatever. I want to say this my mouth she's a good woman in God eyes, because she knows the God, she serve's no it supposed to be We not only she everyone! Then it be you can't tell me nothing. She right you can't tell no one nothing who knows it all, don't want to hear you or listen. Women don't say you can't make her, so will say fair men or man stop being hardheaded and listen. It will come back. No, you don't. I want to teach this. I will bring marriages together pray positive and love. God first not wishy-washy teaching what people want to hear, but what God says. Women your men cry to not in front of you sometimes or most of the time depending on the man. We are different but believe me he's crying inside as fuck up. Jeffrey was only towards Cleopatra he cried to. He was a cry baby to her. When she cried all of it was real mine was fake all of it. If she says until this day, I didn't say that. It will be a lie, because one she came back to apologize. When she didn't mean it, because she came back arguing right after the apology back and forth. She was bitter and angry. If God know we are all hurt, cry and mend hurt one another. Who is anyone even me to tell someone don't cry! Cleopatra lied to because she was injured that she didn't forgive me or herself. This come to reason that she can only believe herself in everything. I was seeking time from her and patience. I kept walking away. I walked away to let her be to herself to pray. I won't be there to do anything aggravating her at all. I even said I am a fuck up. I owed her that much do you hear me women? Guess what? The goal was to destroy me right back ladies. I'm not saying your agreeing I'm just asking, because I feel women who been through this and men you go through it to feel it to. Let someone know how they can deal with it. Women you're not going through it alone you're not in this by yourself and you're not only independent, because everybody needs somebody! See I understand even an accuser needs help and a provoker there lying to. It is a nasty, hateful act, mean and accuser needs help not only a man that cheats on his woman or wife. We all need help in different ways and areas in life. This don't always be love and don't help the relationship really the marriage. For the woman to defend herself being angry and bitter. She takes her bitterness, anger, they have taken someone else down with them. The women feel like they all clean all in the clear and beautiful. You can have a beautiful face on a woman. It can be on a handsome face of the man, but the actions, ways and doings tell it all both together not one side! Falsely accusing and provoking is an aggressive behavior and act. You're telling your man I don't want you no more you fucked up you're never going to change. You're going to always be the same, so why you get back with before telling him this. When you're with him this then after your telling hi m this back up and still tell him. This destroys hearts not only men! Cleopatra never ever recovered from me. What I did to her, and she lied to me. Most people are afraid to hear the truth when women gather the devil shows up and sit there, pays attention in the corner of

the room watching, listen and whispers in every one of their ears just like Eve. It going to be a lot of readers especially women saying what this man knows about a woman. He doesn't know anything at the end of the day. When you do tell a woman the truth. You hit them with low the blow, child please you don't know what you are talking about, anyway you don't nothing about no woman. Where you got this information from somebody had to tell you this or that is. Your opinion. Really, I don't care. I can't come out with no book called a Diary of Mad Black Man that wouldn't be right, because me woman will say your holding on to something you need to let go. It's the past and you need to move forth. God created marriage for not to hurt or envy. God created marriage for pleasure and forever like Adam and EVE. He created them and they chose to do what they wanted to marriage. This why it doesn't work today because both parties reject God plan. They do what they want to. See you can never satisfy a woman because the cycle on her brain. She wants to be a mind reader. Then it he doesn't do this when it really means do that it changes. She changes the woman everyday as well as her hormones constantly even before or after her period. Even before it comes on her mind, brain, body, and everything changes. She can be a nice witch, a bitch, moody, cranky, loving, aggravated wishy washy, tired, build up it's, so many ways you can't explain right women or woman. She even changes her outlook on herself on things. She changes up so much she will leave you at the starting line. If you can't hang with her, Jeffrey can hang with Cleopatra. She met her match I met my mines. She just always wanted to be right and win the woman! One day she will dress sexy the next day she would dress regular. She changes up the woman loves to read and find out things some be nosy. Well I will say most women is mysterious finding out something is her key sometimes and can be easily irritated. I learned that women score higher on test than a man, because of their brain. How they think more, because she wants to be right all the time to tell the husband/man what to do. What he or them is thinking right ladies/ woman. Her fight a lot of times like I said in one topic is beat a fight or argument with silence, attitude or it could be ignoring you being funny or sarcastic, joking or no sex she has a lot of ways of defense she can even try to use God leave me alone I'm praying right now. She can make up any little thing to be left alone. She can say just leave me alone, but I know she know I know we know a woman is not going to do that. Her ways are unknown. She will say that is not for that then what is it for, because you have million and billions of ways and changes! Her manipulations can be smooth, quiet, she doesn't want you to know who she is or where she is coming from at times. Women are aggressive in different ways. She is overly sensitive and emotional. She has high levels of stress and low levels depending on what she's going through. The woman also is aware of what's going on focused on herself as getting back up when she falls of going through things in life. A woman can avoid conflict and bring it right or wrong. She is easily turned off see I learned that when it's time for her to make love everything in her mind is shut off she only focused on the husband/man, her, and the mood and orgasm. With Cleopatra Jeffrey played one time he said baby you are putting it on me she slaps me and said stop baby you are messing up the vibe then he said to Cleopatra you said I act like you don't be putting it down, so I went with your flow. What you wanted she wasn't satisfied on that. Now like I stated when any woman is bitter, angry, unforgiving, revenge, vengeance, and most of all rude. She refuses a man's advice period. As I got ready to be a real man for myself, God, and family, because no matter how much increase I gave and showed in our relationship she was not interested in me. She was not ready to risk conflict when we forgave one another. She wasn't even motivating, helping, or encouraging me. It was raging hell in her from bitterness. She was too angry to see it. I also loved her and always was proud of her to have strong desire to do more for herself be more independent and better her career. She was bickering with me more and more for me hurting her. She was holding back for the person she wanted me too only be for her not us. Now when I say what I had to deal with as a man in a relationship since women have a lot to do and listen to I'm a pain in the ass trying my best, doing chores, washing dishes, washing clothes, stressed out, dealing with daily issues hers, mines and the children. Also dealing with her family problems and mines with my crazy family problems at that. The consist headaches which goes with paying the bills emotional stress. I always had duty to do I am this complete loser and fuck up. She drained the life out of me on days, so women do you only go through this in a relationship and marriage? The worse thing is being blamed for things I didn't do! See I'm letting women know your not the only one that feels unhappy or happy sometimes, let down and the whole world or your world is turned upside down. You're not the only one full of emotions. You have some men more emotional than you at times. You're not the only ones feel or experience depression, loneliness, mental, physically exhausted in life men do to just as much as you. Then you have these women that say I'm unhappy all time, because of this man that made me this way. It's his fault all his fault I did nothing wrong in this relationship or marriage. That's someone that's perfect. The quiet woman her best quality is being silent and it's her strength. She observes and listens to different situations and makes her decision on how to respond to another thing. I have learned about women that called their period different names. Their period or menstrual cycle the names are called Susie, period it's that time of the month, friend, on the rag is the old school women I mean elders other names is curses, or a curse. Aunt Flo, Auntie, Army, war, mother nature, bloody Mary, monthly visitor, moon, sharp weakness, change up. Another thing I learned about every women period is not the same it can be months heavy and month light changing up on the woman life stress, healthy life, depression, sick all kinds of ways. I understand the different between a man needs and expects of a woman needs. I seen some women, so angry come out loud and say leave me alone my period on let me be. Another thing I learned from the woman is that she knows when her man is sick, she knows when he wants to eat sometimes. What he is thinking you just can't get in her mind, because she's the encyclopedia, the dictionary, the wrong, the brain, the laptop, the IPHONE, all calls in and out and knows everything. She will tell you she doesn't know everything but mean different at times. The woman brain is a brain that function that's stays boost of energy. It's like a race at the starting line the woman is the gun the starting line the bullets and she goes off. It could be in a good way or bad. She leaves and you be trying to catch up you will drive yourself crazy even walking away talking a breather and coming back at times she not satisfied! She wants more and more. Don't mess with most of them when their period is on because they be mean, tired, aggravated, frustrated and over withdrawn. She takes days off work. She can't work some women they can't call out right quick. The woman wants it to be quiet and left alone depending the mood and the woman. Did you know how many times I looked at Cleopatra pad to see that I love her enough to go buy them for her and to do my best to show that I love her enough to go buy them for her and to do my best to show that I understand her experience women only thing. You see men especially black men they mostly he got seven children. He bit on women, he is on child support, he drinks, he does drugs, he doesn't have a job, he's in jail or prison, he's gay, he's a dog or tricking, only he fornicates and have the flesh in him, he doesn't have no time for the Lord. Is its good things men do? What I never felt the pain and cramps women go through that is very hurtful pain you can't even imagine. I didn't experience from certain women that I've seen with my own eyes that they can be a bitch. When their period comes on this is not out of disrespect this be actions. What comes out their mouth the number one important thing in a woman life is God. A real woman does not need to feel loved to have sex. What women want girl chase, because its God vice versa for a real a man what men want boys chase a woman wants and will love herself and feel loved and free a real man to love her. See when I was happy when Cleopatra forgave me, I felt free I was friend to her thoughtful, supportive, considerate, listening, hearing, understanding, accepting, non-judgmental, uplifting, and encouraging. I was also a loving man exciting, energize and hyper with, so much stimulation I was a challenge. I loved a look at the heart. My heart physically, my romance was affectionate, sexy, fun, and different. I was a provider being all these things wasn't enough. Jeffrey was becoming what Cleopatra wanted him to be. It was God first then her. It was not easy especially when I messed up. Jeffrey gave Cleopatra what she wanted. You don't have to ask God for nothing he know I did my best for everything above. I made sure she was everything upper and higher than anything. I was high myself. I was crazy in love still is today because she asked me. You didn't find a woman yet? All these years it been two years. Well did she even find a man even though that's not my business as she would say. Ladies on break-ups, divorces and separated. I loved her she said I didn't because I wouldn't have done the things I did. I agreed! Never did I say

the sins and wrongs she did to me was that love? I didn't say she's still God child. I hope she just would of saw in that way. You can't make nobody love you or see you in love until they choose to. I just see when a man does something wrong its different, everything changes up. She took me for granted at times. She couldn't see the man I tried to keep my woman. She didn't even know to hold resentment against me judge and unforgiveness that was her power against me. If I can hold this in my mind and towards him and bring it up. When ever even at the right time to hurt him like he did me. I won anyway, because he can't never ever win again, he's a loser. I'm now in control of this relationship. Now since he controls it my time am I wrong? No, I'm not. This never gave her soul comfort never did heal me, because we were not one in our own home. She didn't want it to be. One that's why she didn't forgive me fully 100%. She did it for her only way to achieve her own moral superiority, but not free or love me what she stopped calling me fat jaws. She didn't see daily dramas of unforgiveness she saw me as only hurting her the only evil person is me in her eyes. It went as I did the most, I did the most sin I'm the worst person. Bringing up the same old thing Isaiah 43:18 Forget the former things, do not dwell on the past. When she talked to me, she never brought the best out in me this don't only go for women or woman this goes for men and man to. This is not man's world or woman. It's God we just living here until our times comes. No matter how long or short you talk a loving person smoothly and naturally will sit there and listen when they love you and care. I admired her I was waiting on that. I made it about her more than me a lot of times she couldn't see that. When I gave a compliment or gave positive things to say being good and fair. I didn't get positive feedback I got cursed out. Now I sat down with like 10 women at a restaurant one day and they brought me something to eat. They just told me to sit down. I look handsome I was on Miami Beach, so they saw me walking with my suit on they were from Alabama, so one lady seen that I had my tablet. She said what are you writing what that is I said I'm writing several books this one is call You Can Never Satisfy A Woman, so they said add this in there that women talk so much add to much on we do we talk a lot every woman is not the same I know I just had to write about these women. So, I was sitting down listening to these women talk they also was saying we talk about other peoples and other things and drama. I said if you talk about other women and people's you don't think well. We talk about one another behind each other back if you are talking about drama and other people, they said all at the same time. We are friends. Well I learned from my mother as a woman. If a person is on the phone talking with you about someone behind their back, they will talk about the person who they are on the phone with or away from. I'm not putting women down I'm just showing you the experience I have sat down and learn off different types of women. Another thing I learned about the woman is that. When she has sex or make love to the person, she with she can tell. If he's been cheating by the stroke and the strength of the feelings and size of his penis and testicles. If its big or small. She knew what is going on before you know she is the teacher testing everything. It does not mean every woman looks for the man is cheating. She knows when its good right and on time. I have let some women know about this book the title and topic they got angry and was offended, because I was telling the truth and telling the secrets. Women have secrets for a reason they don't like them to be told but want to find out the man secrets. You have some women that can't handle their alcohol when they drink. I seen this woman that was drinking. She just was standing there and she just peeing on herself, because one she had a weak bladder. She couldn't hold it anymore. You have women who drink and be happy some drink, because of problems. Some drink because they are addicts. A woman is someone who's independent and be there for her husband and children and back him up though thick and thin. A lady is the beginner she in that stage of being a woman. The bitch does not care. She does not respect herself or other. The whore will sleep with any and everyone. A classy woman that's a woman of God will feel God and herself not pleasing others first to like her. In her mind and heart, she will not feel slutty that wont even e in her head, but I can say I see a lot of women on the streets who went from losing their dignity and self-respect. A real woman will keep her head up standing strong. It's complicated to satisfy a woman even thou they have much confidence in themselves. I learned that certain women don't have children to defend them being a woman this does not mean that. She would not take care of them. If she had children, she just chose

not to have any children. A woman mind never sleeps. She can love until there's no love anymore. She can be there in a relationship when it is over you are thinking of a master plan. Really several, because a woman mind never sleeps You know I agree a woman is left behind of the role of a lot of responsibilities they must pick up and a man to. What hurt me the most was when I got saved, gave my life and soul to the Lord. When I stop being of this world and still was treated, put down and talk to like I was still living in it. It's a big difference between living in this world and not being of this world. It wasn't all and only about her hurt and only about her hurt and only her and her children. I'm a man my feelings were hurt a lot more than I admit saying sorry for me and her just being better man. We both are human beings and emotional creatures in God eyes a lot of times. We look at and see what we want to and our way. It was times she hurt me on purpose and by accident and swear she was the target and victim always. When a Jeffrey did all that he could do for Cleopatra that he couldn't do anymore his spirit felt crush, so women you feel men crush your spirit, so don't say bold or be harsh and think what did he do wrong or men? See when she rejected me on making love that hit my heart, mind, soul, mentally, and started frustration with emotional strong pain this because hurt feelings but he was a cry baby. The next thing was money if God says in his word better or for worse just because I'm not making much as my wife or less does that matter if she loves me? I'm shit I'm a fuck up, get your no-good sorry ass up, even when I was trying. Even when having her mean attitude towards me she so bitter to wear looks actions respect towards me is this mother fucker is not known well he should have done what he done he's not appreciative or giving credit for shit not no more for what he has done to me. Jeffrey told Cleopatra thank you and love you more than she did after she forgave me, she chose not to celebrate the best in him. Instead, she was pointing her finger at me every day and the worse thing was she provoke me so damn much she pushed me back to the streets. I asked these one day. It was two of them I asked can you satisfy a woman? It was a joke they said it at the same time, Hell no!! I said why? One said she wants too always be right. The other said she always wants something. A woman is not satisfied because it's all the man's fault a woman is very fickle. The minute you figure her out or something about herself she's going to switch up. It can be a fact, or an opinion any conversation or something that was done right or wrong. She will change up it's her nature women always mean the opposite at times of what they say it's a natural reflect back-n-forth also women are prideful they just don't admit to it and are so dramatic. Don't doubt your husband from things from the past of your personal insecurity's, family members, friends, and certain people leading them astray Cleopatra did this to him, but Jeffrey showed her that he genuinely cared and love her so much. Women are complicated creatures. A woman has her needs, wants, likes, and say or speak on she's going to be heard being stubborn. It even makes them at times impossible for them to just really talk about or focus on one thing. The woman changes up every day in certain ways, shape or form. A real woman looks on life that's what fits her the best. Not only does the woman be focus on how she dresses and look she wants the car she buys to go with what she's wearing depending on the woman. Jeffrey learned from Cleopatra she was and still is multitasker all by herself. She did get carried away, but I only did that to her in her ways, thoughts and vision of negativity not just only hurts and pain I done wrong. She was crazy and insane, a Leo but only times I made her that way come on she's a human. Cleopatra was a woman that was constantly searching of Jeffrey happiness even with him making her laugh, smile, giggle, blush and kiss him with a hug. Then tell I'm so crazy a trip, I'm just too much, a hand full, I'm something else, what she's going to do with me let me know if I left something out now. Now what was she? I don't because she was the innocent one, she was good not bad. A woman doesn't even at times because she's difficult or her mood swings or changing up. A woman will give hints and signs like Cleopatra did to Jeffrey he knew it because he will say what do you need or want baby? It was not about sex it was about me being a man of God stepping up more to understand to how she communicates. She was the strong black woman that got straight to the point I was listening it was just a doubt in the back of her mind about me was filthy, because I gave her so much attention and I was like I'm uncomfortable where's mines. I complimented her on her on everything she has done. It was like leave me alone, ignore me, but I still made her feel appreciated. I told her the clothes she put on looked

beautiful, her hairdo was nice she was a beautiful woman, and I will let her know even with my sins why she was being holy and perfect she was the best thing that ever happened to me I loved everything she did even when it was wrong. I was hurt because she was a part of me inside and out. I knew what she was comfortable with and not I had to we was in love she taught me some of them things I learned things on my own watching, this is why I knew what would get her angry or not. She still was angry from the past pain and hurt I'm the man she was sitting back always watching to make a move on me at any time when I was not doing nothing but her mind and negative vibes knew it all and all the time it was not true. It was not God, prayer, positive, health, and doubting it was mixed up and confused and the woman will tell it as what you did to her only and let's hear her side. Men please listen to me women change up on there emotions and feelings and who they are this don't mean there bad. We can't live with them or without, God puts us her not only them only God knew everything about. Cleopatra always like to have fun she was always looking for a new idea for of lots of excitement from me because she could not stay mad until she could not truly forgive me. She wants it now then changes up from time to time. A woman loves to experience other things that interest her. Even when a woman has made up her mind about everything it still changes because her mind does not rest it's just like when I was around my mother with my aunties and other women I got jumped they was always right and never wrong. Experience is one of the best teachings. The experience in life myself and being married two times and in several relationships with different women I learned and observed them. I was just waiting for the right time to come out with my book. I had a friend and his name was Walter he was a son that was raised with a single mother and became a Lawyer. He felt and lived a life that if he did the right thing that he wouldn't go through things that black men period in life go through almost every day. In society he seen lots of black men go through things from different cities. All kind of clients that was black men go through divorces doing right and good for their children and wives taking everything from them the system, judges, juries, and society was on the women side. This black man lived a decent life. I'm telling you it's a true story so change this look, think of it as no kind of a negative way. He was never on the streets on knew about the street life. All he knew about was being a Christian man, getting an education, being a good husband, father and being a good person to other peoples that less fortunate he became one of the top greatest Lawyers and thought of representing people from the streets. Walter thought by living the life he lived there he will never be mistreated by the law. Until one day he went out to eat with some friends of his somewhere black some were white so he remembered that he left his wallet in the car, so he told everybody he was going back to the car to get his wallet. As he went to open his car door the police grab him and slammed him on the car he was screaming I'm a Lawyer I know my rights what I do wrong they said shut the fuck up and arrested him on speculation that he was a black man about to break into a car. He had on a suit, but they did not see that they saw a black man. They took him to be process fingerprinted and stripped him naked and made him squat so they can check his anus. Walter told the officers you can't do this to me because I'm a Lawyer and I know my rights and the police response was our bitch now nigger. He sat in jail for the rest of the night. Even though the state dropped the charges against him tested it and take away the hurt, humiliation, and the pain he went through because he looked like the black man who burglarize somebody else car. I told Walter and women especially blacks that a black person in America has no chance in being in a positive light. No matter what the up bringing or situation he comes from, because he's a black man he's still going to be treated unfairly and put down not just by the society, police, system it can be other things women you only don't go through especially what a black man goes through. It is the most everyone has a story to tell and a testimony. We all go through it. Walter told me daily he has clients mostly black men that come to him constantly for representation against the mistreatment from police officers using their position to abuse and hurt them daily, but he would have never thought that one day it would happen to him because he was a professional Lawyer live good and stayed out of trouble. He thought how he achieved became successful and he thought who he represented or became which is a Lawyer will change all that but reality sat in to make him realize no matter what his situation was a black man in America. It's just a matter of time where

they get you and emasculate you and to make you feel and treat you lesser than you are Walter thought he was an exception to the rules because he was a black Lawyer. He always saw it's done to a lot of black men but when it hit him it hurt like hell a pain that hit him, he did not give up, but he was so angry. I felt where he was coming from I been there seeing men and women raped just as much black young men in foster homes, shelters, false prophets raping men and family members abusing them they being neglected just like women even worse it goes vice versa but most are not giving attention to men like there doing the women. You even have the women saying the only thing they go through worse is the police and make that as an excuse not to go any where like my situation. I been out of prison 27 years and I thought if I changed they would treat me different I started voting and only doing this for me a change makes a big difference if it got worse just like when women say and men when are you giving your life to the Lord the devil comes more and more. Well what do you say to the black when he changes his life. When I was not a criminal any more or a bad ass it even made me feel like shit. When Cleopatra told Jeffrey you always in some shit people was looking at him judging him from his past what he did wrong instead of asking him what happen. Now I'm not the man I use to be anymore!! It's more things that's hidden that black men go through and not giving credit for like they should be fair and no one owes anything, but love that don't give people in this world to put women higher than men or men higher than women no one! Another thing is no matter how much you tell the woman your sorry for what I done wrong for cheating she will never give you a chance back 100% faithfully, honest, truthful and be stating it will never be the same like it use to be or ever be the same way like when we first met. That's what she feels, think, and believe what she going to get out of that. I want a woman any woman to please and love herself for hurting Cleopatra Jeffrey knew he had to give up all the power to win her back that happens sometimes vice versa: not all and only for women. I'm not angry or do not like women I'm just trying to get out that men go through just as much as women cannot be satisfied. If you find a woman that does not love herself where do you think you come in at the same thing goes for the woman finding a man that does not love himself.

The woman can't do everything and so as the man! I have learned the other secret to on the woman. How she will buy a dress, leave the tag on it, then take it back to store for refund on her purchase. Another thing is and don't say women that's a woman. It was a brother name Roger his lady walked up to him complaining about money in front of other people. So, he stood there quiet she said speak the he spoke. She said shut up then he you told me to speak. Now you want me shut up, which one you want me to do come on now. She said your trying to be funny, so he shut up. So, then she walked away saying I don't want to talk to you no more. I have nothing else to say to you don't call me its over. She walked away angry, frustrated, upset and she got in her car slam the door and pulled off. So, now on this situation some women will say she was wrong. Everyone is entitled to their own opinion, so women will say what he did wrong? Men will be men regardless. A woman will say I don't ask no man for anything. I don't need nothing from a man. She wasn't wrong its something he did. Now if the man did this to the woman and it was reversed the world would be coming down. He would be everything, but a child of God, no good, a dog, rude, disrespectful, no home training, no father role model or figure, no manners, don't know how to treat or talk to woman, have all kinds of cycles a sinner, very cruel, nasty its others, but guess what she called him then wanted to talk to him. He said I thought you didn't want to talk to me anymore. Now women would say if he would just shut up. She was probably calling to apologize. The same thing goes for both parties. Did the man have to taken through all that? I know some women would have said if he would have just given her what she wanted. Then guess what she came back and said I'm calling you why you not answering your phone don't you see me calling you. Is this a woman being a woman or only this type of woman? Every woman is not the same, because Jeffrey went through this with Cleopatra. She would get on the phone fuss me out then apologize then fuss me out again. She would even stop talking to me, which the role come out into the mind games. Who he thinks he is? I'm not calling him first. He is going to call me. Men have +ways to of their ways. Men being men, so is that a woman being woman. A woman she's never satisfied. Women been telling me and so is a man not satisfied. Some women

done got in to if with me debates about this book. I'm writing most women said it's true you right about that women. I didn't even know; some scream their statement was you not lying about that. See I need to explain to the women is that there are supposed to be no secrets, lies, mind games towards your husband/man, no hidden money, bank accounts, friends, girlfriend, or boyfriends. If you agree because marriage is different from boyfriend and girlfriend. I'm not talking about paper I'm talking about the bond, because if you take another thing to another thing what do have? Ladies it starts enemies, curses, intimacy, drama, thoughts that are negative, because Cleopatra just looked at me coming home from work with mean, angry and bitter face. She asked me who I been listening to. I cheated yes. I stepped away from God commandments then when I repented God made me pay for all that I had done. Cleopatra added more on to God plan with her evil thoughts, bitter cruel heart and she was blind to see God was punishing us both. We both was out of line in our marriage, but she was to selfish to see that you right. Women when you tell men that's hardheaded you can't make no man do you right or treat you right if he does not want to. You can't change him, make him do nothing he does not want to now vice versa. Can you women say the same thing or be stubborn or selfish. He made me be this way. I never was like this. It was all his fault everything! When Jeffrey got saved and then Cleopatra told him I forgive you before we got married then took all problems home saying I should have never taken you back. You right why did she? Did she love me women? She was angry at the time then why she forgave me? I am trying to figure that out. She is a good, loving strong woman. What am I? Just only a man! That's all! Women will say you broke that trust that's hard to just give that back. I agree it is on life of sins everyone does including me. Cleopatra didn't know her frustration of bitterness was her walking up to me confessing she was wrong, which she would turn it into a fight more of her not letting of the past. What I did I did not want her to give me her trust. I worked and earned my trust that I didn't get. How can you tell someone you forgive them and don't, because you must do that to make trust possible again? When you go to God first, yourself, then yourself, the other person and then use excuses every time that forgive, forgive, forgive, with no actions. This man fails and messed up me, myself yes, I'm getting on me. I got up clean myself up and shit. Jeffrey thought his spouse Cleopatra was going to choose to forgive, encourage me and help him for us both to start fresh of rebuilding trust. She did not encourage me she hold on to I was a failure and over my head and used everything against me she could her children, her family, using it in arguments. The truth is better than a lie I'm all these things but no I'm not I love I have a great heart and a great passion about myself she said if I did not want this to work I wouldn't have took you back now would I? Yes, she said that, but she didn't show me she was the one wanting everything granted to her. Jeffrey tried hard to do complete Cleopatra and he put that on his mother's grave he wanted her with God's grace and mercy to walk with him through his past and hers together to heal one another with God first he could not do it all by himself either. Everyone is wounded, hurt from sins and what someone did to them not only women. This is not no excuse for adultery, lust, fornication, cheating on their wives no this is for all sins. Today in time we just want to be stuck on one thing and use that towards someone to keep provoking them as a target, but eventually we are lying to God ourselves and the person that did us wrong. Yes, I know, because I done it no one is perfect. Cleopatra helped Jeffrey with the past then soon as she gets angry it didn't come out in Gods way it came out in a provoking, hate, anger, then she thought it wasn't a lie. What she was doing and telling me that I'm going to stop bringing this up, stop throwing anything in my face. It was like she was looking at me as if I were doing dishonest things in front of her. She shows evil actions and expressions at me. You have certain women agree with this party sad and happy that make it last forever. He shouldn't have done it in the first place, so how do we make the relationship or marriage work? It gets worse and show's we are ready to break up. My prayers and love with God I were told it was all fake and my sins were even worse. Even her I know the God we serve don't look at that or say that these marriages today don't want to include God. They need to watch how that gets you. suppose to heal one another at times. Cleopatra wanted Jeffrey dead because she will tell him this. Why this happens to you in jail, and this came back on you for the way you treated me. Do you know they almost let me die in jail, because I went in more than

seizures? Then if I would have died what would the women have been doing. What you women will say of course her husband, so she didn't mean what she said she was just angry at the time. She loves you. I wish she really see me as a Christian. Just like she saw herself falling short of the glory of the Lord. The woman has her bipolar moods sometimes especially when they can't get what they want they get upset, angry and stubborn. Some of these ways can't keep a man home. It doesn't always be the man fault. It is the woman ways, and she don't know how to talk to her man. Especially how some women act differently when their period come on beware get from around them and let them be. She highly in her irrational moods back to bipolar. There would be times women can be distracted and go into depression. Sometimes it elevated their moods. Its evidence that it presents differently more in women then in men. It is all kinds of things with women it is their guilty pleasures such as shopping, sex, with or without consequences. A woman can be bipolar in ways, and it affects her emotions. When you think she over here she is over there in the state of mind, emotionally, spiritually and physically. Women want to talk they like to detail and explain. In a marriage in a relationship. When a woman trusts a man, she will open her mind and feel him out by what he says and do. The adage Trust is earned. You must get out there and work your show with action. If you are feeling this person you going to show them how things are done for them. You are letting them know. Trust means a firm belief in the reliability, truth, ability, or strength of someone or something. A woman can listen to what is being said that they will give their all for the person when they are a relationship or a friendship and you as the person believe them they have your back until the end. You rely in the person to be with you through thick and thin, the good or bad in your life this shows you have a friend. The one thing you should do is know and love yourself. When a woman regains her trust in man she plays this mind game with trust and really do not trust a man or anyone. Intrigue means you're interested in me because I feel curious about you. I am fascinated about you and want to understand, it could be a romantic interest or just a friendly interest or just special. Intrigue you could learn a lot from woman or man in getting to know them and things about them. You have the curious eye and feeling that makes a woman want to get with that man and learn more about them. The woman is intrigued movement in relationship. They have a fascination for a man to get know what they are about and what they are really looking for in woman whether it is the looks or the personality. When you are intrigue you must have an open mind as to you woman/women what it is you really want from the person. As a woman we should know our worth however we stay curious when we get into a relationship. Not trying to turn you off but ask yourself are you movable, unstable, both or not? Do you have a bad attitude or good one, or as it's known everything is a man's fault, When it comes to a woman and her sins right and wrong is all on demand and the man made her that way as most women tell it for example, the woman feels like there's only cycles with the man but not with her she would tell the man can no one make him do what he don't want to do Cleopatra will say Jeffrey made me this mean, bitter, angry, vengeful, nasty evil woman and take it to her grave. Now correct me if I am wrong the woman must have the last word it's either her way or the highway. If it has too hot gotten out of her kitchen where she says she want something and agree on it she changes it anytime when she is good and ready. Now is this before or after Cleopatra gets cheated on or she does the cheating? Jeffrey believes that everyone has sin on having sex, lusting or fornication just like a woman seeing a taken man it could be a lady and say no I cannot sleep with you at all, and you are in a relationship or vice versa for the man as well saying he is a man he cannot do that but going to say no. Oh well if she were a woman, she would not open her legs. Like for example the story with Bathsheba, David and Bathsheba was wrong. They both knew they were relationship. However, Bathsheba was for herself and fulfilling her needs and desire for selfish reasons and so was David, getting what they wanted out of it. It was all hell in the end! Now when Cleopatra tells Jeffrey to get from around her because he is aggravating her. When Jeffrey leave's Cleopatra wants to know where he is at and wants him right back sometimes. This goes for other women as well depending on the situation and the type of woman she is. When you are having too much sex and making love too much she needs to marinate, because she is sore, you are doing it too much. This all we do make love or have sex. It is good before it starts while you are into it.

Then when the man is resting, and the woman changes her mind to say I am ready. You can say just my back is hurting or I am tired darlin'. It is like this from the woman who you are sleeping with or why are you tired and worn out? Are you cheating with another woman? woman's time. Playing mind games with a man now these days undercover. Then when Jeffrey is talking to Cleopatra she will say shut up you talk too much. When Jeffrey is quiet, baby what are you thinking about? Then Jeffrey will say baby you know I am thinking about you. One way or another from the woman like this, Cleopatra will say Jeffrey you are thinking about that woman you cheated on me with Vanesa. You are lying with your lying ass, and you cannot be quiet to yourself! You can be watching your football game or a peace of mind with yourself she gets to know what is on your mind, because what the woman for sure as a fact as she says you cannot tell me what is going on in my head, but she can tell you up and down front and back backwards and forwards top to bottom telling you off good with a thing or two. Then Cleopatra can tell Jeffrey about church and tell him to stop cursing. We just left church spirits cannot be around her but only on Jeffrey. Now when Jeffrey speaks to Cleopatra about God, it is not spiritual she comes straight out and say, so you are speaking straight from the heart now? Cleopatra says I know you are not telling nobody about God all the hell and sin you put me through and our family. When Cleopatra is sinning God is still with her, but the devil is with Jeffrey and the spirit is in the room and everywhere Jeffrey goes. I have been relationship two times and I have seen it all, done it all, have dished out, took it in have received and until this day everything is still all Jeffrey and only him. Jeffrey did no good, no love, no nothing now this is true, I am not talking bad about women I am just telling it like it is. A fact not an opinion. When she goes to the mall do not distract her. I learned from a woman guess who, well two women and many more Cleopatra and my daughter Anita. Do not ask her are you finish what is it or to hurry up if you can handle it you will get fussed out there and all the way home probably until the next day. Anyway, when she goes to the mall or anywhere to shop do not aggravate her, because she must assess the situation she will be there for hours, and hours come to you to get your opinion or fact that is when you give it. You are not right some of the times, but she came to ask you anyway. Now when Cleopatra and Jeffrey are getting ready to go out it is the same thing, but it takes hours for her to get ready like I said she is a woman. She is emotional, loving, caring, sharing, independent, and respects herself knows love therefore she gives love! I said you can never satisfy a woman. It is never enough for her when you take her shopping she wants more. Purses, clothes, money, car etc., or it can be small things as her man to give her. She wants everything her way, she wants a man that she can trust. A woman has been hurt so many times and done wrong. Some women have a vendetta to settle! When she is ready, and God knows what she is ready for. Some women PMS every day when the period comes on or not every month for Some women have an attitude for nothing a lot of times. In today's world no matter how hard you try they will not be happy. They will find something, because the next day it will be their job, if it does not be the man, or someone else fault or someone pissing them off. It just never their fault or their wrong! A lot of women cannot handle the truth, because when you tell them the truth is still a lie. If you have cheated on them you would never get another chance, she will tell you she forgives you with her mouth but not with her heart. When the man she is with is for real, he is still a dog. She will call herself a Christian, or whatever God she believes in answer him to his face after all the years they have moved on telling him, I still see you as the same negative man because you hurt me. What are you going to do about it? She will walk up in your face while your crying looking at her feeling the pain, she felt what she is taking you through. What you have taking her through as time has gone and passed by. Then it will have something to do with her mother or father or children. She will be unhappy with herself and take it out on others. She has the nerve to tell you only men do this in the world! When her period comes on sometimes, she is in between happy or angry mood swings and she say you cannot tell her shit! Cleopatra and Jeffrey got their daughter Anita a dog named Smitty, Jeffrey told her this is your responsibility and I let her know if she did not take care of the dog I was going to give it away or put it out. Then I explained to Anita about handling her responsibility with the dog. It is the new world order. The woman children who you are married to, so it is the children and mother way now today. Then they sit down and talk with one another as partners or family when the father is not around I never been part of the mother-in-law, brother, sister, son, daughter and Cleopatra is one big happy family, looking down on Jeffrey! Now you know by being a woman it is certain things she will be picky on. Jeffrey brought and got plenty of purses for Cleopatra. The strong black woman, and do you know what she said? Why you got this one? I wanted the other one like this next time, Was not it a surprise! Now you see this man right here, in any form and that know me cannot talk about me or call me. It is what Cleopatra talks about, they talked about Jesus Christ. He still loves them then and now until this day, forever and eternity and I love them in the same way. Cleopatra (THE WOMAN) Jeffrey help shave the hair on her vagina he even went to go shopping by myself to buy her sanitary napkins by himself. Some people look at me crazy shit I did not care. I loved my woman. Who said all men are the same? Jeffrey even washed her vagina and gave her a bath come up with the rag I know how it goes, and for some of our women tampons are uncomfortable, so some women do not use them. For some women it hurts and does not feel good, but you see, you had a man right here who took care of his woman. It was times it took his woman braids out her hair and washed her hair for her and remove polish off her nails and toes, that is right. This man did that! Jeffrey even took care of Cleopatra when she was sick however she did not give me credit at all. Please let your man be a man and give him his space, do not pressure him. Why is that? Most women will say all men are the same negative or positive, because if you always see a man that way only you will always be by yourself, you know what some women say today my son is my man or her baby, then becomes your child, then grown up, or if you have two or more. Whatever God blesses you with your son is not your man. You are saying that God do not say that. Some women say fuck God I will deal with it. Some women get in that shady way, but some women be so mad that they do not know what they are saying and do things just for get back of pain for so long and still come go back and forward to God then leave then go right back. Some have told me that in my face and never came back to apologize, because themselves and false prophets. Women themselves or that have friends, or they own mind have told them that they do not have to apologize or come back and ask for forgiveness. Well, God said, go to him and repent on your knees, then go to the person and asked for forgiveness. Forgive yourself as well. I hope the women will not say I know I am not talking about God just like everybody else has the right to and have the right to praise him! Some for prophets, brothers, sisters, associates, people have told a lot of women do not listen to men! No, God said, do not put your trust in man or woman! God sends brothers and sisters drunks and all kinds of peoples so do not take the word of God and use it all up on men! Use the word of God as a doer for God's sake. Also, to do unto others as you have them to do unto you. Not for tic or tac or get back. You will only be hurting yourself. You will only be putting a curse upon yourself, so much build up inside! The woman will always have a reason to have all the time, she will have a plan, A, B, and C and not let you distract her from it. She is always right. If she does not go after what she wants. She feels like she will never have it. She is going to tell and ask because she know the answer to the question before he or she says it, with her hands on her hip or her mouth or lips poked out with her finger pointing at you or depending on the woman and the topic is about really the conversation she feels like if she does not ask all the time. That answer will always be no. So, she got to find out her mind be running. She is going to step forth. Because she says no one is going to have her in the same place (child please). Be careful and be alert. She will always come with the <u>A. C. T.</u> A is Accepting her thoughts and feelings because you cannot have none of any kind of feelings to express like her, because you are acting like a damn woman and you are too damn emotional, God did say we all have feelings. Yes!! C is for Curious she is the only one take valued directions to know something or find out something bad or good your direction is messed up some of the time or no time or most of the time at all if you have cheated or used her or made her feel in some type of way. Once you made one bad choice or decision it is on you when she decides that is her choice. One it is none of your business I said I was sorry and do not go there or it can be a beautiful charm of fragrance of words, actions, body gestures, looks, silence and ways that she will make you change on her apologies because your mistakes are nothing compared to hers. It is all about the woman in her book & diary it is all about her love the

way you love her and how to love her, but you still did everything wrong, so she got every right and its advantage over you to do this until you separate or die. T is for her Tolerating what the man and people in life put her through until she has sat down to herself and thought of the wrongs she has done. She acts like the husband/man even though she is the woman. As a man says a woman should stay in a woman's place. Now if you lose your job and you are trying to find one be prepared for unexpected It is not better or worse, no more in her eyes. It is aggravation she is doing it all by herself, so she got this. She feels like only she been through a lot in her children. Her mind is a beautiful garden. They are flowers that grow, but the man has weeds and get from around her, because the man is disturbing and aggravating her too much. She says he is weeds and going to kill her flowers. Two queens cannot be in one castle or a whole bunch of women cannot be in one house, well like my mother used to say, an all-whole bunch of pussies cannot be in one house". They will get tired of one another! Cleopatra said Jeffrey talk too much, so when I shut up and did what Cleopatra said of not talking then I was too damn quiet. I was not talking, but I have learned that we cannot live with them and cannot live without them! If the woman is stubborn she is now acting crazy it is all on the man! Now men have done a lot of crazy things. There is no excuse for them suffering the consequences. They reap what they sow and that is vice versa but not in the same way towards woman/women. Do not be around here saying everything is all on the man and you did NOTHING!!. Every person that has walked the face of this earth has sinned. I learned that a relationship is a give and take. Is this still wrong you cannot never satisfy a woman? I even ask lots of women why they feel like a man cannot satisfy them and I got different responses. What have they done wrong? They said nothing. Have they ever pushed the men, or any man they ever had away? No matter what the woman tells you, her words and ideas can change the world, she is the educated one and in the woman darkest or her light. She can always be found not the man. She will always say, I did not say that at times but her actions, attitude, ways, personality, she reacts differently. As I learned from the older women and Ms. Germ number one, as myself and it goes like this, A woman is to always be recognized. A woman is proud of herself. She respects God, herself and others, she is aware of who she is, she needed to seek definition from the person who she is with, nor do she respect them to read or lead her mind. The woman that she is quite capable articulating her needs and wants. Women/woman are hopeful, she is strong enough to make all her dreams come true. She knows love therefore she gives love. The woman is a gift more emotional than love itself. She recognizes that her job has great values. A woman is a good creation smart species and always independent. The woman will make her own money and would not let money make her! The good woman will give her tithes and offerings in church. If the woman love is taken for granted, it is known that darkness will come into the light and God will take over. A woman is someone has a pure inspiration, a strong, powerful, doubtful of endurance. The woman knows that she will at times have to inspire others to reach the potential that God gave herself and all women with that she knows her past, understands her present and move more and more ready for the future that she no God has for her. A woman that has God in her knows God. She knows that God world is her heaven spiritual eternal playground but without God in the woman life, she would just be played with. Now the woman will keep God in mind constantly and she speaks it. Then most women say men have them this way, because he started back doing what he was doing before. He is going to stay that same man please encourage that man do not kick him when he is down and trying to get up. The woman will say also with bad and good times when the man is doing right that he still deserves this for what he has done to me, so she is unforgiving, so if she cannot forgive on them other things in her life will be a hold and stop. That is what God says they can continue to play with it if they want to. I see there is more gifts for women than for men. Now is that right? Yes. For a woman what she has been taking through, and especially the black men now what they have been through? One. When they are first born. The strike is there black. What they must go through in America not being raised right in a struggle. There is no excuse, feelings, or love for them, but that is for women, good or bad. God says we are all wonderful gifts being born in this world. Now Jeffrey will give anyone a gift or feed someone whether their right or wrong. That Is the heart that Jeffrey has? So, people that is ignorant saying well everyone is not like that, you right. This is one of the reasons why relationships are not moving forward and not forgiving and not having a good heart. Especially relationship give-and-take, better or worse, richer or poorer sickness and in health until death do us part. Now a lot of people that do not like me they talk about me. Now I know Jeffrey is not telling anybody how to love and about love. You do not have a mind like a woman as what is going on today with your rights or wrongs while you are getting it all together about yourself. Everyone is going through something even what you are going through. Most women know how to hide their emotions when they are going through something and can keep a smile on their faces to cover up the pain and guilt even being innocent, Women want all the credit even when it is not due to them. Women I love you all and pray for you do the same for me. just like in the bible when its everybody must go through a painful near life and death experience to make them change their ways." God did not say the woman or man ways! You cannot change someone if they do not see an issue with their actions. Do not do this as a get back to hurt someone and keep your wall up vice versa. I heard women say the reason why men forgive quicker than women do so they can keep dogging and get over on someone feelings just like that. That is not true on every situation, because believe me you are not going to make him, but it has been 10, 20, 30 years and women have not let up on forgiveness is not hard for their family on their side with the cycle even on mines. Now "a person told me are you writing this book for yourself. I said no I am writing for everyone, even me. I am still learning." Jeffrey could not take the blame for everything. I cannot stand up in front of our Lord and Savior and ask him that, how will I look, I will not do it, because my heart is not like that, so is Jesus, do not let no one tell you that your heart cannot be like Jesus, how are they going to say that when Jesus was the one said be ye perfect love and forgive like me. If he does not, then he hated me, brother and sister. I have sat down. Let men, women, ex-girlfriends, ex-wives and people curse me out family members also and I have accepted their role vice versa with me doing it back to them, but the woman says it is FOREVER!! I hear some people say if a man cries or hurt over a woman he is weak in his feelings or should he have the right to feel weak when he is hurting over someone he genuinely loves yes or no? You know when I was growing up. My mother loved me, soft, strong, humble and hard, but she could not teach me how to be a man! Now I did a lot of wrong things. I argued with women, and I would beat on some of my girlfriends. We got into arguments, fights, some beat me up and I walked away. A lot of times I was wrong and had to many women, but I did not deserve another chance. I cheated, lied, bullied, sinned, I even cried, I was scorned and in pain. This is for a woman, and this do not mean men put your hands on a woman or woman put your hands on a man. Nobody has a right to touch anybody, so what are you going to say you know that is not going to happen. We got to go through life with many issues positive or negative. You have a choose to make a choice in life to live like that in misery with company or happy which one is better for your life? Now a woman should not say he deserved to die for ever that is a miserable, bitter woman. She just broke up with a man from many years ago and brought it to the next man, bringing old grudges from the past in the relationships and wicked spirits right along with her! It is not only the man on all wrongs wrong sweeties there are two sides to every story in the marriage or relationship. You know a lot of women do not understand this or what their mothers went through. Did they have curses put on their daughters and sons. They do not know a lot, do they? They can tell you, but do not want to accept it. The woman says she is blessed whether she is with God or not, mad, angry or happy. Not true, because God does not say this in his word. You cannot be bitter and blessed at the same time. Not if you have a Godly heart. You are not a woman that act like a fool. You know what people have done to you, but you will forgive again and again, because you will have a beautiful heart just like your face, or is your heart going to be wicked forever! Both parties want to be in love with someone who deserves their heart, not someone who plays with it. Sometime women want to tell you women who does things like put their hands on a man because they know that their brother is going to always believe them before he believes the man, that is why there are so many men who get abuse by the women and sometimes take it so there will not be no problems. She is taking you through a lot. If you are thinking of someone today or not at all rebukes that and still say a

prayer for them and stay prayed up, because you do not know what they are going through when it comes to a woman. Just like for you my sisters. See, it is time when the woman thinks that she is losing her mind, but she knows that all she must do is get on her knees and pray to our heavenly father and for a godly man to come into her life and change it around completely. There are times when the woman feels like she cannot go no longer. But God keeps her moving, so as the man. At times she wants to lash out on those who she felt done her wrong. She lashes out on those who have been in her corner from day one like her partner meaning the husband/man, but God keeps her mouth shut. As well as the man. Some women think the money just is not enough, but God helped the woman to keep her lights on, bills paid and a roof over her head for her children. At times when the woman thought she was going to fall down God lift her up and the same way for the man. When the woman was weak God kept her strong the same as the man. The woman can go on and on, but we are sure we hear her as well as a demand or cry some hold it in putting on makeup. The woman and man are both blessed. Men pass this onto the Women and Women pass this onto the Men. Both parties are kept by the love and grace by God, so what God does for the women that he does not do for the men. There is no such thing as 60/40 God is fair that's why relationships go through their ups and down listening to other people instead of God! See I learned things from women. They are not dogs. No one is a dog! Mark a great friend told me never be ashamed of the scar that a woman has. I have been through it with some people abuse, lies, people cheating on me, telling me different stories. The man is tired of people hurting in so many ways, however he still feels the pain and manages to deal with the problems that his woman brings to him meaning if the woman has been hurt sexually, mentally, emotionally and physically abused she will not know how to love correctly but the man still stays around to deal with it out of love for God and her. Anyway, it simply means that all what the women were telling me I was to stay strong with whatever I been through that hurt me, so please women teach yourself that! The same advice that you can give to your child and others you should follow. I can tell a lot of women the past should be left in the past, or it can still affect your future. Live life for what tomorrow can bring and not what yesterday has taken away because tomorrow is never promise so you should not let what hurt you in the past have a hold on your life in the future. God says every day is a gift! In life. Women you will realize that there is a role for everyone you meet, people will learn something from you, just as you will learn something from them, even if you both are selfish at times. Most woman will say what can A MAN teach me. He is considered as nothing however some men learn or was taught by a woman about women. A woman can teach because she is kind and not the man. So, everyone you meet they will test you, use you, love you, and will teach you, but the ones that are important are the one who bring out the best in you. They are rare gems and amazing people who remind you why it is worth living for. See Cleopatra did not understand that she hurt Jeffrey, and he hurt her. Jeffrey & Cleopatra hurt each other so bad they both played a part in the relationship. It made her be on top and leave me on the bottom. Every day of living is a second chance. Jeffrey taught Cleopatra family somethings. She cried on my shoulder about many different things concerning our relationship and family. It is the people in your life that will turn their backs on you when time get hard. The ones who would do anything to see you smile and who love you no matter what those are the ones in your corner. Just like God does! But some women do not understand that they will push the ones who are there for them away for the ones who do not give a damn about them. I personally am going to stay away from people who are broken, complaining, still have hate, bitter, man or woman problems, sinning, jealous, childish, foolish and stuck on stupid and still do not want to change, because I had the same problems. I am no different than these people. I have been there done that I am going to pray for them, go up to them and tell them I love them. Encouraging your spouse in the everyday of living in prayer and happiness. False prophets say you cannot push that spirit away flea right now Satan! Now most women tell men see you did not want to listen, God do not like ugly, all this came back on you, and you are reaping what you sow. False prophets will help them to. People who are not doers of God for real. When you tell her this you are not a believer of God, then will change she wants to take back what she says to you that the Lord says it was just for that time that is only for her and to use against you. Now, with you

telling her two wrongs do not make a right she has the last word!! You cannot make her listen. Now her charm and warm personality is what comes in when she says two wrongs do not make a right. At times sorry is not enough for the woman and you changing it be her that must change to trust you again! Now you see our eyes are fixed on what we do not pay attention to but when we do it is eternal. Jeffrey learned from Cleopatra an educated woman that and did not get no credit. When I had to prove it to myself before others. I stop creating misery, harming her, and myself, pouting and complaining. I read scriptures she gave me and read on my own. I stop trying to be like other people. I created my own success. It was and still is subjective. I am special and I have the power to do better. I loved myself, because at once I did not love me more than anyone has love me accept God. I learned without telling the woman. I told God back what he already had told me on my knees with our communication. In context whole chapter 10. The thief come not steal, nor with the intention to kill, or destroy. He come that they might have life, and that they might have it more abundantly. I thought I had all the answers, but I realize I have not lived long enough to confront all the questions. Do you know how I got the wisdom, I prayed? Women says wounds do not heal well. So, they uncover their wounds in God's presence and allow God to gently heal their injuries, insecurities, and do not do it in a way of ignoring, being rude, sarcastic with the person who have hurt you. What I do not understand is that a lot of women say their family members have their faults too. They say their family is like music, they have some high notes, some low notes, but always a beautiful song but the man note is dead always like him. A woman will tell you quickly. You cannot change how she feels about you, so do not try just let her live her life and you live yours. You heard her you got the whole world and everyone backing her up and you deserve what you get in return. Every penny! She is going to sit down and give you a lecture, how to change if you going to be around her, because when she is fed up. It only goes like that for her, right? You cannot force a person to show you respect, but you can refuse to be disrespected. See people living by these worldly lectures, God said when a man finds a wife/woman he finds a beautiful soul, a good thing and the love of his life as Christ loved the church. A woman said in front of

Cleopatra and Jeffrey in relationship counseling that God says a wife/woman must be submissive towards her significant other and stay humble in her relationship. She left that out when I said that is true and said the other part God says she got quiet. I asked her man friend Is that true, his response was I am staying out of it. See relationship go by 60/40 rule. What the world says is not good to talk at all when the woman is speaking. Let her have all the say so and be quiet. I know when to speak and not at all. That is not a marital relationship that's control, and police patrol of probations or parole people cannot even say what God says using was better for their selves. The woman that is bitter loves revenge. I have kept and walked away from some women false teacher who have said I do not care. I am going to talk! See, it is a way how you handle each other after you have heard that woman or another man or person have heard her that is it. It goes like this, give, but do not allow yourself to be used. Love, but do not allow your heart to be abused. Trust, but do not be naïve. Listen to others but do not lose your own voice, and to the woman you can do this in a humble Christian nice way as God way not your nasty rude way. So, girlfriends, yourself and others can tell you while you are doing evil back and say girl we feel you. You will be hurting God yourself, your life, everyone around you and getting back at the person who had change themselves. See before I wrote this book, I believe, so I prayed. I listened before I started writing I earned before I spent, I thought good before I started writing I did not give up on life. Now some women where are you all at on this educated man and I am living, because I have one life to live before I die. I even looked at the woman and said do not listen to people who tell you what to do. Listen to God that encourages you always to keep you where your heart is right. I got cursed out, so I ask you what is that? The woman will back her up for ever with her rights and wrongs and say what you did you do to her. That is all your fault, because that man is not for you, what happened? Now when Jeffrey have done wrong to the woman, Jeffrey deserved what he got back in return Jeffrey was sorry and all the get backs stayed that way for years coming from Cleopatra, but Jeffrey can say one thing no one in history has ever been perfect to death from swallowing his or her pride. My woman could give me knowledge, but I cannot give her none, because the truth requires change. She wants to stay in the past and do not want to tell you are still negative, so she should tell herself right there. I lied to you, about making this work and letting the past go. Cannot go anywhere, because she is the one bringing the past up, so that is not being foolish? Jeffrey was apologizing for things a lot that he did not do wrong, Cleopatra lied right in Jeffrey face by getting this done in her way. Whatever she wants with a straight face child. Please? Whatever, I did not do nothing. She does not need help you need the help, because you made heard that way until eternity. I know women that need help men to, but this is about the woman so she can be at peace and her mind can be free. I have brought my woman exercise machines to work out on she was not satisfied and did not work out. She said she wanted it when she gets it she does nothing with it. It was a waste of money. I did it because I cared so she can be in shape. She says I want to go walking and I chose to go with her for the first time. She says make sure you help me out and stayed on me when working out love. I said OKAY. Jeffrey was told he was being humble and nice for what he has done. Cleopatra then changes and says leave me alone, I am tired and aggravated. Then Jeffrey gets fussed out for being considerate, concerned, helpful, by keeping her on track and healthy. Then Depending on the type of woman saying help her to stop smoking. When you tell her baby, you going to get sick. She comes out and says, now I know you are not trying to tell me to do something, because I cannot tell you nothing especially about the other woman. The other woman that will always come up in a conversation that will be so petty against you of her being smart. Playing on your intelligence when she really confusing herself, because she still with the person she says she is going to work out with. Common sense will tell you if you agree to make it work. That is why a call to make it work is the key to a healthy relationship, of responsibility is being responsible where you can act on your own without someone supervision, her attitude is success. It is not just independent woman paying all the bills herself however her husband is included as well! Not a lot of women and people will say I know I am not talking about women. How I have treated a lot of women yes, I have. Women have treated me bad, but not the ones I cheated on first. There are women and men that have cheated on each other. Does he still supposed to pay for it? After she has forgiven him?

How much time she needs after she has forgiven him and says it is over repeatedly. Yes, it is because it is a hold back on your heart, God's heart and the person you are hurting. How can love still to be in your heart? After you said you forgave this man. You are bringing it right back up saying it is not enough, it is more time of you being selfish all for self! You know Cleopatra look at Jeffrey with a straight Christian face, humble, sweet, kissing him soft and put her hand on Jeffrey's chest and say baby that is the past what my mother, my children, and I have done to you, please forgive us that is what God will say please, and Jeffrey says okay you are right, I love you and at that time I do not hear her telling me. Do you need time? Jeffrey feels Cleopatra hurt. It is not right? I know what my family did to you and me as well. We are no good, because it is wicked when a person calls themself a Christian with love and be loving with the heart for their sins, but Jeffrey gets it throwed back in his face for what he has done. Then Cleopatra makes changes the love for her family and children staying strong but love she have for Jeffrey is hate! Then says she does not feel that way, it is entirely different. Jeffrey will never understand a woman's world. Pain is pain. Everyone has been through it in life! See it be times along the way when a woman is saying he cannot be forgiven. She will say it with her mouth, but not with her heart, soul, mind, body, and spirit and with action of love. Nor is it shown after she say she has forgiven him all those years! The woman will have many worries and concerns on where you at? Where you been? Who you been with? What are you doing? Why can't you answer your phone? Why can't you stay on the phone? Why are you lying for? You are lying! Big concerns that do not go away, and the more she tries to free her mind of the negative thoughts while you could be lying next to her calm doing nothing. The more the woman becomes very persistent because she is visualizing the image of the past, thinking hard and staying focus. When you will say something or ask something she will argue, because the past has her mind locked and chained! Forgiving another person for yourself. You will move on from the past and release yourself from negative emotion and thoughts. Jeffrey has even built-up Cleopatra mind by meditating, holding her, bathing her, rubbing her feet to help clear and free her mind. I was trying to get into her mind I was controlling once when I got right, I started helping. I laid down with her in positions, so for a fact so she can be comfortable for her to be relaxed with or without me. A long day of work, I even sat back, and she brought thoughts into her mind and not let them pass through, just engaging them and it cannot be as well on a TV show, in front of the pastor, myself or anyone. You can ask Cleopatra if she hurt Jeffrey and paid him back with the pain, guilt and be hard on Jeffrey after she told me she forgave me. Cleopatra disrespected me many times in our relationship. Jeffrey said that she sinned against him a lot. She would say no not one time taking up for her children first, then herself and family, because it is my fault, so I am guilty as charged. Just like being born in America while the fire is hot. It is good to exercise with the woman, because it focuses on the body, and it takes attention and aggravation off her mind giving her a happier mood for herself, if she makes the choice. Jeffrey told Cleopatra letting go of the past allows you to focus on the future,. It helps a lot. Women chooses more empowering thoughts. I will hope women do not say oh he thinks he knows us! He did not know nothing about a woman. Jeffrey do not have any knowledge or wisdom that is what Cleopatra will say. She only had it! Even though I am writing about you cannot satisfy a woman. I will stop feeling guilty for everything to make the woman feel good. I was beating myself up by making her feel good, because she did not care or appreciate me. I felt trapped and powerless I had to go ahead and read myself, she needed space. I freed her mind and allowed her to tell me while I was looking for a job, I am not paying bills or doing shit. She is doing it all. Cleopatra attitude was unpredictable leading her to tell Jeffrey that is right. However, I am all wrong on everything, her mother, children, and myself seen what only I did wrong. I did not know good in this world. Most women say no man do! Now, when you make the woman smile and laugh she feels better. How long will it last for? She wants more and something else, even when I was tired and worked hard. I was about to fall out from working so hard. I did not feel like it. I still did it, because I said God, she smiles and changes how she is thinking! The woman, well most of them never have behavior problems. She is going to let you have it, telling her about her problems, you better going somewhere CHILD PLEASE! Just like how some women feels like they never are being heard or listen to. She was neglected, and still is, because she cannot forgive. How that man feels like how a woman feels emotional and she had the nerve to tell a man he has never been neglected at all for him to suck it up, accept it and be man about it. Stop acting like a woman, so what your feelings got hurt be a nan stop being a punk or acting like a damn woman. Where did God say this at? Nowhere. Jeffrey has brought a lot to the table for her and her family! Jeffrey have repented, and blood is still on him with Cleopatra's unforgiveness. Now I do not have nothing against women that I cannot get any credit or props. They want credit for something they did not do, feel and know that they are entitled to something whether it is right or wrong. They are not always right. I am not downing women I am telling them its men that are trying their best and they are not given any credit for it! Now, a lot of women will read this and say I had of lot of bad experiences with men, so they are saying it is all my fault. Men stand up for their women if they are right or wrong, because of what they have been through in life. Now, that means letting the past things go. I started writing even let go all the regrets I had inside. I even let go, so I can honor myself and my choices I made in life. I let go of the criticism and judgment I had on myself. I worked on me to love myself. Jeffrey gave Cleopatra (THE WOMAN) by giving her space to herself alone with God. Jeffrey will get calls on his cell phone from Cleopatra who cursed him out and said, you do not love me, because if you did you will be home with your woman. Cleopatra will tell Jeffrey get your ass home now. People will say you let her talk to you like that. Yes, I did not put my foot down, because when I did at first it did not mean nothing or solve anything from the past. What I did was I stop wasting my time trying to help fix something that I knew it could not be fixed by me for the woman to be happy. By her not putting her 50% into our relationship we both got hurt in the end. As well, to be fixed you know you have doctors, therapists, psychiatrists, counselors to tell people we understand the woman more than the man and the help is more for her than for the man. Jeffrey provided for Cleopatra when he fell on hard times, she did not help lift Jeffrey up when he was down or stood by his side? She put her foot on his neck. Jeffrey had surprises for Cleopatra her daughter and son. It could not and would not go through because of Cleopatra (THE

WOMAN) saying Jeffrey did not have anything to offer to her. Now the woman will tell you do not scream your scaring me and the children. The walls are thin in the house, but for her children, home, life, her ways, self, and you, right or wrong. She can say her children sees what you are doing. I am doing wrong, but her wrongs do not matter, because her love is important and more different than yours. You are a dog, slop, and a pig! I did not know when grown children disrespect the parents in relationship in a home and one parent let it go and one parent reprimands them. What does that say about the family life? Jeffrey provided for Cleopatra even when he fell on hard times. She did not help pick me up or stood by my side. Some women feel like their children cannot bring bad spirits and be wrong. It is all something protecting them for the wrong reasons. When they are wrong, and she is to. Now for the right reasons. Yes, fairly, now these times and days they are right for everything. A strong-minded woman would not bring up the past she would love, forgive, walk away and try again. Persevere no matter what! Whatever she goes through in life, not in a 1 Way her Way in the world with the one-way attitude, kiss my ass, I do not need your help and says it sarcastically so rude. No, that's not God's love that is her love. Can you receive something good from this negative energy attitude it is not welcome at this time? Smiling knowing God's knowledge, wisdom, positivity, joyful, graceful is welcome here and having fun! This is not opinions only facts. I know a lot of women who would tell me that. That is your opinion writer, know this is facts. I am letting the women know there is nothing wrong with enjoying things in life, even though they will say we know this already. You do not have to tell me this, so stay attached to it. Do not be off and on moody, cranky, mean, movable and unstable with a nasty attitude. Both will not work together! Jeffrey told Cleopatra being grateful allows her to live in the present and see the blessings in front of her right now! Now women have told me get your damn GED, go back to school, do this, do that. Why do you not need this goal right now? Isn't that right? They are saying that they are not our mothers but sometimes they act like they are our mothers. When a lot of times they be coming at us like this. Let me tell you something right now please does not say it is forever, or Jeffrey what did you do to make Cleopatra act in this type of way? You had to do something because she is usually not this way for nothing. I am letting women know you can learn things from men. We learn things for women. We all are human beings because learning does expand your mind. We learn something every day. I learned something from a wise man, woman, drunk and a fool. It helps you achieve a more enlightened and informed point of view. Not only is it not all about you but you still try to make it be all about you right ladies? Now see the tongue is deadly, especially when a woman talks how she talks when, what comes out of her mouth and do not know her husband, man, friend, fiancé, ex, or whatever. When she talks she do not care, her talking can be worse than a hit, anger, abuse, sin, a bullet wound, murder, a stab mark it says the tongue is deadly. It can kill because the woman is affirming it all the time by the way she acts towards the man. It is always going to be her way or the highway. She acts sometimes negative and positive all in one, so things can work out perfectly, so it can be her choice. Seeing things from her perspective is different from what a man thinks. Do you hear what I saying listeners? I hope you can understand and visualize what I am saying in a positive matter. Not in her way it is the highway! She is listening, hearing, and discussing opinions, facts, differently from our own open mind and help me to see it in her perspective. She is being stuck in her own ways! Therefore, she knows it all. She is the dictionary and the encyclopedia. I am not putting the woman down. I am being real and upfront. She says she got her wall up for many reasons that a man will not understand. No, you choose to keep it like that God can be that way and will not be bitter and nasty and rude towards no one. God is a jealous God. Also, God has made that person reap what they sow. He does not hold a grudge at them all day. God disciplines them and does it, because he loves them, man or woman and after the person knows this, because they have a mind of their own. To pray to God and be at peace with him and there self and their relationship that they have. So, the woman can make you pay forever! She will argue, complain about the past was something said constantly. She does not know by being foolish and ignorant. Sometimes it is not the man that is bringing her down it is herself and that is a bad habit. She will be so angry where her emotions set in. That is negative and a bad feeling with her past experience's spreads, influence her

thoughts and actions in a bad way. So, this cut off everything of her negative experiences, and it stops her from being successful and say no there is no wrong in me or sin at all. It is the man fault. Anyone can be easily influence by negativity, learn how to stop it and deal with it. Apply this to your life. I did. See I am judging myself ladies! The woman knows that God is the positive man, so if you know that do not treat your man wrong for what he had done years and years ago. The woman knows she is the encyclopedia, she is the mood. Now the woman will tell you quick you are the reflection of her, but when you tell her that her job is taking care of you, there is nothing to be said after. This is one of the reasons the divorces rate is so high. The woman will bring up something from the past, present, so it will never be a future. She can feel impressed with herself. After all, who does not like being wrong and never is. The woman has set it up that she is so much better than the man and play the same game repeatedly, with the egotistical touch. Instead of acknowledging, being honest with herself, her real intent, she is just using her ways and what he did to glorify me, myself and children but forget him. That is what Cleopatra said what Jeffrey talked about too much? When he is hurting many times. Everyone says you understand her! Now it was time I had to prove everything, I stopped! Now rather than the woman seemed to accept the humbleness of your changes and seeing that she is no better than the man, that they are merely a reflection of who you really are. Jeffrey and Cleopatra used to spend enormous amount of time and energy proving who is right and wrong going back and forth with each other instead of trying to build up each other. I stop that I said let us do it her way. I overheard this! Let us do it with her selfish way, let us do it with the 60 percent way! Let us do it her way and her children way, Jeffrey said I am going to do it God's way. It still did not work. It was not God it was Cleopatra who Jeffrey could not never satisfy. This is the woman rule. We would have a good relationship if Jeffrey were not cheating. You are the man and head when she wanted hpm to be. It was Cleopatra's game playing on Jeffrey's intelligence of get back. I have improved my attitude towards her and showed her unconditional love. I gave it to God to handle it. I love her more and more sensitive and open. I dropped my ego for her. It is that Cleopatra let Jeffrey do it all by himself. Jeffrey could not do that; it was too much for only Jeffrey to take it in! Of being the man in control no longer participated with mind games with Cleopatra. Then I had more time for me to see my wrongs, learn from my mistakes be a better man of God not perfect, stop more time to listen, love, share and be loving to a much greater smarter extent, then you have known in a relationship and marriage. I stopped using, inflated or deflated myself to use her. Do you hear me, ladies?

Chapter 2

See all of them games the woman was playing I got from around her because she did not deserve me. What gives women the power to feel there always right. I was ready for loving the woman being with God, open, vulnerable and interested in her! Women stop saying you do not ever need a man ask God to send you right man. God made man and woman. God did not tell you to live alone forever. Every time when I was with the woman in a relationship, sick, constantly nervous, upset, aggravated, because of problems at work or her personal life. Her good times and failures, problems with her children, gaining or losing weight, never satisfied with self. Do you see what I am talking about? Headaches, heart pain, cold, not a happy woman, jammed nerves in her back and ribs, she did not sleep well, falling asleep in the morning and tired very quickly during the day. Our relationship is on a breakup mode already. She is supposedly doing good because she sees me as a negative person in her life. When I see her beauty, I tell her how beautiful she is even with the bags under her eyes and slapping herself on the side of her head Itching, mad, tired, stressed out, when I am act on something, I am either right or wrong, because I cannot never ever get that respect. No more. I messed that up for life, so I never got a chance to correct it. I fell asleep next to her and hugged her shoulders and she pushed me away many times. When I am right she said, it is hard on her to accept the truth. I admit it I know it hard on her. Bringing her flowers, kisses and compliments, surprise her and please her every minute, give her lots of gifts and lived just for her. I spoke in public, only about her. I incorporated everything in her direction. I praised her in front of everyone, even on her job. She blossomed. She felt like dying. I prayed with them for her and water her to bloom backup now. How did my woman lift me up and made me look in public around her family and children? When I did good! Now, don't make her family look bad pulled them to the side, but I'm dirt. I am put in check in front of the mother and children in our house. That is grown and her coworkers like I am a dork. When I go to church on praising God. False prophets have told me not to act out like that in church and I be feeling good for God. They have women screaming, shouting, and hollering. I am not praising the Lord for the women, men, or pastors. I am doing it for God. This is the only one I must prove something to. God says love one another and stop gossiping and talking about one another. I never got nothing good to say that's a lie. God does not say that or treat no one in this way! Cleopatra always said to me, just like Mr. Rickey, Bishop Howard, her mother and her children say, she can tell me what everybody say about me. I had to stop playing games and go along with the flow! Is it okay to disagree on things with a woman, but not all the time! Because it is the man responsibility to make a woman happy just like the saying goes Happy wife happy life. In all she has her mind made up already. Now a real woman does not want no pushover for a man, I agree. It is true in life. Nothing is handed to you on a silver platter. Does a woman know how to keep her man? Does she run after him, not when he is doing wrong, but she will when he is doing right, because of these days and times? Lots of women are saying I do not run behind no man. I have fought every woman I have been with for satisfaction. We all need adversity without it we cease to grow. So, when the man stands up for himself and demand the same kind of love, respect, that a female demand it should not be no problem. Then the past comes up. Until this day I seen one of my partners, because I have been relationship several times and one of women brought up what happened 15 years ago and thought some women will agree and say that is right girlfriend tell him sister. He is not about nothing; now when Jeffrey comes back at her with something that the past like Cleopatra that is an instructor. Ask her for a ride. She said no because I don't want you around my children and what you did. Her daughter is 24 and her son is 17 she can bring up the past, but I cannot. I'm a big-time sinner now. Women do you all understand and feel my pain on that? Where's the sin in that? Are you all going to correct your sisters or you all going to say keep on? We feel you girl. They have been doing this shit for years continue to do it. When you all say I deserve this. God is not doing his job. You women are letting your anger out! You are being the vengeful, angry, animals, wolf, bear, tiger, lion, cougar, and anything that comes to correct. There is no understanding at all. Now all women want a man that they can trust. I know I messed up on that, and I fixed it the women said it was fixed after she forgave me, and it was not fixed. She lied so that's get back after getting the problem solved! One thing that I did go off on no woman wants a boring man. Some of these women know what they want in a man. They want the man to be what they want them to be, like one of my women in the past told me putting me down all that talent going to waste. Why you won't be an artist? I told her because that's not what I want to be. I told her I want to be a model and actor! Then when a lot of women break up in a relationship. They act like they are not lonely and do not answer your calls, but you to talk to them on their time. See, I have learned that a lot of man have hurt a woman and vice versa. Mostly, the woman can have it altogether and be looking for something better, or be all to herself with her children, or just by herself alone. In the end she will be only hurting herself and the person who is trying their best from the changes that they made and corrected. She will be lonely and be with her man lion Poseidon. She will be telling him a lie and swear it is the truth and saying they are satisfied. When they are not. She does not give a shit on how you feel. I have self-confidence now and I'm very happy. I am attracted to myself, and I do not need no one to tell me. See therefore you can't be around angry, bitter woman if she's not happy with herself, or how can she seek for the relationship to grow. Now my backyard was dirty, nasty, filthy, stank and smelly. I cleaned my yard. However, Cleopatra bought the trash off the trash and put it all back in the yard plus some extra trash. Also, in the front yard too. I am a failure forever in the woman eyes not in my eyes or God! If I didn't have God, I would be in a mental ward somewhere, because we drove each other crazy. Let her tell it. I was the only crazy one in this relationship. I was the one blamed for all wrongs in the relationship. Now Cleopatra heard about Jeffrey before she in a relationship with him. I thought going to another woman would make it better. It made it worse. Even though the woman was pushing me away I realized it was same sad song. I had to be happy with myself. She didn't care for me no more, because if she did, she wouldn't have kept throwing the same thing in my face, the same past things in my face. I'm not going to say what the woman said. That's why I don't talk to you because you keep talking and bringing up the same thing. The woman uses that only for men and power to hurt them back, especially men. The women blame men for everything. My woman was spoiled rotten and selfish really calling it temptation. Her way of getting thoughts out my mind and have me focus on something that was not the problem was by her starting an argument with me about everything I did to her and the past. Look at this confusion is something. What Jeffrey do not understand is why Cleopatra would show him with actions and tell Jeffrey her mother said this and that, when it was good or bad for her children and herself if it was right or wrong, but when Jeffrey said baby, your mother said this, she was saying do not tell me what the fuck my mother said she is two-faced you have something against her? So, is that not a curse or a cycle? Cleopatra will use that at to the best of her ability to make herself look good. Get me back to make me feel like shit hurt peoples hurt peoples using the past against them. She thought it was good and happy when it was breaking up our home, the entire relationship was already broken up that does not mean her mother was a bad woman. A woman sees things her way, especially cycles of grandmothers, mothers, aunties that stick together against the man, then say he's trying to break us up with the love we have for one another. How is that when this man tried his best. Love and did what the fathers did not do for their children. That I did so just like I must answer to God as a man. A lot of women say think and feel everything that is going on in the relationship. If they tell God sorry and don't tell their man, it's all right. To a woman have shown contrition and stop blaming everybody, but herself. Jeffrey words was enough, God was not enough to Cleopatra from Jeffrey, gifts, being on time, praying, singing, being the best man walking away, helping, roses, a card, letting things, even cool off and cool down excusing himself and blaming himself correcting Jeffrey was not enough for Cleopatra. The Bible on bitterness holding on to, or showing feelings of intense, a strong rude, nasty animosity, hatred, anger, a resentment or vindictiveness wanting to get back someone. In other words, that describe it on merciless, unforgiving, holding a grudge. Bitterness is also described as feelings resulting from something that is difficult to accept! The woman says I will get even with him! The woman says this, Cleopatra says it in her mind, heart as well. Silence. Okay I forgave him for what he did to me that would not be fair. He does not deserve to be forgiven I am going to carry on a little longer. He will see what he has done to me, and things will happen to him, because God do not like ugly. That's why it's going to continue to happen. Now the bitterness can be also directing when we do not forgive ourselves. Even though God has forgiven us. Now the woman carries on the load until she says in her way and attitude saying to herself. I deserve it, but I am strong enough to take it. I will just carry on this thing and deal with it myself. Self-centered pride latches on to Cleopatra heart. The forgiveness of God, me, herself, and others. Just like when Jeffrey looked at Cleopatra. She said fuck me to me and her children came out her vagina and if they are right or wrong. She is going back them up. She's just going to deal with it with God. She didn't care! She didn't know that it was the curse of the devil using herself, mother, me, daughter and our marriage. She sat back and laughed and never apologized. I had bitterness and anger to once until I got my life right with God. Cleopatra said it took you time right, so now it is going to take Jeffrey some time you got to wait like you had me waiting. God don't say these things, we do out of hate, pain, hurt, and of the world, because God wants us to love each other and others like this. It is unconditional love because bitterness causes bad things to happen. No joy, no love, no peace and always trouble. It also causes diseases that was my fault to! We are also affected spiritually when bitterness is not resolved, and how? By an inability to accept God's love. It causes you to doubt and forget your relationship with God while you still be saying you love God, you are a Christian, lying at the same time, still bitter and have not forgiving at all. A lot. You do not know this when you become angry with others and yourself and bitter, unforgivably you are telling God you are that way to him as well! Jeffrey told this to Cleopatra what God says. It was presented to someone an offering however you must remember your brother or sister has something against you, so you leave your offering. Then you go back to brother and sister and leave your offering. Reconciled with your brother and sister. So, the Lord not only tells us to go to the others when we're bitter or unforgiving, in any sin towards them, but he covers both angles and tells us to those who are bitter or angry towards us. Jeffrey told Cleopatra. This, she told me she can and only have to go to God and you cannot make me forgive you if I do not want to and the pastor said that I can go to God! I did things to myself and doing the same thing as listening to false prophets we all sin. Let's not continue in it. There's also something else, forgive and forget, because how can you forget something negative that's stuck in your mind? The Bible says God remembers our sins no more, so how can God forget something when he is omniscient? You know what my woman said, because you are not God, that's not God's word he said be ye perfect and do not be of the world and do not remember sin. How can God know everything and still love, forgive and forget, but my woman does not and treat me evil here is a fact and the truth? When you forgive and forget, the forgetting means you, like God, he says be just like him. Do not hold that wrongdoing to the offenders account the charges have been dropped that is not easy for women to do. It is worse than the system because they drop your charges when your found not guilty but bring your past back up to hunt you! God forgets all the charges against us and make sure they are closed and dropped. God knows about everything before we make a choice to do so, but he would never bring up again something that was in the past unless we did it again. That's what we are to do to. Leave it right there at the altar because if you don't you will bring curses, spirits, witchcraft, demons and other things along with you that will be following you even in your sleep. Even when you wake up. Cleopatra said that only followed Jeffrey and he would not be a man and just own up to my shit one time. So, what going to counseling was for? Why are we in relationship for? Why are you accepting me back? Why apologizing to me for bringing up the past? Nothing, because she already had in her mind that she wanted to take me back forgive me, be in a relationship with me and her heart, soul and mind was not right! See her as a woman who came back to me, reel off and control in order. A strong woman who fights, anger easily, not in love with me even with everything I have done positive not one thing against her. She did things against me the entire time I was doing good this she said you went back to your old ways laying in the bed next to each other. It could be a whole week straight right in front of her face, so she was not confused and wrong. No, because she's a woman and she need more time. Right women? I'm on your side right or wrong! Did she truly really forgive me? I am a human being, a man. I have friends, myself/man/men/husbands are emotional to creatures that have feelings just as much as women do. I am someone special. She would have forgotten about offenses and never ever brought it up again. Do not dwell on the past and do not let the past dwell on you. When Jeffrey talked to Cleopatra. I was trying to understand her you blame this all on me and you brought the spirits back not me after you as God to bring me back to get married. So, this woman did not know she got something rich back it was God me in her not rich by our careers or money. It was supposed to be for richer or poor's sickness and health to death do us apart. You got what you ask God for her eyes. She did not mess up because I messed up first woman/women/wives. I know it takes time to get over when a man/men/husbands hurt you, but you are not stupid, you know what part you must be I am not blaming him, saying, you could bring a backup, throw it in his face and he have not been nowhere around. Kiss him. He kisses you back, you both romantically hold one another and embrace one another that after the forgiveness later down the road of years to come. You say I got him and now it is payback! When Jeffrey hurt Cleopatra. She said you made it this way! When it first started, I understood hurt was her major problem and she cut everything off from me. She had every right to. She was hurt. She didn't want to hug, touch or caress with me until she got ready to satisfy herself sometimes, she will include me. When she wanted satisfaction. Being angry most of the time. She said I hurt her so many times that she is not going to ever love me again. The way she used to. In her words to me. In her words, only I hurt her so many times that she is cool and coldhearted. I learned from her a lot of things, you can learn a lot from a woman I tried to teach her let her tell it I can teach her nothing and she is right. I cannot teacher nothing if she does not choose to accept! So, she thought, and just damn knew for a fact if she withdraws herself from me. She won't be hurt again. Jeffrey said Cleopatra holding her hand softly let us pray together. God was telling me so. God could heal us both at any time. God could have healed her heart if she would let God. I told her, so she can live again from the heart, and she loved me. She always told me that is not love that do not go for the woman/women/wives they love no matter what their love is courageous! Man/

men/husband are about games most of us are as women say. This is for women that are bitter whether it is the truth they show a lack of at times concern and only care about themselves. It's all about what they put in, they are sensitive and touchy have such feelings. They tend to avoid meeting with you as they at times show a lack of gratitude at times they would usually speak with words and actions of empty flattery or harsh cry do not let me add on their body movement at times you can see it and if you do not catch it you will be pacifically throwed off also. The grudge crutches against you a loan, time they also find it extremely dive to forgive and forget. A woman be the sweetest thing in the world at times in life, then at times in life forget to share or help anybody sometimes end up moody extreme, extremely hot and happy one minute, and the next minute you know they are angry. Bitterness gets worse. It starts a little seed of hurt, but it grows into a dangerous thing. Many people can be heard, persons bitterness or anything, I have learned, try my best to be kind, never give up, say please and thank you. Do my best and have manners, love, all the time, have a great damn heart with big dreams and constantly continue to dream bigger. Leave things better where I found them, keep doing the right thing. Forgive always tell the truth and work hard keeping my promises. Pray be a leader, respect myself and others, always be responsible these other things make me a better man. Now what kind of move. Now what kind of mood the woman is in? She would tell you happy, angry, sad or you got me acting crazy like this. I am crazy in love with you, see how you got me acting about to make me lose my mind. But you can't act crazy or get drove crazy by the woman! To woman/women/wives. He can't act like that. There is no need for you to act in that way you're acting like a five-year-old child. You could tell a woman that vice versa. But will she have received that. Be careful don't get fussed out, curse out, or put in your place! You're just a man with emotional needs, affectionate, cries, and want to be healed. No, she must be satisfied, of it all. She is the focus and only the children. I'm trying to find it in God's word in the holy Bible. I don't see only women feelings only. Some women have picked up the Bible and used it in their own ways of her, bitterness, unhappy and carrying the Bible like a piece of luggage, like one woman or any woman would say do not do that. It reminds Jeffrey of what

Cleopatra did to him or what Jeffrey did in the past but when you said you are hurting the man and it brings up past things on her it is He's hurting from another woman that hurt him. The woman would scream say as a strong woman and with attitude. Do not compare me with no other woman you have been with because she is her own woman she does not need no one to stand up and speak for her for the respect she can stand for herself at times she would tell you out of her mouth. You are not your omen what your own thoughts and thinking she always must do the thinking for you. Most of the time. She knows it all pleads no debate; you will not win with woman/women/wives! She can show you in many types of ways that she knows it all. She will say she don't know it a bit being told most of the time or sometimes I don't think so. A woman can show actions that is rule, smooth, selfish, rude, nice attitude, her way, her vocabulary in her eyes of her mouth and tongue that it goes down just like this, you deal with it or not. Just like my partner. Cleopatra told Jeffrey, so I don't care! You know I see my mother, my aunties, niece's, grandmothers and my sisters say a man is going to be a man, so is a woman going to be a woman. No, you cannot get into my mind, you do not know what I am thinking about you cannot read my mind, you do not know me, you do not know what or how I am feeling, but she damn shows knows the man. Real good. Man/men/husbands/ shit they been doing this for years girl. Now can I ask you all a question woman? What hell you all been doing for years? I got the answer nothing because you are learning everything from the men. So, you did nothing wrong at all! See, the woman knows the man good now. Jeffrey didn't have women and Cleopatra tell Jeffrey you just had bad experiences with women and asked Jeffrey what it was what Jeffrey only did wrong. The woman was never wrong, so when you read this book. What a woman says he crazy, he came to me nothing because is not he could tell him, he got some nerve. The women are stuck in their ways but getting in their way you better stay in your lane and stay out of their way. They even tell me all the woman I have cheated on. I got the nerve to tell someone about women. Also, how I have treated them, and everyone changes everyone takes time to get it right like a mother child or her mother or family brother sisters relative family members love is love is a commandment so I can love if someone hates me. False prophets tell Jonathan these women that you can't make no one love them instead of telling them we want to break this curse, pray and rebuke it in the name of Jesus and leave it at the altar, instead of were going to pray as well, to encourage more men to come to the church. They say they are no men in the church. Don't down men don't down women. God don't like that. I never said that there was, not good women. We can live with you all that we can't live without you all! Where does it say in God's Bible, you can make no one love you or wait on it? No, that is how we make the choice to treat people at from his heart. It's a choice, a man or woman shouldn't abuse it and use it against it towards anyone back and forth I feel a woman scorned. Yes, I do feel a man hurt! I just seen one take their frustration out on their children. It takes time. Yes, it takes time to get over when someone has hurt you badly, just don't use it by getting over on the person. If you know what I mean like my friend back in a day. Lisa, her husband cheated on her with her friend. She was angry at him for many years and left help with the child. They both had together. Now see how she is using that vengeance on him herself and their child, when she can be praying and loving not being sarcastic, she was supposed to have a forgiving attitude saying I forgive him, but I don't want to see him anymore. That's his child and her child. Not my child now is that God's way and commandment? That's her way vice versa on a man to man that do this to. Now bitterness and anger, malice, unforgiveness brings sicknesses to. When a sickness comes on someone, they blame the other person than the other person blames them back then it goes back and forth. No, your body your soul. I got mines right don't blame other people for your wrongs and actions that even goes for me. See carrying on with wearing your body and soul down including the person you are with your soul mate. It's all the man fault everything right? I have seen women say it with wrath, anger, clamor, crying, shouting, screaming and evil speaking and talking about God. God says, be kind to one another not leave the church. They curse your man/men/husband out, then when you get in the house did look straight into his eyes and tell him it was right by you and God, but then you say right in the man face. That's right, I said it what you going to do about it. False prophets tell you that's the devil and be humble be calm to the wife but the woman/women/wives you hurt her, she needs time to heal she's different because she's a woman, they don't teach this more now today and be misleading the people. It's like everyone wants to live, but no one wants to die. People want to go to weddings, but most of all not by standing up for their relationship and keeping them together! I would like to tell false prophets stop misleading women. So, the pain could come out in the way God says. Counseling a marriage is prayer first worshiping God and letting the husband and wife know what to do, that God says do not telling him one thing and telling the wife another that is confusion when really you're turning them both the same thing you're just switching up. So, for Christ's sake you have forgave us and being kind to one another. The false prophets are telling the women right in front of the husband. That's right, he did you wrong. Now he must pay after the woman has forgiving him. How are you going to reap what you sow? After God has forgiven you, and you have forgiven yourself and ask your wife for forgiveness. She has said I forgive you now let us move forth. In the past I have told my partner it is your time to suffer the consequences like a man. No god did not say that. See how fake leaders mislead you. Jesus said you will suffer if you do not forgive your brothers and sisters and God will unto you on forgiving someone truly from the heart and they won't forgive you. Holding onto long-term grudges. If you don't let, go of it where will your relationship go? Now the not so Debbie had a real calling woman will see. I let it go. Godly, damn, and suck her teeth and roll her eyes, will bring it up sometimes change it like getting you back by not making love to you. Getting back to Smitty. She said she doesn't play games, what is that? Everyone has play games during time in their life, not the woman, because she is the mind player, the mind reader, the educator for, she will get back at you by not speaking to you and when you want to have a conversation. She will lie and say nothing is wrong. I just don't feel like talking to you! She would not want to communicate or compensate, but she says you can't make her do nothing she doesn't want to do, but when you do that to her. That is no way to treat a real woman. It is the woman that get more credit than the man. Who wants to be treated like that, she will tell you already that you are grown ass man, do not come the same way at her like you always have to be the bigger and better person, because you, the man or husband? Everything falls on you that will be pressure on the man, don't you think? I understand now it's men that took women do a lot and its men that's been through a lot. Mothers have neglected their sons gave them up, abandoned them, so how does that feel for a man? A man word doesn't count. A woman word does. When women are fed up, no man can't be fed up as well. Respect is to each other and others. Now Cleopatra has brought Jeffrey clothes and she dressed him appropriately, which she always kept Jeffrey together. When I bought her clothes. I don't have it together and I got to give her the money. She gets the money she wants to give it back then when I don't have no money. She's mad. You can't never satisfy the woman. I'm not saying bad things about beautiful women. I'm just speaking out the truth that's been going on facts, not opinions, because I don't want to confuse myself and other people. When I know what I'm talking about. Now the woman is good since the woman will read this, some or most and say I had something bad to say no I'm writing from knowledge, wisdom, love, and my heart, but not at all periods with my private part. Education stands here leadership understanding to. I would like to hear women facts and opinions. Listen and respond. Here it goes. A good woman will allow the man that is in her life to respect his freedom. Still waiting for her and still have a better idea. What look for now. When at times the man betrays her trust. She can't hate him forever. All real woman that I've been speaking to. They have class, some women move past petty foolishness can work together that are not jealous because they're better than that. See some jealousy and protectiveness is natural in relationships. It is important the woman and man understand. Both partners are secure enough in themselves and with each other to know where to focus their energy. The good woman has love and respect for her man or husband. Fair is fair. Not a woman way or man! The good woman has an attraction to a man who want things to last forever. We all know is not going to be perfect, but do not use that to keep getting into disputes, arguments, back and forth. It only stirs fire to the flames and then break up, because you get tired, you both get that not only the woman! How long will you stay in a committed relationship with someone that told you, forgive them and keep bringing it up. What they have done wrong. If you could trust them, or believe what they ever say again to make it work, how can you construct a solid lasting foundation with them? You can't! That's why you played yourself because you didn't keep your word as well as your promise. A promise is your word, and you couldn't keep it to the ones that does this. Now to my woman I was always being compassionate, supportive, and encouraging towards my woman because it is the biggest part of building a successful relationship. Cleopatra says Jeffrey do not have it. I'm nothing, and I don't know how to do that and never will. Now nobody wants a person who is a downer all the time and will not support them in their endeavors or in their time of needs, struggles and trying hard. Two teammates can work together they can create wonders that are so magnificent. See Cleopatra. The woman got my name tattooed on her neck and I got her name tattooed on mines, but she was so smart on everything else and could not see that just was done on one thing that she also had in her mind that she wanted out of our marriage. I even got inventive in my search and wrote down my rights, wrongs, goals to keep my relationship intact. My woman looked at that as it was not enough, that is not good enough and you took me through too much, so did this woman waste my time? When I did good in her eyes, no, I didn't, because I still was the same shit I was when I was doing bad. How can you take the bad and put it with the good? What you're going to get out of that. She doesn't see what you put in is what you get out. Help me grow. I helped her grow. You can't never satisfy the woman. A woman has matured and a vision always for our future. Jeffrey even sat down with Cleopatra. What is it you want? She said nothing. She's good. I knew the love was gone. She stopped calling me baby. When she starts saying nasty things. I just like calling you Jeffrey was wrong with that. With that attitude, not sincerely! I'm being intellectually challenging and having the ability to hold real loving discussions about important topics about how to keep her happy, constantly. I even learn that a woman improve herself every day, not to be perfect on certain things she improves herself on certain things. She is not perfect on everything she does. She will improve, but not be perfect. My woman was determined in our relationship that everything every chance she gave me was determined by her as though she was not at fault on nothing period and that I was at the mercy of change giving as though I was never in a position to determine how many chances I have gave her, she is saying. I don't have a right or chance fairly as well as her. That goes to show how unbalanced and selfish – he was controlling me in the relationship, and I did control her first plenty of times then stopped. Now she never understood me, listen or heard me out. I never saw any woman as a price tag. It was about the dignity and about me carry myself to show respect to my woman. It doesn't matter what car she was driving. How much money she was making where she lived what she was wearing. I was looking at the woman respecting herself closed legs. Now women. What do you say about this man? It goes both ways. I put effort into everything I did. I paid for breakfast, lunch and dinner for her and the children. Women that's reading this, will say why did you bring that up? Because I'm a proud stepfather patting myself on the back and proud of myself and happy for myself that I did something good! Women are proud of themselves being mothers, right? So, I can be proud or happy of what I tried my best at? Women don't want the romance to wear off, don't never let it go because if you do, it will be boring, empty, invisible, shady, uncomfortable, and no love will be there. Now a woman continues to do what she knows attracted her man in all the time even if she been with him for years. It will show she cares about keeping him around. When Jeffrey satisfied Cleopatra. It wasn't enough. It was never enough because when I got that right. Something else came up, did something else wrong, when I fixed the wrong to right than the right became wrong, the right is wrong, and she still will be a beautiful strong black woman. The woman feels like they are rejecting they don't see the wrong they do when the man tells them at times, and they reject the man. No one deserves that. Black men and women were in slavery but at times a woman can't see when she to be slaving the man and holding him accountable on stand as he has a background, so he can't work for her at all. No more, because of his record don't that sound and seems just like the system. She holds her wrongs and don't accept no man telling her she's wrong your psychological things, especially mind being full of contradictions and don't want to admit to her wrongs until she's ready to. The man is wrong for his wrongs and wrong for the woman's wrongs. See, I can admit I'm wrong yes, I am and there's no excuse!

Now you tell the woman she's wrong knows you better not you got another thing coming, everything comes up from the past. Now a woman knows this she raised her children right and tell a man, he did not he's no man, so don't teach her son nothing but she can't teach him how to be a man that was my job, daughter or children not nothing that she can't teach them. She got this. She could give her children love so God gave Jeffrey love to give to them as well, Education we both taught them everything mostly and all Cleopatra wanted all the credit for. So, women you can learn something. Now a woman is a queen on her throne who have mastered herself, she is not perfect but with her ways and attitude sense of humor she has! She is complete she comes to full realization that everything she needs to fulfill her mission can be found within. She's uncovered her powers and she know how to use them. did you hear what I said, and you feel where this man is coming from? Oh yes, I know this man is very intelligent. She is no longer on the path, she has come the path, you can't never satisfy her, because two Queens can't be in one castle, two bosses can't be in one house. My mother and grandmother love one another but couldn't stay in one house together. They had to get their points across together and only point they got was out the door. Cleopatra and her mother Pam were just alike and tell Jeffrey I do not know what I am talking about but got him down packed. It's one woman going to sit on her throne as she going to get what she wants. Therefore, Cleopatra's mother would be in the couple's business, because what they have been through and experience. Now the Queen that's the woman on the throne can't be satisfied, because she always wants more and more and never, she will be happy, but never satisfied. Then the woman will always look for ways to make things better. Never will take her suggestions as complaints or criticisms, but only her desire to make the relationship or situation the best it can be. Now when I grew up and became a man was it good. No. Out of disrespect and no love it was too late! Now when the woman calls you where you at? I'm out to the store, you are lying. Everything is a lie. She is all about the truth, honesty and trust always only in the relationship. The unsatisfied is always right and sometimes confused on what mood she's in, misinformed, rude, stubborn, unchangeable, senseless, but never ever wrong! The woman is quick to misunderstand

and always have something on their mind, but they quickly misunderstood their man or lover. Having sex or making love. She doesn't like quickies only if she going to work or something. Then when you not doing quickies it turns it to you doing it too long, you are hurting me my stomach, the woman is so smart than the man. She will do research better than the government and FBI. You can give her what she asks for, need and want it will be never enough. She even uses her imagination to blame men for everything she asks for a good hard dick or fuck. It hurt to hard you got her sore, stop baby and sometimes you will get fussed out. Damn you trying to rip me open. My damn stomach killing me, demanding and never satisfied. Now she will get her organism and be satisfied then next time one wants it not enough, woman make up your mind, do you know what you want? She will also be proud, but never satisfied. The woman also feels confident and loved because they know their man still wants them. Then it changes up. Questioned start baby do you love me? Am I gaining too much weight? I'm I too skinny? How do I look? Does my hairdo look good? And sometimes I will get this answer, you are lying in a good way for real! Your being honest! Serious baby! You sure? Come on? Please satisfy yourself and man or husband. Stop complaining. You did not complain when you watch the Time of Our Lives, Here My Children, Our Life to Live, and other soap operas when you watch them. Don't be like that forebear lady on. A woman once told me don't carry all that luggage forever. Anger, rape, unforgiveness, hurt, pride, guilt, no love, fear and she still a bag lady on all the purses I bought for her and was not satisfied on the free one's, so if this woman said you going to hurt yourself carrying all of them bags like that. She is the main one needs to stop and the abuse bag that's easier said than done. She got some nerve! Still complaining about my ex-girlfriends, complaining about everything and come with demands. You're pushing your man away. It could be patience, love, support, reliability, devotion, it is never enough for them. In it is frequently in every way there is in making them happy. it is only impossible, but should never be attempted, because a 'woman told me you are trying too much and too hard. An older lady slows down and when I did the woman said, why you stop? What's wrong with you? you are acting different. you have change, who you been around? Who have you been talking to? What women been around You? Then if you tell her something, she taught you that you both agree on it is I do not know what the hell I told you that, oh lord you right whatever, let it go. Women like to believe and like you to believe that they can get along perfectly with or without a plan, but the truth is they cannot. Everything must be organized, arranged, expected, and planned, and this I just the beginning of their quirkiness. Overtake their pads and make up in their bags everywhere they go that's a lady. She is beautiful you just can't never satisfy her. Its bad things ridiculous women can do in the relationship, but when you fart in the bed its nasty, when she farts in the bed it is okay, so what then the man does not like an unexplained outburst of emotions woman as well as meaningless fights irrational in general. When they get overly jealous over as superficial men but force each other to lie about it to keep men off the trail of the truth. Now you have some women use their period as an excuse to be an absolute Mrs. Bitch excuse me of my French well should I say in a woman term. Then tell the man with mixed signals. He's stupid as hell did come back to him and ask him baby do you love me let's make love or tell him I love you baby, and the woman strongly plays the victim while becoming viciously manipulative. Now she will say you have problems expressing your feeling Chief, Capt., Major Lieut., Sgt. and Corporal. My woman was chasing me when I heard nasty and screwed her over, I admitted to it. I rejected her off what I've been through in the past. Then I started being there, that she rejected me. So, she feels like because she did cheat on me with a man it's different. How is that? Because it's her way. Take it or leave it. You can't satisfy her. Is that not getting even with you and making you pay extra like you're on her payroll and she feels like she could cast you out anytime. Then women will say the opposite of how they feel and expect us to know for a fact, then when something is wrong, and you ask them about it. Then they say, I'm fine! Communication is extremely important. So, if something is wrong, talk about it. Then when you tell them they're beautiful. You must get question about it. They are good women with bad habits they have long conversations without mothers, fathers and family members sometimes friends. The reason why the women bring up the past because there holding it in the relationships are not good with blaming, jumping from topic to topic, avoiding, sarcastically remaining silent, name-calling, manipulating, threatening, lying, secrets, denying, controlling, false accusing, running away and being selfish with you or the other party is wrong. Bringing up the past is the most part of their toxic arguing repertoire! Then it comes a part weatherman is afraid or scared to ask his woman/women/wives or girlfriends anything because he's not certain of knowing that everything he said or did from the past will be held against him. Even today, right women? The woman other needs are to feel and be safe. By nature, is it the women security seeking creatures? Bringing up the past is the way to control and be safe. They know if they keep that in their mind, member past hurts and betrayals because they're not working it out on being positive. They are putting a curse and being cautious more and more aware that something is going to happen again. Then the man is always filling attack and deserved it forever, she will say that's not true, but actions will come out differently. See cycles goes on and on like Cleopatra told her mother do not talk to your husband like that you are hurting him mom now. When her daughter gets married look at how she talks to her husband any kind of way by seeing what the mother does being raised up and living in the same house together. Women loves to make emotional statements, passionate, connection and love when she focused on the past. Every time she looked at the past, she looks at the man and see a dead-beat no-good pig in the graveyard. Sequencer always feels unheard and invalidated no matter how much you try she's going to hold up her wall. There is no love no more vice versa, as I hope they can't take that there is no love. That's not romantic! That's being rough and hard right women? Her insecurity dies even more. Then the man, because been there. The feelings and no heat with a crazy woman like to argue to get her point across to get back at the enemy that you have become to her, so he withdraws and hold back more. She does not make the situation any better, because she's pushing him away as well. It also makes you feel crazy. I took a breath and step back and did not try to listen to the of the woman of her emotion that she's expressing, because I respected that the woman feels heard and loved. See the woman is always the smart one in the relationship. Now correct me if I am wrong, to the educated women, if you are constantly bringing up the past or thinking about it, especially after the issue was resolved then forgiveness was not expressed, case in point a lack of mutual trust and I left out respect in the relationship. Now a woman would say don't throw up in her face. What you have done for her or her children, but she can because a woman that can do that, because she is a mother. Where it says that the devil says that! I have been through this, and it hurts to have past mistakes constantly thrown in my face. The woman doesn't want you throwing nothing in her face or bring up the past. If there is one thing I refused to deal with is a woman throwing guilt things against me, and they are so smart that there is nothing positive or productive to be gained from remaining in a toxic relationship of a woman that cannot let go and let God. They tell the men. As a man I'm responsible for every woman that I've hurt it in the past. There is no fighting fairly with the woman. This of agreement with her. Emotions are real. If you ignore someone emotions you will not be worth being in a relationship with them, so how can false prophets tell women about the men acting like a woman. When they express their emotions. Now Jeffrey has the woman ever felt the men need of emotional safety net, not Cleopatra, absence of drama, nagging, and so on. And if a woman makes an emotional statement which comes something in the past or not comes in the form of an attack, because she feels hurt, angry, bitter, and unforgiving and insecure. Then that's her problem. She must find a way to deal with her insecurities in emotional outburst, not anybody else! Women love to bring up the past, because she's flexing her muscles, she lives up, your good. Then she knocks you down and brings up exceptions. Using guilt as weapon it is a way to punish someone in its a reason to stay there for you to be afraid. Now Cleopatra has said to Jeffrey you hurt me it does not matter to me; she demands that what hurt you did to her. Never could compare to what she has done back to me. Is that not evil? No, not in her eyes and in other women eyes, because she's blind to see what anyone is saying. Now when you satisfy her, and you were a liar. Still all once after you have been giving. That was. She says I'm forgiving you sweetheart. I'm going to change this time for real, I promise, I'm not going to hurt you again, torture you, and put you down anymore, but then women will say remember isn't this what you didn't her, so she is just paying you back for what you done to her, she made a promise to meter that it's said and done before the man does anything wrong right back and do it again. So that was a lie because on word of her tongue. She said she was going to stop everything, admitted it was wrong and sin. So that was a lie, and she used him and played with him and cheated, because she lied! I was a liar. Once and that is not good, because if you lie, rob, steel, cheat, abuse, mentally, physically, and come in all kinds of ways abusing people. Cleopatra never sat down with Jeffrey and really discuss the resentment she did to him, she told Jeffrey that the past and you still bring that up about my daughter, Jeffrey, my mother and Jeffrey said you never listen or understood or heard him out. She cursed me out by her cursing me out. That is what she was doing in the relationship. I admitted sincerely from my heart. She did it when she got ready to let it go in a nasty way after we broke up and I got a divorce. There was no more king, she said that's all you talk about, but she told and talked her pain out used it abused it, and then I said that's the past, I forgive her for God myself and her. I treated my woman like the Princess and the Queen! Now what she tells her man he is trying to separate her from her children. When the man loved her, stood on the corners innocent sweating taken bullets getting shot, robbed, beating and saving her son life more than one time. So how is it I don't love her children because the woman is confused and angry! When I cheated it was all about control and I stopped. Cleopatra cheated back holding a loyal man hostage and make Jeffrey suffer of unforgiveness to gain power for the pain. I took her through then started going back and forth! The woman feels like well were going to be angry forever, and says it's not like that, you don't know what the hell you are talking about. When the whole time she's getting even. Women families have taught them. Blood is thicker than water. A man come and go. We going to remain here until death comes while he's gone. So, with all their sins, fighting, arguing, fussing, blaming, one another drama and so forth. How is that different from a marriage? That's a relationship. That's a family as well. Going through rights and wrongs? The new generations and false prophets have changed it. God remains the same, and his word is just us acting in that way. I see us because I have sinned to. I'm not perfect. Family is not only about blood is about God first love. If the people in your life who want, you in theirs. The ones who accept you for who you are sinning, rights, wrongs. The ones who do anything by any means necessary by only God to see you smile and who love you no matter what. I know this lady. Once she had a son who was killed, sold dope, robbed, beat people up and I loved her son, but she did not discipline him only during certain times. I am a son or with any other woman I cannot be loved in that same way, because they have been taught and raised by family that is biological only. We can go through it. It's okay to be the other people they different. If that's your husband or boyfriend is different, you don't need him. He's a sinner and a liar and no good he doesn't work at all. You and I'm a son of a mother as well. As then vice a versa. Now the woman will say I forgive you. Then interrupt you when you're trying to explain the truth from your heart. Then speak to you and accuse right there in your face, have not did nothing and will not give without sparing your feelings, be so angry. Will not this person will be praying without ceasing. Upset will not asking you a question without arguing. Will not share, because she will be pretending off the past. You can't satisfy her because she will enjoy then have something to complain about. Forgive you with punishing you. And make a promise and won't forget no more one on the run. Now the woman has eyes, and you can't ignore as well as beauty. If Cleopatra she would have seen what a mess Jeffrey was, how moody he can be, and how hard he was to handle. She still didn't want me. If she loved me, so why I loved her always like this. I even spoiled my woman and treated her like a queen. She was happy, but never satisfied it's never too late for the woman but the man it is. You're a coward, your everything, but the child of God it's too late, so if a woman says you right. I have been hard on you. Well, to everyone in this world we live in. Our love it's a commandment. If they don't look back. I will pray for them and forgive them and leave them, it's in God's hands. I will pray for them and encouraging not to give up and keep on pushing them. It is never too late to mature; we all can heal from what's been holding us back. Free yourself it's time to grow in places we are afraid to grow now the part of a relationship is about missing someone is that you never really know if they're missing you just as much, but the woman pretends like she does not miss the man and be coldhearted and show off need towards him. I know I became a man. When Jeffrey got saved in Cleopatra the woman was so blind that she could not see and knows it all. She knew I was saying before we got into the relationship, because a man gives his life to God automatically sees his woman as woman with vision, because even though my woman was angry with me as being the bigger and better person, her love, faith and support, perspective challenged me every day. Sometimes all day long. I was not great? I am A man that told my woman to and allow her to push me, to pray with me and investing me. Now! When Jeffrey asked Cleopatra the woman sweetheart. Do you think and feel like I messed up your life, she said yes? After we were in a relationship and she said it with anger, vengeance and wrath I knew in my heart, soul and spirit with God that it's better or for worse, richer or poorer, so she said you asked me and I told you the truth, you shouldn't ask me that if you didn't want to know the answer. Then you shouldn't have asked me that you bought it on yourself, with a deadly tone, putting a curse on her relationship, saying that so then she said, I'm an instructor, my mother and my sister both have cars. Everyone has a car and money, but I'm broke and dealing with you. Now if God says, for richer or for poor if had nothing She still supposed to be in love and help one another. Lift each other up when we both fall because we are together. So, right then and there. That's why we got into relationship know I was with her because God said to and love her as Christ loved the church. I held my head up high when my woman or no one was there and tell me I wasn't nothing I deserve to be treated right. I am with something special, not just the woman. Like today, with women wearing cancer shirts for themselves and children. I'm a cancer survivor, my father died of cancer. My grandfather, and 14 of my uncles a lot of men die from cancer. But the system is hiding it, I'm a testimony. Jeffrey loves himself he was fully and totally committed to Cleopatra needs (THE WOMAN)! She may not feel that way for unforgiveness and bitterness that was in the back of her mind as she was watching and looking at it was already in her head as the same way for woman/women/wives I messed up bad. I replied! I asked for forgiveness from God. He forgave me. I asked for forgiveness for myself. Jeffrey forgave himself when Jeffrey went to Cleopatra to ask her to forgive him, she said yes, she forgives Jeffrey,

but lied so as women say today you got to know and feel where she's coming from. She's a woman. She needs more time to get over her hurt and in God eye's she just hurting herself! Now when a man greedy, selfish, bossy, controlling, cheating, lying, be over everything, very mean, nasty, overly demanding, distracted, abusive and it don't take all these things to hurt a woman/women/wife not saying all these things have happened, but it could only be one of these things any woman will break down. I agree, but when these things happened to man/men/husbands the women get off easy saying I'm sorry. Does he deserve this until she's ready to say when she so or I say so! That messes up both parties' dreams, goals, and future, however God see's us as one. Within our hearts as any relationship that we both pray and say we don't hurt each other again. We are all not perfect, but we try to be we can be. I was wrong and apologized. Cleopatra apologized to Jeffrey and started right back again, then so many women say you done wrong Jeffrey got apologies and fussed out! I hope and pray one day woman/women/wives could walk up to the man and say I have been abusing you with words, criticizing you, putting you down, insecure, bold and bitter, not listen and hearing you, not respecting you, and most of all blaming you for everything in our relationship/marriage, please stop for real not just say it, do it. Then something comes in your mind, or you feel in a certain way, blind and the devil has trick you and you feel as you know for sure he is doing something wrong and it is you and you feel no certain kind of way that will not push him away, a lot of women will say he or you were already like that as a man every sense you dogged and cheated on me. Women do you know when you do not pray with and for your husbands/men/man and all you do is call them dogs and curse them out and he is trying his best not to go out. You know I see human beings have a lot of animals and have insurance on them to some of the pets every now and then turn on them a lot of risk they live for them the owner treats their animal wrong what happens? That let you know right now respect Is due to animals. You know, God send prophets, or it could be anyone to say let go and let God. You know us as people's, we hold things in our hearts! Beware of women who don't take responsibility for their bad behaviors. Did Cleopatra (THE WOMAN) treat Jeffrey like a king when he deserved it when Jeffrey gave my life to God like David and his son Solomon? No! When you're in love. There is no sex there is making love that's not the first thing it's about in your marriage it's about God first, Women try to use certain powerful words out or in the Bible as well. If your wife Is not a believer In God, and the husband is still a believer In God and pray for her and him and his job is still not to leave her. Now if your husband Is not a believer In God and the wife is still a believer In God then she one another. Don't look down on your husband because he sinned and continues to pray for her husband but don't use this as a tool to leave or towards you thought you was different and holy than him calling him out of all kinds of names but the child of God and still telling him you love him, saying he's the devil he don't have god in him because if he did he wouldn't have cheated on me he can go burn in hell all I care. A woman loves to make love with and to her husband. She doesn't want a two-minute man because she could pick up fast and quick when she's not getting her love. Same as man woman. A woman will fuss you out quick. She must be satisfied and when she does it's a change up because of her hormones and her nature she's a woman! If you give her an hour of love, she wants more you give her more she's sore. She wants to stop this then start right back, Depending the woman she is and the mood her ways will still not be known. She is good and bad complaints being in love. WATCH OUT NOW she's smooth, she will catch you off guard and you will fall for it, and you will say what, YOU CRAZY! Then change telling you. Hurry up screaming slapping you or scratching your back she says, She's love. It was good and it feels good, and it felt good, because you have her mind gone. You can do it to and so good too much and she screams saying baby you wore me out that's enough putting her to sleep then at times when you both wake up when the man comes with love she says no her stomach is in pain. Then when she gets up, she says I want some more. Then you say baby, I'm tired and remarks comes out like this. Oh, what's the matter you can't hang no more! The woman you sex or making love as a weapon sometimes, I'm telling you how relationships are sometimes you can never satisfy the woman! She loves to play mind games. The big mind game is making you wait one out of a million and one ways! Leave you with another chance to text or call and calling you back-to-back then ignore you. Then, come right back and talk to you. The biggest mistake women make that kills a man's attraction and one reason he pulls away, not praying with him or talking with him asking him is everything okay! Being sweet with words, communication, and body language that will help and make him listen and feel more attracted, and don't do things that push him away. Say things to him. That's inspiring and romantic. The subtle energy shifts you can't do today that will draw you to him, how to raise your self-esteem and feel so much better about yourself, so he will want to get closer and closer to you. Don't use the wrong words and actions, so you can always keep him attracted. Share everything with him and you both. You are partners. Anything of what they did in the relationship, and sat back and thought, No! All the things are his fault. Spending hours thinking of him and you together and stay your thinking of yourself and what the wrong only to you. Cleopatra (THE WOMAN), but then Jeffrey change before she let up and walked out. Women grant your man his wish and hope are not all and only about yours! Just like on a good day! Jeffrey's woman Cleopatra never thought from her heart. After forgiving me why he's acting the way he's acting? Because it was all about her and her children. I was not a part of their family. Now a whole bunch of women will get on me stand up and say do you blame her for how you are treating her and what you've taken her through, no, I don't. I'm looking at what she said of forgiving me and moving forward like she said. I let the boss make the arrangement. Now some women are different, they will say you don't let nobody make the arrangement for you, your crazy! A lot a woman feels like they don't bring the trauma and drama on how they make men feel, oh yes, drive them crazy and run them away. They express their feelings at times. And most of the time express them in a way that is judging critically and then the man feels blamed, concerned, boxed in and pushed away by not showing him love. How to share and embracing him in the right way at certain times. The women have several demands it's called. Get back or get him back. The man needs his woman company, touch, affection, and you will feel compelled to open his heart, act, and get it, Now I have this question's women asked us, does arguing and getting back makes anything better? Does that make a relationship forward a woman who has good sense and educated now can Cleopatra (THE WOMAN) think back to when we first met, no, it is too late for that. I can't tell her what to think or when to. We will focus on strengthening and building one another. It made us both extremely attractive to one another more. So, what happened to the woman who attracted me, in the first place? I messed it up, me, myself. Did Cleopatra ever think with effort and say to herself, Hmmm, I'm going to find ways to bring Jeffrey closer? No! Getting her man back, No! Surprising ways to help bring him closer? Nonomino! She maybe thought she have of looking at my flaws, wrongs, and sins, but not her actions towards me! Trying to inspire me? No. Did she tell me she felt and create more intimacy? No. Now Back to lovemaking now the woman would say I like it on my back. Then when you do that to satisfy her. She wants something different. She is just like lovemaking in different positions, different change and different motions please do not take this the wrong way is not all about the sex it is saying a woman is like light switch. She turns off and on! See, she is more to she wants to turn you over then get on top, then pound, bounce, jump up and down, side to side forwards and backwards, circling motion around and around good, and satisfying being she wants it from the back. Then when she's sore she wants to stop and rest, that depends on the on the woman because some women can be sore and still want more, get more and take it all and some with extra when she does stops, it's time to change it up again, then when you want to change it sometimes it's a problem, but it's felt so good pain! I have been in several relationships with different women that hurt so good it's hard, I even heard them say feel so good pain. They had me confused. I do not be trying to figure them out or put them down. I be saying seeing what action is that you hello can't satisfy them. They want more and more! Jeffrey got into an argument with Cleopatra (THE WOMAN). About that telling me you got lazy and worn out you can't hang no more. This is a real statement from my heart. I was not worn out from the making love, I was worn out from the bitterness, vengeance, demanding, hatefulness, and get back that Cleopatra was coming at Jeffrey with that was wearing my body out and down. There was not enough strength in me to make love. I was stressed and feeling low. Can you woman/women/wives understand and feel what I'm coming from and a man's point of view, what you will have been. We can't go through it as well as men? I don't have anything against women. I love you all! I'm telling you my everyone has one to tell and I wouldn't call it a lie because we all have been there in way. Then when Jeffrey did make love to Cleopatra because she decided to let me back in again. She said baby I'm sweating you trying to kill me from the back, damn. I said, laughing at her from the back. No, no, get your ass up then slap her on her on the ass real hard and you said I couldn't hang any more, I said get up, get up and she be worn out not wanting it. When she says stop baby ok please it feels good. Then when we stop, she you put it down good. Then have her finger in her mouth falling asleep and saying stop picking at me that's not funny baby. I say you the one said I could not put it down no more. When she gets up to go to the bathroom, I slap her on the ass, and I say come on its morning time it's time to get some more. She looks at me and say you make me sick you got my stomach, thighs and back hurting, Then I say but you just told me you like to be fucked see, you can't never satisfy a woman. When she sits on the toilet to use the bathroom, she says baby you got me sore and my vagina hurting then she says come here she slowly kisses me, and I kiss her in her happy lovely way romantically. Then it's I make her so sick, but she doesn't know she hurt me sometimes and don't care and will say that's not true then why in the hell she says it? (I DON'T CARE) and women that's not all on men that we made you all this way on all your wrong and actions of sins! Then she will give me a soft kiss and not giving me one changing when she gets ready and still tell me baby, I love now women is that love? Even making love together and put it all on me like always. It's the men fault right ladies. It's just like spending money in a good way you never get tired, the woman is never satisfied, then when I kiss her while she's on the toilet she says shit I want some more and I say but you just said no but then she says I know what I said, Lets go I want some more penis, don't do it too hard. Women make up your mind. Then when we get back into the room and lay on the bed, I lay on top of her then I go slow she throws it back slow then I go faster she go's faster. I go harder she throws it back harder, then she says it's good it's good then I say it's good and she says you putting it down and I say loud I thought you didn't want any more you just had to feel this hard penis again, she says give me some more I want more you like looking at this ass when I change the position? I say you know I do, Then after we finish then she lay on the bed and want to get her vagina sucked, licked and with my mouth close on her clitoris with my tongue wiggling on it and after she has cum so many times then I say baby your vagina is swollen and sore then she say, I know what I said, Shut up and suck your clitoris and slap my head I then laugh and shake my head she's going to drive me crazy, because she don't know how she want it, I'm giving it to good and giving it to much. I'm not doing it enough, it's not enough or she's not in the mood or is! There are times when me and her are not in the mood. She's never satisfied. My woman tells me it's something I'm not doing right then change it and say you doing a great job then changes again and say back one she said first, see how a woman change? Is all woman like this every one that has been hurt can't let go of the past, which is a true reality and can be a deadly trap and we all know it takes time to get over, but it lasts for decades of not forgiving. In the Bible it does say forgive and forget false prophets and taught to forgive but not forget. God didn't say that the people have said that, because I didn't know in Jesus' time when they forgave one another and that was it! That's why today they called it the new world order they trying to give orders over God and all they can do is try I know God gives us orders to follow and give his orders not our own not man or woman. He gave his commandments not men or women orders. Now why is it that the woman gets angry and say all we good for is sex that's all you want to do. As soon as you stop that then it's another problem! The other problem is just lying there and not doing nothing. You're not putting it down no more. They still complain they best friends that are women know everything then they will say I don't have no friends. We'll they are telling their pastor, mother, son, daughter, friends, another man or hole family something, because women love to talk yes, a real woman know when to speak and when not to speak, but when they do. It comes out, then women say they don't cheat and if they did it's because all men started them to, they been doing it for years. If no one can make a man cheat like women, then the pastor says for the women then it goes both ways. If the woman is cheating. She's cheating on her on. Then why women sleep with married men or sleep with

men that have a woman, because that woman is not thinking about that man or woman, she's thinking only about herself just like Bathsheba she's being selfish. 1.) She's being for self, 2.) She's all about her getting what she can get out of it to fulfill all her needs, but it can't because she thinks she's happy when she's not! The big deal that was a lost was she used what she had to get what she wants. If it's God knowledge and wisdom to get whatever a woman wants. A woman is said known, action to be smarter than a man on game now everyone has common sense. The woman is smarter and professional than the man. Everyone is made different! Some women pluck hairs from there chin, shave their legs and pluck hairs from their nose. Another thing they do is check and smell his private parts that is only if that man has been cheating or a health condition, the man clothes, the pillow, blankets, sheets and checks his phone depending on the woman and relationship because a woman can be doing slimy secret things, be guilty and blaming it on the man/men/husbands at times. The woman wants to read the man mind, but just like woman and women have told me you can't read her mind, you don't know what's going on, but could tell you what a man is from A to Z, from the top to the bottom, inside out. Then you will have the Christian, or any religion woman say I don't do that the devil is a liar, now you do somethings or a lot because you're not perfect even Mary and Martha weren't satisfied, because Jesus let Nazareth die to see how strong they faith was! Now you go the first date with a woman. The man will know if he is with a lady or not and take things slow! Then when you keep going out having fun, and she wants to get laid not all the time depending on the woman then after that night she keeps calling or texting you vice versa it had to be something I did, or you did right! A real lady it might take up to 2 or 3 months if I'm wrong depending on if she's still holding on to her past relationships. She was last in, or something holding her back that she's keeping to herself she's a virtuous Godly woman that's it's only her and God leading her or she's bitter to holding it in that herself can take care of everything and no one or nothing can help or stop her from making up her mind! She is feared and scared of respect to move into a new relationship the wonderful secret I know is that the woman must work on herself/me getting me right before she does anything. Jeffrey wishes Cleopatra would of did that with her heart and everything before she got back with him! A lot of women do this!! Some women like shaving themselves some women do not, but when it is clean you are going downtown at times yes you are, some women let their hair grow hairy on their vagina, very few, because a lady keeps herself clean have to keep panty liners, tampons, pads, extra lotions, body oils, perfume, spray, all kinds of etc. to keep herself up, don't forget her makeup, lip stick, lip gloss, nail polish and extra panties! Don't never ask a woman about her weight or age, but she can ask how something looks on her for an opinion in the mirror she can only say and think to herself in her mind as a woman because their certain things you can't just know that's personal! It will be a problem if you ask the wrong question about her, Think first! When she asks you what you think baby and you tell her you're lying sometimes or get her daughter opinion or someone else when I took my woman to buy shoes not on everything! If I picked different shoes especially the black heels I picked out for cleopatra at times she didn't go with my say so by asking me what I think or should she get this then when I say yes it's hmmm then why she ask me several, several of times that's a woman can't be satisfied. A lot of women told me and off my own experiences you can satisfy a woman, but then they said money, shoes, clothes, cars, God, sex, love, children be well taking care of on time. Then I ask them when you do get everything are you satisfied? Then they said they want more! They want everything then when they are relaxed and want to themselves, they still love when they men come right back. Then it's something else! Women love to keep secrets. I must tell you that there are some secrets women keep from the men. I will admit men do it to women do it the best. They don't say what they mean they mean what they say can change that or this at any time both ways never satisfied. They are possessive with the ability what they want. A woman's heart is deeper than an ocean of secrets. They save memories from things we won't even imagine a woman can't stand to suffer or pay certain consequences that she knows she can be dead wrong for and can get out of it with a sense of humor with a blink of an eye! Just say I forgive you that's it. Even when most women don't even admit it. This does not mean they will not be in love with the person they are with. They still will show their love giving it from there heart with action, let you know what you did to make them smile and be happy especially the little things that count. They just remind us how good it is to feel loved in the right places and all those details that are still a part of our past have helped us as men become the wonderful person we are today. I give them credit, but men do their part to of inspiring them with happiness, connection of feelings, romance and protection. Men or women didn't teach me everything come on now! A scorn woman that tells you that she forgave you and it's been years ago and still holding on can be a bitch. Not as sleeping on you or opening her legs. If she does do that to the ones that do they know what they are and who they are about just like no good men that are ho's, Women with anger, frustration, malice, short tempered, nasty ways, bad attitude and yes she can be a bitch! Now I give women their props. A real woman can handle her own not having pride saying she doesn't need no one help at all she adjusts and gets the job done still you just can't never satisfy her. Now if a woman wants to forgive you vice versa. She will invest in her man, learn from him, see him win, support his vision and be in lov e with him daily. What Jeffrey cannot understand is how Cleopatra let her daughter Anita disrespect him in our house and say why you still getting on her? Then she kept disrespecting Jeffrey, Cleopatra will stand back and don't do anything. When her daughter Anita was wrong because they were friends, she was afraid of her daughter that she will lose her, and she was 24 years old. Real women get there and make their own money and a real man does to. When they get together and involved, they share what each other has. A lot of women say the man supposed to only take care of the woman and everything, where do it say that, because when Jeffrey was in a relationship Cleopatra brought him clothes, shoes and watches so does that mean Jeffrey was a sorry man, because she brought Jeffrey something or give him money sometimes not all the time. It is women who bring their children from the other relationships and do not see that big, huge responsibility falls on that stepfather/ man/men/husbands that is seriously on him as well! Blended families can be incredible after all it can be challenging for the man, but the woman does not see that in the same way. However, there is one person that does which is God! The woman can see her and her children. The devil torments people by reminding about the past, and don't want the person to remember why the relationship ended that's just on the men wrong and actions right women? The person does not want to deal with the feelings and always run-away period. Then the devil is perverting or poisoning their memories because they are making a choice to let him or whatever the spirit is regardless of what happen, and only thing the woman focus on is the bad things and looks only at that man! Cleopatra (THE WOMAN) focus on the bad things bringing it into our marriage. It happened early too. The emotional scars from the past and angry, arrogant, dispositions! Do you all know that unforgiveness can be an invisible umbilical cord but comes with hard core rage of actions that connects us right back to our past sins that opens even more spirits back which we repented for our own selves before we even meet someone. It is that unforgiveness feeds more bitterness to the women than it does to men. This do not sever the cord for the sake of the relationship and do not want to learn to take captive of the painful past thoughts from the past I feel you women on the present! Men to with God's help! A lot of women do not want to take steps towards forgiving those who have hurt them, it can be healthy letting old feelings go. People wonder why they be sick. Most women need to forgive and thank God for the good in their past and ask you to help you forgive the bad in your past so, you can determine to live in the present and not sarcastically, with love and sincerely from the heart just like Jesus.

Chapter 3

Now Jeffrey asked himself why he keep living and loving Cleopatra (THE WOMAN). Clearly when she did forgive him or love him in the same way. One of the serious problems were that as much as he knows that he can't force her to love him. He couldn't force himself to stop loving her and she will always say that she couldn't forget what he did to her in their relationship she tells Jeffery over and over that she can't change that fact that he did her wrong when they were together. It will only be one thing straight to the point suck it up and be a man you did it all. In the woman eyes and God's with her only she can see but as you are being the man your blind! I know it is more than just this to it ladies when the more for that man is going to come in? Some women love to go to bed feeling upset. God does not want us to lay our heads down at night or at any time with us going to sleep upset while the other party is laying right next to you feeling unloved and unwanted. Now a of woman will say you cannot read their mind or tell them what they are thinking or what they are talking about to you or no one, do not judge them do not care what you say, but Cleopatra (THE WOMAN) knows what Jeffrey been going through. She knows when I am right or wrong. My blood pressure up or down when I am happy when a mad, sad, judges me talk about me to her mom, points the finger at me, blames only me, etc. but she did not do one thing wrong. What is in my heart for her and her children. I walked a good path being my own person not being what someone else wanted me to be for her. Her opinion or fact for me was only hers, it was not even shared. It did not matter at times that I hurt that is why I was the better man to the woman. I could not satisfy her! When a relationship is ordained by God. You do not have to force it to work, but the other person must relate to God also! A woman does not want to switch up the positions depending on only what it is or her. When she is about to have an orgasm and please her man this is what I do, I always keep the toilet seat up after you use the bathroom. Keep it clean and smelling good for you woman. Another thing I learned good about women is they never roll their eyes in the same way, it is based on what the feeling what they are thinking about what they are sayings, emotions and I like to use the word attitude actions mean a lot just stay quiet and watch her when the woman sits back she observed off my experiences and my learning. I had to stop talking and listen, watch and stare she is a wonderful homework assignment! Now it was times when Jeffrey was with women and Jeffrey was in a relationship with Cleopatra (THE WOMAN), when he asked to make love to touch or rub her. She would say no. Then I would okay I will do it myself, then when I start to jack off because she would not give me any love then she will say, come on baby. See is that not mind games women? Some women or most that's right girl, make him pay for what he did let him go without for a while. Give it to him when you are good and ready. After how he treated you, do not give it to him all at one time. It is other things right women? Now, when Cleopatra wanted some loving now. It was clear as day. What came out, I was you sleeping with somebody you been around that other woman I know, and you know how she made me feel the other night looking at me straight in my eyes, knowing she slept by me. Now she will not stop talking shit now she wants love all back over again. And she is not confused it is all about her feelings and not mines. I am acting like a big ass baby or a little child, then it is a dispute of her throwing it in your face. I do not make love like I use to no more. Then she changes quick, come on now baby, I am sorry! Now she can fall asleep on you, but you cannot fall asleep on her. You are going to get fuss out quick, especially while she is talking to you right or wrong. Then she walked away from you when she really did not mean it and wanted to stay, she just trying to prove her point. When she says do not think or be negative at all, but she could sit back and say he going to cheat, lie, and do it again because I know him. He always going to be no good, so are you not going to get what you ask for? Yes or no, please answer this! Or all the women going to say that is not true. Every woman is not like that. Now when a man finds a wife, he finds a good thing. So how can the woman blame the man for everything. I even mean for her sins as well. As I have done my research and read my word. The words of the King Lemuel, the prophecy that his mother taught him. What my son? The son of my womb? And what, the son of my vows. Give not thy strength

unto women, nor thy ways to that destroyed King's. It is not for kings, Lemuel it is not for kings to get drunk. Not at all. Lest they drink, and forget the law, and pervert the judgment of any of the afflicted. Give strong drink unto him that is ready to perish, and wine unto him that is ready to perish, and wine unto those that be of heavy hearts. Let him drink and forget his poverty and remember his misery no more. Open thy mouth for the dumb in the cause of all such as appointed to destruction. Open thy mouth judge righteously, and plead the cause of the poor and needy, who can find a virtuous woman? Humbly love your husband humbly love your wife. You must love your wife as Christ loved the church for her price is far above rubies she picks up where her husband cannot she is his backbone and the husband pick up what the wife cant's and it shall not be throwback to each other face. The heart of her husband does safety and protection trusting in her, she also trusts in him, God is love. He tells them both to stay not to go because love, but a woman that fear is God and God does not hate or evil love does not hate marriages. It always loves good and right. She is in love with his love, he is in love with her love, so that he shall have no need of spoil. She will do him good and not evil all the days of her life. She seeks wool, flax and work willingly with her hands. She is like their merchants, ships, she brings her food from afar. She rises also, while it is yet night, and give meat to her household, and a portion to her maidens. She considers a field and buy it. With the fruit of her hands, she plants a vineyard. Everything the wife would do would be for Christ. She girdeth her lions with strength and strengthen in her arms. She perceives that her merchandise is good, her candle goes not out by night. She lay her hands to the spindle, and her hands hold the distaff. She strengthened out her hand to the poor; yea, she reaches forth her hands to the needy. She is not of the snow for her household, for all her household or clothed with Scarlet. She makes herself coverings of tapestry. Her clothing is silk and purple and smooth as love of the clouds in the sky in heaven. Her husband is known in the gates. When he sits among the elders of the land. She makes fine linen and sells it; and delivered girdles unto the merchant. Strength and honour are her clothing; and she shouted, rejoice in time to come. Wisdom: and in her tongue is the law of kindness. She looketh well to the ways of her household, and eateth not the bread of idleness. Her children arise up, and call her blessed; her husband also, and he praises her. Many daughters have done virtuously, but thou excellent them all. Favour is deceitful, and beauty is vain: but a woman that fears the Lord shall be praised. Give her of the fruit of her hands; and her own works praise her in the gates. This wife would be in love with Jesus Christ. that is how I know Jesus would send me this wife because she will not waste her time looking for love in the wrong places. It is not the women I want this is the woman God will send to me! I could not never satisfy her! It is okay to love something and someone, but do not be no fool. Now women still say this, only go for them. Men are human beings to because what person does not care for someone that is sick. Cleopatra (THE WOMAN) told Jeffrey it was not her concern no more to see about his health, because she is not my wife no more! God already has your life laid out how he wants it to be, but don't say you're a Christian and don't do and treat someone any kind of way and still say 'you are one that's not right on God eyes, because he says so. You know I am a man I tried my best. The woman I tried my best to satisfy I still love her children when I told them I love them I showed it with action. I was not perfect I do not say it with habit or to make a conversation. I said it, because they meant the best thing that ever happened to me, and I shared my love with them as a family they did not show it back! Love your enemies, do good to those who hate you, bless those who curse you, pray for those who mistreat you and I see a lot of women get on men for what they done and their wrongs and tell the men about God, Cleopatra used her children to hurt Jeffrey and continue to hurt him while Jeffrey keep doing good and walking away and believe God is okay with her actions, and Jeffrey tell this to the women who don't want to forgive life is to short, so wake up in the morning with regrets, so love the people who treat you right, forgive the men and women. We believe everything happens for a reason. If you get a chance take it if it changes your life let it. No one said it is going to be easy, sometimes women do not understand that their actions and words will offend men, and plan to do it out of so much malice, bitter, hate, anger, unforgiveness and to perceive things with malice. Now when you do right or wrong, just because she is the woman is she is amazing with the love about her

knowing all her man flaws, failures and faults and yet they chose to love us anyway. But they say as women we do not love and like them as they love and like us, that's not true, because God's gift of love is for everyone. I am going to be man Jeffrey made some bad decisions, paid a price for everyone and still paying for them until this day from Cleopatra, that is still does not mean I am wrong. This is for women who have not let go in their heart. Now these decisions women have made they know what they are doing, quickly they would say do not tell them what to do, they got this under control or its I know you are not telling me nothing and you can get your own self right and your act together. So forever until she feels like it right you will just be a crew up that cannot tell her nothing, but little do she know she was so smart to where she made choice to take you back, and mad a promise to God, to you and herself that she will make it work. What man having been through this with a woman let go of the past and move on by your side. Instead, she is putting you down, holding you down and broke a covenant with God to love you with forgiveness. Together forever, the perfect relationship is one made up of two imperfect people who are held together by a perfect savior. THAT'S JESUS, when Jesus was in Jeffrey and Cleopatra (THE WOMAN) had the devil in her and Jeffrey will walk away every time after Jeffrey gave my life to God and calm down. Those curses came upon her children and our relationship, and it still would be my fault. You cannot satisfy the women I done sat down and stood up with humble discussions, because I had to learn and see that arguments were sin and evil. The arguments were to find out who was right or wrong. We had to decide as to what right and come to some type of agreement. When Jeffrey tried to find out what was right and the problem from Cleopatra she would say I am not going to argue with you, talking with her while she is angry, nasty, screaming, even nice calmly with an attitude. About 30 minutes later she will say I am not going to argue with you, but just did. I had love with my whole entire heart, because when I fell back, I had gone back and learn from my mistakes. The reason why I did was to love in the right way and know what love is. Now love is God and when 2 people touch souls, spirits, honesty and trust helping one another with mutual respect. Love means also that differences can be worked out. A true relationship is when you can tell each other anything no secrets, no lies and I did this when I was given my second chance. Now women please give your men certain things the streets cannot give him, and that's positivity, respect and a peace of mind! Do not say okay I am let you have this, no give it to him, because you know women it is not right to be angry forever to your husband/man/men and become more spiteful, jealous. You drive the man crazy and makes his life a living hell and use the children she has had from other man towards you, by hurting you more and more making your life compromise and stay consistent, so that of you will be comfortable and a lasting healthy relationship with the children. A real mother will get along with you for the sake of the children and both of you. Jeffrey had to learn on his own that ships do not sink because of the water around the ships sink and get in them. Do not let what is happening around you get inside you weight you down stay up. You know I was not Cleopatra or her family choice, but I can honestly say I am a great choice by God and so are they. Cleopatra (THE WOMAN) said Jeffrey did not have no money, so she was doing everything on all her own, she could have done better if she would have never got back with him Jeffrey slowed her life down. She could have had a car and she was important, but I was not. I never pretend to be someone I am not, because I am good at being me. Now the things I have done in the past that people have not forgiven me for I forgave them, and I ask God for forgiveness for the sins I have done to them. That is why I am proud of who I am today! I may not be perfect, but I do not need to be. The woman did not take me as I am now, she lost me. I have loved her and shown a true sign of growth in my life. Now I have cross paths with people who have hurt me, and I am still nice to them. Now women do not give them their all that is a lie, because they have transformed their energy into one another and its real, even on bad times. They are both surrounded with love and Inter feelings, inter reacting with God, love, praying, trust, downfalls and pouring feelings within yourselves back and forth of eye drop of a tear. The pores from your skin, sweat, goosebumps, and chills rise. Know that the man is surround by his worth, his rights and wrongs, he has spiritually insight in him as well do not leave him empty handed! You would not want him to leave you empty hand with your rights and wrongs and spiritually, would you?

Women let the world make them hard and life they let pain make them hate and bitterness steal their sweetness not all only just on men. Women listen, forgive them even if they are not sorry and showing no action, because holding on to anger only hurts you more, not them well that depends on if both are still together! Now women are beautiful you are beautiful you a girl the blooms like a rose and not a badge of shame, very glorious it is so beautiful that all you women are masterpieces created by God from man. To the women I say surround yourself with people that makes you to be better and move on with your life with God first, I am talking about after you have gotten your life right and start back loving yourself and God's way not your (CHILD PLEASE) way. I want to tell the women that I love you will, because yesterday is gone today is almost over and tomorrow is never promise. Women was given special gifts from God the 4 gifts that God gave you females was more and more, but I am going to let you know what the 4 gifts are. 1.) A key for every problem! 2.) A light for every shadow! 3.) A plan for every tomorrow! 4.) A joy for every sorrow! A man will put in work for a woman he genuinely wants. Now when the man wants the woman to listen and hear him, she is right no matter what! Now see then you some women stand back, disrespect they man and then let their children disrespect stepfathers that raise them while they are always saying the mother is doing a perfect job whether mother and children is right or wrong. The mother with her children stands their and lead as a family pack and jump into stirring variety of problems non-biological parenting. Then saying she a good damn mother for all her trials and tribulation of her hard work she put in raising her children, and do not know somewhere down the line she made mistakes raising them wrong in some ways not meaning she does not love them and cannot see this in some ways for a man! This is a relationship between a stepparent and stepchildren the mother and father Cleopatra (THE WOMAN) backing it up. Like Cleopatra (THE WOMAN) and lots of other women that are not satisfy come into relationships with emotional damages and curses, because when things go wrong, they do not know how to fix it they pull off other spirits from there up bringing in the past. Things like wives not forgiving their husbands talking in a disrespectful way, mothers and fathers only being there, treating each other any kind way.

This outburst of communication and do not want to trust the man ever again saying it cannot and will never be the way it uses to be, because you cheated on me, ever again! It will and can get deep decisions related to the step or biological children and they confused putting in their head some of what in your head that to you done broke up everything and no good. At times, the woman is doing it and she cannot ever be wrong, because they stick together right or wrong, because me, my brothers, sisters and mother did it with other men. My mother was in relationships with different men good or bad times it was only about her and her children. We thought it was a fun, happy, sad, disappointing, hurtful, helping mommy pick at the man thing, but as I got older, I learned and realized our mom created some of the problems she was not a saint woman. See it be a lot of women that say they do not care, and it just do not only be for what someone or the man took them through it be their nasty ways as well. A lot of women put the same curses on their sons and daughters like their family members done them and down to their relationship, and do not know it with debates, fights with words, arguments back and forth, you cannot tell your mother not to talk to your significant others like that, now that your raised up telling your man friend nasty things and talking to him any kind of way, where do you think this comes from? Only him and his action from sinning because he is a no-good son of bitch! Now women will tell men about their cycle, but women do not have one, until they speak to talk about their past life story when their good and ready nice, but their angry they do not have no cycle, so when women get angry they do not have no cycles? Tell a man quick since I brought up your cycles now you want to bring up mines. She was raised up proper, nice, perfect well educated or, not right? Then they say to men what the devil spirit has taught them and has accepted from him like Eve did from the serpent, (SAYING) he does not love my children like I do. These are bad attitudes of troubles that are petty, unnecessary and say screw you all that got something bad to say about me or my children and all you did was tell them the truth they just could not handle it. Some women say I will just deal with God, because you might not be my husband/man forever, but my children will be my children for the rest of my life, and it comes down to a choice and chose my children. That is a dangerous mistake to make in a marriage, because God says its him, husband, wife and children not children first. God had a law for relationships if cheating that they are committing a major sin. God says the two shall become one! Not one-point-three or one-point eight, but ONE. The only two people can be one is if both husband and wife surrender everything in the relationship to the Lord. That means mind, soul, body, spirit, home, finances, assets, pray, decisions-making, and children. Withholding anyone of these things refusing to give it up, BECOMES an IDOL! It threatens the entire relationship. Then the woman says he cannot, or I know he is not telling no one about God. How he is no god and sinned and treated me how he is no good and never will be the man he used to be, but me and my children is going okay with the Lord. He is the sinner, and he is going back to another woman again. He is going to keep lying and doing the same old things that the knows how to do best. I am a Christian and a great woman of God, because I am blessed and I have the holy spirit in me and I do not care what no one says I do not care, because I know I am right! Now false prophets will tell husbands what spirits that have on them in front of the wives, and we need to rebuke them off eight now in Jesus' name. A man of God does not supposed to act like that. You are the head of the household you suppose to love your wife as Christ love the church. When she brings evil spirits, anger, hate, pain, demon spirits, if she has even a good spirit at times no one can tell her right from wrong depending on the woman she is. She is God's gift their no wrong or no sin in her or her children. Without pray you cannot make her change, because just remember a woman will forgive, but she will not forget, because remember when you were like that, so now after her forgiveness she is telling you your reaping Certain women say God is not telling him that, but God is saying that about me, no demons or evil spirits never used her or came upon her. what sowing in so many ways actions come to and just imagine as women say just think about what you took her through. That is a tit for tat not forgiving! Coming together and waring it out 50/50 or praying for each other to break the curse and combine as one. Now she confused and coming at her husband more. God says relationship involves trust, but the main fact is what work and faith are you both putting in, not the man only. When you marry somebody, it is imperative that they become Co-workers of God, yourselves and children along with you if you did not trust yourself and children with the man you married then should not have married him. You were holding him up from moving on with his life. Did the false prophets tell you that or your mother? It could be co-workers, friends, women in church, family or things that is still stick in the mind. God wants us to have the agape love for one another that he has for us. This is the same way the woman, man and children really everyone supposes to have! Love is by choice and commandment it is the greatest gift of all. It means doing what God will do regardless emotional or circumstances. Now women are saying men are too emotionally today, so what are you telling God when they say that about their husbands! Love is God fair and equal. In the relationship the biological or non-biological parent supposed to still feel right to that child or children, because God says so there is no favoritism. The false prophets have lied and did not tell the truth of God's word sing that if it is not in order honoring thy mother and thy father. Spare the rod spoil the child otherwise these that are evil will drive wedge between a husband and wife and bring witchcraft and curses. When Jeffrey became a man of God, Jeffrey parented the children with Cleopatra together. Jeffrey follows Gods law, possession and did trust God operating as a team together it is just that Cleopatra (THE WOMAN) was not on Jeffrey team this is not to say every woman is like this a woman cannot be satisfied. Then will walk up to her daughter after I walk away and hear her tell her daughter what I told you about talking to him like that and disrespecting him. That is why it kept going on, because she never handles the situation right then and there. She felt like she had the right to keep disrespecting me and walk up to me and say you saying something against my children? See women these are the principles of respecting your man this is not control this what a man wants. She was getting on her not in front of me, but away. Cleopatra wonders why her mother is locked up in the room watching TV all day every day. It was not all the mother fault or the Stepfather but look what her daughter is going through a cycle! A real woman cannot even change a man, because his bad action she loves him a man must change himself, because he loves her! Well, a woman once told me that (BABY YOU CHANGED) I been hard on you I am sorry, and before something comes or anything aggravates her, she is back to the same shit the past. Tell me quick you're the same old person. In a relationship I told the woman it was women out there trying to talk to me. Do not tell a woman everything she would say do not ever lie to her I agree to that, but there are certain things you cannot tell or show woman. Jeffrey knew it was men who looked at Cleopatra and tried to talk to her when we were doing good or bad. A lot of people do not understand that is when the loyalty comes in stronger, because you would be tempted. You know how I know I changed, because the woman that divorced me that was not satisfied, and selfish push me to my limit. I knew because I pushed some of them as well. Jeffrey thanked God and himself for learning about himself, Cleopatra never did. I never have time to hate anyone and never will, because I will love to do it. If I intervene in something God does not like, and I made a big change. I wanted more than anything to be accepted by God. I stopped feeling down and out. Jeffrey stopped living in the past only reason he talked about it, because the disrespect of the actions and words Cleopatra (THE WOMAN) used towards him. Jeffrey stops feeling like he was failure Cleopatra (THE WOMAN) told Jeffrey right in front of her daughter and son that he always was a fuck up! I stop thinking that nobody did not want me, because Jesus loves me and stop thinking that I could not do anything right! I learned to love a woman with God, not with my private part like God loves everyone. You know women that do this when your husband /man/men /boyfriend has done something wrong do not look at him forever and fall asleep with him every night or look at him in the morning and always say, think, bring something up. Where you at? With your ex-girlfriend? Or your ex-wife? Or with your friends with women? Or listening to your ex-girlfriend? Or with your baby mother? Or asking women for money? Or sleeping with else or someone new? Or a roommate? Or fooling with her or with someone? She still calling you. You calling her? You do not know what is going on? Man, what is going on? Fiancé? Some ladies who like you. What the hell you done into or did wrong? I am giving you a warning. Do you want to talk to me? Are you at her house now? Are you going woman? You going to be a bitch? What are you thinking about? She does not even have to nothing a question mark can be in her mind that do not mean she not going ask something else. Tell me one time did she say let us pray, come here so I can tell you I love you, let me hold you, I miss you. Let us make peace I am by your side! Amen, that after all you have been going through you are going to quit, just like that. No way you going to fight like crazy until you break through! You would not give up on God, your children, your mother, brothers, sisters and your family, so God also says do not give up on your marriage! Jeffrey cared about Cleopatra, soul, mind, spirit and body, because he would pray with her and today not caring what women say stop saying out your mouth to your husbands/man/men just because you read the Bible, that don't mean your living by it anyone can read the Bible, but don't be a doer of the word, because the spirit comes in all shapes and forms of life stop saying this if you don't have anything good to say shut up. Pray! Women being evil these days with her saying just because saying let us pray that do not mean you living by God. You cannot no one pray if they do not want to but use this as tool against anyone for being mad at yourself or what someone done to you or getting back at them. Now if you keep saying, but/but keep holding feelings inside that is hurtful you can bring that towards yourself and other people. If woman wants to pray or not, she got God watching over her. I remain her soulmate crying out for her soul. Lord knows plenty of people cried out for mine. When Jeffrey met Cleopatra or when any man meets a real woman, Jeffrey saw a woman with a beautiful mind that was good for a lifetime and still will say a good thing about her today instead of talking about her bad. I mean this from the bottom of my heart. We both missed something good, we both are lifted not only her he does not know where some women get that from! I know Cleopatra is a good damn woman. She was hard to get I could not run game on her now this how you know she was too good to be true. This goes for women to the worst mistake you can make is walk away from the man who stood there waiting for you. Never leave loyalty that do not take you seriously when you had done right or wrong and make mistakes and want you to take them seriously no matter what. Jeffrey knew he was a good friend Cleopatra. I am kind and still doing my absolute best that I can be, I am not perfect! I have told a lot of women I am not ashamed what I have been through, because God use my story everyday it is his

glory to give to me to tell others, men have told me their stories as well. So why will Cleopatra (THE WOMAN) will hate for Jeffrey? You know you do not have tell no one you hate them, and you can say out your own mouth that you do not hate them. Women can show their actions expressing how they feel about you with behavior aggressively angry and body language gestures with their eye contact. They would feel and know only thing brought this about and made her the woman/women/wives she is not confessing to her wrongs as well as man confessing his wrongs! I found out cheating on a woman was not being the man they expected me to be it was not easy, a lot of things in life are not easy, but me learning from my mistakes made me the better man I am today. So, God put me into a challenge being faithful. I see women that are lonely, angry, and feeling despair and forget that God hears every pray they keep saying, but their mouth, heart and with switching sides of attitudes that change. I love you women that is going through it when all things fail in the relationship with hopes and faith you get back up and try again. I will do it for you sisters. Men/brothers I love you as well. Women lift your men! Can women regret their wrongs and resolve the issue? Or just always be right all the time. It is true your husband is not saved if he cheats on you there is no excuse. When you sin towards your husband and he does not cheat, and you talk to him any kind of way is that being saved? So, after you have taking him back and forgave after so many brought it back up threw it in his face are you saved? We all know there are all kinds of sins. Women are your sins different than you are man/men/husband? Men are your sins different than you are woman/women/wives? So, both sides cannot judge each other only God does that, so no one cannot say who is right or wrong on either side. Let us love one another for love is of God. We love him because he first loved us. I do admit a no-good man can cheat with a bunch of women but will lose his mind I know them spirits are serious, because I been their done that. If a woman does the same thing it will go for her to. One thing I do know mostly I got to give credit for a man cannot take like a woman can of being cheated on. Women and men separate common sense from bullshit and bull shit from common sense and its according to how we think. Women, please explain to me why you cannot never forgive a man sincerely? When will you as woman ever trust a man again? It tells me you cannot be satisfied on accepting the man apology and began to heal the scar on your heart. If God can forgive us for men and women sins when will you forgive? However, she lies and says she does. Women I know and you do as well a real man will take care of home. Instead of ripping and running trying to impress the streets. When did I give all you credit with hope, faith, and the women that love the Lord? Now women men are human beings to. What do you give them credit for, nothing I did not get my second chance, but a woman deserves that? We all mess up, can I get a kiss forever, be nice, friendship. I want to be cuddle and an apology and I need love to! I need. Most women be unselfish, and she said I do not need no man and be with one the whole time! A woman wants a stable man and she need to be stable herself. All a man really want is good woman by his side. Men have just as hard of a time trying to find a good woman as woman has tried to find a good man. A good woman is comprised of much than being a woman, who keeps a clean house and put a hot meal on the table for her man. Many women say they want a good man, but have you asked yourself, if you are a good woman, nice, sweet, not with an attitude, and understanding, encouraging, supportive, and motives. Now a good woman is not quiet with no input. She is full ideas to help improve your business, outlook in life and overall health. She supports her man ideas and motives him to accomplish his goals. A good woman is a good listener. Ultimately, she can change you without trying. A good woman makes you a better man. She keeps him honest-a man is not allowed to lazy when he is in a relationship with a good woman. When you put a man down while he is good than what, so you expect from him? You are not respecting him. So, if you do not respect him do you expect respect in return? Cleopatra did not encourage Jeffrey when he made an honest living Jeffrey was proud of. She did not know how to talk to me to tell me things being down on me and did cater to me in loving feminine way. She used to provide me with mental stimulation. She did not see potential in me anymore, and stop treating like she used to, the most capable and deserving man in the world. I did not even exist in front of her anymore, because I can tell by looks in eyes the way she was staring at me. I even begged to stop treating me like she was treating me. Anything is possible, when I did mess up and

she forgive me as she say she did then she changes and started being insecure with herself and me, jealous over other women. She was quick to put me down and the other woman who she kept bring up who moved on with their life, just because she thinks the woman looks good and provide competition to her own looks. No man wants an insecure woman who is always messing up his business deals, because she thinks he is flirting with or having sexual relations with women he is in business with. Women often look for stability in a man. What they do not know is that their characteristics as a woman that cause the man to become stable. Most relationships are temporary, you know they will expire any second, minute, hour, day, week, month or year. If God is not involved it take three to make it work not one. False teachers have lies, we all have lied. It takes three 1.) God! 2.) The Husband! 3.) The Wife! If the wife is forgiving, she makes and pushes the man to build a future with her. The good woman will encourage the man to think of his goals, plans, and make sure they are in alignment with what you both want out of life. A good woman does not require that you buy her expensive gifts in order to obtain, or maintain her affection, and to be a caretaker for her children. It is not all about money with her, it is all about you and the heart you have for one another. The two special people you are together. You know, never tell some you forgive them and do not be mean with your heart. Especially women they will say why is you bringing up the past let the past stay in the past. Cleopatra said you make me sick, aggravated, and cannot stand you! Now when it is for her she needs and wants all the time in the world, even after she forgives you. Then you can break up and get back together and uses you with that. Then you say I am woman I am different you have understood a ˙woman needs more time than a man does. So, when man does everything to win your trust back its takes two to get the love back after forgiveness. So as not giving the love back as the woman you do not become a liar and set back the man, because he has moved on with God while you are tearing down the home God and he has built up more for you. Then why did you give your husband/man another chance? Just know you must go back to God for another chance! That is not for a get back. That is saying love thy self as thy neighbor do unto others as you want them to do unto you. It just does not take the negative saying, the guilty man person he caught guilty and convicted it takes God and both parties! You brutally beat the man up constantly and in your mind, it keeps going on. He cannot never ever get away with it or nothing, so how did you expect both of you to move on? Now I am a man, I going to put myself in the woman shoes if she were to cheat on me, I could not handle it. Yes, I am putting myself in her shoes, so I will not tell I forgave her then bring it back up in her face. I know my spirit, my mind, myself, and my heart would not be right or honest, so I would not set back the relationship and not be blessed! Now the women are not putting up with your behavior and it is not acceptable, but when it is the man, so what! You are getting him back and it will be all and only his fault! Cleopatra and Jeffrey made up it was not a kiss up or make love, or lovey dovey, because I broke her heart. It was a meeting to decide if it was worth saving our relationship to give it one more chance with marriage counseling. Cleopatra and Jeffrey were with the pastor, his wife and other couples in the circle and Jeffrey heart got broken back for breaking hers and Jeffrey admit as a man he reaps what he sows, what goes around comes around and karma is a bitch this was before she forgave. God paid me back good she did to then she did things to me after God did his job, she was so angry and bitter she tried to take God's place and over did it and did not think she did. It was not even a start to see God and each other again. It was just her, her children and only about what my no-good ass did. The old past relationship was not dead, she was in a graveyard digging up more skeleton bones, so how could we build up one another? She even fights for it she kept feeling insecure and angry did not receive the pay checks I brought in from working, 1.) of the reason was it was not enough, 2.) pride 3.) she did not need me anymore or want anything from me. Came to me when she was calm then ask when she got ready to. To women, if you are ready to forgive or prepared to change you ae already a setback yourself holding back your life and that dangerous, and bitterness and be in anger and pain for years. Cleopatra was taught things in marriage, as well Jeffrey. It has its ups and downs and struggles. She told me I was evil and because of me we broke up, so since I was breaking and trying to find a job she did not want no broke ass man. Tell me she never lived like this, and she could have had a better life then being with my

no-good broke ass. So, women if I slowed her down she did not marry me for better or worse, richer or poorer, sickness and health until death do us a part. After for forgiving me she got married for the wrong reasons, because her heart was not right and time heals all wounds, but if you do not help yourself you will not help the relationship your wounds will not heal it comes with in self first. Jeffrey improved and showed Cleopatra he was not a cheater anymore. Still, she made an excuse of saying you cannot make me talk to you, so what, I do not care anymore! So, did she sincerely forgive me? No! Did I deserve what happen to me after I was forgiven repeatedly after 6 years! With God, pastors, family members and others even begging her children I took care of to talk to her. That is not enough love women? No, because you cannot satisfy a woman. I am ready to hear it ladies, how many times I cheated? No! Are you honest with yourself and her? Did you go to church? Were you seriously in love with her? Are you still lying? All men say the same shit. YOU WANT YOUR CAKE AND EAT IT TO! No men and you do not know what you want? Now she is coming something like this, child please I am not tolerating you, you do not have no business or anyone about no damn love. You do not love your own self, and you not God. How much bills have you paid? Did you treat her like a woman? Did you put up with her children? Did you try to separate her from children? Did you take care of her and her needs? Did you cheat on her after you got back together? Did you really love her? Did you beat on her again? Is it something you did to keep her this way? You the one that made her like this? There is no forgiveness all men the same? How many chances she gave you? You do not deserve no chance once a cheater always a cheater. Child stop running game. You are a liar? Sad stories? You do not have a job? What led to this? It is all kinds of questions. I was a keeper not a player! I never treated her as a booty call. I gain experience from women and with them, but a lot of them be hardcore as they have not learned anything from a man who is on T.V. or a millionaire or has high education you can learn something every day. A lot of people say you cannot compare with a woman's love that is not true; love is agape. Now amazingly simple, women are saying Ladies: THIS IS A GOOD MAN and men are saying MEN: THIS IS A GOOD WOMAN. What they both supposed to do? Looking at what

God says do and wants God and his will, and it goes like this. GOD'S WILL! God will be to love each other; its commandment loves your wife as Christ love the church and wives be submissive and love your husband. God will be acceptable God watch you while you watch one another and the children as a family not separated. God will be kind to all needs. God will you both pray apart and come back to always pray together, the devil will try to come in to destroy and tempt you both, but he will not. God will bless you both financially not say ever who makes the most money, better or worse, richer or poorer, sickness or health until death do us part. God will be that you do not lie to one another or cheat on each other, because its God commandment and no committing adultery, because it a commandment. God will be watching how you appreciate one another, and each other intelligence. God will be you looking at both of you to be proud of one another. God will watch how the wife build husband and others up and do not tear each other down. God will never disrespect one another. If you do its prayer and forgiveness with love actions. God will be if you do not have him involved in this first both of you together you both will be played with! You know I stop trying hard to search for love, because in the end at the right time love will found me in God's way. You know when a relationship is ordained by God, you do not have to force it to work. See some women say they want a Godly man soon as the fire comes some want to back away, run, hide, get angry let God make a man out of him, before you try to make a husband out of him then when he does become a man of God he get took through the hell of what the man took her through that's not fair after forgiveness that's curses, diseases, get back, hell, stress now the women can tell all the men that, but want accept it back, because you can't make them or want them to do they don't what they don't want to. Excuses is a sin in Romans: Jeffrey is satisfying Cleopatra the best way he could, because she deserved it, Jeffrey called her my sweetie, baby, love, sweetheart gave her hugs and kisses and prayers and meant it. I did it to not never let go, but she already had let go lying to God, me, herself and others going on with her rules of the devil words instead of God. Like women say once he does it one time he will do it again God doesn't say that or believe in that (THAT" S THE WOMAN WAY OR THE HIGHWAY). All

these talk shows, man, woman, book writers, putting in their heads that if you hurt her you cannot earn her trust back anymore it will never go back to the way it used to be see that is negative already women stop doing that for God! I stop cheating when she was crying about the struggles, her mother, her children, me, her job, bills, problem, pain. I cared and held her, sometimes I said I told you are being selfish she told me you do not have to tell me nothing already I know that I would be the best communicator, listener and teacher when she was first. Some women and false prophets are saying karma is coming back on you now after she forgave you. However, the woman says you deserve what happens to you. Jeffrey was never scared to be feared by my family, friends, or anyone to have Cleopatra in the spotlight, why not? She is my everything! I let her know every day how much I really loved her. But she still was not satisfied! It was the finances to pay the bills because she would cry instead of going to God! Now when are women going to say how fair he is, I need a good man! Now some women will say she is perfect in God eyes. She is special. She is better, but when the man says this. She says child please. You need to sit down some where no one not listening to you. You cannot tell nobody nothing. I cannot read a woman mind, but they swear on a Bible they can read ours and know us front or back, top or bottom, but you do not know shit about her she says with an attitude and be back in love with you the next second, minutes, hour, days, weeks, months, years, you on her time. It is set for the relationship to fail, but in this world for failure, we live in it today. It is all on the man, I even did this. She does not deserve me I am no good she needs to stop thinking about me, I was begging and thinking about her I hated myself, I wanted to suffer. I stop thinking about me and thought about her what she was doing and where she was at. Now did she say the same thing about me when she put me down after forgiving me and God's way No! You have other people, women, and society saying be with a woman if she is fickle and unfair, but not to be with any man that treat you wrong you do not deserve that girlfriend! You deserve better, but a lot of them are saying he deserve it. Men been doing this shit for years. Jeffrey wanted to understand, learn and grow, but Cleopatra would not care, listen, or observe or give Jeffrey a chance or look at Jeffrey as a human being. There are reasons also why men get tired and fed up that lots of women do not realize! It never good enough for the woman. The more the man is being good the more problems he run into, and ladies do not say child please. Or it is only a few good men out here then be vice versa, because women mess up, just as much as a man do. Sleeping with married men not saying the man does not have nothing to do that, we going to talk about the women now, and what the men go through be a woman and keep your word after you have forgave your man and you both are moving forward open your heart up and trust back honestly don't let your mind say one thing, but your heart say another or your mind change back and forth, because you would be doing that the man you're in love with you would be hurting him back and forth and getting him back for something happen in the past God say let go of the past. The women say it to the man and for others be hard to accept it for themselves. You Are Never Satisfied! You talk to your man like he is your child and then your attitude is stank, funky, bitter, angry, rude, disrespectful and do not want to care again repeatedly you bring up the past. How is this a Christian and being Godly you are helping the demons and spirits come, and do not feel like he does not deserve a second chance. You heard that it was said you shall love your neighbor and hate your enemy. Do even the tax collectors do so? Jeffrey dealt with it like a man, but Cleopatra (THE WOMAN) did not have enemies in her household. Jeffrey prayed for Cleopatra whether he was doing good or bad. I prayed for her welfare I got the point more than anything. I do not change people, and neither can we, but changing is making us bitter, angry, unforgiving, and we cannot pray like that and stay the same way. Women do not try to use God to keep treating your husband/man nasty. She is saying you cannot change me, because she is giving the devil more freedom to break up your home, and the attitude from the woman comes from work, bills, money, situations, angry at family members, not having a car, financially stable, or her children not coming together to figure out how to relieve stress. It is all on you the man/ husband, so do you think women men do not get tired? Especially with your bad attitude, the things you say out your month, bringing up the past all the time. It is okay for her to get from around me. When you get from her and walk away from her pettiness you wrong before you

left when your gone and when you come back if she has not changed her mind. She will not talk at times because her action will show she does not care! You are right she does not care, so how does she expect the relationship work out if she does not care. In her eyes there is no love, but tell you quick, fast and in a hurry that you need to go to God. Now women feel like they cannot shut their man down like Cleopatra. Her daughter told her that all the time, Jeffrey's stepdaughter said right there in front of everybody, Cleopatra would say I do not care what you or he say. So, my children come first, so by my woman putting me down they follow her, but she taught them to see my wrong doings. Believe me they watched her as well, so she taught them something that they are going carry on in a cycle. Now see watch this women Cleopatra laid by Jeffrey side in bed at night and told Jeffrey her mother talked and treated her stepfather in nasty ways sometimes. Now if this is a daughter of a mother saying this see what Cleopatra was saying the same thing the cycle went on. See when you tell your husband/man/men always to look in the mirror at only themselves all the time and never tell yourselves what does that say about you? Will you check yourselves before you lose your man? Especially in the tone the way she speaks to him it be disrespectful and ineffective. Where is the love at? Fussing with your man/husband that leads to a fight, it comes verbally, mentally, and crazy. Words can cut his heart it is worse than having a blade or gun in your hand. It feels like you are holding a knife to his throat threating him and it be deadly, killing his health, spirit, soul, peace of mind, showing him a lack of respect will only cause conflict and shut him down. Now some women will say no he is just a weak damn man! You know how Cleopatra (THE WOMAN) that Jeffrey satisfied, she accepts it. She spit in my face telling me I forgive you I just cannot forget about what you did to me harsh and cruel words. A lot of women when they go through things in relationships and marriages one of the things that comes to their minds is that it will never be the way it uses to be like when we first met! It will be its over than it will change, or she will change it baby let us move forward, then most of the time there is a disagreement from the past of man has done. Instead of loving your man you bring up the issues from the past year ago and do make them a part of the issues of present. Women how is that love bringing up the past? Oh, I know love him, but! Being a strong WOMAN is not only one thing based on standing up to a man, because when you do things like this to your MAN you are truly downing yourself and your relationship. It is a fact now women can you handle that. Then the man knows it is not true it is a way for a woman to control and always have lead way and push all buttons intentionally. That is not love this is one reason why he leaves. Now the woman has time for work and to go out with girlfriends, to shop, eat, entertainment and time for the pastor. To listen to them and they listen back they even have time for the church organizations and committees, and Cleopatra had he no time for her relationship and committing to her man. When I or other men want loving sometimes women give all kinds of excuses what about our needs. A woman has a lot of complaints it could be for good reasons or sarcastic angry mood reasons about what is hurting her. The stomach, headache, her feet, period, back, so she will not have to support her husband wants and needs. He will be hurt and broke down when her hormones or nature changes then she becomes like a lioness. Cleopatra is the queen, LEO! Women say these words I am aggravated, not now, I am just in the mood, I am frustrated, I am sick, you are bothering me, help me with this from work, oops I did that been there done that. Women can your man be the number one priority? I feel men who do not become first in woman life who they love, they be last or have wait. So, women do not push the men over the edge! It goes like this nowhere I am not doing that I am just being a woman! You know at times woman use the statement I am just being a woman to get by or get away with what is they want. A woman can be moveable most of the time, she is on the move. Unstable woman we already know what you are about! See a man cannot say but, but a woman can. A woman should know her place, but I interviewed lots of women that talk about men, and they said to me they did not do anything wrong. You have a lot of women who cannot let the past go, be empowered, being hateful and envious of one another. A lot of women say never chase love. Affection if it is not given freely by another person or a man it is not worth having. Can (THE WOMEN) stop abusing men on forgiving them? I fought for my relationship and was standing in the ring all alone. When women get hurt or not and they say they forgive they are not trusting your

words or actions anymore when it is over its over! Both parties need to love each other every day. See what a lot of women do not understand is and know it is after you forgive him of what he has done the best way to fall back and love all over again is self and God with your lover. To treat him in the same you did when you first began dating a fresh new start! When Jeffrey told Cleopatra (THE WOMAN) this he got cursed out there was not no God coming out of her month. There was a rage of the devil spirits coming out her mouth off her tongue from her heart that was already in her mind, the mouth of the tongue as a two-edge sword. You might as well say she was spitting in my face. My love for her I expressed deeply, but she did not believe it, because I cheated her emotions were sins within herself of not forgiving me telling me she did, but her actions were totally different. An action of boldness verbal speaking in a rage of fire saying I forgive you and I love you does not mix! Not showing love or forgiveness does bring on rage women. Women from my heart feel this poetry please respect me on expressing the way I feel and where I am coming from for you to say well we must hear her side of the story, because I already have told it all like she would have on her side and you all would have understood, because a woman knows a woman! All day ever day my mindful love was different she knew this that is why she kept coming to me on her own with her words saying I am sorry; I am sorry I will not bring up things again. Then change and say all you want to fucking do is have sex, that is all we do then she would say things like I do not care, and I do not give a fuck, you are going to hit me, you are running up on me. Women I felt her she was having flashbacks from what I did to her in the past, but we could not move forward when she came to me and told me she prayed. She prayed to God first then went to the pastor when I came back into the picture, she told me God answered her prayer. So, all those nasty words and actions was supposed to stop under God's order after we got married. They are teaching today only the head of the household is the man and everything falls on him and he is held accountable for everyone sins and actions. I wrote from my heart, and I put in the good things with the bad. Good things men and women does. Can they say the good things men do a lot? Women have been brainwashed about men they are good for nothing! Every family have cycles I met a woman that do not have at all, and she wonder why she cannot forgive, because she has a mother that is the same way. Mothers your children are watching everything you do. Even with you doing good or bad. I hear and see a lot of people say do not argue with a woman or debate with her if they are right or wrong. You will not win or be right that is being selfish or stubborn, getting a point across in their way or the highway. There are no rules or rights when you are talking at times, she got it all under control! Does God say this? No! When it is over the women does not forgive or forget. Like everything I do wrong to Cleopatra almost? Years when she was wrong, she would say all what you had done to me and took me through and my children, trying separate and break us up and did it to me on purpose to hurt me, because I hurt her. Did not see all the times it was a curse she could not see it and she with her mother. Some of those spirits her mother was trying to get her back to live with her she was getting me back while I am doing good I deserved it and she see it, know it, but know she is sinning and did not care. Someone that have so much vengeance in their heart does not care therefore they say they do not. God is watching over me for bad as she says but looking over her for good. Years will go by, and she would say I am to compare what you did to me to what I did to you, and she would say you did it all. So, she is not letting God in her heart she is controlling everything. Now truth matters when she sins even if she is lying right or wrong she is a woman she is all good, but mines does not! It comes to the part where Cleopatra (THE WOMAN) has the mind, self-knowledge, she is doubtful, game being angry with herself and Jeffrey very indeterminable, she loves to manipulate the argument, because she will be right every time, because Jeffrey slept with his ex-girlfriend. It was wrong, now Jeffrey followed Cleopatra (THE WOMAN) on her education that help him, ideas, patience, humbleness, even gave her my plants that Jeffrey watered from my heart, she knew her actions came with demands and do not have one good thing to say about Jeffrey or give him credit for at all. She wanted her facts and opinions only they meant something. Fuck mines I cannot teach nobody shit. I got some nerve trying to teach somebody anything. I am a fuck up always as what I was told! I know and bad women talk with each other women have meetings together, because they have the correct answer if there right or wrong, she is the one that runs everything the woman! I admit I was foolish, nasty, and dirty but no one needs to be treated like shit after forgiveness when they have changed their ways, my life and I got better. When I changed I got knocked down? She always saw in me and saw dissimulation in me every day on almost every situation and occasion, so falseness, unfaithful, treachery, ungrateful, hate, angry, the boss, the past, careless, etc. on and on with no satisfaction and want more and say more, in a court of justice women are found guilty of perjury then than men. Can they all take an oath on that? Therefore, God says that women are not allowed to have control over a man she can speak and teach in church, but not hold office or authority over men. They naturally lead away from the truth. Now women are going to say, you want men to fight us, control us, tell us what to do. How to dress, where to go, what they should do, no I am not saying that I am saying do not be a movable, unstable, bitter, malice, unforgiving, moody, your way a woman can be nice, sweet and spoiled also spoil your children most of the time or some depending on the woman. The truth did not matter no more, because the man, (ME) I lied! So why did she take me back and said we are going to make it work. I am forgiving you then say I do not know why in the fuck I got back with your ass you make me sick, and I was her husband when she told me this. Now sisters and women will say that is right look how you treated her! So, I deserve to be treated like that under women authority and rules. It is not God's will to women that think this way. Stop calling God's name you feel, think and act out this way on something at times that is not even true you are cursing yourself and husband! God does not agree with that, and you know that, just like not taking your husband mess so you think God and your husband going to take yours? So why you keep doing it, because the man keeps doing you wrong then if he is why are you still there? If he changed and you are doing the same thing to him. He is doing good for you; the woman is doing good as well as her children you do not deserve that? She thinks he does. Then you are really saying in your heart and mind with actions your better. It is ok to say your better, your pushing, your trying, but do it in the devil's way only God's way. Like a family, women, men, people they feel like that if they do not lie, steal, but they curse only when they think they are better than anyone else.

God says no profane language that is a sin. Now this family feels like and says we got jobs, education, we know God, but do not forgive there better than the other family that is trying to look for jobs and have not found one yet with an education and that family sins as well to. That is not right women by God when you put your husband family down. If a man is trying to date my daughter if I had one it will be ok because he is going to school or looking for a job. I will not put him down because he went to jail and then got out, changed his life and then say to him you cannot have my daughter because you been to jail. Now when President Obama says band the box and give ex-convicts another chances the women want to stand up for the man that's president, so please be the same way with husband/men/man in God eyes first in the same way. With men in God's eyes not just a president in the oval office. It is some men put men down when they try hard. Like I knew this one family that this man named Charles got out of prison and he was looking for a job working at a hotel. He met this lady and met her family they judged him for his sins, wrongs and never look at there's. The girl's name was Cynthia she told her family she loves him they will have their ups and downs the family will say I told you so, not to be with him. She will throw things up in his face telling you this and that. She will make him feel bad and he will say we will your mother and family are good. She would say my family got something and what do you have? He would say you got with me, and we would go back and forth on and on because I knew I would be right there looking at them. He would come to me and say she did this and she will say he did that then her family will talk about it in her face. Then she will go back to him and tell him all what was said it will hurt her, but when it was good terms she will go against her man and then go back to her family side. What I am trying to say is they both had they rights and wrongs, ups and downs, but not one time they prayed together as a family and had God included. It hurts a man like me to get God included and a woman tells me in my face and treats me with nasty actions saying (IT'S TO LATE) your time ran out. If you would have did it right from the beginning. It would have been right we would have never been in this situation period but tried to use God and say erase her sins, children, family sins, and so we all mess up screw him let us go! We have family that pray and tell men they do put their mothers in place when there wrong, children, and when they are playing the same game and cycle the mother taught them. Now when a woman catches in a lie, like Cleopatra (THE WOMAN) when she caught Jeffrey in his lies, Jeffrey made another lie to cover it up. See I was being a man when she was with me! When I caught her in a lie you do not only have to catch her in a lie saying cheating, because you are going to say men cheat more than women do or I am just trying to find an excuse to get out what I did. I am talking about women lying about giving you your trust back and you earn it, lying when they say they forgave you and they have not and been lying saying they do not check your phone and they do, lying when they say I am not going to bring up the past no more we are moving on. Lying and saying I am not going to be angry, malice, bitter, and hateful anymore, lying and saying there going to trust you while you are doing good and making an excuse saying they cannot never ever give you a chance, because if they feel like if they do he will do the same thing again and never will get it right, and that is not true you have men have achieved goals done right and changed. Lying when they want to make love and tell you no, when they want to and really do. ARE THESE NOT SINS? Will this not break up a relationship? Can unforgiveness break up a marriage/husband/men/man hearts and home? Ladies answer this question on thinking with God, peace, honesty like you want anyone to treat you and ask you in the same respectful way! A woman that walks with God and will always reach her destination! When husband/men/man does his sins depending on which sin it is, because a woman and can see everything then her look at him he is not walking right with God. You know I have not heard women say that about men I am not coming down on women I am just speaking the truth. Everyone you meet comes with baggage you just need to find that someone and stay with them forever to deal with it vice versa. Men need to be respected as well as supported, valued and loved just as women! What hurts it so much is stop saying you hurt her that one time she will not never be the woman was when you first met her stop it. I say stop now ladies because that is a curse and trouble right there. I could not even explain myself to my woman, Cleopatra! THE WOMAN! Negatively speaking I was fuck up and an ass hole. I knew there was difference between an ass hole and being confident and assertive. I am a strong survivor powerful black man and the woman who I love did not tell me this. This does not mean everything is on her or on me or us. When she told me, you damn right everything is your fault. Then I woke up she is not going to change she is going to be stuck and set in her own way and her mother's way! She is not going to help me or make it work! I loved her daughter so much that I protected her because with my love she was my own daughter, and from the evil world. I loved her son Troy so much I gave him back when Cleopatra told Jeffrey to give it to him, took him for walks, talked with him, dropped him to school and picked him up, and Jeffrey was still a fuck up! She was miss using me because I did it to her so she use her children back towards me because she knew that will hurt me. Women will do that to men to get what they want it is a manipulation tactic! It is just that she did not really get over it truly after she forgive me, she told me. She got over it, but she was not honest and loyal. The women will say as well with Cleopatra all the shit Jeffrey took her through he broke her heart do you blame her? This what you women and Cleopatra would say. Then she should not get back with me and leading me on! Jeffrey had to learn, to love himself before Jeffrey loved my woman, Cleopatra! I do love myself, I am happy mentally, spiritually, emotionally, and a good conscious. I still love her until this day. Now after she forgave Jeffrey, and Jeffrey got right with Cleopatra (THE WOMAN) gets the curse on her relationship Jeffrey brought some baggage and a lot of cycles to off my father and mother to my relationship, as well I am not perfect.

Chapter 4

Like when Jeffrey will let Cleopatra (THE WOMAN) know what her sister Nancy did to me and curse me out for reason, sometimes and for things Jeffrey did in the past. Cleopatra will just sit there and not do anything, no respect. Now if I was disrespectful to her mother, which I was not I only spoke up on the sister to her I will get fussed out saying do I have something against them. I will get jumped and I will let the mother know what her daughter Anita said and did to me. She will say I don't know what's wrong with my daughter Anita, Nancy and she will say the same thing for Cleopatra (THE WOMAN), so I had no one there to back Jeffrey up when he was right. Her mother and the son! A lot of women will back this up and say look what you did, you deserve that, what did you do it's all your fault. How do you expect her to feel, look how you did her she's getting you back and you deserve it? Especially with Cleopatra telling Jeffrey, I cannot deal with no man that every time I hurt my man, or my children hurt him he goes running to another woman instead of saying let us pray. Let us go to God but she would say God is for her and her family. She will say to me shouting and screaming that God is not for me because I'm not like every other man. I'm the devil and no good, but I'm still a child of God! Where does God say that you are right that's an angry woman that me myself created forever right women? Women is women not disrespected some women PMS EVERYDAY with attitudes, some do every month mood swings or is that all women? Some go to spas, a lot of shares, some do not, a lot of trim, some don't. They have their ways that are not know and the ways of a woman will never be known, as the Bible says an adulterous woman, because my grandmother said she haven't met one woman who hasn't slept with a man who was married or if he was not married. The woman knew that the man she slept with had a woman, so does not mean that the man only was an adulterous or committed adultery the woman as well, because the woman was thinking of herself just like Bathsheba. My grandmother was honest she said she slept with married men and men that was not married, so she was in sin busting hell wide open as she said on her on actions of sins and self. When she was living, she said she had to repent for herself, sins, ask for forgiveness from the people she hurt and slept with. She knew because on judgement day it was going to be only her in front of God, not the man she slept with or the woman being there, ONLY HER! Just like I sinned myself on Cleopatra! Like Cleopatra (THE WOMAN) slept with me when I was in another relationship. See we all sin no one is perfect. I can take the needle out of my own eye; Women & Men take it out of theirs because God is coming one day. If you don't be here when he comes when it's your time you will see him any way on judgement day. Me to! I'm not keeping it my way it is God's way the truth and the light. Now even a Godly sometimes you will beat yourself up. Sometimes women are different on certain things, as men on certain things. The woman does not deserve or wants to go through physically or sexually assaulted or abuse men as well. They have been through these things in life. If it was not a woman, it was family that took him through this I am a prime example and others have spoken on what men been through as well. Now what I said some or a lot of women will say go sit down somewhere that is excuses, let that go that is different that is the past. Now women go through things differently where they see as something worse in life for them! Every human being cry, hurt, weep, cries out for mercy, prayer, past hurts, cycles, everyone, children, men, women, Moses, Peter, John, Jesus Disciples hurt, cried, and prayed that was men. I do not have anything against women or men what I do is come with facts is which is everything is not the man fault! We all fall short of the glory of the word! We need to teach one another, pray, and help one another, not only be seriously focus on only just women. FIRST GOD! Now if a woman says I know he did not talk about God no woman of his sins that he slept with and his no-good self, yes I did just like to who every one that is like you that have sinned. God forgives you with love and I pray for you. I keep you all encouraged! To the one's keep seeing me as if I'm that same old person and others in this world that get treat this way. When you do that look at yourself in the mirror please God is not pleased with that. Does that what God see in us? NO! So, when you talk about someone just know that you are talking about God because God says do not do your brother and sister in this way. That

comes in sin when I need God and you do as we'll his mercy is with us all day every day. See woman/women/wife one day you will tell your man/men/husband that you do not give a damn or care. Really you just do not know you are telling him you are not my husband and I do not love you or care anymore. Then it comes where you will say the wrong thing at the wrong time on the wrong day. See you will be so angry that anything comes out your mouth. When a woman is angry, she is not being a wife she's being negative and thinking of all kinds of negativity. See she say wants it to stop but it goes back and forth because the man now can't take but so much, but she only see's what he did ONLY. Now what woman would say out their mouths to push there man away that hurt them! Jeffrey seen a group of women talking one day it was 20 women. They were talking about men. I was selling purses to them. Jeffrey said can I ask you women a question and they said sure, I said I hear you over talking about negative things between all of you about your men together. Just gossiping, why are you all not praying for them? Out of 20 women most of them said child go somewhere that we are not trying to hear that. We speak about men the way we want to you need to go somewhere with preaching to us, we are not in church take that to the church house. Then 3 of the women said you know what you're right. Then 3 women said come here, So Jeffrey ask them may I please ask another question then 3 women said what? But before I could speak the other women said, WHAT. They said it real loud. So, I ask the 3 women what you do wrong to your men. What sins did you commit because I have heard what your husbands done wrong? I ask did you cheat on them. 3 of them said they cheated on their husbands like they did to them, the other group of women suck their teeth and start rolling their eyes. So, you all didn't do nothing else to your husbands? and all of them said No. They said what's your point no relationship or marriage is perfect, So Jeffrey said OKAY it takes two, so you all did wrong and sinned to, right? 17 of them walked away saying you all crazy if you sit there and listen to him. You have 2 or 3 women that's the ring leaders. However, there is one woman that's bold and brash. Some women are walking away from the conversation. When your involved in drama it can be manipulating or misunderstood with women. The 3 Women who stayed with Jeffrey came up to him and asked him can we pray with you. I prayed with those sisters that remained with me. You see God uses men, women, drunks, children, animals, all kinds of people, for anyone to put them down to hate them so much? Cleopatra did things that made Jeffrey feel so bad that I really felt like a dog for real, feeling like I was horse crap, and times I wanted to go out into the streets, kill myself or let a car or truck run me over. She only felt only in her ways she felt like only the woman feelings are important and special. Today you would look at Cleopatra and she will say I did not say that. She would always look at Jeffrey's actions not her own! What Jeffrey said do not make the same mistakes me and Cleopatra made in our marriage. For better or worse, richer or poor, in sickness and in health, until death do us apart for marriages and relationships. When getting married and guidance from God. The husband and wife hold the Bible and reads together. This shows a unified front in their marriage. Prayer changes things as we know between man and woman. Between one another man and woman we are a team that could have made it without the curses right there listening to those evil spirits from the devil. You can be listening to your mother, your father, friends, associates, children, sisters, brothers, co-workers and anyone because it can be yourself you're listening to those spirits in your mind. WOMEN LISTEN TO GOD! Now do you see the things I put in this book about good things about a woman. I am waiting for books to come out for men trying their best! Do you know I seen some women that have done men wrong? While a man is trying his best to make her happy. However, the women only see whatever she wants with no remorse in her heart. She sometimes uses the children if they have some as a tool. Then when the women see the blessings that God gives a man, they think about what they could have been doing in the relationship. This is not the man who cheats on a woman then go find another woman and leave their children, don't put them in the same category. Like a no-good husband that cheats do not put him in the bucket that has change. Now see women a lot of you do this, do you make the change and truly be ready for a change when you take him back after all the years you been together? Or do you just say it and mean it, but it is only in your mind tells you different. You feel in some type of way that within yourself only your feelings are not acceptable or fair but to you it is inside and openly. Women do you know you can say something which it can be nasty. Some women feel the man has push them to be the way they are today! Women and men change it's the emotions and different types of feelings she feels that she can't control that overtakes her body that she doesn't know how to let go and let God. Doesn't God bless the man for changing don't God tells you to treat us right and keep no record. So why are a lot of women saying when they get angry but you're not God. Is it that much hate in your heart to call out God name and not love your husband/man as you call on God, in front of his face, because if she screams at him and he cries out constantly saying I'm sorry please stop I'm begging you saying it repeatedly? A lot of women say they have forgiving their husbands/men and they are not a child of God. A husband/man can be telling his wife/woman God says forgive humbly then the woman changes it by saying shut up there is no God in you that her way! What God wants the women to see is that God has molded her man from what he used to be and where he came from. Jeffrey accepted the bitterness in Cleopatra voice even when I satisfied her, and she did not accept it. The woman says God do this and that, but not telling her man that when she letting the devil control her anger! What I am today I have God on my side to pick me up all the time. I got a hold of myself and saw the big picture in life. It is true I do not have no mother or father, who taught me some things about life period. They were not perfect either. Only God our father in Heaven! It takes everyone in life to fall to get right back up. God is their brothers and sisters to I still help. People have spit on me, used me and done me wrong, because of my kind heart. Jesus did the same thing, so did his disciples and others that is living I love give love who give God grace and favor to all the glory. God make all of us wait for a reason at times. It is for a reason and season not only for men, everyone! I have sat among other men and women and in front of God, which I confess my sins, wrong and doing by repenting. I have a lot of women who done this. Or just told the other women that they talk to that it was all his fault, told them bits and pieces, but not everything. There are three sides to a story, your, his and the truth. Women can be selfish and say he hurt and dogged me; however, I did nothing to spark his behavior towards. The other women say I feel what you are going through, because

Cleopatra (THE WOMAN) always came back to me to tell what people say. Also, what I was not supposed to do. What other people say has nothing to do with our marriage. We are in our own house and not theirs. I prayed for them, you and myself. Did you tell them the sins and the evil you did, because you called me back with evil intention not with a sincere heart with love saying I am sorry and do you forgive me. I would say that is not with love from the heart, because all things cannot be all my fault. Especially if you apologized to right that is common sense. You know when I was living with my mother, I saw how she talked to men, she would put them down, cursed them out, criticize, falsely accuse, mistreat and use them for her children. She was a mother who also sinned and was not right in everything. I did not understand, because I was a child, when I became an adult, I understood how it felt when I became a man. Especially in my own house raising someone else children. It is not easy can mothers and women understand that? If they understood only themselves that is being selfish. No one understood and felt what I went through. I am sorry! Its two words from the heart. Do you know Cleopatra do not know is when Jeffrey told her daughter Anita to leave his house for disrespecting him? Anita called Jeffrey on the phone to apologize for her boyfriend behavior. I cannot make him apologize. Her mother did not know she did that. The mother, daughter and friends were going against Jeffrey, so how was I wrong for the daughter apologizing to me? Because Cleopatra says Jeffrey was wrong and mistreated everyone. Do not do evil for evil, but when we were in the counselling the false prophet said I was wrong, evil and a sinner for a man to do his woman like that. Calm down and change you reaping what you sow. You must be the better man and walk away. Then when Jeffrey changed and became a man of God this is when Cleopatra got back at me by not forgiving me from the heart. The pastor did not stand up fairly to say do not throw stones or be disobedient at your man. God works on people like he did me. Jeffrey could not make Cleopatra change and she used everything that she could against me. Cleopatra kept telling Jeffrey what God was telling her. The seed was planted in Cleopatra mind you cannot make me listen or change me. She kept saying it constantly. The pastor wife told her husband that Cleopatra must give Jeffrey the lead way in their household.

I earned trust already with God and another woman told him that! Cleopatra (THE WOMAN) did not tell me that! Then when Jeffrey told Cleopatra she was selfish and unreasonable she cursed me out. When the bishop told Cleopatra, she cannot be selfish sometimes she listens to him. When I told her that when she came home, she said to me I wish I would not have never told you that cursing me out. Now who did not want to hear the truth. After the divorce, the Bishop sat next to me in his truck and told me you right son. The Bible do say forgive son, move on and find someone else get a divorce. When I did my last woman wrong, I broke up and in a new relationship again do not God say do not break up? Man, they can say what they want to, GOD IS AN AMAZING GOD! I was not perfect, but I tried my best and went the way Cleopatra (THE WOMAN) wanted me to go. I did everything to earn her trust and most of having her back that does not love. I am just playing games, so what all this writing for games. I write from my heart. My heart is hurting just as much as hers. God knows, because both of us cry out to him! We know how things work together for good to anyone that is for love of God, to anyone who are the called according to their purpose. I still will be called a liar, no good and dirty. Women are important men are important God is number 1. People better start forgiving faster, getting better for God and holding on to doing sin in this world is getting worse. What I don't understand is that a mother, a woman can say she's going to back up her children if they right or wrong because that's what a mother supposed to do. It's a damn shame that they do not back up their damn husband or partner to the one's that does this I'm disappointed with you all. So, you women that do this to your husbands say this is right! That woman does not honor her husband. I am not that biological father to Cleopatra (THE WOMAN) children. Now god says she cannot do that, Cleopatra told Jeffrey to his face she can do whatever she wants to me! When I am in a relationship with Cleopatra (THE WOMAN) her children became my children, and I became their father. Just like their mother's rights or wrongs, good or bad and sins as well as mines and theirs. She didn't instruct the children to respect me fully when I got my life right with God! Now if Cleopatra would have let Jeffrey earn her trust, respect him and resolve all issues we wouldn't have went through this. Cleopatra and women will say how so, you cheated on her, yes Jeffrey did. She forgave me, took me back and said let's make it work so then that's not on me. See in the first place if she would have kept a clean heart of forgiveness her mother and grandmother they could not forgive something they went through in life. Not to speak bad against them, I'm just telling the truth of the cycle following Cleopatra generational curse on her not to forgive me. What will she say about me like a dog? I am different my situation, the way I did her, and treated her children there's no forgiveness! Forgiving someone is forgiving! No matter who they are. Now a woman that say to her husband I back my children up whether there right or wrong. I'll just deal with God she's not honoring God's or loves God! When Cleopatra moved out, she told Jeffrey baby you are trying your best! Then Jeffrey told Cleopatra you were supposed to tell me that when you were in our home or bedroom in love with God as a family in front of our children. Instead, you waited until it was too late. Now can most women back me up on that? Like they back up one another. A lot of times Jeffrey cried, and Cleopatra did not care about his tears or prayers, cries to God. Jeffrey spoke to Cleopatra; she did not listen it's just like a movie. One thing Jeffrey can say Cleopatra cries meant everything in the world! You know Jeffrey learned even more things about families, no one is perfect, they argue, fight, ignore, even stop talking to each other at times but in the end, family is family the love will always be there. So, why Cleopatra (THE WOMAN) didn't see me with my goods and bad forever? When a woman is being satisfied by a man she never gets tired of shopping, buying shoes, or wearing high heels or buying her hair. Now I must give her credit on her hairdos, because it's not the hairdo making the woman. It is the woman making the hairdo look good for herself. She is a strong woman she's just not satisfied. She's going to shop and not drop it's not all about that in her life. She never gets tired of getting beautiful because she wants to keep herself up. (YES) that's right I'm talking the women keeping yourself up I'm proud of you and that learn something from it. She's going to sit in her tub and relax. A woman is just never satisfied. She's on time, loving, emotional, romantic, have ways of being a phenomenal woman, her beauty, her smile, sense of humor, her destiny, (POWER), control, her mind, her respect, always keeping her head up, observing always, planning a plan before it is put into place and speaks to it into existence. It is in her mind already she has marketing and public relations in her. She is building a tower and an investment already; her beauty is captured from God taking the rib out of man! The woman loves to be massage. Wants and be the best she can be in what she is doing to achieve her goals. Her prayers are serious with the Lord she can't be satisfied because she is the mind reader, she is correct on everything, right ladies? She will say that's not true reading this book to the ones that say that, but the ones that do will say that for the ones that are women are real women of God or fake. Women who are of the world and not of the world, humble women or attitude women that still will say (THEY CAN BE SATISFIED) and they are not mind readers but tell you quick she knows what you're thinking about! They all still will say that's not true, so why you must win every argument because you're the woman, and that's just the way it is can you be the better man (WOMAN) sometimes? Mostly every conversation must be right all the time and get the last word! This is the part I like when you say (OH) you're trying to say this, or what are you trying to say I'm not good enough for you to listen to what I have to say. You are telling me no baby before I finish my statement. You Yes me all the time. While you talk about me it is still (NO) (NO) (NO) in Cleopatra mind your saying yes, she really does not want to hear nothing what her man has to say. Is that why (WOMEN) you don't listen to your man in the first place! A lot of women might say I do not know what I am talking about. I had some bad experiences in my relationships with women. All women are not the same, but it said men is right ladies, or their going to say you met the wrong woman it is you not them. As I talked to men and women married or not, they express to me that's it never a 50/50% split in a relationship. However, they say it more a 60/40% relationship unless we are on T.V. around millionaires, billionaires on shows with fame they will say 50/50%. So why are so many marriages failing not because of only MEN! It takes two. Women say men push them away, they go to their mother house or sister or girlfriend, daughter, or hotel or better yet a place to clear their minds. They do not want to be around stupid, ignorant men, so it works both ways. Do you know women push there men away a lot? Women have you sat back like you watch T.V., get your paycheck and set up appointments that is of importance to you, but have you thought about what you do to your husband or man to push him away? Not saying your bad women, just saying what about your flaws. Then your crap you do don't stank only the men crap stank. Everyone has bad in them and some change for the better. We all need change. We need to work on ourselves every day, I know I do, and I am working on myself. I fall, but I get back up, dust myself off and try again. I admit I messed up a lot of times repeatedly. I realize I was lying to myself until I started getting things right by working on me. I know I have plenty of things to still work on. I am a real man, and it takes courage to say I know God applause me. I thank God for that every day! A lot of women will say that's your opinion. Everyone is entitling to their own opinions your right and I am going to say the truth. Not to tell the woman what I want them to hear as well as the men. I'm going to tell them the truth that's how people be confused, because people are telling them what they want them to hear like politicians, false statements, false mind sets, false new world order, false lies, false pastor, false leaders, false teachers, false marriage counselors, and false doctors that got degrees just a come up to tell you anything to have you coming back. I would never get a T.V. show or a radio station or have plays on T.V. to take up for men or women no it's going to be right vice versa only right, fair not buying people or buying fame or selling out or my soul, because love, caring, helping, listening, hearing, doing, and understanding has nothing to do with involving in what's or pulling someone in, just to like you to make money and be all about yourself and taking up for men for what's between your legs. How they feel putting it down with sex NO!! It's what's in their hearts that's right, thinking with their mind, righteous and positive respective Godly gentlemen and women who are nice, sweet, happy, submissive, humble and not all about themselves being selfish we must hear both sides, both stories. Its women will say and lie. If you ask them what they have done wrong to their man, because how he have hurt her years ago and still say no, no, no she's right and she did nothing wrong and it was him. He's to blame for everything until she breaks up with the husband/man and still be holding on to the hurt for more years and takes it into her next relationship or just live alone miserable for a longtime aggravated

let down betrayed misused, abuse mistreated, no trust, upset, hurt I feel her (THE WOMAN) (THE WOMEN), but there not the only ones go through pain: I will not be taking up for them putting them down the men like lots and lots of women do shows the man the man is always to blame! This goes for women and men before you speak to one another think before you speak to one another with positiveness. When it comes out it don't come out with force, cruel, control, or sarcastic or rude words are deadly and vicious, show each other action with love how to treat one another. Tell each other with action how much you love one another every day in the morning and at night. Even calling each other during the day If you have job or businesses to say I love you. Don't just love one another love all of Gods children and may sure prayer be involved all the time. Make sure you talk with passion, romance with God in middle. When you are hugging and kissing don't leave out faith, God loves this and knowing you both love God you will continue to do this, you can learn something for one another and teach each other something every day. Especially compassion in your heart. You have hearts, smile, pray, cry, get emotional, and most of all have God in your life! If you want your relationship to grow and be good worker don't quit your job. You can be each other bosses in good way women like there men nasty, freaky, sexy, handsome, horny protectors, a hard worker, responsible, on time, hot gentle hard at some point and time if you know what I mean! Men want their women looking beautiful, nice, sweet, prayed up, good mothers, good looks, not about her what's between her legs or what she got to give and only thing he is looking from her is respect, love, a good cook, that's the way to his heart. Women want a man that know how to cook. He loves how his women dress and carry herself as a woman. A real strong woman does not want no other woman to have what she has. A real woman does not share her man, only Ho's does that. A real man does not share either. Dogs and cowards do that! A real woman will have her man heart and his mind by treating him with respect and love. She will keep the upper hand and have his back when need be. She knows in her man eyes she is fine as wine, bad to the bone, beautiful and nice. Some women don't like to kiss with lipstick on and some do! The woman knows how deep her love is as well as she will make and have the man full of joy even if he is sad. That's why he can't live with or without her! She thinks and knows she can read her man mind if she's right or wrong. Her mind is an energizer, Duracell, battery charger, a map, a phone, text, a dictionary, a professor, answer, question, period, stop sign, teacher, leader, mind reader, encyclopedia, class, group, counselor, going overboard, technology, but least she is not last the silent person! The fastest track runner in the world with her mind she will give you a head start she more than every woman she knows she's natural. A lot might say I don't know nothing about no woman, I can't tell I wrote this book, didn't I? THE WOMAN THE WOMEN! YOU CAN'T NEVER SATISFY A WOMAN! Now the woman is feminine and a good charmer with perfection. A woman fragrance on brings out her charm to. She is full of sunshine with her smile, which is light and bright. She will bring your tears from joy to sadness, from sadness to happy! The man is associated with the smell of the woman fragrance. It's impossible that any man when she walks up to him, he does not give her a compliment on how she smells. The woman trusts in God, believe in herself, follow her heart, listen to her intuition and she know she feels everything she does is right! The woman must be comfortable. I know a lot of women are going to say he say this then he says that about women he doesn't know what he is talking about hmmm! Whatever, when they read this book. All of you must do is look in the mirror every morning when you fix yourself up YOU! THE WOMEN say one thing then say another it is what it is. It's just like men deal with it. Now I have been relationships with a lot of women are they going to say, because you are a whore I will never tell them that judging them saying just as an example did or was you married with the man you have in a relationship. Your child was a bastard, because of the father. No, I wouldn't do that. That's just a woman being a woman she changes up with mood swings. Women mostly feels that and know her for sure that the man pushes her away, but it's vice versa. WOMEN MAKE BIGGEST MISTAKES THAT PUSHES A MAN AWAY AND KILLS HIS ATTRACTION. I'm a good man with a good sense of humor and happy I'm able to laugh at myself at times. I have flaws I sinned, but I'm not a sinner! I can't get away with nothing, because God see's everything, so women please don't say go ahead with that please! Some women have full control over the unity. Now I tried to teach certain women this never lie when you say you are going to forgive your husband, mate, or fiancé, because when you lie on forgiving him it will never free your mind women or self or life and every situation you be in it will set you back and you feel uncomfortable by taking that out on the person and yourself. Then you say you gave a chance to, which you really didn't give him nothing and never forgave him. Men do something for your women often even when her days she's not in the mood and does not want to be bothered I know sometimes it does not to do nothing and sometimes there is no credit, but God will give you credit when she does not give you nothing. These pretty women out here love their men vice versa. I hear lots of women saying you men made this woman angry, nasty, evil, she was never like this until you hurt me! So, what did you do to make your man angry, upset, hurt, and push him the hell away? When are you going to think of that! Now the Bible states that the ways of a movable and unstable woman are evil. I'm not doing or starting no debate, argument, trouble, or back and forth with women on this point of view, because I know lots of women will say I'm not right or shut up, really I don't know what I'm talking about so most of what I'm saying about you women? We know this is the evil woman. She gives no thought to the way of life; her paths wonder aimlessly, but she does not know it for she cares nothing about the path to life. She staggers down a crooked trail and doesn't realize it. As Gods word speak, my son, attend unto my wisdom, and bow down thine ear to my understanding that thou mayest regard discretion, and that thou lip keep knowledge. For the lips make keep knowledge for the lips of a strange as a honeycomb, and her mouth smoother than oil: but her end is bitter as warm wood sharp as a two-edged sword. Her feet go down to death; her steps take hold hell. Less they should ponder the path of life, are ways are movable, that they cast not know them. Hear me now therefore, I see children, and depart not from the WORDS OF MY MOUTH. Remove thy way far from her and come not near the door of her house: this is not for the good women this is for the evil women. All of them still can't be satisfied. The good woman (YES) I'm talking to you that's reading knows her man favorite meal like the man that's goob d knows her favorite perfume and what she likes to wear. She knows the best way to his heart is his stomach not what's between his legs he knows that to. He likes everything his good woman makes and cooks. There's a lot of ways women to show your man you love him. It's not all about you women or your 60%70% it's about you both. Making it work together communicates having a long, wonderful life with each other. You both will do whatever it takes to keep one another not just the man only! I had to fight and fight to keep my woman. A lot of men do this woman you're not fighting by yourselves. Let your man know you think of him all the time the way he will love to be seen and prayed for. Do you tell him he's a good and strong man which you always love having him by your side in your life and he's doing a good job? Do you let your man vent, get air and think? See Cleopatra (THE WOMAN) family fights, playing mind games, plays with my emotions, feelings and I get told I'm acting like a damn woman. Didn't want to talk or listen to my problems and hers but had to listen to her made an excuse that I didn't have to listen if I didn't want to, so you don't care. You know at times a woman and tell you what your caring, feeling, thinking and don't be right all the time that's how some arguments start but you will bring up something being stubborn or selfish to block your husband/man keeping your brick wall up dangerously! Women, please learn from other women that do this. Men must let their guard and wall down just like you do women, like what I'm talking about on my topics. Jeffrey had his wall up on Cleopatra not forgiving him or caring about him. Jeffrey had to forgive Cleopatra so he can be at peace and ignoring her sins and ways. Then it was going on for so long Jeffrey threw in the towel and said he couldn't take it no more. One thing for sure Jeffrey did come back to try his best and put in his all! Cleopatra made Jeffrey feel like he didn't have no say so, no love and caring in our relationship, (YES) he was feeling like shit! Never ask me one-time WHATS WRONG? Come here I want to hold you it was none of that, so we can talk dear, but I did get cursed out still on the job. The ex-mother told me she gets on her daughter about where she's wrong at in my face. However, you talk behind my back in the daughter Anita face. Why? The daughter comes back and tell me that's how I know. If the daughter is coming back to tell me that she's talking about our relationship, herself, me and her mother what is their accomplishing. RIGHT WOMEN YOU ALL KNOW HOW IT

GOES! It will be sometimes Cleopatra will come to Jeffrey crying he say that's your mother baby. She will say my mother say and do wrong things sometimes. Jeffrey says you say things behind her back, but that's still your mother. She will then say don't tell me nothing about my mother she be talking about me then she will take up for her mother to get back at me saying, you got something against my mother see. See how misery loves company. Therefore, the mother, sister, auntie, daughter, and Cleopatra stick together what's wrong and use it against me and others but can't take doing it towards one another if they are right or wrong. I always gave up something a hug, a conversation and the truth when I got saved and married it's the small things that counts. People are blind on that, and I pray and hope they move that darkness away. I'm still trying to realize how can I break you up from your children when I put them in a house, clothe and fed them. There is some men and women out here that's not doing anything for their children. When I still could not find a job at night I went to the gas stations to beg for money and sometimes went to friend's business restaurants to beg for food as well, so before leaving or home a lot of times about getting fussed out about cheating with the woman I cheated with in the past. How was I cheating with the past woman or any woman when she will follow me with the children in the car sometimes saying I'm sorry baby come back home? I know women because I hurt her, she a woman she gone feel that way and hurt people so you're behind her 100% because men hurt you! Then times she will get out the car walk up to me, and say come on let's go home why you out here asking for money you don't have to do this, I will say (YES) I do, because you are pressuring me about your paying mostly all the bills. I'm not making enough money and throwing it up in my face about telling me your daughter don't want no broke man like me because I'm broke. Being angry saying she don't have no money saved up and no car like her mother and sister, so then she was all about money and materialistic things, because every day I'm looking for a job. I can't make no one hire me but however I'm trying my best. She acted like she was married to her mom, daughter and sister and trying to prove a point as a mother when she's dead wrong she still gets the credit. She was more a friend only to her daughter not God first and me that's why

I would walk into the house with hundreds of dollars then the mother would look at her daughter/friend and say look how much money he made today. I'm bringing this up because Cleopatra was not appreciative! It supposes to go God's way that's what a lot of peoples say but don't do. Now tell me something ladies. Now as this woman moves out then she sits on the porch and then tell me after she moves out with her children that I help raised. She told me I tried, It's too late for that now. Right ladies? After the pain. Really, I learned from everyone getting hurt not only women. I never got any gratitude from Cleopatra after she forgave me I got cursed out when doing a good job and saying in front of people on her job in front of the custodian worker, so I don't care; I went to job interviews she is not being satisfied then be nasty and say go pick my children up, not our children (HER) children. I was disrespected in front of people, while I was on a leash that's why I told the mother your other daughter disrespected me, and I told Cleopatra they wouldn't say nothing at all. I was getting jumped for history things when I first came into the relationship I got disrespected for nothing, so if your mother did not like me when she first met me why did we get together because Cleopatra said my mother don't like no man I get with. What does that tell us I protected you and your children. When a young lady came to our door one night being raped what did this man do? When your son was choking, and I saved his life what did I do? When we had gotten robbed me and her son what did I do? I told the robbers tried to kill me and let the son go. So only mother's love, care, do, and will die for their children only not so God does not do favoritism! She didn't tell me she love me for that only thing she told me was don't tell her mother because she doesn't want to hear her mouth or in her business. For that I admire this man God does to if I would have died for her children but if I were dead and gone thank God, I'm alive would it matter? Why would I want to separate someone you all up for being a brave man of God? The mom called me a thug from my past that's another reason why she didn't want to tell her, and I had her grandbaby life in danger. Now when Cleopatra was in the car with her son Trevor, and they were robbed she told her mother everything. Just like me leaving the children home at times while I take Cleopatra out to eat or certain places the mother or auntie will go get them from our house and take them to the mother house why we are out, then when Cleopatra will go to her mother house and the auntie and mother will get up in my face and say leave them there again and watch what happens. Sometimes Cleopatra will talk sometimes she won't but when Cleopatra left them there and I was not home nothing was said at all because she's the mother of her children, right women? IT's a shame for her being with me or around me I'm shit, but the family is good with God, smart, and loving thinks God all the time. I don't see where God say that I'm not his child, everything is my fault and the good works I done. A man has feelings to. She didn't know if she would of gave thanks to her man will keep us together, she right she didn't care anymore. She was saying I don't know why I got back with you. She didn't want any advice I offered. I was a problem in her eyes or her children, which I was wrong on somethings, just like she was. No parent is perfect, but she was wrong with things concerning her children than me. Jeffrey couldn't tell Cleopatra nothing about her children. She let it be known to me my children. My mother did the same thing with her children. Mothers have a lot of control, and they feel like it's right, because just by them being the single mother it makes it hard for them, so they can use that to do or say anything to back them up and their children. Jeffrey wasn't allowed any freedom by Cleopatra because she used my past constantly against me. She was saying my ass don't love me, because if you did you wouldn't have walked out on me. When Jeffrey walks back home Cleopatra would have an attitude while I'm lying beside her. Some women would agree with her ways towards me. They say she couldn't satisfy herself, so how was she going to satisfy me. Women I'm not taking what Cleopatra (THE WOMAN) did to me I'm saying we go through it to. Your man appreciates you, however when do you focusing solely on him by making some eye contact with any interruptions, because you don't like to be interrupted ladies! Now some women and men may say let it go, I have. I am merely making a point clear man are not always the blame or his fault for every situation that goes wrong. It's just like news channels and T.V. shows the black-on-black crimes. They show black men killing each other and it is said statics they 75% in prison maybe more. However, the government, billionaires, millionaires are the white republicans that run the White House and system for decades of this USA. It's happy fun in their rich ways of thinking saying at least we do it in the rich way whether your wearing saggy pants, your black robbing, killing, stealing, but your white dressed in suit with a high position your no different black or white a robber is robber, a crook is a crook. You see therefore 75% of officers is not locked up, because the same system that locks you up get their own out of trouble by paying money. Do you know how many officers got off with locking up black men for false charges? They are killing black men they haven't locked half of them up yet. The news channels report lies for them because they all work together POWER, CONTROL, AND MONEY. I'm not trying to make this a white thing or racist thing it's true. It's crooks that have been getting over for decades. My point I am trying to make is that it's not always the men fault whatever color he is women do wrong to. We all have sinned sometime in our life it matters of you understanding and take ownership what you do. I respect all the women and men to grandfathers, grandmothers everyone. When someone say everyone is not like you, I move away from them, because I don't want negativity around me, I'm not on that level. They are not going to show everything officers do, because they supposed to protect and serve. It's a business and investment jails and prisons. Like Odama said the children in Baltimore had evil in them when they riot, not one time just once he was evil! People going to say you know he not going to say that you know that, because the of the situation he's in. He is black, everything bad is happening. These are the last days women, so it's not men only. People need to go to jail that do wrong, but women don't treat your man, just like system and government does don't keep him in jail or prison for something he has done years ago. Why are you still accusing him like he is before a jury in the courtroom and your judge pounding on his head, holding in contempt? Guilty, Guilty, Guilty. You know your home, marriage, relationship can be a jail or prison you both will be locked up and incarcerated! Don't drop a bomb over your man head every time you will cause an EXPLOSION! This is what happen to most of men like when they are pulled over by the police a lot of officers are not satisfied. I still respect the law because it's what God says. They pull you over then when you give them your license and the officer go look it up they see what you have done in the

past your record or you skin color stupid things then come back, and you are judged by your record. See this is what happens in a relationship. Women lot of you want to be your man probation or parole officer, so you can have control. Now even if it's a good day and good women it's not all on the men ladies. It's not only for you women it's for men to. When someone loves you, they just won't say it you can both tell how the way they treat you. A couple of women told me that the way their man treats them is on attitude they give them, so now I see most of the women have attitude's period. Is that in the blood line or nature a lot of women don't know, well they do know that the past should be left in the past otherwise it will kill the relationship. If you forgive your man, then is the healing process to look to grow and move on. It can kill the future of what you are holding on to. You have your wall up and you need to let down start to heal for your hurt by men, well men have been hurt to not as much as women. As ladies yes, they have it, it's just been hidden! I got comfortable with letting women disrespecting me of things I had done years ago. Now off their things they did years ago, LET IT GO YOU STILL ON THAT? That's the pass! The one who who's bringing up the past THE WOMEN want you to forgive her for all her sins and wrongs, but still hold on to yours. It's you got me. So, I'm getting you back. I knew this man named Benson and his wife did not see him in 12 years, when she saw him walking with me, she said you look handsome Benson, are you still a hoe? Benson was married moved on with his life and had 3 children and preaching. Now was that right to say out her mouth, so other women will say you don't know what he took her through, so she's going to have that in her heart forever or when she feels like it's time to let it go and curse him out. He spoke to her and said God bless you he did not say you know your sinning of the words that coming out of your mouth, because it would have gotten started. Right, you strong women out there? I learned a lot of this from you. Women you mostly do the checking if you know what I mean! Now when the woman makes the man feel miserable and he has changed he can't go get a room or go to his mother, sister, auntie, or family house. When he comes back home, he's the same thing when he left the same old thing, (WOMEN) you don't think that's that same old thing in your mind? It is to the point where he hurts are you telling

God he deserves this or are you telling him he deserves this? I believe it's both because what you do to him you are doing it towards God! Falsely accusing him. When I hurt people, I hurt God. Now when he does not want to accept this and come into his own room most women are nagging him, jump on top of him and let him know you going to give me some today laughing with him, but just cursed him out. Then women say lots of men give the best sex and love in the marriage and relationship. Is when you make love you get through arguing or fussing, because it be good that's the make-up sex and love the devil is a liar. It is just like alcohol once you to get a taste and drunk or drink once you stop the problem and situation is still there not God! Some women say all I need is a good fuck it will be alright some say a cold shower or a hot one or bath there good or she wants a drink or her vibrator there's different kinds or just one. Her toys to play with and your right that's what you are doing with yourself because how long that last for a certain time because when that wears off then what? Moody time whatever mood you're in WOMEN because every woman not the same. Make-up sex or love does not solve the problem when you're not getting along. I'm the man saying that ladies a man, not you this time it is me! This is my true words if you have problems or anything you can ask it is respectful. If you know me you can say as you feel love is here and God is not confusion, misunderstanding, drama, wrong, manipulate, gossip, stories, lies, conning, hustling you, telling you anything to wheel you in, criticizing or no negativity! So, I know women are to say, what kind of women you are talking about, because I'm not that type of woman. Women do that than those type of women need to stop that and let their ways, or the past go it don't only be cheating it can be most, some but not (ALL) I'm sorry women I can't agree with you on something that's not right. Especially that makes common sense! A lot of women are going to say shut the hell up (I KNOW YOUR SMILING) or got an attitude of this topic or depending on what your feelings are, because God made us all different (BUT) we are still all the same in his eyes and we are still human. Now I do not understand false teachers telling women if he does you wrong it takes time for you to heal how long, because it's up to her to let you know the healing of the Lord touch her and make the choice to allow that to happen. See the false prophets are

not telling this to the man that change there not giving fair counseling. Women that don't forgive, don't tell or listen to how you feel or how they feel how you will get curse out, but they will show you by the way you treat them. ACTIONS speak louder than words, so sins just don't come with adultery it also comes with other sins to. In the marriages that are curses only the women had enough not men, right? The way Cleopatra (THE WOMAN) her bitterness and bad behavior changed the person she uses to be I can take credit and most of what I did then when we got into a relationship and all things was good, she got bitter that was not on me. All people have cycles and bad habits in their family no Cleopatra family if anyone going to say something about her family it's going to be her. Not with me Cleopatra knows everything about me and my family. Her family don't have the willingness to break their cycle. They have a lot of excuses and talk like they the victims of every situation every time. It has been times as a man where I have been hurt so bad where my whole-body cries and I feel weak. My heart beats with warmness, Jeffrey can't say a word at all just like when Cleopatra is in front of me talking. Jeffrey mind was set on his pain and Cleopatra the woman pain where she didn't ask me am, I ok. What could I do to fix this I couldn't do it by myself? I stop being a player, because it was not winning the game, but when I when I grew up and became a man. I realize I was losing my woman heart and love. I did good for 6 years not pushing her to forgive waiting patiently until she came to me and said it! I even changed my actions, my tone, my looks, my ways, to tell God myself and the woman with satisfaction. I learned my lesson it did no good! Now women you want me to feel what you go through and pain God first really for a fact, we'll feel mines as we'll and husbands/husband/men/man! I love sister Sonia the poetess that she writes about brother's, sister's, history, the truth, knowledge, wisdom and a lot of peoples can't handle that! Especially myself at one point of time sorry for that many of times women don't say I don't have no business talking or saying nothing about women. It's a freedom of speech you got it as we'll as a voice to be heard go for its women! Right? I learned a lot from different people, so you can learn something every day. Men are dogs and no good to most women. Now you good women you are you put God first, yourself second and you. The good husbands are providers and love their wives like Christ love the church. You strong women out there I know your purpose it's to love God first be virtuous, love your husband and stand by his side always intriguing the woman purpose is always fascinating, arousing her curiosity and interest in herself and her husband. What she believes in is compelling to appeal highly and strongly. Her plan intrigues her and do not wonder if it works, she knows it will. She knows she will be heard and notice her looks of beauty will be drawn to herself and even other capture it. VERY STRANGE. She has all kind of powers it can be good or bad and force it does not all only come from men cheating, sneaking ways of plotting and using her imagination she's a woman. Can trick, treat and cheat I mean this a good way with fun ladies. Don't take this in a wrong way love to entangle her purpose of qualities are so high she will blow the man mind. God said the man will never be alone, so he gave him a helper, help mate (THE WOMAN) I love our women what more do they want? They never get tired of buying shoes buy more want more. The woman purpose is also to be relevant in behavior, not slander or slave to much wine. They purpose is to teach what is good, so to teach other young women to love their husbands and children. The all-purpose woman & women knowing their purpose and place nurturing of their child always have compassion. The women for all purposes first supplication's prayers, intercessions and thanksgivings be for the family for the husband is head the king, God is in his high positions. God will lead them in a peaceful and quiet life. Godly and dignified in every way. This is good ladies, and it is pleasing in the sight of God our savior, who desires all people to be saved and to come to the knowledge of the truth. For there is one God, and there is on mediator between God and men, the man Christ Jesus, not for some women to say I know it's a God angry or happy and tell their mate you're not God child, angry at him for what he has done in the past vice versa towards the man to. The woman purpose is to also learn quietly with all submissiveness I do not permit a woman to teach or to exercise authority or stir up over a man; rather she is to remain quiet. For Adam was formed first then Eve; and Adam was not deceived and become a transgressor. A purpose is to also submit to her husband and build him up with encouragement and consolation. Yes, submitting to one another out of reverence for Christ.

Wives submit to your own husbands, as to the Lord. For the husband is the head of the wife even as Christ is the head of the church, so also wives should submit in everything to their husbands. The woman job and purpose are to be supportive and do her husband God not evil. She is the woman she's meant to be I love you all sisters no color, no race it's from the heart, no game, lies, plot, schemes, scams, from God even the brothers, men! The women purpose is to be honest, modest, and chastity. The husband safely trusts her! You women I give you credit for being afraid for the Lord that give you more meaning to your lives from the Lord to yourselves and your husband I got to give men credit and encourage to push them and a hug and trying in this cruel world! Her dress that she's wears out in public as an all-purpose woman does not never draw attention to her body by being over or under dressed. No, the attraction of her beauty and anointing and the Holy Spirit God with her. It's what it's all about, and to women who feel that they not satisfied of the men who hurt them that they had to go out to be a prostitute or a lesbian, mean, cruel or bitter don't let that bring yourself down low that you go away that you think It will be better then be in a worse situation or go to another man that brings worse things in your life, your too beautiful of a woman to do that to yourselves. God loves you, but he hates what you are doing. I'm not judging you I'm telling you God's word not using it against you do you love yourself? So, you wouldn't do that? A real woman will ignore confusion is not selfish, she wouldn't be the one always telling someone what they better do and what they should be doing to get their selves right. She will be working on herself and doing better, getting better and not doing her thing doing God's everything! Now the all-purpose woman of God will repent, ask forgiveness, stop bring the past up, confess her sins and accept Christ through faith. The Holy Spirit will give her strength, courage and direction to fulfill her duties and with that inner ornament of a meek and quiet spirit God will see, not her saying she forgives have God then back arguing that's the devil. She will tell you in your face arguing with me I got God! Therefore, when Cleopatra (THE WOMAN) said screw God when Jeffrey told her that God comes first, him, you then our children. Not our children first, she said Well, just deal with God and that she will. She never ever came back to me to apologize or ask forgiveness. It's the cycle her mother taught her and agrees on, because when you tell them they tell you where you can go, what you can do and they can't even tell that to one another, so what tells you. See when the woman doesn't really forgive this put her in a way towards her husband for freedom to treat him and do him any kind of way then it's turned into a power struggle and a wall of her having full control it only leads into bondage the selfishness, bitterness and ungodliness of many women is without excuse then there's no time to listen or talk, because of her. Frustration cannot be understood towards you in the relationship and marriage. The women that been hurt and can't forgive is REJECTING GOD FIRST, THE HUSBAND AND THE MARRIAGE. The children are laughing, smiling, because they are saying we got our mother when the devil is laughing with curse upon everyone in his hand. There's no sweetness in the women it's all gone and when you continue to pray go to God and say let's pray. She says as the devil with the thorns on her head you can't make me pray. Then when you ignore her, only focus on you and go to God she still does not come, because she has not fully forgiven you it takes two, just like God & Jesus as one, but everyone situation is different, but still if God is not included then it does not matter. My woman stopped being a home keeper, she stops loving me with actions, but kept telling me and saying it teaching the children with the husband. The wife is warm hearted person in the household, just like I said every marriage, relationship, man, woman, husband, wife have their share of ups and downs, rights, wrongs, good, bad, adultery, fornicating, sins, lies, false accusing, but when the evil steps in and one person is handling it alone with God and others gives up now it's your time. No false prophets and preachers say that not God! Now today a lot of women want to choose a career over God and their marriage and get ready for God when they have the time to. Why would any woman trade this noble place for some dollars earned or for some coveted position? God order say's for better or for worse, richer or poor, sickness in health until death do us apart. Not your children saying towards your husband that you don't pay no damn bills in this house with your tired ass. While I am looking for a job. Now Cleopatra (THE WOMAN) said why you still talking about this let it go about me and my daughter, about what Jeffrey did, and she did not forgive. I changed and I got step on she used her children towards me to get back at me. Women don't you feel this. See you don't only go through this and it's not easy to raise someone else children. I went through this! Now Cleopatra (THE WOMAN) was telling lying beside me in the bed. I know it's not easy raising my children I know they mess up and lie sometimes so if you know that when you be in front of the children, the only thing you have in your life, when I say something just like she does as a man it does not mean nothing. I'm always wrong see that's a curse right there a cycle and no respect towards me. It's cruel and my soul is feeling it running more to God as well towards woman/wife! Cleopatra said to me like this, (YOU'RE NOT RUNNING FOR JESUS YOU'RE RUNNING FOR THE DEVIL) and no matter what women are going through Jesus is with them even though we know is with us all but not when she's scornful, bitter, and angry. Even when we all sin God is with us! In certain ways a woman's role beyond her home. In the Old Testament & New Testament of Godly women even have responsibility in the kingdom of heaven with God, and in the house of God, today in church to do their responsibilities within the church. Her love, gentleness and compassion she is a living example of that which becomes godliness. Older women are to teach the young women that the word of God be not blasphemed. The Christian women have the cares of a home and family. There are definite guidelines for women's behavior in the church. In like manner also, that women adorn themselves in modest apparel, with shame fadedness and sobriety: not with braided hair, or gold, or pearls, or costly array, but which become women professing godliness) With good works let the woman learn in silence with all subjection, but I suffer not a woman to teach, nor to usurp authority over man, but to be in silence. For Adam was first formed then Eve, and Adam was not deceived, but the woman being deceived was in the transgression. Notwithstanding she shall be saved in childbearing if they continue in faith and charity and holiness with sobriety. This is a true saying if a man desires the office of a Bishop, he desired a good work. A Bishop then must be blameless, the husband of one wife, vigilant, sober, of good behavior, given to hospitality, apt to teach; Not given to wine, no striker, not greedy of filthy lucre; but patient, not a brawler, not covetous; One that ruled well his own house, having his children in subjection with all gravity: Now I know lots of women pray for they husbands/men/man, cook for them and stand by them as well blow his mind as well to just don't do it with your games at times and you women know what I'm talking about and coming from. Only focus on God and one! You're not perfect we know it will be times you put him down talk nasty and dirty towards him not all on his sins and actions all the time yours to. Don't play games, protect his dreams and give him strong wonderful space to grow at times like you say she's a (WOMAN) so for him he's a (MAN)! Nurture him, love him with his children or yours, honor his mother, be understanding have realistic expectations of him. Let him lead. Accept his flaws. Praise a pat on the back and prayer for his strengths and respect him. Be his friend grow with him. Enjoy life with him.

Chapter 5

Cleopatra (THE WOMAN) in her own skin the mother teaching her children mentally, emotionally and spiritually. Jeffrey put him thoughts into them as looking at them as God's gift. It's not about how they see me or how I see them it's about God sees us! This is the mountain in the man this is deeper than love itself. I believe in women and men they are God's gifts! You learn something every day about life. In a relationship not only, women can have freedom of expression and that's how T.V. shows, false teachers set it up only for a woman, men have freedom of expression as well this don't mean the man is acting like a woman. If the man does not cry or hurt how can he not have feelings as well. It's a lot of women that are stubborn and want their own way and they say it's all the man! The women be stuck up and with a stiff neck making the man suffer in God's eyes the stubborn woman or wife is as guilty as anyone who worships the devil, Satan or evil! Now girlfriends that I had in the past did not understand me. Now with Cleopatra (THE WOMAN) Jeffrey tried his best giving his all to satisfy her. I feel you men out there how is it all the man fault. If you are the woman who being one way minded, you wanting and having your own way without regard to your spouse ideas or feelings? Women cheating is not the only adultery, stubbornness is an iniquity and idolatry, because in the word of God women it says, though has rejected the word of the Lord, the women feel like when the men has done them wrong they have said they have let go and let God. What they are really saying is that I'm letting you go and only letting God in! Women the heart is deceitful above all things and beyond cure. When the woman is being bitter, malice and inflexible to your spouse is FOLLY. Do you see your ideas from their perspective? No because if you did you will not want it your way or the highway! If you're always negative about him and your guilty you leave your man or husband with a crap of horse shit on him with feeling; A spirit of control, rejection and putting him down. Women stop carrying the suitcase around with the old dirty funky same clothes and saying that's why you let his ass go. Did you ever whip your own ass of filth stank and funkiness that you were wrong and didn't never ever came to look to see it? I know that as a man even my own shit does not smell good! So, when the women that do this says you, you, you, it's one finger pointing at the man when four is pointing right back at themselves. The woman is saying she's right and you are wrong. The women feel like hurt, pain, sufferings that they only been wounded, (NO) both man and woman have. America has the highest rate of divorce. A lot of women have become feminists, rebelling against God's word by not obeying their husband and stubbornly demanding to have their own way. The conflict of unforgiveness creates a two headed monster or however the wicked spirit comes informing that's a witch, a woman, who's angrier than the devil because he's laughing and she's listening to others instead of her husband. This is woeful evil sin. To women that reads this book don't be angry at me or yourselves to the ones that do this. Cleopatra (THE WOMAN) said and felt like she never disobeyed God in our relationship it was only me. You know when I got my life together before I got into the relationship, I told her not to bring this into our relationship. She took me through abuse constantly, emotional, verbal, educational, psychological, financial and spiritual means. When a man is Godly help him more it's important to do so. Cleopatra (THE WOMAN) was not the helper. She was rebellious of what Jeffrey did from the past that she said I forgave you for and did not mean it. She was always an opposing force with little harmony, happiness, in our relationship she was an uncontrollable stubborn woman. She would say good for me I deserve everything that's coming to me and until this day she's telling me I got saved. Now during women P.M.S can be mood swings that she or you as a man can't even imagine herself being with God or the devil because she can change at any time, we all sin this is about the woman thou! Now the women that are with God she will have mood swings but out of 100% the husband is going to get 60% percent wife. Now if she's with the devil he's going to get it all the bitter, attitude, stubborn, her way, my way, no way. Real women don't walk out of their lives I have learned that on my own God loves all of you women, men to, we are all God's children. Women I give it to you, and to the ones who's reading this book she knows God is first and her husband who she is married too. It is her environment and a sacrificial, loving, sensitive, emotional man, but some false teachers say that's a woman God did not say that in his word people just say certain things in certain times to get there way or get there point across, take up for someone, tell them what they want to hear or just make someone feel good and it be fake the whole time! Men Jesus gave up his life for yours so give yours up for your woman I did it was not good enough I was put down, not forgiven and went right back to my old ways, because I gave up on my marriage don't make the same mistake I make you will be making one of the biggest mistakes in your life. I learned when going through tough times go to a room and pray and you can go get a room at a motel with time to yourself. Jeffrey did it when he was with Cleopatra (THE WOMAN) and Jeffrey went right back to her after leaving that let you know he was serious about the relationship. Jeffrey wanted it to work and loved Cleopatra, because if Jeffrey did not he would have not tried to make it work even she did not even lift. She said I do not come first in her life her children do. When she said I was trying to break them up from each other, why because someone between her family or friends told her that and going with her own negative mind, soul, spirit and vibes! Jeffrey risked his own life for Cleopatra's children because when the girl ran to our door that night screaming and crying banging on the door, I let her in while she was bleeding. So, someone told Cleopatra she told herself that I was breaking her up from her children, but she was in a relationship with me. Do you see what this man did for Cleopatra's children? So, this still means that I am full of shit until this day no matter what she is and so is her family. I just want to know can women tell me it is not easy to raise someone else child. Is that not a big ball on the man back some women would say well he is not no man if he got to talk about it or bring it up, and why not? He goes through pain as well! Then this is when some men get attack especially stepfathers don't tell women what to do with their children! I love them all even Cleopatra the most who Jeffrey broke up with. Really, Jeffrey loved Cleopatra more than he loved himself if you can imagine what was happen I could not believe. I went hungry so they can eat sorry to women who say only this that only they will go hungry for their children to eat I don't think so because I'm a man I did it! When the mother said you do not Jeffrey do not stand out here and beg for money. I said yes you told me that but behind closed doors in person with God, myself, your children and you put down. So, when I get out there I will say you was arguing with me in the room just now, because you were not satisfied, you did not know what you wanted, and you were aggravated because most of the bills was on her. I could not get a job. Still looking for a job every day in the hot sun! I gave Cleopatra (THE WOMAN) my all and everything into her. Jeffrey put Cleopatra needs first and he tried his best. So, what her daughter Anita and she was saying, I did not try hard enough! I knew God said better or for worse, so I hope she knows what she's teaching her daughter. Yes, I told her daughter that was my daughter when we were together. I told Anita to let God send you a husband/man that believes in him first and doing something for himself, has a great education and treats you `just like he wants his mom and women in his family respectfully to be treated! He needs to be in church. Now this do not mean to every single woman out there that forget and say to their husbands when times get hard, (WHAT YOU TOLD OUR DAUGHTER) now look at your sorry ass now you can't find no job, but even though you trying to find one. She is on your case because you cannot make nobody give you a job or hire you. Women remember to teach your sons and daughters what better or for worse, richer or poor, sickness in health until death do us apart means, please tell, show, pray, put in with work of action because if you don't you will be bringing cycles and curses. Just notice some families cannot take, go through these times because we were not taught the struggles and pain which is what they parents going through. Then the woman be in so much pain she asked God why she had to go through this, they always think for every situation it is on the man. It is all his fault that this happen in the first place I can agree on somethings or most depending on the situation and problem everything situation is different. I cannot say everything that is common sense. So, this do not come from some women sides of their wrongs and actions on their cycles? Telling a man that everything is his fault is not being selfish and admitting to your wrongs as well. (YOU KNOW WHAT THAT IS?) That is being women who cannot fess up to what they do wrong in the relationship. If a man is doing everything to satisfy you. So why you cannot satisfy him each day? Do you as a woman think you always right about what you feel is right! Cleopatra and other women got on me about me about my ways and cycles women cannot take this criticism because 90% of the time they think they are right and 10% they are wrong until they feel as it is time to give in! See for breaking a lot of past cycles I had on me I got a thank you then I got curse out before based on nothing no evidence at the present time or moment, but it was one thing to inform you women things from the past, however the cause is from rehashing the past even more when will she let go? See I did not get a kiss, smile, love, or hugged not even a thank you that means a lot when someone change for the best it's not only for God and themselves, but also for you. You every thought about those women? NO! You had different thoughts, lukewarm, curious, doubtful, fear, and you say that God is in control when that is nowhere in your mind because these thoughts would not be in your mind! The other thoughts are in her mind that she is indecisive back and forth flip and flop, unknown she thinks she knows herself on this but do not. This does not mean she is not a good woman or lost respect for herself her concept on somethings is screwed up! A woman can be a dreamer to. We go through things in life, but God sees how strong our faith is everything is a test. We do not want all women to say yes, and all was it only that it because of I am, or men is bringing women down! It is all his fault! Then you have lots of women feel and think that they husband do not deserve no second chance, or her full total love and obedience but God says so. Her responsibility is to be the best wife she can be under God not for her children only first out of envy from past disputes. No, It's God Husband/ Wife and children. Jeffrey sat back because every time he put his foot down as the head of the house in God's way and not in control after he changed it did not mean anything to Cleopatra it was all about her. Did not walk up to me or call me sincerely with love and ask Jeffrey, Love do you forgive me. See these cycles come down from women in her family cycles that has not been broken and yes, Cleopatra (THE WOMAN) told me about so many of my cycles I had to get them right, so what she was waiting on? She had me on hold her man. See some of the gestures and attitudes she will give me her mother will to. When Cleopatra could not get what she wanted she will act in the same way her mother will. See I could live with her, and I couldn't live without her she's still a good woman. I have seen good men and women in great relationships. There's good in all of us! You know Jeffrey even sat there and looked at his queen in a loving way, Cleopatra (THE WOMAN) will say WHAT? I won't be saying nothing the whole time I will be in the mood of the time of gaining respect and trust that I was already supposed to get when she told me she forgave me. Jefffrey completed his test with God but not with her the time being was a test, studying, quiet, and learning because this is what you go through after a woman has been hurt and done wrong it's just that in return what I've learn from and got it together what's the outcome return from Cleopatra (THE WOMAN)! At the same time, I communicated with her and shared what was on my mind and heart. Don't even try to get in a woman mind it's like falling in quicksand. She asks I did I even did what was supposed to do! Now today if she were to sit here and lie then say no you did not. I will say just like any man say ok darling to give them what they want not for a debate to come in. So, why did she take me back forgive then marry me and after marrying me she brought the past back up? A lot of women can say they forgive they men and say I did, I did so if so, why are we all arguing about something we both supposed to move on about because someone is holding hurt inside hurt people. You can say the past is the past but if you are bringing something up it never left so you cheated back on and on lying to your soulmate not of him making an excuse to get out of what he's done he's caught! He left his trail, you got him and made him pay then he must suffer the consequences more & more. See then you have women say I see you are for your mother, your father, children but not for me then when the man comes in and speak standing up the past must be brought on him so the WOMAN/WIVES/WIFE can get of what she or them did wrong towards the MAN/HUSBANDS/MEN! The scriptures in the Bible on forgiveness goes for the man and woman. The women say we do forgive but you men go back to doing the same old thing no most of that old thing be in your mind woman and it be hard to let go. Do you truly give that man a chance just not only cheating women you can say or most of the time, some or most but not all you can say what you want to your grown that is selfish because even God do not blame us for everything! Our own actions and wrongs held accountable for then we repent God forgive us he does not come back and say you did it again be thinking, nothing be done God do not do that. See you can be talking with your man and bring something up from the past or petty then he cannot speak at all even he gets a few words in, but I thought you let that go, then you be like shut up or walk away even get loud! He can ask question like, I thought you? The woman will say WHAT, OR WHAT YOU SAID? It is time for her now she got him where she wants him yeah now what the arguing starts. It does not be nothing for him to say your anger comes out then he walks away that mean come back or stay don't go she is in her mood! She is swinging which way to go she do not know she's more than just upset. Woman/women/wives you supposed to be loving your man/men/husbands I do love him, but he did this, that, and I don't know if I can ever trust him again so if you don't know YOU DON'T CARE enough to accept his apology and completely move forward and heal! The love is still there you just be in pain not only for the woman man to. The trust can be giving back to the man if you honestly clean up as well of what hurt the man has done to you when he's clean because if your heart is not clean then how will you be able to let him back in then you would be blaming him for your bad heart that is not being clean he did his part! Trust is earned by both parties involved most peoples never say this it's 1 not 2 because cannot do it all by himself! Women if you can forgive a lot that do not want to do this you will not be satisfied with God and within yourselves and others, but Cleopatra walked up to me with a sinful heart towards me and say baby will you forgive my family, children and I isn't that what God says Jeffrey? I will say yes. When Jeffrey did forgive, Cleopatra argues with me, and I say you bringing up anything on me what about forgiveness? Then she will say and use that I forgive quicker than she does and that's what wrong with men today they think we just supposed to forgive them just like that. A lot of women use this treatment towards their men today. She had love for herself, God and her children to touch me on my chest humbly to touch me on my chest crying, me holding her when her mother took her through things, I said go back and love your mother forgive her. She would cry, scream, holler and that same love for God and forgiveness she did not give to me one bit and I was her man. Cleopatra (THE WOMAN) told me all we do is fuck good then change it and say that's all I want to do to her. Do you know how that feels? When I'm lying beside her she tells me get your ass up and do something shit I'm paying all the bills, at night this is what a wife supposed to tell her man. Jeffrey did make Cleopatra feel low so low you can imagine, but then I got my life right with God and she ask God and prayed to bring me back to her. Her prayers were answered by the Lord, and she was not satisfied at all. It was I did this wrong, I did that, I was on her children, on her, on her mother and her sister. I was a fuck up, lazy and a grown ass man that did not want to work, started shit I was all these things, I meant her no good, I can say she was special and still loved her but could not say one thing about me. Like loving her children spoiling them like she does by giving them things right back because the bad cleaned up and changed, she brought the change back like I did not cleanup she wanted all the credit, because her mother. I didn't know where God say a mother supposed to do right by backing her children up when they are wrong sinning towards the husband or anyone! A man will give a woman another chance, but will a woman give him one? I was caught texting, calling woman, flirting, lying, cheating, with another woman I did it all. When I was abusive verbally, physically, mentally, and evil. Jeffrey stopped it all and changed it all came to a complete stop Cleopatra put a time on our relationship because she said it was too late. I shouldn't never do those things and she don't care anymore. Now for me and her because she told me that she forgave me honey for everything and said to me I mean it from my heart. She didn't from the very first start. I believe with women on the stand she has every right to do that and say that, but not on God say so judgement on his stand. In our relationship she treated me as she was the God, she was bitter and scornful. The woman is unpredictable in a good and bad way, because they mood swings at any time. Then I got a headache the woman wants more and more, now a real woman I give it to you all no one can keep you down the more she prays to God the higher she grows, and she be spiritual and lifted. Now Cleopatra (THE WOMAN) does not ever put on herself. My woman always makes her moves and always in a situation out there in the world. My woman knew how to handle things and walk away from issues she lived her life with her head lifted-up high and knew what kind of people to be around and did not ever compete for attention was a plan and educated all by herself and loved, but you know she did not say one good thing about me. I am a child of God! We gave one another everything however we hurt each other. It really hurts the most when Cleopatra (THE WOMAN) says everyone played a part and was wrong. The clincher was I was told this on the after math of the ending of the relationship which means the break-up. We met up one night was supposed to be our last time seeing and touching each other in a hotel after making love and I was laying on top of her and she was holding me tight when she said this telling me good-bye, but meeting with me on more occasions. She can say that and change it in her way in other ways for women towards God and her man that it's only my fault and only the children are chosen! When I ask the son, Trevor did I ever tried to break you all up as a family and did I ever let you get into a lot of bad things, the son said no you didn't try to break us up and you did let us get away with a lot of bad things. We stuck by each other at one point then Cleopatra (THE WOMAN) gave up on me and wasn't there for me through thick in thin anymore. She supposed to stick by me no matter what comes along. Cleopatra stopped fighting for me. What she didn't realize was the one thing she would never have done to me I did to her, and I didn't realize that visa versa. A lot of women say something against the children. No to women that do this don't use your children as a weapon because your children can turn on you with that spirit that you are using against someone else, that's called taking advantage of someone and using your children as a tool and weapon. What goes around comes around! To Cleopatra (THE WOMAN) I tried my best to satisfy that don't have nothing good to say about me, she doesn't know God created me to put something in her to make her feel better and special like he did her for me. I gave her my heart, smile, my love words, prayer and encouragement. I satisfied her so much it was too much. The beauty she has and power. Her brain is a computer and she use it better than technology she knew when to shut it down on me and when to open it back up when to use it for experience and when to bring virus. She gave me life and then took it back. She gave me respect then took it back. My thing is ladies come can you say, because it is something I did. But I cleaned it up! So why is it when a woman does wrong, a wrong is a wrong it's a sin it's different for women. Ladies stop saying that and looking at if it's like only that one thing, because that's not God way that's evil. The woman that I satisfied is a mother. She was my partner no she still I take that back she still is all my love I put in! I gave her respect with her ways, sins, rights, wrongs, good, bad, and her best. She is more a better person. She is a strong black woman. She used the word strong as good as I have seen her learned on her own and with me. I was in love with this beautiful woman. Can you imagine so many things were place on the relationship man I tell you? This is knowledge for other women to learn things. Now she is a strong woman in good ways as saved, blessed, believing in God, loving God herself, her children, me, and everyone. Cleopatra (THE WOMAN) is a good strong woman that's crazy as hell that walked in all purposes for her opportunity's. A woman who carried her weight and mines that could fight her own battles, build her wall up all the time with a plan. I love her when she was strong, good and bad! When she's a woman that showed up for work on time and can defend herself. A strong woman with a good attitude and say prayers and was on me hard to pray. That's a strong woman that's an instructor a woman with class better than any woman. A strong woman that couldn't be defeated, who has compassion and lay the Bible on my chest or beside us to make love soft or strong. This how you know when a man loves a woman, when he can put up with her rights and wrongs, love her for her bad or good, still want her back and go through whatever it takes to get her back! I have got to be a strong man to put up with her as well as she was putting up with my shit, take care of her and her children. I tried my damn best, because for her and the children the other fathers were not there so why was I? If she says I did not love her or her children that is a hurtful pain to me because all the sin she done she is still a loving woman of God and still love God, me, herself and her children but I can't! Now the woman can't run game on me or have a sense of humor or be smarter on this. It's a part of every woman that's inside of her when she's being strong will, rude, disrespectful and nasty. Now I understand you women when the man has treated you wrong, I agree with you but when he has gotten his shit together and you're using the same old shit against him time after time you're being a strong angry evil MRS. BITCH! Now you want a man to handle the truth. You want to get on him about he can't handle the truth from you women at all. Now is it time you women can't handle the truth, don't want to listen and this is the strong woman paying you back. When you have not done nothing to her at all or she's still holding on to the past to say I'm a strong damn woman with anger and you can't know a strong woman with unforgiveness! This is the rude, nasty, evil strong woman, who uses the past for the present on and on and feel, know like that she does not play a part in it at all. When the relationship breaks up, to stubborn, selfish to see, blind and still saying I can see don't tell me nothing or I don't want to her shit you got to say. I didn't get into a relationship with Cleopatra (THE WOMAN) for her money, because I had my own money just like she said they could never say until we broke up only she can say (BABY I DIDN'T FALL IN LOVE WITH YOU FOR YOUR MONEY). Now she can put me down with her daughter, mother, son and anyone that she had in mind and say they don't take care of a grown ass man who is a man going out there every day to find a job. If my ass didn't have no job and I'm trying to find one I'm still not shit with Cleopatra being the leader and her children following her. Now the strong nasty rude woman can say and do you wrong and have her children involved in the issue. The mother is laughing and think it's cute to the ones that does this. Let you in a disrespectful way she's in charge as a strong woman. Instead of being a woman to be nice, back you up, help you and stand by your side Cleopatra (THE WOMAN) said you want me to be like them dumb ho's out there in the streets that you were fucking on me with, and it be towards me. So much anger, hurt, unforgiveness coming back and forth apologizing. I'm telling her the same thing she told me thinking she's perfect. Jeffrey wanted Cleopatra to treat him as said a good Godly woman supposed to treat her man, respect not in my way only God's way. When I say God, I mean leading the holy spirit to her in mind, body, soul, thoughts, and in that way! I never had God in me, so if she can be strong and right all the time on that and think, feel, see me always never having God in me so tell me is that a Christian? Can you please answer that, because no matter what someone says about you your still God's child no matter what I love her? She didn't even tell me God loves me! I'm not making it out to be she is the one that's wrong at everything no she never woman up to her wrongs! Like she gets on me all time strong woman putting her wrongs and mines all on me. I'm not holding in anything I'm showing marriages, relationships how everything is the man fault even until this day. When she cursed me out saying dirty words to me for no apparent reason. This real man didn't let his woman walk away ask her, I ran her down. Now they say you don't suppose to do that when they wrong. See therefore divorces is so high in this world not just only for men sins and wrongs. I didn't let my treasure go for another man to have. I fought, fought, fought and fought saying I cause this on myself listening to her, myself, false prophets, mother-in-law, the children, when I said that's it I'm getting tired of being taken advantage of something happen 6 1/2 years ago. It's good to talk it out, because if you hold on to it then what winds up happening you wind up breaking up, arguing, always angry when a woman wants to talk, she wants to talk happy or angry. The false prophets are telling them, friends, family members you can't make her talk to you. If she doesn't want to then tell that and uses that against the relationship. Instead of them telling the positive thing, pray and respect one another. A woman just does not only deserve respect, loved, prayer and man due to the strong woman that's mad and rude while you are telling her good morning I love you and she's telling you move out the way. The women that do this be strong, bitter and don't know they poison their marriages. The false prophets and teachers agree that it's okay. God don't agree with that. That's the woman who's doing wrong to her man. She has someone backing her up saying yes that's right let's get him. Like when Cleopatra (THE WOMAN) uses to stand there, and other people got on Jeffrey in front of her for what I did to her in the past. She says she forgave me; she would stand there and stand behind whoever it was getting on me about my past. Cleopatra would say yeah, yeah, yeah that's right it all your fault, so you never forgave Jeffrey however she loved Jeffrey over again with a clean your heart, so you don't have to deal with God on that no, because your different than me. I'm a no-good man that's shit. Jeffrey can say Cleopatra is special and a good woman, but not back up her wrongs to be a slave in a chained relationship! The woman is never satisfied she carry all kinds of things in her purse the woman, they want bigger house more money. A woman could repeat the same thing over again P.M.S. or not repeating the cycle and feel like something is wrong with her sometimes when it's nothing at all. The woman is always curious about herself. She will always have A DESIRE FOR MORE OR SOMETHING NEW! I know women lead their lives by following their desires, plans, dreams and goals HER CHOICE IS NEVER WRONG. I can't stop her from wanting! Sometimes she happy sometimes she's not half of the time. It has something to do with her family, then next day it's the job. I know Cleopatra (THE WOMAN) when it's the time of the month she be on all kinds of levels especially with her hormones, unhappy, happy, cranky, stank, funky, attitude, ways be like don't mess with me right now. Cleopatra (THE WOMAN) always came at me. What is wrong with me? Did I do something wrong? Not her! She loves her family but can't stand mines. Cleopatra (THE WOMAN) will always be the gift from God. No woman will ever be satisfied. Cleopatra (THE WOMAN) would cook for me when she got off work barefooted in the kitchen. Jeffrey would cook breakfast for her and the children. I love her to because she has hope, smart, and she nurtured me. She believed in me one time I never stop believing in her. She used to fight for me, and I can say she still is a good woman and deserves nothing less from me. She is a person I hope one day she can tell me that! The only sin are not only adultery, lust, flesh and fornication ladies. Check this out these six things THE LORD HATE: Seven are an abomination unto him: A proud look, a lying tongue, and hands that shed innocent blood, and heart that devised wicked imaginations, feet that be swift in running to mischief, a false witness that speak lies, and he that seventh discard among brethren. My son Trevor keeps the father's commandment and forsake not law of the mother: bind them continually upon the heart and tie them about the neck. When the guest it shall lead us; When they slept, it shall keep thee; and when thou awake; it shall talk with thee. Now a woman can repeat something like it's a new year. She's doing this and that time for change and wants more, but soon as you get out her or tell her the same thing humble and calmly it's a fight, it's a debate, its wrong. Love does no wrong to a neighbor there for love is the fulfillment of the law. I am praying that one day to all the people who can't forgive hopefully one day that do! The one's that can't forgive because I was here once hug yourselves and other you will fix the broken pieces in your heart! When they come on one accord with God. For women with the tongue can they really sit in front of there, husband, man, boyfriend, fiancé, and say dear GOD, I deserve my tongue cut out! I am guilty of saying mean, angry nasty things. I am also guilty of telling lies, not forgiving, I am guilty of falsely accusing others. I ask you to please forgive me for all my sins to you Lord and to the person who I have hurt standing right there in front of them? I repeat that I have done these things. I need you forgives. My tongue is my worst enemy. Please help me clean up my act. Please how to teach me how to control my tongue. Please hear my prayer and forgive me in Jesus' name: Amen. I do not like a woman that talk too much, I will not marry one that do to, because a meek quiet spirit in a woman, she needs to know her place and when to hush, because the Bible says so not me. Everything does not require, a response my grandmother told me, A WOMAN MUST BE SEEN BUT NOT HEARD! When a real Godly woman knows her power, she doesn't have to do a whole bunch of talking she even know and learn her powers more when she doesn't say nothing. Know how to use them wisely and Godly! I'm telling it to myself as well as the Lord teach me to have a humble quiet spirit! I want to measure my words and I'm still working on that a lot of women need to keep quiet. (See your getting angry that's alright you are going to get delivered). Some women hear a conversation going on you just have to say something or add on just shut up. You will get anointed if you just keep quiet on your fasting: Without talking sometimes God is working on your mouth do not talk to only the Lord! If someone walks up to you and ask you, how are you doing? Do not say something rude be polite. When you ask you how are you feeling Love? Just throw hands up to the Lord and wrap your hands around his neck and hold him tight. You got get in God word find out what he hates what he likes and don't like. All you got to do is present, just yield to God. Then you have a joyful woman. A woman that knows her power don't have to do no talking not saying she do not have to speak at all and she's under control, it's just that she knows her place! She's still never satisfied she wants more. Life is too short for people, friends, relationships, marriage even for your own self to argue and fight one another in mind, spirit, verbal, mentally, physically, ignoring one another, get back, friends count your blessings value your love one's and move on with your head held high and a smile for everyone. The woman that can't be satisfied always remember she will give you something greater, as well as something beautiful nature a baby, she will make a house a home, she will cook for you, she will give you her heart she doubles what she is given to her. She just wants more and more she's never satisfied! She also deals with stress, burdens, she smiles, screams, sings, cries, be happy unconditional and knows what she's worth. My people are destroyed from lack of knowledge, so why does the women want all the knowledge and wisdom? Please don't say I have problem with women, or I just haven't found the right woman or what women I have done wrong to, because no man or woman in a relationship, marriage is perfect. The woman has all the education which is not true it's only one person that get all that's God it is not the woman just because she's the WOMAN. It is the heart that matters Jeffrey had Cleopatra (THE WOMAN) tell him numerous of times that I was jealous, because she got an education, and I was a fuck up. She got that from her mother and when Jeffrey asked her son did I try my best of taking care of you all was it true? He said yes therefore I told her to stop talking to me like that in front of her children, because they won't ever respect me, because how she disrespected me in front of them, so what the mother did wrong they followed her. When I did right it didn't matter because my past or any skip hop mood I made or what I said I was wrong. I'm not taking this out on everyone or someone, another thing is why a lot of men that are married the mother-in-law does not like the husband or don't get along with the husband or the father-in-law see these curses. The husband be married to his wife not the mother-in-law and the mother is not satisfied. They say we just want what's best for our daughter, so they live they life for them and still make some choices or decisions in their lives just let go and let God. It's like the daughter is in relationship with the mother and they are best friends, not by sleeping together. I don't want women to say so what do you have against that and them not sleeping together just all in her business! No one was there for me to back me up when I was right, NO ONE! Nothing I ever did was right or good in me, and to the woman that do this say I didn't say that men I feel you. To men who been through just as much as women hurt and pain I understand. I feel when your woman comes in your face and tell you that what she took you through and shit compared to what you took her through! Everyone has a story to tell as well as a testimony and been through trials and tribulations. When a man makes an excuse, he's ignorant lazy, stupid, making excuses from the past, he's blaming others and hurting the wrong people for what he's been through. Now with a woman don't go there it's different from her in life she needs all the time in the world and has an excuse for her wrongs. If it's all the time in the world she needs it, she can do it, and if it goes like that for the woman power and control. If you got a problem with it that's just how it is marriages are not broken up on husbands/men/man! Now you have lots of women to look up to T.V shows, movie stars, soap operas, they listen to them follow them and tell their lover or friend this is what this and that person say when they can't listen to the person who's in front of them who they are in love with. I'm not putting the movies stars, T.V shows, soap operas down that are successful and rich, what I'm saying is that these peoples have lives and are in relationships they get divorces to and listen to other people talk in their relationship they have it just as much worse. Half of them do it for the money. Don't know who but that what goes on in life! Take it or leave it. Women have you ever felt what men go through. What they go through in life especially black men. I don't put women down for being motivated, smart, nurturing, beautiful, right, wrong, ambitious and more than she's all that and some. Jeffrey always told Cleopatra that she thought she was the only one would go without and her children can have it all. I did the same I will go hungry to feed the children and her. Women say you don't get any credit so you throwing that back up in her face you're not a real man because if you did things for her children it was from your heart, but I was not appreciated! See when a mother does it and be wrong it's ok Cleopatra (THE WOMAN) doing it was good in her eyes when she was wrong in her eyes she said she is the mother it's her job what she damn does for her children (MY CHILDREN)! You know how it goes women. No one cannot tell a mother who. How to take care and love her children they are her babies even growing up. So, as a woman say not being satisfied, I didn't love her children? I love them more than their real fathers did, because they did nothing for them at all. So, when I was their father I feed, took care of their needs, show them love and affection, I was taking them to school and holiday shopping. Around the holidays we would put up and decorate the Christmas tree. I would not miss a birthday for the children. I prayed, protected and die for them I'm not being a father and a mother. My mother went through a lot with men. She was with, different relationships. They were wrong and she was wrong in a lot of things she did. If I write down or sit here and say I love her for that I will be lying. I don't back no one up for doing wrong not even myself, and a lot of mothers teach their children that if I'm wrong back me up no matter what, but if they do it to one another it hurts. They will argue with one another in families thinking it's alright when they are confusing the children themselves and bring a cycle. When they say I got the nerve to tell someone something of the wrong I done, the same way they are telling someone something of what you do. I don't see all the bad and wrong in you whoever you are! I see that in a lot of families they jump back at them telling them you don't tell me this or that I'm grown so, so you are drama I'm not going to listen to you when you just talk about me in my face and talked about the other person earlier. So, you done talked about me to others and you're going back and forth with me right now and these same women on this level will say they are right. They go out with their family but when they get hurt by the crap that they dish out and receive in they are not going for it and still angry, hurt and upset they are miserable misery loves company, right women? I have a friend name Thomas he said Jeffrey my woman sees all kinds of women. She sees and say certain things about them, don't be worried about them and be happy. So, then he said the grocery store they go to all the time a woman that works there spoke to Tommy and his wife Eva. Eva spoke to the lady back everyone said hello, the lady's name is Ms. Warren. So, Tommy said Mm mm and sucked her teeth and Tommy said she only speaks with me and a nice conversation. Tommy said every woman you have met you have never got upset, angry or caught an attitude he said sweetheart you would never get angry and be satisfied if got God and one another. You have a husband/man as Christ love the church and honest to you and you be submissive to me, so Eva said it's nothing, but still had an attitude with Tommy. So, when Tommy came to me, he said Jeffrey, do you know Eva never got upset about no woman until the other day this lady Ms. Warren started talking to me at the grocery store. I don't understand brother. I said brother listen women can be funny at times especially with her intuitions that don't mean she's a bad woman at all she's a good woman made from you and God gave her to you, but I sat back, and I observed. My woman didn't say anything and women period, just like women observed men from top to bottom! So, I said to Tommy you kept asking over & over again what's wrong? What's wrong? All the lady do is speak to me leave it alone Godly then suck her teeth then be sarcastically smiling and sometimes looking curious. Jeffrey said brother Cleopatra (THE WOMAN) observed me and other women observed me as well knowing my sisters, I told him women are strange I said your woman is a woman so she knows how women think react and what games they play but she sees something knows what's going on with that woman that she says your being man that can't see, because you are just a man. Some nasty women will say that man was dumb or he's just always thinking what he got between his legs or say something like they probably fuck before or still is you never know girl watch his ass. That's not right to say for every man in this world but I say your woman is going to keep that to herself if she hasn't told you all this time. She sees something in that woman you can't it's a secret woman don't tell on certain things in their head not to be said in their diary. Watching with their eyes observing. She wants you to know what she wants you to know and tell you what she wants you to hear not it being bad that's a woman being a woman! I told Thomas she's going to keep that to herself just leave it alone because if you keep bringing it up then it might come to a problem you just have to let a woman be. Even if the other woman Ms. Warren is not doing nothing wrong or bad at all. (WOMEN) if she has her reasons one out of plenty of rules women have, they have their reasons, and your woman has hers. Some women look for things some mind their own business. It still comes out where they all are being a woman to find out or know, or see or think more and more, or be fascinating, confusing, be challenging, or a woman that's too smart for her own good. Then say (NO) you men can't handle a strong smart woman that's to some men not all. I'm talking about women who's to damn smart for they own good where they swear, they know and tell everything. I didn't tell you baby, dear, honey or in an anger way or nice I don't know everything, but at times how she comes at you, talks and her tongue, speech, voice, opinion or fact must be heard. She is saying and knowing everything with her mouth. She's just not telling you I know everything. Then you have a lot of women say what you could do for me. I was doing for myself before you came into the picture and I can do it now, why would the woman say that to the man. When they are in love with one another they need one another, because if not they would be owning their own by themselves! Is it about the money? The Cars, materialistic things? The house is gone. The businesses are gone. No more going out. Because if that were what it was about that's why you're not together to the women that say I couldn't take care of no grown ass man that was married to listening to their mothers of their cycles, because they lose money, houses, and didn't know the one in front of them was important than the material things. Let it go to their heads. A lot of relationships have broken up on this marriage. When your man is trying to find a job and he can't find one. He is trying extremely hard to get a job. When you pressure him, because he can't find a job calling him lazy by calling him that in front of the children, they feel that they can say the same thing to him. What you call your man who is trying to find a job. When a man is on his grind to get job and going to interviews everyday keep mind woman, he can't make an employer hire him. You must keep encouraging him that a door will open. When Jeffrey was in relationship before we broke-up Cleopatra (THE WOMAN) said I don't take care of no grown ass man. When I came home from my job search early during the day I would beg and ask people for money late at night to feed Cleopatra (THE WOMAN) and the children. Then the daughter Anita would say what the mother said I don't take care of no grown ass man that's looking for a job every day. Cleopatra (THE WOMAN) would ignore my feelings and pain saying Godly you still on that you haven't let go. When we were together and broke-up. When you hurt a woman, that pain stays forever for some who do not want to let go. Women, please give men more credit than you do. Men are happy to know they have a woman who can please and impress. I bragged on Cleopatra (THE WOMAN) I loved her that much when she wasn't with me, I stood up for her. A man wants a woman that a lover not just sex or a provoker on the past. He just doesn't want you to stimulate his mind in good ways. He wants you to stimulate his spirit as well. You are already the sunshine he wants you light, bright, sunny and he wants you dark in the bedroom with the stars with high heel shoes with you saying baby look at my heels. I never put my money, job, business, or career before Cleopatra (THE WOMAN) in that case I should have been married to the business, but that never happened, but when the business dropped money got tough Cleopatra (THE WOMAN) was married to her job that was first. I still was by her side and helping her. Happy Cleopatra happy life, but not doing it the spoiled, selfish, nasty way for women it is God's way! Like some relationship when the women say jump the man say how high go do this go do that. No, it's respect for both parties a lot of women use the past off what the man has done to her. I got to have every damn thing. He must do everything I say for what he done to me as he owes me and he's a cash machine or a push button! Jeffrey went for it for what I did to Cleopatra (THE WOMAN) I admit it, but she went overboard which she got that from her mother Pam. You know the thing that hurt its so bad Jeffrey got from around Cleopatra (THE WOMAN) that wanted to fuss, argue, with him and I walk out crying out the door. Time to myself with God then she would call my phone and say you don't fuck love me, because if you did why you walked out what I'm doing here by myself? Can a woman ask herself that when she's driving her man crazy sometimes? Then she will change it and say I'm sorry not in a sincere way come back what you want me to do beg you. No, it's how you ask it is how you talk to someone. My opinions, my facts don't mean nothing forever! Someone told me I shouldn't have hurt her. She shouldn't have hurt me. Everyone has been hurt. The thing is can everyone forgive truly not say it then bring it back up in the household, they live in. The woman thinks the love is still there, because she forgave this man, but sick to her stomach, because as soon as she thinks about what he did to her everything comes back up hate say this eating back up the vomit and pig slop. I'm not putting everything on women

I'm saying it is not right and fair in God eyes to say it is all his fault you don't know what we go through; Women use this when you need to. I feel you, but after you forgive don't keep in your heart, because you never forgave with every action is a reaction, because if I did not do nothing to you how could you ever respond to me with a reaction whether negative or positive, look at yourself, baby look at us now. It's all me. So, if God does not all you and not all me, what make you say that out your mouth? To the one's that say to the other spouse pointing the finger. I never said it was all Cleopatra (THE WOMAN) fault, ever did I? No. Now correct me if I'm wrong if someone is blaming someone else for their wrongs, your wrongs and everything is that not being selfish. Now I have to say something about women who are healthy and big that's okay. Keep yourself up looking good, your beautiful and good looking. Keep your head up, my aunt told me that big healthy women who can do things that some slim women can't in many things and ways not talking about making love or having sex this is about respecting woman/women. Auntie Debbie taught me some things I had a lot of nasty ways and did I tried to satisfy my woman is so many ways. Cleopatra (THE WOMAN) I fulfill all her desires, even her demands! Her needs of expectations in her way as well, I was a part of something that I fixed and wasn't apart, because it was all about her desire. I loved her that much, even with certain conditions I was on restriction and couldn't say nothing. If she were satisfied it wouldn't be this then after I got this right, I was wrong on something she brought up it didn't go her way even when it did. I have seen a lot of relationships say let the woman be right even when she wrong! Now if a woman sees her man upset or hurt or crying, I never knew where God will tell you to tell your man stop acting like a woman. This man with a brain with perfection I push myself in pain having seizures constantly pushing myself until I almost died fighting for Cleopatra (THE WOMAN) and her children. Her daughter Anita was put out of my house at 24 years old for disrespecting my house that's tough love! She grown so get your own. All you women right say she is not going to disrespect her mother, because she knew her mother will slap her and don't play with her. She not going to play with me I couldn't put my hands on her. Jeffrey discipline was leave and get out, and Cleopatra (THE WOMAN) telling me what other people said I was not supposed to do. Well, she should go marry them and move in their house and let the daughter curse them out! Can women understand my hurt? Forget me is what her family said to me. Cleopatra (THE WOMAN) accepts her Grandmother Ms. Anderson, and her brother Clyde treated me like family and told me when I was wrong, and it was there respect of how they had done in a way of real true love. A real woman knows the respect and caring of speaking to her man. She loves him dearly so much believe in him no matter what, always encourage and leave him in peace not leave him frustrated thinking more on what he needs to do and get right. Jeffrey just wishes Cleopatra did this after she forgave him, stood there and let her daughter Anita disrespect him! Jeffrey wishes Cleopatra were strong enough to forgive someone who sorry, accept it with an apology and actions. Do you know all of us in life was raised in ways on both sides (HUSBANDS/WIVES) (WOMAN/MAN) and what I'm getting at is a woman can be raised on a part on a good thing in her life, see it and don't at times. The man she's with can be letting her know what she needs work on. She's too busy stalking him down from his past mistakes not finding her guilts within working on her. Then the man can have his woman telling him what he needs to change up on and he reacts in his way of being hardheaded, so it goes back and forth that's not no win that's a lost. I know been there done that and others have I feel where you all are coming from. There is no communication it's aggravation! See Cleopatra would never receive anything from Jeffrey after forgiving him when we in a relationship it was lovely then the devil came out. I gave her and her family the gifts and golden heart I have. I see, hear and watch women say once if you lie, cheat, steal, take, use, abuse, or betray a woman one time it will never go back to the way it used to be it was before. So why do you claim you know, have God and the blood of Jesus in you so that's only for you? When a woman or a man has a forgiving heart please don't mistreat them or use them as dogs saying you can't forgive just like that, and it be years down the road. No, it's a commandment from God not them. God will make your enemies your foot stool. Women don't be angry, bitter and hateful. You know I respect the women who say the man started it he lied, cheated, abused, and he done it all to me I can't take it no more, so I must relieve all and extra back on me! What God does not like or tolerate is when you say you forgiven and you take him back, but he goes through the anger of you really, truly, sincerely. He pays for the punishment double triple and more with you putting a leash around his neck pulling him with the chain then he becomes a yes man, and ok to everything and it's right, right for years and years which took him through pain and cruelty and punishment! Now women don't want this done to them or no one. Pressure is serious for women who let it get to them. God says for better or for worse in a marriage and in his Bible. Cleopatra (THE WOMAN) as soon as the bills start coming in and my business drop, Jeffrey couldn't find work it was either was she's leaving, or she can't put up with this anymore or I'm leaving your ass. You can tell by the attitude, actions, arguing at me about going out there. Coming into the house after looking for jobs all day going right back out then come back and forth because I could not be pressured on I cannot do shit right. I'm trying don't push a man more to where that a man leave home! The best marriages are 2 servants in love as one with God in the middle. God is there and the heart united. Healthy couples live to sacrifice for and serve each other. Jesus says, so women please say I don't know what I'm talking about I got sense because the word of God does not lie, he uses us all to tell it and speak into others! Some women that do this, stop telling your man (YOUR NOT GOD) you can't tell me nothing or you got some nerve to tell me anything get you right before you tell me something. Sorry then said to say he do be right it's just that you are afraid, feared to let your wall down or you give him your all back again! You want your man to listen to you and respect you? Especially if your right or wrong if the wife does this or the husband it's not right, because one or the other can take control of one another because it's two bosses at one another negatively not helping. It's not both of you it's the devil in the middle! Women tend to listen to other people instead of listening to their husbands. When your following other people's advice and not your own instead of following God you can make big mistake! Women want their men to listen to them and they will say quickly don't tell me nothing else about what someone else said about me, you or us. At times, a woman listens, gossip or make it up in her mind and bring it back to her man she can be right in front of him! A woman will quickly say you my husband when she feels the need to say so good or bad what's going on in what mood, I'm your wife then fast she will say you are under control, or you some control. A woman has taken your past and used it against you, her ability to have force and attack to always when she's losing her husband. See how you say it woman a man wants his cake and eat to, so women you don't have to cheat to want your cake and eat it to you got your ways! When I hurt Cleopatra (THE WOMAN) then got myself right with God and didn't push her to come to me to say I forgive you man. She really was being angry giving herself all the credit the best only mother and father, the best bill payer, only one taking in all the pain and struggling herself. When she doesn't know, feel and see we are both taking it in at the same time. We were married, because God word says that he knew his son was going to be crucified and the disciples was sitting there arguing about which was the greatest. Jesus got up from the table to let them know through good or bad times, rights or wrongs, because no one is perfect. He made an example and showed them that the servant his the greatest of all, rather husbands, wives, brothers and sisters about who is the best who did this sin and who got what who or is needed and all need to follow each other. Now Jeffrey was not a man that wasn't perfect I wash the dishes, the car, ran errands, washed clothes, and picked up the children. When she came in from work, I rubbed her back and her feet. Cleopatra found fault in everything Jeffrey did. Jeffrey strived to do his best to satisfy Cleopatra (THE WOMAN) constantly looking for plenty of ways to keep her happy but no matter how much Jeffrey tried you can't make no one happy if they choose not to be looking at you as permanent shit! Jeffrey had to give benefits to CLEOPATRA because she is his ROSE. Women or men just don't come with excuses it is both of you. There's no excuse for wives to say to your husbands I been at work all day you can't find a job I'm tired I got to deal with these children, and other things now I did not say a woman don't deal with these things in life. Like needing assistance on love and help, with I'm saying what do you know what your man wants or needs, what you to do and stop he have a right just as much as you. All that boyfriend/girlfriend games women supposed to get the most out of it and men got to put it down as well that's call growing up! That's a negative way of thinking and actions coming with a bad behavior because someone higher is fighting for the relationship, he's tired and people is following him. Jesus was tired, but he still did his job walking with everyone, with the cross we follow him in, sin and falling short of his word. Now some women follow celebrities and other people. When they have debates right or wrong and vote, so vote for God your husband yourself and listen to each other problems, debates good or bad and come to some type of agreement like you do on your job getting your paycheck! Like you do for politicians, your girlfriends, your hairdos, nails and feet! Just like you tell me to get off my butts. A marriage God says it's for a lifetime not a couple of years you get bored and then run and say that's it. Cleopatra (THE WOMAN) even took advantage of my humility but the better supposed to be both parties not just only the man serve today tomorrow is never promised. I stop being stubborn, prideful, and stop refusing to serve Cleopatra (THE WOMAN) until she started I was doing with her or not, but I messed up and let her get to me with the pain, hurt, bullying, unforgiveness and went back out there getting her back angry at her, myself, God being with the same women. See I'm being a man my wrongs, my sins, my repentance forgiving myself and Jesus not keeping no record now if someone does, they must deal with that with God. Why I have moved on in my heart with a cleanse heart. You know I see a lot of women today and they think they have it all together in this new world order now! The women know they fine and ok, child, please right? What about your marriage that's about to end? Ask yourself that question right now I was an ass hole once that's not cool, funny or right. Men listen to me, when God bless you with a good woman treat her right women you all need to wake the hell up to! When God bless you with a good man treat him right. Did you see the situation with Mary? Her husband cheated on her and for better or for worse then worked it out. Even when women are cheating men can't handle it, they work it out some just leave because the situation on a man from a woman cheating on him is insane for his mind to handle! Women, everyone goes through hell not only you, I'm not saying your bad I'm saying into days society, the courts, the system, the child support, how the woman do this take advantage like I said everyone goes through hell but don't stay there.

Don't torment yourself by reliving the pain repeatedly of someone else, good peoples with good and bad in them go through it to, because at times we do wrong things even when we learn from our mistakes. It's who did the most or less this and that who's good and who better than who in the relationship! It's good to let go but do it with hate in your heart, blaming someone else or everybody for everything! Even today I do wrong, and I don't blame others for my flaws on everything that would be stubborn, selfish, prideful, disobedient, foolish, negative, evil, cruel and all about myself! I will have a big mouth. You know I seen a Caucasian lady on T.V not to make this racist or prejudice. She was a Caucasian lady in an auditorium, and she was a professor talking with Caucasian men or women. Then she said I want every Caucasian person in this room who would be happy to be treated as in this society in general treats our black citizens. If you as if you are a Caucasian will you be happy to receive the same treatment as our black citizens do in this society, please stand! Then she paused because they were crying, and she started back talking to which she said to which she said you didn't understand the directions! If you Caucasian folks want to be treated the blacks are in this society stand! Then she said nobody is standing here that being said very plainly that you know what's happening you don't want it for you. Then she said I want to know why you are so worried to accept it, or to allow it to happen for others. The point I'm trying to make is just like men look what they go through in general especially the black men! Like I said everybody go through something. Women you are not the only one goes through hell and I understand them lots of people came to me and I have prayed with them. I went to lots of peoples who have prayed for me as well. You know what I don't like is people like to dish out but, they don't want to receive, like Cleopatra (THE WOMAN). She wanted me to receive her rights and wrongs and then tell me when I get a little say in (I DON'T WANT TO RECEIVE NOTHING FROM YOU)! When someone told me off like pastors, other people, her mother she stood behind them yes that's right, yes and when I humbled myself with God speaking to her with love she told me with hate in her heart you can't make me receive! Society has told some or most women a man supposed to handle everything. These men go through pain to there not superheroes. When men are not in position to do certain things how they get handle and treated, do they get the same help as does women? Everyone needs help I did not say lazy that's a sin. Jeffrey would cry and tell Cleopatra (THE WOMAN) everyday please don't do this to me I would beg her, but to herself as her thinking and feeling on her mind concept that be wrong it's all about get back. It's right because now like most women you see how it feels. So that's selfish repaying someone for what they have paid for and I'm feeling that way but as a woman she's feeling different no way and right confused. I'm going to tell all you women first, then myself, brothers, and sisters God already knows you know this already some will say then why are you telling it because it feels good to be positive! Jeffrey was in jail when I was with Cleopatra (THE WOMAN) I got jumped, beat up, I had 10 seizures I got pepper sprayed was put in the hospital came back to jail and went into 7 more seizures. God already made me pay for my sins and my partner forgave me before I went to jail. The Police beat me up I got out of jail and went right back because that was a violation on my probation for a year I still got arrested I had to plea on one charge for not paying my taxes and was innocent on the other charges. When Jeffrey was away I picked up the phone to call Cleopatra she was crying saying is you ok is you alright screaming to God me and herself I said OK it had to take almost losing me to bring in love. Then getting out of jail Cleopatra (THE WOMAN) came back oh this is not over. I'm blessed I'm living even times she cursed me out on the phone bringing up the past and telling me other people asking her on her job why I'm incarcerated? Because she told them oh yes, Jeffrey paid for what he did to Cleopatra (THE WOMAN), and she felt like that wasn't enough. Now I was and use to be a thug. God is who guided me, and I transformed myself to a better man. I am not the man I use to be, just like Saul he murdered Christian People then became saved transformed to a man of God named Paul. People called me all kinds of things in the streets. Then Jeffrey changed when Cleopatra (THE WOMAN) scream at and curse him out and Jeffrey was beaten for no apparent reason. My rights were violated I was a thug.

Chapter 6

Now Jeffrey is a change man and look how the system still treats me as a Black Afro American violating my constitutional rights and other rights as well and Cleopatra (THE WOMAN) with them as well cursing me out of the jail. When Jeffrey was at the window getting my property with my nose bleeding and head busted in pain, she is cursing me out saying I am always in something, just like the officers did beat me up in police station going in there to file a complaint on some officers that violated my rights and in America the police station is open to the public, we the people meaning everyone. Then when Cleopatra (THE WOMAN) gets home she says baby I am sorry I was wrong for what I said to you earlier, just like she did me when she was moving out when she told me she was sorry for putting me down all the time. I am trying best as a good person! Now freedom for me and men, don't you think it is too late for that? I was supposed to get that in front of God, children and her with respect. She told me when she felt like it but when I really needed it, she did not give it to me. When I told her constantly over, over again that I loved her and still do now! Cleopatra is a good great woman, mother, best friend, confidante, and most of all number 1! She did not say one thing about me good. This is to the women that are dead wrong, selfish for themselves and what they can get just like a lot of men do as well. Everyone has been bad in their life as a child and an adult, but the women that want to get the or man, because she sees, she wants what the other woman has and selfishness for self! Like Bathsheba with David in the Bible, women that do this have their, sins, games, ways, power, mind, control even when the man do give in it is wrong for you to do! Paul knew the older likewise, that they be reverent and behavior also leaving as a priest for God, the older women the already learned to love their husbands, learn to love their children, being reverent, Godly, modest, appear wise and charge them with seeking out and meeting with every younger in the church. As God says bodies presented as living sacrifices, holy, acceptable to God, not conformed to this world, but with transformed and renewed minds, and bodies that are temples of the holy spirit glorifying God in your body in spirit which are God; no longer living for me, but Christ living through them! God says the women is supposed to present themselves to him and live their life the way he told them to as a walking temple of as a consecrated priest of God, as a living sacrifice and as a bond servant of the Lord. It is not slandering, a nasty tongue, Paul talks about this speech saying it is a spiritual qualifier or disqualifier. This is a problem we all will face. In the same way, their wives are to be women worthy of respect, not malicious talkers but temperamental and trustworthy in everything not the woman saying I was this way once, but he messed me and everything and I did not play no part in at all! So, the finger is pointing only at the man forever. This is no excuse for a man to get away from his actions of wrong doings and you to as well. Women right is right wrong is wrong, you can twist change it put in what you want to or not but as adults we know right from wrong! It has been going on double time and triple time with getting back added on more and it be vengeance, envy, pride, pain, hurt all balled up inside until the woman say it is enough and really it does not be. See a woman says let go and let God of past issues but when it comes to a man doing wrong to her it is different, how so? The system, world, false prophets, other women, men, feel and teach this. God says with all sin is forgiving for after you repent and ask for forgiveness. Not but, not this way, you just do not know, anyway, whatever, now that is excuses because you have gone to God and back to the person falsifying not only what you told our God, but to yourself and the person you say you love. What is love? It is sure not that because that is not pure, kind, peaceful and has nothing to do with another chance that is your words of saying, (YOUR CHOICE)! Tells us that a tongue out of control, indicates a life out of control with God, yourself, and your loved ones and cause destruction. In the bible the source of all wickedness, especially of an uncontrolled tongue is hell, and Satan is the root of all gossip and sin, all harm talks and all slander. If you are damaging the reputation and love of your husband, you are a tool of the devil. The devil does not use only the husband he uses the wife as well really all of us. So, women do not use the devil saying your husband is the head of the household, so all sins fall on him because his sins and actions. When we are held accountable for our own actions, mistake, consequences we make in life.

Not saying husbands do not do this I am talking about women. Satan is a false accuser and so each time a wife does this she incites a believer to do, so that she is doing Satan's work. Satan is the ultimate source of all evil, the root of all wrong behavior and sense in the Bible says the tongue can cause great evil, Satan is always close at hand. Godly women never are to surrender to the devil. What the woman says out her mouth is true, honest, just, pure, lovely, and respectfully from the heart and soul in the spirit of Jesus Christ. Now when Cleopatra (THE WOMAN) said this when she put her hand, on my face, and on my heart, she controlled me with the right spirit of agape love. She will say baby calm down do not be loud and I will calm down. When Jeffrey tells Cleopatra something, she would bring up the past and say you are acting like a damn woman. She did not say that when she first met me. She was sweeter than any fruit you can imagine, nicer than a rose blooming, a butterfly flying to land on top of the rose in the sunshine and in a relationship and the wind blowing god's breeze! Cleopatra said Jeffrey I forgive you; the devil did come inside of her because a partner does not supposed to say that off her tongue that is does not love Jeffrey. Women that do this stop telling your men he does not know about love period, because you a woman your different than him on love from past experiences, seeing him as a no-good piece of same old shit, and you lay next to him every night or some, most then sleep with him then turn around curse, fuss him out before he gets out of bed and knock on the door. He did not go nowhere to cheat he was with you right there, so you are telling him he is wrong for what is in the back of your mind, and you made love with even before he left, (YES) women your something else to, A TRIP! God loves you and your husband, and the commandment is to love one another, and others do unto others as you want them to have to do unto you. See when a woman gets angry or bitter if it is for cheating or anything depending on the woman situation and problem, at times she would say do not tell me nothing about God and curse with and about it letting you know that God was not in it when you did what you did to her so do not bring him up at all. Now when she is ready and changes God is in her now, she is ready to tell you how, what, to do in the word of God. See some or most women will say or believe I do not know what I am talking about, crazy, a fool it will be good thing to said on good parts. How do I know all this, and it is true? How do we know if you are not lying most men are dogs and is the same because I remember it all I would not be writing it if I did not! I never too old to set a goal, a plan, dream, and keep going not caring, worrying with someone putting me down saying their never wrong. You know God does not like and hate when you pick on people or someone God hates sin. Teach the women to be reverent in the way they live then they can claim the younger women, I believe what God says it is never too late but in life all of us take chances to try to play with God we all done been there and done that. Women are not giving up on life. Women have been through things such as sins and divorces so do not give up on your husbands! You have a loving wife, the sage wife, the happy wife, the angry wife, the teaching wife, the mother, the foolish wife some or most times women please do not say, child please what women he been dealing with, it is the women I been running into or me because no damn marriage or relationship is perfect you know your husband/man like the back of your hand, but do you have you in check in your ways! You also have the mourning wife, the spoiled wife, her private in her about her and what she does, the angry female dragging woman, the tree woman to grow woman to grow and build and the wisdom wife. Do you see I am writing not negative I am writing from my heart even if some or most do not agree with what I am saying I am stating the truth, the facts about a woman/wife? The life is open on the personification of wisdom as woman/women/wife. The woman/ mother/wife and elders teach the young women and their daughters. If someone is doing right or wrong, as a message listen do not put them down or talk down to no one saying there the devil, pray for them with love to flea and rebuke the devil away because you have been there in that stage once if it was not like that same person way it was a pain or way of struggle period. Jeffrey never looked at Cleopatra face period as using her for money. I did do her wrong sinned, lied, cheated, abused her that is enough. When I was with her, and I got my life right God I looked at her soul I felt and knew what it was to be with God to look in his eyes and Cleopatra eyes as well to seek everything there was for our destiny! When Jeffrey was with Cleopatra, she showed him passion and gave it to him from her heart but then when the devil came to use her to bring back the past that is when her mind changed. She did it all right as she speaks from her mind, mouth, and the relationship that is only her and not me. Tell me something women? When your married and the first person does the wrong and then the other person comes back, because hurt people how long does this supposed to go on? Because you are digging a grave deeper for one another. All the years I knew Cleopatra and still see her passion of love and beauty is still growing with her ways. She sees the good things Jeffrey have to say about Cleopatra. She has not one good thing to say to me or about me. Women please when your man has not done you right, work it out do not work it out to get angry that is lukewarm because you change at any time, moment, mood you are in not as meaning evil my saying is just being a woman blowing a man mind driving him crazy! EVEN THOU A WOMAN IS A BIG HUGE PANEL. I understand if a man has hurt you. Then you take him back then later down the road you forgive him but why do you bring back up old past things? Isn't that like letting your own toilet in your house stay backed up and keep overflowing with the same old shit? Because you do tell him he is not shit, full of shit, doing the same old shit. Or you got something else on him he forgot to lift the toilet seat up or out it back down. I know to some women I need to go sit down somewhere or gone somewhere with that or just shut the hell up! This is not an insult this is the truth I am not God I am the messenger. With you would be opening doors back up that God and you agreed to close but it do not be God it be you because you bring back up the past that do not let you both last, and you have not fully kept your commitment, you be angry and say, (HE DID NOT KEEP HIS COMMITMENT, SHIT!) PROMISE AS WELL so what the hell. Did you really give him a chance to? Or you just said it and jumped on his case or back being hard on him. Then back fussing with then you say, because he damn deserved it God did not tell you that, women that do this in your own state of mind is telling you a get back is fun and evil. When you sit down, be calm, think about things while in your surroundings to yourself and fake like you do not want no part of dealing with him ignoring your husband not responding or calling him knowing your ass miss him. Some women play games give a little take a little back when you say, right? You know who you are. I know Jeffrey got back at Cleopatra (THE WOMAN), but you notice something funny she said she never did this to me she a saint then. However, getting back at each other did not make it better or worse now how many women can say this getting back at each other is the right thing? Then Cleopatra (THE WOMAN) says when I get ready and feel like it you cannot make me go to God and ask him, am I doing things right? Watch what God tells you because God will tell me that is not right to do to no woman. I will say to God I know that is not right he does not have to tell me which is why I repent because I know it is right. You do not have to tell me but with action I am waiting. It is shown against the spouse and the woman comes in saying we will then you know and see how I feel now! Wisdom is the way of thinking and movement a lot of things and more work together. In the Old Testament and new I found out knowledge and wisdom with God. Cleopatra (THE WOMAN) who Jeffrey tried to satisfy extremely hard for her heart was hidden and built around with hate that Jeffrey had to go to God get himself right to find her. When Jeffrey did Jeffrey was forgiven and spit in his face then coming back and forth with apologies. I know women this how you feel when you be treated in this way I agree, what I do not agree with is forgiving someone letting them back in and you get married with them then years later bring the past wrongs back up so this mean I never was forgiving for my sins! God even made me reap what I sow even she added on extra and more her grudge, hate, vengeance, pride, negativity towards me! How can you say you a Christian marry your man that you have forgiving then say you been hard on him and let nasty things come out your mouth? That is not Christian as God word says. You are a doer of my word only things that comes out of your mouth is helpful for building up others even strongly loved with encouragement with one another. Women love to say this is from their mouth. (NO) It is God own meaning God has it now if it is not God words, spirit, good, prayer, love, communication and prayer it is best not to say nothing at all but when you say the opposite negative things to your husbands he is this and that, then I am sorry to tell you sister's that's not God coming out your mouth that is the devil and he has your soul and spirit! Like I said like your pastors tell you in church over again I am going to say it in the same way their wives are to be women worthy of respect, not malicious talkers but temperate and trustworthy in everything. Another thing is with these women with these different color hairdos and the way they are dressing. Women I tell you this because I love you bring attention to yourselves by the way you dress not judging. I also want women to dress modestly, with decency and propriety; Not with elaborate hairstyles; but with good deeds. Today at these times lots of women are saying they are saying they are no strong men at all. That is not true would you want the men to say there is no strong women. Godly wisdom in the lives of younger women. Women I lift you up to push for things you think sometimes you cannot do the devil is a liar, YOU CAN IF GOD SAYS YOU CAN I FOLLOW GOD. They say I do not have a heart I am no good. I was once like that once, but I change, looked in the mirror, before you speak on someone pray for yourself and others. Cleopatra (THE WOMAN) is a gracious partner. This is a test for the women get wisdom read these scriptures. Once reading the scriptures think about what you are learning already to know, see, need help on and could lead the message to another sister. Now what have this man that is a man of God have taught you? With this message God has given to me to give to you. A wife of noble character is her husband's crown, but a disgraceful wife is like decay in his bones. She is blessed who has believed that the lord would fulfill his promises to her. In the word of God, I read a strong humble loving woman knows she has enough strength for her journey, but a praying, women know it is in her journey where a shell gain her strength with the Lord and be a loving wife. Then you have the evil strange woman for the lips of a strange woman drop as a honeycomb & her mouth is smoother than oil, but her end is bitter as wormwood, sharp as a two-edge sword, her feet go down to death her steps take hold on hell. Their women I love dearly from the Bible that are still women in Heaven until this day. You will know me, and you find me, where the boldness of Esther meets the warm, closeness of Ruth, where the hospitality of Lydia is in line with the submission of Mary, which is engulfed by the tears and praying of Hannah. I will be the one drenched in Bible verse waiting for you. Do not rebuke an older man harshly but exhort him as if he were your father. Treat younger men as brothers, older women as mothers, younger women as sisters, with absolute purity. Give proper recognition to those widows who are really in need, but if a widow should have children or grandchildren, they should learn first to put their religion into practice by pleasing God. The widow who is really in need and left all alone puts her hope in for pleasure is dead even while she lives. Give the people these instructions, so that no one maybe open to blame. Anyone who does not provide for their relatives and especially for their house has denied the faith and worse than an unbeliever. I do not want no one to be like me or they said I need to be like them, be like Jesus do what is right. A kindhearted woman gains respects, but ruthless man gains only wealth women do not use their word against them forever cleanse your heart let God deal with you and it! Get back after forgiving after your mouth but not with your heart being cleanse, because then when the woman says I forgive you husband and do not mean thoughts come to her mind she lets and allow ways as a wife where she can influence his heart she is really lying telling him that he cheated. Then saying we going to work it out when she is not doing God's way. She is doing her own work, way, plan sheet, work schedule, her own advice, her details, diary, master plan, and it all be full of hate brawled up inside and people are influencing them that it is ok when they already have in their heart, mind, head, soul, eyes and speech. I say all these things because she looks at him, she sees negativity and unforgiveness is hate. She is not recapturing respect for him no more it is over. She does not know when she is saying you cheated so she been said it was over she is saying right there after forgiving and laying bed going to sleep angry. With him and everything else she is telling God it is not going to work and tell you in your face at times she still loves you. She says shouting out confused and do not know she is telling you it is not going to work not God she talking to, but little do she know she is telling God first because she still married to you and in God eyes but not in hers because she is so angry that she uses that pain and hurt as her defense to always be right and never wrong, and then there is no price like love. Now when Cleopatra (THE WOMAN) curses me out tell me about myself she knows God, top to bottom, up and down and the Lord still going to bless her. She knows for sure what she is talking about and not wrong at all never without a doubt. Now when you tell her something, she will say to me, God do not like ugly Jeffrey and tell me God is not Going to bless me because I am always doing her wrong. I cannot get no more blessings from God because what I have done wrong to her, and this is a title for me forever. Hurtful words are sarcastic and since the tongue is deadly control what you say to anyone one day come to you that you do not want to be hurt. A lot of people say words are nothing that's not what god says a tongue that deadly that speaks wickedly is evil two edge sword and picking at people. Some women and people look at that as being petty, nothing in their eyes then when they are in the shoes of the person they have hurt, and it falls on them then they will see. I know I have been there and its people still telling until this day what I did in the past that I am not even around still saying I am that and they are the ones coming out with their mouth evil towards me, I still love them, I help them when I can and still say I am a no-good person see when you have a good heart that do not matter because love covers all. What Cleopatra would say is I did not say you did not have a good heart I said you do not love me then changed it and say I am not nothing! This why the world is the way it is because there is no love in a lot of people heart. Then I will ask one question, if I am all these things why are you even talking to me? Is it to me used? No. As Cleopatra would say then I do have good in me because you have love it is the other things she holds in her heart. So, God can replace the love. God can put the love there if they can receive it. They can pray all day long and talk about God also how much they are doers of the word. If they do not let go and let God like they tell others and me, use that advice for themselves they will be doing the work of the devil. Now please read this and be fair do not be angry or have an attitude everyone is entitle to their facts, opinions, their own beliefs and what they feel think or say God gets the last say so. Jeffrey misses the Cleopatra that would accept him for the crazy person he is for loving me for me and still is with my crazy self until this being my best friend giving up on me, was making me laugh every day, my careers and choices. I miss so many things that I cannot even explain because it is so many of being in love with Cleopatra! Jeffrey tried his best in the world to satisfy Cleopatra because, not just with her behavior mines as well. I checked myself for both of us, so I put both of her blames on me to keep her happy to give her what she wanted to start all over again. You know when you hurt a woman, she hurts you back and it continues. Then it is all on the man and she wants the credit that happens at times of being the better man for the woman, but lord knows they have run the 60/40 out! Then I was very honest I would go to God crying and the pastor going to Cleopatra did not mean anything because to her I was shit, a joke, a liar and did nothing for her at all she did it all see no she was selfish it just was not enough I could not afford her. The men that were supposed to be the fathers of her children was not in their lives, I picked them up from school I loved them and still do to. I gave them what any child would want and its children out there that do not have it at all from some parents they never seen or had it and that's LOVE! I wonder how they can teach their family we sin but we a family and still love but when I sin or make a mistake I am not a loving person or a part of their love and is not included or fit in nothing in their family! I apologize for my behavior and make amends with God first then her and she said I did not I only went to God. I felt so bad where I let her know everything I feel badly about and when she did appreciate it I still felt her pain, but I was going to take insults, criticism, torment, and blames for past sins I did. Still holding things against me years ago like I am on trial already guilty in court. Every word, move, thing I say or do it is my fault. The next thing I did was just change more and more. We know a woman is different she need more time and Jeffrey gave Cleopatra that for the Lord, me, her, and the children. Her needs that I was meeting and understanding them, but she did not receive them. She still needs to make it work, and I took my time patiently to bring more enjoyment. She said leave me alone do not touch me at all even with walking with her to the park. Then she said stop that, then I will say sweetheart why you would stop, and we are married? That will turn into an argument, and we will be right there in front of one another. We will not be around no one not even the woman/women she is still falsely accusing me of. I would walk away! The reason why I turned my back because I get fed up with. It was because of her rude, disrespectful, attitude, angry ways and behavior. She felt like sometimes because she was an instructor that she was always right. Then tell me I was jealous because she had an education, and I did not then come back to me and say Jeffrey I am sorry. Women tell why you do that? When is your husband/man telling you did something you do not want to receive or listen then come back to him and correct it? You do not think that is using the silent treatment to get your way? Ignoring his feelings? Crazy head comics? Self-obsessed? Is she crying wolf? Not accepting the blame. Judging your husband/man openly? The big thing is when you make him question his self and his sanity because it gets very intense, right women? See women when you are in front of your husband do not be cruel and nasty with your behavior and stop saying to him, (I KNOW ALEADY) you do not have to tell me nothing. She knows that already, but she would say she do not need his advice depending what mood what situation. She got it all together she is like what advice he can give me or what he can teach or tell me. He had that chance already this solution also functions as a second chance for the wife. Where she can do whatever she wants to think during it the subject in all its aspects. If she thinks their bad behaviors towards her husband in her mind, she will react in ways at times she would not even know, because she is over control by her own self. Actions and final decisions will not change and go back to good manners unless the choice comes with action in doing with love! How can her husband keep walking away constantly if he keeps getting hurt? See what I am telling women is that men do not only do this, let the past reflect on their present and future, women do to. This as well, so just think beautiful women you could not move on with the present and future, because of the reflections on things from the past. Women say it is different because of personality, life experiences, gender, she is more open minded more than the man, goals, dreams, letting their emotions take over their feelings, she goes back and visualize over again that woman/wife/ex-wife/wives/baby fathers, it is all still there! Do you see these false prophets, teachers and leaders are telling women it takes only the husband to get the family out of any situation? If something goes wrong no matter what it is it falls. When he complains or getting upset, he is not manning up he is acting like a woman. See this is not giving good spiritual advice Godly that is being misled to women by what husbands they should have. How someone is going to tell you about their husband/man they damn sure do not want you telling them about theirs! It is 3 all in one not only the husband he cannot do it all himself. Is he staying by his self? No, that depends on the woman and how she is treating him it is not all about her, his feelings are involved to, because she can be right beside him. She can be annoying acting like she does not even care or have a husband that is invisible. When really, she is the one, because she is to blind to see that they are still married not by paper but by God! Now if she gives it a chance then it would come together, because both is on one accord the train would be pushing with two tracks what would the train be? It will help for and with one another not a chance then soon as he does something simple by wanting to make love. She would say that is all we do good is fuck that is all we have good in this relationship. You put the curse right back in your marriage then people be around you or you hang around will back it up there miserable like you. Tell me why they do not have no husband/man or no one and by themselves it was not only because he/they cheated you had something to do with it as well every relationship is not the same! She would say right, no! What will God say about that? You already know! Then a lot of people say they do not know, but they do. A drunk man does not tell tales they know what is going on. Let me tell you something women/wives that do not give they husband a chance. I am talking God's way and not my or your way. If you continue to insist on your way and arrogance, not caring about guidance and your husbands find no other way just like you give up women when you are tired and fed up, you do not think men do not get this way as well everything has to be about you! You are backing your husband/man back into a corner and he cannot breathe, focus or think straight it is not that he is weak minded he cannot be tired of your shit waiting for you to get your shit together swearing you do. Then his solution is he is nothing down, hurt, neglected, frustrated is he abusive? Yes, he is. Now if ladies look at that, just as much as they want to look at their abuse it will be 100%100! A woman/women/wife is going to feel all types of ways and feelings of being abused and mistreated I agree and there is no excuse. I ask you women how to do your husband/men/man been abused by you? A lot of women say not like how he/they did me or us. So, women your abuse to your man was seen in God eyes stronger for you than it was for your man? Correct me I am not wrong, or I cannot make an excuse for my sin's actions or wrongs, I am just asking a simple question are you going to let your emotions take over this question or you going to come like God will? Only God can say what sin is worse than what sin not man or woman husband or wife, so let me know please what is worse on your husband/man over you? See when Jeffrey was in the bed at times with

Cleopatra (THE WOMAN) he cannot compare his relationship to everyone else. There was no love, affection, communication I do not understand because she is being a woman that is just how a woman is she been hurt so much that give her sometimes she will calm down and come right back and apologize, she is a woman that is what we do, some might agree, some do not. Some might say that is her, I am not that type of woman but every woman in life has been hurt so you been here. I am bringing out the truth telling it just like it is. So how is there love when you tell me you love me then cross me out? I do not understand that women then make me understand like you want others to understand you! So how are you going to tell me I cannot make you give me anything. Something that you do not want to but tell me as job and a man of God I suppose to stay doing that, but you are not? A lot of people say stop telling Cleopatra (THE WOMAN) she is this and that and love her, especially God! What God says for both parties in the relationship now and today there making it mostly, 70% and that day of partnership. Some peoples will say it is not what they said or want it is what God says and does. See today it is a shame that false prophets can mislead their sheep and then all that listening it is hard we all have been there then you must start over, this also comes from everyone does not belong in your relationship or in your business because it becomes a problem you start listening to others! It does not even be God speaking to you or those peoples that be bad spirits to break up your home. Before in the middle and after always about God, husband, wife and children some people are confused and say the children first, some peoples say the wife first, I was trying find that in the Bible and never will because it is not there! The woman uses these verbal words that use this by their demands like what are you trying to say to my children, they do not come first? This is what biological & stepfathers go through man it is not easy to raise someone else children. I am going to put father & mother like Mary & Joseph with Jesus, because Joseph adopted Jesus they did not bring no papers to court do you know a lot of elderly peoples did this back in my time growing up and the time before but not today, it was more love back then like Mary & Joseph. God is still blessing me with my love and gift I have he already has and more to coma I speak it I claim with faith always with prayer. Cleopatra (THE WOMAN) my love will never die or fade away, if I told you that it did I surely would have lied because I am not going to sit here like women do and pretend or fake like it is something not in my heart. I will not deny or keep my feelings suppressed it is her that I still love the most and the best. It is plenty ways A WIFE can bless her husband with this love I hope and pray she get this love again we can be together because she did not have this love after forgiving me. She thinks about me, because I think about her after our break-up, I remember her beautiful face, big eyeballs and her father nose, she remembers my fat jaws and call me Jeffrey? I hope we can be together again she need to get her love back. Can she remember how she fell in love with me? I remember how I feel in love with her. A woman just does not like to think about some things or most things in about their past relationships it can be good or bad because they can use things to help themselves or hurt themselves depending on the woman. When Cleopatra first picks me up in her car and said get in. Jeffrey said I can be crazy, and she said boy get in now! Also leaving the song I was singing on her voicemail and her just being her! A WOMAN! You know I valued my woman of her substance, because she respects and always had value in herself. She submitted to me, respected me and was submissive when I did her wrong, I did the children wrong to because what you do to the mother it reflects on the children vice versa. When I changed God said she was to give me my respect back let me have the lead back, being the head and I did not get it at all periods. A lot of women will say that is what you get I do not deserve a good woman like her. She is a lady that is there saying he say she say do not have nothing on God Saying! I changed myself because I loved her, she could not change me, I had to do that first for God and myself. She just believed it was a change in herself, her family, her children and not me because I am shit in the past, present, future and forever because only what I did to her wrong. God did not tell none of this in this world that is cruel that we live in God said son I forgive you not for someone or anyone with a cruel heart to say, do not put God in it now! I do not keep no records I have a forgiving heart and do not hold no vengeance, grudge, no wall up I will take care of you if I have my last dollar. See I am not going to sit here and say I do not have sins just like I just told you my gift and my heart you have your gift, heart and love to so I can hear your story. I am being real who wants to have God first then get married. The secret is with God husband and wife. Never belittle your man. Never talk down to him. Never ignore him. Never let or make him feel replaceable and you do not have to only cheat on him to make him feel this way it is men more emotional than women. Never play down your need for him, never cause him to feel embarrassed, never look away or text while he is talking, never manipulate him, never boss him around, never laugh at his mistakes and faults all the time, never put no one before him, never be inconsiderate of his feelings, never tell his personal business. NOW WOMEN YOU DON'T WANT THESE SAME THINGS AND MORE IN RETURN? You want more because you are a WOMAN, you want more and more! It does not matter if the man you are dealing with is your husband for years, your boyfriend, your father, your grandfather, this is how women should always respect. The decision you make with your mate is right. Not now back and forth, because tomorrow is never promised, and life is too short. If you are living for your future, you can already be prepared! You choose and be better or worse! False prophets have told wives their marriage that it is all on the husband and for him to change it all because he messed it up first. This is not so! God says in the bible, can two walks together, except they be agreed. A good marriage requires to not only the man, but both are committed to the same purpose. They both walk together and be committed together for the same purpose. They both know what the purpose is not only just the man, No. If the man knew it all he would be the encyclopedia, but men leave that to the women think they know it all not meaning or believing that is true that is how they are! We know men are not that, but women are damn good at it! Women will say they do not know it all, but you cannot win a debate or be right she will say I did not say that! They shall love the Lord by God with all their heart and with all their soul, and with all their mind. This is the first and great commandment and the second is like unto it thou shalt love thy neighbor as thyself. A relationship with God is one of the reasons to be successful in your marriage and relationship with others on Christ, because the devil wants to destroy what God created but cannot, Relationships does get targeted and tested by the devil it is ask by God permission just like Job was tested! Most women think it is most men and adultery are the mostly only the number one sin with their attitudes saying that is the men fault. I learned that attitude makes a difference and reflects leadership. A lot of women need to learn from this. Most of them would say you do not have to tell that they know already in there good or bad mood! Some women feel like if they had more money or better man, marriage, education, health, car it is all good and ok but if she does not have God, a nice humble spirit and attitude you do not have no control over your own self! See this is what you tell your husband/man fair when he is loud out of control, temper tantrum and disrespectful towards you right? This will bring on sickness on both parties. The wife wants to blame the husband then he blames her. Some of you women want to put all your blames on the men. We will ladies look in the mirror, ask yourself what it is I need to get right on me. What I need to work on, check me, (ME)! If you focus on your husband/man, everything his fault, he knows it is not and cannot keep putting up with it then who is, you to tell someone off? I learned this from a woman, so you are too good to learn from man off his mistakes and sins your closet need some cleaning as well. You are saying every day, every night and all the time you never played a part in your marriage so let that go. You should pray in your space, don't go through crap on him pray for him because you cannot do both back and forth, what you get out of that? When you do wrong, sin and make mistakes you do not want no man/woman or anyone to keep bringing up the same old things. How do you think they feel? They feel like same old thing, but you do not see that you see and eye for eye! You are not going in Gods way you are putting it in your way calling and claiming God you think you are doing right but you are not anyone that believes in God or not knows that we all fall short. When it comes up to a woman getting hurt then they hurt the man back that is understandable they do sins against the man there is no sins counted there is get back constantly, repayment, charges, fines, penalty's, fees, a ring match, then the attitude of anger brings on sicknesses. Then the woman will say you brought this sickness and curse on me, this family, because you cheated, and she was angry, bitter, and the man was telling her to stop but could he make her listen? Like myself I would let peoples get me angry. Every single time I would blame them when I sometimes started it, sometimes it was so petty that I could have avoided it, but I learned the hard way I learned from my mistakes! This will cause me setbacks, shut my mouth, stayed and realized it was me sometimes that need to just walk away I was right smiling! Women, a joyful heart is good medicine, but a bitter crushed spirit saps one's strength. So, the attitude does make a difference. Stop looking at your circumstances. I see Pastors tell women something I have seen plenty standing right there, and they listen or in women's bible studies or get togethers because plenty men in family were Bishops, Pastors, and evangelist. While at home their husband's arguments start up fights, disputes, verbal words, then when things get lots and taken away the wife says no good husband it is all on you and your fault you let it get taken away. Never say let us pray, the wife keeps her eyes on the things that are taking away that God can replace instead of praying with the husband to get things back every time Jeffrey told Cleopatra (THE WOMAN) God is telling me for us to pray 3 times a day. She said angrily with wicked heart you cannot make me pray with you if I do not want to. So, all that time went by of years she did not want the relationship to work, because I could not hold it together all by myself, but she did because of making the most money and she said it out her mouth I am paying most of the fucking bills. So, women tell me something how can you still have God which you still do and say a man of God supposed to be there for his wife if she is a believer or not but when he acts up or you act up he is not a man of God? She listens to the pastor. When the pastor said to me that's not God in me. When the pastor says follow your partner`. She did not want to do that. See confusion, this why the next woman God sends me it will be a secret. When God sends me the special woman who will be wife, he is one I will talk to and be thankful for. I will be living by myself, taking my cold showers, pray through the night, take a bath rebuking spirits that do not belong. WOMEN I FEEL YOU! Women you are not the only one has gone through this I feel you. I am a witness for men as well. I cry to and I am alone with a wife I am married, but I am a good man! Cleopatra (THE WOMAN) she did not know with her attitude and her anger while her saying I am hard on him a lot and blaming him for everything all the time until this day she does not know that it is foolish and confusing. It was a goal when she affected herself, God, me and the children. Women and men just do not hurt their children at times you to as well. The children have their eyes on them they see what you are doing, at times they use things against you to get what they want and get their way. What they want you to be teaching them things. It brought out the worse in her. She still is a good woman to have no amount of love, positivity, God or trying more satisfying of positiveness doing thinking, saying or anything would change our situation. Cleopatra would hide a lot of things behind her mask of optimism. I wanted us to have a positive outlook on life. Jeffrey really put so much into Cleopatra (THE WOMAN) which he did wrong, and she did him wrong. No matter how much Jeffrey put in her eyes he never tried or got anything right. I never succeeded at the job no matter how hard I worked, I was never good enough, and I never got or was given a chance from God in her eyes. Judging me on my sins really both of ours. Everyone makes mistakes. Jeffrey had an angry, bitter, malice, hateful, woman. Jeffrey even learned working on himself for God Cleopatra (THE WOMAN) and the children. I can do better next time. I did not get a lift or standing by my side holding my hand saying it is going to get better. She always had a negative vibe and told me in my face yes you are a fuck up and yes, she could not go further in life with me. Jeffrey asked Cleopatra would it work out for us and move forward. She said if it was not for you, I will not be where I am today. Then she said Jeffrey you ask me a question I gave you an answer! Now that is not the devil using her. Like he used me to cheat and to do other sins I did. She says and feels as a woman my cheating, abuse towards her is getting me back from what I did to her so feel her pain now for what she holds in her heart! We are not even until she says so. Her negative mind was focus on me, family, children saying screw me. I am no good even better or worse, richer or poor in sickness and health attention just for only her. Cleopatra (THE WOMAN) refuses to do things for ever unless I am doing something for her first always. Cleopatra will tell Jeffrey I do not need you while she was with me, I can take care of myself I do not need no man. Then she will change her mind and say thank you for giving me this, so it is some good in this man but how can it be good in a man you love that you the one keeps changing up on in with your mind, ways, tongue and aggressive gestures to Jeffrey! Then why come to the husband/man that you called a liar to his face and put him down? Then come right back and say she is a woman who hurt from what she has been through including the hurt from you, so that is an excuse to continue to hold a grudge over my head. Some women say, YOU DAMN RIGHT. For what you men took us through. Women and men, we must ask her that and it still will be my fault on every sin! So, she said why waste her time on someone like me that is wasting her time on what I did her wrong. Cleopatra will talk to Jeffrey when she gets good and damn ready. God says be ye kind to one another. Whether they seem appreciated or not. The woman does not the only one who needs to be satisfied. The man to! Women your attitude can make a difference in your life. This helps you on a lot of struggles in life when you become discouraged in the day of distress, your strength will be meager. Now women do not say I think I am holy or perfect, I know it all or I am using God, or I got some nerve telling a woman anything. I learned from man and woman as a human being who God sends my way all the time and still have more learning, teaching, accepting and humbleness to do. I am still learning more and more, and I love it. Now it is a project that makes me better! I improved my situation with the strength of God which he gives me especially when he first wakes me up! Jeffrey told Cleopatra (THE WOMAN) just like she taught him as well, but I never taught or teach her nothing. The Bible and us praying will improve our outlook on life it did for both of us and others! So, the look to God in the Bible kept her from spiraling downward, and her behavior. I messed up bad that as a man I did think that and felt I did not deserve Cleopatra back but with and through the faith and works in God is possible, I just wish & hope it would have been the same outcome for me! I am not an animal we all have bull crap in us and have done wrong. My mother always said everyone has come with some bull shit but when I ask her that don't you come with it? She will say I do not bullshit I do not have time for it but then I will say you just said everyone she meant everyone accept her. Right women? No one is perfect! We must continue to be made new in your mental attitude. We all can be made new again in our thinking, making a change, we can continue like the scripture says, All the days of the afflicted one are bad, but the one with a cheerful heart has a continual feast, and when Cleopatra (THE WOMAN) told me I was a screw up, a fuck up and all negative things but not one thing godly to say about me. She did not have nothing at all to say good about me. She wanted a car. She is, an instructor and her mother have a car, but she did not. That let me know it was not for better or for worse because when her mother Pam told her something that was right or wrong at times, she did not want to listen because all the gossip and the mother talking about others. See women when your around gossip it is something you get addicted to because if you did not you would not be around it period your just in engaged with that relationship not your husband/man! Cleopatra said Jeffrey do not and will not listen to her mother because she is two faced and talks about everyone. When her mother told her what she wanted to hear it was all good to make her feel good, but just did not know she will tell me things in my face behind her daughter back I am not talking bad about no one I am just showing you women areas you mess up in and blame your men for everything! Women if you see everything negative towards your husband and marriage there will be no one together it will be your selfishness, because your both still in God eyes but God will see the problems that is destroying the marriage because he is not involved. You know God can be there it just be us ignoring God he does not ignore us we are foolish at times. False prophets have taught women only the man brings the wrongs only because, he is the head of the household. Women if you see negativity you should pray for positiveness in your life. You do not pray then come back doing the same mess you did again, because you of your husband faults. It is in your eyes, emotions, feelings, ways, thoughts but in God you are sinning you are going back and forth with the devil! Just by you being negative how do you want to help someone to try to work it out, do you know why? Because you are thinking of yourself of what that man might do again, or he is not going to try. So, it is a fact on moving forward with someone you are willing to take back and make work? Women you cannot make something work if you do not put nothing in and believe in God, yourself and the person who you forgave to let back in your life because if you do not you are playing from the first start and all what you invested into was gone before you said let us go for it! Now women when you forgive and say but I thought you still be thinking about fear or something you heard. What I just hear that I said something which throws you off with everything else how to deal with consequences, situation on how to handle and work things out with honest love. Jeffrey knows it is not easy it was not for him for Cleopatra getting hurt by me. What she went through in past things in her family and cycles myself as well of what I been through with Cleopatra and my family cycles, self and life! You know when you cannot let go of past hurt or grudges, revenges overtake your body because not do you block out the person that hurts you, you block out yourself, God and other bless things that God has instore for you. Then when you be to yourself sometimes thinking what you let God do was a blessing for you to move forward sometimes it do not be that because you have not fully changed on getting you right! Women do not pick on your husbands it is not funny or right to pick on anyone or provoke him. If you keep on seeing everything be negative, you will feel afflicted off and on. Then you will be in front of him saying baby I love you then you change; I cannot stand him you will change back and forth because your mind is controlling your thoughts. Woman you are not thinking before you speak, or your heart is not fully cleansed you just talking not loving talk is cheap right? Every day will appear bad, evil, dark and you will be blind. Women do you know when your husband/man walk into the house you both live in he sometimes feels that he is haunted in his own house and uncomfortable? Some women do not even know how to say I LOVE YOU! Some women do not speak or say WHERE YOU BEEN AT! Then the relationship will be over, the devil will laugh and say I got both not just the husband/man. It is her blaming him and him blaming her and they both would be wrong on getting a divorce, not just (THE MAN)! We all will keep a cheerful heart and feel joyful that is why I am hyper all the time of my testimonies why God still have me here. When a bad thought comes to my mind I push it away then pray, because if I let the devil take over I will not move forward on God eyes, goals, blessings, dreams coming true, the future, peace, knowledge, wisdom, obedience, laughter, life itself will be a dark blind filthy place for me so I make the choice now to put positive and good things to fight against the negative. It is like having a job that is paying 50 dollars a day at the labor pool. I looked at that as I am thankful at least I have a job this all I got. I did not do that I said positive things and Cleopatra (THE WOMAN) was angry, because it was not enough. She was not angry for nothing how am I going to be lying, cheating and with another woman. I am in the hospital in pain from the jobs when I changed while she is cursing, angry and thinking only of her job first instead of God, herself, husband, and children me loving her saying go home I will be alright you have to work tomorrow, so you will not lose your job. Her job was more important than losing her husband and until this day I still have them health problems which are worse now and still bless to be living! Even when I had seizures back-to-back still getting up to hustle and work. I learned to think of something constructive. Cleopatra (THE WOMAN) taught me that, but when I told her it only applied for her until she told herself off not letting no one else at all. There is more happiness in giving than receiving. Unselfish giving brings deep satisfaction to the giver because we were created to do more than simply look after our own needs. Experiencing the joy of giving can do much to help us cope with negative circumstances in life. I did bad and there's God in me. I did a lot of things in God eyes for someone or anyone to tell me I am nothing at all, helping peoples with their daily needs. I could not do it all, but I tried my best this is how you know parents raise their children up and spoiled so much to where they do not know how to tell them no at times. Then mothers feel way that you have neglected their children because the way they been brought up on their raising from there parents of what they have been threw or past marriage relationships. When you tell them no at times when you are disciplining them your wrong at times, but when a biological mother is telling them it is different because they be training them in ways they can see and cannot. The child knows and watch, the mother what does to because some use their children to get what they want out of men when they know the man has a good heart! If the mother is right or wrong, she can do the that. You have women and people say today those are not your children so she can do that it was not like this in the old days. All women that do this is right knowing they wrong in God eyes they just being selfish saying they just wants what best for their children and them. That is not in the Bible that is in the world. Like Pastor Jim Everett says children breaks up marriages to and romance is not only for a wife. It is for husband & wife there trying to change and add on to God's word but cannot, they will be judge! I know I tried to do it once when I was of the world. We all have relationship that are together also are friends.

When Jeffrey asks Cleopatra (THE WOMAN) to forgive him she did not love or forgive him. She did not give me empathy, patience, and rewarding me from her heart sincerely. Now women do you all say we going to give the men one breath of air, or space even a chance, NO! You all know who I am talking about with you stank and funky attitude. You are not going to say we know we get on men nerves, (NO). You are going to say the men get on yours and aggravate the hell out of you. Most women will feel and say that they put up with men all the time. Is that at times on some or most occasion that is just a woman being a woman? Not only does she change quickly and constantly like a light switch they turn off and on, but she will have one on her man/husband turn him off and on when she wants to, she has her special powers. Now let us not talk about a woman split personalities it can be repeatedly. She will have her times and moments she just will never be satisfied. When I got my life right with God when I was married to Cleopatra (THE WOMAN), I began the day with a blessing from God telling her I love her and doing it. Thanking God for waking me up starting my soul day with spirit walking with the love of God that feels good I am telling you. Knowing that more blessings and positive sharing the goodness with Cleopatra, shinning my smile with hers inspiring myself and her even when she was angry even on happy days in her way of being stuck and selfish. God was with us both still is until this day and she helped me reach my goal at times I just kept praying that she would do it for us by letting go of the past hurts. Women do you know when you let that control you that hurt breaks up you with your man? You will say it to. He can be coming from anywhere then you will come straight at him about something, and you just know it is the truth when it is a lie, but you are really looking at the past lies he told you and treated you on so that makes you insecure even more! Cleopatra said Jeffrey was nothing but a known good fuck up and we will come from having dinner from a restaurant and I taught her children nothing and I was a sorry ass man. Cleopatra (THE WOMAN) use things against Jeffrey every day when he was in love with her relationship and until this day, she cannot get over 15 years in a relationship with him and 8 years along of them being togethers. Where does this happens at in other relationships? Show me I got to know from women with attitudes or just women period in general? Show me I would like to know this is you fooling yourselves, because you only hurt yourself even more of holding pain inside that is a truth of being done to you. You are doing back to the person by getting the person to get even, what does that do to you and your problem? Nothing! It is just like you walks in your bedroom and you take money out your husband pants and go somewhere and he does not know, because he cares and loves you. Then when he wakes up, puts on his pants, get in his car, go to the store, puts his hands in his pockets and call you. Then ask dear did you take some money out my pocket, you answer back and say no lying to him not all, but some women have done this. Then he asks you where you at, you lie to him and say you to the store, but you are at your friend house or somewhere else, because your mom will call him and let him know where you are at. She is right there beside her. Now he is hurt, disappointed and do not trust her to some point. Some women will say that is not nothing they can go in their man pants anytime, get what they want and do not have to tell him anything. When he let her know that is not right, she will apologize depending on the woman/wife time, feelings, moods and situation. Then he will do something to her to hurt her back, because he does not trust her now. See now if your husband/man takes money out of your purse and it is so important that you needed that money for a reason. Women please do not go there some of you saying a man/husband should not be getting, wanting, taking or asking for money from his woman/wife that is foolish they are married, but if when he does do this how would you react? But see it is both parties on how to deal and handle the situation as adults not to continue to fight back in all kinds of ways that do not resolve nothing but a major problem! It creates more problems and pain for your life and others. Like I said attitude makes a difference, because of your behavior, but Cleopatra (THE WOMAN) said it, because of me and all on me. She did not do one sin towards me. We get together she will say I did not say that back to what I was saying before Cleopatra (THE WOMAN) kept saying I do not want to pray with you. You cannot make me pray. If I do not want to! Now I understand that if God was leading her on that, but for her to say that to me every time. I ask and say baby let us pray and she got on me as well as telling me I am the man and the head. I am not using (BUT) for an excuse. Women do this a lot after being hurt and do not mean their forgiveness, because their heart be too bitter. As God say in his word defraud the nit one the other, except it be with consent for a time, that they may give yourselves to fasting and prayer; and come together again, that Satan tempt you not for your incontinency. So, when false prophets tell husband and wives, you cannot make no one pray. No what they should do is God say and word not saying. God word and saying, but if God do not like that (There is no carnal minded!) God says come together as one. That is what a real prophet will do come together right now with 2 or more is together and God rebuke all anger all bad spirits. All wrongs, rebuke all negative, bad sayings, bring more prayer, love, peace and joy not what a pastor, a wife, or husband want to say their way or a negative, because what God put together no man or woman separate, so when someone says every day I do not want to pray you cannot make me pray today the devil is using them that is an evil spirit. We pray on and rebuke it. Women do not want a man around that does not pray, do not have God in his life or evil around her life, her children, the same goes for a man! Correct me if I'm wrong what's the difference from lying, cheating, stealing, killing, adultery, lust, fornication, evil, flesh, gossip, drama, witchcraft, gambling, unforgiveness, not doing unto others as you want them have to do unto you, bitterness, hate, malice, vengeance, grudges, jealousy, bragging, adulterous, greedy, falsely accusing, thieves, homosexuals, unrighteous, drunkards, revilers, hate his brother or sister, is a murderer, blasphemy, profane language, what's the difference? There is no difference it is all sin not honoring your mother and father, proving your children God says. Whoever keeps the whole law but fails in one point has become accountable for all it. So, what person say most sin is adultery on man, and it is all the man faults? Now if you see man, woman, husband, wife, brother, sister sinning. If anyone sees his brother committing a sin not leading to death, he shall ask, and God will give him life to those who commit sins that do not lead to death. There is sin that leads death. I do not say that one should pray for that. All wrongdoing is sin! The unrighteous will not enter the kingdom of God, so do not tell your husband or ex he is not going to heaven, and he is not doing right and you cursing him down off your tongue instead of praying for him. Now I have seen curses over Cleopatra (THE WOMAN) family of grandmother to her mother. Every family has this. This is a fact a cycle needs to stop period and prayed for like Cleopatra (THE WOMAN) schooled me on. They had issues in their relationship and past curses down. Like some of these mothers, women sleep with married men and past curses on to their children and family members. Like with David, Solomon and Bathsheba. That was not only a curse on David it was on Bathsheba and Solomon as well on to Solomon's son. The curse was on the whole family back to what Jeffrey was saying Cleopatra (THE WOMAN). Then she learned from her mother to have anger against her husband and being rude, very nasty and then praise her mother and other women these days with attitudes. I ran away from Cleopatra (THE WOMAN), because of her attitude, behavior, nagging, disrespectful. If she goes at it with her mother what she is going to do with her own husband. She says no you beat on me and cheated on me, but when we first got together, she did say my mother do not like no man get with. That is not a mother love on that situation that is being miserable, angry, she without a man herself and think of other things inside of her mind. When I got my life right with God the mother said the same thing and the daughter, she does not like no man I get with, so is the mother married to me or the daughter to make the choice, because the cycle has been not been broken. The daughter wants to wear the pants and the dress. It is a cycle. When I was nice, I was talked down and put down. It is not all Cleopatra (THE WOMAN) fault, she put her faults on me. I am not going to say I did not blame her for things I did, because this man can admit that. A strong good man can handle a strong good woman not strong rude mean woman, who says she forgives her man. Then have a nasty rude, bitter attitude and violent behavior that she speaks out nasty you made me this way. So, Jeffrey says like this demanding respect a man feels uncomfortable and unwanted, anyone I mean anyone who has got themselves right and together do not deserve to be stepped on. Cleopatra (THE WOMAN) is angry when we were living together that she was confused. When I told her things, I would tell her sweetheart you said this and with a strong woman evil spirit and voice she would say I know what I said. I know you not trying to tell me nothing you do not know shit after what you had done to me you have no say so. How can I get respect from a wife that do not have respect for herself or husband disrespecting him? She said it was owed to me for her to be disrespectful and everything is all my fault. Cleopatra (THE WOMAN) her high class beauty with her smile, her eyes, dreams, goal, she still my queen. Her kindness has me weak in knees in ways to still be in love with her. I admired her being patient and going through what I took her through hell and back. She is a person. Can I ask her, am I? I cannot see good in her or her actions, but I see is her bad actions, which I do not see nothing. After all she do not see nothing in me or my worth, but bullshit! The Bible gives the word from God speaks on the beauty of women. Cleopatra (THE WOMAN) has all kind of features. I seek to found her because I came back as God told me to. Now to women it is not right or fair for women to be raped at all. I feel the women pain who spoke up or keep silent about the situation. The sex offenders that are out there are nasty, no good and need help for what they do to people. The ones that repent and get there life right with God they are forgiven, but not by how society sees them or persons they did things to. Now men there is many who have experience rape, abuse, neglect and was betrayed by people. Now I watched a movie called Addicted where the woman was raped as a child. As she got older, she became addicted to sex. She had a great family, her mother, good husband, son and daughter, but she secretly was sleeping with different men, because of her addiction. Some women felt her pain. Some women said it was right because we feel where she is coming from. Do you think it was right in reality? NO! or the movie because this matter and situation happens every day in life. Now women do understand their men. Now women can you understand men in this situation that goes through being raped constantly. Now the system is not going to let this be known they are going to keep it quiet on this on T.V shows, movies, in society, church, schools, programs, etc.! Now a love an excuse and I am not blaming them it is (THEY NEED TIME TO GET OVER THAT) everyone understands. Now for men get over it you are a grown man stop complaining, emotional, you sound like a weak as man that is the past and that is why he cannot move forward with his life. See there is mostly no one there, no one to listen, hear, communicate with or understand not even help as much it is as it is for women than men! The point I am trying to make is like you go to the store, holidays which mostly everything is for women, but for men it is mostly nothing. There is no 100% for both sides men or women treated today. Do not say the women get raped more than men because men been raped just as much as women. Do not say women have been abused more than men have been abused by officers, feelings, provoked, pressured, foster homes, the streets, schools, detention centers and the system. We have human beings struggle period in life. Now after the movie addicted what did the mother do? She walked up to the husband gave him the Bible, said forgive me, let us make it work and he went there to make it work. Cleopatra (THE WOMAN) told me to get help for a lot of things like therapy, psychiatrist, join a therapy group and when I did there was no help. I helped myself there was no group therapy or any help. Cleopatra introduced me to therapy when I went there, they said you are doing good. I did not have a help mate at the time. Now this woman had a sex addiction why? Because she was rapped as a child now do you think lots of men have this problem by being raped or abused? Women take this problem out on others and themselves being feared and victims. It is right because what they have been through suffering and pain, but the rule for most women is men cannot never do this! It is not tic for tac or men have this excuse just, only when they are a dog, there nasty and they want their cake and eat it to. It is not that, because they are dead wrong. I am talking about the same things and excuses women go through on most thing, they feel men go through that and feel it to. A lot of women have told me that when a man is emotional, he is weak depending on her mood and the woman but then will change and say some men are more emotional than women! So, then some women prefer to be with ruff necks that is what they like that's hard core not romantic, because when he is changes to be emotional then at times the woman can change by nature, gestures, feelings and moods that she just feels inside that is comes with a strong thought process! Some women do this. What is wrong with a man telling a woman he loves her every day? It tells her do not argue, do not fuss calm down, you do not have to scream or yell, do not catch an attitude, what is new, listen, hear, feel, understand, do not walk away, baby let me hold you, you do not have to roll your eyes or suck your teeth do not say hmmm or whatever, anyway. See when a woman/wife know her man/husband is emotional and loves her having their ups and downs and she rolls her eyes at him sucks her teeth and walk away that times she just does not want to hear it being disrespectful towards her man. Cleopatra said to me these are mostly women things that they do now I am going to go to the woman, and I am going to stand up for you women and after I do this think of yourselves and getting on you. When you are talking to your husband/man/fiancé/ boyfriend him he does not roll his eyes, because he is a man, but if he is doing body gestures or things that your emotional on that you do not like that he does that gets to you then it is a problem. It does not even have to be body gestures it can be something you are not comfortable with. Well, it does not make him a coward or weak it is all about love in the relationship. When Cleopatra was talking to me she wanted and needed my full undivided attention along with respect and a decent conversation, but the woman does not feel right when the man is watching T.V while she is talking to him and he is saying what you said, give me a second watching the T.V talking to the T.V. When is he ignoring her that is not right is that a man or woman thing? Or a bitch thing? Or an emotional cry baby thing? NO! That is respect communication on giving one another attention. When the women are talking right or wrong and the man looks up in the air looks down to the floor with his head any movement the women reflect off that, because she feels rejected by the man actions. When a man cuts her off from talking screams and yields at her, curse her out that is `11 and tuck it in and be a man. Now the older woman did not do this in the Bible Eunice, Ester, Mary, Martha, Ruth, Sarah, Anna, Hannah did not do this. They taught the younger women in the Bible how to treat and be towards their husbands/men. Now to what I was saying the women today do not know what the world has come to these women today, just as the same as the men. God 100% Do not put it all on men God know if a man cheats on his wife that is adultery and cannot keep doing it. God will fix him good. Now God knows and sees this man has repented and forgiving him. God did not tell the woman now let us get him together you go first God then I come in, or now let us go together hmmm, yeah let us get him Lord that is right I am on your side and with you on that. No do not twist and change God words and spirit because you cannot! We all need to be worked on I know I need to work on me I also need to meeting people who is with God and needs him because I am a work in progress, so I am working on me more to find inner self. God is healing me more, being passionate and loving no matter what man or woman judge me on. It is agape from God love as I love growing more relationships with him every day until I leave this earth only memories to have in my mind that are positive. God is building my empire more because the last time I did it myself and it all came down. I tried to do it all over again it came down because the devil was there saying come on, I am with you we can do this together, but he tricked me. I went to God and found myself. Now what I was saying about a woman does not what a man do to her and how she feels about it. What she cannot stand and do not tolerate when a man looks at her in her eyes and says I do not care or so what she feels she is not loved at all. That right there cuts her off from everything because she feels neglected. I am on the right-side God not the husband or wife all God is in the middle. First & last and begging & the end. I am going deeply about prayer now. The Husband/ man is the head, and the Wife/woman is the help mate, tail and backbone the one who ignores first husband or wife go to God in prayer first fast because we know a marriage is not perfect. Whoever ignores who first or you are doing it to one another both feels afraid and then go to God and cry out to him, because if the husband is not a believer or saved and all he wants to do is argue and fuss like it says in the word when the husband is not a believer the wife must not divorce him. She must love him and still pray for him, and this goes for the wife/woman if she is not a believer now I am 100% I cannot give the woman 80% then give the man 5% nowhere does it say this. Even if a woman does wrong now today, she is still respected as a mother and a woman of God or not to say I am 100%. A Godly woman 100% no matter what so a Godly man is. Now the next movie I would like to talk about is Not Easily Broken. Women will say that is just a movie this is the real world I am just not talking about a movie not God that is true. How many marriages on both sides not only the man the husband and the wife going by God 100%? Why is that their marriages are failing because it is not involved at and only just the husband come on now ladies. No together as one! Not the husband way or only the wife way or women telling her in her ear or family members that's right girl has him under control and in check you got it girl. If she is listening or not those are spirits of negativity around her. Just like she tells the husband she does not want them negative spirits around her to pray and rebuke them away real fast because she does not want to be caught up in the rapture with the devil same way how your husband feels. Not to stop from being around them, because that is the first thing the woman will say to her man when she is pissed off. Especially when she is holding on when he did something to her in the past or she did something to him and they still are going back in forth when she thinks she is winning when the devil is laughing. Like the movie Not Easily Broken did you see how the wife treated her husband talking to him any kind of way? How she pushed him out there to be with another woman. Now in reality this does happen but is it right? NO! It is, not right? Because it is adultery to cheat or sleep on your husband or wife! When a wife provokes her husband it pushes him away, pressure him, put him down, and not encourage him or stand by his side this is what pushes him out the door. Women do not study this or look at this hard as what am I doing to push my husband/man away! What am I doing? The woman needs to walk up to him and say let start over and do it the first day we met God included. A lot of women will say (YOU) all men hurt us and we going to pay them back. We cannot give them a chance, because we were hurt too much every time, we give them one chance they hurt us. Women do you really study, think, concentrate, take time patiently on the word chance or do you react before you think and just do what you decide? Because you can say you want your man back and get him and do not be working on you loving him so much and still be hurting inside it is a love hate relationship with her! I know too many women not everything learning from you other women life and my own experiences! Women do not say something with your mouth and do not do it with your heart because women you have mouths after mouths of one tongue. Now leaving church when you get home, and your man needs love you bring the past back up. When your man is talking to you in a loving manner you bring up the past again and he has really change but your selfishness does not feel so you feel it is a no way! So, if you are looking at him saying you dog and you can be doing that without speaking or just being quiet your looks can be treacherous, temperamental, sarcastic, sensitive, curious for whatever

reason she chooses and feels. What are you if you are in love with the same man bringing yourself down, because while saying with your mouth (OK) let us say it is a chance but your actions, attitude, your disobedience and heart is not saying that? So, you say, because he broke my heart, do not tell your man with a broken heart and go right back to him with a wicked, bitter, malice broken heart, because it is not going to work it may last for a while but not for how long as you think it would. So, do not go back to the man until you get yourself right and work on you before going back to the one you say you love, because you are going to blame him even more piling up more shit on him. How does that make you look and feel at the time woman you will say I do not care give a damn or do not care anymore and still be with that same man! That would be picking, poking, pointing the finger telling him you hate him and cannot stand him with so many actions of disrespect and behavior and you know it is not right by God and you show out and off any way. Now when a woman loves Cleopatra (THE WOMAN) she loved me in so many ways and feelings Godly with her all. Jeffrey gave her his all, but she felt like I did not need anything in return. Jeffrey do not care what no one thinks or say he loved Cleopatra. I came with respect, a natural order and it begun when I first fell in love with her believe is not the word God is! She was then and now still the most important person, place, human all in one I do not care. No one can tell me what my heart feels, but God like a strong woman color does not mean nothing or anything the woman is standing up for what she feels herself, her goals and dreams and what she says period. I stand up as a man of God! We all fall short of the glory then women say to a lot of men child please or whatever you the biggest hypocrite ever. Now you tell the woman that YOUR NOT GOD, WHAT YOU TRYING TO SAY! She will not accept on her sins, that does not mean she will not admit, but not when you ask nicely or say only mostly on her time! I have seen a lot of male pastors tell the wife listen to your husband AND SHE SAYS no, no, no! But listens to other things the pastor says, but not that, so is that a clean heart? No! Tell you quick in your face the pastor said this. I saw the pastor in church tell Cleopatra (THE WOMAN) that you need to listen to your partner, and she said NO! As Jeffrey loved Cleopatra and her children but not supposed to put our relationship last this is another reason why Cleopatra was attacked by the devil. The devil used the children to against us. She did not say our children she said (MY) children (HER) children only when I did a financial thing of taking care of them. What a lot of women do not realize is that when you push your husband away and put him down, even when my stepdaughter Anita was sitting down doing her mother's hair and she would be fussing me out. Telling me right in front of her children I do not know why I took your ass back and her daughter will tell her you are putting him down just like Cleopatra told me she uses to tell her mother Pam the same thing when she talks to her husband any kind of way. Now Cleopatra and her daughter, is doing the same thing that her mom and her did is that not a cycle? Cleopatra is acting the same way towards her daughter when she is only correcting her, but Cleopatra will tell her daughter Anita to mind her business and stay out of it then need her back for certain reasons to use against me and manipulate! Cleopatra will sit right there and say so I do not care about this relationship or you. Then the woman says in her heart and mind he pushed me down, so it is his turn to be push down I am hurt. There are times as much now to let him see how it feels and this do not make it no better and the woman wants to be the only ones teaching this, but do not accept this as much when the man is in pain you still can learn. You must make a choice on your own and make that decision smart and right ladies do not make up one wrong that come with your force army base killing. If you do not get angry with yourself see a lot of women do not realize that is married that when the wife pushes the husband away and put him down the children look at it. If relationship/marriage is not all that important then these cycles rub off on the couple and children. Cleopatra her father and mother cycle rubbed off on her, as well as my father and mother in my family. Who has the right to tell me only it is all my fault? Women are quick to say God and our marriage come first which is true, then they come in and say oh you are leaving my children out over and outburst with nasty words of harsh aggressive of disrespect. Some go through worse whereas the children ask their mother to do you love dad more than me? Then some children ask fathers do you mom more do you love me? Cleopatra's daughter Anita use to ask her, mom do you love my brother more do you love me, Cleopatra let me know this when Jeffrey came into her life. Cleopatra said no I love you both the same this came from the fathers not being there and at times feeling left out, jealous, not enough attention, it is being more to the other child, or the first child being spoiled so much, or both given the most attention to someone else, and feeling left out feelings are important women not majority for you! I know I am 37 years old I been there done that and experience it so I wonder how children today how things should and suppose to go. When the parents already lived the life, they are just coming into. You know I ask my mother the same question of her at times being the mother and father and my father being the mother and father that do you love my brothers and sisters than you love me? My brothers and sisters did the same thing wanting more debates of someone getting more than the other! We will be upset angry and hurt we was young we did not understand, but when this be this way when you become teenagers, and then some of these cycles come into as adults and mothers and fathers do not know everything, and they be wondering where these affects come from in their children therefore we all have been ways and brought up different! Jeffrey told Cleopatra about her children, but Jeffrey could not tell her anything because he was a thug from the streets because my past sins cheating on her brought everything back up on me, she cannot have her children around me now. I am a dog, criminal, a sex offender, a ho, a user, a robber it is her like calling me that in some way, but it is not it is her actions and behavior treating me just like the system! Cleopatra will get angry start an argument when Jeffrey just talking to her about her daughter Anita respecting our relationship and she just snaps, go off and says you got something against my children, knowing that will get to me because how I was raised up. I cannot make children throwing that in my face using that for what I did to her. Then come back and say baby I love you, but you are leaving our daughter left out and you giving my son, me and you all the attention. Now Cleopatra can say this, and the man have no say so because when he does then it is a major issue or a big problem! Not for women though for the wrongs or rights to get out and get away from everything. Not what we been through with men hell and back as an excuse to cover up it up all. On relationship/marriage women, HELLO, LISTEN, HEAR! When you walk in the house from a long day of work you walk up to your man/husband, he asks how was your day? Then gives you a kiss. Then you ask how was his you both agreed right their God was there then you two as one then you go to the son our daughter and say we love you. The husband does the same thing towards God the wife and the children. He does not walk into the house and walk pass the wife and run straight to the children when she walks up first how would that look? Feel? Ignored Cleopatra that was bitter would say it is not all about making love and that is all we fucking do good and right then change it and say that is all you did you cannot fuck like you use to no more! I would look at her and say that is so rude, nasty and selfish. She is my wife married to me, so I just stop being emotional of that ignoring her let it go away like it was never said. What will God say about that since Cleopatra (THE WOMAN) said I cannot talk or do not have anything to say to her at all because anything that comes out is bullshit and a lie. For all the wrong that I did, and she is right there nothing for me to say I would be setting myself up that is why the new world order in these marriages, do not say nothing wait until she calms down she will come right back and tell you she is sorry! Cleopatra has it all to say and more to add on! See this is where cycles come from and out of the women because it is deep generation curses. They feel like they are owed something see children be included in this at times and it be dangerous. Every time I sat there and told explained and showed Cleopatra that I was not trying to break her up from her children she said yes you is, then come back and apologize to me for saying that then change her mind, words, gesture, attitude man a woman is incredible. Listening to Cleopatra's mother telling me those are not your children negro the grandmother even says (MY) children see the cycle, and a lot of times I understand they was not my biological children, so my responsibilities meant something to God, not to Cleopatra that is good enough for me! I still said to the children go with your grandmother or mother after I was disrespected by the grandmother and Cleopatra. Then my son Trevor would cry and say I never believe I will have to grandmother no more and as it all was said this was all on me and my fault. Now see this is the truth and Cleopatra could not handle the truth I am not leaving me left out I could not a lot of times to, but I be damn when she told me take it like a man that I need to stop being a coward and take the blame for everything! Now when Cleopatra wanted to stand up for respects when she got ready also when I told her that is respect for God, you and others. Cleopatra was not respecting me, so her mother was not. Not only because what I did to her daughter while in a relationship, she was already disrespecting when she first met me. While in a relationship it was ok then Cleopatra outburst with the past, so she was not ready for relationship then the problems and our wrongs. Now Cleopatra (THE WOMAN) can say you did not want my son to be with Jeffrey she never said father, because the mother taught that in her marriage like my mother did raising us up in her home, so this don't tell you of these curses go on and on but you let Cleopatra and her mom tell it I'm change and say you don't want my son Trevor going anywhere with my partner and I will have my suit on wanting to go to my son graduation. Then Grandmother will be going with the son while I am sitting down by Cleopatra arguing with her mom telling her she is miserable and how is it still my fault then on everything? I was hurting bad, and I could not say nothing but feel, look, stupid when I been telling Cleopatra what been going on, but I lost that respect and had to earn all trust back. Now Jeffrey still must wait but Cleopatra corrected her mom, but she is not correcting herself on her relationship to be back equal! I took Cleopatra's son Trevor to get haircuts, get him shoes and clothes, when he will go to school and get back home, I would ask him, what did your classmates say about your hair cut? He would say everyone like it. Then he will say I liked it to, then he says I liked it to. A lot of children at school said where did he get it from, they want one to. I also asked him because it made me feel proud to give and let him have something I could not have when I was growing up that the emotions of love are an awesome action. Now I will see the bad texts in my stepdaughter Anita cursing me out to her friends and what the grandmother would say about me. When I would tell Cleopatra, she will say very disrespectful you had no business going into her phone you fucking deserve that because you went through her phone, and you got just what you were looking for. I cried! Then I was a cry baby and a woman and bitch for that. Then when I see the text messages in my stepson Trevor phone she will curse me out but when she got in her mood to handle it she did, was that not confusing because waiting on someone to respect you is a limit that they can take right women? Every time of 22 years of a relationship it was all and only my fault. If Cleopatra's mother sits in a room to herself and watches T.V. is it all the husband fault and deal with misery behind closed doors on both sides. I see plenty of marriages, divorces, relationships and on everyone everything every sin, fault is on the man. A gentleman is letting people know the faults on both sides no favoritism or sides taken he shows where the husband is wrong and sins and the wife on everything. Now when the husband does wrong it hurts and reflects on the marriage, they both feel it, because 1 the wife is feeling more pain and the husband is wrong. Now when the wife is wrong if she cheated or not it could be for other sins the husband will feel the most pain because she was wrong! Parts of this world have taught divorces and the peoples that is teaching falsely that the woman/wife needs all the credit and attention. God did not make the rule or commandment so all wives husbands and false teachers that say this do this will be judge accordingly to his word. I knew what love when I met Cleopatra. Love I must explain it to you because it is seriously deep. L- is the mouth that I open to speak life and brought a life together. O- is the hands that open doors for opportunity on doors that was closed before and in both of our lives. V- is unbelievably valuable and God that brought us from the dust of the ground that we were not allowed at to stop buy, sale, lease or even rent it, but gave it away freely to everyone expecting nothing in return. E- God put E last to connect the L the O and V together simply, because everybody that is old enough will discover it is very essential! I know and mean the most ingredients to this thing called life, so as I close this chapter what I am saying is do not love for granted, because it may grow legs and walk out your life and you will be crying to God every day, hoping and praying to God that it returns the same way it left. Take the Lord with you in everything you do, and it includes the Lord. The world does not exist when you have God. A picture perfect, marriage is two imperfect people who refuses to ever give up on each other. Do not do what me and Cleopatra did we got a divorce I filed for it because I could not take the false accusing and criticize when I got saved and married, I got pushed right back to women. People hate me because they cannot figure out or understand me what I have been through in life and marriage. I am still being blessed. When the other people say things like this and that is going to happen to me speaking bad against me, God open other doors even more, because a lot of women will tell them in they face or behind their backs they cannot stand and do not expect anything never good to happen for them after how they have been treated after years. Cleopatra did me this way and still doing it until this day. Now god says do not say these wicked things out your mouth to no one and the woman be quiet to say we will you are not God. What God says win you do someone wrong, then you are doing it towards God to. Women that are angry and bitter do not think like that it be so much malice in the heart because of the man. They even say I am sorry for blaming you for everything, but the sin of bitterness and malice take control of them then they do not have control of themselves to handle the problem. The little I had and the strength I had I left Cleopatra (THE WOMAN) she did not appreciate me at all she got stubborn and turned into a gold digger instead of leaving it in God hands. Cleopatra was angry, complaining saying why am I in this situation? Meaning only herself. When God says for better or for worse. She did not appreciate that rare ability. She said I forgive you, but I cannot forget about what you did to me in an angry cruel wild way. She learned a lesson as she said switching off and on not to ever trust my ass ever again but still come back to say I love you baby, yes, I know women that is a woman. She said I fucked up bad. Cleopatra told me she will never ever get close to me again, so she cannot let her forgiveness be God's way it has to be her way thinking it is God's way by just talking and changing up like stories that's soap operas! But lies and says it is only his fault and it is only just all on him for the cheating part. Cleopatra let it be known and said actions coming always like you women say gone girl or that's right girlfriend it must be her way, her attitude to forgive me, because her behavior was foolish, petty, uncalled for and unnecessary. Cleopatra feels like she is a teacher her behavior is always good, excellent, right, and correct you can be good at things and need more work or others we all do. Tell what marriage is perfect and only has faults only on the man. One of the things women says is if you do not know ONLY WHAT HE DID! There is something left out is not it, it takes two as one many people wanted me to change I guess they wanted me to be a doctor, a lawyer, they loved the idea of me, but could not handle the reality of me however I accepted them, like my mother-in-law she wanted my stepson away from me, because I she said because of my past I was a bad role model for him. My stepson Trevor is smart, intelligent, bright, well educated, have a great sense of humor and persistent these things are true. Everyone has a story on me in her family and they think they know me 100% percent bad and not well, they have nothing good to say about me, however I forgive them. God has a lot of good things to say about me. Now Cleopatra would say my mother do not like you because of how you did and treated me. When I first met Cleopatra, she said her mother do not like no man I get with so she should of woke up she was blind! So, the mother does not have a forgiving heart you know our race on forgiveness is awfully bad we all been there! Just like you know how the curse has passed on but as to treat me like a dog and call yourself a Christian her mother and family. Cleopatra looks at Jeffrey staring him in his eyes holding his shoulders and say Jeffrey you have a good heart forgive them. Cleopatra cannot forgive me and teach her children and the cycle is bad and they all take time to forgive one another in their family because how they were raised. As her family to put me down and blame for everything I am not ashamed of what I been through right or wrong, because God is using my story for his glory a lot of people will not understand only God! God is for everyone that is why Cleopatra (THE WOMAN) only told me the bad negative things she sees me as and I was only in her eyes. God is going to be with me always and never leave me for anything. As we all fall short of his glory she never sinned against me as she says and feels then change it and say I did not say I did not sin against you then I ask her then what she is saying, she would say it was my fault so she cannot answer the question that she is guilty on the answer she do not want to give being selfish. By God not me being perfect I still love Cleopatra. Not only her me as well I almost went crazy in our relationship she did to. Thank God I am still here so is her with life itself a blessing from God! I could have lost my way I am back on the path with God. I do not want to give up on something or cannot go a day without thinking about Cleopatra for better or worse and we are not married, and it still feels a change of time. I do not stress because God is going to change everything by faith, I speak it and claim it! I can be a man and say I betrayed Cleopatra trust she pressured me on things as well, provoked me not to have no freedom, no air, everything Jeffrey did was wrong he did get it right, for God, myself and Cleopatra. What hurt the most was the teacher did not give me a good grade or believe or like my effort. Her looks did not draw me to her it was the attraction of her smile, her spirit and respecting herself draw me to her she was and still is A PHENOMAL WOMAN! I begged her to lets to do things back together again she was honest until I hurt her. She could not be committed with a liar, but I did get myself together I started being more compassionated, supportive, and encouraging towards her even with her lying on forgiving me still accepting her bitterness, pain, evil and angry attitude with only accepting her needs. Cleopatra is a beautiful woman I cannot let her go and someone you can take on the world with. A woman that you can give the world to that's high mountains looking down at the world! One thing for sure moving forward I will not let no woman tell me I am a piece of shit; I am not worth nothing and put me down and tell me while she is with or not I am not going to ever be shit. Especially being a husband, I am someone special who committed myself to the Lord and if a woman cannot see that then it is something wrong with her! I was treated like horse shit. I give myself credit and God does I tried my damn best if no one does and that is all that matters both parties do not suppose to let the love or romance wear off. Both parties not just the husband/ man or all parties! The respect for her was around, because everywhere we will go a lot of women will say that better be your wife. The people that will know I am her husband that will be happy to see her. Did she know how much I put in I believe she did she just did not care because she felt all the pain, I took her through no matter what I did could not make up for her pain and hurt. See that is selfish because it was all about only her, so if everyone knew her how could it be all my fault? In other words, Jeffrey can say good and great things about Cleopatra. She always strived to live a happy better life even with bad times. Even thou her mess ups, sins, actions and faults she does not know with her being angry all the time she was the one who see the best version of myself and looking at life differently and changing some of my bad ways! Cleopatra feels and says Jeffrey did not help her with anything or teach her nothing now we all know in the relationship it can be break-ups and if you married lead to divorces and separations, but we still learn things and help from one another especially learning something every day. I did not get a DIPLOMA or DEGREE, but it comes from the LORD! Men have a hard time just as much as women finding a good relationship it goes both ways it is crazy women and crazy men just like Cleopatra told me when she first met me, I can be crazy to! Now women you say your man have done you wrong, lied, cheated do you really give me a Godly chance of forgiving him with your heart being cleansed? Does your mind say one thing and your heart is still not healed and in sin as well? Cleopatra (THE WOMAN) kept saying I should have not moved with you right in my face right after we were in deep relationship. Me lifting my heads up walking away, so can she see the curse that she seen her mother talk to her husband any kind of way and said to her mother do not do or talk to your husband like that. He has feelings that not right and a sin and don't know the mother is teaching her as the wicked mother or witch with the wand let me tap you on your head, so you can do your man this way when he's doing good not bad, so I don't want Cleopatra (THE WOMAN) to say I did it, because how you treated Jeffrey for 15 years being together that will be the only thing Jeffrey say. It took my mother 14 years to get over the past then go to my father and say I'm sorry for blaming you for everything, didn't walk away and say it still was you. You did more than me. Cleopatra (THE WOMAN) was quiet, she helped, but stop listening to Jeffrey period.

Chapter 7

A good woman with help will try to change you, but a bitter woman won't make you a better man. She will make you feel like you in a garbage can with all your dirty clothes, old baggage, filth, spit that's not taken out, every time the garbage man comes to pick up the garbage it would be outside, because the bitter woman will add things in the garbage and pile it up more and more. So, what do to she expects to get in return or back. When she is selfish like a quote said, an angry woman feels I'm going to get what I want. I'm a strong woman with all I dealt with and what I'm going to say you never ever changed. When it was her who never changed for real in the first place, with the beginning of forgiving me. When she's forgiving, she will make her man honest? He will be loving, humble, the sweetest man in the world. She won't listen to others, that my sister, mother, daughter, son and my pastor said this about my man, because she is a strong woman. She doesn't want what her family, my family or anything someone has to say about her only. When she's selfish and only about her not US! Tell me quick, who you been listening to? But tell me with a quickness you listening to this person and that person, me, and a add on. What I better and need to listen to, because if I don't, I'm considered even more headed and negative. Now when Jeffrey did ask Cleopatra when you gave me your man a good promotion just like she does her job, children and family with good bad rights or wrongs. It's either she can't answer that or it's an argument but, will have all the questions to every answer and answer my question with a question, have her own questions and answers always letting me know 100% she knew me and everything I'm talking. I told lies but not about everything a lie is a lie. Cleopatra always Jeffrey you were always trying to preach, and no one was trying to hear that shit he was talking about, but she can preach and tell it all, because I'm always the fuck up that's not shit I'm always the garbage can. When the last time she encouraged me to make an honest living that I can be proud of? I can't remember the last time she talked to me in front of her children respectfully with love and know in the way how to do it

that's very important you know just saying negative being on me hard and putting me down. How can your woman say she can admit for being hard on you then come right back and you haven't done anything, and right there in front of her and she starts an argument up? Is that not Bi-polar? I guess that's just a woman being a woman, every woman doesn't do it, in the same way it still blows a man's mind! When I did some things, I did to Cleopatra it first started, she was insecure and jealous I made her that way. A real man owns up to his wrongs, sins, and mistakes and changed. I tried to teach her no man wants a bitter, unforgiving, insecure, jealous woman that's always pressuring him about the past. There are ways to be jealous for your companion, but not out of hate or evil with confusion. You both want each other attention not to share it's just so amazing! Always getting on the man when he sees he has a dream, future, goals and plans. Do you think you are helping by always hunting him down on his back constantly? Because if a woman is doing good or bad, she doesn't want a man messing up her dreams, future, goals, and plans. Women when you think in your mind, we'll the mind is already there it's the thoughts that you let come in and take control over you, your husband/man and don't have no common sense of what's happening or going on, but you swear you think you do! I never said your thoughts don't be true I'm talking about the one's when you go overboard taking charge over everything in your way of it can never go back to the way it uses to be. You will take the man back once he has cheated on you, used you up and have done you wrong right? Then say and want to make it work after all what he has put you through asking for forgiveness and you giving it, but it's not over because remember you both are in this together because if you weren't you would not have taken him back and he wouldn't have accepted it if he did not want to. See women this is not mind games psychology this is the truth, but the messed-up part about it is when you took him back you weren't really for sure you were thinking both sides, mindset, personality and the woman because you took him back and he got back with her so what you both get out of that is what matters. Did you take the man back, say and put actions with negative behavior saying, (BUT), (IT NEEDED MORE TIME), A WOMAN IS DIFFERENT FROM A MAN), (I OR SHE NEED MORE TIME

TO GET OVER THIS)! Then where was starting fresh and forgiveness was at? Women keeps a lot of things in, will say it's over and that don't be true depending on what it is. A lot of peoples say when two peoples forgive one another it takes time see that's bull crap right there. See God knows and us as well know the times come in when no forgiveness and the harm is done to one another or someone then working it out going through the battles then when you both come on one accord to forgive then it's all left behind! Now when we say we forgive, but we are not through hurting yet and there's some other things to be let out or I, she, me, you, us was not finish, because see that's after not before so you backed up on God's word and each other this where confusion comes in when we can't get what we want out the deal. A woman that thinks a man is flirting, having sex or dealing with another woman, she is not showing any trust in him. Also, she is not let him clear his head. I was the man when she first met me. We all know every relationship is not perfect as a couple we go through bumps and bruise as we taught each other. In the relationship I was in we both was wrong for sinning, complaining and doing things unnecessary to each. All she had to do was look at her mother situation. Why she's locked up in the room, watching T.V. and lonely. Its deeper than that knowing it wasn't all the husband faults. While she locked up in room thinking about God, herself, him all those years whether good or bad thoughts. Therefore, the mother said to me if I would have put my husband first on a lot of things before my kids he would have still been here. Then Cleopatra (THE WOMAN) would say I don't want to her to be my mother, because she shows two faces. No, you don't want to hear the truth like you been saying to me that you can't accept just once. So, her mother, just made that up, her mother has her ways, but she still can advise us on relationship, she's an elder and with her wrongs it's all good in my mother that I learn from her some things that my real mother didn't teach me. They can learn from me some things they weren't taught. We all can learn something new every day from one another. Someone has done someone wrong that's why everyone must repent. So, don't look down on no one and feel or say. What can they teach me all what they have done! Well, we all need to look in the mirror at ourselves please don't say I'm making up an excuse to get out of what I have done wrong to blame you all, what I have done is gone and past! Right is right wrong is wrong. If it is wrong don't just tell the women don't go backwards that goes for men to. Don't tell men to go back to then threw up prayer for them as well of yourselves and they do the same for you. Jeffrey brought all his wrongs, filth, sins, his past, negativity, lies, abuse, everything what Cleopatra wanted him to do then I had to go through consequences of burning, perish, suffering and die it does feel this way! She did say that's why what's happening to you is happening, because how I treat people. So how do I expect to be blessed. Then say I didn't want nothing bad to happen to you, I'm sorry then go back and change it. Tell me I'm Carnal minded and I'm not a child of God or Christian as she says and speak from her heart or I'm not God or a pastor, you be surprised the things can come out a woman mouth. A lot of women feel her and its right that must be dealt with by God not the women way. When I felt this way of hurt some people told me to leave it in God's hands, continue to pray, love myself, her and others. Now that was and is the right way. A woman with love, wisdom, communication, understanding, forgiveness, power, grace, mercy, a sweet cleanse pure sincere heart carries herself with a humble spirit how to treat, speak and handle others. Cleopatra (THE WOMAN) was not gentle and quiet that's why I kept leaving and sleeping in my car. Instead of having humility in front of us we were just suffering from the past. I pushed her with soft and tough love to push herself and me more even with her good and bad times giving up. I had my dreams to, because she was a woman I met with a blessed spirit and vision. She never compared herself with others until she didn't mean her forgiveness from her heart and that was not on me it was on her. She was the one who came to me asking me for forgiveness and telling me she will never bring it up again. Cleopatra always told me to stay humble and didn't think at times ever that she needed to be humble! Her and her family would think they were better than me and deserve better than everyone at times. I owed her everything for what I did it was not enough love to show her it didn't mean anything to her, because if it did, she would of saw one thing good in me and I didn't get loved for that. We know at times in our lives we make the same mistakes we struggle and sin at times and days are happy I have hurt people, but I have not made others fall, so I can get to the top and if they need a hand to get to the top with me and there trying I can and will help them. I would say therefore this or that happen to you smiling, laughing, or making fun of them saying yeah you deserve it. I want great things to happen to and for you! God says forgive your enemies and love them. There were things that I found in me because I found God! It was said do not let you adore be external the braiding of hair and the putting on of goal jewelry, or the clothing you wear but let your adoring be the hidden person of the heart with the imperishable beauty of a gentle quiet spirit, which in God sight is very precious. I am also working on me even more to be a better humbler person I need it women pray for me as well as for your men! It's hard but I'm not giving up. God has faith in me, and I have it in him. Jeffrey wants to say to Cleopatra right now your fabulous, wonderful, lovable, special, a mother and a woman of God. Now I want to ask women a question? Are you humble, not forgiving, not with a clean heart are you respecting yourself and God? Or your home and husband even your children because some women feel like they can do this and if some wants to accept it or not, they don't care they are going to do what they want to do that's benefits them. Now I'm a great man of God I'm just getting better. There are good women out there that are pleasing to the mind, soul, body, spirit and the heart. I don't put women down I encourage you. Now when a woman does not talk a lot all the time this gives the man chances to sit with God and himself to think he reflects on what has or have not done and going to surprise and be the sweetest husband in the world even more. When a woman/ wife is screaming, yelling, cursing him out continually getting on him what this does to him is makes him feel like he's a child. It was plenty days and nights Jeffrey couldn't stand Cleopatra, but he couldn't live without her and still constantly tell her I love her tried my best for many years! God had chosen all type of people to be holy and dearly loved, clothe yourself with compassion, kindness, humility, gentleness and patience. Bear with each other and forgive one another if any of you has a grievance against someone. Forgive as the Lord forgave you and over all these virtues put on love which binds them all together in perfect unity. Let the peace of Christ rule in your hearts. Since as members of one body you will call to peace and be thankful. Let the message dwell among you richly as you teach and admonish one another with all wisdom Psalms, hymns, and songs from the spirit, singing to God with gratitude in your hearts and whatever you do, whether in word or deed do it all in the name Lord Jesus giving thanks to God the father through him! You know when Jeffrey was in jail Cleopatra or no one knew what he was going through he paid for every sin right there being beat, hurt, pain, bleeding, crying, praying for everything he did to her and my family, see I'm not perfect and she did not do one thing wrong to me as she say, and other women says. I was praying and God came to me in my sleep letting me know spiritually and sending people to me, I reap what I sow for the sins I have committed. Cleopatra added on more with her over dramatic, emotional, dangerous spirit that was not with love because God is Love! She punished me even more so can you tell me; how did she truly forgave me? Letting me know when I got out after making love to me after she was backed up for so long and missing me man the love was serious! When Jeffrey was incarcerated, Cleopatra was crying and cursing me out, see the devil was not only busy with me he was with Cleopatra as well, but she's perfect as her actions shows, mouth, gestures and her mind thinks. We all in life have learn when me, you, us are all hardheaded when I got home I got it to she wasn't finish with me either I'm going to ignore her or I'm going to let her stand up for herself. Jeffrey even forgave Cleopatra on the way she was treating me, I said did so much to her I'm going to take all the shit and put it on me. I'm the man, but I learned a lot and woke up, I'm a child of God not a woman treating me like a pig. It's not right to pick on someone or make fun of them when there trying. I learned being married and with God. Faith it does not make things easy it makes them possible. I see and know that it wasn't Cleopatra being pretty didn't make her keep me. Me being a real man myself wanted to stay with her keeping me. I was a wise man and still is to put me down as a fuck, a thug, and ghetto and lazy even though her saying that out her mouth, because a wise man can always be alone a stupid ignorant man is a follower in a crowd! We should always humble ourselves therefor under the mighty hands of God, he may exalt you in due time. Casting all your care upon him; for the careth for you. Be sober, be vigilant, because your adversary the devil, as roaring lion walketh about seeking

whom resist steadfast in the faith knowing that the same afflictions are accomplished in brethren that are in the world. But the God of all grace, who hath called us unto his eternal glory by Christ Jesus, after that ye have suffered a while make you perfect, establish, strengthen, settle you. To him be glory and dominion forever and ever. Amen! Whoever does not love or forgive his brother or sister does not love God? We know already God will not forgive those who don't forgive others or themselves! I don't understand when a woman is right or wrong, she is strong but when a man is right or wrong, he is controlling. In her mood depending on the woman, she is and time of the situation being a woman. With a man he's all these kinds of things out the woman mouth at times he's controlling, he should not talk at all that means in her time shut up, because with Cleopatra when Jeffrey just spoke on with what he said or felt, what's right or a statement I'm always disrespectful. If I don't say anything at all I'm ignoring her, I'm not romantic and I'm a party pooper if I cry or expressing my feelings then I'm called a bitch. Then I'm acting like a cry baby or a woman. If I'm happy, loud or outspoken I'm making a fucking seen but Cleopatra could act out in any kind of way she wants and it's all, because of me for every action she reacts off or on! She would listen to a false prophet telling her and herself that it's ok to disrespect her man with her behavior behind closed doors. Now I'm going to explain a brawling woman and women, please don't say only just men make us like this. It's all and only the men fault. They are no good and dogs. The brawling woman who says she forgives her husband and does not truly, honest with a clean heart. She argues at him constantly of what he did years and years ago it doesn't have to be years it can be a forgiveness on a week or same day or whenever and brought back up being married to a brawling woman years and years or a short time! A brawling woman is in a wide house she argues most of the time because she's miserable and complains over money, bills, pettiness, work, you the man, financial things. Then tell her man she had her own before she met him. I don't need you/him! Tell you I had it all before I met you while you're married or not arguing over how she says the man says he's never sorry when he shows and says it a thousand times but she's to blind and selfish to accept, receive and acknowledge it! She can't say sorry her own self holding things in what he only has done! She even argues over her children saying, (THESE ARE MY CHILDREN). Now women this don't leave your husband/ man left out telling him that in his face maybe not times to yourself, but words can be hurtful to someone's heart! The brawling woman as you can see gets on the man for any little thing when he is not being lazy and trying his best and it's still not enough of satisfying her. She argues over stupid, petty simple things. She puts all the bills and frustration on him. She feels like it's all her responsibility paying most of the bills, you have a low income, and she feels that it's not enough money. Like Cleopatra an example, she's said screaming right in my face while we were struggling Jeffrey didn't you say you didn't want our daughter with no one with someone who did not have a job or nothing? When I was out there trying to find a job, it was hard to find one, because of my background being an ex-convict, but I did not let that stop me. Right in my face standing there made me feel less of a man that my own wife would put me down instead of encouraging me to the next level with prayer, love, guidance and help for better or worse richer or poor. The brawling woman also gets on her husband/man for things he did not by. He would get her things that she wants however she felt she should be there, so she can get what she wants and pick everything out not get surprised. Cleopatra constantly correcting me pointing out my wrong doings and faults even when I was trying to do right. She even got on me when I wasn't praying enough or reading the Bible, but I can come in with God and I have no right, whatsoever to say one thing about God to her, because how I have sin towards her! She even had the nerve to say to tell me about constantly it was only my attitude, ways, and behavior but her ways all together and in shape. She even got on me about my language/English! Reminding me every day up until now of my failures and sins towards her. Cleopatra (THE WOMAN) love this it was turning her on of get back put at the same time she was not happy women learn something please on your times like this with anger in you on way! The brawling woman is a fighter she doesn't have to use no hands her blows is her mouth, body language, feelings, when the husband/man masturbate when she's not giving him attention or love. One of the best brawling woman ways is (SILENCE), I don't know, walking around naked and you see her expression of not wanting to be touch! She is a fighter and so many ways the devil uses her to complain and bicker with full of contention and bitterness. Anything and everything that's not up to her ways and standards is a cause of another fight in the ring for her to nag and complain until she gets what she wants or her way stubborn and selfish. The list goes on and on! She will say when it's time while sitting on the throne as the judge in her courtroom with her gravel in her hand with always order. As a God to say when it's time to forgive and move on when she feel and say it is. It's an excuse as her saying and with bad behavior with action you can't make her do anything. Now I'm ready (Selfish) for self. When she is brawling angry, bitter, cruel she is not with God and false prophets have told her they are still Christians when you tell them the truth they get angry, just like when people told me that robbing, stealing, selling drugs, beating people up and me going to church going to church at the same time is not a Christian. I got angry and was making excuses I realized I had to stop and confess to my wrongs, sins, and actions! Not only was I tired and fed up I was not doing right by God's order. Also, God and people who I have hurt and sin against this goes for men to. Women don't let no woman tell you that you are a Christian, and you keep sinning towards your husband and still claim to be saved and a doer of the word! A brawling woman is not happy she's in love alright with misery and hangs around other women who are the same way. It is a sadistic joy for the devil, because misery loves company for all of them that around together flocking as birds not just certain people only men, that family or my family we are not perfect. Every family has a cycle or curse that has been broken, still need more prayer and once broken things open for a renew life. I know form myself, my family we need the prayer, but the brawling woman will stay we got all together, we don't need nothing at all. The brawling woman will dig up the old sins that's in the closet and beat her husband up every chance she gets with harsh words and her foot on his neck like a dog pointing. She would say don't move until I tell you as if I was her child. She nitpicks for something to fight about. She thinks a physical is different from an emotional verbal fight against you. There always an argument with Cleopatra saying that's nothing in comparison to how much you did to me. What she is doing towards her man so she could heal her heart of pain without thinking about she is hurting God, herself and others. Cleopatra still has her man they are still as one under Gods eyes, however the devil is in her heart and mind, because she does not see love anymore. Think about its SIN can ruin everything if we let it not only the man! WE! US! TOGETHER! As ONE! OURS! LOVE! ME & YOU! The brawling woman is a wife who argues and quarrel over everything! The brawling woman wants to tall her husband about the word of God, but don't want to listen at all. Cleopatra would say you didn't want to listen, so you can't make me listen showing evil to evil, tic for tac, sin for sin, confusion, manipulating! A continual dropping in a very rainy day and a contentious woman are alike. When it rains it would saturate the flat, sod roof. Thus, during heavy rain, the roof would leak, drip, drip, drip! Because the roof was often sod, long after the storm was over, and the clouds were gone, the saturated roof would continue to leak. Drip! Drip! Drip! A contentious wife is that roof. She nags, complains, and when the argument is over, she keeps bringing it up again and again. Then tells me the man why you can't let the past go when it hurt that have not. Can men tell their women that today like the elder women listen? When the husband walks away the wife argues with him on the phone. Where you at your ass does not love me, because you wouldn't left me here by myself. Now like women say listen to man who wants to be around women who's angry, abusive, talk too much and torturing her husband. A brawling wife and a Christian wife are two different people. False teachers said they are the same they are still Christians. Living right by God's word, l and have faith. I never knew or seen where it says a husband can keep cheating on his wife and be a Christians that's a lie, the devil is a liar. So, can you tell me where it says a brawling woman is a Christian and says I'm better than others. No! It's time for prayer, healing, and anointing of God over them both to be together and right with God. Women cannot be a man towards their husband. Your place is being a woman of God! A lot of woman or man are not taught to be a wife or husband. If you want a righteous home, you can't do unrighteous things towards one another being married or out in the open. One God, one marriage, one accord! You know a lot of times in a marriage or relationships the woman says God is getting the man back for what he has done to her.

Really most of the time it is not God, it's the woman. It shows her anger, blind, upset, and bold to know, understand or listen or hear what's going on: Life is too short to be angry, vengeance, evil, bitter. And with malicious in her heart, so be kind and understanding. A woman will say can she really back it up, after she says she forgives and stop being a brawling woman. All I wanted was family, friend, food on the table, a roof over my head and that will make me the richest man in the world to have a woman like Cleopatra (THE WOMAN). People out here want more, there's nothing wrong with that but don't let that take over your home when you can't have what you want your way when you want it! Jeffrey understood Cleopatra tears as a friend, also love her enough to make her smile and know it. No one knows our relationship like God me and her tell others to mind their business, because they can't tell us nothing only if God was leading them. I was not perfect neither was her we both was angry and took each other for granted at times. Cleopatra forgot when I said let's go out on dates. Let's not stop that or get bored I even said let's try something new, I never ever stop saying I love you not even until this day. I reminded her how we fell in love I wanted to always end an argument with her to make it work with her it didn't because she had too much hate and bitterness inside of her I would come back, and she will be angrier at times. I couldn't compromise because she wasn't willing to do it fair. She wanted to do it her way so we could grow old with one another in the same moody way. When I first met her, I became her best friend. Does she remember that? No, only negative things! Me and her are answering services. Now if you ask her, did she leave me at peace? And truly give me a chance? Because she told more than one person along with the pastor, I really been hard on Jeffrey, so hello where is the chance? This does not mean everything is on her on me we both played parts no marriage is perfect; I'm still trying to find out where is that written it's all on the man. Cleopatra even bothered Jeffrey with my moments, checked my phone, stop cooking and feeding me. Especially when she uses to give me a kiss after she put the food in my mouth. Women this goes for men to when you supposed to be given another chance, I rather be single than waste my time on somebody who take me seriously and believe in me that I changed! When they are getting better and doing better, I rather be in a relationship with God than be in a relationship with a brawling woman who's miserable and angry. I rather be alone, than feel alone even when I'm thinking only about the past. What I've done who can't move forward. Jeffrey have learned with Cleopatra was not all about sex I will watch movies together with her and she will be angry when I say let me hold you, then she will say no! Let's caress? No! Then she will decide to put on the black high heels that I brought her naked on the bed and want to make love or have sex when she was ready. The best time with her is when we laid together and she said baby read these scriptures and lay on me naked not making love not making love, just enjoy God's company! I learned that an unforgiven woman that's something can stay in her mind until death do us apart! (BECAUSE WE ARE APART AND SHE'S STILL THE SAME WAY). I know women she's that way with me but no other peoples, because she wants no remembrance of us, moved on and want nothing from me, because when a woman leaves and move on and fed up that's it. Not just because of me but women have their facts and opinions. I'm being patience with my heart that she comes back I guess women will say I'm crazy she not taking you back boy, just like you tell woman/women don't take him back he's no good. I wanted so bad I want it on my time I'm being honest, but I know I can't and won't get it like that, because I'm putting a curse back on me for the devil to kill steal and destroy! I take time for God on myself even for Cleopatra saying it's not her concern, but why is she still getting on me. Real love eternally requires a great deal of sacrifices, patience, and discipline woman/women will say where I showed that at not all but some especially Cleopatra, but she's the woman so she shows the most love. Hello women! Your heart deserves the best even when you're too impatient to give that. I'm talking to someone! I'm proud of being who I am. If I don't love me I would I respect myself and speak up? I can't do anything without being criticized. I love me! I'm handsome and wonderful inside so when people and women say I'm shit my love all rubbed all that away from me. It doesn't exist all God and me is standing there with open hearts, at the same time with our spears and our amor suits on the full amor. Life hurts you know what I'm talking about now when a woman is hurt from way back, from the past and holding it inside until this day a lot of women do that and still be in front of her soulmate and say it's all your fault. Then say when it's not true and the man could be with God and the woman will still say, because it's not true. See peoples in life can say it's just words yes, but then when it hit them, they feel it no one likes to be falsely accused for something there not or stop doing! Sometimes women you think you don't push your man away. Some do depend on the woman being selfish, saying he will be right back I got this. You are seeing him as the same person when he's around you most of the time and you're telling him right in his face, you dog, liar, and you this and that some say things like I wish I never met you and you going to burn in hell. So, he still is not going back trying while you're pushing him. How can a woman treat her man like a human being if she's not giving him a chance, disrespectful and not treating as a human being? Then the pain she has for him she lets it just sit there in her heart for years and years. A lot of women say they give it to God, but then in their heart it be bitter, lies and then look at the man and call him the devil looks at her then she tells him he is not God! All he is doing is letting her know is what and how God says we suppose to conduct ourselves in our relationship, but she feels of how he hurt her so much from the past there's no chance! It just doesn't be the woman it be the devil spirit with her building walls of insecure, shame, fear, untrustworthy, force of everything on her husband/man then will say he made me this got damn way. You're the reason why I'm this angry ass woman and you can't make me change my mind, so what! Then it comes in where she will say I don't care anymore so the whole time she's saying it's over she does not want to be with you. The devil uses the women to keep it in the darkness and secrets and to be quiet about certain things to keep in of fear where he can come in and kill steal and destroy the marriage, so then it stays in her mind that's a bad choice, because how can she let the healing of God in. Especially when she keeps the wounds hidden deep inside! Women when you open your heart to God and to your husband don't close it back then over something petty and not worth depending on then you bring the past back up on him. Don't bring yourself in to the light with God shining as your words the way you talk to him and leave yourself left out with God that's carnal minded, because seeing both of your sins everything and pains as one. Now I owned up to my own behavior, especially actions of what peoples have done to me. A real woman/wife/wives will understand they will fellowship, but no-good woman/women/wives don't see that as pain, a lot of them see that as grownup be a man, and stop acting like a child, a bitch, a ho, or a pussy depending on the woman the things that can come out their mouths off their tongues. This is only to the ones that are bitter that do this and the same false teachers right or wrong that are confused right along with them as well, because they tell them what they want them to keep coming back! We don't know their relationships, but do they talk to their husbands or wives? Like that we don't know, so they will agree that it is right in God eyes to talk to the person you're married to in any kind of way. Stop looking at always only who hurt you and who did you hurt come to an agreement back with God, because I was still repenting and praying on things that I took the blame from Cleopatra (THE WOMAN) and for feeling other women been through with men and taking other men blames not just my own, because I'm going to tell you something when a woman is hurt she's going all the way in. I just couldn't keep taking the load on me. I'm being held accountable for actions I did not do anymore! People are going for self-forgiveness. They believe in there on ways that God forgives however they get it mixed up and not be a doer in their own way don't lie and say you have not done this. Do you know we can do a sin at times and don't know we having to be human beings, and someone must tell us at times we don't want to accept and do? With our thoughts we refuse to forgive the other person that hurt us it can be me or you, but just ask God only forgiveness and be so angry at the other person that sin towards you your feeling like just, because you told them you forgave them it's ok fine and alright, but in your heart, mind, silence is saying an action only you keep in envy of mentally, abuse, spiritually, physically and health wise. It's a paragraph, diary, dictionary, encyclopedia, repeating science that continues to go on in her mind, because the woman think she knows it all! I did not say she do I said she thinks the process of her mind and her thinking. You see marriage today don't bring both problems, pain, hurt, and give it all to God. One wait on the other and the other spouse does the same, because they feel the other has not paid off their debt of what they have done instead of erasing it they right down more add to. It was too much to bear Jesus went through more than that. That's why he died on the cross for our sins and forgave us. When we ask for forgiveness and forgive others. The painful scars have been a testimony to other marriages, healing and prayers out to them not to give up Jesus does not like divorces. I want to be prophet to others to heal their pain. I understand I have been there, we been there! Women give their lives to God and stay positive so you can be a blessing to others. You know its people that give their lives to God and go back and forth and sin I'm one and a witness to tell on myself can I get another? I have done it plenty times I know a lot, but let's not put them down let's pray for them, Right woman/women/wives? We all have been their own sinning and falling short on the glory of the Lord. I knew a woman that was married to my friend and when he got saved, he lied to her. She kept telling him you're the biggest want to be Christian in the word get out of my damn face talking about God. Instead of praying for him healing be brought in and stay there. You shouldn't keep bringing it up it's old. She goes to church to, and I was there while she curses him out in the church, yelling, screaming and very disrespectful to him and the women was holding on to her while she was angry praying for her ignoring the man this is what their teaching in some churches, yes. It couldn't tell her ever what she did wrong because all her moves, wrongs, sins and actions was because of him and that he was a no-good liar. What should he ever have to say about God that's how she feels, see and talk to her man? She said in his face he's still a Christian and a child of God but he's a dog and I can't stand his fucking ass, but I still love him he's so crazy. He's a trip and I don't know what I'm going to do with him! A woman is a work of art, and a masterpiece Cleopatra is this woman I'm talking about. She's beautiful in every way, especially her eyes. She brushes, combs and wrap her hair before she lays down to sleep. I used to love help Cleopatra change her pads and throw them away most men don't do this and then I would go to the store, however before I walked out the door she would kiss me to let me how well she appreciates and how thankful she is towards her man! I love her soul it's the most beautiful part in her. She's so serious my baby is alive. I like and love when she's capable and passionate, She's God finest work of art. She's pretty! Everyone looks at her everywhere she goes because she's natural work of art. Even her heart has art and her smile, and I love her nose and her big eyes they are art as well especially her big, huge eyeballs. She's a work stronger than fiction. I feel her jealousy, pain and envy towards me it's a wound to her inner self love, because I lost her trust. She did not take the wall down fully after she forgave me. What the devil spirit will use woman/women/wives it's what you expect you hurt her it takes her time to get over it. How much time? There's no time after forgiving someone and moving on. That's being very selfish to the other person you claim you're in love with. Cleopatra put a while on her heart and anything you can imagine but she never forgave me. I didn't mean to hurt her heart and she kept the wall up. However, I didn't keep my wall up, or get back at her because the change was made to God then to myself then towards her it didn't mean anything. So, if a woman says that's right and good how can she say let go and let God? I can tell you because she says one thing and do something different. Cleopatra have so many arts of herself I can explain because it's greater than love itself now that's an awesome amazing woman, I see why women love roses and flowers! Some people say they can't, but I can. They are marriage rules by God not by others. Women I have something to tell you I live alone by myself now satisfying her again I call her when she says, Jeffrey I'm wrong. Even when Jeffrey called her, I would say I'm wrong when Cleopatra was the one wrong being the better man on that. She's right when I'm sad even when she's happy bitter or angry. I still have her picture when she was a child and mines. I called her by her first name she says I don't like to be called that. When she's negative, angry, insecure, sad, happy and joyful I looked in her eyes and told her no one in the world is right for me but you, no one! I would call her before I leave home, when I'm at work and when I leave from work, so how is that a cheating no good man? Even when I didn't have a job and was looking for work, I would call her when she would upset me, and she was upset I called even at times I upset her. When I was down, I would come to her down she said I was acting like a clown but when Ronald the clown came to her school she smiles and laugh with him I was not happy or laughter in her life anymore. When we have our talks, I will always tell her how sorry I was and how much I loved her. I would let her know what looked good on her and what did not. She still was satisfied to a certain extent because it was more, she wanted or something different corrections after corrections! Their where times when Cleopatra got off work and Jeffrey will hug her and crack her back and she will say baby that feels so good moving away softly and slowly kissing me! Then a 2 hours later she will come by me and say to me baby you act like I'm this angry evil woman. She will say it, contradict herself and twisted it again and say you made me this evil bitter ass woman that I am then come back and say I'm sorry love. Women, please tell me what is that? That's just being a woman. Mind you this is still Cleopatra and I love her. When breaking a woman's heart, it's wrong it must be healed and conceal her pain, but she can't do evil and don't forgive, to the women say yes, she can then where that get her? A woman knows how to use the pain to get away with everything I was not ashamed of the pain I came back like a man for something special a woman that's beauty to get another chance. Jeffrey faced her standing their face to face being falsely accused after hurting Cleopatra he understood how much he can take. What women don't realize is they don't let it all out they are thinkers and doers will tell you quick, you don't know their mind or what their thinking or did but can tell a man she knows him more than anything and how he is, who he been talking and listening to. She feels and know what she knows and what she is talking about you can't tell her anything! Her God doesn't lie to her but since you are the man that's the dog there's no God in you but when she's sinning or not, she has a God on her side. Jeffrey stops trying to fix every problem with Cleopatra himself it was wearing him out and running him down which is why he walked away and slept in our car or own the streets with my brother watching him do drugs on the sidewalk talking to me. Slept by him nights on the streets when he prayed for me. When we do wrong to one another that does not mean we have no good in us. While Cleopatra was home and Jeffrey was talking to her I did not tell you to go out there you chose to do that, I just don't want to be with no sorry ass man. When her children and her hurt me, Jeffrey would leave then she would call me and say get your ass back home. See she lost interest in me, she stops knowing how to love me or understand all over again she was not ready for that all over again. Then say your ass is acting like a woman you want to be out there then bring me in the house a fuck my brains out punching my chest while I'm on top making love! Now hear me good ladies! I left and slept on the streets because no man wants to be in the house that's saved and a man of God with no brawling woman. No woman wants to be with an abusive, violent, arguing man she will be a fool so what will he be? A fool as well and the woman will be perfect these days now. Marriages look at yourselves, then say look at us now. Also, where we are for the future. Now being with a single mother and raising someone children is not easy some people will say, yes, it is. So, as a stepfather helping her raise the children together. Jeffrey respected Cleopatra for canceling dates with him when we first met because it's not about getting between a woman's legs. Her children came first. When we moved in together, Jeffrey still put them in a home with a roof over their head which was supposed to be there father job, but God made me this man to do this job. Cleopatra gave me her ass to kiss when times get hard. Cleopatra and her children where my priority Jeffrey was patient. It was not about no money it was about God love and the family with the responsibility all in one package. I loved her with respect being responsible stepping up to the plate being a man. I did this with all mothers that I appreciated and sacrifice that I made for her and her children when I first met her and her children. I was consistent with everything I did for the family I knew how she felt when she was taking me through a lot as much as I was taking her through, when she came to me and said I forgive you. It's special and kindhearted to forgive with love the ones that you have hurt and the ones that hurt you back to everyone leave everything you can't solve yourself in the hands of the Lord! Now this same woman that Jeffrey love Cleopatra, she is a masterpiece, stable all by herself. See that's how you know when you love someone that you can still be there for them, help them speak good about them and not talk behind there back or in their face nasty, not saying I don't have faults and wrongs that's just my heart and gift that I have. Everyone heart is not that way and if they be evil and say because or, but, then they need to go pray and cleanse their heart and let go and let God and it will happen with trust, faith, and believing. Jeffrey prayed for Cleopatra to do this.

Women don't tell your husband/man when he sins then he goes to God get on his knees prays, repent ask God for forgiveness and come towards you tell him things God is not going to forgive him just like that, or you think you can get off just that fast or like that, oh you think what you did to me I can just forgive you and all the time has pass by! See it do like this with women that be selfish and have all the time in the world and it be too late to forgive tomorrow is never promised, so like you tell men they need to forgive, check themselves and get it right. Cleopatra (THE WOMAN) is unstoppable with bitterness, malice and rude with a brawling wicked attitude. She is still very successful after all she taught me all a lot of things, I just never taught her anything because her heart is not clean out and a wall up towards me people say that that person will just be angry at you. Honestly when you have not forgiven or hold something in against anyone your heart will not be right with God so that spirit will reflect on places you go because when you get upset, sad, angry then that comes out that what's in you then people will get that same treatment! Stress comes from trying to do it all on our own so when Jeffrey told Cleopatra to put it in God hands and walk away, she cursed me out, hung up on me, screamed, yell, catch an attitude and this does not get us nowhere and there's nothing wrong with her period it's only me. She is still telling me Jeffrey leaves it in God's hand which is what the same thing I told her. She had it all together Cleopatra would say I don't want to be your wife no more, being a father or mother is one of the highest paying jobs in the world. Since the payment is pure love, Jeffrey just nominated Cleopatra for the loveliest, caring wife and mother award. I love you Cleopatra! Men take your time with the woman. Now Jeffrey learned a new thing from Cleopatra when he does things, she doesn't like it because it aggravates her. Now when I get better you can't see it because no matter what I do she can't stand me for what I only did, everything she did was right to do in God's eyes, her eyes her mother eyes, her children's eyes, so what's in her eyes is negativity always. Now when I tell her something, she says you make me sick then hang up, then calls me right back says baby I'm sorry and can't have her way! I'm learning more and more things from women and Cleopatra observing, standing back I'm never better, good or nothing I'm the same old shit stating from her. I can take that they talked about Jesus Christ. Who is the person I'm nothing at all, but her family is loving, Christians, and saved? A lot of women will say they have bad spirits and sickness from the husband/man/men they were dealing with. It will never ever be their fault when there wrong a lot of times. Until this day Cleopatra is telling Jeffrey what to do, how to do it, where to do it, and balling up her fist at me when I tell her something. I can admit I been hardheaded a lot of times as a man what is not fair when Jeffrey let Cleopatra know you're not always right and it's not acceptable what she's doing of treating me wrong it's put right back on me that I'm still the one that's not listening! I can't make her listen while she's rolling her eyes in the air fussing me out that's a strong woman with an attitude that I can't handle. Right women? It's found to be a strong woman, but don't go overboard things in your husband/man face and in the air towards people as well to be strong with disrespecting, bad behavior, wicked, rude, angry, nasty to get what you want, how you want it in your way that does not make it better that pushes your man away. I have heard and seen a lot of women say girl I got him doing what I say now, on lock down, he is writing all the checks, he knows not to play games with me, he knows better, I got him on schedule and speed dial these are things that will make your husband/man leave, because I know a lot of you women left men for this same bull crap. I'm with you on this, so what's up with you? Emotional, love, God and health are good how you relate with each other yourselves and God determines how you relate and get along with one another! God will heal you of your scars women but must let him don't say your healed in the blood of Jesus, but in your heart, it still hurts which it means you have not 100% healed. How can a healing come upon your soul when you chose not to let it when your talk is cheap to God and yourself, it only wants what it wants, because healing is a choice for God not to keep making an excuse to keep using someone continually of what they did to you years ago? So, if you say, I'm going to let go when I'm good and ready to ladies what God let me forgive you and keep blessing you while you continue this? No! We know God is not going to rule in favor with that. God will not say that so don't tell men to keep making excuses and you don't tell yourselves that, that's for any sin. Healing transforms your life it's a special kind of grace women. It can happen any day, time, and place it's better than being helpful and giving its God! Physically, mentally and spiritually don't let it be too late. Can I say that woman? Do you like to hear the truth? The life and love for life is beautiful and short. Women don't ever think men don't scream, yell, cry, shout, pray be pushed away, provoked, used, lied to put down, step on in that case God would have only created women. It's a process for a man to heal to. Women and men say life is hard nothing is hard if God is included, because God will fight the battles for us some time, we feel that God is not there, and he is taking too long. I used to feel like that, but I stopped, because God took his hands off me. I went through to many situations in my life. I felt God made my faith go away and me calling God a liar to his face which was not true he really fights my battles. I had to ask God for forgiveness! Going in your room by yourself with God present to pray is your healing. Coming out the room with the anointing staying on you and not rubbing off. You become a target even more by being tested and you're doing right by God, but God will always be standing around you as your bodyguard. When you get angry you don't tell God to his face you don't need him anymore to his face, I have seen this. Women your attitude, actions, ways, and spirits say it all. Your mouth says something good, but your tongue can be that deadly switch. Take my advice it's important that I help enemies, because I have sinned against God, brothers, sisters, and sinners who have not done me wrong. I stop saying I'm not a fool to hold in my heart against something or someone to get back at them with God on my side no it's up to God to do what he does. God can say I want these enemies to come together. God could say this or that or never evil negative or bad because God hates sin. When I tell them, I leave it in God hands I leave it with love and peace. God does the rest by doing that with a cleansed heart, God will bless me more God is going to take all the hurt away only if you let him. If people be mad with God and don't know and be praying to him. Women live with being broke down for years become accustom and addicted to it. Women pray just like men just well as children. Women sit there and say when is God going to take the hurt away, why? Did I have to go through all this? Just like men say to God as us being equals. Women must choose to let the hurt go and let the healing begin not back and forth. A lot of women don't realize when they say they forgive, and they don't they be lying to God and themselves. God will walk with you, you hold his hand then let go, because something comes up then you forget about God, yourself, husband and love. You can't build a future because thoughts and many things about the past shows up. The woman be quick to say in her mind, soul, body and diary! That it's different from her and other women when God commandments don't say none of that. Healing is coming back and standing healthy again. Jeffrey didn't win back Cleopatra because she would not give me a chance or let me love her again. Put away your anger women and open yourselves up to the healing and love from God not I got God then I don't need him no more and I can't stand him no that's not GOD'S LOVE!! Women if you don't forgive you will have yourself in prison. It's like you're paying your way out of bondage yourself out of your own mess you can't forgive and being locked up God put locks around you, but not angry, bitter, malice, hatred, and get back locks. People can be selfish they only think about themselves. A forgiving woman can talk to her husband, each other feelings it a relationship correct. It will be no embarrassment or discomfort prevents them from shaking. Women have manners and respect for your husband. You don't have to be aggressive and non-communicative because no one can make you do what you don't want to do even interrupting him. This does not mean he will control you women. All I am saying is being a loving Christian calmly and directly humbling him and you. I didn't like to be corrected many times. A lot of women think this is only men, people, marriages, relationships feel like as if the other party won't give in then I won't! I like being fair with give and take, I gave more still until this day I want to satisfy this woman by God's grace I will be rewarded it take two, because the man can't do it all by himself or the woman either. A lot of people in relationships say you can't make me pray with you or I'm not ready to. You see the devil love you when your week because God says come together and pray. Well, the devil will tempt you that's only if you let him. False prophets tell the women that you can't make no one pray if they don't want to, that's true, but don't use it against marriages. People therefore marriages are failing. The false prophet will come back another Sunday and say pray with your husbands or wives. Pray with your husband to block out the confusion. A woman sees the good in her husband. She emotionally in love with God, herself and her man! She will only look at the good and the situation. Now women things in this book will refer to you or you can learn something from it if you choose to because you know you have the best mind and conscious of your own self to add on, disagree, or have your say so. I have learned something from everyone and still learning more until this day it's to do so because you can know how make better choices and how to deal with life, yourself and people! Can you learn something from this book? If you can't you have not forgiving and still you be hurting, scared, feared, and your always have a negative impact on your relationship with God, yourself, your husband, and others. It can be damage in all of it, but if you don't let God in to fix it then you can't work on or choose not to get help to go on with life. Do you know when it's women that do this to themselves, they say and feel the truth of men hurting them so much from the past they go with 10, 20, 30 years with no one by themselves locked up. Absolutely true and still blame all men held accountable from it. It will be a failure nothing happens without God's permission only when it's going by his word and a doer by him only. Jeffrey paid attention to Cleopatra I don't care what no one says. I observed and learned when the woman is asking question. She's not trying to find out what's going on, or the truth a lie or all kinds of things that her mind it's curious and a calculator. It's also trying to know more, find out, figure out already know, pray and know everything. First, women say I don't know what woman/women you been messing or that's the wrong woman, well I have this to say you play some roles out of this if it's two or three as a woman because every woman is not the, can I get a last word in ladies? NO! It was written and said that using anger as an excuse to sin gives the devil and foot hole, unforgiveness, speaks off the wicked tongue hurts. Don't listen to the devil women like Eve did. Refuse to listen to it. Listening to yourself, others and the devil not being on one accord, for better or worse, richer or poor in sickness and health until death do you apart. A lot of women listen to what peoples say or you married the wrong person that or those people was not there on that day. So, they are miserable of their lives of what they been through listening to yourself sometimes when it can lead you to do the wrong, evil thing and swear we know everything. We are caught up with us on ballcap on ourselves, and emotions instead of God. Instead of both parties saying we are not doing that anymore. They are still focusing on what they have done to one another. What they are doing thinking evil from the heart being hurt so many times that there's no room ever for forgiveness and still laying right beside one another telling each other I love you and there's no action! Again, from most women it will be said that's game and foolishness. It is always someone going through worse than you. The devil attacks us in our hearts and minds for victory, but that's why there is a God that is the way the truth and the light. If you want and chose to live of the past, negativity, stubbornness, selfishness. Just remember you must learn to humble yourselves there for under the mighty hand of God, that he might exalt you in due time. Casting all your care upon him for he cares for you. You know a lot of times marriages we can say God says this and that and it don't even be God saying nothing it be us trying to use God against the other person that hurt person to get back, confused, or get what we want. Do you know you can be so, hurt you can be doing something sometimes and you will think, know and believe off your own actions and emotions that it can be right or wrong we are human beings this happens at times in life! What we trying to do is put it all on God towards and against others with envy, jealousy, pride, hate, bitterness, karma, hurt, wicked, evil, drama, and most of it all is to get even and revenge. Do you know one sin can open doors at times for lots of witchcraft and all kinds of demonic spirits to come in. A lot of women feel like words, actions, being used, disappointed, abused, neglected, being left alone only hurts them. Now you can give your woman all the money in the world, houses, love, roses, shoes and clothes give her everything. When she is unforgiving and told you, she has lied and did not mean it from her heart all that what we have done won't matter, and it's only one thing God. The holy spirit can come in and stop things that's in her and that's God! You can give her the world it won't matter she has to choose to let God in and what and want the help, but one thing a lot of relationships don't do is work together. They will say they know but don't do, because a lot of times one person would do it and the other person won't then it would switch up and change that be spirits. It's called things that you have to stop and give up that you don't want to like the things you be having fun off. That's getting back while you are laughing but at the same time you be angry at yourself others and the person that made you that way instead of compromising. It's not your ways and wrongs as well women know their rights and wrongs but, at times man when the debate comes it's over then the game comes with, don't debate with her just say your right all the time. Go right along with the program to feel and keep her, agree with everything really being a (YES MAN) she's saying and being happy, NO! Women don't go there with what's wrong with that, because God don't say these commands of marriage man & woman make this up. There is something left out how the man feels this why it's us not the woman only her emotions reactions and ways of nature, life and love only. You must give up a lot of negativities to move forward with your relationship. One person can't say I'm going to give up everything that I don't want to that means that there holding in and then come back, and the other spouse does the same thing it just be moving backwards instead of forwards there's no coming together as one in that that's games! Jeffrey showed Cleopatra that he learned that our love was not based on sex, it was about God respect, trust, honesty, loyalty, courage, but she didn't give me a chance as women say IT WAS TO DAMN LATE NOW YOU WANT TO CHANGE! It's a lot of things Cleopatra could not see and did not want to learn woman/ women Jeffery know he could not make her, nor she could not make him you can't make no one change but, how long was I going to sit there and take that crap off a woman. I changed for the better man of God, myself and family I did had to prove that to everyone I hurt included God. So, women I don't have to put up with it or take any mess? Cleopatra told me she did not want to listen or talk but then come back and say baby I want to talk Jeffrey will you listen? Then when Jeffrey sits there and she speak and respond right then I'm a liar, I'm still with the other woman, don't walk away I'm talking to you! Women this is to you in your relationships and marriages don't judge your husband because they sin, and you see it differently than you and judge them accordingly to your law and way God them like you 1! It is said the pain that you've been feeling, can't compare to the joy that's coming.

It's a lot of good women going on for themselves men to add value to both of their lives not all the credit only to the woman. Admire each other both of you have greatness. You will hold each other when you're up or down, two people will hold and have the heart to go through it all and be there that's love. A submissive woman will carry the load for her husband if he can or can't it's for better or for worse. Especially when he's trying! She knows how and when to pray for him and speak to his spirit if she always cursing him out and not praying with him doing it then change this is putting a curse on him. Jeffrey let Cleopatra know this and he was a fool, because his past could not teach her anything. CLEOPATRA (THE WOMAN) when I say WOMAN, I mean it with (POWER), because that's what the WOMAN is! Cleopatra was so angry with Jeffrey and blaming him for everything that she was pulling him into destruction. Cleopatra stops praying with Jeffrey and start playing mind games with him I know women you did it to her so, how do I expect her to feel? So, she got me back I paid more than a penalty. What was next for me a rope around my neck to be hung or death? Women you all have different magnificent, quiet, stylist, great since of humor nice secrets! What made Jeffrey fall in love with Cleopatra was I had to earn her not buy her. She is a real woman I just could not tolerate or take her stubborn selfish ways. I want to say a lot of times shut the hell up and be quiet, but I was scared because I learned from past arguments with a woman you can't even win don't try to you will get knocked out before the round is over. Only the Bishop, Prophets, Pastors could say that to Cleopatra, and it's not even her own man that she listens to. A lot of women and people will say because you hurt her, then forgive him or her like me. They say you don't understand I need time, how much time years and years. If tomorrow is never promise who is to leave get sick, old, or anything life too short for all that crazy mess and tell the man quick he the one needs the help go to God and ask for forgiveness. Then get on your man even more and try to use the Bible, God or anything you can that is necessary with your POWER & MIND observing more and say the man is the head and everything falls on him. It's two as one not one as just the wife only because what he done. It is not 20/80 or 30/70 because therefore marriages are the way they are today. God is a fair God of no favoritism or not a changing

God. God designed Cleopatra to be what she is special. Cleopatra is a lioness a queen of the jungle, a Leo that has too much in her to be playing childish games. See good and bad in me and her, but she only going to tell the bad in me. If I'm telling her what her bad things are, she's going to let me have it. She's going to do the telling and for me I'm doing the writing of this book. She will let me have it some more. Her mother and sister would be telling me I got some nerve only, all what I did, and they are holy only saved. A lot of times in life people will never understand something until it happens to them, I know because I hurt God, myself, Cleopatra, people, family members and friends, but I repented. The excuse of Cleopatra and her family sins was because of what I only did wrong. Like Cleopatra's mother Pam she got on everyone else for their wrongs and sin but never said one thing about her or apologize, so Jeffrey knows where Cleopatra got that from! I am only held accountable of my charges that have been dropped by God. Jeffrey love Cleopatra through her flaws and didn't change her. As her man I still supposed to love her with her bad ways to. I have tried my best to heal her wounds when it was rough, good and bad days I even spoiled her. Some men or women would come with saying that's where I messed up at or shouldn't have done but you would do anything to please and get back someone you absolutely love. I found the one for me! There that bends down to listen, I will pray if long as I have breath. Wisdom in a woman terms as God is, she is submissive, humble, kind, forgiving not only on to something from the past. If she can trust in me again, I can teach her how to love me like she taught me her emotions, (EVERYONE EMOTIONS ARE NOT THE SAME) hidden within herself. She doesn't want to let me back in. I had to let her back in. It was not safe or easy it was trials and tribulations it was both of us weeping and moaning at times! We can fear only God. Cleopatra could have learned to love me all over again. Jeffrey can admit when he first met Cleopatra he thought in some ways with his penis, but as he got older, saved, repented, got into relationship and she forgave me it was not about that anymore because he did realize his penis is not what his heart could not handle and that was lose a special woman again that he will regret in the end! When Jeffrey slept in his car at night on the streets, in family members' homes on the floor crying, because Cleopatra was falsely accusing me, arguing with me, and fussing with me. She didn't know how and what I was feeling because she was looking at herself, her job, her children and saying fuck me and here relationship because fucked it all up and she did not do nothing wrong. It was only about her since I cheated and never be forgiven. Women let me tell you something if you think junk you think negative, you will always constantly be having thoughts and evil doubts that's always wrong about your husband. You will never try to connect with him if you're always this angry, mean woman! You will be disconnected. Every time you make a call you will be hung up on or if you make a call you will be hung up on because of your attitude and you right you won't care like you say. So, if you don't care how do you love God, yourself or husband with that kind of attitude and behavior? It can't go your way only because of the past of what he has done to you. It's not him it's you that can't seem to let go, but you're blaming him still over again he can't get away with nothing. How would you feel if you changed on anything and someone or your husband kept pressuring you, provoking you, falsely accusing you, insulting you, harassing you about the past, and pointing the finger only at you? Don't say I would not do this, because I'm a strong good woman I don't play mind games and Godly only a childish woman would do something like that, because I lot of you have done it. You just don't want to own up to it until you feel like it's time, or calming down, or your sorry with your charming ways I'm not saying you are bad woman/women/wives, because we can't live with you, and we can't live without you! Isn't that the truth? You will be tired, fed up, aggravated, because the first thing the woman would say is you still holding on to it, or same old shit depending on the woman/women and that's the past and you haven't let it go! Somethings for actions and uses. Now here comes the bougie and sidditty woman like Cleopatra and her mother at times two bird of a feather flocking together thinking and coming with there's nothing wrong with them at all! Ready for anything and perfect there's no cycles, no curses, no repeats or wrong with them or their family in their minds and reality they feel and think they don't do any wrong. There's no such thing of their wrongs in their vocabulary because they are highly educated and feel think and say can't know one tell them they do no wrong at all.

Cleopatra looks at me today and tell me Jeffrey I still got to tell you this and that, but I say one thing I don't know what the hell I'm talking about when it comes to her, and I been with her all of them years putting up with her. So basically, Cleopatra is saying I can't tell her shit. The mother is the bougie one she carries the cycle from sister and past it down to her daughters. Cleopatra's mother is perfect for the T.V show Mr. Charlie's wife. It's the truth someone must let them know because they tell it all without leaving nothing and adding on more. However, it's lie's and swear everything be a truth. Now Cleopatra is bougie but mostly Sid ditty because she is similar like the mother. Cleopatra never called me a fuck up or called me nothing in front of her mother that right there put certain things in her head and told her misery loves company. This really is deep now when the grandmother comes around. They treat me as a family member she does not be with the drama or past things and when they get out of line the grandmother stands up for me and put me in line as well fairly and right. She treats me like family and put them in order and says stop and then they do it and be bougie and Sid ditty and quiet. Now sitting high in the penthouse, when Cleopatra gave her mother's number to her grandmother then she called Cleopatra's mother to see how she was doing. Then the mother called Cleopatra and why did you give my number to your grandmother? See the cycles? Cleopatra said because we all need to come together as a family but there's no cycles needed to be broken in their family. What does that tell you? There is a point in time in everyone family that someone doesn't no better. The Grandmother would call me her baby, son or Jeffrey however Cleopatra being bitter I'm everything but the child of God. I am this or that to Cleopatra but the mother like calling me Jessie she's bougie and that was not my name. Now the sister is lost to her offspring none of them have a man and live in a house with a bunch of dogs and women together. I wonder why? That's another curse but we are not going talk about that with the father and mother. They will always other what no one say about them when they get slick, sarcastic and be rude with someone because they always right there saved but gossiping and telling others off most of the time. No one can tell them off. They can't tell their stories they can't tell their flaws but could tell some or others off quick. They can't accept no stepfather, but the stepmother is in play wrong or right with God, but not us. What Cleopatra is seeing her mother do and the mother, her, will say what about my curse and me I'm not nothing. I said plenty of times I do have curses, I did wrong, and they have not admitted their wrongs towards me, because the mother taught them you never tell them anything about themselves to the family in front of other peoples, but they can, how does that feel? You only tell other people that by their actions, attitude and ways. Now when the mother pulled me to the side, she told me Jeffrey if I would have put my man first on a lot of things, he would still have been here so seeing why she's by herself? Now see how Cleopatra's mother walked around with a lot a pride and could tell her daughter she was wrong on how she was treating her husband and closed in the room for her actions and wrongs missing her marriage. See it don't be all on the husband/man/men women and you know this you have your pride of silence as well! You don't miss our water to your wells runs dry women this don't only go for men doing you wrong this goes for you to when you're wrong. See Cleopatra's mother said it I put my children first on a lot of things against her man then Cleopatra said I don't want to hear that shit about my mother be saying she talk about everybody behind they back! However, she listens to her mother on certain things. Cleopatra only told me what she wanted to hear. Now what they going to say on Judgement Day? They gave it to me judging me, so they are no better than anyone else. My Stepdaughter and son they were hurting, because their father pretended to be there, but I was hidden. You know they were perfect and couldn't stand up and say I'm hurting. I'm I wrong as an addict of hurt and pain? When I called the mother to pray with me and sent her text messages of scriptures to read, she texted and called Cleopatra to tell her to tell Jessie to stop. But the mother can tell me about the word anytime she chooses. This is what the curses and cycle Cleopatra do to me. The other family members do not mess with anyone at all. They prefer to remain neutral party and they do not mess with them, because of their wrongs and sins they don't have none. Now the mother comes to confess to me, but never in front of her daughter, God, Cleopatra and the grandchildren, because she wanted to take up for them and love them being, they are family. Cleopatra's mother never treated me the same as family and love me as

God says and do. You know we have a whore, streets, game, profane language, money hungry, mind playing woman. My point I'm trying to say is every woman is different, so don't say women that read this, She Not a Woman if she's doing that. She still is a woman who hasn't grown up to give herself respect. All women are not the same, but play similar parts the same way, because a woman is woman. No matter how you cut a pie or cake, eat it or let it sit it is still a pie or cake. A woman is just like a dessert that's in different flavors, sizes and quality. You have the woman that wants to be satisfied with another woman, because they understand and relate to one another. Then the woman says I gave you sex, my love and vagina. Well let me tell you something ladies and not in a disrespectful way you must want to give it up and open it up to let it go in, it can't go in if you don't open up. It is not all about sex at times. If he's a two-minute brother on the first try why would he get fired, because he didn't satisfy you. When you are satisfied and you get it right women please you complain about your worn out, your sore, your stomach is hurting, you can't walk and some of you fall asleep bent over. I have had sex and made love with different women in life, and they be satisfied, yeah right to a certain level or extent because of their nature and hormones. Some women smoke their cigarette when it's over and be please, but then come in say you wore me out, she says her vagina and nipples are sore. I guess when she's hot and it's going on, she's not thinking about that's then when it's over she wants more depending on the woman she is. One woman told me she had it done good, but not like this before, because the other man did not satisfy her like I did. I completed the satisfaction of the sex, but she still was not satisfied because it was something change in her mind with her thinking, moods, throbbing, high style vibrations even thrusting the drive is going more faster than you think! The woman MIND NEVER STOPS THINKING and her moods swings changes much as well as her body, her ways, thoughts and shopping and millions of other things! She shops so long because she must accessorize, catch the deals or get what she likes. Observing the woman Cleopatra as a gift is a gift what Jeffrey have experience. You must get into a woman's mind, act like her, be around her, think like her, to get to find her out and know to seek to know where she is going and all about. You know some when like it in their rectum because some women I was with in the past introduce it to me and say I'm going to show you something, yes women are something else the most! This woman I had sex with she told me her rectum can cum I did not believe her when I took it out it was no crap that came out. Now who taught me this? A WOMAN named Victoria. She wasn't satisfied either because when I licked her vagina back and forth she screamed, hollered and Cumming back and forth so much pleasure and excitement, then after that she complained and said you got my vagina numb, sore and licked me wet. A woman can be satisfied in the moment, for that moment then outside the next watch now she changes fast! Then she told me you don't made me cum so much I can't no more I'm wore out, tired, and dried up. She got vagina dryness yes women I know! Just like her rectum was she was working my ass, but I was wearing her out. She was saying baby that's right cum with me it feels good open my ass baby. Yes! Once we were finish she said baby that feels good and tongue kiss me she knew how to flex and relax her muscles, then after a while she will say you got my vagina and rectum sore but it's a feel so damn good pain feeling baby! Vivian told me what I was trying to do rip her vagina open or her rectum open. Once it was finish then it was baby you got to let it calm down. Then you have the woman/women that is the manifer, knows and ready for the man/men that plays games, prepared and ready to have her guard up to. Play him before she gets played, she does the same game and thing the men do that cheat on their women! They are called womanizers see vice versa. Both human beings only difference is one is a man another other is a woman. The man is the male, and the woman is the female which is God's creation. The woman that's the manizer uses men for herself, selfishness, pleasures and then say I don't need a man but was with one for her satisfactions that did not last long. Then say you gave me your everything I don't owe you anything but took it anyway. Now we already know these kinds of women are of the world that do these kinds of things. We can't all be put in the same category with the Christian, Godly, Motherly, Warrior, teaching and master mind woman. You have women that love their jobs and their careers more than they love their husbands and when the husband brings it up he got to be jealous when he's expressing how he feels being left out of time, affection and attention being given to

him and you are together. Now when it's the woman it's a whole different ball room and game getting more points, credit getting put up on the board for her, because her time is serious, valuable, patience, important and a fact! That is another curse on Cleopatra's family Jeffrey did not love Cleopatra for her vagina I loved her. I'm attracted to her beauty, her heart and awesome feeling that she has for herself now the real good woman/women that's out there will anticipate her man needs but it would hers for herself than for him, she will accommodate him before anyone else. A man loves when woman is thinking, respecting and loving him and already knows what he likes, loves and don't have to remind her or tell her what it is. See women men are emotional more than you at times! Women don't ever go to bed angry with your man and a man does not like a nasty attitude woman. He wants to stay and keep a woman who words towards a resolution. Women getting in the last word all the time and holding your tongue in at times and accept the wrong even when you're not at times that's not easy for you to do. See you see when Jeffrey told Cleopatra not to go to bed angry, so spirits and grudges won't translate in our marriage. She will get angry more, will walk away and say I will stay to myself, and it will still be on me after forgiveness. Now Jeffrey as a man was getting over the hurt the pain and so forth even more things I can't explain after me and Cleopatra broke-up her trying to curse me trying to put it back at me, because she told me after all the time I told her she said to me on the phone and in the text that I still have in my phone today, she said Jeffrey if you don't forgive me for the wrongs and sins I did to you, you won't be able to forgive and open up your heart to and for the next woman to come in! Now women what does this sound like? A different thing to you owe you don't because you all haven't heard her side of the story or how she feels and where she's coming from? Like she said made her this way forever. Now women/men/marriages do you feel where you, me and yourselves are coming from? She did not see herself, the bigger picture, the better persons to set aside self-centered bitterness, malice, negativity, all she saw was me, because she told me, her man+ that she was supposed to been driving a car her mother got one her sister got one and she don't have one and could have been moving further with her career if it wasn't for my ass and shit, fuck ups and mistakes. What you put up in the air it will transform or transpires in your life! Women when you always must get the last words that's petty and selfishness. How is it that you're controlling with telling someone the truth they just can't receive it then want to use reverse psychology. I'm pretty sure you won't say this to your man or plenty of times. See holding back women brings back spirits to and holding in, because the woman can say a lot of words with silence, attitude, actions, body gestures, touches, hand movements, expressions and looks! It will be times Cleopatra will smile at me, it will spiritually Godly and a lot of times it will be wicked, evil and uncomfortable because I could feel she could to but just like she said she did not care how I felt. With that said the false prophet told her she was right all the time man you don't know Cleopatra like I do, like women know one don't know your man like you do. Women you always have something to teach and learn to respect your husband/man relationship in the same way. If you're on a funky stank, baggage load one day and still want love and respect as a woman because you're a lady then give it the same way back to your man if he's stank and funky sometimes as well a marriage/relationship is not perfect. Don't let your panties he stank, and you take them off and rubbed them all in his face like there smelling good, fresh and his boxer or draws are stank 24/7. We all smell at the end of the day from moving, working, walking, body movements, even talking because our body is movement and in action. Do you want to see a woman get or be pissed off? Jeffrey always showed an entrance in Cleopatra because she's something special that attracted to me and great quality. I feel passionate as a man of God and a great person. I know women that are real, know where they want to go and don't give up. They are some women in their comfort zone. I found my woman, I even prove to God, myself and her and can and did change and required a lot of effort. God gave me blessings and credit myself as well, she won't but I will for her that's a heart. I appreciated that woman who I was in love with to which I did take her for granted in a lot of ways so did she towards me. My taken her for granted was not refunded back to me from her heart you can refund things back without money or fame because GIVEN IS COSTLY! I knew I wasn't going to get it from the Government because nothing is free, but God and love so when you mess up on things like this you must clean up

after your own shit! I got it from but not from her. She got back at me
from hurting her two wrongs don't make right. I guess that's only for
women for everything else it's right? Let the world and society tell it.
We only must go by what God says. Cleopatra was making mistakes
that was turning me off and pushing me away, using my past, her past,
the children past, the past, everything to put the house, and the baggage
on me she never thought what Jeffrey am thinking how I am feeling,
where I'm coming from, here me out, what did I do, or what can I do
to help. A fuck up can't do anything if that's all you call him and see
me as I know I'm not that but from a woman that I love does she know
how that feels to be called that? Until this day Cleopatra will come in
front of me and say she did it all and me right and I was the one fucked
up. Then she would change it and say I did not mess up Jeffrey you did.
Then go back and say Jeffrey you don't listen so what is it? I can't stop
whoring, taking out my money, lying, fucking with that same woman,
give my life to God fully, continue to stay prayed up, leave her children
alone, find a job, be a real man, pay no bills, fuck like I use to, respect
her or anyone including myself, know how to talk right, stop talking,
not saying nothing, drive right, could not be responsible, could not take
care of her children right, not listen, not understand, I could not do
anything right. Therefore, I withdraw from her period. She will say it
was only women and being a ho! No one wants to be around a person
that insults them as all negativity and no good in them Cleopatra didn't
know the critical mistakes that was literally killing her man entrance
see there is hidden reasons a man will commit to one woman but not
another is listening, hearing and understanding. I was begging her to
let's get it right and be with her more and more. When she was a sweet
woman, WOMEN I KNOW I made her the bitter woman so after that
it must continue and on? Women I see you out there especially the
strong-minded women, you are the warriors, the motherly love that
you give is like and is the love Mary the mother of Jesus gave to him.
You know you can say what you want to say you can't read no one's
heart you can feel. Cleopatra (THE WOMAN) don't know of the
curses that feel upon them self-righteousness, see women will know,
but they won't tell on themselves about their curse, because their either
angry with themselves or their man, or just don't want to talk about

some things. Is there something wrong with me? Yes, in ways I'm not perfect but I need a woman to pray for me and encourage me not keep her foot on my neck smothering me. A person that's willing to admit there wrong and take full responsibility with giving love showing actions is a blessing. The congregation in Corinthians these ways some of the first Christians in the first century that was first sinners praising idols, worshipping witchcraft, demonism and steeped and they were not happy campers. These peoples gave their life to God and became prophets, teachers, pastors, bishops! See no one is perfect. This goes for everyone know the no that the unrighteous shall inherit the kingdom of God. Do not be deceived by fornicators, idolaters, adulterers, effeminate, abusers of themselves with mankind, thieves, revilers, extortioners, shall inherit into the kingdom of God. And some of you are washed, sanctified, justified in the name of the Lord Jesus and by the spirit of our God. It's not all about sex all about women it's a time when your backs up against the wall with each other and you are both sleep it's a warm love. As a woman period you are all entitled to change your mind an anytime I can vouch for that girlfriend sometimes when women ask a man something it be, because it's a reason it's not always right mostly in her eyes SHE'S VERY CURIOUS! Different reasons like being noisy, not trusting her man, something to know and find out, just her mind comes somewhere else. I must be myself I can't be the other person because that job is already taken. Anything that's worth having is worth working for. I want to tell you something (MOSES) version of the ten commandments, when the women were playing the father's well and they were laughing, talking, playing and having fun the oldest woman walked and investigated the trees and looked down and the other women said what are you looking at and she changed even her voice she said it loud. (A MAN)! She was the oldest and the elder of all the women and they all walked up and said what a strong man. It was Moses he protected the women of the evil men that came to interrupt and bring trouble that was called Lydia. Another thing a lot of Mother's needs to learn and parents instead of buying your children all the things they never had teach your children God, prayer and all the things that you weren't taught growing up. We all have been taught somewhere in cycles, I'm telling it even on myself so when you tell me

who am I to tell something just as you are to tell and learn as well even myself. We all are human. I will be myself because I love me. I'm just being me I learned to stop forcing and trying to make someone love me, because they want me to become and be like what they want me to be. Never really love me because through the struggles they will still be with me and have my back and I'm not with the ones that did me wrong and I still help that's the heart. By not being myself as doing wrong, sinning, backstabbing, getting my way and doing wrong to others that's evil. Being myself as being happy a lot of marriages give up on one another what the other person has done to one another. Instead of moving forward to be with the Lord what you really invested in all this time the direction, the vision of the big picture and passion for one another. Instead of looking at all the good and positive teachings you look at the negative. Now to mother's, grandmother's aunts, nieces, great grands all women don't stop teaching your family, children and loved ones, but don't look down out your nose looking down on someone they can't teach, say or do anything at all. You can do your thing because it's your family, get angry and they try to get away with it, because God sees everything, just like he's watching me, he's watching you and everything, everyone, everywhere. I even heard my mother tell people don't tell her shit or anything about her children when someone came and told her something she will be stubborn and say what did they damn family teach them or you, and won't admit her wrong, but was quick to tell someone about their wrongs and like she said their shit! She still did good and love with a good heart and took care and in other people children my dad to. You see marriage is God/Husband/Wife and the children not the children first then God and the marriage that's not in order. False prophets said the children comes first in the marriage. See when the men have done the women wrong or the women have done the men wrong they go running to their children and false prophets speak and tell them things, hear things and accept what is being said as the truth is the gospel and be gossip at times! No! They supposed to run to God. Now at the jobs I worked on I ran into all kinds of peoples but the right person (GOD)! I had to go through high hell gasoline draws high waters and back. In the marriage you give your best to one another, they listen, they think about each other all the time they are in love. The kindness and romance are there. When cheating is involved and financially the bills get worse, children, jobs, struggles, hard times when they stop putting it in God hands in the marriage and want to do it all themselves. Then the woman tends to turn towards herself, mother, children, friends, work, gossipers giving them all the attention and time. Then she deals with her job and the man gets push to another woman because he's not being treasured, (THE TREASURE IS NOT ONLY ON YOUR SIDE WOMEN) it's both. Sometimes the woman goes to another man. When the children leave the husband and wife looking crazy because unforgiveness and damaged is done they have spent all those years and the only thing they look at is negativity and it will never ever be the same as it used to. The spouse is not even the last thing they look at it only be about themselves. Cleopatra invested more time into her job, mother, children, family than me. Then quick to say you want me to stop and forget about my children. See that right there, I did not say that the devil used her to say that a woman at times can be so hurt and bitter where she will be tricking herself repeatedly and it comes from different people's family members co-workers and even spirits in church talking to her instead of listening to God. Just like the man was not listening to God now she's not but it was not them both to her it was only him in (HER EYES)! Cleopatra uses a lot of things as an excuse to forget about me completely of making it work if your hard on me how is there a humble spiritual chance with the love from God? I hold things against you: you have forsaken the love you had at first. Consider how far you have fallen! Repent and do the things you did at first. I want to tell this to women when you fall in love with your man, then loose that love it's never the love it has gone away because you say and choose for it to be. If you say God is in control and in place of all things you're not feeling, pushing, working it in with our God with your husband you're a false witness! If you have transferred your love somewhere else like your family, job, etc., money, unforgiveness, bitterness, malice, hurt, pain, elsewhere, places, your mother, Christ only for your sarcasm, your career, other people and material things. Like Cleopatra her washer and dryer it was before me and that's a hurtful thing and not to throw in her face I brought it I just feel so not loved and unappreciative that's more

important than me. Some women will take the dog and love the dog more than the man. Now I got my stepdaughter Anita a dog and the dog left with Cleopatra, my stepdaughter, my stepson and she called me saying Jeffrey the dog passed away our relationship did to, but she loved the dog more than she did me. Like her mother Pam when she divorced her husband, she said the dog going with her and that dog passed away, so it's just curses together that are no cycles and wrongs, sins of no wrongdoing to their men/husbands! God is first the marriage is second and then children.

Chapter 8

A woman loves to share her thoughts with her husband in their marriage. Communication Is the key with God sensitivity, care and emotional support not blaming the man for everything. Then you have women in relationships that argue about money, sex, not valued by the other, not caring, some women will say to their men that they don't care about their children anymore and it be dead wrong disrespectful, cruel and coldhearted so bitter that you can't get a conversation out of them. Then say you don't give a damn about her no more. When he's doing his best as the man being there. Then the woman will say there's no help anymore I'm the bread winner, so it's all on her what she will feel, say, think and be more sensitive in a behavior that's unnecessary. Can it be fair? It's called putting yourself in that other person shoes. Ask yourself women, what must it be like to be married to your ways and self? Examine your attitudes and behavior, because it's all not all and only on men only to women that think, say, feel in this way. If it's not you then it will help more to learn more. I can learn from you, and you can learn from me, that's if we choose to. We all can learn something every day because a woman comes a different background as well as the men. Sometimes the woman will use that against the man, because the woman uses harsh words against the man 100%. You suppose to sacrifice for one another not only for the woman only than yourself it takes two not only all about the woman. See with Cleopatra (THE WOMAN) she felt like and showed actions that she will exit me out on all things, because I hurt her, and she put a wall up forever. A woman wants to hear security and see it in a man's words as well in actions very emotional because women are strongly emotional creatures. The man wants love, friendship and respect. Sacrifices go both ways. See false prophets and teachers have taught women and women friends also women who don't have a man or miserable will say teach and put in the air and the woman will take and receive it in with a dangerous mistake and choice. Listening to other women or people, women while you're married that can explode your marriage! Like women saying girl he's no good listen to me, instead of going to God for help for therapy, help, counseling, forgiving, that's all spiritual, mental, emotional, physical, help you need! Then when your husband listens to you now in these day's he's accountable on trial with you being the jury and judge and he has not done nothing wrong and then the wife would say, who the hell you been listening to? And her word stands it supposed to go like this. You both may or may not communicate at the time and need to let it go but some go on and on. We need to come back to God as when we first met, I'm talking to myself and all marriages. When me and Cleopatra first got into a relationship, we vowed to take care of one another needs. A woman does not want to judge on the way she feels same way for a man, but it could take one to be selfish and then the ball drops when it's worse than it's even darker! Where does God say that it is more love and giving for a wife/woman than for a husband/man I never seen it. Women to your bitterness past pain for instance, refusing to forgive someone can manifest itself in how we treat a husband today and say he would never treat me like this again. She will move from God and think she still have a relationship with him and is bitter. Now when the husband stands up to the wife who says she don't forgive him. He stands up doing lovingly respectively like myself I made up: my mind to be heard and refuse to accommodate the dominance. I even step back humble myself and put my hands up to feel Cleopatra (THE WOMAN) pain only reason why it didn't work, because every time I kept trying. She kept putting me down. She even said out her mouth she can't see good, because all she sees is negative, I'm done. If she spoke it the changed didn't mean no good relationships are not a legal system or government system. See it has that today. Once Jeffrey and Cleopatra (THE WOMAN) would have turned to God's word together everything would have been ok, but when the false prophets told Cleopatra (THE WOMAN) things like you can't make her pray if she doesn't want to, don't worry about her focus on you. She listens to that she even starts saying it and using it against me we will still have been together if we both had prayed and worship together. She was overwhelmed, gave her attention more to the wrong things, forgot and didn't see the things I was great at and that was important I did. You should never put your husband or wife down. Women who give up on their marriages for their children even though they maybe loving and serving their children often find that they have nothing left for each other. Once their children no longer need them. This is another reason why in divorces have increased more. Woman a lot feel like their children are more important than their marriages. See what a lot of women don't understand that do this when you don't put your marriage first you will be living with your mother that doesn't have a husband or marriage. You will not realize and be blind. I don't have my mother same ways we are like one another, other aunts, sisters, and only we tell the husband about his cycle and ignores hers. See the devil starts to turn the woman heart back toward her relationship and marriage. You remember the good things, negative things, bad things and forget all about the reason why it ended. The devil woman/women of bringing up the past of the other woman and it hurts the husband and wife. Jeffrey told Cleopatra that she was letting the devil poison her heart more with her mind, soul, to dwell what I did to her in the past. Anger and unforgiveness stood in Cleopatra mind and heart and it's still scared. I'm not saying these things to say everything was Cleopatra's fault and only on her I'm saying this to say she said and put the relationship, break up, sins, faults, all on me. Unforgiveness is like an umbilical cord that connects you to your past and feeds your spirit with bitterness set yourself free. I learned more and was taught more as well a woman wants to be satisfied is affirmation. She wants to be appreciated before making love and after I told Cleopatra she is beautiful before when and after we made love. A lot of times I got fussed out, but she still smiled and said it was a feel so good pain. Sometimes about a woman myself, you, we, I can't even understand them. I was a great lover and still is for Cleopatra with great intensions and my confidence! Now I was always focus on her because I paid more attention to her, treated her and made her my number one priority! I was by her physically, body, mind and spirit I was not perfect. This man right here understood and did it. Jeffrey gave Cleopatra soft touches inside and outside the bedroom and positive encouragement she can say out her mouth that I never did her good or did nothing right does not mean that's that true. I'm not a dog I'm a human being I'm somebody and someone. I could not pray with her because she did not want on choice from things in the past that she thought that still was happening. On a

spiritual level with God, it wasn't about getting in the bed it was about God, me and her. I even brought up topics she would not know that I would talk about and talk to pastors about in counseling. I was being the better communicator, but I was still shit in her eyes and I couldn't understand that! I even showered her with all the love in the world. I showed her I was thinking about her even when she was angry because you know how a woman is her mood swings change up because she will say (I CAN'T STAND YOU)! Then change and say Jeffrey baby I be missing you. Like when we got a divorce and went to get a hotel room to make love, she would grab me and say, I do be missing you I just be so angry. Now can Jeffrey say to Cleopatra and some, most or all women out there, do know what she wants? No because I know that she was no sex or screw thing, but a real woman doesn't do that no because she still right in her eyes no matter what. Now I would like to share this with women it was this man name Mr. Vernon Coleman, and he had a daughter, and he was married to his wife Marjorie Coleman. They had a child it was a girl, and her name were Cynthia Coleman. So, when they brought the child home and then the mother passed away, she died with cancer and the father was left with the daughter. So, the daughter mother family felt like the father could not raise the daughter, it was the two sisters of the wife that pass away named Renee and Claudia. So, they took the daughter away from the father because they said and felt in, they own words that in those days and times that a man should not raise a daughter by himself without a woman. So, the father stayed by himself, and the daughter went with the aunties. Now women tell me is that a woman, system, right or wrong thing? What's going on in this world? Because this could not happen to no woman everyone would have been on her side. This man worked hard and now today this man is 78 years old. Are you women going to ask question or say something negative like what he did for it to be that way? What happen? Or was he truly there for her or had some problems. I believe some would say that's just one good man out of a whole bunch that don't shit for their children, he probably was a sex offender or a pervert, but every woman is not like that just like your men are women! Now you see you have women that will ask plenty of questions and say plenty of things. Now if the woman would have been going through this right or wrong don't take her damn child because a mother love is different and unconditionally, but now today they are getting on woman/women/mother's but look what it had to take, even taking advantage of child support. Now Mr. Vernon he was hurt and knew a lot of men who went through the same thing he went through, and a woman know her face is beautiful. I to know her face is beautiful just remember your man/husband face is handsome you don't only have a picture frame for you, your together that's what make the picture comes out! Now a bitch goes from worse to worse, but a good woman will always be a good woman. I must keep wrapping the good woman up and opening the presents, because I will never be a fool to throw away a gift THE WOMAN! I learned how and always will continue to learn more about how to touch a woman in plenty of ways that do not have nothing to do with sex, only love, comfort, understanding and protection. Now women it's not only and all about you it's about life itself. Women have your man or husband dinner ready, prepare the children for rest, so you have some alone time with your man/husband. Women you should not be bitter when you forgive our man/husband and truly mean what you say, be honest with yourself to know that you want to forgive and don't keep bring it up. Prepare yourself to reach your goals of making the evening for you and him by listen and minimize the noise. You have given him the attention he needs and watch the relationship grow. Women, please think before you greet your man/husband at the door with negativity of problems and complaints. Now a woman does not deserve to be treated wrong in the relationship neither does a man. Cleopatra not forgiving Jeffrey and angry with a mix of love and hate. She had no trust or respect for me, which it felt like a heartbreaking war. You can show your woman how to laugh all over and again, have a great sense of humor, even seducing her more keeping the positive and cheerful. You can be straight and 100% honest. Being open and truthful about every aspect of your life and hers winning her heart more. She is ready, prepared and wants more honesty. Don't ever hold anything back from a woman and don't underestimate her. The woman observes what you do and listen to what I say. A woman hates a liar, especially right in her face. Also, she hates a hypocrite in all forms being an outrageous flirt with your woman. A woman loves when her man entices her. When

you are available to give a good thrill and all the love in the world to your woman/wife. She can get enough of the thrill and love because she never satisfied and wants more if it's not this or that it's something. Her excuse is she just being a woman, and they will say to the man what about you all. At times we have a woman that is unhappy more than the man this is not all the time depending on what mood she's in, because she can change anytime. When a woman forgives, she will never forget the betrayal, because she is holding in the hurt inside. She does not feel God, she just says it and have mix emotions, it's not my words it is the truth. It's bittersweet she has set the rules Cleopatra (THE WOMAN) she hates Jeffrey. It's still in the back of her mind like a dark room with blood, heat, aggravation, malice, and negativity. Now Jeffrey heard Cleopatra (THE WOMAN) say I forgave you, yes when we got married, but change her mind. She was angry I shouldn't have never taken you back and went on with my life. If Cleopatra have told me that in my face being, we were in a relationship to me I should have moved on with life. A lot of women at least she told you and was honest about her feelings, which hurt and pain inside of her. If it was the other way around you got to do it God's way the right way to work it out, to move on, let go and let God. The women say it's not easy but, tell you when it's the other way for them sinning, they family, mother, children, its different. I understand they was taught back up women and family if there right or wrong, but don't do that against one another and still be doing it towards another and looking down on other people like that have it all together. When it comes to them by them being different and having special hearts from what I'm seeing! Women are the necks the men neck the woman is the help mate. A woman is strong and small they all come from very strong women of generations that are opinionated. They are not pitiful. They don't carry cry women are very indecisive right of changing the mind every second. They are and encyclopedia compassion is all in them and all around them. Wisdom is the principle thing, and do you see this man that give you this knowledge that right this book to you. A real woman always makes a decision that matters to her. Now when the man gives her a reason to feel otherwise, if he's wrongs at something that he has done to her but that does not mean for everything, the actions that he does wrong is on him. A woman is an over thinking and carry on so painful baggage from her past telling her husband/man what he needs to stop doing and let go and she's not doing anything to make it no better. There are women that are dealing with so much in their lives and no one would even know it, because she will smile and deal with it. If she's married or in a relationship the man will see, and she will swear up and down you can't tell her how she thinks or what she's thinking about or going to say or do! It's not all about showing the woman it's all about showing one another. I heard a lot of people take off for women when there right or wrong, and say when women are angry all the time it's something the man did wrong or what did you to her? Was she this way when you first met? Ok then. Or did you cheat on her? Or it's something you did? You did! You did! The man did, the man is no good and then and later down the road. Then you have the false prophets come in and pray or not and start off with negative things like, where us are men today? Women are here more than the men. We are all supposed to be praying, fellowshipping and worshiping the lord, we both can do dumb things in a marriage. Sometimes men and women as sinners make false assumptions, miscommunicate, manipulate and say nasty mean things to one another it's not served by your woman or wife it's served by one another. Instead of following God's word together we follow false Godly leaders and family leaders. We will sometimes put our hope in listening and following other people instead of God and each other. Women you can push your husband/man away by putting your job, texting or being on your phone, being on your laptop, shopping, arguing, reading all the time, saying things like I don't care anymore or what he says, watching T.V, quiet all the time, nobody language with ignoring him sarcastically, making a list up on him forever. So, you women that can't forgive of bitterness that wears out, because divorce with the devil hate with the fake love he stirs up and you help it, because eventually the list of wrongs, negativity quickly to a list resentment then to bitterness of evil to unhappiness in a corrupt life and forgives immediately. Cleopatra kept saying it's over I don't want to hear it or you, I'm done I shouldn't have never gotten back with you. I didn't forgive and I should have moved on. She was even saying it was a broken relationship already leaving church not wanting to fight just talking and not showing she did not want to fight for our relationship when I prove to the Lord and my relationship, when I proved to the Lord showed I myself and the children I changed. As Jeffrey got older, he got wiser he learned and saw in Cleopatra the inner beauty she believed in herself she stops believing in him. I did a better job than the fathers that left their children, messed up and sin not judging them I step up to try to be the man not a perfect one! Just like when women stand up as good mother's right or wrong, I'm damn sure going to stand up for myself and other men and give them the credit they deserve that they fully don't get! The women deserve it to I don't know one left out if God don't do us this way and tell us not to do it to one another then I got to stay on my job. Women and men deserve credit not only just women. Cleopatra is capable of anything even when she puts her mind to it, she is a beautiful teacher, she's a leader and she's bright. This woman is a LOVE YOU ALL by herself. She is confident all by herself all by herself especially by her experiences moving on and staying strong sinning or not I can encourage her. Cleopatra will always be the woman I know to stand up strong and be determined to rise even more. Then you have women who say things out of their mouth and say, they didn't do anything wrong, and people will back it up and say they know they wrong they just being a woman or women! I selected plenty of women to give surveys on my book and ask different kinds of questions about my book and themselves then watched what came out of their mouths they will be on their own actions and judgement, concerning their ways inner thoughts that a man never knew I also been named misconception man forget about them. Women you do have seductive traits you all have. You love to seduce men their eyes also give off a under handed agenda. Cleopatra (THE WOMAN) told me she may be ashamed because I made her that way, so if God says to forgive, she said she did. When a woman who make her husband, a shame is like showing rottenness in his bones and false prophets and poetry men agree with this the woman with the woman so, they are calling God a liar to his face to stand up for something that's not God's word. Give not the strength unto woman. It's not all the men it's not all the women. People are afraid to be married today. It's not like it was in the 60's/70's/80's somewhat 90's both are afraid now this book is not all the men fault or women and will not end on everything to women and put down the men to encourage women more. Everyone has been hurt sinned against, done sinned so no man or woman is higher than no one, but only the true almighty God! I see this couple that was married 45 years we going to look good together and regal together bad days, good days, clean days, dirty days. First thing someone would say to hype women up is what he is saying with an attitude and don't know what that couple is saying. When things be done in God's way it's the 50/50 which is a 100% good winning chance, not your mother way that's why, you're by yourselves like she is you have women in this situation. Listening to their mother's saying they are there for them, but still arguing with each other going back and forth. What kind of life is life is that to live? Not your father's way either but see the apple does not fall from the tree and you're following the same cycle. A lot of women feel like struggles, intimacy and no one communicating with them understanding only their pain everyone goes through this! Then you have women that share their business with other women like their mother, friends, brothers or anyone like they were sworn enemies they still come back and talk to each other in times of hurt, crisis, pain, unforgiveness and only when it's mostly bad when it supposed to be and only should be with God. False prophets try to teach women things how is he going to tell you something about God when he's not right his self? The same way he tells the woman, she always has a good spirit and listens to the wife. Now when she is a believer or not, when the woman talks, she can be in the open and talk, devious, jealous, in any way. Women I'm here to tell men can write their problems and pain on paper just as much as you. See what a lot of women can't see is that men that have been through rape, pain, mental abuse, lied to, abandoned, used since a child feels a lone in this world as well. He can't love any of the women he so desperately wants to connect with, because he can't trust them. The men are afraid they will abandon him. Overwhelmed by his fears, he retreats emotionally and physically from the world. Now women go through this, and the world is given to them but, ignored to the men but not by God. It's just as complex with men and women. If it's ok and alright for women to be afraid of their heart or life or talk about their failures and seek help for one another, why men can't do this as an equal open heart as well and help? God open you hears so you can hear man and woman should be together keep forgiving one another however he will have enough if he keeps forgiving her is she keeps bringing up the past on him, like in the same way if he keeps cheating on her. See what today what couples' is don't realize is you both feel in love not one person! However, the man has had enough. I would like to say something to women who can't forgive, God says forgive everyone even yourself it would be husband desperately changing, he works harder even be sweeter even the wife can't let go of the past to forgive. Then the wife does not realize she's suffering because she did not forgive. It's hard to do at times, it's a personal thing sometimes but women you must not excuses and put off doing it again any longer. Forgiving is the most important thing because if you told your husband sitting after making love or whatever you both was doing that you wish you would never have gotten back with him after you forgave him that's wicked and evil. Cleopatra said to me in her own words as if it was a Godly thing, but it was her thing and way that God put together. Putting away the pain and suffering us, yourself and everyone. I'm sorry to women that and men I'm not ready and you can't make me be so there is no God, love, communication, doing, trying or understanding that's fight debate and argument! It is an excuse you use when you choose not to do and understand the real love of forgiveness. You need to look at the real reason why you don't want to forgive, and most women don't want to because they afraid the man will do the same thing over again and is feared by him and herself and feelings to be hurt again! Cleopatra (THE WOMAN) stayed angry towards Jeffrey for protecting herself, children, family and allowing her time. When it runs out not God and tell me to forgive her, children, mother, sister and family, but won't forgive me then tell me in my face she can't (FORGIVE ME LIKE SHE FORGIVE THEM), because they did not hurt her like I did! She wanted to see more shame and guilt on me before I can be forgiven. I asked her haven't I been punished enough? She will say angry, HELL NO! Then come back and kiss me and say I love you Jeffrey I'm sorry baby. She will say no on a different change of times in her ways and moods swings then curse me out and change again and say baby let's make love I want some penis. Then say I don't care what you say or remember, is that not confusing or contradiction? Then will have the nerve to say I'm just covering or hiding what I have done wrong, and I can't stand up and be a man about what I did wrong! Putting out the same guilt, shame, sins, as the husband getting back constantly isn't necessary only for women as it is taught. Very much so and on this pain is taught to use by certain women at times to get what that want. Cleopatra was stuck in the need to always be right and see me as shit forever as if I'm the only one in the relationship. She must continue to see me in this way to feel good about herself as she's doing a great job by get back. It is ok to cry and be upset, but don't be angry at the whole world, yourself and others. You can be angry of course we are human beings, but not constantly on and on that's not getting us nowhere, but into a death trap or fall into a whole you can't get out of! Jeffrey told Cleopatra forgiving does not require that the other person be punish or repent first when you're continually making them suffer and pay for something yourself have not gotten over, because yourself is miserable continually saying over again he made me this way I'm like this, because of him and you talking about you want it to work out and want help you're not helping your complaining and venting explosively! If you wait for that you will only be hurting yourself, husband, others and family. I got cursed out but when the bishop held Cleopatra's hand in church saying forgive your man, listen to him and didn't know I was watching both in God's house doing good by walking out she was shaking her head saying no, no, no! Humble not arguing with him looking dead serious. Women that do this to forgive you are not perfect either get off your high horse. Your wife and husband did wrong but you're not perfect. You may have not made my mistakes or my sins, but you have sinned and did wrongs. This is for us all. Jeffrey was bad towards God, Cleopatra and our families but I'm not less of a person than them. We both have the same values no matter how many mistakes we have made. A lot of women say men don't know how to love. Women listen without interrupting and speak without accusing. Answer without arguing. Share without pretending. Enjoy without complaining. Trust without wavering. Women forgive punishing. Promise without forgetting. The woman always loves to keep her passion for God always focus. She has confidence all the time. She stops believing. A virtuous woman that's a woman of

God would listen without interrupting. She will speak without accusing, will give without spearing, answer without arguing, share without pretending, enjoy without complaining, trust without waving, forgive without punishing and promise without forgetting and always be a helpmate. Submissive where do one find this virtuous woman like God says. A bitter woman keeps every opportunity to keep old wounds open in her mind knowing that anger, hurt, bitterness an unforgiveness will continue to roll the damage forward it will never be a time to heal if she chooses not to pray let go and let God. Then tell her husband she owns him in so many different ways and curse him out forever not just by mouth you can do that woman, you also can by thoughts, remembrance, imaginations, gestures, and thinking quietly what's going to happen to him next? Let me see, or guess! Cleopatra showed me a lot of things she just thought while she was so angry and still is that I don't know any better you can and will be in this way when you can't get over past things! A woman is soft emotional love from God the rib from man and she do not suppose to let the world or pain make her hate if she's a woman of God! A lot of women said they was sweet until the no-good men made them bitter and push them away. I can understand that not for years and years with you saying you want to try and help make it work after you forgive then that's a different thing because God is in! Wives you do know that you can push your husbands away. I could not promise everything and be perfect I'm not God. One thing I did is that I tried, I was worth it, something, someone, somebody a human that's God's child to. Jeffrey loves every inch of Cleopatra and still do. If she couldn't say anything nice about me why she didn't just pray for me then come back and treat me right as she prayed? You want me to tell you what a false prophet taught her that by praying for herself, family, children they fall short their God's children I sinned, and I was the devil. I gave her my time, attention and my love from the heart. It was good when the money was there when the money left it was miserable, see how marriages be it's the times when it gets hard is you going to stick stay and fight the battle together not only the man! The right woman wants your time, love, smile, honesty, effort, security and you choosing to put you both as a priority. Jeffrey wants to say this to the bitter woman and Cleopatra even when you say and talk bad about me in my face and disrespected me there was a lot of times I was good to you, but you will never tell me that and this is for men that go through this to. I'm not afraid to start over again no matter what sin I have done, because God knows it's a new challenge to rebuild and what I need. See what I said rebuild women so when you forgive or change your ways of doing wrong just know what rebuild means! Because when you both are the contractors on the property, laying out the plans, the man picks up the shovel and you knock it out his hand you're not helping or trying to give him a chance to start over so the building will never get up some of you women help then when you think something is going wrong or is happening that's not you, just let your mind take over so. now something you let shocked your brain. You can't focus swearing you know what you are talking about then the building is halfway up, it catches on fire and fall! I want to tell men that a woman's face is not about beauty it's her mind, heart, and soul. Relationships you do learn something as it's grows. Do you know that every single person you have sex with leaves their spirit on you? Some men and women have awfully bad demons that why it is not good to lay up and sleep with everyone you meet. Then you wonder why you carry these bipolar tendencies or ever since you been dating this person and you lost more than gain. He or she has put a demon in you that its whole focus is to make you blind by the sex and not by all things. This is for the men and women that do this, but when you with God together great miracles happen to people. Who knew that God loves them? You put your relationship in God hands not yours, because if you put it in your hands it going to go back and forth and crash, because you're going to point the finger you're going to thin you're the God and in control. If you tell your man I'm getting you back for what you did to me after you forgive him then years go by, and you continue to do it so is you not doing to him what he did to you. No sin is greater than the other, same thing go for the man vice versa. The reason why Jeffrey wants Cleopatra (THE WOMAN) back is, because God never tells me <u>NO</u> GOD WILL SAY <u>YES</u> BE PATIENT IN THIS TIME NOT MINES, JUST BE PATIENT. False prophets will appear more and will receive a lot of people. It isn't over until God says it is. I'm not the most important guy in the world, but really God believes in me, but do

Cleopatra (THE WOMAN) say, feel, think that I'm not anything or nothing? Couples a lot are not raised up on both sides to know when struggles come to go through thick or thin love is commitment, the feelings are good or bad, right or wrong it will never be perfect. Satisfying the woman is holding her in your arms, but she's not satisfied still, because when her mood swings change for every reason in any relationship it goes for everyone who have been taught wrong to the man what did you do wrong for her to feel and be this way. Prayer and God makes marriage last not a paper, money and what someone says. Now people get upset especially women and say when angry or not to their man you're not God, but leave the husband left out sure we love the Jesus wants us to. Therefore, Jeffrey let Cleopatra (THE WOMAN) know in front of her. I'm trying to communicate, I'm loving our relationship, I'm respecting you now, I'm loving you, I know what love I'm showing it, doing it, giving trust, patching up what I did wrong and wounds, I cut and heal with Jesus changing my heart to do so now. Showing reasons, I was continuing and trying too hard, because Cleopatra told Jeffrey I should have not got back with you while I was saved and coming from church arguing with Jeffrey mean, bitter and angry, so what she was telling Jeffrey I wish I wouldn't have never started with you or forgave you or fell in love with you. We both had the best of each other and took the rest out of each other. We couldn't show love to one another, because falsely accusing back and forth. I needed a hug I needed to be cared for. I couldn't get it because I fucked up. I shouldn't have and that's on me forever as women has been taught. If Cleopatra (THE WOMAN) told me in my face I'm choosing my children over, you. What will God say on Judgement Day for her like he will for all men he will forgive, because she, her children, family never came to me and ask forgiveness for the sins they did to me, but I went to all of them and ask them to forgive me. She cursed me out, but to forgive her as a woman, mother, her `children, her family we don't suppose to give a reason we want to, because it's the right thing to do so, we can be forgiven not to forgive and use people against one another to make a choice out of it. These sins are ways of lying to God and spirits distracting us from our families a lot of women be blind and don't see that. They see themselves what they been through, children their problems, they come first and that's it. Then say God told them this, God did not say this, because when men do it in this way Cleopatra (THE WOMAN) be there as the help mate to tell them let God and let go, rubbing and holding them. Women go through this after years and years because they allow this. She feared that I will do it again without giving me another chance, because she will bring it up and I didn't even do it or nothing I would ask her to prove it, what did I do? First thing she would say is you starting the same shit and turn it on me using me from what I did to her. Then when mornings we wake up, I will say let's pray and when we go to bed at night. She will say you can't make me pray when I wanted to pray. She felt like she was neglecting God, why wasn't she? She did not pray with her man at all so, that's not praying with, God and him, now if a man wouldn't do this with his wife you must pray with your wife and love your wife as Christ love the church and pastors, women, men, getting on him in the church, but the woman is free she can do what she wants to and get back at you, which it is wrong and vice versa in the marriage today. Now an attitude shows how you really is a woman, do you look at your attitude? If you have a bad attitude it stops all kinds of good things in your life with the relationship with God and blessings. See Cleopatra attitude was her way out not God's way. Me a lot of times to when I was hardheaded. We both were ungrateful at times and we both had attitudes. I deserve her bad attitudes because she's a loving woman, her children and whether her children were right or wrong the wrong that was evil still look and was good in her eyes over our relationship, because what I did wrong and I was never right one time. So, she uses that against me and said so what. Different poets that's men say things like this is right no matter how long it takes when a woman take you back all the things you put and took her through receive it back no matter how long it is. Now where God says that at and they don't had God know where in it! We all come from bad back grounds from somewhere in our family. The cycle is not only with the man it's with the woman to! A woman with a good attitude precedes and predicts success, favor, and promotion with love even more. A bad woman/women attitude precedes and predicts failure, disfavor, evil, rolling her eyes not caring, sucking her teeth, angry and demotions! This does not mean that my attitude was good all the time either, NO! It was bad a lot of times and who taught Cleopatra (THE WOMAN) for her records Jeffrey didn't teach her a damn thing! Pride is an attitude to. God loves us too much to push against we are headed towards the wrong direction. God always have a message for the church and us we fall out of love with our God, marriage, one another, and our selves. We forsake the love we had at first. Suppose to consider how far we have fallen, repent and do the things we did at first. Today false teachers use us, we, divorce, divorce, divorce. This must stop God says it's never over with him, I said it was over at times, you said it was over at times. We all have given up in life and fallen but gotten right back up. Did God say negative things that it was over? NO! WE DO! Marriage is not easy it's a job and responsibility, but success is always possible when you work hard and hold one another hands and do God plans! God created marriage and for it not to fell it takes two. Ladies when your husband/man help him, don't push him down and step on him. When do the same as sinning or not hurting him, you want him to back you up and it's his job as well as yours. Now a good woman is loyal to her husband she will never bring him down. Now I made Cleopatra (THE WOMAN) angry, disrespected her, treated her bad, she did not forgive me she just said it. Now hate is in her heart it's consuming her, because she is saying she will curse me out, she doesn't care about me and continue to say and do it. A praying man is a powerful man I prayed, and I got ignored. Women you don't suppose to hate your husband no matter how much they do you wrong vice versa. Then when life gets hard you want to give up on your marriages when you don't suppose to do that if you don't have much you still supposed to give. Forgive all never stop praying for yourself and everyone else. Women pray with, for and over your husband. Pray what the lord guides you to pray it's you and God connected its God time and the relationship you have with him. A wise woman/woman know the love important of speaking life into her husband/man. If Cleopatra loved Jeffrey, believed in him, encourage him, and would have been my peace we will still be together. She kept putting me down because I had no money, no doing, no more businesses, I wasn't nothing to her there was a lot of other things to. I never stop fighting for her love it made me do some crazy things still do until this day. I never stop being friends with her after we divorced but she can't stand the hell out of me, I kept my word regardless of what I didn't keep no secrets only ours together. Cleopatra knows there where things her mother did not raise her right on or teach her and that was how to forgive, the man or the woman don't suppose to control. When the man has done wrong and starts controlling, he's wrong, but then when he's forgiven it comes back on him more than seventy times seven than God because all the woman see's is bitterness, hate, and revenge! The woman or wife can use against him and towards that you controlled her so bad so you can never get or earn another just again and if you do it won't be the way it used to, so it won't still be right in her eyes, (THAT WON'T BE IN GOD EYES RIGHT WOMEN)? Just like the system due to black men innocent or guilty. Jeffrey got his life right with God for Cleopatra to accept me back as well as her because if she did, she wouldn't have taken me back, right women? It's that she lost trust, faith, and hope and let the devil use her. Cleopatra said she forgave me it went back God me and her authority, but Cleopatra was to blind to see that an unforgiving woman that's scornful by not doing it by action all about love. We cursed each other in our relationship, me and her had to bring God back. When Jeffrey got saved and repented came back to Cleopatra and got married, she brought everything from the past back up that's like going to all the graveyards in the world and digging all the bodies up. See the bones come back worse and when I mean they come back it be worse than what the husband did because it adds up and brings more spirits that you can even sleep in your own house. I stop saying I was the boss, and I only was saying Jesus is the boss and what Jesus says Cleopatra, woman, women will take that it in as being hard broken that is an excuse now you want to talk about it's too late for that. Now was you talking about God when you were fucking that bitch? You did not bring God up when I caught your ass in all those lies, did you? Forgive me for the cursing but this how it goes. Cleopatra will listen to what the pastor says and me she just did not agree on nothing I did or said she will change and switch up in so many moods that you or I can even imagine. Then when I told her it wasn't fair and right, she will say, no you trying to con me or hustle me! Reverse everything and her rude disrespectful reactions to me on all things. When Jeffrey said to her we are partners we are a team come on now baby, Cleopatra would scream and say I don't know why, or she moved back in with your fucking ass with (MY CHILDREN)! I gave honesty because I know and did it in front of her let's pray before everything and she will refuse everything about me inside out. Then she would use her rudeness behavior or selfishness, pride, mean attitude and use the right to use God over me of her leadership of getting me back of the woman I left her for in the past before we got married not after, before! I was a liar I was everything but when I gave money, took care her children and made love good depending on the mood she was in at times when she feels to say baby you a good husband, DAMN WHICH ONE AM I? So, when Jeffrey did things righteously and Cleopatra ignored him, because the devil spirits was passing through in the back of her mind because the woman be lukewarm feeling good one moment then the next don't bring it over here. Cleopatra evil heart of bitterness wouldn't let her move forward now a real woman of God will know that's unnecessary and very petty a woman that's drama or getting back will say it's good you left him it was over any way he fucked up. I finally got it right it says summit to one another. Jeffrey was thanking God for myself telling him Lord I'm better than what Jeffrey use to be Cleopatra kept her foot on my neck. Encouragement: Let all bitterness, wrath, anger, clamor, and evil speaking to be put away from you with all malice, and be kind to one another, tender hearted, forgiving one another, even as God in Christ forgave you. We need this relationship that need this, I need this, you need this trust in the lord with all your heart; do not depend on your own understanding. Seek his will in all you do, and he will direct your paths. Fathers are plainly important as mother's, God design's, creates, blesses and heals, defends, forgives and loves us all. When we sin why do we feel like at certain times it's a difference? I see that woman/ women feel that cheating is the worse sin of them all most of them. Jeffrey told Cleopatra's daughter Anita quick, she thinks she knows everything, and she grown in my house. If they were tired of me, being harassed by me being the parent then move out! Cleopatra the mother Pamela could say it, because she's the WOMAN/MOTHER she been doing it before Jeffrey came along and for years, RIGHT WOMEN? Jeffrey knew it was not all about sex when he gave his life to God, it was about God first, himself, woman and children SEE IN ORDER. I don't know what they are doing and talking about today. The best part in the relationship was God, Us, the children, laughing, happiness, holding one another, enjoying one another company. Cleopatra was just to blind to see it. She will say how can you know her behavior and don't mines being stubborn for her actions and wrongs blaming them on me. See when a woman/women get hurt when the years go by, she feels she has the audacity with power to take control over everything that she's going to get what she wants no matter what no matter how you feel! I stopped explaining myself because she only meant something not me and she was important, and we gave her that extra fulfilling a woman wants everything and was she satisfied no because it was more! A woman is a beautiful thing she's worth saving she loves, but it is not and only all about her I see marriages today and the marriage be only the woman/wife, God will not be pleased with this he is not some women will say and WHAT" S WRONG WITH THAT YOU JEALOUS? HMMM! It's life and nature in the man to the king and queen lion bows down to one another it's LOVE! There's no damn whip appeal thing that's games. I agree when a woman/wife/woman/queen is hurt she cannot share her trust to the husband/man that her it can be for men to because both sides get neglected, Ok women we'll you say well the men do it first most of them do no excuse, but it's not your job as a woman of God to make him sacrifice and pay like he's your slave and you're the owner! It can be for every or anyone that's let down or treated wrong but when a woman says she forgives you are saying you're you are ready to accept the trust back from the man within yourself and to love all over again! It would be a close relationship with lies back at the man and plenty of women will say he or they deserve it after she has made him pay constantly! It takes time, courage, help and love not getting one another back that makes it worse women say that do help because she's venting and letting her pain out yes FOR HOW LONG because is not only watching the husband ways and behavior! I had an addiction of a lot of problems I told on myself I'M A MAN! I got help to!! That's just like someone on drugs so when the person gets off drugs and they are human beings, be off drugs for 8, 9, 10 years and then they go around family members they have done wrong, and they JUDGE

THEM. Because they think of the past and say, what you came to steal? You want a hit? I don't have no money for you. Now the woman doesn't have to be on drugs she could have been a prostitute or a stripper or whatever sin she was in of stealing in the same way she walks up DON'T JUDGE HER SHE HAS CHANGE! Like how black men that get out of jail or prison and be JUDGED no matter what color he is any man that walks the ground on in God's earth! I'm one of them so I know and how does it feel? Only ones that go through it or soul is good or not no one is perfect! They have changed and the ones that do judge they be doing more wrong than anyone and can't look at the flaws. DO YOU KNOW A PERSON THAT CAN'T FORGIVE HAS AN ADDICTION? And do you know why because it's they can't and don't want to choose to work on continue to get on and be on the same old thing! They have taught the women that if they keep doing this they will never change, and they are always right. Women says men do this more than them and then men say women do this and that more than them, EVERYONE DOES WRONG! We all have good and bad in us and have sinned now Cleopatra will say don't try to get away or out of what your ass done wrong to me. They are different types of addictions WOMEN and MEN. Like sex, drugs, alcohol, lying, cheating, using, manipulating, fighting, drama, falsely accusing, unforgiving, abuse, violence, controlling, getting back at someone, bitterness, living off the past, cycles, bad behaviors, gambling, arguing, debates, anger, malice, vengeance, resentment, strain on the house hold, bad ways, provoking, worrying, depressed, low self-esteem, addictive behavior, no trust, blaming one another, drama, adultery, sneaky smart secrets, a certain life style, THESE THINGS ARE BAD HABITS that somethings in life we been through that we couldn't stop doing and it was hard! A lot of women said it was for men only cheating, abuse, not taking care their children and it was all the men fault and they did nothing wrong! NOT ONE THING! And they say this for real I didn't do NOTHING. Persistence you be surprised how far it can get you because likes things slow and easy and for a man to take his time. She has all the answers she will say I don't have all the answers, but her mouth, ways, and actions will show differently. I know women want to be told the truth and not lied to about anything. Women don't lie I heard a lot of women told me they lied all because every reason was because the man made me do it and we get it from you all. A woman is concerned and nice my part is for a lot of women when you prove yourself it does mean that you prove anything, because she does not change the thoughts in her mind and uses against men it could be in good ways or bad ways because the women mostly let the man thinks he has everything under control. She uses everything to win right or wrong in order to get her point across she will talk too much about herself she's a woman. You can and will be truthful to her and agreeable about everything she says however she's happy wants more! She never runs out of gas. A woman is great what is a man? Women know they want to be in control of everything and the situation at any time or sometime at least. Most of the time they think that they are even during times when they're not. They use constantly different kinds of communications to test and feel out the situation with the man. She can't never be satisfied only a certain time, moment, extent, switching up anytime any day with her mood swings! A woman likes when a man is being natural being himself. A woman can also have different types of attitudes bitterness and unforgiveness can be an addiction as well if you can't control it or stop it to women that do this! The woman knows everything, but she does not know the bitterness poisons the relationship. A woman could say she know but don't know when you help her to stop and understand she will curse you out. So how is she telling the man she doesn't want his help and have not looked in the mirror at herself, because the man is helping her. She is not helping him to help her because she's not helping herself let things go out of her heart that God can could control if she let him as well! Most women can't let go of the past and things and take to their graves. What does this accomplish not anything? In a marriage give your doubts to God if you don't you will never resolve them. God is gracious to us, God is always there to your doubts, but you have false prophets, teachers, leaders that lie and try to use anything they can. They will say if the husband or wife is not a believer still be there by their side. If they don't this continually doing it over again, back and forth and then use the Bible against your marriage, because they take this and use this against one another as sword to hold to each other necks instead fighting together they be fighting against one another. It must stop somewhere. When you doubt you are looking in different directions not one as one or one accord it is God and one! Then it can be disbelief, no understanding, aggravation, hesitation and lack conviction, because they can't decide one way and God arguing because it be so much confusion! Cleopatra said only herself until this day, I'm going to say it and still do it so is she not telling on herself? Women will think men can't go anywhere because they think better than them. Jeffrey told Cleopatra she will never resolve the matter with him if he was always the enemy in their relationship, if you don't hand it over to God she said I know you're not telling me about God all the wrongs and sins you done to me. So, there was no positive or good she saw in me when I changed just because I changed does not mean she changed her thoughts, vision, her looks, especially on the inside, her heart, her memories and cold-hearted feelings. So, it was all a lie, because when I changed not overnight it took some time so did hers she needed more time, because she's a woman and more emotional and as a man I took the 60 of being wrong and gave her the 40 for being right! She got extra time, years, and it was a lie back towards God, herself and me. She was not honest with God or herself. Women will agree with her and say he still deserve the punishment until this day! What did you did you wrong to her I know right women? The big thing will be what do I have against women? No! It was just that woman and women out that push they men away. Every woman is not like that and the same! God made every woman different everybody feelings get hurt or done wrong to and sinned against one another. So, we all should react like women do of unforgiving? Be bitter, mean, nasty, for what we been through in life vice versa men and women. So, when men get cheated on, raped, abused, domestic violence tell me how did men get raped more than women in slavery time they lied they should act nasty forever? To come out with a writer like myself had to deal with a lot as much as a woman because everyone story is different. Raising someone else children is not easy then women want to trust the girlfriend, friend, mother, words, her boss, and tell her husband/man what the people said about him to his face and behind his back and still lay beside him. They can go listen to them, because it's bad on you and them all about you all because your miserable together. As soon as the man is doing with the women doing with, they friend or they're wrongs and then it's putting you in check, who are you listening to with bringing up the past with it's on now. They will say who you been talking to? The same people they have been talking to have problems like them and want them to be unhappy just like they are. They will listen to them all day, (THAT'S TRUE) A FACT! We will talk about Jesus' scriptures all day and don't do them. Our faith comes by hearing the word of God. Many times, in my life I have been standing in the same spot in a place of doubt between of all kinds of directions what I understood and between what Jesus was saying then I changed and walked to God's direction. I refuse to stay in a place of deception. Jeffrey chose God, Himself and Cleopatra but she said I didn't, I did, I tried, on and off, I was right, I was wrong. I overcame a lot of things she said she was not in a relationship by herself but didn't back it up by holding my hand with God walking with me. She kicked me on the floor more, so I was dirt. It wasn't no love for me until she chose to give then take it back away. Every relationship/marriage needs input if it takes 3 God the husband and wife. It takes two human beings in their relationship for it to work. Everyone deserves respect don't when you go work hard for your money and you go out to eat you give respect women, you want great customer service and assistance and your order correct so what you think your man wants you know he love surprises just like you respect is even do to a dog. Women your man can't do it all by himself. Then the woman says it's all on a man everything. This is what pushes a man away and he does not feel important period because of the disrespect and neglected! Sorry to tell you ladies this does not only goes for you it goes for him as well. He is left out and ignored. He is a human being like you. No relationship can go with only a husband or just a wife it must be both, it's just like a car you run out of gas, because you just driving it around all the time on E just like your man you put your foot on the brake when you get ready and take off when you want to with your mouth, ways, actions behavior and more. It's a husband wife and children not children wife and husband false teachers, leaders, T.V. shows, talk shows and other things have influence. Women the most they listening to what others say instead of God. A lot of times arguing be in your car while you are driving the marriage already be out of gas and the woman

has the right to say and feel it's all on him, he must take the blame for everything. She speaks things off her tongue as if they are fair when it is deceiving, wicked, evil, and the right to call herself a Christian. The devil sit's back and laugh, when she says you mess up our life, I shouldn't have never ever got back with your ass, my children came first not you. I would say God comes first and our marriage and the children and she will say loud WELL I JUST DEAL WITH GOD THEN I DON'T CARE.

Chapter 9

A lot of women will say she did not mean that she was just angry, upset, hurt and at to some point where she had to let it out and express her feelings, not with God being talked about like that that's just hate! Cleopatra will say I am not a real man, go find a job, I don't care, whatever, sucking her teeth and rolling her eyes saying I wish never came back to you. I was the one messed up her life, she said to me all the time I want to divorce you, all you want to do is fucking have sex and that's all you want from me and think about. Cleopatra says I know I'm not trying to tell me what to do, what's right in you for all your fucking up you don't have a job and you're not trying hard enough that's what this is, and that person said about you, I will never believe you ever again you are a compulsive liar. You are a cheater, no good, you are not a Christian man you might as well be the devil no matter of fact you are because you know a woman tongue and mouth of words change! Now when man or men say all these things to a woman/woman, and she has hurt you can you be right or wrong in my hurt or men? How you suppose to tell a strong woman if she is ever wrong, she deserves everything? But not for man when he does wrong. How dare people do this give more credit and it is valid for a woman than a man. Remember you must be judge by God even myself. So, watch what you say, your actions how you speak and what's behind. No man can do it all by himself in a marriage not everything. My brother told me marriage is a 60/40. Sixty is for the wife, forty for the husband. The he said man what I go through you just don't know or understand. Cleopatra's children ignore Jeffrey like I'm not here at all with the children Jeffrey had from her don't ignore him. Her children are follower of what she does to me. Women and men what Jeffrey went through with Cleopatra (THE WOMAN) is hurtful and a show of unlove. My brother wife is ignoring him to. I told him remember when you said the children always come first, I brought it up to show him, tell him, letting him see by action what is not right. Jeffrey wanted love and affection from Cleopatra (THE WOMAN) was supposed to forgive me, forgiving is

love so when she said baby, Jeffrey see you changed did she put action behind that? No! Her mother didn't teach her to forgive and be by my side to encourage me after the storm going through it and when it's over then thunder comes, she holds as a spear in her hand. A lot of people even women will say I can't make her change, but when it's the other way around and the shoe is on the other foot then alright that's enough God has had enough. Everyone in the church knows the sisters understands the man is the head get on your job, she will get a show, a band, a bishop, a prayer, a person to listen, understand, hear her out all the way, a stadium, a hall, auditorium, poetry, affection, family, mother, father, stars, talk shows, movies, feeling their pain they will listen to the world. Cleopatra did not crown her king only God did however God and Jeffrey grown Cleopatra he fought the battle with the blood, and she didn't pick Jeffrey up when he was down, but when she was down it was Jeffrey job to pick her up. I wanted her to build me up because their where hidden battles I fought on my own as well as women do as well as women do. Do you hear, understanding, and hear where I'm coming from? Some things on my own she did not know about because we did not have a relationship with God at times and women say, it was wrong and sinful things and have you reading then say we didn't say. So, what are you holding in or telling on yourself or something that you keep inside to yourself and don't want to share, get it out, communicate and keep it all balled up in your heart? How is this going to get you and your husband on the other side of the road, or the fence, or the bridge he can't do it all himself? But do you know it's a lot of women today feel as if the man should! Some women have ways that are like I can't even say or explain they can't either in their times on their moods depending on the woman. Also, a man being and putting it in the right way like women saying I will tear his ass up 8 ways till Sunday if the man if he does not act right, she got all kind of ways I just had to put that in there! I'm speaking from the heart! Tell me something woman/ women/wives, when you do wrong, sin, or hurt your man/husband, cheat, lie or whatever sin you do when you don't dog or cheat as much as a man do, I ask one question what should be your suffering and pain for you to go through, and I have your answer right here you ready, THATS ONLY FOR GOD TO ANSWER JUDGE AND LOVE

THEM ON! Not every woman in the world but most in times of day and now. I wouldn't know that God call a good positive thing not bad like men making you this way, right? I wouldn't lie. A single mother is a serious thing, so men be real with her serious and up front so the same thing with your man's women that are loving man's and father's or stepfathers. Jeffrey loved Cleopatra and her children so much he cried as he right this book so much. Now deeply in love with a woman who children's father's that did not step up to do what I did I stepped up and got pushed down. I hurt a lot of women very bad in the past it wasn't right to take what I did wrong to women in the past see things come from my past experience I went through that I did not forgive peoples on so women what you think will happen to you when you don't forgive! For what I got taken through in the past with my father, mother, and family did to me, and I did to others neglecting me, so I took it out on everyone, especially women. This stem from the abuse and rape I endure from family members. Also, my mother leaving me with my dads' family. See so many stories be told to men being raised up they don't know who to trust or believe, yes they get raped mistreated and abused and who is there to listen, help, talk, pray and treat them when there being raise on this way from a child? I want to say it is no excuse to hurt anyone I'm making my confession when you get a certain in life to grow up and understand when you know right from wrong and is an adult! Why can women go through when they get hurt plenty of times from hurt, pain, and suffering putting up with life in the world forever. Women you think men don't go through this what you go through? (NO)! Some or most would say stop being a baby grow up and stop dwelling on your past move on. Jeffrey let Cleopatra know I am somebody and she change his heart and his mind was not empty. Love is in it but, it was too late for Cleopatra for Jeffrey to get it right she was unsatisfied. It's never too late for the woman, however you got to stay on point and time! When Cleopatra put Jeffrey down even, so he still showed her I'm going to be someone anyway, because God showed Jeffrey how to reach out more to him, myself, Cleopatra and the children even when the devil used her to treat Jeffrey like he was shit. Like he used me when I did her wrong, but Jesus picked me up anyway. I knew sometimes the things I went through when I was married it was God guiding me to be strong and take me to another level. Cleopatra couldn't see that Jeffrey she could see is that and say Jeffrey was a fuck up and always be one. Jeffrey deserved everything that's coming to him even until this day. God guided me forward not backwards. He is lifting me up higher in is heart name with his great works! Jeffrey says that, believe and he already, Jeffrey says the same for Cleopatra a good woman who he still loves. Look me in my face right now in my face today and say I'm not shit but then call me back or text me to say I'm sorry and curse me out then say I love you Jeffrey please forgive me. I know I'm a mighty brave man that's a courageous man I love being spiritual immensely and care deeply, but I am not perfect. My behavior now comes from the heart that is in divine order, pure and heavenly. I have my generosity and a good heart my kindness is gentle. When I had all the businesses and money it was not about that, because I knew this man with his time who found a way to spend good time with, she meant everything to me I didn't look or care about her butt we were looking into each other eyes smiling at one another I was showing my dimples and she was blushing. I looked at her and her children to give them something that I did not have fully which was LOVE! I wanted to see what was ahead of her I wanted to see the future. What messed us up was both of us and her daughter Anita, we stop doing things that we use to do when we first met in the first place! Now I would like to ask women these questions? Why did you sleep with married men when you knew they had a wife? Why you slept with a man, and you were not married to him? Wasn't that carnal sin? Why did you lie? Why when a man got a divorce, and you knew you was in it involving yourself waiting to be the next wife for the backup plan? What are you going to say? For your action, wrong and sin, oh he made me do it, WE get this and learn this from the men, because you are better dogs than we are, you taught us this, you men been doing it, so these are excuses right? EVERYONE HAS DOG IN THEIR OWN WAY. ALSO BEEN DOG ON! It comes with sleeping around on someone, like the way you talk, treat people, principles of respecting yourself and others, IT IS NOT ONLY ABOUT SEX! It can be from handling situations in a peculiar manner. Controlling and abusing someone with words of authority over them. Men have been doing this for years, then women will say men made us react this way and the way we are today, GET BACK! As a woman she need to be held, get laid and needed some sex. Now what God what say about this? God's word is bond to everyone in the same way we know that, but in the world how a lot of people react on it don't seem like it because they want to do it their own way. What Jeffrey couldn't understand he made peace with his past so it wouldn't change his future or have an effect on Jeffrey Cleopatra brought back infections because of her unforgiveness and her mind, thoughts, heart, the way she looked at things in her own way not changing at all. Cleopatra wouldn't let the past go so we can walk into our future together. She kept saying sorry bringing all kinds of things back up then curse me right back out and speaking bringing the other woman back up continually. What people thought about Jeffrey and said about him is none of their business Jeffrey stop caring. Cleopatra (THE WOMAN) said I don't care or give a fuck anymore, but she will say my mom and people are telling me things about you. I know myself, you're doing the same shit, looking at me with her devious look with her cat eyes slowly with bitter spirits, talking about me behind my back and in my face, but she was just quiet the expression on her face looking at me angry told it all with her body language, movement, feelings, and ignoring me. Basically, Cleopatra will change up and say who am I talking to. I would look at her crazy as she's the crazy one after she tell me she loves me, because I know I did no such thing, but by what I did from the past of her putting me back in denial throwing it up right back in my face. I felt from my own wife I'm a failure, I'm not trying, I am not shit, because I'm not trying hard enough. No matter what I do or say even fix it's not good enough for her! Sometimes educated people with a higher level of education will think some people don't have common sense. I have street smarts and Cleopatra has education smarts. She wanted to be the head of the household when I myself the man will come out and express my feelings and say you do what I say and not as I do. She threw up in my face because she knew she's making the most money and the bread winner in the house. Women you can't be satisfied because we always want more and change at any time. See every time Jeffrey got paid, he handed his check over to Cleopatra, but she felt it wasn't enough she seen her mother do these reactions and ways in her marriage. The same way how the mother did her is why they couldn't communicate together, so how would she treat her own man. Women don't know cycles how they dad and mom did them could reflect on their relationship/marriage to and what they did not have at the time to teach them! Cleopatra will throw Jeffrey check right back in his face and tell Jeffrey she doesn't need shit from me. Life is too short to be hurt and punished by Cleopatra (THE WOMAN), because financial Jeffrey didn't meet her standards the day that man walks out the door you don't know when you will see or hear his voice again in life. Women we know that we are hard to please and satisfy in life. What do you think? True or False. Cleopatra never wanted to give Jeffrey a second chance to be the head of the household, because she was taking advice from her mother or other people. Now see her mother will be locked up in the room watching T.V. The vicious cycle and ways of why Cleopatra was never wrong like her mother going back and forth arguing. She knew all the answers I couldn't know because I messed up cheating. We both would smile together. We are quick to listen, slow to speak and get angry. She looked to get back at me for my wrong doings. She showed disrespect and insults simply to hold her own to prove her point. Now how is that? I don't have a problem against women no I don't and for men that read this book that can learn a lot. Just like I had to learn a lot. No one is perfect some women can to. I'm hungry to learn more about the woman. So don't say I have problem with women. What's wrong is that I'm hurting just like anyone else. I know how many of times that I've done right. When I was given another chance by God, but my woman found her man cheating. Then the husband in the movie put the baby momma and wife in their place as to how they act. He told them both to learn to respect each other. The wife said it about time you speak up and they came to an agreement to come together. In the next segment of movie part 2 the wife did not forgive the husband. She kept arguing with him for every little thing. So, to all women that's hurt, evil and angry they need to take to listen to your husband and learn what the problem is. When Cleopatra (THE WOMAN) say I forgive you Jeffrey went to speak with the pastor to inform him Jeffrey was not having an affair with any other woman. The pastor says to me I know you are not doing wrong. He said you need to go back to your woman and pray together. I did as I was told. Cleopatra said get a damn job. Cleopatra said I am doing all the work and you the one who messed us up. Jeffrey cried and accepted what she said in silence. It was very hurtful at that time and things was spiraling out of control. When the pastor asked her is, he still beating on you? She said no! So why are you angry? You need to stop listening to your mother because you run home with the same issue. Jeffrey knew ladies he deserved what was being thrown at him by Cleopatra. When I became a Christian, I stop hating people no matter how much they mistreated me. I stayed humble and whatever or whoever was saying negativity things to me I would walk away. When she walked up on me as a real man thinks I remain positive no matter how hard life was or is today. I gave my all and still do even though it wasn't given to me. I kept in touch with the ones who have forgotten me and forgave those who has treated me wrong. I never stop praying for the best for those who I love. Jeffrey wanted to save their relationship, Cleopatra did not, because she was hurting and did not accept his apology, she gave up. She believed in the 60/40 rule. When she started speaking her feelings and lashing out that she made a mistake taking me back and moving in with me. I took a long look at Cleopatra, and I said do you want this relationship to work or not? Even though she said I am not your woman. When Jeffrey realized Cleopatra needed help, he begged her to get it and Jeffrey asked her to pray with him. She said NO! Cleopatra when she was in the mood of love, she would put Jeffrey favorite high heels, say baby it's time to make love. I would look at her while crying inside with hurt thinking about how she is ready to make love to Jeffrey after saying nasty things. Now women ask yourself would you push your man/ husband out them to be with another woman? When the man or husband is loving, caring and would make love when you want. Can you ask yourself if the man sincerely want to be with you and no one else while he is putting in all his effort to make the relationship or marriage to work what are you doing? He is saying he can never satisfy a woman. However, I will try my best to satisfy her in every way. God see's everything what she did wrong back to me. As you women read this book. You can see as the inquirer encounter or interview with several women. I get a key account and testimony from several women on their ways, characteristics, nature and life whether individually or collectively and. Cleopatra (THE WOMAN) didn't know when Jeffrey was disrespecting her, made her angry, cheated on her, Jeffrey stops repenting and ask for her forgiveness, then Jeffrey let God deal with it, but she didn't do that vice versa. When she said she forgave me with hate in her heart. It is consuming her because she did not leave it in God hands! Now today a lot of women say their children come before the marriage. The number one then the marriage must be second, if your job comes first, if you back accounts come first or having cars and materialistic things come your marriage will be at risk! Period! No matter how busy or important you are marriage takes priority. Cleopatra (THE WOMAN) told Jeffrey he would have a car and money. Everyone else is saying I'm broke, my mother, sister have a car, but I don't. Instead of God and us, Cleopatra was looking at everyone else life and not our life together to live. She believing what speaks to her in for better or worse, richer or poorer. You must help one another. God says a husband and wife as two become one. No one spouse can dominate the relationship or control the money or make all the decisions. Husbands and wife, men and women, are equal when you in a marriage, which you should work as a team. You don't get married then when one person goes broke you want to separate where is the together in having each other back? False statements and people can mislead you women and men to believe it's all given to the women, or to the men, but mostly the women get 95% of the credit! Two people working together are better than one, because they have good reward for their labor. For if they fall, one will lift the other, but woe to him who is alone when he falls for, he has no one to help him up. Again, if two lie down together, they will keep warm; but how can one be alone? Though one may be overpowered by another, two can withstand him. And a threefold cord is quickly broken. These things are serious with the husband and wife with God first! Love, sex is not in the way of wrong, but you know what I'm saying making love, communication, concerned, care, trust, work, faith, prayer, help, responsibility, tragedy and time with one another alone. I understand you women that are hurting for what men done to you pray for them its right to not like it, but don't hate them? Because when you hate anyone remember how can you love yourself or God? I heard women say they can love God and hate, can't stand, don't like that man, because he is not God. Instead of false people teaching them to do this. You can't make them change. They need to say, pray for them, yourselves and others. I'm not going to use women to buy a book, sex, to like me for only talking good about them and only them. Love me and like me for me from the heart vice versa. Now its right to say that when a single mother or a woman is raped, abused, suffering, struggling in pain, sick, surgery, life or death, cheated on, molested, used, going though cancer or mental, physical, saved with Christ or not, problems, hurt, put down, let down, homeless, it's hard to understand her pain she needs more time! Right or wrong? But when it's a man and he go through this is it any different? What I have seen from false teaching, favoritism people? Yes, because he is a man and stronger with much strength within him that he can get over things fast. How is that any different from a woman strength. Most people have hurt and struggle with the pain in life. God can speak on that so, all these people that are out for fame, publicity or to take sides. We can't do the works that God can, but we have no right to put men or women or anyone down and say this side or that side can have more than the other. Now we have Cleopatra (THE WOMAN) that says we can be friends, go out and want to get laid and all she wants is to be friends with benefits. Now this is where she has a God man friend and can't even see it, because she's doing her. What she thinks that is safe. Now stars, millionaires, billionaires, and T.V. shows will have their opinions and says saving today's topic is about women. You will have them say that's not a real woman, because she must marry first, don't judge her like that, men been doing this for years and not talking about the man, but include him in vice versa. See I'm fair and caring I'm somebody take it or leave it! Women will understand some girlfriend circles will be into their conversations about men. Even in the real world today not on TV shows or movies. Now soon as a man says we just friends that's all the house coming down and hell is busting wide open. Here it goes, he's no good, that's game, he got all kind of hoes, he going to use you, he is taking you away from your children, he going to have sex with you and leave you, he's not about being a friend, child please! Whatever! See you when I see you with an attitude, sucking teeth, when it's time to free his mind and just be friends, it's a problem. A woman is just never satisfied.

Cleopatra (THE WOMAN) came over to Jeffrey house to have sex with him. She said she was HOT and MOIST, she misses me not being rude or disrespectful to me, was she being a hoe or coming for a booty call.? To women, me or men, NO! Cleopatra (THE WOMAN) was still getting over the divorce. She realized that getting the divorce was not easy. When it's my time and it's me, because I'm a man I'm full of Bullshit, I'm this. Some women like to flip and flop, they change many things and still not satisfied, because she changed, and I did whatever she requested to satisfy her, and she still wasn't happy. So, don't be quick to say to the man why didn't say NO? Why didn't lock the door? You weren't a man, it's all on you, because you're the man and you know better. When Cleopatra (THE WOMAN) asks for money Jeffrey will get cursed out because she felt she had the right to do that, but that don't make her right. Cleopatra (THE WOMAN) when Jeffrey talked to her she said he will be appreciated of what he gave her this time okay I'm sorry. The woman has an excuse for her wrongs, because all her wrongs she feels the man made her that way only. Can I say that for men I think it's going to be said like this all of them like that, because a man going to be a man! Is a woman or man any different? Now you also have a lot of women who take pride in their appearance. You can't force someone to respect you, but you can refuse to be disrespected. Now women, is this a take up for? Things we all do needs to be 50/50 fair. It will be hard times. Women are saying today that they are making men pay forever that hurt them. You both will stick by one another man and woman. When you care for each other through the bad and good not just when it's only happy, easy and good days only! Jeffrey did become a real man, responsible, because she said thank you, Jeffrey surprised Cleopatra, planned things, Jeffrey got gifts. I even humbled myself a little. A real woman knows what she knows out of life. She won't give up and she will keep going until she gets there. The woman will also offer her heart. The woman is loyal to her man who expects no more from others than she is willing to give. A good woman will bring good gifts by her smile, support, caring and understanding that brings all joy. Jeffrey loves Cleopatra herself (THE WOMAN) did this then when Jeffrey only did all the sins in her eyes, wrong and was the bad man it was all on him, but she was always the good credit score changing woman. Now come on do you really think or believe everything was my fault ladies and gentlemen? What marriage/relationship is perfect? I know that are good women out there who is not proud of themselves and is you should be proud. You respect yourselves and others you are aware of the power, world, and who you are! You neither seek definition from her man, nor do you expect to read your mind. Women you are quite capable articulating your needs. A good woman is already strong. She recognizes that her strength is weakened by attitudes that suggest that she doesn't need a man at times. I know and we all know that is not true. I, you, we, need lots of loving. A good woman is hopeful she is strong enough to make all her dreams come true. She knows love there for she gives love. She recognizes that her love has great value and must be reciprocated. If her love is takin for granted it soon disappears. A good woman has a dash of inspirations and a dabble of endurance. She knows that she will at times have to inspire others to reach their potential. You know when Jeffrey first met Cleopatra (THE WOMAN) it was also a reflection on himself, because Jeffrey didn't bet her he waited for her even if that had taken forever a man knows a good woman when her see's or meets one. That's if he has grown up or not, he knows a good woman the bad one doesn't know what he has until he has lost a good woman, or she has walked out on his ass. The man that knows and do the right thing will get surprises he can't even imagine. Now woman let your man be a man and watch the surprises you will get it will be things blowing your mind courageously and insane! Cleopatra was not like other women Jeffrey have met in life even though every woman is not the same she was one of a kind in her own special way. I did not talk about no sex it was about her first then her children it was all about the (PACKAGE)! Some men don't accept some do, just like women but I did. If I wouldn't have, I would have been a coward, so I took the responsibility it doesn't be easy not only for you women myself as a man raising two different father's children is difficult! I didn't call her out any name when I first laid down with her. I became equal with when she said come here and put her hand on my face and rub me softly and told me I will like for you to meet my children. I treasured her heart that's what made me a man. I achieved more together with her I finally met someone in my life that made me feel like somebody when we first met. Women they are large and in charge that's in fact because even if she tells the husband/man he is she's letting feel that way when she knows in her mind different with love it's her unique special way of love! A lot of women run things today, then say it's not like that. Trust must be earned but when a woman messes up, she can say with and do a charm, touching way, with words, looks, body language, serious movements that the man will be caught off guard that he can't even imagine. A woman does a creep to it's called the silent, happy, cry it's one that's Godly and unconditionally and one that is game! Eye contact comes in usually. See when a husband/man messes up then do right to earn his trust back because the woman says she's willing to accept him back and she just say that but she's not meaning it as woman/women/ wives would say. She's a woman come on now you know she didn't mean what she said because she was emotionally going through her stages, this is true to some extinct not to go on to pressure someone and back you both into a corner. Why did he to do to me? You see I must get mines this gets nowhere but selfishness. A woman knows she put her man down like shit when she's mad but she's not thinking because she's in denial not to communicate until she feels if and it's when so to do it when she's ready to. You are on her time now. This is especially important to your marriages and relationships. How are you going not to never forget what you said and done, but you said you will help and forgive? In life we say let's forgive but don't know what it means and how to treat it with God and great behavior in our hearts. Now today it's different for against a man on forgiveness, how angry, bitter, malicious, revengeful, hateful and treacherously I see women on how they react! Now a real woman of God that's virtuous will know what this mean does it God's way and will not use it to her power of ability to control every situation the conversations, opinions, facts, and the matter of everything that she can't let go of something she has no power or control of doing by herself on her own. Same way she says God help my husband saying back for herself! It can be times when she needs it more than the husband/man does at times telling him he needs God majority or all the damn time. Jeffrey even realized that a lot of times my greatest accomplishment was keeping my mouth shut going back in forth with Cleopatra or any woman! You are a real woman I give you my credit all of you saying you pick up all the pieces, rebuild yourselves and come back stronger than before just don't do it in a JEZEBEL WICKED YOUR WAY SARCASTICALLY. Doesn't it talk about women who talk too much? All kinds of manipulations in Proverbs? Men I give Men credit as well for doing a great job and being stronger. I will not sit here and give women everything and all the credit. Jeffrey satisfied Cleopatra (THE WOMAN) but to her it was not good enough he still did even more with God, love understanding, listening, honesty, affection, communication and patience it had to take that, because if Jeffrey did not get right she wouldn't have got back with him would she? Any woman would know that common sense. The time was perfect when Jeffrey gave my life to God and to get Cleopatra back. She did not communicate in prayer for or with me but will tell me quick in or out the spirit in her spiritual realm gets on me about everything good or bad and still me I need to pray by myself and when she said so. I could not tell her or any woman/women/wife to put, fix, or even put in my mouth to say that God and the holy spirit is not with her I had another thing coming and problems with another battle to fight up against so like you women say, DON'T GO THERE! STAY IN YOUR LANE! She did not want to listen to me then choose to change then want to listen this is before I changed and went back out to the streets, so women don't put in your mouths why did she act in this way or what made her this kind of woman. She did not do this for nothing it had to be something to make her act in this way, oh yes, I'm respecting you women so please respect me back in the same way as well thank you. Cleopatra will say she sorry it's her fault it's all on her when she humbled herself then change minutes, hours later saying, expressing, back and forth to Jeffrey I'm not shit but a ho and a fuck up then apologize. Guilty expression a woman will keep inside at times, and you can't even see it at times but at times it will show. We both with God was supposed to make things better she felt like she was the only one fell hard and down for her husband/man and she did the job well done and correctly spotless without one damn stain. She's all the cleaner's bleach, pine-sol, fabuloso, soap, ajax, and I was the GERM! To her I was pointless and reckless see we all do right and wrong. Jeffrey destroyed Cleopatra in a lot of ways, but Jeffrey came back to Gentrify her from my actions of sins towards

God, myself, her and the children. I don't give a damn what no one say about me because God know what I did it's just that the woman did not accept it. You can't make no one change or accept something they chose not to I tell you something when it's two people in love it's a totally opposite difference. When you get someone back it's not you only it's both of you and you feel like you the one should get all the credit for it because you have been hurt the most so when you take that person back and you stay stuck in that way you don't have nothing in you to love, give, help, share, talk, time or a bond! When Cleopatra partnered Jeffrey, she was telling God first it was too late before she told Jeffrey, and she did not know this because she was to bitter and scornful to. Then tell me changing when it's time to make love or she's come or want what she wants to please and satisfy her needs lying beside me change like from Mary to Jezebel saying Jeffrey that's not true because I love you but I'm sorry to tell you, you are not God but then still talk to Jeffrey any kind of way. She kept saying it even when we got back together like the arguments she had with her mother saying to me IT'S ALREADY OVER AND IT'S OVER at the time she or women feel like they don't speak things like that unto existence, after the sin has been done and forgiven for or arguments start before it that don't even be true of falsely accusing. Husbands, wives, ex-husband's, ex-wives, man/men, woman/women feel like they can hurt each other in any kind of way and for a pay back where we feel that we are venting out expressing ourselves in a right way making us feel that for that time being we did something but we don't really truly know it's not about that it's about the person who you're in front of that you have to spend the rest of your life with! Not continually hurting one another because we are not next to God and this is what false prophets, teachers, T.V. shows and people taught them/us by listen at times because we feel lonely and hurt quietly inside or out going to looking for the wrong people accept God! They are confused instead wanting and finding out the truth they want to stay in denial believing a lie because how they have been treated wrong or have treated someone wrong. Now a real strong woman will walk away if she knows and feels she is doing all the work in the relationship and fixing it on her own and you think a man won't? Now when it's the man, will she not be pushing him out and away? Like Cleopatra use to say when Jeffrey sat in the living wrong I wish I would have never ever got back with your ass in front of her children, disrespecting God, Jeffrey, herself and the children she felt like that was not disrespectful to God in her no she felt like that was her being angry at me with God and they both are punishing Jeffrey for what he did wrong to her a lot of women feel in this way to when they are hurt! I have seen it with my own eyes. Family members being married, friends in different places from what I've seen even in church. She didn't even know by my tears as a man it was a lot of hidden battles I fought in my life. She did not know she became a fight to put up with not only her and women myself as well went through this. She was always angry, mean, bitter because her world was, I did all the damage. A damage hurt woman will think emotionally feel this way but if she doesn't try herself to get out and want help where would she be? Some or most women will say stuck with me, him, you or us not both! It depends on the husband woman and the situation because everyone is different, but it is still one way with God not ours, so women and men stop playing with yourselves! All kinds of excuses on both sides are unnecessary your husband is not only making excuses if so then he will be the only sinner and the hardheaded one something you would never be. Come on ladies I know that's not true. A woman that will never forgive she will never want to be your friend, is that right to say? She is a woman how would she ever be your friend if she doesn't believe in you. Cleopatra criticized and rejected all the time, God created Jeffrey to. After forgiving me was it, he's thinking something good, he's in love, he loves God, he believes in me, he entered my life again, NO! It was she choose to be an evil woman. I became a man I have lots of fun with her at times, but she will not put in what I put in because she felt she could do what she wants to pay me off. I prayed when she didn't even when she said screaming at me saying I did pray I just did not want to do it with you her own husband yes I deserve this for what I did to her, right women? Don't feel sorry for me no I don't want you all to, go with God and if God is not in it, I don't want no parts of it! Jeffrey had a good time with Cleopatra when she didn't want to know she's a woman. She is God's child in spirit. When Jeffrey was with God he cried out even when Jeffrey cried without Cleopatra being there with God believe women it's not you only that cry out the most everyone cries to God! I know she did not still let the past go and still carrying the load and admitted it but did change herself to see things in God eyes only her own. Women a lot of you need to know or thought about your husband/man can carry a couch and refrigerator all by himself. Do you know how it feels to carry the load all by yourself? Yes, you do so what how do you feel and think about your husband/man in this way. Never sit back while your spouse deals with hardship. Offer to always help one another, because if you keep pointing the finger getting back at one another where is the love in the marriage/relationship? There is no love there are two people having guns in separate hands pointing at one another moving around slowly watching who's going to shoot first, so sad to say some marriages already be dead and broken up or the other one be shot and still living crying for helping but be liking the pain because the battle be fun to some people then they hurt in the end still when it's over like I said we all are not the same! It be a divorce, nowhere, set up, anger, destroyed, strife, get back, war, all these things are a get back, really you are stabbing each other hearts I hear some women say well he did different, and he started then the husband says well I ended it. Yes, the devil this coming in and we are letting him to kill, still and destroy our marriages but the devil is a liar in Jesus' name. Being faithful does not only means you are cheating I want to be on the number one list of the marriage is not being a believer and a doer of our God now that's a cheater! Not the husband/man/men first. Men cheating is the only thing based on to stay focus on is for men not to cheat. You got to believe in one another, embrace each-other be safe to one another especially for each other burdens. No matter how we do wrong God values us anyway. We are God's children, and we call each other Christians, but don't treat each other as God say. We will feel like I, you, we, or families must be treated in a certain kind of way because we are not close to God if your Pastor goes out to save souls God gave me and you that same love, holy spirit, trust, faith and soul! Where does God say if your husband or wife cheats, they are forgiven but they must repay when I forgive them, and you do the same? No, we just had on and judge and try to change God's word against one another it doesn't be God it be us that choose not to change. No this is what the devil do he uses people to say, you're not God when they really look at the person as a sinner and there's no other chance for this person or whoever have done wrong and sinned. They are angry at the person and swear up and down they know what they're talking about when truly they're first mad with God, because God word says in his word do unto others as you want them to have to do unto you and love thy neighbor as thy self, so you don't love God. Women do this to screaming I do love God I love you to I just don't like what you did to me there's different ways to show and express hate without saying in words correct your behavior women. Some women don't even tell they husband they love them they love them back they just have sex with them and go to sleep, be on the phone with them and he says baby I love you darling and you saying back and be like yeah I love you to hanging up fast! We all been in here in our own ways of marriages, problems, situations, even the pastor and his wife done been through there things this why they share their testimonies with God present for people's souls in marriages/relationships, it also be women counseling for marriage with God first, men, you must choose to want to accept that group of love and help for God and one another! Who is different a man or a woman don't say different in judging or in the way you want to let's do it in God way if you chose not to then that's your choice God is always there to answer when you, I, or anyone knocks on the door! The husband is and wife give it to God together. I'm going to tell you what Jeffrey went through doing wrong and sinning towards God, myself and Cleopatra, Jeffrey got his nose broken, beaten by officers, Jeffrey got slammed to the floor, choked, going into multiple seizures, almost dying, pepper sprayed in jail, and jumped in different cells by inmates, after Jeffrey was pepper sprayed because they knew he couldn't fight back. I busted my head open having a seizure bleeding again. Then my stepdaughter Anita said to Cleopatra's mother why is they doing him like that in there? Cleopatra said to Jeffrey see your daughter Anita do love you when she came to visit Jeffrey when he went to jail because she been asking about you your stepson Trevor to. Then she had the nerve to tell me this is happening to you in here because how you did Jeffrey and treated him and you reap what you sow and you know why Jeffrey took that in as a man because he was praying to God every night asking for forgiveness from him for his sins and towards Cleopatra, my children and everyone family members as well. When I got out of jail, she told me right in my face God did not forgive me and he was not finish with me all the time and I was not going to accomplish anything. Just like she spoke in my face moving out then coming back saying I shouldn't have told you that. Women you say don't let a man tell you something then come back and do the same thing again, so not as a get back what was Cleopatra doing to Jeffrey her actions speak for itself! Then change and say God is making these things Come back on you. I took it like a man to. She was incredibly angry with me and was loving what she said what God did to me, because she was envious at me. Who would want these things to continually speaking over or to someone or anyone like this in the name of God? Saying that they are saved and a doer of the word only one God calling him different names which he is but still one God! Forgiveness is important when I did not forgive my father when he was young I did not forgive my father for the sins he did to me, and hurt my feelings leaving me and my mother I was incredibly angry with him and did not know what my mother did wrong I thought she was all innocent for everything. I felt everything bad that happen to my father he deserved it, that was not for me to judge or decide but I did it anyway. All of us have done this in our own way not God's way and try to use God on forgiving the person in the way we want to. If Cleopatra would have really forgave Jeffrey, we of still be together right now! I'm also going to say this to every beautiful woman who don't need to dress half naked to get a man's attention, NO don't do that. Our generation today is becoming more and more so busy trying to prove that women can do what men can do that woman are losing their uniqueness. Women you are not created to do everything a man can do. A man can't do everything a woman can do. Jeffrey invested in Cleopatra because she is a good woman. See a woman that is no good is a bill. God, a wife and family is the best thing a husband/man can have. What a lot of women don't realize today is that there loyalty is tested when her husband/man has nothing and trying to find work, and other things when it gets hard when it's a struggle, yes he have you there for that and he feel in his way as a man that he still have to do what he can't trying his best putting his all in because he loves you just that much. Now woman/women/wives you love, provide, teach, guide, and encourage your husband and children but then some of you today be your children friends, let them do what they want to then you don't get on them because you are afraid they might run away because that's all you have or something that's bad experiences you went through with your parents. Some of you women sit there and do drugs and drink with your children a lot of you hold up on their wrong doings and tell others or someone quick about their children but no one bet not tell you anything about your children you raise. It was not like that back in the days that's a cycle came in to. Then you think about the wrong your husband/man has done in the past, and you use the children against him, and it be years ago. Then you think what you think he's thinking and tell him what it is getting him back in that way to you have so many tricks up your sleeve and say you a strong woman you don't play mind games only children that. Instead of perfecting the ways of being a good woman to your husband/man to move on your showing off and out in bad behavior way that you can't even recognize that you think is comfortable, correct, right and in order and you got this. He doesn't have no say so or anything to say after what he has taken you through and done. If you told a bitter woman that's scornful let's not take life for granted, in a blink of an eye anything can change at any time it would be her changing because her mind is not stable so forgive your husband/man. Love one another and love each other with your hearts with God first. Sometimes when a woman is not ready to commit with her attitude you will get curse or fuss out quick. Ladies please don't feel, take or say I have a problem with women, no I do not. I'm saying look what goes on now today in this world we live in with marriages/relationships and women. A real man will sit down with his wife/woman and admit his fears and don't hide anything from her but not tell her things at certain times not to be said or told to a woman. Some things are not to be said! A woman is very curious! If she's not wanting to find out she's thinking about it or insinuating this why she's smart and on top of everything! Cleopatra was giving Jeffrey everything he wanted but Jeffrey guesses he don't deserve nothing at anymore not even her love or respect. Jeffrey, let Cleopatra down but it's a shame she did not do nothing to him Jeffrey express how he felt in all kinds of ways expression of feelings by picking her back up. Trust is something easy to break, easy to lose and something hard to earn back from anyone not just from a woman/women/wife, but don't use the person that's your husband/man/men who earn it and now you want to take them to hell with you because can't truly forgive that's something you have to deal with God! See there won't be no trust at all not even with God or with one another at all I'm not too afraid and speak what a lot of men won't women as well! Women keep your classy-style I give you credit. You have a lot of women say that men are no good, liars and dogs. How many of you are praying for our men and treating as God say they are men of God's and they have done right or wrong, so you think that you are doing good you have swept them under the rug. When they are in the wrong instead of putting them down tell them something encouraging like you will give a homeless man on the street a dollar that's on drugs and some of you will respect that person on the street than your husbands! Do you know I been to a lot of churches and while service is going, I done heard plenty of wives in church argue with the husbands and look at them in a certain way and do anything they say? Jeffrey lied to Cleopatra so because he lied every day that goes on from the time we be together Jeffrey will be a liar he knew just because someone talk about you and say something that don't mean it's true they talked about Jesus, when you have proven yourself right to God and marriage there's no need to be petty like that towards someone you love. Then lied saying she was sorry for lying to me so how to fix it with her is bitterness so let's lie to one another back and forth, then come back again and say I been so hard on you blaming you for everything and she won't curse you out any more, so women I'm taking pain just like you have and my owns looking up at the ceiling about to go crazy walk out in the streets and let a truck run me over and kill me sometimes wanting to commit suicide. Yes, women I know how you feel to be hurt now I see how it feels because I was hurt to. I'm taking blame for men that messed up to women as well because I want not to make the same mistakes over again. It is for God has not given us a spirit of fear & timidity, but of power, love, and self-discipline and of a sound mind, for us all not only men not only women, us all. Women that do this, can take responsibility in yourselves for your own action instead of blaming everything on men especially the black men! Everything is pointed at the black man/men. Women when you can't forgive you are so argumentative find anything and everything to argue something over accept something positive. In fact, you all don't consider it a good time unless you been arguing with someone over something. You argue over petty things even over you on actions, you hide behind of God to do that with (ONLY GOD CAN JUDGE ME)! Then you define yourself by conflict and not by who you are building with holding grudges Cleopatra did this to Jeffrey, and the sad part about it was she was proud about it. She was proud to be loud, argumentative, rude and turn around and that foolishness a strength and the word of God getting back at me. Cleopatra then will say you can't handle me I'm too good and strong of a woman for your ass and call this right, but if Jeffrey was doing the wrong or right what is she doing? Now if the shoe was on the other foot how is it that she more human than I am. When I didn't want to argue with her and walk away, she will say, you can't handle a strong black woman. This isn't just a culture shock this goes by the way women handle conflict and the way the rest of the world does. No matter how petty or inappropriate the issue was she found a reason to fight not fist fight with words, mentally, physically, emotionally, using spiritually in a way she thinks is holy. If she couldn't find she would make one even if she knows she's not going to like what she sees, hear, get out of it. She doesn't care because she got to get her point across. The goal to her is to never come to a resolution, I fucked up, and that's that. Cleopatra goal was to come to an agreement because Jeffrey mess it up too many times that only goes for him, her family, her children and ask Jeffrey do I have something against that, because I got my wall up against you Jeffrey. The goal is to just vent this never, ending, vengeance of hate, anger and rage. Now when was the last time Cleopatra admitted from her heart, she was wrong, sitting down and clothes her mouth? Now that's a controlling thing being throwed in my face so she can use my past as a steppingstone to get away for what she's doing to her husband wrong! But from only her side of the story Jesus knows she's only right, pure, and she has the only good spirit not me. Cleopatra and other women that do this as a hold you do not lack the character to stand down for bad behavior even when it's destroying your family as a team, because something you can't let go and making an excuse forever saying you made me like this, but you can change just like other human beings and sinners as yourselves. Cleopatra continues to fight and arguing with hate in her heart, yield to her and a lot of her arguments was backwards, misguided, and downright petty. Now she's continuing to say I'm putting her down for all the wrong I did to her mostly plus the fault I have to take of her doing to me. She is never ever wrong and would tell me until this day all what I took her through, and no one understand what she been and went through as a woman and only a woman can feel and understand where she's coming from! You know she don't even feel that she put me down and most women will say for all the wrong I had done wrong who would blame her. Probably all women will say it I know what I'm writing on based on a true story of what I went through men go through as well. The solution is to be quiet, nice, virtuous, humble, gentle, communicating, conversations with love period. Close your mouth when speaking at the wrong time when you shouldn't have vice versa for the man as well see I'm being fair not on let's reel women in or men. If you spend more time listen and hearing your husband/man out instead of battling with him how Is that going to get you anywhere, as a woman/wife he wants around him. Then talking to him you will peep game not looking for game to be ran on you. Isn't chess, checkers, football, basketball, hockey, ping pong are games? So, if you don't play with your team mate together you will lose then let the other side win. See God is the ALMIGHTY, THE ALPHA AND OMEGA then the husband is the manager, the wife is the coach the children are the players so let's go out coming in and win. This man right here, myself Jeffrey was not telling Cleopatra (THE WOMAN) the instructor what he wanted her to do when Jeffrey got saved and became a Christian 6 years ago doing good but to her and other women will say and feel SHIT what we been through with you all ass that isn't nothing, because she/her/the woman/women/wives might be feeling or going through something else, and I thought it was only men hold things inside and women tell them baby you can't walk around all your life holding in what your father or mother, family, someone did to you, you have to forgive so you can move on with your life. This is nothing against women this what's going today what he has seen, experience, saw others go through. Jeffrey was telling Cleopatra what he expected from her as a woman she never asked or listen. So, if she never asked or listen or hears me out, I was out voted. Cleopatra was in my heart but Jeffrey was not in heart she will scream and say you is in my damn heart you don't know what's in my fucking heart, now what women or someone will say she loves you she was just mad at the time, so let's say Jeffrey called her a bitch or told her I don't love you any more, said to her that's why Jeffrey slept on you or I'm going back to that woman, will the volcano start to explode? Will I get to say I love her? but it was just that I was mad at the time. No, I will be a no-good ass husband that don't know how to treat a woman/women/wife I don't even know why she got married to someone like me! Women told me I was not take the blame for everything that's easy to say when you're living with that person, and I will tell you that's easier said than done and I got that from a WOMAN! Cleopatra has so much built up inside her she was too busy being a hate monger and a spoiled selfish brat. Black man/men/husbands in general are tired of it everyone has their rights women are the law and power, so you don't feel men have there's. Now you don't feel like men don't get pushed around or away? Women lets us know wives submit to your husbands as to the Lord as well let the wife see she respects her husband. I know a lot of women will say you don't know what the hell he took me through, and I put up with his ass with, SO YOUR JUST INVISABLE! We know about his no-good self, let's get him! So, what's your penalties and consequences? I'm not speaking bad or wishing nothing no one deserve to be treated unfairly and no one has the right to blame someone for everything and leave the other person out there all by themselves. Cleopatra said Jeffrey cheated, lied, he used her, Jeffrey hustled her he did everything there was, but the Lord say to do so, why should Jeffrey say sorry to tell you. When I get right the relationship will go nowhere, because it still takes God and the two to become one, not just the man only getting it right then it's all good fine and dandy with him and God. Now what happens women when you don't want to accept him after you have forgiven him? Now you have problems after problems to deal with that you can't solve, because you your letting the wrong person deal with your scared wounded heart you can't heal and you think it's you doing all the work, that's another problem right there you be driving yourself crazy trying to love your husband thinking going to run out there after another woman or someone else blowing your own mind when you are the one not letting GOD handle the problem of your inside of a peace of mind, heart, body and soul! Cleopatra will tell Jeffrey in my face several times over again that he created all this mess. So, if God walked up to Cleopatra and say stop forgive and move on, she will say ok. Don't God say go to your brother's and sister's ask for forgiveness when you have sinned towards one another? A lot of peoples will say we'll you know how peoples is you can't make no one forgive you, and this is true this is how they hearts are because they will scream and yell and you saying you want me, you, us to forgive just like that I did not say that, and it can be years down the road it doesn't me the person sometimes it could be yourself! So why you can't listen to your partner? Cleopatra responded well to negativity she was miserable like her mother Pam the cycle was transforming bad. She will tell me with her hand on her hip pointing her finger in my face saying with her provoking what you going to hit me? Then say for number 1 you are not GOD, 2 you deserve what's coming to you and for what's happening to you right now you haven't seen anything yet, 3 when I get ready, when I say so and I feel and choose how do to so I will when I get good and damn ready to. So, Cleopatra told on herself right then when she gets ready being selfish, so women being this way you will not bring on my more hell and bitterness? Women and men are equal it's not all about you women. You don't suppose to get caught up on he said she said women not even in your own minds, because you can make up some he says she say thought up of your own in that mind of yours that you have by listening things in your mind that can be negativity we all think bad things at times. It just a man can't tell a woman about her mind she just knows she has a mind of her own! See a woman mind be ticking and she will think until or already have there what to say out her mouth she knows her words could mean something of love and at the same time be dangerously challenging, walking away works until sometime of point because when you arrive back its way she brings in something else up in to get what she needs to say, want and to find out. She's not satisfied because she will dig up more it does not have to be always wrong let's just call it curious! Like I was with my sister one day in the hospital and my fiancé was there, but she arrives late, and did not call no one to let us no she had an appointment and was dead wrong making excuse after excuse and finally said OK both of you I'm sorry. Then when my sister walked away and said I'm going to the restroom I will be back. Then my fiancé walked over to me laid by myside and ask slowly, SO WHAT WAS THE CONVERSATION ABOUT? See my fiancé was in her insecure factor on her own about my sister in her own actions it was no talking behind no one backs it was emergency for health reasons and concerns. A woman doesn't have to be insecure just for sex, no it can be life, what she has been taken through, took someone through, can't admit to her wrong doings, holding on, past rape of abuse domestic violence and what parents have taken them through, could not succeed to their goals in life that held them back it can be plenty of things even forgiving themselves. Anyways just that fast I seen how my fiancé reacted off my own sister every woman not the same every woman has had they days times experience off insecurities. When you look at someone and see everything is wrong about this person when I see them there's one positive thing to say. So just ask yourself what is good to do with or for this person? Then if you say you can't pray for them or with them is there not something wrong with your spirit and soul? Because did send me, you, us to do his duty if you don't choose to do so then you back up yourself and blessings and say someone is speaking bad upon you. God is telling you what to do and sending others to tell you like he send others to the peoples to come tell you and me as well and using me to tell others, so God uses us all. Women sit down and hold your husband hands at times he needs this stop telling him or them if it were not only for us women you don't know what men that would do nonsense there's only one person gets all that glory and that's God! Just like a marriage together as one saying, doing if it were not for God what would they be. Women don't worry yourself or your husband this does not means I'm controlling, lesser, lower than a woman or I'm telling women they are just for listening to their husbands and don't worry them or themselves! Your equal and this is the right thing to do in God's way! It was said you submit to one another in the fear of CHRIST. Husbands, submit to your wives, submit to your husbands. Respect your husband like you will do the Lord, not saying to your husbands well the Lord

will not do us no wrong being angry, bitter, and throwing in his face with vengeance the Lord will do you no wrong instead of hugging with tears from God with joy of praise. You both have done God wrong and your marriages. Do you both have God and moving forward, or do you have one do what I say and the other do whatever or when you get ready this is confusion and God is nowhere in that. Women when you say you did nothing wrong! Your lying guilty and wrong because I don't know one marriage that is perfect! God is in agreements, facts that goes according to his word and doing not but and or if! God says respect and do each other like you do him. Jeffrey told Cleopatra (THE WOMAN) respect him as you will do the Lord don't worship Jeffrey only worship the word of God I speak and teach she will say I can't because you cheated on me and dogged me out so I can't. Do you see this women speak into existences what you say what your husband is and treat him as continually, constantly, there's no love nowhere in that it's pushing him in the streets away from you he's uncomfortable this is why he get from around you and you will say, I don't care look at what you did to me or he will come back it be psychology, mentally, physically with blows you can't see coming and can't even imagine. I have seen women break up with their husbands and say I'm sorry for the way I talked to you, treated you and put you down after the divorce it had to take them to break up and divorce so one thing comes in this world of life is a man is missing out because he knows when he got a good thing until it's gone. Women don't respect your husbands on the way of the past what you been through, or your mother's way or experience talking with you, or what she been through with her marriage now she's divorced, or the way your friends respect their spouses, not from by watching T.V., movies, respect in the way God say. Why should I? I heard a lot of women say this, because says so just like when or if you cheated, lied, sinned, provoked him, falsely accused him, ignored him, disrespected him, control him because you got your get back and had to have get your way, used him it doesn't have to be for money only it can be anything like sex when you feel like it. See what a husband/man needs and wants from a woman is GOD WHICH IS LOVE AND RESPECT. Men gravitate to the place where they get honor and respect. They run from any place where they see trouble or disrespect this don't make him no coward this makes him a stronger man to become a better man to believe in himself, just like great things about you women right? So, it's about God and us Jesus walked with everyone. What does this mean for women? How do you honor your husband? If he does fail, fall or mess up sometimes he's imperfect not most of the time because you love him, he makes mistakes at times. God knows, he knows this you do as well. A lot of marriages fell because women try to change their husbands from making mistakes and what they want them to be pressure them too much and tell them what to do. That's the wrong approach. You certainly don't want to allow self-destructive behavior. When necessary you should allow him to make a mistake. For men, some lessons are learned than failure. Please let God be the enforcer for your husband not God holding on to you to get back at your husbands. Husband and wives are equals. This means you can say whatever you want to say, no. You can comfort your husband when necessary: Love, I don't agree with that. That's wrong because a woman wants all her man attention, security and love. Once you have confronted him, leave it in God's only person is worthy is God, so why are you saying you did not do nothing wrong? It was all his fault man/men/husbands. Please stop focusing on the past because it would only back to the start line starting all over again when you have a backup plain with the devil skeletons and bones, black, dirt, mud, and darkness. Then you won't care thinking it's 50/50 you got pay back when you want it to be finish and stop but spirit you have inside is not prayed up and your mind is saying different then it goes back and forth. First thing is he did it to you, he should have never done what he did, and we won't be in this situation I feel that and respect that but for how long will you have him under your command until? You can't answer that yourself because you are angry and unforgiving! God is first, marriage as one husband and wife and things come in communication one, spirit one, children all one, personal growth one, more romance one, making loved one, Intimacy, Spiritual growth. Meet your wife needs Jeffrey did for Cleopatra when he got saved and was her partner, your woman supposed to meet your needs as well. I put in the love and security. Who is sensitive and understand and is emotional Jeffrey was too emotional more than a woman most of the time to Cleopatra even she said that to him without respect and love I'm glad there's a God that do? My heart soft more and lovable as well as praying. Then I wanted us to communicate I couldn't do it all by myself God was first I needed her, I wanted her help she loved unforgiveness so much that she would not genuinely love me all over again. It was I talk too much. My leadership was not right because I messed up. Now I'm going to speak on when women break up their marriage and homes with bitterness and hate, saying making me a stronger woman leaving this man and this marriage made me feel better when at times she's leaving when her soul, spirit is not right. Do you have a clean heart? Before you divorce your husband or after was you still mentally, wickedly with spirits that you thought was Godly but was sarcastically fun, but you did not have no heart to give love. Grudges, hate, when you were in your marriage and then got a divorce. Do you know some marriages/relationships are still going through this? Husband and wives are debating on which sin is worse than the other now in these days and times instead of forgiving one another and praying. God don't say things like this for marriages to go back and forth. Man and woman are saying and doing this then you have these women now today want rich men for their money or a rich husband. We charge them that are rich in this world, that they are not high minded, nor trust in uncertain riches, but in the living God, who give us richly all things to enjoy. That they do good, that they be rich in good works, ready to distribute, willing to communicate; laying up instore for themselves a good foundation against the time to come, that they may lay hold on eternal life. It's not your job to bring about change women. DON'T NAG, don't become aggressive or fearful. Instead, pray for your husband and rely on God to change his heart and mind, pray with him too. That's what it means to have faith. You rely on the holy spirit to enforce change now how you want it your way or the highway. Honor where you want your husband to be not where he is now! HELLO. He will rise to God and your level of honor. Men will do anything for honor and will become their fullest, healthiest selves when it comes their way, by giving him undeserved honor, you always speak positivity into your husband. When Jeffrey spoke it's too late because Cleopatra let him know in my face, she shouldn't have never taken Jeffrey back no matter what he said, see the devil had her blind where she sees things her way where she can't wake up because the evil spirits have her bound in control. Always think and see what you first saw in your husband because you would do because you would want this for yourself as a human being, love, and a Christian. Think about things that first attracted you to him. Then honor him at that level and help him rise to it. Cover his faults and focus on his strength. When Jeffrey and Cleopatra were partners, and he took each other for granted on somethings and focus on bad things about each other at times instead of God. That's because the devil wants us to pay attention to the worse qualities in our spouse. God wants us to think about our spouse's best qualities. That's why prayer is such a critical discipline for husband and wife. When need to remind ourselves everyday about the good things our spouses do. When we remember these, we realize that the good out weights the bad. If honor and respect is a greatest man needs, does he receive these from you? This is the Bible call for you as a wife. Respect your husband in the same way you would respect Jesus Christ! I messed up my leadership before I got into the relationship, I can be a man and say that. Do you truly forgive? Or you just say it and don't mean or do it? Holding inside all kinds of things that kills your own inner self and spirits. All marriages and relationships have bad times, bad days and failures. The woman/wife/wives will say you betrayed me, this marriage and children first most of the time it's hate and vengeance, not how can we fix this will tell you fast God was not with you when you were cheating so God is not and will never be with you. It's no I don't want to hear it it's over! It's not most of the time how we going to leave it in God's hand and when I mean deal with it I did! Then the woman comes in and say but you don't understand she even tell God this, depending on the woman because every woman is not the same. A lot of women can't let go and let God on forgiveness it either be divorce or break up something from the past by not letting things go! It was gone out of Cleopatra's mind, soul, spirit, tongue, skin, chills all over your body even the sweat. I know it was hard for women to forgive, can you really let go of all the negativity of bad feelings, emotions, that's negative about your husband? Especially his misdeeds not seeking revenge towards him all the time holding a grudge, or are you viewing him as good God's love in truth, life, and light with you both or you just going to keep fussing and cursing him out? So, women when you don't forgive you start pushing your husband/man away this starts distance between one another. Cleopatra (THE WOMAN) said she did not care leave her alone. It started more hate, anger than it starts hurtful negative impact or your health. Then you are the woman to tell your husband/man any place, day and time about how he she should and the way he should take care of himself but if he tells you just one thing he can't lose that privilege which has ran out already if you say so! Then the woman doesn't see no God she becomes bitter as the God with her wand in her hand on her broom stick as the witch she has her on book of words of God to use towards you and change up in her! A woman will make an excuse to get away with her wrongs and add your pass wrongs on it for her to get off and you can't tell her anything about her health problems. She's the nurse, doctor and the back up! Women you make forgive a hard thing to do not because of him all the time it's the way how God says to forgive. It's a way how you and the husband supposed to do things not just the husband because he's the leader that don't mean he does not need help and do everything by himself. Women when you express yourself after the forgiveness take a good look at yourself and make sure that you sure this is what God is telling you what to do not your mind saying one thing and your heart saying the next. How is your behavior? Are you looking at yourself? No! Your just too busy watching your husband next move and running your mouth. Your mouth can get you in something that you can't get out of as well ladies, things like he's going to do it again saying that woman, that bitch, you, her, she did it, you did it, you! Where is God? A lot of woman gives the devil the power and glory and say God was not there when he cheated so he's not a Godly man a look at the husbands and see the devil! God is nowhere if don't tell the truth or forgiving and being honest with God, yourself and your husband with true feelings, they are likely to be resurface making forgiveness difficult to do. How are you going to express something to your husband/man by attacking? Then saying it's too late but you chose to take him back with your face down whiles he's trying to do his best, no what you really need to be saying is that you are late because your guilty. You are not going to admit your wrongs or created any of these things in this relationship. Cleopatra always focuses on what Jeffrey did, and every time came out with negativity out her mouth, so it was in her soul, mouth, heart, mind, body and spirit to think this about me. Instead of her coming to pray with me focusing on how God want us to be and feel together explaining how hurt, anger, disappointment with both is and not bring up how foolish I was. I'm not going to tell you my wrongs because she always brought up how disrespectful and a fuck up, I was. Everything was my fault, so Cleopatra was worthy right? She will say I'm not saying that then come right back and change and said I don't mean that then she does. When I say everything was my fault, I mean it. When she wanted to talk, she was always special and holy and had the spirit on her side even with the bishop etc. When Jeffrey speaks, he got cursed out, when I'm quiet then Cleopatra comes back to Jeffrey and say she's sorry, wrong, and forgive her. How long did that last getting back until this day with I'm a coward and take the fault for everything like a man. When Jeffrey expresses his emotions, Jeffrey act like a woman as Cleopatra said plenty of times. Tell me don't every relationship on both sides man and woman express themselves in their emotions? I took ownership for what I had done as well as Jeffrey took the blame for Cleopatra's wrong and everything! The only way it would have been right if Cleopatra would have own up to her wrongs to and we would have been on one accord with God! She did not see I agree with her 60/40 first I gave 100 I had to because I messed up bad, I gave her all the credit, how much do a woman want? When it supposed to be 100/00 50/50, she never agreed with me after forgiving me because she said all the pain and hurt, I did to her. I was never giving anytime, respect or credit to accept my point of view of seeing things God's way and my point of view fairly it was all about only her. It helps to hear, do, feel, and say I want to make it work, I love you, let's pray, I'm sorry, best of all let's give it to the Lord. This was not said, mostly she brought the past back up for making excuses why she did not want to make it work and that was my fault to. The way she talks to me putting me down and her actions, didn't even want to touch, kiss, hold or hug me until she was ready to put the black heals on or wanted sweet dick Charlie! Cleopatra felt comfortable because she was all for herself, her feelings, what she wants and can get and did use us together because I deserve the get back and take it like a man! Jeffrey asks Cleopatra to please stop when he walked up to her she said and what you're going to do hit me? After Cleopatra said I forgive you after calming down from being so angry, envy, and let's move on I will say are you sure and for real this time? She said yes and I said OK I believe you and we kiss! Now did she break my heart, trust and God's vows on marriage with in herself and in front of our children? YES! BY GOD, MYSELF as well and much towards OUR CHILDREN because they were following her cycle like her mother's cycle she's following now. Now by her words and what women been through and I took her through hell no I'm wrong forever it was and will be how could I do this to a good woman not looking at what I have changed into be good! So, what all the sorry was for then? Jeffrey knows he got this lady just like Jeffrey kept saying sorry to her so there's no excuse for him to get out of my wrongs that Jeffrey was forgiving for that God is not making him pay for but from Cleopatra (THE WOMAN)! Cleopatra knew she was dead wrong she knew she was guilty but did not and will not confess and admit to it she's just being a woman, right? Now I say this not to put her down I say this to understand where I'm coming from her license was messed up she don't have a car she has a sr22, she lost her apartment that she told me cold hearted sitting on the porch in my face that I thought she could not get her own place and I did. This all happen when I wasn't in her life, and she moved out living with her children and had to get another job. This is a strong black woman that says she don't need no man. Now women will say it's dead wrong that I'm talking about her, she's got her mother she does not need me women please learn something from this. What I'm saying God watches us all and see what we all do wrong so we both mess up in our relationship and God made us both pay not Cleopatra she lost everything because Jeffrey even her mom throwing her out was my fault and things on her job, but you know something women she did not listen to me when Jeffrey told her she came after the fact and then said you was right! So, don't this sound like a woman like you all say certain things a man be hardheaded on. When a husband or wife is down the other supposed to wake the other up! My job wasn't enough money for Cleopatra she did not want my little paycheck she will give it right back with pride we are not married, and Jeffrey still helped her after we broke-up and Jeffrey will never say he don't need her help, yes Jeffrey does, and any one God will use and bring. I will never say I don't need anything from anybody because you don't when you will need someone help! I'm going to tell you something this lady told me one day. Her and her husband had a car. The car broke down, so they needed me for a car to get around in. I could have been like that husband was rude, nasty, mean and a get back like he was with his car, but I didn't and the excuse for people are everyone don't have a heart and do the same thing as you. My car got into an accident and the husband and wife got a brand-new car. The husband was angry, because he didn't have a car and how others was treating him and his wife when they needed a ride, I helped, but it wasn't enough for him as a man, but I did my part. So, when my car got into an accident he said no I couldn't ride in his car, but his wife came to me and said when I had my head held down she apologize for her husband not giving you a ride, because Lord knows I don't know when I will need someone. If you're moving on and forgiving don't do it out of hate or anger it's not forgiveness. So, I'm teaching and saying that when you get hurt and then you forgive and don't mean it you have not put them in harm way or let it go away with both parties really, because you both need to regain control over the situation not just the man/men only women. If you are not ready to trust your man or husband or wife let them know, because you will be cheating. You will be lying not sexually or adultery you be lying about trust to start over again to build something that you both promise on to love forever. Forgiveness that Cleopatra (THE WOMAN) could see then was blind open her eyes then closed them all, because of me will Jeffrey be right and said she had every right to blame him for everything. She played no part. Forgiveness works when see that your husband is good now and his heart is clean is yours now to of forgiveness as the woman as your job on your side there's two sides. If you always judge him every day all the time and nag him, if you personalize the problem, that is you view your husband in a negative light, rather than viewing his actions, positively, forgiveness will be hard to come by. Everyone sins, makes mistakes, NO ONE IS PERFECT. Even Christian or whatever God religion or God you worship caring, loving people do hurtful things to. Women say you just want me to forgive you just like that overnight, NO! I didn't say that because it's not easy it takes time don't do it. If you not ready and don't do something you don't mean to do if you truly ready. If you both being 100/100, 50/50 forgiveness is the right thing to do and very appropriate response. This is more than a value because I know when I lost something good. A woman that was the best teacher in the world and taught me things that no one could. She stayed on me that was good I wish she can say the same about me I am the shit only in her eyes. After she lied about forgiving me, she only put her own needs ahead of mines. She didn't look at what our relationship was worth saving she looked at I shouldn't take you back in front of her children back and forth saying it sinning. Then say forgive me I'm sorry for saying that then when I got tired I will say stop because you don't mean it if you wouldn't bring all these things back up that's in the past, you're not being honest when you can't forgive. Your unforgiveness pushes your partner away. Two married people working together can be one because they are sharing change is never easy for anyone we fight hard to hold on to a marriage. You can learn something now the longer you don't change the more you dig your grave and it be hard for you to make a change period. It's all about each other in the relationship not the woman or the man. I walked away plenty of times crying of pain and trouble. Jeffrey took Cleopatra (THE WOMAN) through for peace of mind and calm down even more, even my soul, spirit and thinking. Especially my lustful flesh with the devil telling me in my ear go find another woman you don't need that she puts you down, your better than that. When I fell, I got back up I went to church for prayer, got on my knees and cried while praying. I asked God to forgive me she said I treated her like shit, so karma came back on me, but one thing I'm not going to do is take the blame for everything when I know I tried my best. Jeffrey knew honesty was Cleopatra's best policy. She was willing to compromise in the relationship. She was open minded and ambitious as well goal driven, all the time she was crazy as hell but that's what I love she was my crazy as hell! I sat back and look at the outside of our relationship. When she was to herself, she had a life outside of her own. She's a woman! This one of the reasons why I was in a relationship with her I fell in love first plenty of other reasons as well and I was right with God the first witness, myself, the bishop and his wife but not Cleopatra because she said Jeffrey would change then say he won't never change and not believe in Jeffrey talk is cheap when there's no action. When she got angry, and she said she didn't do things that she didn't mean God can forgive for her sins and they are gone away but mines are not and will never be forgotten! My sins were worse than hers like she said and felt feel only her on this, right women? You all feel where she's coming from and understand her point of view knowing only what she been through because you are all women you been there or been through worse with a husband/man because you all are women, and the men are left out stop blaming men for everything. I'm writing this book based on experience from what I been through in the past relationships rights and wrongs and women have giving facts opinions, life, from men and what I have grew up seeing as a man not only what I brought on myself but what I learn from my good and bad. Jeffrey learned more stops being a child and he was taught from Cleopatra from the advice she has given she did not only do the teaching Jeffrey did to. A lot of women feel like a lot of these men are hardheaded and there not. So, you don't listen? Then make bad mistakes I know a lot of you will say we did not say that we just know how to make better decision and think right than men and make better choices. Cleopatra is the instructor they educated her own different things in college, and she learn things on her own but how she sees things and know for a fact she knows everything. Now marriage you suppose to serve one another now don't let the woman be scornful, bitter she will make an excuse for her madness, anger and wrongs at times it will be all the man faults. You have women that will go out, mess up, cheat, and a man won't know a woman never stops thinking and the man won't know what's going on she will have more game than the man then tells him for her actions that she learns from the best him. Don't make an excuse for a woman, because what she's been through all her life forget the man, he deserves it right or wrong, right women? Depending on what type of woman/ women/wife she is. Please stop making excuses for women, because women are different last time, I check the holy spirit is different and perfect is God! Sorry women men don't get driven crazy only you, now who said that? Women, poets, writers, people trying to get points to take a side one sided. I don't think so I'm not jealous women or mad at what they are doing some things they have twisted that don't go right by God and anything to tell you what you want to hear. Cleopatra did not forgive Jeffrey from her heart. What are you going to say women because I broke her heart, so why she can't forgive me when she gets ready to see that backs it up and come back with it's being done back to me what I did to her so accept it like a man I now God is not confused man and woman is? We feel the women pain. She needed an excuse because me and men been doing this shit for years because all men are the same and made an excuse when you get caught in your shit. God is not not sleep only on men ladies especially when you be so bitter no, he sees everything on us all on everything I'm judging me first. I even did a good thing, so are women going to say what do you want, you were already supposed to have your shit together, do you want an award, credit, a trophy, it's not over it just started. Jeffrey put himself in a woman's place Jeffrey thought about and felt her pain, the things she wants back in return with entrance because it does take a lot to gain back a woman trust, respect, and love back that's why Jeffrey stood back walked away from my baby Cleopatra and went to God. Jeffrey also went to different Bishops, Pastors, counselors and churches they are witnesses she did not care but one thing that did make Jeffrey feel good was if no cared God did and still rewarded him and Jeffrey say that from the heart with love not to put Cleopatra under the bus or down. You cannot reason with a scornful bitter woman her way is never wrong and always right because she changes up so much. She wants her cake and eat it to not just a man because a woman wants her needs and wants to depend on what they are and the time she has HER WAYS TO! Sometimes you can't live in a glass house and throw stones because the hurt in the heart that you can't let God handle to give back to someone that wounded you it's best not to go back to them if you can't handle the test you're fooling yourself. Women you will say no I fooled myself of coming or going back off your own tongue and word and do otherwise. Cleopatra told herself forgive him, no don't forgive, give him another chance, no. Don't these spirits do this woman? They do the same to men when it's time for him when he can't keep his dick in his pants, and he still goes out to cheat. Now if Cleopatra's daughter Anita told her she bringing Jeffrey down and she got to forgive Jeffrey what does that tells you? Some or most women will say her daughter can't tell her what to do she's the mother she raised her that does not mean she does not know how her mother is feeling. Now I get it women when I was like that once or lots of times but where does a stop and ending comes because if we use it back and forth against one another we are playing with the devil and trapping ourselves and getting what out of it? NOTHING! So, women gone head be my guess if you are grown and that's your choice to go out that's a bad reputation for your children, daughter, son on how to handle their marriage. Will it be one way when the man messes up, it's him watch out blaming him for everything because he will cheat first because he's a man that's what men do look what your mother been through. Women it's not only cheating its other things in marriages that will break it up only if you allow it and don't have God that's important it's a responsibility a job God, spiritually, mentally, physically IS THERE A GIVE OR TAKE POINT? Meaning between the husband and wife, WHERE IS THE BALANCE? Is it only for women of what hurt pain and suffering they been through? I know we praise the same God! Women you say, think, do, and know if it's too hot then get the hell out of your kitchen get and stay out your lane if you can't handle it. Well as you say heated up and angry with your strong powerful attitude MY KITCHEN. So, women now for you with the shoe on the other side on the man foot when the kitchen get hot can you stand their heat! In a relationship woman/women/wife can you live a balance relationship with your man/husband. See the words that comes out of a scornful woman's mouth that scorn other's things like, MY CHILD, MY CHILDREN they are going with me, when I leave. Then your man is no good he's shits, and no good for nothing, then he's just like every or any other man. In this world that we live in we all the same in GOD EYES in ways I can't even explain not saying do each other any kind of way. A POSITIVE AFFIRMATION doesn't get so angry that you, me, or we sin. Also it says not the sun go down upon your wrath. Women is not only hurt when she lay down on her pillow to sleep. Everyone has problems not only the women. If you are a woman that STAYS bitter, wrath, anger, clamor, evil speaking, not kind, rude, unforgiving, what's the different to God? Tell me please! Now to women this will be different in their way, how they will put it and see it. Now I'm going to speak on the woman from the 50's, 60's, 70's, 80's, how today a lot of them new today coming up their feminism has changed back in them days. Women would have stayed with a man that's a hardworking and the same age as him or older. A real man that will say not just jump in bed will say I want to meet your parents respect himself, her, and family as well and introduce her to his family. These women stayed to themselves did not talk too much mind their business and stayed out of people's business. They did not look for fights, nag, arguing, drama, they were women with class who move forward. These women had clear purposes of understanding a woman that's 69 years old will not get with a 20-year-old man in those times. They're doing all kinds of things today. Everyone is not the same but back in them times it is today a lot of people have changed. Now Cleopatra would say I did sin but not like how you did me wrong and Jeffrey cheated she did nothing! It is better to live in a dessert land than with a quarrelsome and fretful woman. A good wife is the grown away from her husband but she that brings shame is like rottenness in his bones. It is better to live in the corner of the house top than with a brawling woman in a wide house. The husband should give to his wife conjugal rights, and like wise to her husband. VICE VERSA not get back the world the devil and false teachers and us doing what we want to and then say in our own way. For the wife does not have authority over her own body, but the husband does. Likewise, the husband does not have authority over his own body, but the wife does. Do not deprive one another, except perhaps by agreement for a limited time that you may devote yourselves to prayer but then come together again so that Satan may not tempt you because of your lack of self-control. Do you know Cleopatra didn't pray with Jeffrey not one time? Women I'm confronting you and standing and Cleopatra it's what Jeffrey did only. My fault only so Jeffrey could not make Cleopatra pray with him! God said this on our vows or did she because when we got married, she said I bring God only in and leave the past behind. Now the works of the flesh are evident sexual immorality, impurity, sensuality, idolatry, vengeance, sorcery, enmity, strife, jealous, hate, fits of anger, rivalries, dissensions, divisions, envy, drunkenness, orgies, and things like these. I warned you as I warned you before, that those who do such things will not inherit the kingdom of God. The women said it was only idolatry. They will say don't focus on your wife or husband and both will be confused because they will be on one another and listening to what other peoples are saying. Instead of getting with God to deal with the problem. As a man I was in sexual immorality, was in foolish talking, abusive, filthy, dirty and nasty but God forgave me! Jeffrey repented and changed Cleopatra said once a dog always a dog treats him the same way. Thank God there for me to give me another chance Jeffrey just wish he can say Cleopatra did the same thing from her heart if only she had peace of it to give. Let my joy be complete by being of the same mind, having the same love being in full accord of one mind! Behold the woman meets him, dress as a prostitute, willy of heart. She is loud and wayward her feet do not stay home. I got to work on this. The woman folly is loud she is seductive and knows nothing and Lord knows a scornful that blames her husband for everything is wrong there's no excuse for him just like there's none for her! I turn better to women because I was hurt, angry, upset, and in pain when I got and learn what love really is and was, so I put myself in her shoes. Women shoes got in the ring and took the knockout for 6 years back and forth and women will say that's not nothing she should of taking you through more on how you did her we were not there, so we got to hear her side. Now witnesses saw me sleep on the streets and in my car Cleopatra said that's you who choose to sleep on the streets but she to blind to see and know why God says it is good to sleep on the house top of your house in the corner instead of in the house with a brawling woman. When I got away and even men, family members, picked at me. My brother Paul when he got married, he came to me with open arms about his wife and stepchildren the way he was getting treated and respected and talked to from his pass sins his wife was making him pay for force and pushed on him. This goes for anyone it is not good or a blessing to sleep around on your husband or wife and falsely accuse someone of something they have not done at or bring up there pass and use the false of the old person they use to be and what they have become now that is so cruel! It's just liked a man or woman who goes to jail or prison they do 10 years and get falsely accused of the same thing buy getting put down and treated wrong by peoples, jobs, and when they really have changed it's hardly any love, respect or chance it's not easy! Then change the system up even more when they get ready it's like the woman pressing charges, dropping charges, bringing them back up and opening old cases on her husband/man. The women that's doing this don't know the system have them program. Then you have people speaking things to these peoples that don't hear them out and say you want someone to feel sorry for you. You have men that teach and tell women that the catering is to be only for them however that's not true it's for both of you. The man needs to be catered to as well, they address a general purpose, reason or feeling to back up women the mouth of the heart confessing what you say women you want a man of God, men you want a woman of faith. Jeffrey looked at Cleopatra why we are not praying together? Because she doubted me all the time by listening to the false prophet and family members was telling her. When I said baby lets pray together she would say you can't make me pray if I don't want to and in counseling Jeffrey told the bishop that Cleopatra is not praying with him instead of him praying for us to pray he told me in front of her you can't make her pray if she doesn't want to but got on Jeffrey to always to pray for Cleopatra and with her. God want 2 people in committed relationship to pray as one. A believer or not still pray. Cleopatra will say right in front of the Bishop and at home you can't make me pray. Then tell me at home why did you take me back then I will leave. Is that not a sin on our relationship and giving up on God? Cleopatra and some women will say don't talk about God now and we just came from church but tell their husband/man quick you just got out of church and you cursing and acting out in that way and you a Christian. Women stop using an excuse of only God can judge you screaming out in your husband face because why you did not leave then it was not all on him, you thought of your ways you just could not come out and admit to them you were guilty but did not feel that way in front of your husband. Everything is not taken for advantage forever women when you are in fear and afraid to let your wall down you're not the only woman has been betrayed by their husband so get up and give the glory back to God and leave it! When Jeffrey was saved and hurting Lord knows I am now, because Jeffrey's misses Cleopatra, she said you want to be a man of God, but you're playing then come right back and say I'm sorry! You can't satisfy a woman, but you can compromise with her, most with are content with it. They are verbal at times. Jeffrey always wanted to sit down with Cleopatra and have the deepest affections for an intellection conversation. The time and ability to sit there and just talk about anything love, her, children, forgiving, but all she says and argued about was me fucking up and the bad I did. I found part of her in me even when she was not perfect and sin, I ask her what she saw in me. Even thou I'm divorce I still make a phone call to her and still make a conversation send love letters to my heart from her helping her and her children telling her I love her and them and she is a gift. Her reply to me is still I'm a fuck up, she still got to tell me this and that I'm still the same way and not in love or don't love me anymore and I'm trying to see if she has a man now! I'm not even thinking those things I'm a real man I'm thinking about the treasure I lost and not of my mistakes hers as well. I lost every privilege as she says come on now being married 7 years and together 14, divorce for 1 year and make love with one another off and on I was just a benefit. Not to Cleopatra she is never a heart breaker and a Christian woman that don't do no wrong until she says she does! She's asking for needs and it helps with one another see the bullshit women it is time for me to say stop acting like children and be real women and grow up. A real woman looks good first for God than herself, her husband, and her appearance is not doing it for attention that comes automatically because she's beautiful she's a woman. She's doing it for herself, she's beyond beautiful and looks good all the time. A husband does not to all the word all the time. The husband and wife take turns and being together strong for each other in the moments when the other one feels weak. Certain people have said a taught it only to the husband. Jeffrey learned from Cleopatra she said she did not learn one fucking thing from him but call Jeffrey up and say are you still doing the grants to help people, because my daughter needs one for her business to open a store. Cleopatra is the woman she knows it all and you can't tell her anything. Kindness don't cost nothing women help your man when they down, don't put your foot on his neck when he's trying to get up. Another thing is don't be bitter, angry and hateful that you feel that what you did not forgive him for after years has gone by you use that in every which way you can. He is doing great but not the hold world, so he wants to control your mind, life, feelings, and emotions is that how your thinking? You women that's bitter, angry or playing mind games even if your man is there with you he's not because you

don't see no trust, love, relationship all you see is self and a dog by you until you change your mind and say oh time to fuck lovable husband. Women if you have been used and you have taken your husband/man back and forgiving him, witness and stated with God present and say you have the Lord then years have passed you by some women don't even wait for years they take charge soon as they leave church in the car, so why would you bring up something that's the past? Why would you bring up something that's dead and gone and won't let you last you remember what I was telling you women about dead skeleton bones? Well, some of you be walking around in your house with those spirits as the walking dead sweethearts your husbands just don't sin and bring spirits home to you, your spirits rub off on him as well don't think your worthy! Now women when a man wants to explain himself when he's right you don't want to understand for what he's done from the past like you say THERE IS NO UNDERSTANDING! But you want him to understand you in everywhere there is because a woman is strange, and your ways will never be known. Women being ungrateful, complaining about the things happen years ago instead of being thankful for what God gave you back because you prayed and asked for you just did not know how to deal with it in your cycle of past things not being taught just like you said that man he could not let go and work on of his cycles see fair we all have something behind us to fix! Moving forward on the good thousands of things God put into your husband you're looking at the negative things these women that have bad attitudes I'm going to tell you something you all are just like cars that have flat tires if don't change it won't never go anywhere. Now when Jeffrey was quiet did Cleopatra care at times it was important because when Jeffrey did not say anything this kept her wondering, thinking, she could not take that because Jeffrey was not giving her the time of day to feed off her negativity she got real deeply curious that pissed her off so when Jeffrey talk too much or was quiet Jeffrey was going to get it either way! The excuse was I deserve to get treated wrong when I did right because I fucked up too much to ever get another chance. It was a lot of times when I did not speak, and she said go do something shit and curse me out without caring saying I don't care no more! Then women will say I want to hear her side and how she feels. Now after she says we are starting over and dogs me out not by cheating but by respect, submissive, trust, honor, obedience, honesty these things or anyone or human has change and the other party has agreed to accept them back with women saying and stating with her she got every right to. So let me get this right if a woman were to cheat on me and I argue with her every day and night going to bed wrath with anger the years later while counseling is over I go to her and say I forgive you. Then we go home, and I bring everything back up in her face, put her down, curse her out, call her everything but the child of God, don't pray with or for her. Tell her she's not shit don't make love with Cleopatra when she asks, but when Jeffrey want to play mind game with her will this be right? Answer that question women and it goes on and on etc.! Now can a man say the woman is not looking to Jesus now, so she does not know how to treat her man and she's not a real woman? She will think her own ways are right, but the Lord weighs the heart. She would make the Lord as an excuse to back her up as an excuse that can only judge her. A real man and a real woman make a team with a big difference together they never give up on each other. God always has a purpose for a woman pain and a reason for her struggles a gift for her, especially when she's faithful, tells her don't give up a guess what he says the same thing to the man. See women that do this is wrong don't allow your friends or your family or your children to get between you and your spouse, don't associate with anyone who hates, disrespects and dishonors your spouse make them clearly understand that you and your spouse are one. Anyone who genuinely cares about you will honor your choice of spouse and will treat your spouse with dignity and respect. Anyone who comes to you to gossip about your spouse is sowing seeds of division in your marriage, protect your spouse position, image and reputation stand up in defense for each other. What God has joined, let no one separate. M The wife be focus on the husband cycle instead of praying with him for him holding his hand telling him what was taught as a man and this etc. We do not have all the skills because Cleopatra's mother Pam she saw her mother do things evil towards her stepfather. She said mom don't do that you are hurting him by the things you say out of your mouth, cursing him out, fuss at her and say please leave me and my husband alone. You want me to be miserable like your marriage and did Jeffrey look at Cleopatra (THE WOMAN) and said bad cycle no Jeffrey hold her and prayed for her while she cried not just that one time plenty of times. It was only me every relationship/marriage have serious problems not only men! If God comes to us with love, then he wants us to do the same for one another. Now in the Bible the Samaritan woman at well. This woman was divorced five times and living with another man. She was living out of all kinds of laws and commandments broken and sin on. Yes, the Lord saw it all just like he sees everything including Women and Men, Husband and Wife! This woman was promise living water by God. God brings life to everything we go through in our marriages, God did not reject this husband or wife we do that to one another, it does not be God it be us! Women say well he started it! God wants us to be fix us and not false teachers to come and mislead us we accept what they be saying instead of following God and the person who we are in love with we be too busy listening to other people! False prophets and teachers be in the church say it's all on the man he is the head everything falls on him in life no one can take the whole load by themselves and carry all alone because in that case they will perfect! I know women that been married 4 or 5 times and don't have their spirit right with God because I done sat down and spoke with them because they have told me they love my heart and spirit they did not give they souls to the lord they gave them to the devil and used men and thought they was God's, and the men were worshipping them. God let them know that they were drinking from the wrong well because I told them, and they told me I was judging them but then came back and told me I was right, but they did go to God first because before you can admit to any wrong God, and you are the first to agree before you share your testimony. See in my relationship with Cleopatra she depended on only Jeffrey to do everything because she said Jeffrey backed the family up making stupid decision and cheating. So how was I supposed to get another chance to prove I'm right? God and Jeffrey knew he was right but Cleopatra thought, saw, and felt different constantly a blind woman only see's what she wants to! Jeffrey depended too much on Cleopatra to their relationship was dysfunctional because we both should have been depending on God but I'm going to tell you something women he was desperately begging Cleopatra for another chance yes I still say and mean it with love. I got on my knees begging her to stop yes, the same thing men has taking you through of begging and coming back yes, she was worth it! So, it had to take that? Yes, I learn something we all do. A relationship with the lord impacts your marriage and your life more profoundly than anything else. Why? Because a husband and wife go through things in life when bad times trying to meet only their basic needs for acceptance, identity, security and purpose. You don't want to get those needs from God when your angry at one another, can't let go and let God take control. God will meet those needs when you both let him not only the husband, but money is also not the number 1 problem to fulfill your needs, work will not meet them, what will meet them is you together if you can't forgive one another how can you go ask God for forgiveness. Those will fail trying to do it their way getting even, but God love never fails! Women ask God to bring the holy spirit and water back to you and your marriage like the Samaritan did we been drinking from the wrong well, it's just like going out there to get a drink and come back home and what happens? This why it's called a hang over your doing this over your husband/man. You will find fulfillment when we pursue him above all else. Most women feel like once you lose them mentally you no longer have them to the one's that feel that way. Strong women that been done so wrong knows how to keep their life in order when they fall, when they cry, when they are sad and with hard timing. A good woman knows to always be thankful for all that she has especially God, her husband and their children she always is ready! Now I got to let women out there in this world who is calling yourselves real women and you are not. You want me to tell you because you won't be dressing mostly half naked for the world to see you for attention so men can attract to you and will not be bent over always lustful in flesh, adultery as well. I don't care how fine or sexy you are that's not beautiful or cute that is for you as a silent humble beautiful woman your God's treasure, yourself and husband. I'm going to tell the truth, or do you want me to tell you what you want to hear? I know something but don't know it all. Nobody is jealous or in your business you women that do this don't have no morals or values for yourself so classy women are jealous of you? Because some women think in these ways. Get out of here. You all wonder why no man has consider you yet that do this because it's fair not no woman's way because just like it goes the reason why the man has not gotten the woman God has sent him yet is because he has not got himself together for God to receive what God has for him! SO, WOMEN YOUR NO DIFFERENT IT'S FAIR, did you just jump right in bed with him, or did you get yourself right for God to send you the right man and was ready to receive? I got to say this and add on you look good for yourself for a thrill but don't possess the qualifications to be his lady then you can pray in love, but then not live-in hate that does not go together that's all mixed up and know you are a woman of God. God let you know this in his word, your pastor let you know, can your husband do it? It's not a joke it's serious. Jeffrey told Cleopatra that he couldn't tell her anything when she was good in ready to talk because Jeffrey said when he does talk he do it too much or I'm talking to damn much, so Jeffrey don't know which way to go she's blowing my mind. Then it be I'm trying to be funny right? No, it just that Jeffrey didn't know better like Cleopatra said, it comes like this (I KNOW WHAT THE FUCK I SAID)! A woman doesn't realize at times her behavior will push her man away it's one way or the other when he leaves he's going to get apology to come back to get what she wants or let's squash this love and make up I miss you or curse him out even more letting he's out there with some other woman or doing something he got no business doing! When the man tries to correct the woman half the time. Did you hear me say past hurts! When you hide secrets of any kind within yourself from your husband/man that you have not forgave him or have some type of grudge, battle, debate even attitude and have not let go and still hiding things deeply things inside in your mind, body, soul and spirit you bring them back really they don't go nowhere they just be kept deeply hold down inside that one little thing that you don't like then all hell breaks loose! It is the fear in woman it gets worse and be more darkness. You have a lot of women saying bold, nasty, cruel, evil, bitter, harsh words your spouse that you and they would of never came back together he don't say that you been doing the thinking for you and him you are the mind reader and thinking. Before he goes to the streets out to a woman that he's not even with a woman or sitting on the porch looking down thinking or he can be walking around the block all night or for hours. Some or most women will say he don't have no business out there that time of night he supposed to be at home in the house with his wife, don't know husband/man don't want to be around that mess he wants to be free and at peace of mind to. You be looking at your husband with an attitude and some of you don't even speak your looks say a lot of things to and he's just saying what, what did I do wrong? It's the way how you're staring at him women just like you ask your husbands when he walk in or lay beside you, what's wrong with you? What happen? You know something's wrong your concern happy, angry, or sad you still love him and don't want anything to happen to him. So, you don't think the same way about you to ask you what's wrong and know when something is wrong with you for God's sake your married! You think you have it all. She wants things to stay hidden to have advantage over you it's all a payback getting more overboard even when she never wants you to be a winner again because of the brick wall she put up you broke and lots her heart. Like my mother said when she was living YOU DON'T WANT TO SEE A WOMAN GET ANGRY it's funny because she never said anything about a man getting angry it was only woman and when I ask her about the man she told her own son it's only the woman and then she will say I don't want to talk about it no more. I saw when I got older when she was looking at me and she was saying it from past things because what my father did to her remembering them because she will smile and say you just like your father! Good or bad terms love or hate the dynamics of a relationship the WOMAN see it as! A woman at times want shame on her man but just don't know she's the one breaking up the home the most not for everything when she is, and she don't want to accept because it's all the man fault everything! Now it's a difference when you admit your hurts and tell the truth some women will say why he lied why should I? Forgive instead of continuing to lie if you want him back to make it work, TRUE! Don't continue to stay in the closet with skeleton and bones and afraid to come out battling with the wrong person all that anger in fight against the devil not your husband not just the devil love divorces the system does to. Women the relationship will improve then you will be satisfied but once you do don't come back to the same crap because if you do you will be stuck in that same mood thinking it's him when you're fooling your own self being moody to!

The man wants to talk to you and humble with God and love and tell him he's talking to damn much but when it's your turn to speak listen to the woman she's important and no man supposed to tell or treat no woman in that way, not a real man. A man wants this to it's a relationship no one gets more than the other! You know the man messes up all the time, because you say you know him more than he thinks he do and more than he knows you. It comes to a point when he does not know anything when you can't forgive. He wants to hear it from you he has a heart to feelings as well. The man wants you to deal with things in a nice way, why? Some will say so he can use me again and dog me? Don't continue with things over again that's repeating in your mind women that you can't control that you are letting control you and can't think straight everything don't be on your husband. Why are you not thinking straight? He can't think everything for you and make up your mind those things be your imaginations, thoughts, doubts, worries, stress, mindless, and cautions all that don't be on him! NO IT DOESN'T, YOU MAY STILL THINK SO YOU GOT YOUR OWN MIND. Now women you don't think you don't to take responsibility for your actions that results from the pain. HELLO! Do not be in denial or deceive. Evil company corrupts good habits in other words if you women be around other women who talk and starts trouble even gossip or be separated or divorce you're going to wind up in the same situation because there not happy there miserable is their fellowship and prayer in that circle? No let me correct myself is God there. So that's not the place you need to be. You will be on an old dusty road all by yourself walking all alone or with them same women. You're going to wind up in the same situation if you don't change your ways and surroundings of who you associate with the people who you hang around and be around. When Cleopatra's sister and mother disrespected Jeffrey most of the time they got away with it because everything he did wrong and the drama they were causing with one another because the mother did not like Jeffrey when she first met him and start texting and talking about behind my back and my wife would come back to me telling me. Then when her mother talks about her and hurts her feelings I'm the man that must hold her and say it's ok but there's no good in me only when the wife says so when she has her needs not ours. Now when she's upset about something then go talk to the mother or listening to her because you can be around family members and be married and listening to that drama and it reflects on your household. When Cleopatra was upset and say you talking bad about my mother when Jeffrey just says she just was rude and disrespectful, and you just stood there that be getting me back from she did not get her way or something from the past that's she's not talking about to God and still haven't let go. When Jeffrey first met Cleopatra, she was a Christian and still is Jeffrey was not perfect Jeffrey was in the world somewhat she invited him to her church and to read scriptures and pray, reading chapters and verses. I was holding on to things from my past for what I've been through in my life a lot of women will say on this I'm not holding on to anything. What my family took me through as a birth, child, growing up with family members, foster homes and things I did to they as wellbeing raise, abused, being raped, mistreated, and put down. I will admit I took that out on every woman I had just like a woman will do the same who take her through suffering in pain, but I had to stop somewhere in my life and stop hurting the people who loved me women forgive and learn on this as well. When Jeffrey was with Cleopatra he took a lot of these things out on her some things Jeffrey made excuses for my wrongs and actions some things they were hurtful what Cleopatra did to me and Jeffrey did to her and was wrong for. I got help just like a poor man homeless or a famous star and a wife sticking by their side. Well, every woman isn't the same some hold out some can't. When you become a woman that don't forgive and say you do but don't show it with action you refuse God, yourself or anything you block a lot of things out! You won't allow your man to complain. You will say things off your tongue like fuck his concerns he did not think about mines when he hurt me so why should I think about his? Therefore, divorce so high it's not all and only men/man or all his fault! Women it's deeper than that it's not all about you. The woman attitude, hate, envy, get back, not in the mood to be touch, no love, this kind of woman will swear she knows it all and got it all together and you can't tell her shit. That's true and a fact. She doesn't even know and swears she got it all on lock down and handling it like a real woman and not coming out with nothing out her mouth with God unless it's about only her and her children there's no

God in her man no more until she says baby I love you. The only thing she is doing is locking problems into the relationship instead of locking the key and giving it to God. God has given the man the rule back over the household in order because the man is back in obedience, instead she is with the lock and key not sharing she has both the lock and key to lock and block her man out and the key to open when she feels it's time to let him in! Now however it takes to earn Cleopatra trust back Jeffrey don't know because Jeffrey was waiting and accepting everything, he could put up with that he couldn't more than her because she said herself baby I'm going over saying but no action. Now I can see earning someone trust back that's fair but riding out someone for years and years that's painful and cruel punishment almost 24-7 because the woman don't see the problems and concerns just accumulated it with her mouth that didn't go away. Then the family talks, starts up trouble, text, silence, secrets, defensiveness and when Jeffrey told Cleopatra this, she said shut the hell up! Past hurts! Then I knew I was nothing to her but a dirty dog. I treated a real woman wrong yes, I did, and she made me pay for its real good yes women she got me back. I deserve it but what I don't deserve is when I gave my life to God and together and she went to God to ask forgiveness and I did as well and did not get what anyone will want, LOVE! We forgave one another then before years could go by she brought it back up and Jeffrey said he can accept that she's a woman she's venting, hurting, crying out, emotional, bitter, scornful Jeffrey did not blame her right away he felt Cleopatra (THE WOMAN) was coming from and that's from my heart understanding in God's, Cleopatra's and everyone point of view of being hurt. She made me pay double time and to blind to see until she came up and said OK then turn right back into this witch walking up on me casting spells like crazy you can't even imagine. It was like it wasn't a sin to her or the devil didn't have control over her she had it all planed out and he was not using her she was saved and blessed! Women, men and lots of people would be saying where God was when I was sinning also where was God when she was sinning. Where was God period because we be so hurt. He should have been there in the middle all the time in our eyes both should have been there. A woman knows when a husband/man cares also when she's caring to even when she's angry she just doesn't want to let him see because she's

guilty and afraid he might do the same thing again. See you must care
for each other happiness and love instead of yourselves and own. No
matter how hard it gets or how painful gets when Jeffrey went through
things with Cleopatra, Jeffrey put her and the children before him,
because she a loving woman. She gave me what the streets did not give
me, and it was positivity and a peace of mind. When Jeffrey messed up
towards Cleopatra, he messed up forever. Women say that once you
break their heart it will never go back to the same way it uses to be see
how the devil uses people. No that's for the women who feel in this way
and say this you speak things that's negative when you claim you serve
a mighty God and what you speak and say it comes into existence. Then
you will have to deal with that vengeance in your heart for the rest of
your life because a woman of God told me the same thing she said Jeffrey
if you don't let go of the past of what I have done to you, how will you
move forward for the next woman to come in your life for God to send
to you? That woman was Cleopatra you see the woman can tell you
something after and maybe or not it had to take her to break up with
the man to get a peace a mind to do so. When a man does this, he has
the whole world coming down on him! You will tell the man quick for
any sin in return if he does not let go and let God it is no different.
Women only sin there is badly adultery. Have you look at your sins and
self, flaws, ways, wrongs, actions, cycles and pain you cause to your
husband/man and yourselves? Have you seen how your tree grows and
been sometimes, and twist this happens in your lives to not only men!
God is the only one perfect and straight. Women due to your mother's
and father's pressure and inflicted by your parent's you women do what
they do. You learn who you are that is shown to you in a positive way
in your eyes, but it can be iniquity a sin! This is not judging women I
never met one person even in the Bible and now today that did not have
cycles now until this day only true one is God. The women are saying
its men! That is a lie. Cleopatra told Jeffrey about my father, brothers,
sisters, family and got on them to but that could not come back in return
no way she was not having it her family and her was acting worthy at
times what person hasn't done this we all fall short of the glory of the
word. I got angry but then I deal with it and got help from God,
Bishops, therapy and myself. Cleopatra ignored Jeffrey on that to there

was not your trying baby there was all Jeffrey was a fuck up. I told her she got defensive instead of looking at her flaws and sins I was only sinner, cycle, a curse person. She did not take responsibility for her sins and actions and tell me quick I don't have to tell you sorry or forgive you it's called I owe her it's pay back with envy and bitterness! Cleopatra forgave her mom and dad for passing along that iniquity in her generations, but you got a man standing up sitting down trying to save his relationship with your help that's your relationship as well, but you can't forgive your man like your mother couldn't forgive hers and you both got what you wanted each other! Forgiving them will have helped our relationship because when Jeffrey told Cleopatra that about forgiving her father she got angry at him Jeffrey don't have no business telling someone to forgive and I'm in sin of what I'm still held accountable for nail to the cross until this day, but she can tell whenever however when and who should forgive on her saying with the Lord! When it was me looking for forgiveness it was all kinds of excuses because I'm the head of the household and it goes all on me. These be inner vows! Cleopatra did it to Jeffrey at times thinking about her mother thinking he was the only one did it from parent to child. She made bad promises to herself in response to difficult or pain. Cleopatra said she will never do her daughter or son like that give my children there things back please don't take them away when Jeffrey was discipling them looking at me at times hurting off what the mother did to her not seeing we have a family and this relationship, our home! She also said she will never live with a man again. Cleopatra said she will never let a man or woman talk to her in that way but she's the woman standing strong with a nasty attitude because she's hurt and got to continue to take it out on her man even the hurt her God has forgiving me and he has moved on with Cleopatra and change but Cleopatra is saying and treating like Jeffrey didn't. This is a woman no one will hurt her again! This will control life women not yourselves you make yourself a Godly control over you and your area. Says instead you ought to say if the Lord wills we shall live and do this or that, but now you boast in your arrogance. All such boasting evil inner vows are very evil and mean because of me all on everything on the face of this earth and I could not change it. How long was I supposed to wait? How long was our relationship being supposed to wait for as long as she says it's time to let go it be marriages/relationships be married 15, 20 years and don't be happy because of this. Cleopatra did want to know or love on that this was not protecting her relationship when she said I did not want to come back or I don't know why I got back with you anyway right there she was plaining to move when she got the money and had a plan but still think about married me anyway. She said I was acting like a child she said I was the one being unteachable this took us to dangerous extremes and the daughter and son was laughing at it with her. You know Jeffrey told Cleopatra admit the negative you did wrong to your husband and repent to God then forgive me for my sins and hurt Jeffrey did to you. She looked at me and said you always talking, and you can't make me pray she never got on her knees with me or prayed with me it was back and forth because she did not tell me. God came first then us and our children. She said my children come before you and I will say what about God and our relationship she said I will just deal with God so was that not spitting in my face or on our relationship? She brought up saying so you saying my children don't come first and not involved? I did not say anything like that she did see what things women can say out they mouths. Came back to me the next day when I was sitting on the porch saying she was sorry but the sister in the car smiling and the next day arguing back with me on the phone all over and I'm this and that. When a man is born is brain is on the left side of his head and the woman brain is on the right side some men think slower than women at times depending how wise he is same thing that goes for women at times when they are stubborn, selfish, and not listening. Men and women supposed to keep themselves humble not just men. A man that loves a woman can see in herself! See you can be a woman with a mind with mostly everything even sincerity and great feelings or be a bitch with an attitude even change to be a woman of class and respect yourself they be the best to deal with and the hardest because they know they work but the woman who does not care or have respect for herself.

Chapter 10

A real woman is temporary she decides and will have several thoughts behind it. The woman is the excitement as well as the passion of life. She is a creative art of all by herself she's wo-man vowel and symbol before man her pride, she's the package, the torch, and the prize with all the confidence in the world and life itself. I have learned a woman wants to know and learn more every second every day. She has to many flaws to be perfect. Then the man tries his all in his self with his strength to satisfy the woman because she has more than one attitude with numerous ways and personality's. Women single is a blessing but there are somethings just not meant be said when you are single to make someone feel bad and be sarcastic over dramatic with it. Women don't go there about what the man did this is about you get on yourself if can't tell you what to do well can I please ask you, you're telling and asking men or your man right? Number 1. The truth, Number 2. Your internal emotions, Number 3. Your slick ways of body language 4. Your tone of your voice, 5. You don't need no man or depend on one to make you happy. Now the man/husband must put up with your shit as you feel like it does not smell bad. Now I'm very emotional about this because Jeffrey loved Cleopatra so much sometimes he would act like her naturally as a woman emotional please don't go there as I'm sounding and acting like a woman because being married you smell like one another, and act like one another. God created us naturally all of it the woman has the man traits in her some, the woman came from man, and we came out of the woman from birth, but I did not act the way she acts on treating me. Everything was on me. The man will try to talk to you with affection, but you won't let him because your too closed minded of what he has done to you to show you your arrogant attitude sometimes. The first Cleopatra would say is, I don't let no man like you determine what I have in, want and need for my life. Wait a minute wasn't we married? It's one, it is giving up the eyes for the us! Cleopatra will change back up then the excuse will be (THAT'S A WOMAN). Some women out there will say maybe or that's her every woman not the same so deal with it! When a man has his faults towards the woman one false move or slip not even a step a woman does not deserve that kind of treatment at all. Now you have men give women what they want and need, and it be times that the woman at the time in the mood she's in if she's ready to give him what he wants and need to receive what he's giving changing up at times thinking and his actions stating what you are you looking for with or without him. You still love him and he's not going anywhere, then states he is driving you crazy, he's a trip, he's something else, he's a hand full, he makes you sick, what are you going to do with him. Excuse me can I ask you a question? What are you? A Godly woman that's it. The woman then says, I'm tired he will be alright, whatever, do you have thought you don't drive your man up the wall, away and crazy? NO, not how you put it in your way looking at in from your perspective, you're too good for that you're A WOMAN. Women let your man do his thing he's free not to do whatever he wants to we know that come on now, even times if it's without you. A forgiving woman that gives her man another chance for real gives her man the space he needs to be himself! She will know who ever comes in or walks up no matter who it is she will recognize that's the passion they have will become more interesting and passionate soon as you have these nasty, rude, revenge, attitude a man is much less or more likely to get crazy, weird, insane, walk away, be tired and worn out, let down, step on, not encourage, walked all over just like being abused and you talking about only what only he took you through have what you have been going through for years it's all about you. There's a lot of ways to describe it getting shit on, bitch at, a hard time, but Jeffrey learned from Cleopatra because at times they were test and a lot of times it was overboard but to her it was just her getting drove crazy and got throwed overboard off the boat and she did not know and forgot that she did not get on the boat by herself! Like she said I admit Jeffrey I've been treating you like shit but did not come with action, love or respect of showing happiness that means a lot the same goes for me as well. A real woman all women shouldn't never be struggling financially, spiritually, or emotionally with a grown man lying next to her. I feel this and understand this that the woman stimulates the man with her mind. Also, she provides some growth in a relationship and stands out and up. I know a good woman when she creates a problem to be solve, calls her man in to solve it, she backs him up 100% and help him not complain when it's not enough when she can't get what she wants, that's all he had to give and she's not thankful! She will never make her man feel unwanted no matter how things get. A real woman enlightens her man, encourages, comforts, calms him down, and love him! Women that do this wrong to your husband/man to much sorry is not good repeatedly, always falsely accusing him because you can't forgive or let go and want him to stay the victim all the time this is a HOLD on the relationship how is he going to lead on this that's your mess up not his! Women no relationship is perfect not one. A relationship works when you both put the work in not only the man. You have women now today saying only men need to grow up and need discipline, we all need that at times when it's necessary or not to learn when we do make a mistake how we can come by handling the situation not only the husband/man being the head. When your man tells you to pray the first thing you tell him is that he has some nerve for what he has done or did and still doing, but when is it you are so different in God eyes? You did not do much sin or wrong as he did because don't work like that of pointing fingers pointing fingers at one another is both soul mates are selfish, NO ONE IS LISTENING! Sin is not making an excuse for men or women or in general period. Your dead wrong but it's not all on your husband/man. Make time for your husband because when he's making up for the negative he's putting in work for God, himself, and you he's special to and feeling good he's putting something back in at times some women feel as that don't mean nothing because, but, or hmm, whatever, we will see and doubting him and herself A HUGE MISTAKE AND DOWN FALL! See your frustration, anger, bitterness, pride, can go a long way because you don't have no control of it, you say fast and quick no it's because he hurt you all the time hurt people hurt people so you're just getting him back constantly. Ladies when you hold on to negative things you don't have no feelings you have hatred in your heart and your eye contact be serious at times you don't want to look at him your emotions be controversial you be in a debate towards him, but it hits you back in the face. When you sink inside there's no area in the heart to love your husband/man because you are EXTREMLY ANGRY! It becomes like a stank and funky garbage can or garbage truck with more garbage that you find more to put and pack in your truck driving around you the driver that's out of about to wreck out and not caring see this is how marriages are today and a lot have died in car accidents fussing and fighting! It can be from waking up first thing in the morning going to sleep or something from the past any little thing you let get to you. Then you have lots of women saying get him girl he deserves this they're also saying we understand we been there and know where you're coming from and what you are going through, how you feel been there done that holding grudges constantly. See you have men have weaknesses that they don't want a woman to know but the woman that is strong picks up on it but WOMEN YOU ARE NOT ALONE. You have women with their fear and weaknesses as well that they keep inside but men pick up on in not only does the man lie you do as well with a straight face telling he can't tell you what you're thinking, feeling, doing or get in your mind! When the man gets hurts, he needs to forgive and move on with his life and stop blaming everyone including his self for past hurts. A lot of women have told me men the say way you expect us to forgive you all just like that and it go away that's not true and a damn lie because you as a WOMAN NOT LETTING NOTHING GET AWAY so you lying to yourself! Jeffrey tried every day to talk to Cleopatra (THE WOMAN) about what he did wrong, she felt we can make it right but when he came in and follow God's commandments it was not God fault. It wasn't good enough for Cleopatra because she never gave Jeffrey no rights for anything to care, share, feel, understand, love or not even an opinion. Jeffrey sinned ok he hurt her feelings she hurt mines as well he was told he was a complete fuck up! She didn't understand realize our counseling was that she didn't ever want to talk it out or help she did what she wanted to do. Woman/women if you are hurt so bad where you can't take your husband/man back and do so don't blame that on him blame that on yourselves because you made that choice thinking one way, but your mind was one way and your heart was not healed so you were not stable in your mind or thought process you were out of order, confused, mixed up, totally you were in denial! Can a woman say thank you to me, not every woman is accepting of it or where I'm getting at or to so if you don't stop what will happen then? A woman/woman needs nurturing not only men it starts with parents in the home sometimes a woman takes that man back because they miss him and they need that nurturing because they do want that man to change so they can get it back so let's say that man does change, HOW YOU'RE GOING TO ACT? Cleopatra did not want to talk it out see women can take men back for different reasons it also can be for the right or wrong ones. It can be for God, forgiveness or it can be her choice on money, sex, get back, the way it used to be, or he used to be, but don't sit back think, and see at the big picture of why I'm really doing this because it can be a mistake that she made and want to blame the man for her mistake because she did not want to agree, believe, trust or have faith in him ever again! Jeffrey couldn't make Cleopatra talk he couldn't make her do what she did not want to do she's grown. Now to you women read this book and men marriages/relationships or whoever this is not to be judged on or go back and judge someone it's something that we can learn from not pick or on someone not back towards me as well. Everyone is not the same we all are different it's based on a fact how you deal with your marriages/relationships treating people in the same way you want to be treated in an awesome way life is not fair and specially not perfect but it's too short to continue to live, speak, claim, and be around or in negativity! Work it out and handle your problems. I see you real women out here when you are loved correctly you become even more 100 times the woman you were before I give you that credit give your man the same he's handsome, strong, leader, he's not a thug and no good, he's sexy and have educated ideas as well! You must know a woman likes, dislikes, her ways, and who she is. She loves to enjoy herself and her life. Well, it's both of your lives together because you are one together. She hates being criticized. She also puts things in order and speaks her mind. The woman loves to investigate and experiment Cleopatra love to do that with me like I was a transformer. A real woman that's strong can't be swayed by a man in any kind of way not only women are ashamed of what they have been through in life as women, so have men in the same way. Something where he came from and been through both sides are a shame to admit certain things or talk about it. Like you have the woman that's the perfect woman, bitter woman, Godly woman, the woman with it all, also the better woman, independent, naive, and the woman that wants to write the checks and control everything! Now I'm going to get on me I'm in my 40's when I was young minded when I was with my first wife I knew something was wrong with me and she did to it's that the love she had for me and understood me because she never been on the streets. I just didn't know how to deal with it and handle it I understood women in ways I couldn't even explain because the love I was looking for since a child that I did not get from a family or parenting now that I got it I'm afraid of it not saying it feels good it's just something so unique. I knew how it felt nasty, misused and abused like a woman feel the same way feeling where I'm coming from and can't use my past for my mistakes I mess up on or a cover up. Don't put me down or sweep me up under the bus understand the feelings I have and where I'm coming from, I was dogged out being raised up, so I did it back to good and bad peoples. Women you not alone men are not either my first wife I was married to me was young, then my second wife I was getting help but not enough still young minded in areas of growing up more to do on me and myself women are you learning things you need to grow up on more? When Jeffrey was seeing things being thrown at him and coming my way coming from Cleopatra and her family misused, mistreated, falsely accused, talk to any kind of way, Jeffrey took it out on the wrong person then when he got it together he was transitioning slowly because he was learning more it's a process it takes time. Jeffrey tried talking to Cleopatra and other women why do they listen to what other family members, friends, co-workers say about their husbands or me. They trust the people who they are listening to, which they have their own problems in life. The way they connect with their own intuition or common sense to tell the man real, quick you don't know shit about life. Then you have the woman put up a front, read this and saying the woman makes the decision. The woman is being incredibly careful what she says as to what she will accept or not the advice given, However the woman won't admit to the mind games she plays or secrets. She knows how to handle her business. She will put up a wall or front and is faking falsely around others, but she is hurting inside and will act like she got everything under control with a mask on. Women knows deep down what her issues with herself but keep it real to let out the negative things in her life. She may let out a little bit of her inner self, so she doesn't show her weakness. Men have weak ways just like women do. A woman will cover up her issues in the open, but they are behind closes doors they feel the pain and hurt. They sometimes pay mind games that is not necessary, keep it real about how you feel. You have some women that think they are holy to the highest level than man. She self-righteous, extremely judgmental, always right, argumentative, then she feels like she can put her lover down, since he commits a sin by cheating, and she is the Christian one in the family, and he is always wrong. Cleopatra says she is the strong woman who did not cheat on her man and did not have sex with no one else. At least I am not worse or bad or sinner period, I'm the woman that's the ideal Christian. This woman brags that's why Jeffrey ran away from Cleopatra when she acted like that. How long has it been since she did this or that looking at me and not her it's all me? She made it be known badly in my face and others to make a point around her putting me down she saved me. When you are holy, it is a lifestyle that will be displayed for the people around you to see, but not for you to point out to others the things in your life that you are doing correctly. No one is perfect and Cleopatra felt like at times. She was close to perfection, because she will come back and forth and say I'm hard on you I'm sorry I'm bringing up the past. I'm sorry, I told you I'll be with God instead of putting God first and our relationship. I'm sorry for turning you away when you told me that. What Cleopatra did was not a sin of sexual acts with a man, it was unforgiveness, bitterness, anger, malice, hate, revenge, envy, jealousy, that she wasn't doing the same thing herself. Then the mother will entertain her daughter and she will entertain her back gossiping talking about me behind my back and to my face being extremely judgmental. The worse kind of religious person is the one who entertains their brothers or sister's business in confidence and acts as if she is supportive just to continue to receive information about her or his personal business. Now I tell you when this woman that call herself religious, her heart is not right. She is hurting people and herself being mischievous, envious, and a back biter! This woman will gossip, especially about the man/men faults, sins and laugh about her husband past sins right in his face openly and secretly laugh about his choices. Everything about him is down and poor even on what his opinions or facts they don't even matter, even his love life she will see he doesn't have love no more period. This woman can't forgive. There are times she will change up that God is for her and not for her husband, because he sinned, sexual hurt her and scorned her forever. It will never be the same in her eyes or Gods it will change constantly, it will be her mind and heart. She displays false, nasty, envy behavior towards her man, which she secretly says she forgive not openly because nothing has change. As humans we all need to be spiritual not only about man or woman God first. Women please don't use your bitterness and revenge towards your husband as a DEFENSE MECHANISM every chance you get. Jeffrey made Cleopatra this way when he was with her we were girlfriend and boyfriend but then we start going to church, then counseling, we were getting therapy, he was praying she was not praying with him, so he was carrying it like she was fair and perfect in God's eyes even she was not seeing it God was because he was not a Christian in her eyes. I was not clean at all, and I begged her not to be this way or take this in our relationship let's give us and everything to the Lord because if you bring it up in my face arguing, fussing, provoking, angry, all the spirits will come back as bones and skeletons it will be worse than the dead itself coming back double and triple! This goes for me, you, us, relationship, marriages anyone take in with God please don't take this for granted. This was about God, husband, wife, children not out order with the children first or the wife first, he say she say that's not in God's order and women not me saying husband/man is in control to take over to do or say whatever it is he wants to. I'm saying in God order! Then in women minds and saying it be that's what happen when you put the/this man first, no did you really put God first with your husband or soon as you got him back God giving you the glory, blessing, what you ask for and you blame him for taking him back cursing your husband/man out using God name in vain or not? Just talking to him any kind of way. A man deserves to get spoiled to not only women and told their efforts are only appreciated women and be made to feel secure. Watching your man or woman every single mood is not coming to make them faithful or trustworthy when you put trust in God to do anything, he does its right women? So that trust, prayer, love, time, forgiveness you put in with God you know as well as God he wanted you to do the same back towards your husband? What did you choose to do? I'm not giving him my everything again, who, not me, I'm not falling for the same thing, tricks, or game again. So, you wasted your time and prayer some go back and forth! Not all the time just for those ladies. See I learn something and more and did things for myself and Cleopatra to show with action that I earned everything back that was shown with action but not a choice that someone did not choose on to change to accept me! It had to be Cleopatra choice to give it. A lot of women would say what do you expect you hurt her so bad until where she couldn't deal with you or anything at all not even God because she's angry and bitter. I had to deal with the same thing when I sinned, made excuses. We are held accountable for our own actions and sins. Like I was saying men listen and learn. I felt good cooking for my family it was breakfast I did not know how to cook dinner at lease I tried. I got put down even for that because of what I did from the past. When I did get paid I gave her the check she gave it back because it was pride and not enough or was it, SHE DID NOT NEED ME FOR MY MONEY SHE HAD HER OWN, but we were married a woman don't suppose to accept money from her husband she has an excuse why or she did not want to take my money because she was independent and a teacher a strong woman! A WOMAN IS WAY BEYOND POINT OF AN EXPRESSION! I got ignored and put down even when I picked the children up from school and dropped them off. How is that a man can get put down especially a black man if he's innocent or guilty if he makes a mistake, sin, doing right or wrong but a mother gets off when she's doing anything. Like if Cleopatra will do something wrong, sin, be angry or disrespect me in front of her children and be dead wrong but she will be right because, what she been through as a mother and being a woman putting up with everything in life what human being doesn't? Cleopatra will use anything against Jeffrey to put him down and curse him out, dogged him out with words disrespecting him, unnecessary behavior that Jeffrey tolerated being a woman as herself being too smart for her own britches. Some things women get away with out of circumstances is the statement and charm of saying I'M A WOMAN! What's wrong with her saying that's what some or most women will say or how you know, you don't know everything every woman is not the same or what is you talking about? See a lot of times Jeffrey walked away from Cleopatra he even did killing with kindness not physically or sarcastically he did it by love, actions, because he was feeling her and his pain together we still one under God that he took her through. See Jeffrey would put his stepchildren to bed and pray with them. When Cleopatra did argue with Jeffrey, he just laid there in tears he was inversible to her. Jeffrey didn't show her his feelings like she showed hers at certain times sometimes our feelings were the same but her bitterness, angry, and acrimony was in the way of her wrongs, ways against my rights and doing what was positive. Don't never feel like you're better than someone else and push them down when they are trying to get up and have accomplish the ability to reach the goal of doing their best and what you ask them for, and they have completed! I sat there and learn her ways quietly at times. I'm going to stay quiet, but it wasn't easy for me to do because I was a hardheaded dumb man. It was breaking Jeffrey down no one taught him this only one person the woman who put up with his shit Cleopatra, but all her shit piled up and smelling good because of me everything! Now she will say that's not true, and it wasn't like that or you still on the same thing, no this is to teach others how to handle this situation. Jeffrey watched Cleopatra (THE WOMAN) he seen, sat back and observed at times he wouldn't answer her calls on nonsense, his fault it was getting to him a lot of times, but he had to put a stop to it somewhere he couldn't stop her she was grown. She going to do her way or the highway. Women drive men crazy to because this woman sure enough did. I drove her crazy to it takes crazy to know crazy right? So, I also did things when she said baby let me do it, I said no it's okay I got it. You see being a real man! One thing Cleopatra Jeffrey loved is the way she cooked, teach and most of all give me scriptures to read. She couldn't accept the truth the same truth she dished out that I gave back to her. We get to point there is only so much you will take before you come back at anyone. It is the man who needs work on anything right ladies. Women study us they know our moves, buttons to push and when Jeffrey got tired of Cleopatra mouth, he would ignore her. Then you have women say I don't have them type games to play I'm a real woman or a real lady want to do nothing like that. Even woman is not the same but in time, day, month, year, season they have done this at her or their time. See when I stopped her, she found reasons to argue with me to rush up towards me to provoke me to hit her, but I raised my hands up in the sky saying NO! She kept saying yes that's what you want to do I left got in the car drove off and cried with God and myself she didn't care about me being to myself with God around NO WOMAN or ANYONE I NEEDED MY WIFE. Do you hear me, understand me and feel me? See when a woman now today acrimony has, man it is serious. It's hell all by itself, judging worse than pointing the finger this goes for anybody, but I'm explaining the woman she's worse than the movie I saw. Especially he words they can be sharp it continues with a dispute repeatedly. She would argue with herself right their talking out loud when she doesn't have a defense or battle to fight within an army. She will talk even in her mind quietly showing anger rolling her eyes with hate. Even opening her big eyes up to see. It's death time to her and ready to throw her bomb at you. She keeps a couple on her. She even has this look when her eyes are closed slowly moving away from you letting you know that her actions that love don't live here anymore there's no losing privileges after separation or divorce or breakup to a lot of women. It makes it worse along with truth as when a woman speaks about how she does right ladies. See it was nights when Cleopatra would sit up, turn head towards Jeffrey and don't say anything while her eyes be shut low looking at him then he would not say anything to her rage would be, what? You going to say something, gone ahead say it! Why are you looking at me like that? Who have you been listening to? When she is doing all these things herself as a woman within herself of bad feelings, false accusations towards me with words. Jeffrey liked Cleopatra walking in her heels he had the pleasure of picking some of heels out when we went shopping together. Especially the black pumps the was loving and happy experience enjoying each other with time together. It was all day shopping spree. Even with children coming along with us. Cleopatra's daughter Anita was just like her when came to shopping. Cleopatra thought everything was all about her. She cut me deeply with her words they were bloody than a civil war. Just like our divorce it was worse than war itself, she thought it was all about her. When you are thinking, knowing, sayings are different from our actions this cause her to act with an attitude or act on what she was thinking as well. A woman does things the way she sees fit according to her and I learned from it. What a woman is worth she's loved by God. I like that the most. A woman body is warm, and I see when she weeps, she also loves to wonder about great things. I love her smile, joy, fragrances, I even welcome her heart. She is so strong she show's other what life is all about. Jeffrey love Cleopatra the educated woman. Now when she went through her sins, wrongs, trouble I told her I loved her lets pray, don't be a woman of worries or fears, frustration, doubts, yes, I had every right to. I smelled like her, and she smelled like me when the wind blew by. I could swear and know she was there by my side feeling her body sex, lust or flesh no by love and passion unconditional. Now no one can't tell me how I feel on my passionate love, ways and purpose I felt I gave, but me and the Lord. I took the time to listen. I did what love is and action is deeper than you can imagine only I can. I forgave and loved myself by founding me, who I was and loving a woman. This is my poetry of art myself within the things I know the psychology that I learned from a woman/woman. I reverse it back towards them, which they can't handle their own medicine they dish out. I was passionate about this as well the women created it. Jeffrey passion was Cleopatra (THE WOMAN) and her children. She knew her children was important to me, so she will use that against me to hurt me by saying things that was not so nice. See women hurting someone is not only a sexual sin there are many other things to. I focused on the love that was so deep I feel like a woman had me out of space, on clouds of joy, tears, blushing, smiles, snuggles, laughter, life couldn't wait to get back to her not feel like someone would take her away, but I couldn't be around her, because it's something special to have a gift you never had before to open up that never can be replaced that's hard to believe and received towards anyone being hurt MEN or WOMEN, but it's true, right or wrong, ups and down, good or bad times. My passion was to surprise, forgive, have a great heart. When Jeffrey was a sinner, dirty dog, shitty liar he couldn't be forgiven, because that's what he wanted to put into words by someone else words off their tongues that was Cleopatra words NO you want me to forgive you when you want me to that wasn't true! No, you want me to forgive when I'm ready to! No, I'm not ready to! Okay baby I'm ready now as this goes on you women do this. No this is true you get everything damn right to do this. Now answer this to the Lord our God is it right? So, when she said that men, that's you, that's all men they expect you and women to forgive and let it go. If you take a long look that is getting back at each other with words and revenge. I never spoke on things or hear her saying I didn't set you up, you set your own self up, because you repented on some things, you went before God and didn't leave it there, you brought back things with the devil! My passions were to walk by your side holding your hand starting fresh all over again. When we started fresh at the starting line she had the gun in her hand up in the air shooting the gun not in the air to my head at me running around the track over and over again as a target doing it on purposely every shot she can get. My passion was to take in just as much as she did even double, because I'm trouble I got myself in this as a man I got to get out of this I understand even triple, I guess she felt no more money, there's no more investment there's NO PLAN! My passions are helping people, retail, sales, her family, helping my family helping myself, but I'm all fucked up. When it comes to her! My passion is music, writing my good heart, forgiving and loving good a lot of people can't do that forgive. It's a lot of people that can't do what I can on forgiving. I had bad sins ad flaws that people can do well that I can't do or trying to work on it and still need more help, so we all are not perfect. My passion is to help children, have some one day if God says so in his favor only it in his hands. My passion is loving people for who they are, what they are going through coming out or going in. Everything my fault but the money for her is not I don't have those faults. I had passion that was wrong to see a man about I can get. Now how many women just say this face to face when there actually wrong? I did things with passion, exciting myself and others free and freedom of giving my heart. See I also learned certain times women can also have strong feelings of passion in a way of anger to act in a dangerous way of bitterness specially in a strong romantic feeling for the man they love! My passion even motivated me I did what I loved thing I was willing to sacrifice. I don't like certain women who feel like they can't be naïve. I had a passion then and still do now is my energy and I have a lot of it as well fire and desire of spirit Jeffrey had in him for Cleopatra (THE WOMAN) my love still until this day and her children. This woman told me at church named Ms. Simms said those was her children to because you put a roof over their head, clothes on their back and food in their mouth as well as put money in their pockets. When Cleopatra came to Jeffrey sometimes and ask for money. Jeffrey asked her sometimes what do you need it for? Because she did not know how to save money, she let me know what It was for Jeffrey gave it to her, to a lot of women and some men or whoever disagree with me will say well why she must ask one that's Cleopatra every relationship/marriage is not the same and Jeffrey was the one good man saving money being persistence and passionate not greedy! Some women don't know how important it is to save they just like to spend not all women are independent t-his is nothing against them this is just explaining on how certain women are and experience learning from them and acting, feeling like them to study them and know being around them as well. Jeffrey had to put himself in Cleopatra shoes feel what she is going through as a woman. What I took her through what she took me through how she feels about her children I learned that she is an exceptional woman when I get my life right. I even stop blaming her all the tie, but can women do that vice versa put themselves in men shoes. Especially the things black men go through this didn't make me. Yes of a man when Jeffrey put himself in Cleopatra shoes it made him more of loving himself of a human being it was okay to empathize he grew up ill to function well on society because he was treated just like women been through what they been through. I have by women that was family members and men and different foster homes I was raised up in. Tell me what and where is the difference? We all have a story to tell it's not the same, but everyone goes through and feels pain! It's not a good feeling but no one wants to go through something like that. Theirs people that talk to women and feel them out more with better understanding than men. All women don't wear the same shoes. Different sizes, brands, looks, styles. Some women don't even wear heels they just have their choices of what they feel comfortable in, it gets deeper that I can't leave out CATCH THE SALE depending on what type of woman/women you are. You know Jeffrey use to put Cleopatra shoes on sometimes being in love with that special person makes you do crazy things like that. Sometimes even when we went shopping, he like it more at home but one thing that it was so important about was what Cleopatra (THE WOMAN) wanted. I would lift her feet up and slide her shoes on her feet and put the strap through the latch and put it on and do the other shoe the same way and she be good to go. When Cleopatra came home at times, Jeffrey will take her shoes off and massage her feet and she will fall asleep sometimes and he will to because we will feel each other love! I showed support just as much as her. Jeffrey like when Cleopatra put on her heel, because of how and the way she walked in them it was more flattering than anything in this world with her smiling at him with love throwing a kiss at him telling him that he makes her sick, I'm crazy and she don't know what she's going to do with him. I know she was in pain a lot of time wearing heels I ask her than sweetheart why is you wearing them? She said because I just do, I'm a woman I like it then I realized it wasn't the shoes that was making her she was making the shoes THE WOMAN! I was ready a lot of times to understand her experiences because she would come back to sit in front of me and apologize for something that I been making up for that she would not give in until she was safe and ready. Women this can protect you only if you have God in it not doing it in a scornful, bitter, angry, frustration way because why do you think you fuss and be aggravated at times you be doing it to yourself at times and still blaming the husband/man for everything. Now Jeffrey love Cleopatra boots she puts on he always looked good on her. No one is perfect I'm a man and I will let no one put me down. I give credit to God, myself and blesses me be back abundantly. Now women that do this thinks it's fun when a man wants to make love when you go down don't put your teeth on him you know what I mean you can make him cry inside and turn him off. When your man wants to love it wants it just as much as you do not play mind games. A real woman knows that everything is not sexual, and this man showed Cleopatra in plenty of ways. Yes, Jeffrey showed Cleopatra as well with action that he appreciated she just was selfish and felt like it was not enough because of what he done off the past he owed her so much back in return! I grabbed on to God, my heart and hers as well, she said I shouldn't have never taken your ass back just arguing at times for nothing and women will say she did not argue for nothing it was something you have done to her. There's no excuse for wrong,

wrong is wrong for anyone they might not accept it, but God sees it. They know but they just don't want to tell you that just want to be alone you can't make them accept or nothing. When Jeffrey let Cleopatra down, he picked her back up WOMEN you think you don't let your women down? Jeffrey gave Cleopatra hugs; he would squeeze all of her against his chest it felt like her soul was in him. This was good to her heart and mines to I can feel the beats in both of our hearts together as a heart goes drawing a picture it was good to be true it was real. Jeffrey showed her he was looking out for her and her children as well. Cleopatra is Jeffrey biggest fan more beautiful than the stars in the sky and the ocean all by herself. Every woman in her life have had different fantasies and love that they have. Women have things inside that they don't want to talk about hold things back and keep to themselves it be lots of things. Jeffrey stands up for Cleopatra and gave her love, credit that she wasn't left behind, expressing education and telling me to go back to school. Jeffrey love Cleopatra she was just being herself and the radiance of the blue sky of her face walking on the beach looking at the water standing in the stand just staring, crying, and daydreaming with a smile night and day or on the docks, balcony of a condo. It's so many things that Jeffrey can't even explain it or imagine that's love saying it, showing it, and feeling it but like Cleopatra said and stood on her word after she forgave him it was too damn late. Now ladies let be for real when you have taken your man back than went through your process of saying I forgive you after so many years there with him then you marry this man, or it can be you already married and take him back. Then you bring up everything from the past and telling him to his face he's just sitting there allowing what he took you through as you add even more. Every time he gets up and you continue to tell him I shouldn't have never taken you back and no text are coming in from no other woman/women period. It's just God, you, her, witnesses, bishop, people, children even the person that does it apologizes, is it still right for women or any woman to say you or any man deserve that? Answer this question please because to any woman those cheats on her husband/man and he takes her back then for years he forgives her is he wrong for throwing it up back in her face likes she's doing it? FALSE ACCUSING is painful especially when someone puts that all in to get back something they

treated wrong, so they had to come to some common sense and realize this was worth having to get back what they lost but you women forget about and don't see the good all you see is you don't forget is the bad he done! Ladies it's not too late to pray to get this behavior together with God. I agree, it's never too late for your children and other things in life as your job and career but what about your husband? It's not too late for money, to go shopping, get your feet and nails done, get you a car, go to work, take care of yourself and business, never too late for you to satisfy yourself as a woman, never too late for loving you and your children but for your husband is it too late you need to work that out in your areas. So, it's made up that woman say and put into action that it will never be the same way it used to be it's not other chance if he did it one time he will do it again and some of you women say this when he doesn't even get all the way in the door not even giving him a kiss asking how his day was. Some women say I trust you but not the way I use to and saying they doers of the word of God I'm not judging this what you tell your husband when he's out of line and order you get on his ass. See the devil like divorces because he can't love period and when you tell your husband/man it can't be the same way anymore, so why are you married to him? Because if you say for God but that's a lie right there because if it was for God it wouldn't be a but just like when that husband/man went out there and cheated on you or whatever it was he done in sin to you to hurt you so he's hurting and waiting. It's just like saying his credit was bad he could not buy a house, car, cell phone not even get a loan because he did you wrong we understand, but when he fixed his credit and it went clean and he can get alone with you but you don't want to give in because you afraid you will get hurt again that's not his fault any more after forgiveness that's something you within yourself have to deal with God! He can't use his credit card because you wipe everything off again and put on there what you want to charge it take it off you're using your power in the wrong way wife/woman/ women/wives. Now when he uses you and messes your credit up and you take him back and he keeps messing up that's wrong, I'm not with that myself I'm against that that's not a man that's a coward but when you have a man that do get it right and you take him back then you bring that up that's your vengeance so you don't trust him because of him your insecure of your trust of self not him. You choose to do what your mind said do not God just like that husband/man at the time with his dick so there's not only sins thought on cheating and adultery there's so many we can't even imagine but we still no right from wrong and held accountable for our own actions and sins. Women get angry and say things that don't mean it knowing their mouth can be deadly as a two-edge sword. It is many things that a woman/women tick there's own self off by not forgiving any little thing pushes their button because in a rage of so much bitterness and anger it can be so petty or anything. Women you won't have peace or freedom for yourself Cleopatra's mother saw her daughter was happy when she was happy when we got together but she was so miserable, and her daughter had to be around her. With Cleopatra things had to be done with her permission it was either bye, I don't care, where I been, and mind my own damn business. Jeffrey love Cleopatra so much when he was with her he showed so much success he saw that when he asked her did he mess up her life holding her back of everything, career, because he was concern even though God knew and himself that he wasn't held accountable for everything. It still really matters to Jeffrey as well not all for the woman because he is with her a strong woman that Cleopatra is would not compromise with him. Some things she would not accept from my teachings of what being taught that her cycles from her mother and father family was hurting our relationship, but it was so funny that how everything was all from my side of my family, father, myself and mother but not one thing from her. It was not for better or for worse, richer or poor, sickness and health until death do us apart. She was just being selfish, and I played parts in it to. If we both came in together and prayed having faith with God and working because relationship is a job and responsibility but when she kept saying I don't want to pray with you in anger she just doesn't know she was saying the relationship was already over like she said I don't want you no more and I wish you never came back. Everyone goes through trials and tribulations! Now today Cleopatra's mother, family, my family, lots of family members, millions and billions of people. Cleopatra's reactions were always better than Jeffrey she was the calm one and the woman to know how to correct and handle all things with him not giving her no advice or letting her have it she going to be one the doing the telling someone off! Now Jeffrey knows Cleopatra a woman of a heart or any woman/women/wife can't get over something just like that it does not happen overnight it takes time depending on that woman/woman, but what about the MEN? EVERYTHING IS NOT THEIR FAULT STOP BLAMING THEM FOR EVERYTHING! Don't just be a great teacher and don't want to be a great learner as well, because eventually you will use your defense towards people and out of control especially towards your husband/man. I love these women out there with their power of strength don't use that as your way or the highway use it as God say like you tell men not to use the Bible saying wives be submissive by not speaking or saying nothing. A woman can talk she just got to know when and how to speak not in authority in God as a virtuous woman! No control vice versa sees both sides been hurt and been through rough times but everybody relationship is not the same. You know as well as Jeffrey does, I'm not an angel and some fathers wouldn't have not done would Jeffrey done for Cleopatra's children and do not bring the children to see how I'm doing sometimes. If she loved me, she would do that. If you loved anyone, they would not get treated any kind of way by other people, family members, friends, or no one love is love. Just because people mess up fall short of the glory of the word and sin does not mean that don't love in times and come back to change to give love because remember when you were once there we all are human beings. So, we are just men and say we are dogs and sin and no good I done heard women tell their men they worse than a pig. You know what pigs are God created them to but don't call your husband/man out names the mouth remember? But when women sin the loving God creatures there sorry, and the charm gets everything out of the way. I left somethings out the eye contact, smile, grin, the touch, grace, lips, blush most of all it's a movement that brushes all things in her favor. A man is not shit at all when a woman gets piss off yes women we do as men can get you aggravated, we know when we don't and it's on you then what is there to say? NOW YOU WANT TO GO THERE! Can a man learn from you and use the same words can you take your shit like a woman and woman up? See a lot of women got on me because of how I did things when I was with Cleopatra, and I told Cleopatra to let me handle that part and she thought I couldn't because she was paying attention to what the women was doing, and the women was jealous they wanted what Cleopatra had. A man that was smart, business minded, a hustler, salesmen, brilliant, potential, a go getter, moving and handsome. I learned where a woman can be so insecure and smart knowing about watching another woman/woman when she is not watching the things about herself to have ready for herself to get right, control, listen, hear, understand to pay attention to things she will lose. That's why when Jeffrey use to look at Cleopatra, my mother, my sisters, auntie's, women, woman and say that's not true and they swear it was all could do is make a face and say you women crazy and walk away because he was not going to win the debate the women and this where the part they mess up at and still think there right to a lot of things to this day and time! A woman can scare you to with looks not to be in fear just drive you insane as what happen? I have this for men especially the black men they go through it mostly the pain, the police, the killing, jobs, America and the system. Now when a black man sits down with his black woman, she gets angry not all of them then when he sits down and talk to a white woman, she gets angry! Not all but some you all know what I'm talking about. Women you're not the only one hurting man do to. It's a lot of anger, hurt and pain inside of black men. What about us not only you women. Women say all the time black women mostly is the ones that have more anger than most women what about us men ladies? We have a lot in common women and men. I had to suffer for what I did I wasn't sincere or forgiving and for the woman or women you can't make no one like or love you for what you do towards them. Now this goes for men, but the woman and women no don't forgive, forget that's enough move on. Jeffrey was the enemy when he did good, he was a liar, a cheater, dog, shit, a good fuck, a bad fuck, because CLEOPATRA (THE WOMAN) CHANGED UP along with being a user, horse shit and a low life pig. Can I say for once A DIARY OF A MAD BLACK MAN TO WOMEN? NO! Then that will be I'm crying like a baby, being childish, finding excuses, or running game. Women will be against what I said of a diary of a mad black man how they been treated by men taking it to their grave not all most but what I said about a cry baby, being childish, finding excuses or running game that's 100% right and right down their alley. I need to let it go right women, I'm hurting, I need to move on, or I want to be able to love again like A WOMAN SAID TO ME CLEOPATRA she got some nerve after we divorce isn't that the hell what I was telling her, but you say men don't listen, so was she? It was a shame she couldn't say or use those words in actions with us forgiving so we can move on baby! I got curse out for asking for forgiveness so dishing out to me and not receiving her own bad behaviors of actions towards me. I have a journal on women I keep, yes, I do. Let me tell you this it was man named June I got in his car one day, because I put in for a Taxicab I got into his car it was a black truck a hummer so while he was talking about safety in the road. Then he said wait a minute man I know you then I said from where? He said you use to sale things a run a ladies and men business and I said no. He said man I use to bring my wife my sons and daughters to you however I did not remember him, but he remembers me because I sold to so many people I couldn't even remember then he ask me what are you doing now? I said nothing. He asks how is that wife of yours doing with your son and daughter I use to see you with them all the time? Then he said you really loved them children like they was your own showing them love and taking them out all the time, I said thanks for that encouragement, but we are not together anymore we got a divorce. He said brother I'm sorry, I said the children are grown now and they are in college he told you both loved each other so he said my wife is a police officer and she was looking out for my safety she put a camera in my car as a black man it's hard out here. He dropped me off to my stop where I was getting out of his truck, he asks for my number I gave it to him I got his number to. So, he said when he goes home, he was going to show his wife the video so she can tell her baby look who I ran into that I was riding in my car. He saw me a couple of weeks later because I could not believe it myself, he saw me at an event that I was at for businesses. He said man I love your spirit I keep running into you and I see and learn a lot from you how you inspire me and lots of people to go out on their own and open their own businesses but that night that I went home I let my wife look at the video. He said his wife said oh that's the purse man how is woman and children doing he said they broke-up baby, so she said I'm sorry to. Then he told me his wife kept looking at the video and it was some women that got into the truck, and they were taking off they clothes naked kissing each other and she is getting on drugs and then the wife said this what you be looking at all day he said wait a minute it's not like that. This what Joseph was telling me when he saw me again he was doing his job so she said for now on I'm going to check the camera and look at it every night you come home then she said man my wife start arguing and fussing me out then he said he just left it alone because no matter how much he tried to explain should not listen, accept, or was satisfied so he said he went out for a beer. He looked at me and said Jeffrey no matter what I said nothing could make it go away but coming back home from drinking a cold one does you know when I came in what she did Jeffrey? I said she apologize, and he said I do you know I said I been there done that welcome to the woman's demands, domain, and to dominate the man in their loving way it blew your mind and caught you off guard he said man it feels like I'm talking to a pastor I said none of that here I just had my experiences with marriage. Now he said the wife said baby let me put the camera back in I'm sorry for everything and for how I came at you, so he said no that's alright and she said why you think I'm going to say or be thinking about something, and he say baby you said that I did not say that then he said his wife said whatever. He said to me he kept it to his self because he knows if he would have said anything it would have been another debate, so he shut up and kept his mouth close and let her know anything. So, we went to the bar to get a drink I told him man I went through some things just like you been through married laughing. Now how many women can shut up like this? Some women would say he shouldn't have showed her the camera, but then he would have been hiding something and you have women call that a lie or secret even games but then if she would have found out in another way it would have been why you hid it from me or why you did not tell me and would of me worse! A woman never stops she keeps going she's the mind reader examining! Women, men mend to. See women when you are scornful and build up with so much anger you hurt yourself more and the man you say you want back in your life if you cheated on him, or he has cheated on you it doesn't have to be about cheating it can be something else. You know a woman can't be just aggravated by her husband/man, children, co-worker, friends, associates, IT CAN BE HER OWN SELF IT BE THINGS SET IN HER MIND something she had there for days, months, years, decades I'm talking about it could be multiple of things! See women when you have vengeance all hold in you hurt yourself that you say it be all on the man/men meaning everything some of it be on you know I agree that some of you women let go because the man keep treating you in that same way. There's a difference we you let go and make and excuse of letting go saying it's better for you because he might do it again and you're in fear of getting hurt again after you have ask God to forgive your husband and God has given you your husband back now your still blaming him and yourself saying you left him because it was best for you to get your life right and be at peace no that's being selfish God did not tell you to do that you did that on your own! See it's your way and God's way. You choose the opposite because you look at what the sins and wrongs the man has done but how long will you hold on to that for? Even if 10 years passed by you still will say it will never be the same again then it's you not the husband/man. It takes two as one just like you be by your husband side when he's sinning, on drugs, abusive, drinking, using, arguing, not making love to you, not home, not going to church, then when he gets right you have giving up on him now. I know it's not easy if you are not doing his sins, you're doing your own and now he's by your side praying. See two wrongs don't make a right so will you both go back in forth and continue to battle who done the most and who's the best or do it together with God? You're not the only wife been hurt you're not the only husband been hurt so stop giving the devil the glory gives it back to God! Women stop saying to your husband's when they change well he was not thinking about God when he did this and that with this woman and that woman you're judging him you sure don't want him telling you what you have done wrong after you have cleaned up your actions and sins. You will tell your husband/man quick don't judge you God has forgiving but it's so funny now today how peoples in churches try to change God's word on how a husband sins are different than a wife sin where is that in favoritism! Then you choose to not be wrong for your actions because you say you're sorry but don't show it with no actions and keep bringing up different topics throwing it in your husband/man face as a target shooting him in the face. You are not sorry because you have not resolved it in your mind and heart of working on yourself to recuperate first. Jeffrey knows he tried his best as a man he open doors for Cleopatra, surprised her all the time with all great nice things and always taking her somewhere beautiful! Now listen as it is true those who have hurt you in the past cannot continue to hurt you now unless you hold on to the pain through resentment. The past is the past. Nothing will change unless you change your man has change you have not changed your mind of trusting him and loving him all over again brand new in a charming comfortable peace of mind, soul, body and spirit. You're the only one hurting yourself with bitterness, for your own self learn more health wise for your mind and soul to be with God to love your husband/man because if you can't forgive him then you can't love him. Women you will be trapped in prison this will stop your marriage for what God intends for you to be. It will be prison bars between you and your husband/man, and you will be looking at him as he is the devil instead of praying for him. Bitterness came with Cleopatra because the bitterness and unforgiveness and so much debating it got so uncomfortable where we were bored with one another because there was no rejoice and prayer and she was to blind to see that it was all on me why she was the way she was only. Cleopatra became so bored with Jeffrey, then she wanted bigger things better versions as it is all and only about her she was the only one important and her children fuck me after all what he has done wrong there was no good in him not one good thing to say about me. God, me, her and the children supposed to be together God says the most valuable things in life is not important money, materialistic things, fame, wealth, can be lost extremely fast if God in its first doing it his way not of or in the world with your family. The husband is the head, but women don't run with that taking advantage of the man as you can get away with any and everything! First Our Relationship with God not just the man because the man can be right and not the woman and the woman can always be right and not the man therefore God need to be in the mist. Do you hear and understand what I'm saying? Stop being control by other people opinions and drama. Some women are being controlled by approval from jobs, co-workers, mother's, father's, daughters, children, teachers, T.V shows, the system, media, enemies, internet, false prophets, he says she say, enemies, gossipers, themselves, relatives, spouses even the devil! Jeffrey understood and still until this day Cleopatra is a strong black woman and a mother of civilization. I'm giving her credit, props and showing the great qualities she has as a WOMAN/QUEEN! Sometime people will take the good with the bad the thing is could they accept it? Life comes from her as well much unity really of a strong intelligent, beautiful, compassionate woman watching my every mood, every step thinking positive and negative which was not going to make things better or bring faith with me to make it work she make think and say she did, but actions was all messed up. It was bringing evil spirits and was not working. You can claim it and speak to it with talking with action with God or you can choose to do it with the devil. It's my choice your choice and who ever choices to learn I mean everyone! I choose God! I'm not using the word or my word towards no one lots of people been through what I been through and their own problems even worse. I understand pray on it if it fails or not continue to pray. You see death and life can be say in the power of the tongue, women you can speak life or death towards your husband in your marriage. The devil will use your mouth, tongue and actions to destroy your home. Good is good, bad is bad, wrong is wrong it don't take a child to know and understand that, but women when you are angry all that angry in you don't all come from a man for every problem or situation in your life. God and your husband love and your children are a family and a relationship it's a strong marriage but if there is no love the word marriage means nothing is just a word sitting there! Women your words can be used as weapons as an army base of all kinds of ammunitions you're at a battle towards your husbands this not making you seem like bad people or women you know where I'm coming from with that mouth of yours. You be punishing him yes it's good to vent your pain what he did to you and took you through you can't continue with this, well you do as an ongoing thing or occasion, but you be so angry you don't care or think about where it gets you. What gets you going to is that you get off good thinking you won the fight and debate, some of you have make up sex, some say let's fuck, smile, laugh think it's a thought of thrill and pleasure but the flesh of spirits of thoughts, memories, comes right back it be an ongoing addiction! Both parties feel as thou they won and have failed because they did not look at the big picture of what's going on with their marriage it's just the fulfillment and satisfaction for right then at that time and don't be realizing we have major problems to resolve in this marriage. At times in a woman life, she can get or be too lackadaisical to some point of time in her life she can be carelessly lazy don't be interested at times until she feels like its women please say you don't get like this at times a lack of spirit or liveliness. When a man is falsely accused this will push him away especially with the words you can and will hurt a lot and that's you fell in love with your man, but he did first because it's the man that falls in love first with the woman before the woman does with the man, because the woman moves slow, patient and takes her time. The woman has a love of grammar that's attraction extremely attention that pulls the man directly to her! When things go wrong or bad the man is wrong, if he's not forgiven then what does that prove when you are saying anything to him or talking to him any kind of way, but I say this any man or woman speak will be judged on judgement day. Have you gone to the person and have ask for forgiveness or told them you forgive them? Or did you do your own thing? Or did you put together something at that time and did your saying at that time just to get over its quick fast in a hurry? A lot of women I have talk to counsel, sat down with and interviewed even said they went to God, but they went to their husbands or ex and the reason why they divorce them because it was all the men fault and I ask them did you all really forgive them? They said yes, I said so you all did not bring it back up after you forgive them, they said yes. I said so you did not forgive them did you catch him or saw him cheating again they said no but they know he was doing it see the women was imagining it, thinking about it, focusing on it, concentrating hard, really driving themselves damn crazy! Women when you are angry, bitter, and hot with anger a heart filled with hate will think and speak hateful words your actions, looks, mood swings, body gestures will be hateful this why when your husband/man tries to touch you slap, push, or brush him off right away. Your husband/man will not your heart by the nature of your ways, feelings he has for you, action, emotions and God records you to not only him he sees both of you so on the day when you both be judge without forgiving and treating one another right what will the

Lord say? WE KNOW ALREADY! God erases everything when you come to him and one another it's called one accord because as one you have giving everything back to God even yourselves! Ladies take full responsibility when you talk and treat your husband/man any kind of way that's wrong and a down fall, because if you don't use the responsibility towards your husband/man that he owes you it all. It be I'm sorry, I got upset, I was wrong, do you forgive me? I didn't mean that, then it comes right back up before he goes anywhere, or he comes back you're letting him have it again and he did not even cheat's you be thinking and assuming things. Then when the issue happens, she not complaining with hell because hell was already in her feeling and thinking in her mind of these thoughts and fantasizing numerous of negativity spirits most of it be scornful and bitter! When the husband/man was right all of them years the woman was ramping, ragging, complaining, nagging, petty, out of control, then saying as a laughing laughter revenge angry way I shouldn't have never took you back and don't know she's telling God this at the same time. See when men cheat on their wives you just did not do yourself wrong, but you have done God wrong first, yourself, wife and family. Now wives when you do your husbands wrong who do you think you hurt? You're not perfect do you think it's a special kind of treatment you get. You tell your husband you have God and the holy spirit curse him out but go in the room close the door and cry out to God hurting sometimes more than your husband and you can't confront standing up looking into your husband eyes putting your pride to the side and say you sorry. You come back out the room the next day sometimes lying beside him with a debt making him pay YOU CAN NEVER HIT THE HAMMER ON THE NAIL OF A WOMAN! See when a woman is bitter and scornful it can be from a lot of reasons like A MAN/MEN but not only that some or most will say most of it. It can be life, cycles, curses, unforgiveness, insecurity, low self-esteem, depression, numerous of things but in times when you do things to your husband out of sin what are you telling God? There's no love for no one not even yourself this is not to blame me or men for past sins actions what we have done in the past or now to make excuses hell no, I'm saying you can't hold clouds over your head saying, thinking, demanding that a man takes all the fault, criticism, and don't want to take in yourself that's selfish and stubborn. This is true then excuses come that you got her angry she has every right to say this and be this way do you blame her, so why did God say forgive for nothing for women only or certain time or things! No, this what people put in there way saying out their mouth and doing with actions. Are you encouraging your man or tearing him down? How can he be cry baby, soft, weak when you hurt his feelings? Some people will go right along with this from what they are taught, listening to others. It is past down like a cycle in the family, just like false information also, it is people that's going through things. They tell you how to handle a problem that they are already going through with their wife, husband, family, job, bad experiences. It is hell and they be sitting back smiling in your face pretending that they are there for you to listen, hear, understand, and love but they be bullshitting. They are going through it or just don't like the man you with or the woman. Jeffrey learned a lesson for not telling people he and Cleopatra business. She taught me this and other things yes the woman did I learned this from the teacher, and I was the student but it's funny and amazing how I could not teach her shit and she could not learn anything from me at all! It was amazing I was not great at nothing or never a great teacher she was and still is a teacher at her job and everything she is the boss LEO. When she got home she never was my student on anything or any given time now what kind of woman and marriage is that of a woman that don't learn something the 15 years in our relationship I was all and only a fuck up. You see ladies when you say things about your husband/man that's mean, cruel, cold that can be lasting when your angry you will say not me, who? Who are you talking to? Who have you been listening to? Whatever? Then it be you got some nerve telling her something all the shit you either took her to or she be going through then she has women that's family members like mother, sister, daughter, auntie, and other woman that's in her ear. A lot of you women been here! Do you hear and feel where the man is coming from ladies? You have your time all the time? You heard this lady what you been going through, so for how long will you hold on to a grudge or grudges because you don't forget? The longer you hold on to a grudge the longer it will take you, your marriage, relationships, to have forgiveness between each other and moving forward first asking God for that forgiveness, then forgiving yourself and then your husband/man. So, the one thing from holding you back from moving on or could be several, multiple, thousands, millions of things because them spirits have you gone. It is the back of your mind that you don't even have control of your own self the husband/man is not holding you back it's the power of your words with action please things before you say and let the fear go. If it is you as the problem look at yourself in the mirror and keep in mind it is repeating itself continually just like you keep in mind watching him to mess up again before he does make a move, please make your move by connected the dotes yourself to your not in this alone you must be not hasty in the spirit to be angry, for anger rest in the bosom. All women are not the same, but I sat down with three women one day on spring break and they all told me as women the whole world is theirs and they run it right along with the rest of the other women in the world and it supposed to be given to them. What's in it that's good I said. What about the men? They said not only for what men has done to us sound and acted like bitter women to me, I still said I understand but I said did you only have hurt, pain and stories to tell? A testimony? God? A gift? The only ones been through trials and tribulations? Other people go through things like men, and they said we are not going to let go of what they did to us we will never forgive them because we are owed everything for how much we been through! I said fairly the men that have been through hurt like you they should have what you have that been raped, abused, sick, used by parents and family members, put down, neglected, use for sex and mistreated, lied to push around and bullied, raised up with no home training, love, attention or food, no home, no role models, no leadership right? The first thing the women said was all that was excuses for men for what happen to them it's different because women are different from men. I said that's not love in your soul, heart, spirit, mind to come off your tongue out of your mouth to say with no peace, but they said with God it is and he understand them. So, I ask them, so you women are telling men don't feel in ways you do? They don't take things out on other people like you their human beings just like you do. They don't feel like you feel at all they said, NO! I said they went through some of the same things you went through or maybe worse vice versa.

Men cry to they just don't show it just much as you do a lot of men it happens to behind closed doors. Then they said those men need to stop making excuses grown up and be men and forgive then move on with their lives that's like that, I said Well you all do the same and like they said we are different, and our situations are different than men on what we go through in life! It hasn't been one thing I haven't been through and other men that have not been, seen or heard, been ignored can it be a diary of a mad black man or white man? Color does not matter any man Jeffrey even laid down in my bed at night not my bed our bed with Cleopatra (THE WOMAN) and said let's pray and with anger she said you can't make me damn pray if you don't want me to pray. Where is love in that can you women step back and take a good look at that? In our shoes, my shoes, men shoes women your shoes are not the only ones need to be walked in and have paths in life. Will it be forever in everything? What the husband/man/men/dogs did? Also, what the women as well us/our relationship or will it be the next level is with God to fix this! See the false teachers have told the women you can't make her pray when if she doesn't want to see that don't even supposed to be said what comes out in God saying let's pray. They watch movies, plays, shows and judge them based on what their marriages/relationships are going through telling you this and that like this person and we should do this and that like they say, or I see and learned on television that's for real and not positive what God told them from the giddy-up. Whatever the actors and rich people or anyone say including me in life reality and peace with God no one should go through these times over again life is too short. If I was to do become a Bishop or Pastor, I will not tell married couples that they should not pray together, or you can't make him or her pray or you can't. God does not say none of this and try to use and change God words on what God lead them to say when God don't be saying no mess like that in the first place at all! God will not tell us not to pray or walk up to your husband or wife and tell them you can't make me pray if I don't want to because God love is not that way! Amen to that like God says in his words coming back together after fasting with praying together and fasting together you will be tempted by the devil not let the devil tempt you and you continue to choose it and go alone with it no that's not God. Now when you start praying and doing God works that when the devil tries to interfere. I done saw and hear a lot of women say there's not a lot of good men in the church or not out here they are either gay, in jail or prison, dead, in the streets with no jobs, taking advantage of the system that's the government, lying, cheating, down low, taking advantage of us women, lazy as hell, not about shit, fuck ups, taking care of women children's and not their own, sinners, telling me everything but God, then tell the men quick we leave them in God hands. It's amazing because I did not hear a lot of women speak on the men that go out in hot suits in the sun that try to look for jobs and can't find one and still try, ex-convicts and looking for work and want another chance, going to church and being told and treated that it's not enough, don't have enough jobs and don't make enough money, he's voting, stop doing drugs, change his life around, stop fighting, going out there every day facing the world, going to job interviews saying he's going to be called and don't be called, what the men did for the community, loved, encouragement. Why I did not her this a lot? Not saying it's not women out that did not do it show it and mean it! Can men reverse this? Please don't say take it like a man don't use game or reverse psychology, can men explain how a lot of men took advantage of child support how women are in jail or prison, how women take advantage of the system and government to back them up, using food stamps, their jobs, or lesbians, using men for money, and they just use the men for caretakers sperm donors, there are no good women, they are listening to other people and women all kind of drama. Now look at this man take at this picture and a lot of women will say that's one good man out of a thousand or whatever number they feel good with saying bad or good look at respecting everyone feelings not just yours. Do you see how some women let the news, system, television train them to think and influence their minds with corruption. Now most women will say of their opinions and facts men been this for years to us. Now it's going to come back on them even harder and worse it will be cruel to say what goes around comes around or you reap what sow. YES! I done heard plenty women say they're going to get that man or them men for what they done. I was doing my research on the female the black woman widow woman spider she sends a call out for the black widow spider, he comes, and they mate together then after they make love she goes and kills and eat him and feed him to the children as well. See you have some women like this really a lot I seen them. The man falls in love with the woman just like the two black widow spiders does then she loses her entrance and breaks up with him, uses anything and against him it's not only thing to the matter is one thing he made her that way come on now. The woman that feeds off the mental, physical and materialistic means of the man and then leave him to die confused really she sucks the life out of him just like the black widow woman spider does, then kills his spirit breaking him down not him being weak it's the woman that's doing it after having her ways, love, sex, mind, thoughts, sense of humor, charm, quietness, smiles, laughs, invisible passions! Yes you have women with serious poison in them as well not coming from just man/men making them this way but cycles from mothers, some parents, family members life and they own way at looking at life on handling things there grown to and know right from wrong! It's just like the black widow woman spider who kills her male lover the woman in life raps her soul, spirit, looks, mind, words, legs, her hands, lips, her heart and mouth around the man and squeeze the shit out of him, so that his attempt to pull out before an orgasms fails and the man blows it inside of the woman vagina and this is not all about sex you know where I'm coming from. Now look at this a black widow woman spider executes this moment doing ovulation to hook her mate with a pregnancy bit. When this is the case and it's over, generally the black widow evolves into a baby momma it be a girlfriend or wife or an ex who causes the man to be whipped. Then the man becomes extremely sensitive and be hurt by it and sometimes she is still having sex with him even at times back-to-back depending on the woman the situation, time, place and mood! The woman can feel or make it any kind of affect I like the word affections; she doesn't have to let the man know every single one. Women you have all been there and done that in your own way or done what you done it's your business you're not perfect just like you tell us men! See the black widow woman sent a love call out and as soon as the male respond and have sex then what happens this is nature. Now women get into this way to they make love then after that the call comes and other things than that. Just like the lions look at nature when the male lion mates with the female lion they have several baby cubs

then who is around to be protective of them? The mother lion queen of her pack and the father king lion will not mess with her cubs because when they get older to mate with other male lions and they are women see that lets you know animals have more sense than people. Male lions don't sleep with other male lions, now the women lions will protect their cubs and stay around them. The only time the female will leave is to go hunt to bring the cubs food all the mothers won't leave because some mother lions will have to stay with the cubs to watch over them. The mothers know the son will have to stay alive, so when the father passes away the son will take over to be the king lion the next one that will come in line. Now I have learned that male lions will fight for their tribes and cubs' period. When another tribe of different kind of animals comes like hyenas, tigers, cheetahs, wild hogs, snakes, hippos the father lions will move fast to protect, but when the mothers are around with the baby cubs the fathers can't be around because they will try to eat the cubs because they smell the blood, but they will not kill the women cubs because they must mate again one day. Now the gorillas that's males send the women out to do the work while most of the time he watches the babies and protects. This makes the mother gorilla at times jealous now you have some women argue, be nasty, happy, sarcastic, and funny. They say bitch I'm the widow already he is dead and gone, you want this no I got this or trying even more every woman is not a black widow not even animals in ways. Only the scornful bitchy woman, the bitter woman, the unforgiving woman, the revengeful woman, the envious woman, the insecure and jealous woman, too much pride and drama woman, the movable and unstable woman! At times in her ways changing up in multiple ways she or no one will understand when she thinks and know she will and can't. See I learned that a woman doesn't want no woman or certain women around their man because she feels that woman is going to take her man or pride, I know women will say quick then that won't be her man then if another woman can take her man there's different type of women that be around you, now you all women so you know how women are! You all are not the same but came be territorial, why? Because not all women know their women friends like the back of their hands you must separate your friends from your man even certain family members, they be wanting him or what you have because there jealous they don't have it. Women God did not put the curse only on Adam but as well on Eve and they blamed it on one another like women and men do today the man works and labor and sweat by the brows of his back. The women bleed once a month suffering from the cramps and pain with labor. This is not pointing the finger at Adam or Eve. No God curse both for sinning and was held accountable for their sins and actions. See when you are sleeping husband/man/men the woman has her legs and arms on you or wrapped around or crossed over on you that means she loves you. While you're sleeping she is already awaking in time looking at you with her smiles rubbing you thinking of things she can imagine and fantasize. She will think and have her mind on thousands of things whiles she's rubbing you multi-tasking at the same times a woman is a work I'm telling you so creative. She has over one million personalities, another thing I learned about the black widow male and woman spider is that the woman kills the male spider because if she doesn't he will kill the babies she had by eating them up soon as the male have sex with her she gets pregnant right away then have a lot of eggs. I feel women pain they feel their pain. No one can feel your pain like yourself because you are the one going through it just like us men do to. Now what I don't like is false teachers, prophets, writers, poets, T.V shows, movies, stars, actors, giving any one negative message because these kinds of people have women and men confused. Then the ones that sit back that do this and say I got them sucked in I have a huge audience. See don't be focused on a percentage of men only one of the reasons why they do this is not the women to change their minds on the way of thinking. They don't be caring about the women or men period they tell them what they want them to hear to keep them coming back this is not only in just men that done there wrong towards women, but also in everything in life that done happen in jobs, positions, women, some of everyone everything even sales telling someone what they want to hear good and bad right and wrong. If God is not in the woman or man, they both will be played with this is what they need. It is good for God to send good men out there because he knows it's a lot of good men and women out there while this negativity is still going on this is not a perfect world, we live in. Women and men will feel and say what they want at times they will first do what they want to at times then add God that does not work and never will. These people want to keep certain women on a wrong way of thinking never to trust again and don't want to cure some help with love you can tell and talking, but teaching to forgive let go and let God in. So, you can forgive yourself, the man, and others that done her wrong in life it was just not only man/men it was others to vice versa on men. Then it be they are trouble over again then make it look like a husband/man with a job 9 to 5 is not shit! Really, they are teaching that if he doesn't have a lot of money or education, he going to spend up your money and mess your credit scores and life. He's not the man for you if he doesn't make this amount of money. If the woman went through something with the father, baby father, or stepfather he's not shits point blank and simple it's all his fault like she's perfect, she is not the only one been through things. We don't want to hear the other men side their bullshit and liars! Then there's women that don't want to give men the benefit of the doubt. The mothers are in front of the children raising them up to hate their fathers some of the children don't even want to hear the father side until they get a certain age like with my father I thought everything was his fault. Especially when my mother will look at me and say you act just like your father you got his same damn ways I was this and that but still showed me love because when I got older I sat down and talk with my father. He admitted his faults as a man but do you when I sat in front of my mother she said I didn't do shit wrong it was all on him but as I got older I seen her ways, disrespect, actions, sins on how she talk to men and people, and I said to myself look what someone had to put up with. I see why a lot of women can't get along with their mothers and they be bumping heads back-to-back. We all do wrong now come on my father said my mother put me down and did things and when he went back home he said he could not see them ways because he was young just like I was, but they came out. See the children grow up, but before they do when mothers it's right and they don't realize the daughters and sons are sitting back feeding off all of their ways good, bad and don't know there getting taught bad until they grow older and feel that hurt pain, them actions, attitudes, ways are not comfortable and right being in some ways confused that this is a good mother and what she had to go throw she can get away with her rights and wrongs but that only last for a certain of time! I'm not saying them mothers are bad don't change my words like a mother can teach her daughter something is wrong and that daughter will think at times it's not, it hurts then when that daughter gets married and have her mother talking to her own daughter that she's raising up, she wants to jump in and she tells her to stay out of it but she wants to jump in anyway because she's the grandmother and she been doing the raising, well experience and no one is going to tell her she's wrong but she still gets told off see that's the part where the mother/women/woman thing is cycles. Then that daughter is feeling like that mother felt when the mother is telling her something right when the grandmother is interfering! It could be both ways. See then it comes in after years and years it's my child, my children by taking a protective mother stand using it towards men or anyone you can even imagine it do be for what's right at times and at times it can be to hurt others hurt people hurt people that God knows that is not right women know to. Some come back to apologize and mean it some don't because they will say it and let the past haunt them. However, she does not care then tell the man he's acting like a child, and he's knows right for wrong, and she got to do what she has to her way or the highway. She knows it's right and don't give a damn how the man feels she comes and say do you forgive me, but it be in hate, anger and unforgiveness and women say how can you say this she's just mad at the time because she won't bring it back up on a forgiving heart! Then it's especially important for the husband/man/men to forgive her, the family, and your family even yourself but for her towards you it's not the same because it's different see stop that that's woman and man saying God don't say that. See these people put so much fear in women to keep them right where they are at that they support things on the way they are thinking. It is a lot of women who are bitter for years and years it still be the men fault in their eyes for those men do you know how long that's been how they feel and you still holding on to that? Some women will say why? They were not thinking about us when they did it. Now the false teachers are saying she needs all the time in the world so give it to her God don't say that. In men there are some women and in women there are some men. Man is God creation, and he took a rib from man to make a woman, so there's no sides on who should get the most it's God right and fair. Another thing is when a man doesn't want to listen to these things, he knows that's not right he is insecure, so I don't agree with something that's not true I'm insecure. Now if I'm not listening or hearing I'm insecure, but that's just like telling women who are listening to these false people that teach that are insecure. I see right through the false teacher's crap. Do you? Now I can say all the women that are insecure, yes, I can but I will not do this because everyone is not the same. Everyone has a story to tell we all been through it, and all can say it's not easy more than all the money in the world. Jeffrey was forgiving, gave my life to God and tried more than known he communicated with her. I tried a lot to talk about things good and bad, I tried to build my trust back with her and stay honest, faithful, be there for us make all the time in the world for her! Leave the past in the past even the worrying and the cheating, the ex-s, having no arguments including walking away from her. Jeffrey didn't expect change right away, because he asked his heart Cleopatra did, she need more time for herself, her heart to heal. Now that is a real man, I appreciated her flaw, rights and wrongs. I was her best friend, I loved her unconditionally even when she told me in my face I shouldn't have never taken you back in the first fucking place expressing her anger letting and getting out everything in front of her children plenty of times. I know I hurt her in front of the children so this must continue of her getting me back of hurting me after forgiveness a lot a woman will say take it like a man I did so how long for? If she wants to, and the women say for? When I did not even do anything sitting down to myself she felt like I deserve that for what I did to her in the past then say sorry God does say I'm wrong then change it and come back with the same thing, but I was the only one mess up a good marriage and a home, a good wife, a special woman, a perfect woman, a strong woman, a got it all together putting up with my only stank shit woman, when I'm and only nothing but a husband/man that's a fuck up and shit. It's only 1 thing what she only been through with me! Every time I was rejected from her for something good only time I was redirected. When Cleopatra said she is a woman that was treated very nasty I learned from her and other women, wives, relationships and myself that women will be jealous in their family of cycles that past on of what their family looks at, handles, been through, talks about, they have and they don't like they can see you have love, communication, gifts from the heart, a good man when it first start, going to church and having God, going out shopping can be very jealous. When you tell the woman that they get upset and angry with you especially when you have done something to them in the past it can be for a sin like abuse, lying, cheated, using, anything and as soon as you tell them someone in your family is jealous and let them know they curse you out and beat you getting angry then the man sits there and mend. Then the woman can tell the man baby I feel like your mother or sister is jealous of me and it can be coming straight from the heart on somethings as soon as she tells you this it's a conversation and important not saying at times it can go both ways depending on the man/woman and relationship. See this is not about back and forth, this is how to handle the situation to stop because these things bring on more divorces and teach more women that we hear only us! I hear sayings from lots of women you can't make no one change, but while you're married to your wife it's true love her like Christ love the church and women have the control and the man is the head, and the woman Is the neck, and she can turn it any kind of way she wants to. Then you have the women friends and family members why you are washing his clothes, why you are cooking for him, and making his lunch let him do them things sometimes you're not his damn maid let him do that his self he is a grown ass man he needs to be doing everything for you get him in his pockets. This be the woman that have no man/husband or do just be miserable because not happy in our relationship going through problems and want you to feel sorry for her and share you over to her side. She is in front of the girlfriend, or it can be whoever expressing feelings of hurt and pain instead of praying she trying to break up your home if you just let her in with one mistake you tell her about your husband/man/self! When your happy you bring all kinds of different results in a man yes same as the man can for her but then when problems come with hard times we both got to hold not one person getting the blame for everything which one is perfect? While your man is fixing himself help him to fix other things and motivate him don't put him down. The last time I looked at myself all the mistakes I made in life, but I look at how God looks in me and shine. How far I have grown from the things I use to do I have grown up in many ways I'm wiser, smarter, with a heart made of gold, because of the experience I'm proud of myself, because it takes a strong man to go throw a journey and hard times in life not just only woman/women. I was just sitting there saying lord I need more prayer now as I did when I was a child in mind of not letting go. Jeffrey needed Cleopatra back he was locked up behind her bars being incarcerated. She was the officer, judge, stenographer, the judge's secretary, the bailiff, the prison officer, the correctional officer, the bondsman, public defender or pretender the lawyer, the boss this was not love this was bitter and scornful it felt like 32 years in prison for unforgiveness and sins that he did in the pass as the crime was never over. She still has it under investigation being the detective and the case will never be closed, because she will have more charges and take some off and put more on like their felonies she will close herself down but start right back up I was filthy and still guilty and this what women would say well you did her this way. She is paying you back. She was perfect, innocent and never was guilty of anything. It was just beating me I felt like I was dating and married to Satan not judging her, woman or women I'm talking about my feelings. I felt so filthy where I was begging God on to let me in on his secrets. You can never satisfy a woman, but its temporary, because the moment she's satisfied, who she is she wants more and now she is feeling unsatisfied eventually, so consistently you cannot satisfy her, because she changes up she's a woman of her nature. A lot of women would say be up front with me or straight up be truthful. Then the woman switches it pays not to tell a woman everything, because just tell her truth. Telling her the truth does not mean she can handle it, especially depending on what it is, when she changes her mood or attitude that she is in what is being said at time. Here is an example if you come to some women and let them know there is a woman who been sending me naked pictures in my phone and likes and work with me on sales and same office. I come to show you darling, which the woman is going to ask many questions, throughs flowing in your mind and say it is good you told me the truth. What come up is you cheated in the past, which I can forgive, but I don't forget and use that against me. You can tell the truth, but she is holding things in her mind, at times she would be holding things in mind, because of the truth you told her. She will be quiet and silent. He is still a man by tell me this information did he do this to make me jealous about the sending him pictures. Does he think I am jealous? Is he doing something? There isn't no woman going to do this unless something is going on between them. She is thinking all kinds on of the things this man will get some of the ways sometimes when he tells the truth not just as much, because she didn't catch him doing anything when you tell her everything it open several doors. Then it be she's a woman you got to feel where she is coming from it be on top of the list about her it is both of you, US WE TOGETHER not only her. Now when a woman has kids if you accept the children you will accept her as the whole package, but when it's the man or men and h has children he's trying to use his against you to have you only what kind of mess that is to say and I see and hear these women my children and use their children on all kinds of ways and things to be rude, disrespectful with no manners. Not all women don't do this, just the one that do. Now women do bad men make it bad for good men. Because in that case do bad women make it bad for good women, because quick, fast in a hurry the woman would say you have to forgive, move on and let that go don't be a child be a man with his feelings hurt. Let him know this why he can't move on with a lot of things in his life. Women are you receiving this, just as much as you dish it out? I'm being upfront and forward! Then you have these women listening to other people what they want their man or husband to be especially when he messed up and so much revenge, bitterness, hate, scornfulness, sin is in you there's no good in yourself to see the good in him, because you don't love yourself, so anything that he tries or do will not mean or matter. Nothing at all he's not even your husband no more or lover he's someone just next to you. Some people in relationships come from different backgrounds. There are times in the relationship that being from different backgrounds you can't overcome who the 2 people are and judge each other back and forth. When really no one is perfect. One is not far from the other. Then you can say things out your mouth to put your man down and say things like you just angry, I got an education, I'm independent and you're not, you don't make as much money as me, my family is different than yours, you just angry that my family did something with their lives and yours didn't, what your jealous of my family and if its right or wrong it is not good to say, because

accepting someone as there is love. One day Cleopatra (THE WOMAN) was sitting with me in a session in my therapist office, he asks did you accept Jeffrey like this before you met him, she said yes. All she could think of was negativity, wrong, bitterness, and unforgiving. The looks she gave and expression on her face show the actions can tell a lot you know. A woman makes up in own mind that you can't change her mind, because it's already made up. She is very emotional which is one of nature's creation. When a woman is force against her will she remains of the same opinion still you can't make a woman change her mind. When she reaches a certain level on an issue or a problem that's when her emotions kick in. She doesn't think logical. Woman is the person to help the man meet his obligation. You have women, men saying today he already supposed to be that way and have it together. He's not perfect help your man. You need help to WO MAN! See a lot of them say they don't forgive, because the man is going to cheat again, lie, fight, fuss, don't work again man, so the man is all a repeatedly fuck up. See ladies when you lay down and sleep next to your man do you know when pray by yourself then with him you fall asleep comfortable in joy, peace and faster, no depression and you live longer in good health and strength that's all the man fault to? A woman has every right to feel the way she feels the way she wants its her feelings they are important. She has every right to feel this way for what she has been through, still going through and holding on to the past. She is not being angry as she says and over exaggerating and that's okay, but when it's a man it's a difference, how so? Ow do a woman ever be in a man life taking pressure and problems upon him and cause more sometimes? No, it's always the man has done something wrong. Now it's time to talk about the woman that's the Lesbian and I have talked with them and learned that they are more affection with their partner. Being they are both women they tend to know what each other want in a relationship. A feminine woman knows what she wants from an aggressive woman. An aggressive woman knows what she wants from a feminine woman.

Chapter 11

I appreciate who I am for that special woman I care about and her children that's my stepchildren. When she says stop saying my children not your children these will always be my children. She will always be my wife. See if she would have appreciated the little things I did she would have seen how much I was going out of my way for her. She saw shit only and a fuck up. My mother always said when you're always pointing your finger at someone like your perfect and have no flaws for fingers are pointed right back at you. Every human being needs to be respected even though you can't make no one respect you or do anything, but you want to stay in that way be mad at yourself don't take it out on the other person who's trying to move on and you're not holding their hand, you're not letting go you must let go. Please give your husband/man space to express himself and forgiveness without making demands on him, getting over on him, provoking him, pushing him away by bringing up he cheated but, but, but can run out just like you tell him your just too stubborn to receive and accept! You would not want this done to you and only thing would come up is BECAUSE YOU WAS NOT THE ONE THAT CHEATED in so many words. The woman will say the man is still on the past when it is all in her mind, emotions, heart, body gestures, soul, and spirit it really gets to the thoughts. The man will say you still is holding on to the past then she would say what would you say is any different from what I did. See right there your confused how you are going to be right about getting back at the man also being rude with a selfish behavior. You are right in your mind at all times until you say enough is enough on letting the man a go to start over fresh with a new life saying you had to get you right to get from around that man when at times you cause bad things on yourself as well and did not want to know or believe it! Everything the woman say is not always right and stating from lots of them it will be said we did not say that at that time being this why at times it goes back and forth. Can you accept your man needs even though you don't like them sometimes watch out now, we did do that but most men are no good and they messed that up I can agree on that for they actions, sins and flaws and what about yours? As the same things you want for yourselves when your right or wrong as I hear from a lot of women your emotional women are different. Cleopatra did not know she was being so angry, mean, bitter, selfish, and forcing revenge putting Jeffrey down all times she was essentially emasculating Jeffrey by taking away her love away from him not showing no actions not seeing his. She knew she was wrong when she was to herself thinking because telling me did not mean anything when she come on her own up to me most of the times because she is dealing with her inner self was not easy so she will be by herself knowing and holding the secrets in afraid to let them out thinking negative always that he will hurt her again! It was not easy for me or her, but she had to be the one to put a stop to the way she was handling that because the way she thought she was doing it was the best, right, good way at all times when she was emotionally killing her soul quietly! I was feeling lower than shit itself as well as my ability to provide as a man because it did not mean anything to her it was not enough, I felt like I was not doing my job. I felt defeated and retreated into a corner with my back up against the wall she would not let me do what I wanted to do because I did wrong in the past, but don't keep treating me like I'm that same person she did not bond with me fairly nor connect with me right it was only on her time in her mood when she felt like when and where it was time to. Now some women will say then why you still were there putting up with that or what you have done so bad to make her be this woman or why you did not leave did you pray? Love is wonderful and when you love someone you will stick and stay through good and bad times, and you just can't walk away like that if you think I'm lying why don't you ask the woman/women/wives we don't need an encyclopedia right ladies? I'm expressing this from my heart do I know too many women? Cleopatra did not support Jeffrey when he tried, she will say out loud and mean, I DID! Where the action in and with love showing with expression, I was full of shit every time. She did it in every way that she could feel like a failure. There was no empowering me. How are you going to bring the best out in your husband/man when all you see in him is a fuck up and coming back and forth to apologize. She wanted and did blame me for everything for the painful past all on me. A lot of times she wanted me to be this then that from me not seeing mines she made me feel. I was feeling lower than shit as to well as my ability to provide. I felt like I wasn't doing my job. I felt defeated and retreats. She wouldn't let me do what I wanted to do, because did wrong in the past, but don't keep treating me like I'm that same person from the past. She did not bond with me fairly, she did not connect with me right, she did not even support me. When I tried, she will say loud and mean, I did! Where was those actions she did it in the way that I was a failure, there was no empowering me? How are you going to bring the best in your man when all you see him as is a fucked up, coming back and forth to apologize? She wanted and blamed me for everything for that painful past all on me. A lot of times she wanted me to be this and that wanting me. What she wanted me to be rather accepting me as I am and encouraging me to become myself. She can sense everything. No, she can't on most things. She is a strong woman. I gave her that credit, but I couldn't sense nothing off her. She did not do what I did. I am considered green shit incredible Hulk, controlling fuck up, she's wonder woman always with the A+. Never falls with the star. This was not motivating me. This was pushing me down with pigs. Women let me tell you something to learn it's crippling and defeating. She got flash backs only just her. As woman you should sit down and ask your man at times what it is you will like dear? What it is I am doing wrong? Because you pressure him to do this and that, make more money, be more this, more that, you want this. You want all these things that is great, but what you really need to sit your ass there. You need to ask yourself is if you're trying to get him to be that way. It would be good for you 80% and less for him or want him to be that way only for you, because he owes you everything in the world. Don't see the good in him only what she wanted to see. Now I learned about the silent woman from being married I needed to worry, because at times Jeffrey was about Cleopatra he already lost she just told him in so many ways and words with feelings and attitude. A woman silence is her loudest cry, Jeffrey knows this, because Cleopatra use to ignore him all the time. She was over thinking and tired of waiting, falling apart, crying inside when she loved him. She loved hard one minute she loved me the next minute, then she hated me. She couldn't live with me or without me I'm only me one man there will not be no man that she ever gets with in the future like him. When Cleopatra was silent and Jeffrey could feel her cry she said to herself he done so many things that hurt me, but inside she was crying to herself and out loud. When I was away, and I could see it standing in front of her. She will say when did I work it out finally you hurt me again. She really didn't until her apologizes. She never showed it she just kept saying it. Her actions were showing force and hatred. She was to bitter for words this is the silent woman. When she took me back and was telling me sitting right there in front of my face, I shouldn't never take you back. It was her telling me I don't want to be married to you ever again in love with you, I can't stand you and I didn't forgive you. I can't stand you. I didn't forgive. When she kept sitting down talking with me. We weren't supposed to give up on one another it was not all about her. Cleopatra had a heart that was bleeding with blood was everything and all my fault. I said most of it yes, but not everything. Some women silence can be loud, some can silently depend what mood she's in. Then some women will say you act like you know me. Like Jeffrey never told Cleopatra she wasn't shit, that didn't mean he didn't mess up in a lot of ways. I like this saying that Robert Mugabe quotes you cannot give a woman everything and satisfy her it goes like this. thing and satisfy it off her it goes like this. You cannot give a woman everything she needs. If God himself gave them eyebrows they shared it and draw their own. God gave them nails, they cut it if and fixed their own. God gave them hair, they cut it off and fixed their own. He gave them breast; they repackage it to what they want. God still gave them buttocks they arrange it to the size they want. If they are not satisfied with the things God gave them. Who are you to think that you can please them? My brother doesn't kill yourself. I did more than satisfying I was a strong man to accept somebody else children and stepped up to the plate and they been other man left on the damn table, so I be damn If I let anyone put me down. No matter it was winter, spring, summer, and fall. Jeffrey made Cleopatra feel special. She holds on to unforgiveness with her daughter being Scorpio stinging me with anger of poison expecting me to die and I was not alive to her. I am not going to lie Jeffrey did Cleopatra wrong, because he didn't love himself. I was raped, so many times. I wanted love I was looking for it and I felt it, but I wasn't showed it, so the sex was to make me feel worse, because that's all I knew. I understood it felt good, it felt bad, it felt uncomfortable, it felt like evil spirits and good spirits. It was confusing can you women understand me? Now you will say I'm making an excuse to hurt women continually repeatedly and not manning up to my wrongs I agree, so what you have to say about this to your women sides is it any different are they any different? Will they say they prostitute, because they been rape, so much their lesbians, because they been beat, so much is that an excuse to keep hurting men? You will say it's not right. She is a woman you got to understand where she is coming from and been through you can't feel pain. Pain is pain. Hurt is hurt. Everyone goes through it. A woman doesn't want to only make love that's not the first thing on her mind. Jeffrey read that experience with Cleopatra he was a man to understand and learn that it was tough for him to do. I thought with my dick. What I mean is I was affectionate with making love. I was soft, had playful intention and cheering her up. The more I showed that the more she fucked my brains out. Yes, I'm a man I said it she put it on me I'm whipped it was good. This is another secret man hide. They feel weak that if they don't tell the woman. How good she pleased him she will be taking over the bedroom and everything in the relationship, not true! Both should be honest, upfront and don't play mind games or sex games. Now Cleopatra initiate intimacy it was more than a need, but then she pulled away, because she couldn't keep her promise of forgiveness. A woman says she wants her man to pray with her because God love. He is the spiritual leader, but ladies and to Cleopatra. How can I be a spiritual leader? She didn't ever give me a chance, encourage me, and put me down? Well women will say you can't make her, so is she not breaking up a home and tearing it down? No! Everything is on the man it falls all on him, because he's the head I know God sees everything. When I wanted to make love, she rejected me selfishly. When she wanted to make love while cursing me out or not, I still made love to her, because unresponsiveness means rejection. A husband that gives his life to the Lord, have changed and build his home back up it don't have to be about money hell no be thankful, faithful, fruitful, joyful, positive, because let me tell you something wives if your husband does not feel and see connection or paying attention and focused on him you will push him away. Then when he goes away as the queen bitter strong woman, I don't need to run him down. What he did to me. Hmmm he got some nerve. He did this to me first he will be back. I got this you're not with no marriage you're with the servant in garden with Adam and Eve punching him in the face. Women don't realize sometimes punishing your husband with silence is punishment enough and bad communication. You all know what I am talking about, so don't go there with what are saying, shut up, stay quiet, we under control, you can't tell me when to talk, No! I'm saying hurt people therefore me and Cleopatra went back and forth. She was so smart to where she was dumb blaming me for everything in our marriage. She couldn't set me free for forgiving me for what I had done to her, so she didn't forgive herself. Cleopatra thought she was the only one always feels sad. She couldn't change me or anything. She was the only one determined. She felt like she was the teacher to change my only bad thoughts. I have sat back, seen and knew that you can learn something new every day with a woman. Today a lot of men don't know how to approach certain women, because these days there is a new generation and old generation. Which do you choose? A lot of women feel the thug men are safer. When they want money, the women feel the richer man gives them things they want in life then being with a poor man with a 9 to 5 job. They want a fool that is rich instead of a faithful man that's poor that is trying. He can show he's trying we got this together. A boy and a real man are two different people just like a girl and a woman. Jeffrey found out Cleopatra perspective. Every woman has one! Cleopatra had needs and concerns. She was with me and wanted a comfortable, healthy relationship, her time, meaning feelings and communication. Cleopatra also in her ways a black woman that loved me and made me slap Monday, beat me up with making love on Tuesday, put me in her hospital, physically, spiritually, mentally, financially on Wednesday call me up on Thursday to let me know on Friday and Saturday she will be burying me and dig me up to take me to church on Sunday. I love the story about Abraham and Pharaoh they both wanted Sarah. Pharaoh wanted Sarah because she was beautiful and sexy. God went to Pharaoh and let him know don't touch her because I will kill you. Pharaoh did not touch her because he knew God was nothing to play with. What God put together no man can separate or come between what was put together by God. A woman is serious about her feelings that is why I had to improve my behavior for Cleopatra. It was showing her how much as a man I was being for the Lord, a husband and father for my family and marriage, but she was to blind to see that it was good and bad, sorry then not back and forth. What she didn't know and see that she forgot I was a human being to. She can't expect me to be perfect in her mind like she said you can't tell me what I'm thinking, but she can tell me quick in her mind as a woman it's just like that leave like that! I'm a man I couldn't help her with every problem! Communication and understanding for both sides not the woman most or all women mostly including Cleopatra know, feel, and say falsely accusing, provoking your man or husband can't push him away. Women if you like this is not just words this is actions towards the person that loves you and you love back. Women don't know that bullying and controlling your man, because the man is doing right, he is not being believed, drained out and can't fight back with love with no true story or faith, because your bitter. Your man like I was under scrutiny, security, he is let down, helplessness and overwhelming right. Cleopatra or women please understand where this man is coming from. Women do you have a family member or anyone who have not forgiving you and it hurts? A lot of family is like this today they can't come together, because there is no real let go let God and forgiveness. Now I feel you men the family will gang up on you and attack. When the other side does wrong, they are looking in the mirror with good things to make it look good. I got this I got that I'm doing it better than you. It's not about that it's about God's love and coming together. Now Cleopatra would say you don't need to talk about coming together. Yes! I sinned I did wrong I repented. What have I got out of that? A slap on the back in the face an eye for an eye, but I say to her she can say whatever. I want to say this my mouth she's a good woman in God eyes, because she knows the God, she serve's no it supposed to be We not only she everyone! Then it be you can't tell me nothing. She right you can't tell no one nothing who knows it all, don't want to hear you or listen. Women don't say you can't make her, so will say fair men or man stop being hardheaded and listen. It

will come back. No, you don't. I want to teach this. I will bring
marriages together pray positive and love. God first not wishy-washy
teaching what people want to hear, but what God says. Women your
men cry to not in front of you sometimes or most of the time depending
on the man. We are different but believe me he's crying inside as fuck
up. Jeffrey was only towards Cleopatra he cried to. He was a cry baby
to her. When she cried all of it was real mine was fake all of it. If she
says until this day, I didn't say that. It will be a lie, because one she came
back to apologize. When she didn't mean it, because she came back
arguing right after the apology back and forth. She was bitter and angry.
If God know we are all hurt, cry and mend hurt one another. Who is
anyone even me to tell someone don't cry! Cleopatra lied to because she
was injured that she didn't forgive me or herself. This comes to reason
that she can only believe herself in everything. I was seeking time from
her and patience. I kept walking away. I walked away to let her be to
herself to pray. I won't be there to do anything aggravating her at all. I
even said I am a fuck up. I owed her that much do you hear me women?
Guess what? The goal was to destroy me right back ladies. I'm not saying
your agreeing I'm just asking, because I feel women who been through
this and men you go through it to feel it to. Let someone know how
they can deal with it. Women you're not going through it alone you're
not in this by yourself and you're not only independent, because
everybody needs somebody! See I understand even an accuser needs
help and a provoker there lying to. It is a nasty, hateful act, mean and
accuser needs help not only a man that cheats on his woman or wife.
We all need help in different ways and areas in life. This don't always
be love and don't help the relationship really the marriage. For the
woman to defend herself being angry and bitter. She takes her bitterness,
anger, they have taken someone else down with them. The women feel
like they all clean all in the clear and beautiful. You can have a beautiful
face on a woman. It can be on a handsome face of the man, but the
actions, ways and doings tell it all both together not one side! Falsely
accusing and provoking is an aggressive behavior and act. You're telling
your husband I don't want you no more you fucked up you're never
going to change. You're going to always be the same, so why you get
back with before telling him this. When you're with him this then after

your telling hi m this back up and still tell him. This destroys hearts not only men! Cleopatra never ever recovered from me. What I did to her, and she lied to me. Most people are afraid to hear the truth when women gather the devil shows up and sit there, pays attention in the corner of the room watching, listen and whispers in every one of their ears just like Eve. It going to be a lot of readers especially women saying what this man knows about a woman. He doesn't know anything at the end of the day. When you do tell a woman the truth. You hit them with low the blow, child please you don't know what you are talking about, anyway you don't nothing about no woman. Where you got this information from somebody had to tell you this or that is. Your opinion. Really, I don't care. I can't come out with no book called a Diary of Mad Black Man that wouldn't be right, because me woman will say your holding on to something you need to let go. It's the past and you need to move forth. God created marriage for not to hurt or envy. God created marriage for pleasure and forever like Adam and EVE. He created them and they chose to do what they wanted to marriage. This why it doesn't work today because both parties reject God plan. They do what they want to. See you can never satisfy a woman because the cycle on her brain. She wants to be a mind reader. Then it he doesn't do this when it really means do that it changes. She changes the woman everyday as well as her hormones constantly even before or after her period. Even before it comes on her mind, brain, body, and everything changes. She can be a nice witch, a bitch, moody, cranky, loving, aggravated wishy washy, tired, build up it's, so many ways you can't explain right women or woman. She even changes her outlook on herself on things. She changes up so much she will leave you at the starting line. If you can't hang with her, Jeffrey can hang with Cleopatra. She met her match I met my mines. She just always wanted to be right and win the woman! One day she will dress sexy the next day she would dress regular. She changes up the woman loves to read and find out things some be nosy. Well, I will say most women is mysterious finding out something is her key sometimes and can be easily irritated. I learned that women score higher on test than a man, because of their brain. How they think more, because she wants to be right all the time to tell the husband/man what to do. What he or them is thinking right ladies/

woman. Her fight a lot of times like I said in one topic is beat a fight or argument with silence, attitude or it could be ignoring you being funny or sarcastic, joking or no sex she has a lot of ways of defense she can even try to use God leave me alone I'm praying right now. She can make up any little thing to be left alone. She can say just leave me alone, but I know she know I know we know a woman is not going to do that. Her ways are unknown. She will say that is not for that then what is it for, because you have million and billions of ways and changes! Her manipulations can be smooth, quiet, she doesn't want you to know who she is or where she is coming from at times. Women are aggressive in different ways. She is overly sensitive and emotional. She has high levels of stress and low levels depending on what she's going through. The woman also is aware of what's going on focused on herself as getting back up when she falls of going through things in life. A woman can avoid conflict and bring it right or wrong. She is easily turned off see I learned that when it's time for her to make love everything in her mind is shut off she only focused on the husband/man, her, and the mood and orgasm. With Cleopatra Jeffrey played one time he said baby you are putting it on me she slaps me and said stop baby you are messing up the vibe then he said to Cleopatra you said I act like you don't be putting it down, so I went with your flow. What you wanted she wasn't satisfied on that. Now like I stated when any woman is bitter, angry, unforgiving, revenge, vengeance, and most of all rude. She refuses a man's advice period. As I got ready to be a real man for myself, God, and family, because no matter how much increase I gave and showed in our relationship she was not interested in me. She was not ready to risk conflict when we forgave one another. She wasn't even motivating, helping, or encouraging me. It was raging hell in her from bitterness. She was too angry to see it. I also loved her and always was proud of her to have strong desire to do more for herself be more independent and better her career. She was bickering with me more and more for me hurting her. She was holding back for the person she wanted me to only be for her not us. Now when I say what I had to deal with as a man in a relationship since women have a lot to do and listen to I'm a pain in the ass trying my best, doing chores, washing dishes, washing clothes, stressed out, dealing with daily issues hers, mines and the children. Also dealing with her family problems and mines with my crazy family problems at that. The consist headaches which goes with paying the bills emotional stress. I always had duty to do I am this complete loser and fuck up. She drained the life out of me on days, so women do you only go through this in a relationship and marriage? The worse thing is being blamed for things I didn't do! See I'm letting women know you're not the only one that feels unhappy or happy sometimes, let down and the whole world or your world is turned upside down. You're not the only one full of emotions. You have some men more emotional than you at times. You're not the only ones feel or experience depression, loneliness, mental, physically exhausted in life men do too just as much as you. Then you have these women that say I'm unhappy all time, because of this man that made me this way. It's his fault all his fault I did nothing wrong in this relationship or marriage. That's someone that's perfect. The quiet woman her best quality is being silent and it's her strength. She observes and listens to different situations and makes her decision on how to respond to another thing. I have learned about women that called their period different names. Their period or menstrual cycle the names are called Susie, period it's that time of the month, friend, on the rag is the old school women I mean elders other names is curses, or a curse. Aunt Flo, Auntie, Army, war, mother nature, bloody Mary, monthly visitor, moon, sharp weakness, change up. Another thing I learned about every women period is not the same it can be months heavy and month light changing up on the woman life stress, healthy life, depression, sick all kinds of ways. I understand the different between a man needs and expects of a woman needs. I see some women, so angry come out loud and say leave me alone my period on let me be. Another thing I learned from the woman is that she knows when her man is sick, she knows when he wants to eat sometimes. What he is thinking you just can't get in her mind, because she's the encyclopedia, the dictionary, the wrong, the brain, the laptop, the IPHONE, all calls in and out and knows everything. She will tell you she doesn't know everything but mean different at times. The woman brain is a brain that function that's stays boost of energy. It's like a race at the starting line the woman is the gun the starting line the bullets and she goes off. It could be in a good way or bad. She leaves and you be trying to catch up you will drive yourself crazy even walking away talking a breather and coming back at times she not satisfied! She wants more and more. Don't mess with most of them when their period is on because they be mean, tired, aggravated, frustrated and over withdrawn. She takes days off work. She can't work some women they can't call out right quick. The woman wants it to be quiet and left alone depending on the mood and the woman. Did you know how many times I looked at Cleopatra pad to see that I love her enough to go buy them for her and to do my best to show that I love her enough to go buy them for her and to do my best to show that I understand her experience women only thing. You see men especially black men they mostly he got seven children. He bit on women, he is on child support, he drinks, he does drugs, he doesn't have a job, he's in jail or prison, he's gay, he's a dog or tricking, only he fornicates and have the flesh in him, he doesn't have no time for the Lord. Is its good things men do? What I never felt the pain and cramps women go through that is very hurtful pain you can't even imagine. I didn't experience from certain women that I've seen with my own eyes that they can be a bitch. When their period comes on this is not out of disrespect this be actions. What comes out their mouth the number one important thing in a woman life is God. A real woman does not need to feel loved to have sex. What women want girl chase, because its God vice versa for a real a man what men want boys chase a woman wants and will love herself and feel loved and free a real man to love her. See when I was happy when Cleopatra forgave me, I felt free I was friend to her thoughtful, supportive, considerate, listening, hearing, understanding, accepting, non-judgmental, uplifting, and encouraging. I was also a loving man exciting, energize and hyper with, so much stimulation I was a challenge. I loved a look at the heart. My heart physically, my romance was affectionate, sexy, fun, and different. I was a provider being all these things wasn't enough. Jeffrey was becoming what Cleopatra wanted him to be. It was God first then her. It was not easy especially when I messed up. Jeffrey gave Cleopatra what she wanted. You don't have to ask God for nothing he know I did my best for everything above. I made sure she was everything upper and higher than anything. I was high myself. I was crazy in love still is today because she asked me. You didn't find a woman yet? All these years it been two years. Well did she even find a man even though that's not my business as she would say. Ladies on break-ups, divorces and separated. I loved her she said I didn't because I wouldn't have done the things I did. I agreed! Never did I say the sins and wrongs she did to me was that love? I didn't say she's still God child. I hope she just would of saw in that way. You can't make nobody love you or see you in love until they choose to. I just see when a man does something wrong its different, everything changes up. She took me for granted at times. She couldn't see the man I tried to keep my woman. She didn't even know to hold resentment against me judge and unforgiveness that was her power against me. If I can hold this in my mind and towards him and bring it up. Whenever even at the right time to hurt him like he did me. I won anyway, because he can't never ever win again, he's a loser. I'm now in control of this relationship. Now since he controls it my time am I wrong? No, I'm not. This never gave her soul comfort never did heal me, because we were not one in our own home. She didn't want it to be. One that's why she didn't forgive me fully 100%. She did it for her only way to achieve her own moral superiority, but not free or love me what she stopped calling me fat jaws. She didn't see daily dramas of unforgiveness she saw me as only hurting her the only evil person is me in her eyes. It went as I did the most, I did the most sin I'm the worst person. Bringing up the same old thing we forget the former things, do not dwell on the past. When she talked to me, she never brought the best out in me this don't only go for women or woman this goes for men and man to. This is not man's world or woman. It's God we just living here until our times comes. No matter how long or short you talk a loving person smoothly and naturally will sit there and listen when they love you and care. I admired her I was waiting on that. I made it about her more than me a lot of times she couldn't see that. When I gave a compliment or gave positive things to say being good and fair. I didn't get positive feedback I got cursed out. Now I sat down with like 10 women at a restaurant one day and they brought me something to eat. They just told me to sit down. I look handsome I was on Miami Beach, so they saw me walking with my suit on they were from Alabama, so one lady seen that I had my tablet. She said what are you writing what that is I said I'm writing several books this one is call You Can Never Satisfy A Woman, so they said add this in there those women talk so much add to much on we do we talk a lot every woman is not the same I know I just had to write about these women. So, I was sitting down listening to these women talk they also was saying we talk about other peoples and other things and drama. I said if you talk about other women and people's you don't think well. We talk about one another behind each other back if you are talking about drama and other people, they said all at the same time. We are friends. Well, I learned from my mother as a woman. If a person is on the phone talking with you about someone behind their back, they will talk about the person who they are on the phone with or away from. I'm not putting women down I'm just showing you the experience I have sat down and learn off different types of women. Another thing I learned about the woman is that. When she has sex or make love to the person, she with she can tell. If he's been cheating by the stroke and the strength of the feelings and size of his penis and testicles. If its big or small. She knew what is going on before you know she is the teacher testing everything. It does not mean every woman looks for the man is cheating. She knows when its good right and on time. I have let some women know about this book the title and topic they got angry and was offended, because I was telling the truth and telling the secrets. Women have secrets for a reason they don't like them to be told but want to find out the man secrets. You have some women that can't handle their alcohol when they drink. I see this woman that was drinking. She just was standing there and she just peeing on herself, because one she had a weak bladder. She couldn't hold it anymore. You have women who drink and be happy some drink, because of problems. Some drink because they are addicts. A woman is someone who's independent and be there for her husband and children and back him up through thick and thin. A lady is the beginner she in that stage of being a woman. The bitch does not care. She does not respect herself or other. The whore will sleep with any and everyone. A classy woman that's a woman of God will feel God and herself not pleasing others first to like her. In her mind and heart, she will not feel slutty that won't even be in her head, but I can say I see a lot of women on the streets who went from losing their dignity and self-respect. A real woman will keep her head up standing strong. It's complicated to satisfy a woman even thou they have much confidence in themselves. I learned that certain women don't have children to defend them being a woman this does not mean that. She would not take care of them. If she had children, she just chose not to have any children. A woman mind never sleeps. She can love until there's no love anymore. She can be there in a relationship when it is over you are thinking of a master plan. Really several, because a woman mind never sleeps You know I agree a woman is left behind of the role of a lot of responsibilities they must pick up and a man to. What hurt me the most was when I got saved, gave my life and soul to the Lord. When I stop being of this world and still was treated, put down and talk to like I was still living in it. It's a big difference between living in this world and not being of this world. It wasn't all and only about her hurt and only about her hurt and only her and her children. I'm a man my feelings were hurt a lot more than I admit saying sorry for me and her just being better man. We both are human beings and emotional creatures in God eyes a lot of times. We look at and see what we want to and our way. It was times she hurt me on purpose and by accident and swear she was the target and victim always. When a Jeffrey did all that he could do for Cleopatra that he couldn't do anymore his spirit felt crush, so women you feel men crush your spirit, so don't say bold or be harsh and think what did he do wrong or men? See when she rejected me on making love that hit my heart, mind, soul, mentally, and started frustration with emotional strong pain this because hurt feelings but he was a cry baby. The next thing was money if God says in his word better or for worse just because I'm not making much as my wife or less does that matter if she loves me? I'm shit I'm a fuck up, get your no-good sorry ass up, even when I was trying. Even when having her mean attitude towards me she so bitter to wear looks actions respect towards me is this mother fucker is not known well he should have done what he done he's not appreciative or giving credit for shit not no more for what he has done to me. Jeffrey told Cleopatra thank you and love you more than she did after she forgave me, she chose not to celebrate the best in him. Instead, she was pointing her finger at me every day and the worse thing was she provoke me so damn much she pushed me back to the streets. I asked these one day. It was two of them I asked can you satisfy a woman? It was a joke they said it at the same time, Hell no!! I said why? One said she wants too always be right. The other said she always wants something. A woman is not satisfied because it's all the man's fault a woman is very fickle. The minute you figure her out or something about herself she's going to switch up. It can be a fact, or an opinion any conversation or something that was done right or wrong. She will change up it's her nature women always mean the opposite at times of what they say it's a natural reflect back-n-forth also women are prideful they just don't admit to it and are so dramatic. Don't doubt your husband from things from the past of your personal insecurity's, family members, friends, and certain people leading them astray Cleopatra did this to him, but Jeffrey showed her that he genuinely cared and love her so much. Women are complicated creatures. A woman has her needs, wants, likes, and say or speak on she's going to be heard being stubborn. It even makes them at times impossible for them to just really talk about or focus on one thing. The woman changes up every day in certain ways, shape or form. A real woman looks on life that's what fits her the best. Not only does the woman be focus on how she dresses and look she wants the car she buys to go with what she's wearing depending on the woman. Jeffrey learned from Cleopatra she was and still is multitasker all by herself. She did get carried away, but I only did that to her in her ways, thoughts and vision of negativity not just only hurts and pain I done wrong. She was crazy and insane, a Leo but only times I made her that way come on she's a human. Cleopatra was a woman that was constantly searching of Jeffrey happiness even with him making her laugh, smile, giggle, blush and kiss him with a hug. Then tell I'm so crazy a trip, I'm just too much, a hand full, I'm something else, what she's going to do with me let me know if I left something out now. Now what was she? I don't because she was the innocent one, she was good not bad. A woman doesn't even at times because she's difficult or her mood swings or changing up. A woman will give hints and signs like Cleopatra did to Jeffrey he knew it because he will say what do you need or want baby? It was not about sex it was about me being a man of God stepping up more to understand to how she communicates. She was the strong black woman that got straight to the point I was listening it was just a doubt in the back of her mind about me was filthy, because I gave her so much attention and I was like I'm uncomfortable where's mines. I complimented her on her on everything she has done. It was like leave me alone, ignore me, but I still made her feel appreciated. I told her the clothes she put on looked beautiful, her hairdo was nice she was a beautiful woman, and I will let her know even with my sins why she was being holy and perfect she was the best thing that ever happened to me I loved everything she did even when it was wrong. I was hurt because she was a part of me inside and out. I knew what she was comfortable with and not I had to us was in love she taught me some of them things I learned things on my own watching, this is why I knew what would get her angry or not. She still was angry from the past pain and hurt I'm the man she was sitting back always watching to make a move on me at any time when I was not doing nothing, but her mind and negative vibes knew it all and all the time it was not true. It was not God, prayer, positive, health, and doubting it was mixed up and confused and the woman will tell it as what you did to her only and let's hear her side. Men, please listen to me women change up on their emotions and feelings and who they are this don't mean there bad. We can't live with them or without, God puts us her not only them only God knew everything about. Cleopatra always like to have fun she was always looking for a new idea for of lots of excitement from me because she could not stay mad until she could not truly forgive me. She wants it now then changes up from time to time. A woman loves to experience other things that interest her. Even when a woman has made up her mind about everything it still changes because her mind does not rest it's just like when I was around my mother with my aunties and other women I got jumped they was always right and never wrong. Experience is one of the best teachings. The experience in life myself and being married two times and in several relationships with different women I learned and observed them. I was just waiting for the right time to come out with my book. I had a friend, and his name was Walter he was a son that was raised with a single mother and became a Lawyer. He felt and lived a life that if he did the right thing that he wouldn't go through things that black men period in life go through almost every day. In society he seen lots of black men go through things from different cities.

All kind of clients that was black men go through divorces doing right and good for their children and wives taking everything from them the system, judges, juries, and society was on the women side. This black man lived a decent life. I'm telling you it's a true story so change this look, think of it as no kind of a negative way. He was never on the streets on knew about the street life. All he knew about was being a Christian man, getting an education, being a good husband, father and being a good person to other peoples that less fortunate he became one of the top greatest Lawyers and thought of representing people from the streets. Walter thought by living the life he lived there he will never be mistreated by the law. Until one day he went out to eat with some friends of his somewhere black some were white so he remembered that he left his wallet in the car, so he told everybody he was going back to the car to get his wallet. As he went to open his car door the police grab him and slammed him on the car he was screaming I'm a Lawyer I know my rights what I do wrong they said shut the fuck up and arrested him on speculation that he was a black man about to break into a car. He had on a suit, but they did not see that they saw a black man. They took him to be process fingerprinted and stripped him naked and made him squat so they can check his anus. Walter told the officers you can't do this to me because I'm a Lawyer and I know my rights and the police response was our bitch now nigger. He sat in jail for the rest of the night. Even though the state dropped the charges against him tested it and take away the hurt, humiliation, and the pain he went through because he looked like the black man who burglarize somebody else car. I told Walter and women especially blacks that a black person in America has no chance in being in a positive light. No matter what the up bringing or situation he comes from, because he's a black man he's still going to be treated unfairly and put down not just by the society, police, system it can be other things women you only don't go through especially what a black man goes through. It is the most everyone has a story to tell and a testimony. We all go through it. Walter told me daily he has clients mostly black men that come to him constantly for representation against the mistreatment from police officers using their position to abuse and hurt them daily, but he would have never thought that one day it would happen to him because he was a professional Lawyer live good and stayed out of trouble. He thought how he achieved became successful and he thought who he represented or became which is a Lawyer will change all that, but reality sat in to make him realize no matter what his situation was a black man in America. It's just a matter of time where they get you and emasculate you and to make you feel and treat you lesser than you are Walter thought he was an exception to the rules because he was a black Lawyer. He always saw it's done to a lot of black men but when it hit him it hurt like hell a pain that hit him, he did not give up, but he was so angry. I felt where he was coming from I been there seeing men and women raped just as much black young men in foster homes, shelters, false prophets raping men and family members abusing them they are being neglected just like women even worse it goes vice versa but most are not giving attention to men like there doing the women. You even have the women saying the only thing they go through worse is the police and make that as an excuse not to go anywhere like my situation. I been out of prison 27 years, and I thought if I changed they would treat me different I started voting and only doing this for me a change makes a big difference if it got worse just like when women say and men when you are giving your life to the Lord the devil comes more and more. Well, what do you say to the black when he changes his life? When I was not a criminal any more or a bad as it even made me feel like shit. When Cleopatra told Jeffrey you always in some shit people was looking at him judging him from his past what he did wrong instead of asking him what happen. Now I'm not the man I use to be anymore!! It's more things that's hidden those black men go through and not giving credit for like they should be fair and no one owes anything, but love that don't give people in this world to put women higher than men or men higher than women no one! Another thing is no matter how much you tell the woman your sorry for what I done wrong for cheating she will never give you a chance back 100% faithfully, honest, truthful and be stating it will never be the same like it used to be or ever be the same way like when we first met. That's what she feels, think, and believe what she going to get out of that. I want a woman any woman to please and love herself for hurting Cleopatra Jeffrey knew he had to give up all the power to win her back that happens sometimes vice versa: not all and only for women.

I'm not angry or do not like women I'm just trying to get out that men go through just as much as women cannot be satisfied. If you find a woman that does not love herself where do you think you come in at the same thing goes for the woman finding a man that does not love himself. The woman can't do everything and so as the man! I have learned the other secret to on the woman. How she will buy a dress, leave the tag on it, then take it back to store for refund on her purchase. Another thing is and don't say women that's a woman. It was a brother name Roger his lady walked up to him complaining about money in front of other people. So, he stood there quiet she said speak he spoke. She said shut up then he you told me to speak. Now you want me shut up, which one you want me to do come on now. She said you're trying to be funny, so he shut up. So, then she walked away saying I don't want to talk to you no more. I have nothing else to say to you don't call me it's over. She walked away angry, frustrated, upset and she got in her car slam the door and pulled off. So, now on this situation some women will say she was wrong. Everyone is entitled to their own opinion, so women will say what he did wrong? Men will be men regardless. A woman will say I don't ask no man for anything. I don't need nothing from a man. She wasn't wrong it's something he did. Now if the man did this to the woman and it was reversed the world would be coming down. He would be everything, but a child of God, no good, a dog, rude, disrespectful, no home training, no father role model or figure, no manners, don't know how to treat or talk to woman, have all kinds of cycles a sinner, very cruel, nasty its others, but guess what she called him then wanted to talk to him. He said I thought you didn't want to talk to me anymore. Now women would say if he would just shut up. She was probably calling to apologize. The same thing goes for both parties. Did the man have to taken through all that? I know some women would have said if he would have just given her what she wanted. Then guess what she came back and said I'm calling you why you not answering your phone don't you see me calling you. Is this a woman being a woman or only this type of woman? Every woman is not the same, because Jeffrey went through this with Cleopatra. She would get on the phone fuss me out then apologize then fuss me out again. She would even stop talking to me, which the role come out into the mind games. Who he thinks he is? I'm not calling him first. He is going to call me. Men have +ways to of their ways. Men being men, so is that a woman being woman. A woman she's never satisfied. Women been telling me and so is a man not satisfied. Some women done got in to if with me debates about this book. I'm writing most women said it's true you right about that woman. I didn't even know; some scream their statement was you not lying about that. See I need to explain to the women is that there are supposed to be no secrets, lies, mind games towards your husband/man, no hidden money, bank accounts, friends, girlfriend, or boyfriends. If you agree because marriage is different from boyfriend and girlfriend. I'm not talking about paper I'm talking about the bond, because if you take another thing to another thing what do have? Ladies it starts enemies, curses, intimacy, drama, thoughts that are negative, because Cleopatra just looked at me coming home from work with mean, angry and bitter face. She asked me who I been listening to. I cheated yes. I stepped away from God commandments then when I repented God made me pay for all that I had done. Cleopatra added more on to God plan with her evil thoughts, bitter cruel heart and she was blind to see God was punishing us both. We both was out of line in our relationship, but she was too selfish to see that you right. Women when you tell men that's hardheaded you can't make no man do you right or treat you right if he does not want to. You can't change him, make him do nothing he does not want to know vice versa. Can you women say the same thing or be stubborn or selfish. He made me be this way. I never was like this. It was all his fault everything! When Jeffrey got saved and then Cleopatra told him I forgive you before we got married then took all problems home saying I should have never taken you back. You right why did she? Did she love me women? She was angry at the time then why she forgave me? I am trying to figure that out. She is a good, loving strong woman. What am I? Just only a man! That's all! Women will say you broke that trust that's hard to just give that back. I agree it is on life of sins everyone does including me. Cleopatra didn't know her frustration of bitterness was her walking up to me confessing she was wrong, which she would turn it into a fight more of her not letting of the past. What I did I did not want her to give me her trust. I worked and earned my trust that I didn't get. How can you tell someone you forgive them and don't, because you must do that to make trust possible again? When you go to God first, yourself, then yourself, the other person and then use excuses every time that forgive, forgive, forgive, with no actions. This man fails and messes up me, myself yes, I'm getting on me. I got up clean myself up and shit. Jeffrey thought his spouse Cleopatra was going to choose to forgive, encourage me and help him for us both to start fresh of rebuilding trust. She did not encourage me she hold on to I was a failure and over my head and used everything against me she could her children, her family, using it in arguments. The truth is better than a lie I'm all these things but no I'm not I love I have a great heart and a great passion about myself she said if I did not want this to work I wouldn't have took you back now would I? Yes, she said that, but she didn't show me she was the one wanting everything granted to her. Jeffrey tried hard to do complete Cleopatra and he put that on his mother's grave he wanted her with God's grace and mercy to walk with him through his past and hers together to heal one another with God first he could not do it all by himself either. Everyone is wounded, hurt from sins and what someone did to them not only women. This is not no excuse for adultery, lust, fornication, cheating on their wives no this is for all sins. Today in time we just want to be stuck on one thing and use that towards someone to keep provoking them as a target, but eventually we are lying to God ourselves and the person that did us wrong. Yes, I know, because I done it no one is perfect. Cleopatra helped Jeffrey with the past then soon as she gets angry it didn't come out in Gods way it came out in a provoking, hate, anger, then she thought it wasn't a lie. What she was doing and telling me that I'm going to stop bringing this up, stop throwing anything in my face. It was like she was looking at me as if I were doing dishonest things in front of her. She shows evil actions and expressions at me. You have certain women agree with this party sad and happy that make it last forever. He shouldn't have done it in the first place, so how do we make the relationship or marriage work? It gets worse and show's we are ready to break up. My prayers and love with God I were told it was all fake and my sins were even worse. Even her I know the God we serve don't look at that or say that these marriages today don't want to include God. They need to watch how that gets you. suppose to heal one another at times. Cleopatra wanted Jeffrey dead because she will tell him this. Why this happens to you in jail, and this came back on you for the way you treated me. Do you know they almost let me die in jail, because I went in more than seizures? Then if I would have died what would the women have been doing. What you women will say of course her husband, so she didn't mean what she said she was just angry at the time. She loves you. I wish she really see me as a Christian. Just like she saw herself falling short of the glory of the Lord. The woman has her bipolar moods sometimes especially when they can't get what they want they get upset, angry and stubborn. Some of these ways can't keep a man home. It doesn't always be the man fault. It is the woman ways, and she don't know how to talk to her man. Especially how some women act differently when their period come on beware get from around them and let them be. She highly in her irrational moods back to bipolar. There would be times women can be distracted and go into depression. Sometimes it elevated their moods. Its evidence that it presents differently more in women then in men. It is all kinds of things with women it is their guilty pleasures such as shopping, sex, with or without consequences. A woman can be bipolar in ways, and it affects her emotions. When you think she over here she is over there in the state of mind, emotionally, spiritually and physically. Women want to talk they like to detail and explain. In a marriage in a relationship.

Chapter 12

We all have faults sometimes we look at other people faults. When we cannot see our own. Cleopatra said everything is my fault and everything in my marriage Jeffrey did wrong! Now you have the lady that keeps up herself with her eyelashes, her hairdos, nails, body and one is with the triple necks. Also talk about the woman who wants to much and do not want to give anything I return being selfish. 50/50 not 60/40! Do not look at your man for the money. What he can buy for you give you. Look at his heart. I was sitting down in McDonalds one day and I see 6 women sitting down at the table. They were from England. The person that was sitting next to me was Mrs. Christy, so the ladies was sitting down eating. We spoke to them they did not speak back. So, Ms. Christine said they was acting snobbish, so other people spoke to them. They were ignoring them to, so I went to the table and said hello to the one I felt had the worse attitude, so I ask her a question what you have to say about women. She said Well me, and my girlfriend are different from American women. I got the one to speak with the highest attitude that was rude, because I knew when I got her the others was going to follow, because I knew when I got others was going to follow, because she was the leader of the pack of the strong women together. She said she was not black, and her friends was not she said they different and England. Well, I was saying to them how is that by the way your attitudes are you eating in a black community and eating 4 different kinds of food in a restaurant that you did not buy the food from that you are eating, so she said my name is Lisa. Then the other friend said my name is Shalonda. The other lady said my name Grace. Then it went down to Cynthia, Rose and Daisy. So, Lisa said we are about her life because it is her life, and she gets to decide how to live it. The average woman is not the same, but they all the same not true not in everything only in some ways. Women it is not the man anger it is both of you. You gave up the I's for the us you are in it together. Do not God get angry. Women holding anger against your husband/man from the past is dangerous you have it in the back of your mind as where he is at.

Where is he going, he is doing the same thing, whose he with, he is with that bitch, hoe, woman, slut, women he cheated with me. Oh! you do not like it, but you love it in your mind, because it is a get back. Do not let the sun go down on your wrath, nor give to the devil, so why you take it there and go to bed with your man angry. If you do not let the anger and unforgiveness go it destroys your soul, heart, mind, husband and relationship for an example Jeffrey and Cleopatra moved and our new home. She was saying after she forgave me that you with the same woman still, you with the same woman still I even went to witness, the pastor they knew, because he was counseling the other person to that was a woman who Jeffrey slept with on Cleopatra and the pastor told me Jeffrey knew. I believe you, because she has someone now, so a lot of women call this pain power for all of them for what they been through. What Jeffrey took Cleopatra though when she said I forgive you; she will come back and bring it back up before Jeffrey started back cheating before he started back texting. Now that is one thing Cleopatra was not taught well on their family cycle is to forgive. See she never dealt with this. She never really sat down with me. I am sorry it ended here. I will never bring this up again. She does not know she cause destruction by doing this. It was all my fault. Her heart was becoming evil, worse and hardened our relationship lost its intimacy. Everything was not left to me. I was the head of the household that does not mean all the responsibility goes on me. That is pressure on the man. Then past and future already in a woman mind that is bitter. I did not say that she or them should not be bitter when they are hurt. I agree, what I am saying after the hurt is there then you claim say do and put in action of helping and working on yourself of forgiveness. Then you say you forgive him, and years go by you say you needed more time to heal. Life is too short and after several times you accept this for as long as I say its time. You do not think you are pushing the man out there. This is how your anger gives place to the devil. The devil just does not laugh with the husband/man and gets him. He gets at the woman to all of you got to do is ask Eve! Her meanness and anger within. Herself deceive me on everything. All she saw was lies about me. When I told her about the truth from the past of me telling her lies. Tell me women or to the reader that can learn something where does this go on in God eyes for anyone is different for a man? Or different for a woman? No there no opinions. Therefore, the God I serve; Jesus Christ and the Bible is so serious about forgiveness. When Jeffrey walked up to Cleopatra to speak with her it shows he was being honest with her. A lot of men walk up to their wives and have their say in matters and it be the right time to speak. It just the woman can be selfish like it will be vice versa for the man. When the wife is in need the husband is there for her. When he says I love you let us talk she will say all you do is you want to just talk. When it is her who wants to talk is quite different experience. A woman has her prerogative about things especially herself and her life. She changes her mind in a second. One they are women it is a thing to be proud, humble, strong, snappy, independent developing circumstance. She would even change her mind even when its unnecessary. All of which have a solution. She makes decisions in and out of heat, she regrets it afterwards overtime. When she is calm or not calm. Especially when she is missing out. She also can be common at times being influences by other women. It could a colleague, friend, family member, girlfriend, church member, associate that has talked them out a good or bad decision or anything and no one cannot make me do anything. I got my own mind, but she will tell another man or any man who have been listening to or talking to or who you been around. Then say you made me this way forever. If I am with you it is all on you! It is like I said that is a woman. She is being a woman that is how a woman is, that is the ways of a woman cannot live with her or without her. The ways of a woman are strange or will never be known, no that is the woman you been talking to that is what the woman will say that read this. One woman told me she just goes with the flow in life. Another woman name Tasha told me she was bitter, evil, nasty woman. She said when she lost her son God changed her and she calmed down a lot. There are different personalities in a woman. A therapist through hard times, a chef in a kitchen, a freak in the bedroom, a coach when you are off your game, she has all of it thinking and watching everything. A real woman would not stress her man out. Like Cleopatra she should divorce before she took Jeffrey back because she did not fully forgive at all. It is that not being a hypocrite, bringing up the past in process trying to make work. She was saying Jeffrey was already cheating when he was not.

She keeps saying I am sorry I am sorry and would come right back with anger taking control of her. She would also come back with you was with her. You were texting her. You do not know how that feels, so I deserve this for how long for as long as she said she wanted to end the relationship. Why are we divorcing? It is not because of me only. Some women that are bitter have times for talking out their toys for their needs. She does not have a man some women do for sexual needs mostly single really pleasures themselves, she horny, hot to satisfy herself. Why do women sleep with other women men? Women say because he is man, no good in some cases, he is a dog, cannot keep his dick in pants, cannot be a real man and think with his mind and be with God. That is true! Something for the women who sleep with men who got a woman. She cannot keep her legs close, she a hoe, no good, disrespectful to herself and she knows right from wrong. The way you get a woman attention is eye contact. Always be a gentleman. Never treat them like objects or talk about them like there inferior. Always offer a sincere compliment. Patience let her make up her mind if she wants to move into the relationship. Do not be pushy, never give her the wrong impression. This goes for your man/husband how to get your man attention. Give him space, speak his language, love at that, do not be his mother, but get along with her, do not push him and cursing him out. Now a man or your man has a say so and a fair side. A human as well as you now listen. It is good for ways to for walking with your man, but no so good at the kill. You women know how to get your man when it comes to keeping him. It is a different story when you got him, the question how you keep him you saying you know how to do that already, but there are other things that you can do to keep a man by your side. Also help him to appreciate you and taking steps to commit to each other. Women do have intuitions, but he every woman is not the same at times depending on the matter of the situation that is going on. She can be right or wrong most thinking they right every time. You can coming home take off your clothes she will look at you and ask who been 1sleeping with? Where you been? Are you telling the truth? She will be thinking it right in her facts, ways or say that she feels you are lying. She gets the last word, her say, opinion or just not saying nothing at all and rolling with flow because she loves you or not, just sitting back watching, homework, testing, looking and observing. I say also starting an argument or her actions will show a sign of not wanting to have sex, playing mind games. Now if she says I am a woman of God she has feelings to. She will talk about it and tell you how she feels straight upfront. Some will say this and that. If I must check him or look at him. I do not need to be him at all that's bull shit because the credit you get is sticking by his side with all his good, bad and bull crap. The thing is do you have shit that smells bad to and know he puts up with your shit and ways to. All these ways! A woman will feel second thoughts about something it is a feeling she may have different kinds the right thing is listen to God and the Holy Spirit because God will not mislead you. A woman is not always right. Sometimes a woman can confuse herself, others and still be right because she wants to be. Now you have women they be waiting for the next argument to happen because of the past there is no peace there is only getting back and it does what? Only make things worse like drinking alcohol the problem goes away temporary, but once you sober the problem is still there. It is better to sit down with your husband/friend/man and talk with him instead of going on with this for the rest of your life. A woman says men do not give up be, so women do not you give up the relationship or marriage. If it takes two with God in the middle, both parties be trying to avoid something that has been happen for years. It has not stop yet. The way plans get hard, stressful and we get upset and angry. It is the way you resolve issues with a fight or argument period! Let your man have a deep conversation with you. You need to open to him, because avoiding him would not help the situation. It can be important things you both need to discuss. See you have women who want to the children first and other things but forget about the husband and marriage. Women did I say forget about your children? Put them away? Forget about them? No! So where is this as you say what you trying to say my children do not come first! Use this as a target anyone or anything to make you look good love do not be in this. This be bitterness, envy, pride and unforgiveness from the past. I understand women the man has beat you in front of in this your children, financially messed up money, cheated on you, lied to you that made you feel less than anything in this world because you put your all in him and invested your all in him, so he has earned everything back! Now if you do that your way ladies what is going to happen? Not nothing, I understand the first 6, 7, 8 years might take longer because every situation is different. Just like every woman is but once she forgives him, takes him back, forgive him again says she ask for forgiveness from God, forgave herself. You have repented asked her children to forgive you. Everyone has forgiven one another, and she brings it up again that makes it right because she is bringing skeletons back worse. Why take something you claim your things to work, and you are not helping you have help because it happens to you, you need time to heal and get over the hurt and pain, but you do. You can use that pain, hurt against the person who hurt you, so there is no forgiveness. Women this just do not go for your children this goes for anything. If you put your time all in your girlfriends, job, career, children, family then you are investing in things other than your husband then it is all about your way or the highway a get back. It is in your mind, you/he should have never done what you done right ladies. Look at yourself in the mirror and ask yourself would God tolerate this? So, should your husband? You feel yes because he was a handful and what he took you though all these years. What have you done NOTHING! Many women are hurting, so are men ladies. You are not the only one hurting and in pain. I see a teacher that called themselves a teacher. Women deserve and need more things than men. If that is true than there is no God and I know that is a lie. Jeffrey showed Cleopatra it was not about the money because when he had my ladies and other businesses, Jeffrey loved her so much and still do for the arguments, disagreement and confusion to go away. I did it for God, her and myself. I even pulled her to side in the kitchen and said look all these women calling my phone and texting me things. All these lies this what we got saved up. Let me quit this business, what I love doing, my dream, my gift to stop this all is that not love? Is that not a real man? She said no keep doing what you are doing I am sorry! I said you sure because I knew what I was doing. I been doing what I like and what I love for years like women love their gifts and independent on so look at where I am coming from and understand me. A lot of you women then like to listen and hear other family members on your marriages. I heard this girl, I heard this girl, I heard that, he did you like this. He will do it again and your man do be doing good if it does not be him always right women. Then it comes more and more remember what he did to you on this day, I saw him on this day, I listen ladies you did not see none of this and you beat him getting angry. You ask him who he been listening to because your wrong and him your feelings are hurt form something from the past and listening to. He says she say now do not go up to no strong woman with that! So, do you think you should come to your man with that? If you trust him when someone does come up to you about your husband/man/ spouse you will walk away after you forgiven him, but you sit there trapped in your mind, if you women been telling men lots for them there hardheaded even me, myself. You have not been selfish, stuck in your ways and do not want to listen and say that's just woman. Men you do not want to make an excuse for wrongs, so you women listen to the same thing. Do not go of what you feel, hear if you do not have proof and see it yourself. When I changed, I put Cleopatra as a wonderful time? First after God because I admit as a man, I was putting her before God worshipping her feeling like I need to pay her back and give her everything. I felt like a slave, but then I had to pray and repent get me right and focus and put God first. Then I put in my effort, laughter, smile, passion and honesty. She was better than my priorities. God had me going while I was sleeping in my car that I did not know what tomorrow would bring so what I have is God, myself, my wife and children so I cannot be angry my wife cannot stay angry too long, she needed to learn how to forgive and love with all her heart. It could not be about us arguing about one another fussing, only about enjoying!! The heart she did not forgive me with she could not do it because at the time she did not see what Jesus did for us. She saw what I only did to us. I looked at her when she loved me all faults and cries when she was fighting battles and crying behind closed doors, I will come and say let us talk, are you alright? Even when she told me nasty things against our vows I still listen because she was a woman that was hurt and burned inside. She protected her king I protected my queen vice versa we stood up at the same time to die for one another like in our yard that day when we got out our car at night. Cleopatra stood in front of Jeffrey to take a bullet for both of us he was ready to fight for her and defend our children. I told her nice things. Jeffrey loved

Cleopatra. Things like baby how did it go today at work? Do you have some papers for me to check? I miss you baby. You are so beautiful! She said things to like calling me fat jaws and telling me my eye lashes is so cute I want you to give them to me, telling me I am so handsome. I let her know my past as a child and how I am not the man I use to be in the streets and changed I never wanted her to feel sorry for me because enough was enough with excuses with blaming everyone else but myself. Jeffrey just wanted Cleopatra to understand who I am and love me for me after forgiving him. Who am I? Special, a gift, love, a heart, good and bad not perfect just like God sees in her he sees me the same we both not perfect no one is. There is no need for revenge being bitter. God just do not give woman chances. He gives everyone a chance after chance who is to say to judge the man of everything falls on him! Now to please a woman man you must be ready 2 days ahead in advance it is not about the sex. When she is ready for that believe you will know she a real woman. She would give it to you in time. She is comfortable to but that is not the first thing on the list. The first thing is God, second is prayer, third thing is respect. I love this because I was stupid, dumb, and a fool. I learned a lot from my past sins, mistakes and faults as acting being, and doing things childishly. Now Jeffrey grew up grown and became a man of God, Jeffrey defended Cleopatra and her children, he made decisions what he knew, what right instead of what he felt like doing. I raised another man child that was not around to do it. I was a good father and man being told I was hard on her children. I sat down and talk to them about education, check on them when they were sleep at night, gave my stepdaughter plenty of kisses, they were sleep at night gave my stepdaughter the cover up with her blanket. Closing her door and his door. Now you have a mother who did not do it for me. Just like mother and fathers who did not do anything for the children. I did not have a lot of children. Mother and father could be doing for their children in this world, but they are not. I just cannot understand what is going on today at all. They do not have and a lot of children I can understand a mother sin. Do a good grandmother sin. I do good with sister, auntie who sins and do good. They are holy than thou and the other men/man is not at all teaching. Women when a man comes back and admits his wrongs, clean up all his garbage. He left outside behind his self. Why do you bring it back up? That is just like when you change your pad you do not want to smell yourself. You do not like when your cramps are doing to you. You want to repeat the same thing with your husband/man/spouse the same bloody nasty pad and you say that different how is it. I agree with hurting. I am back and time to get over but how is it I agree with hurting him back and time to get over but how much time to get over how much time is your overtime. You do not like how your job treats you just do not forget your relationship and marriage is a job to. You can get fire wives/husbands is that something to be proud about? You are not giving up on these jobs, retirements, car, materialistic things, paycheck, money, but giving up on your marriage. Sometimes a man can be weird, but he also let you know and show you that you can rely on him by being consistent in both his words and actions. I also admit I been through hell, struggles in my life and I let them struggles bring me down limit and define me, but I am a man who have tried, seen through a lot of things and still until this day I know with my life myself I have accomplish many things from where I come from and what it used to be. I appreciate the good in life anyway. A woman that has children to raise and is pregnant once she has the child it takes 30 days to let her body build back up. Some women are different it can take longer than 30 days. Now if a man cannot respect his woman or women he just does not qualify. He needs to respect you on every level on your personality, your values, your emotional needs, physical needs also important the general outlook regarding life, your flaws and your past. He will go out his way. A lot of people say if a man cries, he is weak. A man who is uptight and cannot express his emotions will not let you in completely. A real man is not afraid to let you in to show you his real emotions. He speaks his heart out I guess I was just too emotional. Now women uplift your men/you man! A woman wants to see action on you loving her not just telling her because you can tell her all the time, but the servant you are not doing it and showing it and what does that mean? This goes for your man/ladies do not think that you deserve all the credit because you are a woman and your special is true, but it is 50/50. I know people do not want unforgiveness, the devil, envy, hate, bitterness, jealousy to run their relationship because God is useful for teaching, rebuking, correction, training, righteousness so that the servant of God maybe thoroughly equipped for every good work. So, tell me something. How can you tell your man he lost a good thing when you took him back? He changed and you said you was moving forward with man/husband leaving everything in the pass and then ladies that do this for you back it up. It is wrong confusion, corrupt, provoking, bitter, says he deserve it. No matter how long it takes her to forgive him and let go of what he did to her. He must pay back. He should not of did what he did, so this got to come back on him that is the way it is. How we will our opinion and accept it. It is not all and only just about you be careful your actions affect other people to mines do to I am not perfect. So, we all need to be careful what we say and do. Now Cleopatra the woman was complaining about all the bad things Jeffrey did good. I never hid my relationship. I allowed her to my house and family house. As well meet her family I was not a shame and introduce her to everyone she is a lady until this day. I was not afraid to show my feelings or affection around anyone. Even her I was and still is proud of her I was not perfect. I had a lot of faults and wrong. Love does not cheat, lie, commit adultery, abuse, wicked words, provoke, hurt, not jealous it was no one thing! Jeffrey just did not beware of the dog he was Jeffrey also was aware of himself of my own bullshit, but is it that the woman is perfect, because Cleopatra swears up and down, right or wrong, left to right, side to side she was not wrong. Ladies revenge on your man is not right when you take him back, go to counseling then year later you say you forgive him. It be revenge and forgiveness. I do not understand how they can teach and say there's forgiveness on every other sin accept adultery or cheating! Revenge is payback a way to settle a score and keep going for as long as you want it because you to blind to see when you have won and when it is enough. It can be funny, harm, especially affairs of the heart and you want it last for many years and no harm done because the woman likes she happy by doing it but be blind close doors or in front of your face acting like everything is ok. Then it be another after another. Then she wants to forgive then get even. The best revenge ladies are to forgive not right away, but when you do mean it do it not just say it, because you bring unforgiveness on other things in your life. When people do you wrong and do not know how to handle it, but you do a wrong you want to be forgiven right? Now you are spending the rest of your life with man the one you dream about, hold, love, kiss, talk, pray and make love with, so in your mind you are fantasizing. What you are thinking of already. What he is doing when he is not even when he is lying beside you or not gone to the store you think about your going to get him back with or use against him. You picture it right there is the attitude, mean look or the smooth look without him noticing and you do not know it come back and get back emotionally because your happy with yourself so how is your relationship is not going to be happy with your man is, he really your man or you just took him back to tell him I wish I would not have never taken you back. The woman is keeping herself from moving on and healing. She will reverse it and says you then blame you for everything that you are not the one moving on. The revenge turns into mold, acid, hate, frustration, aggravation, it causes a cycle that continues and never ends. It poisons you ladies that do this and the man at to people that live around you the woman does not seek anything but get back. She becomes so moody, cranky, mean, bitter, and say she still love herself her man/husband and do not be she is quick to let him know if he is the opposite of him what he got to do. What help he needs. She cannot be treated this way. You cannot tell her nothing because you made her this way. She plans so many ways to plot revenge! Now a woman has sinned but no matter what happens in the life keep a good heart. A heart of trust and patience. Do not let the darkness of other people harden your heart. She said tell other people this as well and stay out of trouble. The revenge from the woman she will say continuing her revenge, have back upon her side thinking this way of people getting into ear listening to other people there is all kinds of penalties you will be charged with. It is in the Bible women. Now if being evil it goes from evil to insanity and cannot even think straight not forgiving anyone is like killing yourself. I understand about making your man know what he did wrong and getting him back because it takes time to heal but making him suffer over and repeatedly, No! Then it will not go away because ladies it will be stuck in your mind you will be spending time every single day for as long as you be together for what he did to me it is hurting you constantly. The hurting part is it never stop it keeps going and going because one cannot forgive and is hurting from the pain that was done to them. The other one that is trying is in pain because they are being stepped on. Now a strong woman will forgive and mean it that is and a virtuous woman. Now if she constantly seeks revenge that is a weak woman. She will be intelligent because she will ignore him. The man does she says, do this do that even after she has forgiving him. He does his duty as a man loss of people still will say no there is something he is not doing right. Something is going on or what you did wrong again or THAT IF THAT'S TRUE! When it is not how that feels? Revenge do not be a road to self-destruction. Who would want to be around you? You do not be happy with your own self. Never take your own revenge, beloved, but leave for the wrath of God, for it is written, vengeance is mine, I will pray, says the Lord. Do not get me wrong each person story will be different. Revenge will also have the woman telling her man what he should listen to and hear but when it comes to him, she does not care because her mind and revenge is that you did not care. So, now why should she with revenge there is no communication, no relationship, no respect, no love, no trust, no reason to continue. This why Cleopatra told Jeffrey I should not have never took you back repeatedly. Before I went back out to cheat on her she did right there after forgiving me for years and years in front of her children disrespecting God, our relationship herself and me. There are no more best friends anymore. Ladies your vengeance and revenge are mind games as well you want to be in love and make love. When you want to be or when it is convenient, but you be angry says a friend always loves, and a brother is born for adversity, it is for good and bad times. This is the time when the women and man, husband and wife together more the devil is tempting. So, you should pay more and full attention to one another to come back and make it right not get back at one another back and forth. Cleopatra stops believing in Jeffrey after she forgave me. She wanted it to be only about her and her children, but what God created us to be for our relationship to one another and our children. When you are angry women after forgiveness that's not real revenge. Revenge starts into criticizing your husband and rejects his differences. You will not remain his woman for long because you do not see him as the person you fell in love with. Do you want to marry someone who is just like you? No! Therefore, it supposed to be compatible because listening to the mother. Friends, family, children, people then you will look directly at your man and beat him getting angry. You ask who he was listening to. When you are doing what you are asking him and your so blind, angry, getting revenge back at him you cannot fix up and help him, he cannot do it by himself. In your eye's woman it is a one-way road, but it supposes be a two-way street. Both parties can hold their ground towards one another but do it in a respectful way by respecting themselves first. Then one another enough to make your ideas heard while also respecting one another with a chance to speak. We choose to live different response like most of the time women you like to hide your feelings like you can read this book calmly and say NOT ME! WHO ARE YOU TALKING ABOUT? Not this woman. You mess with the wrong woman, every woman is not like that or the just think about it when your angry, upset. Want it your way or the highway holding on to something that your angry excuse of letting go years ago and you have not. This person than gone on with the situation and you have every excuse in the world. You hide your feelings instead of talking about it. You act like everything is ok. You got it all together, but your behavior is rude and wrong. When you reject your man when he is doing right because you are not satisfied by your needs. Turn your heart away from what he did years ago that is opening confusion, drama, manipulation and blame him for looking him straight in his face with bitterness for man and woman, no matter how cool, talented, educated or rich you think you are. How you treat people tells it all, even if you are broke. See I became aware of my own bullshit that a man because it was in my mind that I changed. Jeffrey knew not to treat Cleopatra like a woman not a dog. It hurt me when she started looking at money because God vows do not say that on relationship. Society got or have a lot of us gone that's not creation that's stupidity. I have learned that a woman body is not public property. Now another thing that is not fair and not right when a woman says and be bold on that if she argues with things from the past, get back or anything that is unnecessary that it is like court it will be held or used against you. I been out of prison 24 years, and I got my rights restored to vote. Do you know how I got treated by some officers and I served my time, but I keep it moving same thing for a woman. See a woman will stay quiet at times but that does not mean she does not notice it is simply means she chooses not to waste her energy on foolishness I agree she has more important thing to do. This do not mean her mind is not constantly going thinking about her man and other things that is a woman. Another thing is women to be held accountable when that day ever come. This is not a history lesson or taking sides it is facts. You do not have to be soft to respect women and women you must be bitter to. I am sorry to tell you this lady you cannot go into your marriage with unforgiveness, bitterness, selfishness, pride, angry, frustrated and no love, because of hurt way from the past there is no 100% that you are staying there together. You are in it for better or worse. Your sonly, not papers, court, he says, she says! Society today teaches, treat and tell people that marriage is a contract. Richer or poorer, sickness and health not my husband or wife lost their jobs, so we change into gold diggers now and one or the another cannot handle it therefore women pick up these cycles from their mother's. It is from generation to generation they have one foot out and one foot in lukewarm false prophets help the women on this to by not praying for the evil spirit to remove and the heart to be changed, so tell me something when some use to sale dope then they got saved and become pastors or bishops did people come back and kill them and they got falsely accused and did they reap what they sow? Like Saul when he killed Christian people then when he gave his soul and his life to God. Did God make him reap what he sows and make things come back on him constantly or period. God do not keep no records! Be there to support your man when he is doing good encourage him do not put him down. I am not going to like when I act like a child and did childish things. I had a lot of growing up to do. I did not understand a lot of things what it to build a forever relationship. Jeffrey learned more as he got older, but Cleopatra could not see that he did not want to be treated wrong who deserves that. See the woman is more complicated the woman brain is smaller than the man, but the woman uses both sides of her brain the man somewhat sometimes uses one side. The woman also has a lot to prove today in society that want everything in their favor. She also has the part when she drops her eyes close not shut but almost and pulls her hair back this is one of her ways of pulling the man in, I learn from a couple of women and watching them in action. I know its women out here who bring themselves down I agree because they feel like getting a man will encourage them first, they got to love themselves first. A good woman conduct herself on how she speaks, act and respect herself when I meant agree. I meant that on the pain they go through not going to another man once they break up with one that hurt them vice versa with a man when he is hurting. Now to the woman and women I am glad and thankful God bless me with sisters because they are giving me and putting me up on ways of women how they think, act, actions, loves, games, education and more and more things. Like the divorce with Jeffrey and Cleopatra soon as we broke-up the next day. When we met for me to give her some money for her and her children. She said she do not love me anymore or is not in love with me anymore my sister says I see that is the bull shit because 22 years of being together and raising her children. If love was not there why she come back just to get money. I know she is better than that she is a woman. She knows you going to keep doing a woman do not have to say nothing at times. She just will be quiet sit back and observe but that is a lie. When she told you, she is not in love with you anymore she is bitter, angry and upset. Women lets be real you are not the only ones that go through and finding disappointment and pain unforgiveness is not nothing lifelong love. All the time you be saying I forgave him I did. I did but when I did, he cheated on me again. He did the same thing. Did you look when you took him back. Did you really forgive like God says so and do it like he commands, or you did your way and blame him that you could forgive him off and on because he sinned, but you are sinning and your blind to see because you are bringing up the sin. He did to you from the past, let the past stay in the past. I am not talking about all the years that done past by that you put in prayer, time, love, fellowship, church, each other. Then after that you felt like it was not enough because of your insides of yourself being selfishness cause that. The reason why Jeffrey wanted to make sure Cleopatra forgave him is because we would not get relationship in evil spirits. I said if you need more time let me know in front of God, me and you right. Now if you need more time let me know. She said no let us move on after the forgiveness after the words because it was not from the heart. I do not care what it sins it is if you do not forgive how will God forgive you. We all move forward. Now to all you people say that life then it will be living in a miserable hell pit and putting your hands in the lion's mouth. See when you do revenge and pretend, lies or any pain or hurt for a certain like sex. It is ranging fun with the devil but the point I am trying to make is how long it last. It will fall apart just like Cleopatra sitting there when Jeffrey was in a relationship to her not around only her children with her telling him. I wish I would not of never took you back. Words are like a two-edge sword man and woman, wives and husbands. The source of love is God. Your feelings change sometimes we fell one another, sometimes we let one down, but therefore God needs to be there. The love of God for God to us fellowship together is eternity. God loves endures forever so why would you pastors tell you to wait for them to pray or do not make them pray. We all need prayer. Always pray, always come together, always love this what has not been taught today. Your relationship supposed to go deeper to God. You have a lot of women I learned from and looked at sitting back observing and being taught and going out with as well as living with them, teaching me something and learning from them. Them being them or one woman by herself just being her. I write this book with my attitude, my education, my opinion, facts, patience, time, and brain! I did this I wrote this I learned that a woman can be a sweetheart but if she is pushed or treated wrong, she become aggressive and be a bitch! Some women get judged before knowing them. A lot of work hard. Do not look for handouts. Do not deal with lazy men. Some are laid back. Do not talk too much unless something to bothering her. She knows when to speak. When not to depending on what mood she is in. She loves her freedom. A real man knows when to give her space and time to herself! I am not bringing in my perspective. I am bringing the truth there is no games. Here is my story, my book takes it like it is receive it just like you give it out. Women are not the same I say this because every woman has different personality and different mindset some or a lot of women say that is just a woman some change it up from when I did my research and homework, some women is willing to settle for less or they may not understand they are worth of what so much they are being taken through. Now women know to be free differently for example if the woman is insecure some may change, they are appearance, some may act aggressively out insecurity and be wrong or right! Women have their different in their own ways, living, personalities, taste, looks, sex, romance, etc. Women have they are aspect of the world. Really on how they want to live there best damn life but if all women where the example. Woman would be life a robot heading in the same direction. All of them cannot live together I am not talking about friends, family members. All queens cannot live in one castle! Hell No! I can admit the queen is the most powerful piece in the game of chess be careful of a woman she is dangerous. If it could be good ways or bad ways! A woman wants to take her time. It takes work to. It also takes effort, unity, love, communication and God with the woman especially unit walking together unless they have agreed to do so. Do not put it all on your man because you both want to be walking down the same path so your relationship will be messed up. You both supposed to have a relationship with God and one another. So, when you love God and yourselves do not be what you want to be. Be what God created us to be. The devil brings things like happiness of money, cars, jobs, houses, diamonds, jewelry. The devil spreads dissatisfaction through these distractions. See soon as something go bad then the devil attacks the woman the woman tells you this you that, why you not looking for a job or you are doing this to much or you are not making enough money and them the first negativity is said. He is the man because he cannot, no let us pray he has a job, he is trying so let us pray for a raise having faith together. Faith without work is dead. One got faith and the other do not even like the idea of being women. Now some women would reply to what I just said and use it as, that is thank kind of woman. I learned that if a woman is not getting enough sleep, she gets moody, if she not having sex, she gets bitchy not calling you out names that is just how it is. The food is a chemical the woman must eat as well as the food is imbalanced. She must eat and rest to be what is going on in the world. I also learned from the woman that she is like an elephant they both never forget she holds a grudge like how she would like to hold God or is the God. Finally met a woman who likes a two-minute brother as she sat in her way her name is Victoria Quinones. She says so they can go on and on, so she wants to feel in some type of way, so she can give her man all the pleasing he needs so they can go on and on. I also learned for women it depends on what type of her moods and how she feels. Women has the game the gift of gab a lot of times women talk to put the man up on his self. Now that is a real woman. I was sitting with this woman one day her name is Olivette Waters. She said she did not realize she pushed her husband away by judging him, proving him and falsely accusing him. She said she pushed him to cheat when she should of just keep her damn mouth closed! Now see Cleopatra will stumble on her own rock. She feels, thinks and shows action that is she is perfect. It is all on me but behind closed doors she is crying out not for me wishing bad on her. She is doing great but for what she has done wrong and her kids being there friends. Women do not use your past sins against men done you wrong years and years ago that is a sinful nature. All I was donor, no rights to tell the kids what to do only she was because she is a woman, a mother get all the credit right or wrong I was only a money provider. You want to do all the teaching and do not want to learn anything from a man that sin and done you wrong, but she knows everything, do not receive anything and got every right to forever. Do not hold things in your heart women have cleanse hearts. The woman wants God, loyalty, honesty, faithfulness, communication, friendship, romance, compassion, trust and she still the butterfly. Cleopatra I am still the butterfly you want me to tell you why because Jeffrey still loves her, she a butterfly because she beautiful, soft, gentle, she was pretty and beautiful to see when he first laid eyes on her, but she was hard to catch. It took 3 months to be with her I can understand that she is worth it she is a lady I took my time, she stayed near me slow fast right or wrong but was not perfect. She was in the light as in the same way of the butterfly and times will go in the darkness on my wrongs or hers. She pleased me as well and did not transform herself in and out of her ways. She could see that I could see as well as she could not! She flew through all the storms. I put my butterfly the color of black, brown, white and yellow. My butterfly is pretty and beautiful just imagine her she fantastic. Now can she say one thing good about me. If she does or do not, she still is a lady and my butterfly. She is the butterfly; she is also the queen bumble bee and a ladybug. She is also the butterfly of a woman of education that went to Beery University in Miami, Fl with knowledge and wisdom butterfly power of a mind-built power. A good spirit to! She is glory, sexy, in her own world magnificent. When she uses to wrap her arms around my neck. When the sunrise and before we use to go to bed at times she was flying around right there. Standing in front of me in my mind that is why I hold tight sometimes. Her heart was always on fire for me of a lioness. She is Leo, she was the lock and key still is until this day. it ay. See I am Pisces the fish fast, smart and the caterpillar. If you know love you will understand this that's how deep love is. It will blow your mind. She was a beautiful butterfly that add so many colors in my life flying on a plane first class! We were two of the same kind changing up no relationship is perfect because no matter how tough it was. She was beautiful enough and strong enough, emotional, loving, caring and walking with beautiful heels on that was black with her nice legs as a lady going through hell and darkness with me and until this day. I am telling you something important darkness yet at times still become something beautiful and it is her she is a lady. To her I was no good, rotten, low life, nothing you want to keep in your house, your desk or in your garden I was always dead. I can be a man I was a fly on crap. I admit I was crap I also was a mosquito. See she was smashing me all the time. She just said she was giving me a chance but doing something different the ways, attitude, doing as well was the most important part. I loved her so much that when I fart it was stank and I use to fart on her and laugh in love but when she farted on me it smelled good because she was so special and the butterfly. I know a lot of people what say man you crazy I would say anything like that. If you are in love you crazy enough to understand because it is just that much crazy enough of to be in love to do lots of things. I loved this woman so much I changed her pads for her and went to go buy her some pads and threw them way. I like when I catch a cold, she uses to rub alcohol on me when I cough, and I use to say thank you baby. I still feel it until this day something that is loved cannot be gone over night. She was a woman that was special, different and beautiful. I knew she was a butterfly because I brought her flowers all the time and put them in the vase with water. She always got on me about drinking water this woman symbolized me in many things keeping herself healthy, beautiful, and always keeping herself up. She always told me to drink water to cleanse myself out and to pray so old can pass away so they can come in. I am a very smart man. When Jeffrey was with Cleopatra everything was not his fault our relationship on everything was not one big lie on everything that's not true especially if God knows and he do I am a witness. See I let her know a lot of times life is too short and you never know when you will go. So, we were supposed to dream together keep the remembrance and joys that come from the little things in life. There are men butterflies does not look good they are both beautiful the men have emotional and feminine ways as well, feelings and cries. He is handsome as well to his woman and self within himself and her. See when the woman sees the loyalty, she feels comfortable then gives her heart she will love so much she will everything up to bound the pledge of duty, obligation, trust and her duty. Faithfulness, communication, friendship, romance, compassion, trust and God first. See the Godly woman is good faithful and honest. When she has her evil side of the spirit that is evil uses her, she is secretly unfaithful then a non-believer this not only always means her this way forever. She is this way of bitter way because of him. Men have a story to tell to of histories of why the way they are. We all are human it has just been taught to women they need more time they are different. We all go through things everyone has a story to tell just do not use your past or hurt against or anybody as a sinful nature. You see Cleopatra's mother Pam did not teach her how to forgive. She told her but did not teach because she sat there and watch how and was raised watching how she treated her man. Now she was miserable locked up in the room watching TV all the time of hurt, pain and not forgiving another and quick to tell someone that is the man. If you do not forgive it will not be good for you to move on to the next person who comes in your life. So, you can move on with next woman but not looking in the mirror. When you were married saying that to yourself and thinking that saying should have been in doing in your own marriage. Right is right. I am not angry, getting back, holding no grudges I am telling the truth of what I experience been through and lived. You know Cleopatra, grandmother just passed away and this lady did treat Jeffrey like family like he was her own son. Jeffrey asked Cleopatra why you did not call me for her funeral she said because it was out of town not in Miami. I said so if I passed away my family what of called you, she said that was

different because we were in relationship no, that is what you wanted to do with revenge, vengeance, not see me in your eyesight because her grandmother would want that. If Jeffrey were to pass away her grandmother would have said pick me up for Jeffrey funeral. See love is a commandment we just choose to do it and give it to the ones we want to and give it when we get ready. Now women can you feel this on both sides? Will this be a bit? A woman is truly the driving force of a man behind every good man there is a good woman and behind every good woman there is a good man because sends the man and woman in his time. This is to men that do this he sees is everything stop doing women wrong. Let me tell you men this story it was this. Man, name Isaac he with this. Woman name Natalie they fell in love with one another and got married they was together for years. His wife took care of him. He took care of her. One day Isiah's father Wilson died so, Isaac buried his father and collected the money from the life insurance he had on his father. Isaac was driving different kind of cars showing off bragging and saw another woman name Ella. He started letting the looking at the money her eyes were wide open. He was looking at her body and letting his flesh take over him. He left his wife and went to the other woman so after he divorced him, and Ella lived together. He went to prison want me to tell you why, the woman who left his wife for set him up on a rape charge just to get his money. He has a life sentence now. He is trying to appeal his case and his ex-wife Natalie know she set him up, now guess who helping him? Natalie the woman who he was first married to. See what I am telling you brothers any race any color stop playing games the grass is not always greener on the other side. He just thought it was. Women this goes for you to that only want men for money that are gold diggers. This goes for everyone one minute you could be down now this one thing I got to say about overly independent women please listen to this. It does not only be your problem. It is pain on yourself and your husband/boyfriend/man and a lot of you have loss me because of this. Your mothers are single parents just like you tell the men that is acting up. You are too strong to listen so then the man come along into your life. When it gets bad and times get hard, he is not a man anymore richer or poorer better or worse, then words come out doing this before you came along. I been an independent woman. I do not need you so why did you get with him if you loved him and gave up the eyes for us because you were not ready for the responsibility of being spoiled rotten or seeing what your mom did in her relationship with her husband. You cannot be the man the relationship let the man be the man stop aggravating him. Jeffrey fucked up and Cleopatra made him pay back over back pay more than the government owing people money and taking it back on taxes and said it in face she went overboard. Let your man bring groceries like I did, let your man be fully affectionate with you. You must sit your ass down and submit. Yes, I understand a lot of you was good all by yourself why? Sitting locked up in the house watching TV so the things women do get that your mothers did not have they get angry at you to break up your home and be in your business. You want the men to respect you, so you must do the same in return and talk to like he is stupid. It is boundaries how you suppose to talk to him and treat him not your way or moms or what people tell you how some else is going to tell you about your man is they going to tell you about there is hell no! Because someone come up your face with that disrespect, you are not having it so why should the man allow it, accept it, take it and receive it? He gets tired and fed up with your shit to. Then you women belittle your man when he is not doing the job in the way you want and like and you being selfish, he is trying his best and putting his all. But I understand girlfriend we are here for you it is not enough. Then you be having children. Women you have sons if you talk to these men any kind of way. How do you think your son or sons going to talk that man like he is a boy? Cleopatra did and claim Jeffrey deserved it every time but come back and forth apologized and said he need to work on it. You right and never did we could not go nowhere on her part and mines! I played a part whole lot. You women that do this going to run every man away that comes along in your wrong with changing your shirt because your man does not like it. There is nothing wrong with getting a hairdo that he likes or getting your nails done the way he likes them or wearing a bra he likes or heels he likes to. See your wear or wearing a purse he like to see you wear you are his queen/princess. He wants to show you off for him and to stand you out. Shoes, get him a bible tell him to read it, told him baby try this on. Yes, you did so sit your ass down yes, I am talking to you I said it! Because let me tell you something Jeffrey ask Cleopatra for one hairdo. I could not get it because that was control letting people put things on her head girl, he does not run you. Really, Jeffrey love Cleopatra. She still is in my heart. I do not give a damn what no one says I brought groceries I feed us as well. I could not cook dinner but I damn sure enough could cook breakfast that was not good enough they all were holier than me and did not. God is not concern who does the most or better. It is the love fellowship and the heart Cleopatra told Jeffrey he had a good heart you really meant even when you are angry and until this day? There is nothing wrong with coming in a certain time because your moms are single ladies and your friends you and your man is not. Who told you something was wrong with that? Your friends or your mother because they still single, women stop penalizing your men for something that happen years and years ago your worse than a referee that is cheating for a team that he likes instead of calling a fair game. How you women to tell other people off. When you need to get yourself together to the ones that do this every situation is different just like every man, woman, relationship do not falsely accuse your man you be punishing him make up more and more rules and add them on out of hate and bitterness and say I do not hate you I do not like what you did to me, but bitterness is hate and for right or wrong will use this for power isn't that control? Then you women put in your unfavorable, unforgivable nasty attitude position as an unfair disadvantage, and make your man suffer, like with Cleopatra. Jeffrey had to learn that Cleopatra was not my property. She does not owe me her soul. I had to earn her back. When I did, she said I should not have taking you back. It was too late I wish I would have never got back with you again telling me in my face. I will deal with God you do not come first my children do and made it seem like I did not love her children. She did all the work. She could not fix what she could not face because she was angry and bitter unforgiveness is wrong forgiving someone is not easy to do sometimes so do we make it an excuse to keep getting back to hurt ourselves feel good but do not know the devil is using us to hurt ourselves and the person who did us wrong or we did wrong. Help that person get through forgiveness. Help that man. Help that woman anymore everyone encourages one another because fussing only does what go back and forth not is you ripping one another heart. Your ripping one another love for each. Even God as well be thinking of self. It is a process it takes time but how it is being handle while is going because it could be backed up or moved forward or trying your best. You both must tell the truth and stop victimizing your man or woman. Jeffrey did not tell you Cleopatra get over it. I do not care no more, or I do not care at all, No! I helped her through that why I was man enough to ask her. If she needed more time because I understand that she was hurt and her children was also hurt as well that's why I ask how much time she needed be I even cared about the heart and her being scorned and her pain soul and feelings including everything life period about this certain beautiful woman and children but she right in her saying her words her mind it was too late to forgive but she didn't mean that she was bitter, angry, upset hurt so it was already over. I know it took me time to forgive so I know where she was coming from just not in our relationship so we can stay in love and move on you cannot be pushed into forgiveness and push around telling someone do it do it. Empathizing, what Jeffrey was doing with Cleopatra. Women freedom is forgiveness be unforgiveness holds hostage you be tied up and cannot breathe and then you say it is because he went back doing the same thing and think was you bringing up the something when he changes you could not see because the hurt pain sin is all you can see. I know because when people lied to me and hurt me in my family and sinned towards me. I kept bringing the past back on them. I could not progress, go nowhere, grow, move on, unforgiveness will put in a place that you will never want to be, but you will be there in a corner closed in. Like times Cleopatra stood in front of hollering, screaming and yelling in front of Jeffrey face you gone do this you gone do that all can say was no, no, no I am not because the actions was not doing anything. Jeffrey did not want Cleopatra to hurry up and forgive him or do it when she said it. When she come to me on her own and said herself baby I'm ready to forgive you when that was said it starting all over again and I'm not talking about me going back to cheat right then no, I slept on the streets in my car, on the side walk, in my aunt house, even people like my Aunt Pastor Ellis talking to me on the phone I just could not be in the house with a brawling woman with the spirit the devil was using it was scary and hurtful. I would pray, pray, pray and pray and they would not go on were. It is saying it is hope, healing and help forgiveness is something we must strive for. Forgiveness must be an emotion before it can become an effort it has to happen in your heart. We do not forgive because we want revenge for what you did you got to be paid back even more, no, you hurt me, no you did wrong, women I feel you deserve for me to be speaking to you. You deserve to touch me, kiss me, hold me, make love to me, until I say so. I think you should pay for what you did to me, but the woman was hurt so she would do this. When Cleopatra did not forgive Jeffrey. She took the matter in her own hands. When Cleopatra was doing it to me, she never he thought when her man had enough, she could not because only thing her mind was revenge. Cleopatra felt I am going to hurt Jeffrey is going to hurt. She did not know how much. I was hurting she never ask what I wanted to talk about, I got cursed out! She was acting off her emotions. It is all in the saying but no doing. Who wants to live in the cycle like that, that bondage like being on a merry go round getting on and getting off at the same spot when you got on at? Women are you learning something it is your pride also. I changed my behavior because she kept telling I am sorry, I am sorry, I am sorry for saying I forgive you and not be hard on you Jeffrey I am going to change and did not. She never forgave me so when I would walk up to her or by her it would be watch out, duck, be careful he is coming I am ready anger, revenge battlefield and this how she was. When Jeffrey wanted to hold Cleopatra and help he could not because he made it this way or her this way. I was man enough to suffer the consequences. It was going deeper, deeper and deeper she could not fix what she could not face the fact that I am, around a man who dogged me, lied to me, abuse me, rejected me, who was not there for me and my children. It was all my fault. I felt like I did nothing. I was crying out to the Lord every night like she was. Then she was always waiting on me as I owed her, so I kept coming up to her saying baby do you really forgive because there was no love and how I was talk to my face as shit and treated like shit. I was nobody. Then she the more highly of herself than me, our relationship, yes, she did, she thought she was more important to me than I was to her where does God say that or teach that. She thought he should of did this, I should have done it was enough because she told me to leave or left on my own fussing me out. She will call me back or come back and get me or curse me out on the phone. I still will come home hearing you out there cheating how is that and I just walked in the door ladies. See unforgiveness. She thought she was on some type of pedestal. She thought I am the number 1 only person in his life with my children fuck him ok. I will wait and wait until he keeps apologizing to me. She keeps thinking more highly of herself. Our whole life got put on hold sometimes because we be waiting for something that a person will never come and do. Unforgiveness is one of the highest levels there is of arrogance and ignorance. Then she would tell me I am not going to prosper until I march myself back to her and apologize. I walked up to her, and she will say hammam. Whatever I should not have never took you back. So, what will her daughter Anita and son Trevor be doing in their relationships/marriages of a cycle. Then she can be smiling and over there angry that he is going to get it in return so, she thinks highly of herself holy that she did it to all of me. She knows I messed up and did wrong. She manipulated me for what I did wrong. She kept me under her foot on my neck. She had me attached because I am feeling guilty on everything. I already gave retribution. I supported her, I ask for forgiveness, I kept doing things, I ran behind her. Yes, ladies she had me on lock down. I am a man there is nothing wrong with that. I came to her with Jesus, the pastor, myself, children and wash hand clean I got used with my back up against the wall. Therefore, the daughter Anita called Jeffrey back and said daddy I am wrong I apologize I disrespected your house. How can a daughter do that but not the mother that is the parent? People will keep you in bondage. People they will keep you bound to them because they know I got something on you. I got something on him I got something on her. It is an unhealthy soul tie. We should have move pass the situation a long time ago but where did it go all on me the man! How many times I had to keep proving I was sorry and kept doing for another man's children and after I divorced her, I am not the man I use to be, and I am sad to say this, but it is true you cannot show that to no woman that does not want to receive. She tied a rope around my neck and drove me around in her car. Now when I take of other women and children, she gets all the credit. Now I do not like when the woman says she does not mis her man/husband/ex and play mind games saying you cannot tell me what I am thinking or feeling because what past sins you did to me you have no right to say anything this is her fool as a gun a weapon to blow the man brains out then she swears up and down dead ass serious that she is right. No one can change her mind it is stuck not many thoughts, so many that it is bigger than you can imagine like Cleopatra would say I am not in love with you. I do not love you. I wish I would not never get back with you, you are sorry, you a liar, you a dog, then come back and apologize about everything then says when I say this you know I are saying I love you baby. I really be angry at the time, but I love you (you are so crazy). Now how many of you women say this and excuses that a woman they change up. Men make us this way all the time. We did not come this way for nothing. I like the way God said do. It loves how we treat one another. It is not only for the man it is for women as well to get across the street on the other side. You must let go of the gate holding on to it. King Solomon was given all the wisdom and knowledge from God. He was blessed with gold, money, riches and wives. He could not understand them and their ways, but he messed up. When he fell in love with a woman who did not believe in God. He did and turned his heart to worship other Gods, David Solomon's father slept with Bathsheba and David had him killed in his army. See Solomon picked up his father's ways I do not agree with this was given all the wisdom & knowledge from God. He was blessed with gold, money, riches and wives he could not understand them and their ways, but he messed up with a woman did not believe in God and he went right along with her and turned his heart to worship other Gods. I do not agree with this or like because God does not. MEN, please stop this that is doing it because it is a cycle repeatedly!! Women let me tell you something a man wants to feel like you trapped him or pushed him away he will not marry you because you broke his trust some still get marry and he be breaking up in so many other ways it is not only cheating. I know this couple that has been married 35 years and they were talking to their daughter, and she was in a relationship for 2 months with her fiancé and the mother told the daughter if he loves you, he will marry you. She told the mother and father she is not ready to get married and he is not as well she was always trying to force them to get married. See when your said, angry, bitter, good, bad, disappointed, sinning or going through a lot of God is defending you in battles you do not even know about. The thing I learned about a woman/woman is that you will remain silent and quiet at times no matter what it can be most or some depending on the woman and the mood she is in does not have time for foolishness and petty things but comes out at times with her actions and wrongs when she does not admit she is wrong. Yes, it has been plenty people broken down not just women they are not the only ones that come back strong this is not anything against women it is facts and the truth no one is perfect we all have down falls. Women I feel your pain when your heart and soul is wounded and have bad passes experiences over and over again it is also not right to carry it on and on in the back of your mind having a smile on your face off and on but hurting yourself and others, inside pretending to enjoy life when you can't really because your bitter, hateful, envy with get back saying life time after time who made you that way the MAN/MEN with get back and revenge. Is this going on in your life for years and years when will you genuinely enjoy your life like you tell the man in different ways in his life. You will say your different than the man in many ways that's vice versa, but forgiveness is the same if your feelings are different then your emotions are going man or woman way not God's way life is too short for that, especially yours. Bottom line, a man must take care of his woman and a woman must take care of her man. No one is before the other where is society coming from it is all about the woman. You women that are in relationships you and your soulmate is in the ship together and you must relate to one another not only and all about you women. Relationships supposed to share together disagree to agree it is not going to be easy even your ideas. Women in your cycles you cannot let your mother's, family members, children's, girlfriends, co-workers or anyone justify the decisions you make for yourself or husband/man that is your decision right in smart positive thinking praying first you do not have nothing to explain to them all that time complaining you can be on your knees praying! When Cleopatra's mother Pam she did not like no man with her daughter because of her experience and her daughters on as well. You can still love your daughter and pray for the best for her but not have negative spirits around her. These things will sink your ship and then the same people will not be there to rescue you or help because they cannot help their own selves from drowning so they must have people down with them and you do not have to say abandon ship there will be no lifeguard some cannot even swim their way out. This is important satisfy your man he wants love and respect! It is like the true story about the ship the Titanic it is a true story with those marriages, families, relationships, children's, on the boat at that time it was unstoppable God had to show them anything that man makes can fail but when man and woman make something together with God is a major difference. God makes things to last when that boat was made of steel and it hit that iceberg it broke in half it was sinking so fast lots of peoples thought it was unsinkable please have God in everything you say, do and actions because if God is not you will sink. Women do not let your insecurities and your unforgiveness be in your way with forgiveness and not forgetting in get back bitter ways provoking. Woman/Women I understand and feel your frustration so you are going to stay that way it may be better for you but not constantly. I been there in some of your feelings we all have them been through worse just like you a lot of things was not all my fault and I created all on my own not everything. Women you are angry at your husband/man watch what you say to him when you tell him that you love him because words can be worse than sleeping out on someone at times not all the time your heart be one way your mind be another. Do not control your husband/man in your silent body gesture ways of rejecting him and in other ways that he cannot catch but can feel. Control just do not come with abuse, fighting, cheating, using, lying, getting told what to do, getting treated nasty. It also comes from pride, deception, revenge, rude, mean, evil, unforgiveness, silent treatment, how you talk to and treat one another it is also curses on one another it does not all be only all on the man! It must come back together with God like when you first were in love. Jeffrey dominated Cleopatra she did it back to me when did it to one another at times when we first met then when we got married it was back and forth, she stood up to me if he were right or wrong even when she was wrong, but he could not say or do nothing for all the wrong he did to her only! At once Jeffrey could not stand back up but when he grew up and got himself together, he felt good the thing it was Cleopatra was feeling the same way or just holding on to the past. She keeps changing her mind and heart off and on is not a change it is a confusion. She did not change her heart to believe in me and no matter how saved I was or how much I believed in God. She could not change her heart from evil, revenge, vengeance, bitterness, I could not change her even when I stopped and walked away, I could not do nothing but cry like she did then I got her back. I was wrong in God eyes, my own and her eyes to right is right wrong is wrong I am held accountable for my own sins and actions I am not going to say her wrongs. There are many controlling men as there are women. See you have women think their better men and men think there better than women as well as marriages, wives, husbands' relationships, he or she become aggressive unreasonable, not treating each other equally chauvinism is a sin. It is a sin for men to believe they are better than men. Husbands and wives supposed to be equal. I told this told false leaders, false teachers, false bishop, false evangelist saying a marriage is a 60/40 the woman/wife gets the 60 the husband/man gets 40 happy wife happy life who made up these tales, lies, stories man/ woman not God and so many peoples are following this and anyone that teaches this period or trying to use the bible or anything or anyone that teaches this have to answer to God if they don't repent and get it right before they live here ashes to ashes dust to dust wrong teaching is wrong, teach right with encourage and fair. This is not of saying for my teaching women that you do not get last say so or word God does same as for Men! It says to husband and wife submitting yourselves one to another in the fear of God. Wives submit yourselves unto your own husbands, as unto the Lord. The husband is the head of the wife, even as Christ is the head of the church: and he is the savior of the body. When I hurt Cleopatra then did not get forgiven for it there was no spirit of love, joy, peace, patience, kindness, goodness and self- control and say right there if she did not love me or did not want to be there then she would not be with me at all then why she is there then? Cleopatra said right in front of her children Jeffrey do not care no more even after we broke up and before we got into a serious relationship and after! The world of fake phony teachers said that this for it is God, a husband and wife to

come back together submitting helping one another. See women when revenge is there then you end up with hate saying you do not but your actions, mouth, sins, do not be nice, you then manipulate, intimidated, dominate of your life into submission. Women this just do not dominate you it dominates your husband, each other! All a woman needs, wants to be satisfied everyone. It is so crazy and incredible I cannot even explain it. One is a loving man that is a husband who has basic needs for security, protection, love satisfaction given from God through her husband. She also wants to see your aliveness, your presence, she needs to see it and feel it. She wants to talk to you about what matters to her and to feel that you are important to because let me tell you something she still not satisfied because she wants more with a smile, a charm, a sense of humor, game, not playing games but mind games as what is going on a woman! Many men, women pull away from you because you put too many and so many demands on him to meet all and every one of her needs. If it is right or wrong, when he is not perfect and cannot meet all the expectations in the world because she cannot for him. We know some women will say why not? What did he do wrong? She is the reason because only you or the man and no matter how long that takes sit back or there and let her put you through no matter how long it is or selfish! On any man, woman or anyone. A lot of women need to find out who you are. Now you have a lot of women say once you break the trust, affection, security, leadership, communication that it. It is over so why you then take this to because you are not ready then when the man is right and your bitter you got every right to treat him this way and tell him when you marry him after forgiving him years later down the line I should of never took you back. Think what did you just tell God yourself your husband and your vows? Or you are thinking still with your mind, your thoughts. Your way, the highway it becomes no understanding, no communication, separation is there no love? It is just two people are in front of each other with a dead rose in the middle with dirt, dust, sand, ashes to ashes, dust to dust with God not in the middle. The woman says, I do not care. He is not going to do nothing but the same thing. Like I have a sister her name is Brittany she has 6 children and for 18 years she has no husband because for all of them the same they are no good. No one see what she said all men are the same and not one good one is out there. Then she will drink and say (shit) I need me a man. Then she will change it and say I need me a Fuck do not judge her or me my book, poetry, or what I am saying I am just telling you the truth. Do not say just listen and hear so she starts giving back to the church. Then she started back praying more asking God to send her a Godly man. She changed it right back to what she was saying all over again. Now women will say or to men that read this book you do not know what pain she is feeling, God fix it all. There nothing that God cannot take care of. The problem is she stuck where is she at because she is not ready. She is not loving herself or ready to forgive of all the old garbage. Her children are grown. Now with marriages gone on with their lives while she still sitting there like mothers out here, I do not need no man at all ever I got God. Please be sure it is with love, pure, kind, peace, forgiveness, No revenge, vengeance, bitterness, only a cleanse heart! It is like you are locking yourself in a box and a room, Like Cleopatra told Jeffrey if he does not forgive her for what she did to him how I am going to be able to move on for God to bless him with another good woman. Now she could have used that for the same term and same way as a Christian for our marriage. When I kept telling her to forgive me, forgive me, forgive me. See we all need to practice what we preach and do it well. Not only men/women to. See my sister was in sin with herself carrying on her shoulders. Pray these things do not rub off on your sons or daughters in their marriages and it be lukewarm. We all have been there and look down at one another when we feel like we are saved or doing better or nicer or even know more and have the floor even myself even at times done it when I did not know. Everyone has fell short of the glory. Women is this covering up for my wrongs. NO! This is what I learned of my wrongs, rights, sins, goods, beds, and teaching others still God a lot of learning, working on me as well. See it is a work in progress of forgiving someone, but it is how it is being done. Behavior your tone, attitude, action, movement, thought, mind, time, concentration of a process of love humbleness, kindness, helping, caring, sharing, conversation, praying, together, within self, hope, faith, it will not be done perfect, it will not be done excellent but trying is better than anything! Now watch this women or woman if you feel your husband

is attached to some other things or detached from you on some way or any kind of way. You feel insecure because the wife/woman does not want anyone or anything to come before is God! The woman catches on faster instinctively if her husband and truly is caring for her properly. Women this go the same way for your husband. Your husband comes second God comes first. Cleopatra told her children this her family. Then she got afraid then changed it when her daughter told her you put me out for your husband, but she did not put her out she sent her to her grandmother's house for not respecting me. It just that Cleopatra was blind from the past using it towards Jeffrey to down him for everything being on him. Sometimes spirits will come by your children in your relationship because she put her foot down and said look my man, your father and you are going to respect him and me. Then she changed up when the daughter Anita use that you put your daughter out for your man Anita was not grown and lived in my house I ask her how much she made doing hair for a reason it was so I can give her more money this why I wanted to know the mother felt like I wanted to know to get in her business, her daughter business, her child, my child, her daughter isn't this the way it go but not God's way wasn't the way when it came to me for my sins and wrongs. Jeffrey did too much sin he was the devil as it was taught and said he was a fuck up, but the mother that was the mother of Cleopatra all her children was good educated Christian children in God eyes. What would be told to me now is that is not true where was the showing and the actions no going to make you do anything but when it comes to them it must be this way and get the top respect. See Cleopatra could not teach her son how to be a man Jeffrey was being a man when Jeffrey asks my stepdaughter how much she made to be proud of her. I was acknowledging her work, her job, her business she got it from me. Jeffrey laid down all his selfish ways to meet Cleopatra needs and his family. Everyone deserved a real chance not a lying chance or a fake or phony one most of my life. I blame everyone for the one responsible for doing wrong and that is myself my wrongs, but I know I corrected myself of my tracks I walked on as a man, was push down and the only people that gave me credit was the two brothers of Cleopatra and the father came back to apologize. I never did anything to the sister. Just was going by he says she say. Never use sarcasm towards your husband it brings on damaging his, your spirit. You both supposed to be sincere. When I made corrections, I did not earn anything. Everything that I corrected or confronted I was given numerous compliments but then the anger and bitterness in her. Cleopatra would come back at Jeffrey on another day fussing him out saying you did this you did that you still doing it. I was changing directions that is what we need sometimes. God gave me a second chance, but she really did not! Women do not put your man down when he is looking for a job is that not enough for you if he is trying? Did you married him for his money or love and God put you together, so he does not have anything? Now for better or worse richer or poorer no more your way. You should be praying with your husband seeking God for financial direction and provision. Also, when the husband wants to lead the prayer it is helpful very much so false teachers are saying they do not have to, but God says in the bible they must pray together. Also, when financial pressure comes. I was a man, a hustler, trying it was not good enough, then thugs will come your way like Jeffrey will come home and let Cleopatra know how he was treated. She will tell me I was a fuck up that she got from her mom because her mom disrespected me right in front of her a lot of times I would just sit there. When the mom disrespected her, I would hold her, and she would cry and let it out. I would hold her and say she did not mean that. She still your mother Jeffrey knew and understood, no love or family like that Cleopatra left me when he cheated. She never came back to me. Ladies stop bringing the past up on your man we all have elements of our past ways, sins, attitudes, wrong, decisions in life period but do not bring it into your marriage with bitterness, hate, revenge and baggage. Then you bring a huge baggage into your relationship with your man like you are on/ a vacation forever. It ruined your marriage looking at your man/husband saying he ruined it he cheated. I gave him another chance when you really did not do it just saying it not sincerely and showing action. Then you will have problems iniquity of nasty, rude, immoral, grossly, unfair, wickedness, sinfulness, the Lord will punish the children for the iniquities of their parents to the third and the fourth generation. When a man does wrong do not hold him held accountable and responsive for everything there is. Pride, greed, abuse, selfish, revenge, unforgiveness, control these things be cycles fall on us doing ourselves. Then it be how do you, I, we resolve the matter of the situation. I had to admit and be a man when I sinned. I blamed my parents, the world, friends and everyone else for my mistakes, my sins but then I grew up came before God, myself the church, my wife, and my children. I admit it was my problem and my fault I confessed my iniquities; I forgave my parents to move on with my life and so I can be free with forgiveness. A woman just not only have a beautiful face she also has a beautiful mind as well as her soul. A woman is everything. She is also a drug not in a bad way, she can have up, comfortable, sleepy, tired, relaxed, emotional, have your mind on a lot of things that is well pleased! A woman's mind and beauty are higher than any education there is. She is calm and be mean. A lot of you women was raised that do not run after your man/husband any man not the stupid, ignorant, nasty no-good men do not put them down, just help them, pray for them like you help the homeless men or women what I am saying is stop saying you do not run after no man when you are dead wrong, you are a strong woman and this and that. Then put lots adding negativity on your mind, ways, and your character is right all the time! A woman is also a treasure she makes you laugh with her dirty mind sometimes it is not only good ways. Jeffrey learned this from Cleopatra I love when use to go out and watch her drink her wine but what Jeffrey really like was when she would share her ideas with me, she got me to see things in life even more better having something so special means a lot it is wonderful and interesting. She taught me how to have gentle disagreements and not aggressive one is I learned yes; I did it was just only in her eyes she was the boss. The teacher, the leader and runs the show. She can teach that we can learn something every day as others grow older, but she says she cannot learn anything from me. I do not have anything against her or any woman I am telling you facts about how it is and the truth. A woman has different attitudes they all have self-confidence. Her feelings, happy, sad, irritated, or energetic or sometimes feeling nothing at all.

Chapter 13

See a man is satisfied with a lot of things in life with simple pleasures, but a woman is not satisfied she changes up so much just like her intuitions I know a lot of women are not going to agree with me but most of these things that I write are true even all women are not the same. As a man get older, he learns more and get wiser and smarter. See when the woman gets in her way and can't forgive her mind takes over her behavior and attitude and say, think, believe and know she can do it all by herself and say with words, expression, feelings, movement, actions and in quietness she can do it all by herself she doesn't need no one else help. Not no man/men the number 1 thing on the list period. The woman always wants more and more then when it's too much it's good then it's too much then it's not enough, so which one is it whatever she says and wants it to me. See women it what I said and how I said it, you take a woman out to eat at times why you looking over there at that woman and the other woman will say we'll what did the man do for her to act like that? As it's known on record that it's only the man/men made the woman/women in these types of ways they are in now in today she doesn't have no kind of ways of her own until she ready to tell them. I had a friend his name was Lucas but the women in school called cat eyes because they said he had some beautiful eyes. I was in the car with him one day with his wife Tessa and he pulled up to the window to get his food that he ordered, I was sitting in the back seat so when he grabbed the food from the waitress said you got some nice eyes he smiled and said thank you. So, when he pulled off Tessa said I seen you laughing all in that Bitch face and he said what, all she told me that I had some beautiful eyes. Now how it goes women happy wife happy life and be quiet and let the woman always be right then she will calm down then come back and apologize this is a woman just being a woman, then you know what some women will say? We'll that's that kind or type of woman/women I'm not that kind of woman and every woman is different and not the same. This is a female nature it can be security, provision it will not be enough just because she will be happy,

sweet, nice, charming, lovable she will be satisfied because then a certain time she changes then goes to self-delusional. The ocean is still blue and the water still wet but the wind changes. The woman is the ocean dry as the sand at times and be smooth wet to but changes up so fast like the wind and a man have nothing on a woman changing she can do it and you won't even notice but lest but not last the blue is the heaven of a spell she puts a man up under that he can't figure out until this day! Watch this Jeffrey use to bring Cleopatra like 20 different purses with the truth she still wasn't satisfied he did not say she was not happy or thankful he said not satisfied because it was something else if it was not missing or found it was something added to the love or list even her mind woman's intuitions even if it was something talk about woman/women observe conversations. Cleopatra will go back change and say no I want this kind of purse with all the names on it of the name brand. Like my friend Tavis and his wife who name was Lana I was at their house watching a football game, so the wife Lana looked at him and said baby go to McDuffs for me I'm hungry, Rule 1 women never interrupt a man/husband/man while watching a football game or a game period back to the story, so Tavis said OK baby what do you want? Lana said I want a number 2 with a large coca cola and 2 fish sandwiches with extra pickles and tartar sauce. Taylor said OK then and ask if I wanted to go, I said no I'm going to watch the game I he looked at me don't want to miss anything. So, he said alright then left. So, he came back with the food took it out the bag and said baby I got everything for you. Then Lana said I know it was something I forgot to tell you to get, He said what? My strawberry milk shake goes back to McDuffs and get it. He said I got you everything now I got to go back again I left while I was watching the game with my friends now you got me running back and forth. Lana started arguing with him just because she felt disrespected in front of the men when her husband but did, she look at he was off work watching the Super Bowl game? He got fussed out because he wanted to stay and watch the game and got cursed out, called everything but the child of God over a milk shake. Now some women will say if he just would just shut up and went and ignored her everything would of went well give her everything, she wants to do what she says, and it will go right. Where's the thank you? The appreciation? At least this man cared, loved, and did his job. Then Lana came on his lap gave him a kiss and said baby I'm sorry he looked her and said you crazy you know that see this woman struck a nerve then calm it down see how a woman have her ways and powers to make them feel see right in actions of love a man can't even see not saying he does not feel and know somethings but not like the woman. See at times with woman/women wait a minute something is not right and she's the one wrong and just know what she is talking about when it's right it's wrong then when it's wrong it's right then that change up to I know woman/women that's just that type or them kind of women. A happy wife happy life she gets the last word, last say so her way or the highway. Do you see at the last minute she changes then she knew what she wanted no she didn't because if she did, she wouldn't want him to go back it wouldn't be no argument? I know make her feel like she's the boss like woman/women tell a man/men certain thing and at times things they want them to hear or believe not just lie or the truth it gets deep. It's her prerogative to change her mind and you know who will say it's ok and give the say so? OTHER WOMEN!! Women don't even understand the concept of enough. She will complain about something no matter what ever you provide it is never enough you can do whatever it is to make and keep her happy it will work, and it won't it's the little things women like the most that counts we'll depending on that type of woman. You know when Jeffrey was with Cleopatra he even made her feel like she was the boss right or wrong even made her feel appreciated he showed her and made her feel like she was important and let her know with or without her he couldn't make it because of herself the special woman she was. I gave her help that was strength now if she were to say I did not do nothing at all not one time all the years we were together she would be lying. I like at times when she changed like the wind blowing over the ocean and the water because I blew in the wind with her even though it was times the storms, hurricanes, lightning, tornados were heavy I was there and not there so was her no relationship it was days when it was happy relationship 24-7 with some days and times with perfection! No relationship is perfect all day every day. Cleopatra dealt with emotions and feelings with in herself that she kept in that she did not want to talk about more than Jeffrey she's a woman it had to do with her being her own woman on her own with everything she did was with her own intuitions she felt like and knew because he only hurt her. Saying out her mouth how can a no-good dog like me ever have feelings even though I'm a man and I think what makes me logic I still have feelings to and hurt I'm as well human just as she is. I didn't do right a lot of times I would take her through things that be so complicated, and I then realized I fucked up and fixed it I'm a man now growing up wiser as a man and putting away childish thoughts, ways, actions, words, abuse, mentally, and negativity it was so simple when I changed me. I learned that what may not mean serious to her saying and feelings I didn't know sometimes it was serious when I just looked at her and said that's not that serious, but it was same vice versa. I even learned to choose my battles and arguments Jeffrey stay there with Cleopatra a lot of times even came back so he can think about her first THE WOMAN, THE EMOTIONS EVEN HER INTUTIONS because he felt so important for her and deep inside what he create is that as soon as he leave she's going to think and feel I'm going to be with that woman, or another woman, or hoe's, bitches, I'm a hoe of her sayings after cursing him out just got through telling he about his ass then come make love to his stupid ass telling me she's sorry. Then say while I'm walking out just for air to think of a peace of mind something a man never can't have at times it comes up being throwed into my face oh you're going to that woman house that you sleep on me with in the past, did you hear what I said? Cleopatra said it out her own mouth THE PAST. Jeffrey stayed there with Cleopatra of the war he started he did not want to cause conflict, but she did not want to be humble at times a woman doesn't have to say anything her body gestures, looks, attitude, ways will throw of things quick, and the man will feel uncomfortable. A woman is confused at times because she has certain feelings, and they will listen to a man to a certain point, but they draw their own conclusions how this man is going to treat her and understand her she also can be confused on herself and her own aggravations now every woman not the same that woman has her own point of view how she feels breaks it down and where she's at any given time. Cleopatra did not want to talk it out or listen, hear or anything so Jeffrey would walk away even when she said you talk to damn much even the times she say leave right now get the fuck or the hell from around me I don't want to look at you or around me most and some of those reasons he don't blame for her in feelings in them ways but he can't blame me for her actions of her petty ways being selfish, rude, disrespectful and not showing him no love why she was this way right women? Because of me everything right? Or you don't know you don't know she went through or heard her side of the story I told you everything and did not leave one thing left out will that be a lie to? Cleopatra did not mean certain things she said at times but a lot of times herself and her mouth will go over board as a real strong woman and still tell me she in love with Jeffrey see she been broke up with him she just did not know how to tell me in the beginning it's over just like that it was not easy then you have women come with we'll she did it for herself because she had to get her right and sometimes peoples are in your life for a certain time and that person was not meant for you see that's games when you hold someone up. I'm being understanding and straight forward it did not work out in all her ways only what she wanted. What she didn't realize was as our God says forgiveness is one of the gates in heaven. She knows but at that time she did not care just like she said and felt. Old things are the past they will gain. Life is not easy don't care about the lost learn how to live through the hurt and don't know how to turn it into good. Don't let it constantly bring you down let it strengthen you. All trials and tribulations don't have to be negative. I would like to tell the women you might think you know it all and have it all together and say I didn't say I know it all and know everything but your mouth and what comes out of it and your mind thinking with your actions coming out in a bad behavior way and attitudes with personality's that you can't even imagine that you're going faster than a fire truck with a house that's burning not knowing you started the fire this what anger does you be totally a whole different person. Then you say on your own I don't know everything I don't know it all even when the man is not feeding into your nonsense that burns you up at times because the devil is not getting him any more now he's attacking you the woman. See the woman don't know there are some weird and fascinating things about men reproductive system. This lady and other women came behind her commented me on how I am reproductive since I know so much about women. Every woman has destroyed a man somewhere to his breaking point and his last nerve beyond his breaking point yes I agree for the men who been through this woman you are not by yourselves with pain that's why the song says no pain no gain and no one's every going to love you like I do! See there men that are trying and that's not good enough for some women I'm going to get to that but you will hold that man down and once you hurt that man it takes time for him but a man can't take getting cheated on like a woman her love continues for that man because she chose that man to be her partner, friend, lover, a quick pick me up it has nothing to do with sex the desire just to be with that man because she knows and feels that man is the one for her but when a woman cheats on that man he can't take that he will go crazy! There are certain things in that woman that man deeply wants. Some women and men don't handle things the same way everyone is different. Now we are going to reverse it now when the black man/men are majority doing his parts of the relationship and the woman is being stubborn I seen plenty of them put black men on child support that was loving parents, loving fathers, and seen the women take the money and get they nails, and hair done think about themselves. Now the system is taking everything away from these black men and taking their License away giving jail and prison time and it has to do with politics to power control and money even thou it's politically incorrect and it's destruction of our men forcing them into crime to survive then the black family gets killed by the mother getting on Section 8 and telling her the father can't live there then give her food stamps and she thinks it's all good but the truth is the father got to pay that all back so they put them on child support and take his check and tax him. Now you have a lot of women paying for that who was doing wrong by that they are locking them up. See now the black man is at his first strike he's at war with America because he was born black I know because what I have been through then with the system, the baby mother, then it gets deeper now they dislike one another and them fighting one another is only helping the agenda place upon our people to break the black family so then they can't equal and united. Black men will always go through more punishment than women to some women and the system his opinion and fact does not matter. Then he will be criticized for just having a voice and standing up for his rights and freedom. Then be attacked for standing for his beliefs, for past things, and for positive and for the future look at all our leaders even for the future he still will stand up and accomplish great many things just notice what he must go through!! They are reprograming a lot of our black women. Like my friend Torrez he's given all his money to his son mother for him then takes him to court and lie on him to get more money me and him had the same lawyer his case was a different situation. Now see into days society and world men are denied showing emotions in their society because all we are known for is to only be strong as what some women are taught at the end of the day men just want support from their women. Some women have taught their daughters in cycles we are not allowed to show emotions because that's being weak or a baby to some women. No matter what you do as a black man you won't be credited for on a lot of things or the good you have done. When I was sitting down talking with my friend Torrez, he was explaining to me that he was by his wife side he was there holding it up but when things got bad and slowed down everybody was calling his damn phone aunties, uncles, everyone from her family no one was there to just say you need this or that, the whole family was calling him. He was like you might as we'll say the world was calling him because it was so much stress, pain and depression on him even peoples called him that his woman family told the business to this why you don't talk to know about your business in your relationship on both sides. I went through something like that with Cleopatra and her family and her grandmother, brother and father were the only one treated me fair because of her spirit, respect for herself, love, and experience in life as an elder! She did not treat her family or me different she treated everyone the same way loved me in the same way she loved everybody else she got on Cleopatra and Jeffrey the same way but got on her daughter the most because she was always at him and Cleopatra be she was married to him and Cleopatra said my mother did not like no man I ever got with and her mother had some serious secret ways as woman with a powerful nasty attitude she will be right at times but most of the time go overboard. Cleopatra will use everything she could against Jeffrey to slap me back in the face with help from her mother and the same one

that was helping her will slap her back with the same thing with drama, words, mentally, manipulating and debating. It was not because of everything being my fault but in Cleopatra eyes, mind, body, soul, spirit, not being a bad woman or everything being on her or her fault it was the way she was acting, and this was not only on Jeffrey for everything because if he did everything and she did nothing that will mean she will be perfect and not wrong one time! The Grandmother will sit there with her daughter and say your wrong don't do him like that he's a part of this family to he even told the grandmother the abuse and sins he did to Cleopatra she said that's not right or good she got on him she even told me if I had the energy I will give you a good slap and ass whipping but God is going to take care of you for what you did to my grandbaby. When Jeffrey told her that she said she forgave me she said Well then that don't suppose to be brought no more if she's still bringing that up then her heart is not right and not clean and she need to work on that with God Jeffrey liked the grandmother because she did not play games, she was for real and straight to the point. Now Cleopatra explained to Jeffrey how her grandmother and mother use to get into disagreements and not get along with one another and she will say they need to stop that there a family so where do the cycle come from? Now grandmother told Jeffrey if she doesn't want to forgive you then you can't make her just keep praying forgive her for her not forgiving you it may sound crazy baby but just do it and when he did it she kept coming at him with the same old things it was old, so nothing was brand new starting from the start. Now I did do get back to that did not make me right I hope women get on this level right it's not a man or woman speech or a take up for thing it's the right thing to do but when the grandmother will get on everyone for doing me wrong I use to open my mouth forget back sometimes and provoking and going overboard sometimes and then I will apologize, and the grandmother will say good job. Now you have women now today will say even ask, what you or he did wrong for her to do what she did? Every single time not some or most every time that don't even ask WHAT HAPPEN? Then it goes for every occasion when the woman is hurt every time every woman is saying you had to do something to her not saying women have not been hurt but what did they cause and start and it's not in there no where it's just all the man fault and they did nothing. Negativity pops right up because a woman is good on nonverbal response SILENT TREATMENT, and he deserve it if the woman is right or wrong it's part of her nature and a psychological thing as well. See women has experience with other men or a man so women see these men today as the police see them with the system attacking as we'll we all look the same, talk the same, do the same shit. The prayer only supposed to come in when they feel like it should when they heart is clean and pure because they will say the God they serve. It's our God we serve really but the woman did not mean that she was hurt she every right to do that then when man comes in like that in this way it's different in woman's way she's different she's a woman. Every man has trials and tribulations he goes through not only a woman and women. Now a man is not strong and perfect in every way they mess up so as a woman like Cleopatra when Jeffrey was down she didn't be a strong woman to back him up and lift him up at times like she would say in front of our children we'll stepchildren when I was married to her he married the package. She will say in front of our daughter don't get with no man who broke or don't have nothing going on for his self and Jeffrey would look at her crying and hurting because she's so bitter, angry so much out for revenge after of her words of forgiveness but not meaning it from her heart it was not just funny laughing at it sometimes, but it turned into tears where she couldn't see it only hers. It supposed to be God first, she did not know or see our relationship was for better or for worse, richer or poor, sickness or in health until death us do us apart and she was using her paying the majority of the bills at the time while I was trying to find a job at the same time while I was on the streets hustling and looking for jobs and thank God he bless me with one working at a hotel and at a restaurant that was not enough for her and her not our relationship. It was about herself, and her children forget about her husband he does not exist and invisible. The money I was making was not enough for her children and herself and it was all my fault this why at times her daughter disrespected me and told me in our house fuck nigga you don't pay no bills in this house with your broke ass, because she was watching how her mother was disrespecting and talking to me not for all things but this situation was serious a real strong woman is going to bring out the smile when you down. Grows with the flow and always maintains flexible if I fall short she back me up if she falls short I back her up not tell me your sorry ass now I forgave you and after I forgave your ass I'm going to do you like you did me continue to throw up in your face what you did now you see how it feels. I love you then it changes I don't love you; I love you; you make me sick I can't stand you. I love you baby but I'm deeply sorry. I smelled like the streets, I love you and then make love to me on top of me saying I'm a trip and give me that soft kiss after she finishes! Then that's nothing change back up saying be a man suck it up men can be so annoying right women and aggravated? What can you all be at times? Before Jeffrey got married to Cleopatra he was paying the rent, the light bill and spending the money for the family and women this is not throwing nothing up in a woman face but when he lost his business money stop coming in then the marriage started falling apart on somethings financially bounds it don't suppose to be all about money just like the women say it's not all about the sex or making love. Richer or poor has to do with if you have it or not I'm here we can work this out together the good times are all good but when times get hard it's that what matters to stick together. We cannot be breaking forever now some people run when they get broke because how they were raised thinking it was not going to be a struggle this where Cleopatra did not go right bringing that cycle in her home letting it follow her from her mom without the father there and seeing things happen attitude and ways of her mother. See Cleopatra's mother Pam was married, so if you were telling your mother not to treat her husband like that and talk to him in that way and you putting him down in front of people and Jeffrey where she thinks she got it from hello!! Money and working hard both brought us hard times not only the woman it was lot of times stressful on me then change to her then both of us she felt and wanted to be all and only about her selfishness she didn't know the pursuit of money can cost health problems, but I beg her please don't let the past put sacrifices on our relationship or our health I got it from her listening and hearing. About money when I was in the hospital back in forth the labor pool job here laying in the bed with her cursing me out and looking at me angry and evil with a bold attitude strong black woman saying it's always a problem with your fucking ass you are a fuck up things from the past hearing even things before we got married came up. She did not realize when we first got married me and her we were not leaving the children out or family members it's that she was not taught certain things just like me but let her tell it she's on point and was raised right and perfect! We were supposed to meet and be there for each other needs not the woman needs only. As me sitting there watching their mother and auntie smiling and laughing with them saying and laughing with them saying that's right girl put him in his place handle your business see these games will kill your relationship and it be dry as weed, grass, trees, forest, roses, daisies or any flowers or plants that don't get no water at all periods and when plants get no water what happens? They die. She had her machete in her hand on my neck with her foot on my neck with her foot on my back every time I grew out and branch out she will chop a leaf off she will even burn my seeds of love of words that she felt like I didn't even mean nothing. Not one day my flower will get a chance to bloom out of my heart of love, So I don't love period!! She does all the loving she's the woman emotional creature. I feel you women when you say the man or some or most men broke that real partnership I understand where you're coming from, but if you choose to take that man back and you forgave him and he's not doing the same thing and your thinking he is when he's not and your treating him wrong and like he's the same old shit what are you going to get if you want to continue to feel like shit and be mad at yourself and at him. That's on you know because you broke the partnership and the promise it's not pointing the finger if one person comes up and be the better person like me I was the better man of God I put all the wrong on me but then the woman came back at me with it's not enough how could it be a partnership? So why she took me back? She said because God told her, she said she prayed and ask God to give me back and God gave her what she asks for and she was not a bitch she was bitching complaining and doing the hold 9 yards that's the difference. See it's to man and woman watch what you ask God for then when we get it we want to blame the other person when it's are mess ups and action Cleopatra did not play no part in this I'm admitting to my parts!! We are held accountable for own actions not blaming one another back and forth

for our wrong doings I mean everyone. If you can't forgive your wife or husband or one another then go to God and learn humble to fall in love all over again with that person step by step with obedience the passion for God and learn more in one another the likes and dislikes. Now you have a lot of women say, think, feel and keep in their mind with a grudge it will never go back to the way it uses to be they be saying there ready but truly they don't on themselves they just be wanting the man back!! Some women it be the love, confusion, security, stability, a protection in ways, having a family with him meaning CHILDREN and other things. Back to me saying that it's a lot of women saying it will never go back to the way it used to be then that's what you are going to get you made the decision already before you prayed already and after you pray then start right back with the same thing or something different but still the same old things because it's the past and your miserable when you prayed you was with God but then forgot about God when you walked up to your husband/man you did not think about God and the prayer you thought about telling him off and all the negative things. See you don't know it, but you take the confusion to him that be inside of you what's the first thing the devil comes in to do after praying? To tempt, kill, steal, and destroy then you walk away calm down come back then say sorry at times that be a continue thing. He tempts the husband to so if the same God is telling you to forgive others and yourselves, how is your thinking and your thought process? How is it you're thinking that for certain people it's different by what they have done no it's that you can't forgive yourself and love do it for God you and that person. You a cycle it's so strange because the same mean attitude Cleopatra had her mother was acting just a like. A generational curse she followed her mother footsteps. Some women have no bills to pay and still complaining and have a good husband/man. Women to you that do this ask God to change your heart and mind, soul, body with the spirit of love. Pray to God to change your ways on the husband/man you love to change your negativity in your mind the way you think about him treat him and see him as nothing and what's in your heart making you feel a certain way. Just like the woman feels all great you feel too as well. Please don't take your husband/man back then constantly continually makes him pay back with hell we know you be scornful but how long the bitter woman will continue that life if she wants to set herself free for God and her to love again not everything being on the man and not looking at everything HERSELF! Take him through tutoring classes of demands of control of spitting off at the mouth beating him up mentally, physically, health wise, strength, spiritually you will be in a dark place with smoke on your broom stick being the witch dropping him off and picking him up when and whenever you feel like it and say well that's how he did me that's not resolving the matter that's boiling hot water to throw on him. You have a lot of women feel like when they reject their husband/man at times it's a mind over being strong and getting back at him teaching him a lesson letting him know who's the boss when she let you know Jesus is her boss but she's your boss isn't that something. I see this on hats, shirts at clothing stores but the thing is how many marriages today truly does this and understand this with God first and know he's the boss? Now today the husband wants to be the boss then the wife wants to be the boss it changes up then when the pain and hurts hit then it's dropping on our knees back to God. Cleopatra was so angry her God she served was only there for her and her children I was not a child of God I was nowhere near her as a Christian like she said yelling at me I was not God I told her I know I'm not God, but God says we don't suppose to treat one another like this. Cleopatra always told me about God on her side she's holy, but I can't never ever tell her because my sins are worse than hers when sin is sin, but she would have told me off real fast and quick when I let her know things about the Lord. Dominating me was so cruel. When I wanted to work hard to meet her differences it was not good enough, she was great and excellent in everything! A lot of ladies will say come on now we know no one is excellent in everything but they behavior, words, actions, body language speaks for itself. Women can you really see the things the devil attacks you with? Today there looking at so many T.V shows, soap operas, people that speaking out negativity on poetry not helping to make it worse anyone can have a passion on gift on something but when they use it for evil and for peoples to get back at other people's I'm not for that. I see men and women speak on poetry and it be fair then I see some that say negative things to stay away from men or women and through mixed signals putting peoples down it be false prophets to tell them not to listen to the husbands for what they did wrong, but he is the head and the man he supposes to listen here and understand you're the woman you owned all the credit. Then they use they bodies towards one another in marriages. At times it can be one thing a tempt that all it takes and then it be petty and things start dropping in the marriage it can be replaced back bringing God in well God already be there it be the husband the wife sometimes both that leaves with their body, soul, spirit, mind, love and everything and can be standing right there blind first two holding hands you don't want to go back and forth the thing is to control it it's not he say she say it's what God says and sees. It could be evil things like not praying together, no fellow shipping, no life, no love, no inspiration, no encouragement, no believing, no truth, wicked words, no sex, adultery, provoking, false accusing, past thoughts, negative family members, being so judge mental, no fasting, no fasting with one another. A marriage is not perfect you go through your struggles you must be on the same page. It's not all about your needs happy or mad it's about both of you!! God wants you to come with your needs together in your relationships. We both worship God you get extreme obedience. You have women they teach they daughters to be independent then turn around and baby their sons creating self-sufficient women and the men who are ok with living off them. Every man and woman are not the same so I'm not judging please don't feel assaulted in anytime of any kind of way. A down to earth woman takes pride in herself keeps her motivation going she also take pride in her appearance she doesn't have to put on a full face of make up to get a man she wants. She embraces herself and looks, beauty, style and respects her own sense of style never stop looking naturally gorgeous or must be a high maintenance boogie woman. A real woman stands out more than anything that is what was beautiful when I first met Cleopatra another thing about a woman don't let her nail break, she will have a fit. A down to earth woman does not brag! When Cleopatra cried and I did to when we were wrong or right being human beings when I cried it was fake it was not pain but hers was important and everything included in with it she meant what she said then didn't mean what she said she just kept changing I guess that's a woman sometime Cleopatra will front and act like she don't love me. You have women that don't let men see certain things certain sides because being taking advantage of, so they must do it back as get back for revenge to judge a man/man from the past now if it's because they are still doing wrong and being ass holes that different. You have women when they do get back and it don't even be about cheating it happens at times in relationships. One of the things I did learn if Cleopatra did anything as a woman when it happens, she did it with power wonderfully successful at what she did it showed greatness. It was so fun when we first met and together it was better than an adventure. I was ready for her challenge. Cleopatra and Jeffrey were more and wanted more of each other it's like planting more and more flowers down in her garden and he were the tools. I even made fun of myself, other things, people to keep her smiling, laughing, giggle and be happy. Bad behavior is not tolerated with no one that does not like drama some women be like most men have a bad behavior problem. Your mouth and what come out of it disrespectful can be a bad behavior as well with a cruel attitude being rude, nasty, angry, sarcastic can be a bad behavior. Everyone one in life have been through there own situations and problems worse and harder everyone has had they tough and rough times. A real woman also never compares herself to other people especially other women this is a down to earth woman and it's easier for her to accept people for who they are she know this already not to drive herself crazy!! What Jeffrey tried hard to tell Cleopatra and other women and men when you judge him or other people's especially in a way that makes it seems they think and show that they are better than you. It's something with in themselves it is something they don't like, and it does not make him, you or Cleopatra, men, women, or anybody feel good. I took my own flaws in as a man I excuse myself because vice versa it's all about everyone with love not only me. Even when Cleopatra thought Jeffrey was always wrong and said he was the devil and evil, the only sinner around her she put me down real low for her decisions to always stand high. A down to earth woman will love hard and soft it will be amazing and don't care what no one says it won't be in a rude way it will be a respectfully walk away because she does not have time for games, petty things, bull crap of what someone has to say. If it's encouragement, then that's ok. The woman has different types of drama she can be a drama queen or inner drama queen a real woman would know when she knows and see a real man because he will have his shit together. God first, it will be seen with action and responsibility, life already in place with plans, goals, respect for himself. You know soon as Cleopatra uses to tell Jeffrey I'm going somewhere if she was in the right or wrong. I missed her as soon as she said the words out her mouth just imagines when she did leave it felt like she was gone forever even if it was, with her family to the store, shopping, going to the beauty store or getting her hair or nails done now this is for myself and to everyone else just imagine how I feel now? It's so much love there I can even explain I don't call it no whip that's games I say and mean it from my heart it's agape! One thing I just wish that when Jeffrey was married after Cleopatra forgave him when she said it I genuinely wanted to hope and believe it came from the heart because she was not the down to earth woman when he left and walked out the door he was going to be with a bitch or a whore or fuck all kinds of women or whatever one she had on her mind. Down to earth woman takes pride in herself keep the woman motivation going she also take pride in her appearance she doesn't have to put on a full face of makeup to get the man she wants. She embraces herself, her looks, her beauty, her style, and respects her own sense of style never stop looking naturally gorgeous or must be a high maintenance boogie woman. A real woman will stand out more than anything that is what was beautiful when Jeffrey first met Cleopatra another thing about a woman is don't let her nail break, she will have a fit it's a part of her beauty and it is taking time to grow back. A down to earth woman does not brag! When Cleopatra cried, Jeffrey did to but not at all the time most of the time. When we both was right or right, we are human and when she said no, I didn't cry she is lying because she loved me she said what she didn't mean what she said that's a front. At times women do not let a man see that side a lot being taking advantage of, so they must do it back as get back and revenge. Even when it's not about cheating on one another it happens at times in relationships. One thing I learn if she did anything as a woman, I knew anything as a woman I knew, and she did it showed gratefulness. It was so fun when we first met and together it was better than an adventure. I was ready for her challenge. She and I was more and wanted more of each other it's like planting more and more flowers down in her garden and I was the tools. I even made fun of myself, other things, people to keep her smile, laugh, giggle and be happy. Bad behavior is a choice and I wonder where some women get off on its only men. Your mouth and what come out of it be disrespectful can be a bad behavior your attitude being rude, nasty, angry sarcastic can be bad behavior. Everyone in life have been through the same situation worse, harder, everyone has had they tough times. A real woman also never compares herself to other people especially other women this is a down to earth woman and it's a down to earth woman and its easier for her to accept people for who they are. She knows this already not to drive herself crazy!! What Jeffrey tried to tell Cleopatra and other women not all even some men when judge me or other people's especially in a way that makes it seem like they think and show that they are better than you. It's something in with in themselves that they don't like, and it does not make me, you, or Cleopatra, men, women, or anybody feel good. Jeffrey took his own flaws in as a man I excuse myself because vice versa it's all about everyone with love not only me. Even when Cleopatra thought Jeffrey was always wrong and was the devil and evil, the only sinner, around her she put me down real low for her decisions to always stand high. A down to earth woman will love hard and soft it will be amazing and don't care what no one says it won't be in a rude way it will be in a respectful, fascinating and lovable because she doesn't have time for bull crap of what someone say or do. Now if it's encouraging then ok. A woman has different types of drama queen or inner drama queen depending on that woman a real woman will know when she knows and see a real man because he will have his shit together and his life will be with God and himself inside and out around him his responsibilities already are in place, plans, goals, respect for himself with God the number one thing in his life. You know soon as Cleopatra uses to tell Jeffrey I'm going somewhere if she was in the right or wrong he missed the hell out of her as soon as she said the words out her mouth just imagines when she did leave it felt like she was gone forever even if it was with her family to the store, shopping, going to the beauty store or getting her hair or nails done. Now this is for myself and to everyone else just imagine how I feel now? It's so much love there

I can't even explain I don't call it no whip on me or her that's games I say it and mean it from my heart that's agape! One thing I just wish that when Jeffrey was her partner after Cleopatra forgave him when she said it he genuinely wanted to hope and believe it came from her heart because she was not the down to earth woman when he left and walked out the door he was going to be with a bitch, whore or fuck all kinds of women or whatever one she was thinking of what was in her mind was confusing staying there miserable. Her feelings were sad, hurt, bitter, sad, irritated, or energetic sometimes feeling no love at all. See a man can see things that a woman can't see at times he can be satisfied with a lot of things in life with simple pleasures, but a woman is not satisfied she changes up I know a lot of women are not going to agree with me but most of these things I write are true about women even of all women not being the same. The older a man gets he learns more and becomes wiser and smarter. See when the woman gets in her way and can't forgive her mind takes over her at times as well as her attitude, actions, behavior, and think believe and know she can do it all by herself and she don't need no one else help not even a man one of the number one thing on the list or men period. The woman always wants more and more. Cleopatra mind was powerful, strong, real smart than Jeffrey always he could not go with her love with God in her heart in the state of mind, mentally, spiritual and physically it was bitterness she was not happy for him her man with him living out there was bad news. What was a trip when she always told me that I was a trip then she would tell me she loved me and didn't mean them things she did and then said to me all my wrongs and rights was wrong all the sins on me? Then tell me no man supposed to do that to his woman or treat her a that kind of way. So, she was not comfortable at all even with herself because of me and I was the devil and only sinner where does that come from? MAN OR WOMAN NOT GOD!! Women, please tell me I know you have a side everything our relationship was my fault right women because every woman I done met done told me they are not wrong they did nothing wrong. Then come back to me and say baby I did not mean them things I said or did to you. See women when your husband/man needs space don't pressure him he's going to go to another woman if your false accusing or provoking him all the time especially when this remains in your head when you think he's doing something wrong when he's not, you're speaking to it in the air in his face and to existence. You will be making your own burning bed for you both. When he changes and you give him a chance what does a chance means? This ruins the man life and heart and run him away you say ok I'll give you time it don't truly be no chance or time because it don't even have to take something to go wrong soon as you (THE WOMAN) don't feel in type of any way you are not comfortable you pop and goes off, so did you really mean your apology for not giving him a chance with God first with action and not the way you want it to be? You can have it your way it's how you do it unconditionally with God's saying and doing loyal. Don't reverse this and say we'll he cheated because then your holding clouds over his head on everything there is forgiving someone or anyone. A chance is whipping there slate clean starting over with a clean start but not allowing the past sins dictate the present a brand-new relationship meaning starting fresh. Now hear and listen to this will some women say it don't go back to the same way again so what does that mean or is? A Lukewarm spirit sometimes with God and then sometimes with the devil time in your marriage. In case of what my grandmothers would say that was married one 40 years and the other 20 on the other one there's no such thing on every marriage it's what you put in. Women you want men to understand your needs, your likes, your dislikes, everything, you ever take time out to think if you're driving him crazy makes him confused and drained out and embarrassing therefore he get away. I have heard a lot of women say if he was a real man he will not walk away he will stand there and be a man and listen, hey that's control like you tell the man hey you going to stay right here and listen to what I got to say a woman look at me. The right way is both parties need space sometimes in their marriage/relationship see when a man has done you wrong and you have took him back family members, friends, coworkers and others be in her ear it's up to her to listen and accept but before she put anything in action she need to take care of your mind set first because I know and a lot of women know so do men that how much that man has to go through and be through to. I'm not going to put no woman above me I will not tell her she right for everything even when she's dead wrong I'm not a puppet or her puppy I'm a human being just like her. You Paul in the bible speaks about saying he is the least among all prophets yet, but God promoted him to preach the word the gospel and he felt the least because he prosecuted the church and killed Christians, put them in jail and beat them up only person saved him was God. The man is not of the woman, but the woman of the man. Neither was the man created for the woman, but the woman for the man. This causes the woman to have power on her head because of the angels. Nevertheless, neither is the man without the woman, neither the woman without the man, in the Lord. For as the woman is of the man, even so is the man, even so is the man also by the woman, but all things of God. Judge in yourselves. Is it comely that a woman prays unto God uncovered? Does not even nature itself teach you, that if a man has long hair, it is a shame unto him? See I'm saying the lady is from the man not the man from the lady. Men do wrong and right women do wrong and right please don't put no one down as your better than them everyone needs a hand to get back up. See it saying a police officer can be good to this person then bad to that person then another person would say he or she did that wow. Same thing for a man or woman. A woman can treat this man good or this woman and be wrong towards someone else same thing as a man he can do this man wrong or this woman wrong and be good to other people's we all have bad and good in us. Women this does not mean try to use God as an excuse to get hurt or get away God see's everything same thing for women because when sin and cheat towards God says touch not my anointing. God does the rest not us wishing, planning and sitting back thinking in our minds evil what we think and want to happen it don't work like see women when you are angry, and you lie to yourself about healing I know it takes time but if you are not sure you're hurting yourself more and more because you're not honest with in your heart within yourself and still you are important. First Jeffrey know it's very upsetting it was hard for him to put his full heart into Cleopatra and her family so women you see it's not all on you it's not easy for no one we all have been hurt and have problems. Now if you go on to the role they lied so I can continue and on to act and be in this way so I can lie to as well it will be hell for both of you, true or not? Where do lies get anyone no matter what it is only for the good though see when relationships go through things especially marriages the problem be that they can't meet each other needs is God, listening, work, time, hearing, understanding, love, appreciation and encourage a lot. If you do be right and still apologize for something your other party or soulmate was wrong for let it be 50/50 don't use your husband/ man wife/woman against that to control from the past or anything starts of confusion, negativity, trouble, problems or failure. How can you both work together to meet each other needs when your focus on what he did in the past and can't forgive him, and he's focus on she's doing it so much to him he thinks negative as well. When both of you supposed to be on the same track of the Lord and moving forward, Cleopatra doesn't care now because she didn't care then when Jeffrey was trying then she would say it and mean with her actions towards him with an aggressive angry attitude with mean devious looks and her excuse always to get out was he made her like this and he been around her a long time and he was around no one or woman he can be to myself and all of a sudden she talking about cheating. Just look at me and tell me what I'm thinking about tell me what I didn't do with the other woman children I was with that I'm going to do with her children, and we are married so don't not even get on her children. No matter what they do she got it right women take it or leave it. No that's the kind of woman I was with and every woman I was with, and every woman is not like that. Now a lot of these women today they going to back up their children if they are right or wrong. I talked to her and when Jeffrey told Cleopatra (THE WOMAN) that she was wrong it was who he been talking to? You been talking to that woman? That bitch? Who have you been listening to? I don't care if you been listening to someone I didn't even say nothing sometimes I would just look at her crazy with a crazy look what's wrong with her I'm quiet I'm silent and this is coming all from her heart and mind I'm paying for something happen in the past before I got into the deep relationship did you hear me paying for same thing, and the first thing she will say and other women not every single woman in the world girl he was not the man for you anyway he wasn't shit. Even after while in the relationship, I lost that respect because of no forgiveness. She had her clock with her dynamite with the tape around it with me and her mostly men she will blow us up and don't know it was her causing the explosion. She was bitter!! Do I blame her yes after she said she forgive me we are getting married and moving forward? I had my watch as well timing myself what time to be home what time I need to pick up and drop off the children and working on me so she can be a happy wife even that wasn't good enough. When you forgive someone, this can't go to his grave or yours forever even though we know nothing last forever in the mind set or relationship this will damage the home. She was thinking always he left so I feel a certain type of way, what is he doing? Where is he at? Feeling confused, feeling what she's feeling straight, uncomfortable, about me to herself even though I love his crazy ass. This is my sweetheart Cleopatra yes women Jeffrey sat back and observed because he knew he was wrong for his actions, and she made him pay good he will hear it until this day. She will say quick I don't know her, but she has me down pack and all together at times you can let a woman know that sometimes what she's saying and how she is acting is sometimes rude and wrong it will make the situations worse and get out of hand it is not only for men being hardheaded women. If Jeffrey asks Cleopatra right now did you give me space one time I'll get fussed out, curse out and ask I'm still bringing that up that's why he don't like talking to you then when he grants her wish then she comes with whatever she wants to out of her back, and he say don't do that than its own don't do what he does and don't get on him he does the getting on. Then she tried to force herself on me, oh you going to give me some sex choking me on top of me but when I said in partnership it been said you are my woman I want to make love I'm the devil dog, don't use anything against me I know what the good book says you can't make me, shit that's all you want me to do I don't feel like it come on now I'm ready when she was ready she was hot and happy changing up at times and mood swings now she is not a bitch at all but in her times she can be one angry. What is that doing ladies? I want to hear your facts and men? God knew and I did when I was doing right going to the Pastor house, the Bishop house, my auntie house, my Godmother house laying on the floor looking up at the celling it's all my fault I shouldn't never cheated blaming me for her still fussing me out for something I stop doing she couldn't see that I had a wonderful great legitimate reason well several reasons to get away from her it was like deliver me from Eva. I know she will be like child please, whatever, anyway he trying to put it all on me I did not do anything. Now today with divorces you don't hear both sides just mostly women it's two sisters it be the lie to both sides have lied if the husband/man said he never lied he is a liar and the wife/woman said she never lied she is a liar they both are liars they might as well say they didn't never sin no more after they both got saved a lie is a lie. You know I've seen that in reality today and in movies and in the pass to hear both parties and the two lovers will listen to other people's opinions like they said the same thing about her so they did not sit down and believe one another because they let the envy, vengeance, pride, selfishness get in the way of something I feel you may not feel the same way or something you may feel I may not feel because you will not agree on everything disagree to agree. Women I know men have hurt you and men women have hurt you, but you must forgive them and yourself because if you don't hell will take over you. Especially in your marriage/relationships and home! See this does not show no sign of respect for Jeffrey when he was trying and doing towards Cleopatra constantly being mad and angry, bitter, malice unforgiving wasn't doing nothing but constantly ending our relationship it wasn't only him and women say give up let it go when they can't forgive a lot of them being saying them forgiving but they don't it just be words and what comes behind if we don't forget beware we are watching no that's your way. Do as God say as Paul, as Rahab in the bible with faith don't walk into these churches listening to false prophets and other false teachers say forgive but don't forget and that's it, No! It's a way how God say forgive and do it right as passing it on like Paul pass it on pass your marriage husband and wives other believers, unbelievers as well because no one is better than no one Jesus walked and was around the believers and unbelievers so give your husband encouragement in God's way to help him move forward with all in love not keeping anyone stuck with hate we want us to have passion for one another. We can't never blame God and you have some people they try to blame God for everything so if you know if we try to do that being upset and angry at times we will do it to one another please stop. You have a lot of people say Jeffrey never did that to God you a liar we all have he have because when he has sinned and hurt towards himself, Cleopatra, brothers, sisters, family members, friends he did it against God because when he hurt them he hurt God. I had to repent and ask forgiveness, so women and men please ask forgiveness, change in order and obedience. See a woman does not want to be played with period as she's a playground so as well as a man/woman you don't get it all you did not invented, or man God did God knows who you are man to. See when Jeffrey left home at times Cleopatra's wife didn't constantly pray, be fulfilled with love, think of us, feel fantastic and ready for me when he walks back in because when he walks back in because when he walked in 15 minutes or 20 minutes later where the fuck you were at? Who was you with? What were you doing? Did you go to that woman house? So, like some women feel and tell their friends girl you don't need your husband it was better off letting him go moving on and getting you together. Cleopatra did not let Jeffrey come to her!! Jeffrey could not touch her or give her a kiss to Cleopatra she will turn away I'm talking about before I went back out there and started back cheating again. I was fed up, but I didn't give up I was fighting for our relationship, but I couldn't do it all by my damn self. No matter how much the man is the head of the household it takes two. I loved this woman so much I wanted to give her more time to herself to invest in her heart and loving her more and the children she cried out and to God she just was thinking of what she wanted to think of and other things I did not mean anything to her she did not care like she said. I still was her man right so under God's commandment and laws and vowels it was my fault that's so not true women. Now when you don't want your man to text you or talk to you at all why you text him any way then when you hear him tell you that he does not love you he's not hearing you out no woman is deserved to be treated in this way. Some women or most feel that they should get or receive more from the man than the man than the man should from them no its 50/50. This why your off balanced. Jeffrey even put his needs, space, time off for Cleopatra time off special and important and until this day I'll stop what I'm doing to support her a lot of peoples done said that I still love that woman. Now that is a man earning his trust back letting you know every place you at when you call him, keep or checking up on him then when he does the calling up and checking up it's a problem after the cheating and no forgiveness because she's still hurting when Jeffrey called Cleopatra on her job it was no problem then when things got bad that he brought it changed he don't blame her but what he do blame her for is when he made progress and correction she did not love him no more! I know I had to earn a lot of things back so I got to stand outside in the weather and still get shitted on I can take that to, but after that don't leave me outside to freeze and die. God first Jeffrey loves this woman lord he messed up she's his Cleopatra and I'm investing his all in her. She always got her prizes I didn't get nothing it was her needs first always and only about she is being deserved. The woman is sensible, practical, genuine, beautiful and love, but I can't not take the blame for everything in this relationship being on me. Jeffrey can't make Cleopatra take him back or say she wrong what she's wrong for and that shit hurts you can just imagine how he feel I'm not going to say I'm a man, I'm going to say I'm someone, somebody, special, one of a kind, something, a human being, Important, a person, I'm God's child, God says I'm God's given gift!! You have the crazy woman as well you also have the woman who have everything well you can say every kind of different woman is one. A woman always wants something it can be emotional an important need of quality time of course shoes, clothes, material things but not letting them things make her. Then you have all these women that want to be rulers because if you look at the chest board of the game the most powerful peace is the queen and what does the queen do, it protects the king. No matter where the queen moves, she can never fall this what Jeffrey love so much about Cleopatra. You know when we got to meet one another and going out and she decided, and I did as well to sleep with one another. I guess the first shot was an over dose because she start blowing my phone up I thought that what it was all about but when I got saved and gave my life to God and learned more I became a man in soul and spirit knowing that she did not fall in love with my penis or sex she fell in love with me being me, my heart, unconditionally and who she was when I first met her A REAL WOMAN!! It was not all about her or me it was all about us because I answered my cell phone at times she came to me, and I went to her see to be chose you must be chosen this goes both ways women you don't do it all by yourself. I love all the nicknames she gave me and she knew what I liked but she made me smile inside and put a big smile on my face because she knew the secrets I felt about her if I held them inside or showed them she just knew and swore she knew everything and was right about everything all the time, but I saw that I didn't play with her when it was time to make love because she was not with the 2 minutes I would have been fired real fast and talked about in my face on the first go round she was a silent woman on a lot of things I admit I made her the woman she became a bitter woman then she should never took me back if she wasn't ready to forgive me to work on her and get her right! See when a woman is in the bedroom with her husband/man she not playing she coming correct and putting it down handling her business you also have women be straight up waiting and wanting you to for real to let her know up front is this a sex thing, and we are just friends or are we in love? I agree the women got the men beat on that see women are high natured and they are different from men in a lot of ways see when a woman is touch and made love to she can't wait forever and she's emotional it's the feelings the woman has especially the attention that the man shows her it's also waiting for the next time if it be one because every woman not the same. Jeffrey love Cleopatra like her to she Is a Lion and queen the Leo a lady in the street but a freak in the bed for her one man. Well, I know I handle my business I am the fish the Pisces, but the making love was not the first thing about our relationship the most thing that made her smile was the small things making love was a part of it. Listen companionship was the biggest thing ever it went deeper she was deeper than ever her all by herself it went deeper than friends we got closer than friends the group Surface sings she knew that song as well as how I felt about it the companionship was even when we broke up with her fussing acting up. Tell me something why did she still call this man I know why I called her that's my secret ladies just like she had hers hidden with the silent treatment at times faking with her mind games. It was closeness together, intimacy, rapport, more than two people for whatever reason that always truly connect. It was association of all kinds of things with and for this beautiful woman, she offer herself with love I did to she wanted all the credit but it don't go like that with no body they can say that with the mouth, emotions, feelings, actions, ways, thoughts but to themselves and God there sorry for what they done wrong because they have common sense and five senses God gave them this even me I went to God for a lot of things I did wrong and right so don't play with yourself stop running and hiding women and men!! The companionship is way pass, deeper, good than sex well a lot put it making love the quality time was great walking, talking, going to the movies, going to the movies, going to church together playing games together, driving and talking to one another, reading the bible to one another most of all hearing and listening to the word of God from one another, enjoying peace and quiet with another, I'm glad Jeffrey express my affection, emotions, passion, love, appreciation, feelings, pain, this showed my loyalty, truth and my actions to earn a woman back and that's Cleopatra she just did not choose to receive it so she have to deal with that with her and God I'm glad we got back together way more than rubies when Jeffrey got her back. God put the grown back on my head as king it's just not the queen that accepted the king back then telling him I wish I shouldn't of never took you back like the cycle her mother pass on to her instead of forgiving and moving on! It was holding wrapping my arms around her neck rubbing her back with my other hand. See she didn't truly connect back to me like when we first met she chose not to I couldn't make her so that was in the process already like her mother taught her what she sat down living with her mother and learn this don't make me be like my mother at times she was not a loving mother this show in some areas that women raise their daughters to be in this raised up. Since everyone is not perfect every time someone brought up what I did to her in the pass she will stand behind up and walk up like they were coming to arrest me for a warrant every single time and she would be behind them saying yes that's right and I will say I thought you forgave me, and we were moving forward? She would say so or walk away and cry. I understand you women pay back right call yourself Christians and doers of the word of God. This part is since the woman or women don't forgive you men or me this man then go forgive them for God and yourself and forgive them for themselves, they need it the most. Don't add to God words or try to change it because you will be judge according to God's judgement of his word. This word doesn't only go for women only or higher for men higher it's equal I'm not using or never can or will use God word it says it if you don't be me then open your Bible your word is right in front of you it's your Bible right for God and you. If I didn't forgive Cleopatra, I wouldn't have a peace of mind this why women be so angry because they did not forgive, they husband/man. Find a better way in God's way to not forget when you forgive women don't do it in your way that's all I'm saying. Men to as well. God gave me that strength to forgive and gave me that belief to give that gift to forgive all and love. Now when we married Jeffrey and Cleopatra was with joy all the time but when the unforgiveness, bad negative words, deceiving, words that were dangerous the companionship lacked up it became loneliness in both of us she was just pretending with her eyes rolling one minute then the next minute listening to her mother he thought he was this she will ask him where he get that from? Your mother I will tell her that because she will be there arguing with her mother on the phone or come back to tell me I wouldn't get into it at all then say I told you that already then so as she gets angry at me. The same mother that's to her that's a mother-n-Law to me I will get cursed out for because I'm telling her the truth about something she don't like a lot of people's get angry at the truth I know I been there so I told her if you getting on your man and you both argue behind my back then if your mother Pam talking about me your man she talking about you and everyone else she's miserable and everything is my fault really I can't even explain it that, that I will not sit here and can't say or think that it wasn't good times in our relationship it was great times and fun in Jeffrey and Cleopatra he would be lying so how he be nothing, shit and a fuck all in one? It's not everything on her it's that now it hurts a woman or man will say well you hurt her right? Not every man or woman because everyone has their own opinion! I'm in love with this woman and still love her romantically with all my passion I have this is no game this is my true feelings, not no one else owns! It wasn't even about sex when I met her children, I was dying to have children and I can't even produce children, so I accept her children. Women, not all seek to say and find something wrong when he lets you know when he takes care of your children and you want me to tell you why in this situation because you as the mother call and shout out your children my children and your babies in front of that man of disrespect at times then children see this and say I can use these two against one another I know because I been there done that now the mother already has a separated life with the father or different father's so that be hard for the step farther the most because the mother been in the life and the step mother's out there to because my mother raise other children that wasn't her children off the streets and took them in. Now you have these women saying oh I made my child or children respect my husband/man but when the shit hits the fan it's over. The mother can do whatever with sin not with God but towards the man even over go overboard on petty things and still be right see the system has taught our women this and cycles from their mother raising them I tried satisfy in every way I could it wasn't good enough I did my wrong, I confessed, I repented I just guess every man that cheats is wanted and sin's go straight to hell judgement by most women, so what's the outcome on women? Husband & Wife don't do this please listen to one another unforgiveness does not solve anything it only backs you up and it be with the devil then it be a waste of years gone down the drain and the devil be with you destroying more for no God, no love, all get back who does more than who even for lack of communication. See Cleopatra looked at Jeffrey and said he talk too much then tell him to shut up then when she spoke it was an ok then sorry when she come right back as a woman to calm down then it's mostly not in front of one another it's when she feels in her mood to say it then say he do say I'm sorry and believe every time it was the right time, and it don't be sometimes. A lot of times I couldn't get one word in because I cheated I couldn't say shit will tell me anything out her mouth towards to win of get backs but did not know she was losing because she was setting herself up more with the devil telling me to my face I can't make her feel good in any kind of way to believe anything I say, so how can she ever have an open heart and still be an angry bitter woman. Her son then tells her you are so mean and angry now the children come in the family in order of God plan that's facts God first, the husband next, and comes the wife, then next is the children if Cleopatra is not listening to Jeffrey what did she learn? She taught everything and had the knowledge and wisdom to teach because she's the teacher but then say I can and do learn something from me but then when I teach and talk she felt and said I don't know anything that's crazy. Now at times that I messed up even when I was hardheaded, but it really hit Jeffrey when he did not listen to Cleopatra when she was telling me to stay from around certain areas and he kept doing it then one time he almost got killed when he walked in the door my stepson Trevor walked to me and said daddy sit down and looked me in my eyes and said why did you go back in the same area where trouble was at? Jeffrey said you right he felt he own son Trevor is telling him this the truth hurts, feel good and bad it be that a lot of times he did not want to accept it, then he walked in the room Cleopatra was laying in the bed and he gave her a kiss then laid by her then Jeffrey said to Cleopatra did you tell our son Trevor to tell me that? She said I did not tell him anything he was concern and worried about you and told me mommy why did he go back into that same area to help people that don't want to be help? Then she said crying I can't tell him no more he won't listen! Our son Trevor was sitting right there and said see dad I got on you it was me not her. I learn to take criticism from her constructively and not fight back with her physically, mentally, verbal abuse, or arguing I just walked away and when I did that she did not change she got worse that's right you going to fuck that woman some women will laugh at this saying, get him that's right I feel and know what you're going through they been down that road, been through that pain and hurt but women I'm here to tell it's not make someone pay for something after they change and you have told them they changed but don't show no respect or appreciation when they have cleaned up their sins. I was not honest then I changed not overnight it took time and she changed the time every time to what she wanted to. So, she wasn't honest back with me that's a cheat right there mentally, spiritually, physically, emotionally it hurts women see that different at times from a cheater as a sinner how and the way they ask for forgiveness as well and say I was, and I prayed and ask to forgive me I won't bring it up no more. A SIN IS SIN! No one can hide or get away from their own actions or sins and blame only themselves. I had my own when she met me can I say she didn't have her own place and was living well until the fuck up man came and messed up her life and her career no I can't say that about her she's a woman I'm a man I'm just looking at this society how it's messed up and what is being taught to our woman & men today I did need her just her I didn't want her damn money when things tough I pray she would of felt the same way about me. I was looking at myself as my personal appearance ok I'm starting over fresh and new for better or worse, richer or poor she didn't see that she saw we struggling I don't have to do this with him so when they was laying teachers off if they would of laid her off I was supposed to be moody, cranky, angry, upset, curse, snap and don't want her no more and argue and say this woman messed up my life or our lives. Even when she said get the fuck from around me go work go do something late at night when it wasn't time for me to work and I lost my businesses the grandmother taught the son I wasn't shit I don't have no education I'm not doing nothing with my life I'm a fuck up telling our daughter things as well and my mother-n-law texting the granddaughter and grandson and saying things right to my face. Cleopatra would not stay on her job keeping them all in place for disrespecting me she was more focus on me and every move I made was going to be negative instead of encouraging me and praying that we move forward she scream and shout I am praying you don't know what I'm doing and when I brought up something about God and our relationship she curse me out mostly every time, then sometimes come get me from the gas station when I was begging for money how she put me down asking people for money to help me feed my family. She will say I'm sorry for what I said get in the car. What kind of wife must explain to her daughter when I walk in the house like she's her friend and partner see how much money he made today look see look what he's doing but she is still not happy with me her own man? I took my time it's called PACE I ask her was she truly ready to get married that was a higher level than forgiveness and letting everything go that's why I ask her if she needed more time let me know for her heart to heal. I made sure to respect her and me that I wasn't jumping into anything fast for her and me it was not happy wife happy life no it was God us as one being happy. If I did not care I wouldn't have showed her she should have known just as much as believing in me a salesman, hustler, worker a businessman, an intelligent smart man. I showed her I cared because sincere strong actions are worth than anything in this world. You know to get respect you have to give respect both ways not just one way she gives I give it's not a one way one does not always get more than the

other because he's a man the head or she's the woman she's different God don't work like that see when that happens to each other both parties feel uncomfortable. Another thing broke us up was finances she did not want to talk about our finance es she wanted to argue about them because she looked at only the things I messed up on there was no working together or with me to achieve goals together to start over to be on the same page it was just fuck me. It takes God the husband/ man & wife/woman to make the relationship last.

Chapter 14

You know I have learned, saw and observed towards a woman a two-minute man once she has made love have sex all in one it has to be done right, on time with satisfaction and long lasting but if it does not be this way that is an insult with injury that will be insulting her mentally, physically, sexually and spiritually. I have known women who have sat down with me and told me the experience of making love with their ex-husbands in the soul of spirit and mood with relaxation saying Jesus this man or oh Lord my God. Jeffrey knew Cleopatra did she called out God name the spirit was there and the soul was all one God was present with his spirit peace of mind body caressing one another. A phenomenal woman knows, thinks and feels when your making love to her she knows I am telling something that is important and for real but not all about that vice versa. It is not all about the woman or all about the man. Every woman is not the same a woman can feel when your love making is right and serious, she will be thinking about all kinds of wonderful great things with her fascinating amazing things you will not and cannot imagine as a man! See a woman see's the little things that counts taking really good care of her she stands there naked in front of her man naked and smiles in her mind and telling you that your great and you keep her happy, some women stand up with the nice dress, lingerie, Victoria secret whatever the husband/man brought for her or herself it is what pleases them both. There is no cost on their minds it is the thought that counts. Together mentally, emotionally, physically, sexually, love, feelings with me all inside Jeffrey made love to Cleopatra with all in him his heart and soul in every way he could to satisfy her first and it still was not enough after unforgiving me. Jeffrey learned by observing Cleopatra on things, but she swore she did not learn nothing from him at all. When he made love to her it was real deep even when two people are married. A woman will never tell deeper secrets because therefore they are called secrets and women have lied saying they told everything that is a lie because they think too much and about lots of things certain things are not to be known. Secrets was righteously between God and Cleopatra everyone is not the same you have a lot of women say that they are real women say they do not do this or that and I am not nasty, but Jeffrey would not do that but when the right man come along, they did it because that woman got emotional attracted to that man brought a lot of things out that some women that woman herself did not know what she felt until it hit her. It can be a touch, conversation, respect, feelings, it is very deep it can be prayer, sexual, a gift, a card, letter depending on that woman and what she likes alike can sneak up on her and catch her off guard like Jeffrey words being controversial with Cleopatra that blew her mind he just did not tell her she did not know every time like you women say a woman already knows yes but not everything! Women play mind games as well at times you have certain women say if a woman is playing mind games then that is no woman and I cannot tell you about no other woman I can only tell you about myself and be the same woman talking about women or something even herself it does not have to be bad, guess what every woman has been here different day, time, and played this role so do not never say never!! Only women can have PMS, Premenstrual syndrome another thing is PCOS as well as a gentleman it is not picking at women it does not mean you cannot get pregnant. It is one of the most common, but treatable causes of infertility in women. Women with PCOS the hormonal imbalance interferes with growth and release of eggs from the ovaries, now can women feel me on not making children because my sperm is not fertilized and strong enough? See women men go through things to. See women take a good look at what you do wrong sometimes think stop and listen do not react say to yourself what did I really do wrong, can you really take your time out to think stop and own up to your mistakes? Being in a marriage/relationship can be hard at times it is not perfect with all kinds of things that can be very annoying like texting, not responding back, silent treatment, arguments, off and on feelings can come in deep within feeling different type of ways also a certain way you are thinking and feeling in some of type of negativity he is always wrong. Sometimes in your mind the problem is him or what he did, but he must always be wrong, and everything must be his fault and take the blame all the time? A woman at times can be thinking and know it is right but not necessarily true at every time it is her mind, her thoughts, her ways, her actions, judging the man when you are judging yourself because it is called being selfish and petty. Thinking at times looking at him he going to do something when he is just sitting there or just doing his own thing and your mind is what it is own falsely accusing him of something because he told you and lie that was false, so you must continue to keep falsely accusing him really, you are holding up the mirror to yourself 20 different reflections, persons, peoples, personalities, double visions all in one! Then you do not want to make love to him anymore or when you feel like it really that is not love that is pleasing your needs when you want some, he made you feel like that so get back tick for tac. It is times when you use love against and towards him out of context and insecurities have become your way of thinking of him constantly you do not give him or it a chance even yourself you may feel, think or even say but your actions show totally different signs sarcastically actions not to even say good job if you do how long do it last for that you cannot control your mind the way of thinking. It is yourself at times of not being happy with a peace of mind in your own world of mind set your way or the highway you set yourself up for failure and then jealousy because envy, the cheating be dead wrong walking away be wrong back and forth. A woman is not the only one or human being in life that gets knocked down and the only one that gets back up and keep moving. Jeffrey did this himself when Cleopatra pushes him down and kept her foot on his neck and said I was going to lose everything and not accomplish anything in life. No relationship is perfect not even the hot sun that shines burning you up because you cannot take too much sun you will get burned up right? Women do not blame men for everything! From the heart Cleopatra is the heart his heart as well the angel's god has protecting her and her children good did happen at times, she is great news. Do you know there is nothing good said about me when you want to see get back on anyone that is evil and cold hearted cruel as well? Now look I am doing good now and who is wishing bad on me or try to do bad against me I hope the best for them. Where does God want us to pray over someone bad or wish speaking bad things over them and against them? Is this a clean heart, spirit, mind, soul or blessings let me know? I will not tell why everything you have going to fall and this what is going to happen to you is not that hurting God and speaking things over your own self that goes for me to. Now when you are a woman of God pray all the time keeping peace in your mind, body, soul, spirit, tongue God first everything stays because your heart is cleaned forgivable. After Jeffrey and Cleopatra got married she did not see his passion, sacrifice, love, strategy, focus, positivity, hard work, late nights with me working, and early mornings, feedback, perseverance, learning, blood sweat & tears, improvement, courage, sadness, injury, listening, hearing, loneliness, commitment, training, bravery, effort, pain, elevation, fear, rest, effort, sleeps, honesty, attention, team, work, support, goals, joy, time, most, test, 70 percent, 100 percent, guts, motivation, discipline, desire, business, plans, dreams, passion and God in me only thing she saw in him and said he was is a fuck up. I do not have nothing against woman/women or Cleopatra you do not put no one down when they are showing more than improvement will you say well I did it to her so it came back on me I can take that so does that mean it supposed to go on continually? Now this a man you do a woman wrong or anyone a man to anybody I agree it is a training process you go through a job a responsibility a workout replacing and putting back together what I or you broke apart it is a class; it is a process it is a while I agree depending, the parties that is involved everyone is not the same. Now when it does come together with both of your help then when the woman does not forgive truly, she tears the house down as well as the husband and herself. Is it up to the husband/man to fix everything? Now in this time it is that way with a lot of women now today some women feel like her actions and sins is the man brought out and made her that or this way yes to a certain point I agree not a permanent hold & grudge forever! Now it is some women do not agree with this on how much they been hurt or some that are just selfish as hell you have them ways and rights that is on you with your opinion's & facts even your feelings but do not use it as a tool and only for yourself especially when you do not want to receive. Everyone has their own journey but do not hurt one another back and forth. Jeffrey have wanted Cleopatra to tell him and show him she did not have a problem every minute on him hurting and harming while I am doing a great job not supporting him or uplifting him as a loving husband should be. Already living in American is hard for myself as a black man having enemies dealing with police innocent so it was like she was doing and treating me like the world was I had to stay safe out here in this world. Being born as a black afro American is the first strike right there it is not easy, Jeffrey knew Cleopatra hold it down as a strong bold soft woman when he was incarcerated and by his side. Every relationship/marriage husband and wife there is good and bad in if anyone tell me their marriage was perfect and everything was the husband fault there lying, I have plenty family members who marriages that was not good and they are still together I know it is people out there can take a lot of punishment, abuse, and go through too much. The woman, well some or most says and feels that they have the positive and love on lock down when you go through rough times you suppose to think and put in actions with the thoughts of the process taking your time. See they do not want to think about when they first fell in love all over again it be both or not at all and what they feel or thinking that makes them react. Women men is not the only ones with bad behavior women you do to we are humans like when you argue catch an attitude and say child please, whatever, anyway and then do not like him and say who you are you are not anybody, but you are with him your just mad at the time. It is times you make a small thing out of a huge, big thing then want the man to take the blame and make an excuse it is just her being a woman, right? Making that as an excuse to get away with certain things that line cannot be used all the time IT'S JUST ME BEING A WOMAN it is not used for every situation to get you out of because that man damn sure enough cannot use that towards you, how would you feel some will say I do not care. Now you can use the past to criticize, nag and bring her attitude rudely with demanding words that comes from cycles of behaviors learning from their moms, aunts, grandmothers, sisters, friends, cousins as well from what they have seen from growing up in hose holds of experiences. Now when they do get married some or most· of them things put a reflection on their marriage been sitting down watching and learning now today children are learning faster, quicker, and smarter watching their parents. Some of these women are talking bad about their husbands looking in the mirror knowing they look pretty but the heart is ugly and say they do not have no cycles at all quick to tell the man about his and what he did need to stop and get right about his cycles. The woman does not even have to meet the father, uncle, or grandfather she can hear the stories from the man husband/man or when she does meets them it is a rap! Now when a woman is hurt, I agree she has pain of meanness, hateful, scornful, bitterness, sarcasm, silence, really a wall up but after she forgives it is over as she says but really, it is not over depending on the person and situation and the woman, but you know where I am coming from when she is dead wrong! Now when you come back to move forward and tell the man out of your mouth and from your heart what God told you then you mean it and you can change it when you get ready because what he did to you, so it continues this turns into so much unforgiveness as a well running dry. Silence can extremely be very nasty on how the woman uses it because she just knows what she does and being doing with her secret weapons that she does to her husband/man she does not want this done to her she knows out it feels vice versa. Please do not do something to someone that you do not want done to you it happens in life but do not constantly jug, provoke someone when there trying to honor you with respect for the wrong, they have done to you, and they have cleaned up themselves! You are treating as there still a smelling no good addiction and it will never go away so when you think, feel, say, and action it in your mind and come out your mouth with words you mean and do not mean apologizing then do not mean it because she is expressing her feelings her anger is taking over it is a get back!! You cannot control, rule, and run everything. The woman don't see at times the ways she be acting out towards her husband/man the role model she will set for her daughter watching her it would be good for the part when it's right and stand your ground, respect, don't be fooled, or used, lied to and played with and it also will bring spirits that the husband/man will tell her what he sees and she will not listen to him because his word don't mean shit because what he has done. Most women feel like no matter what they do wrong the children still supposed to listen to them not saying she is wrong and be right. What I say right or man to a woman at times and it is the true and get mad at it because it is that and do not want to cooperate at times in her ways as a woman what do I mean by that mood swings change up? See then the woman those babies her son on mostly everything it turns into MY CHILD, MY BABY, MY KIDS, MY CHILDREN, ME ALL BY MYSELF and then the children be stuck in ways to follow that in ways it be bad spirits all the things the mother/woman been through she uses everything she has been through she can use those children raised up to hate they father a lot of women do this. I have seen women with sexual frustration never will I need a man or get a man ever again do not need things or ask for things and the daughter be looking mean and the son right along with her some cannot move on with their lives because what the mom has been through, and they stay there. Some love the mom no matter what it is and be hurting and just do not want to tell the mother or the mother does wrong, and the children ignores her at times because of her attitude and ways. The fathers see how the mother communicates as well to. Like Cleopatra she repeated a lot of her mother's bad habits with hers as well and only looked Jeffrey and he was the only one had some in her eyes he did that to her at times as well I'm not perfect others in life had did this at times in their lives repeating some of the things of communication, as we all in some way observed as a child whatever way it was some kind of wrong we all have done and watch and learned from someone or something. Jeffrey can admit he was verbal, abusive, aggressive, controlling, jealous, and wrong he got his shit together though because he wanted it to work with Cleopatra, he just did not walk away just like that. It just was not enough for Cleopatra she did not say it is too late she lied to God, herself, me, the children and relationship because Jeffrey did this before we got into a partnership and begged her not to bring it in, so you do not think about marrying someone then say it was too late because you messed up too much this is what a lot of women do. That's like playing the card game spades that's reneging to go back on a promise or commitment, yes I got cut, I got held up and criticized by my fellow lover as well as my partner, friend, and soulmate I put my security in just like the woman with God especially when Jeffrey got into a partnership with Cleopatra because he got saved and was changed into a clean creature he felt good and happy he knew Cleopatra was happy to had to think and be positive but was she? Until this day Cleopatra is the most gorgeous, stunning, beautiful woman in the world on this planet the love of Jeffrey life and he will take her any day, time but we all know she will not take him back? No, and people will say why would want someone that does not want to come back to you or want you any more or wants to be accepted because investing 15 years of a relationship is not that easy 1. Then 2. It is not that easy to let something go you love to walk away from your heart loves. 3. I still love her and is in love with her. 4. God knows this! Cannot never play with God or lie on him. Jeffrey learned to let go still of Cleopatra because she would have control and power over him as a woman!! See what Cleopatra problem was when she stops putting her all in God and doing it her woman way, she started worrying about Jeffrey and every move he was making and what people was telling her and listening to them because if it were fully on God, she would have not even let what people say or what he did in the past bother her. Look at me when I am on a pleasant humble day and scream and yell at me then say to me aggressively (WHO THE FUCK YOU BEEN LISTENING TO)? The good thing is that I have not gone anywhere. Then see did not understand by damaging our partnership by not making love to me and with holding it. If Jeffrey was all about Cleopatra needs, she was selfish and stubborn not our needs because it all about the way God wants us to meet our needs for each other as one not what people say or want what we should do for our partnership. If God created this world by speaking to it into existence so why Cleopatra did not speak to it to existence when she took Jeffrey back and in a relationship because she lied, she did not trust herself to trust him over again. She had to forgive herself then forgive him, but she lied because her thoughts in her mind you are not being fair or right. You do not deceive God is not mocked for whatever a man sows that he will also reap. Yes, I reaped what I sow in my home. What I did and this goes for the woman God watches all. Everyone sin towards one another is friends and confessing towards the devil not God because God nowhere in that, the devil is in the middle camouflaging as if he is a friend. He is laughing while you both are angry with one another. No sin iso greater or different then no other so how can you forgive this but not that, so you have appointments, dates, times, schedules, days when you feel like it. When have you got time and ready to forgive? Therefore, a lot of us where we at because we cannot forgive ourselves and others.

Sin for sin back and forth to anyone towards you or others is rebellion against God. Adam and Eve was tempted in the garden of Eden. Now Cleopatra felt it is she so nasty, rude, disrespectful words and putting Jeffrey down and disrespecting him. Her words anger, being mean, hateful and bitter was not sin and I was not God I was just a man, and she could get back at me. She said off her tongue, but you are not God, but you heard Gods word you sin against one another you sin towards God only me the man the head! See at times when Cleopatra said that is okay, she was thinking a long time that Jeffrey will pay for her mistakes and mines. Then just always she loved to say whatever that mean forget you then. When she walked up on me after forgiveness provoking me saying go ahead go ahead do it, I dare you. What are you going to do this was the double dare you starting trouble setting me up for trouble she was starting because she was so angry and bitter not permission do not do it or what? Nothing means to her something and I always to be worried about when she said fine. This is the word in her way used to end an argument when she knew she was always right, and I needed to always shut up. I was not a puppy to play with to agree with everything she is right because she is the woman everything I dealt with her and her family and children I cried up and myself to sleep and as to her if it was fake and bullshit then came to apologize, the go back on her word confused and blame the Christian on me a person will blame you when they are confused because they do not know what the hell is they doing they cannot think straight or be focused so I was not broke down or picked on or got stronger it was all and only the woman. Cleopatra was compassionate and nurturing mom bonding. My compassion was expressing towards her and her children. Women say they are compassionate than men. That not true because when that woman is with that man she sees and shows everything to that, and she shows back. It is comfortable that he can trust someone finally with his secrets, hurt and pain, He been through to sit down of what he been through in life with work, consequences, battles, broken promises by family members, being let sown by mother, father, foster homes, not been given chances, showed his improvements and been let down hardly deep, facing his circumstances in life. It is the person everyone is different, but we all hurt and go through some type of problems, pains, hurts in life. I have nothing against women or men do not give one more than another God does not do this. See Cleopatra felt and knew she was on a higher holy higher level of God than Jeffrey. She said it with hate and anger. Every time I said it with love baby God do not say that and we suppose to forgive more on be as one God comes first then us and our children and forgive. She will scream yes but you not God yes but I am your husband so what are you telling God then woman? See it is measured in the law in marriage. What have you sow? What have you reaped? Because Cleopatra knew and felt I am the only one sinned, reap, sow and deserved everything back done Jeffrey and pay for sleeping on the bus stops and away from her when she argues brought the past falsely accuse him curse him out this was not a sin this was a get back right women? I am still looking in my bible to this day and reading where wives can do this to husbands, and it is not coming up! You should give and it will be given to you: good measure, pressed down, shaken together, and running over will be put in your bosom. So, with the same measure that you use, it will be measured back to your husband over and repeatedly. Being bitter again when he has stopped it has come on him so God will handle it in his way not yours. God will have the mercy not you or the man the husband or wife. Jeffrey wanted to have sex and make love all the time, but Cleopatra taught him how to be affectionate. Jeffrey met Cleopatra needs he was just waiting on her 50%/50% 100% /100% but she made him overpay with her hot on his back with her whip in her hand or as if he were tied up to her tree and her slave. No one needs to say I am holding on to something no real prophets no where I am coming from and real lovers, from no communicators, human beings, people, adults, men, women I am being for real. A blind man can understand and feel where I am coming from no one deserve to go through this. Therefore, it is so many divorces. On women they get angry you tell the truth is truth God truth is the same for everyone. We all have the fair love that we owe to our spouses, so a woman does not get no better and even to a man. Both sides decide to do what they want to well I will wait on him no I will wait on her. No, he owes me no she owes no we owe God it is already his. We go to him he answers anytime it is said for where your treasure is there your heart will be also. Women when you are not bitter and give your husband the attention and care they deserve then you are sowing into marriage and your marriage will reap the benefits, just like you put everything into your all to your career, education, plans, money, house, credit, scores, children, future but do not get it twisted you cannot put the past on your husband and these things and expect your marriage to grow. Be in your marriage as your BUSINESS. Now if Cleopatra would have reaped love, forgiveness, trust, honest, forget as a testimony what she would got back. It is a two-way street all in one with God first. See I know a woman because she becomes strong of her strength, purpose, dignity, and love in herself. A virtuous godly woman always has her God given passion with an awesome bold spirit that has power or lots of compassion, a woman will fight against expectations and bounce right back always know she is and what direction she is going before she even gets there because she knows who she is. Now I hear all these women I am independent, I am independent but yes, they know when ask for help, she will follow her own path and a strong fighter. Every time she falls, she will get right back up like Cleopatra. She did not let me, or no one influence her decisions. It is times a woman can be balanced, and it is sometimes she cannot depend on the woman, the situation or problem she in even what she is going through good or bad! Now I said a woman cannot be satisfied even to a certain level. It is something wrong, she wants, says, it is something! Now a virtuous woman is all about her faith she believes in whatever she does she lets the faith guide her steps. It never ends with a woman she even helps with the cause. I spoke with a lady named Melba one day she was with 3 other women. She said that she does not want to say sorry to her man or apologize because she stiff neck. She said that is going to be a down fall in a relationship. The 3 other women that was that was with her said the same thing. Women I know these kinds of women, because every woman is not the same another reason a woman is never satisfied because she wants the man to do something better the next day after and after. You have a lot of women once they find out their man loves them the woman takes control. Some men want them to. They like that one that do Jeffrey liked that in Cleopatra. She was to blind to see it at times. We were just a like. It is just that she was perfect in everything and her kotex smelled good. A woman also loves a man that has much respect for his mother and knows when to stand up to his mother in a respectful way. If she is going overboard with disrespecting his wife. He will take care of his wife. You have a lot of women hold on to their sons the most daughters to even far hers and feel like they going to get taken away and they are grownups living their lives. Women also change with age they change in there 30's, 40's, 50's, 60's, 70's their bodies also go through a change especially their mind set but other people will look at them and say girl or woman you are still the same you are not going to change for nothing or you have not changed one bit you still that same person but the person they tell know they have change themselves because no one knows you more than you than your own self. Cleopatra was very baffle when Jeffrey carried all the groceries in the house at times, baby you do not have to do it all then not him "she" would change up on a different day when I am carrying some of the groceries angry and aggravated. She will say help me then I will say I am not at all women say just shut up be quiet and help. It would be better much better this way and vice versa that is not happening with disrespect towards the woman I do not think so! She felt that I can turn mostly anything into a sexual thing but if I said something to her about not wanting to have sex, I am having sex with someone else or going to right now as we speak lying next to one another. How crazy, yes so stupid or dumb. She will think when I am leaving because I am walking out yes. You are cheating because you are damn sure not sleeping with me. No not arguing I want to be happy, romantic, loved and humble like the woman you are pushing me away. Now to her talking about anything or any problem. It is important she a woman but when I want to talk, I talk to much I am less of a man I am not shit when she is talking to much do not tell to be quiet. She is a grown ass woman do not control her. Who you think you talking to watch out? If you not listening! Jeffrey knew at times when Cleopatra would scream at times and every time it was his fault, she always had a lot on her mind. Now Cleopatra always had to get on Jeffrey for washing his hands. I admit I only washed it for special occasions. Now see when Cleopatra asked Jeffrey questions, she can run her mouth and there is no stopping her. I always tell her the truth. A lie is a lie we are all done lying about something. It done been a lot of times after she said she forgave me and went to counselling more after the forgiveness. She will still see me sitting down there thinking about good things it does not be the answer I gave her, or she want to hear because really you tell the truth. It is a problem because the woman cannot handle the truth, or it is something you done to make you a liar forever and the woman right and perfect. See now it will never be the top perfect answer for her because when I did what I did that I should have never done. She would not of be this way, she is now so it is all my fault. I can imagine how many women are like this then come back apologizing knowing they wrong and they over doing it. These women need to stop having the ability with the power to hold grudges and always right all the time as a mind reader and remember everything you said but wrong about what you said remembering what they said and did because they do not add up to what you did to her so she can cover up all her wrongs, sins, shit, dirty laundry under the rug. Jeffrey like and love the obsession Cleopatra had with those shoes. Women think too hard, plan to hard and love hard to put everything into the way they think and plan before it happens. Now when it does not come out the way the woman plans it. They have a way to lash out if its mentally, physically they are lashing out and when we are with a man, he is the backbone as well as the protector and provider. When the woman looked up to him, she really loves him she be so much in love with the man she be out of space not bad, good! When that woman realizes on that man, they look for everything good in him to be right not perfect. They know as well as much as the woman knows vice versa. When hearts are broken a man gets broken down to the woman can break a man down. It is not always women he had to always do something wrong always only him. Jeffrey knew himself when he broke Cleopatra feelings her heart in so many ways actions were coming at him in talking, verbal, attitude, anger even movement brought him down. Facial expressions she had so many, and the change of the mind came more and more bitter and bitter it came in her mind with an attitude that danger could not face. She had he way to break her man her husband down even with the things. She said things she knew that would get to me and hurt me. She knows I love her and still will do and say these things and turn everything around on me and blame me for everything. It did not have to be true. She knew it was not true and it would turn the situation on me all on me in our relationship. She knows it broke me down bad. Get back yes this made it better right women? Every woman is not like this woman, but it is a lot them are. She knew she ruined my life. She was hurting bad and continually constantly getting me back. It is like a record playing over and repeatedly. They do not mean to do this they be angry but do not stop. At first, Jeffrey thought that Cleopatra did not mean this she just angry. She does not want to break up and she want me to feel it that it but no she showed me wrong. Cleopatra thoughts were deep when the pain was involved nobody around her is or was going to be happy not even herself and swear up and down with Jesus Christ and the bishop telling her she was happy. He was telling God was telling him she was happy that is a lie because I was the one living with her not him. She was my wife just you women will say vice versa my husband. No one can tell you about women not only for you but for your husband as well. If you love him help him build together his thoughts is yours as well, you are not the 60/40 smarter one. A good family that man wants not only you he is the leader when he got it right do not keep him locked in the cage or up against the door with a gun up under his chin, yes you be that angry. I know I tried I even held her up. I was the one to make her feel strong. When I tried even more and harder there was more hell raising. She did not want to hear this or that in her mind the plan was already made so when this man put it in motion and became a man of God, he wanted Jeffrey to be for Cleopatra. She was blind with apologies back and forth and for being hard on me so damn much I even put my motion in action. A woman that Cleopatra is still is. She had so much expectation and belief especially being in love with me. I even put more time for this woman. It would have felt better to get the encouragement from her than the bishops back and forth other people vice versa. It was supposed to come from like she wanted from me but the most important aspect when Jeffrey considered in Cleopatra is where is when restoring her back on course, but she would not let me especially with her woman hood is love, trust, respect, understanding, honesty. The considerably basic thing was God therefore I got saved and repented that was not to enough that is only for her, her family as Christian because to her I am m not a Christian, she got a real man because she prayed and ask God to give me back to her after I messed up. Watch what you ask God for, and she lied to herself and God because her heart was not ready, so the bishop ask her this what you wanted. She said yes, I prayed, and God gave him back to me. Now do women know what they want every woman is not like that so is not every man we all are equal in God eyes when I looked at her. I did not see no sexual needs I saw God; love her children I was a man I slept on the floor because she lived with her mother. I even double check myself I even was feeling what she was doing, going, wanting, needing, asking, and saying. Even when she was not talking or saying nothing at all. When she was so angry so how much I was supposed to take? Jeffrey valued Cleopatra when he was in relationship. I treated her with kindness and respect. My quality time was myself, my woman and the children. I was too tough on her children as she says at least some man was, thank you Jesus because he blessed me, she ignored me on that. What I do not understand is that she can be tough on her children and tell me to stay out of it. When she is hard on them, she is the mother. She is the parent. She is the woman she is perfect. Like Cleopatra mother she is perfect. You cannot tell her nothing and this cycle is in Cleopatra. See when we became partners, she said it right in front of children in our home with his spirit peace of mind body caressing one another. A phenomenal woman knows, thinks and feels when your making love to her she knows I am telling something that is important and for real but not all about that vice versa. It is not all about the woman or all about the man. Every woman is not the same a woman can feel when your love making is right and serious, she will be thinking about all kinds of wonderful great things with her fascinating amazing things you will not and cannot imagine as a man! See a woman see's the little things that counts taking really good care of her she stands there naked in front of her man naked and smiles in her mind and telling you that your great and you keep her happy, some women stand up with the nice dress, lingerie, Victoria secret whatever the husband/man brought for her or herself it is what pleases them both. There is no cost on their minds it is the thought that counts. Together mentally, emotionally, physically, sexually, love, feelings with me all inside Jeffrey made love to Cleopatra with all in he his heart and soul in every way he could to satisfy her first and he it still was not enough after unforgiving him. Jeffrey learned by observing Cleopatra on things, but she swore she did not learn nothing from him at all. When I made love to her it was real deep even when two people are married. A woman will never tell deeper secrets because therefore they are called secrets and women have lied saying they told everything that is a lie because they think too much and about lots of things certain things are not to be known. Secrets was righteously between God and Cleopatra everyone is not the same you have a lot of women say that they are real women say they do not do this or that and I am not nasty, but I would not do that but when the right man come along, they did it because that woman got emotional attracted to that man brought a lot of things out that some women that woman herself did not know what she felt until it hit her. It can be a touch, conversation, respect, feelings, it is very deep it can be prayer, sexual, a gift, a card, letter depending on that woman and what she likes alike can sneak up on her and catch her off guard like my words being controversial with Cleopatra that blew her mind I just did not tell her she did not know every time like you women say a woman already knows yes but not everything! Women play mind games as well at times you have certain women say if a woman is playing mind games then that is no woman and I cannot tell you about no other woman I can only tell you about myself and be the same woman talking about women or something even herself it does not have to be bad, guess what every woman has been here different day, time, and played this role so do not never say never!! Only women can have PMS, Premenstrual syndrome another thing is PCOS as well as a gentleman it is not picking at women it does not mean you cannot get pregnant. It is one of the most common, but treatable causes of infertility in women. Women with PCOS the hormonal imbalance interferes with growth and release of eggs from the ovaries, now can women feel me on not making children because my sperm is not fertilized and strong enough? See women men go through things to. See women take a good look at what you do wrong sometimes think stop and listen do not react say to yourself what did I really do wrong, can you really take your time out to think stop and own up to your mistakes? Being in a marriage/relationship can be hard at times it is not perfect with all kinds of things that can be very annoying like texting, not responding back, silent treatment, arguments, off and on feelings can come in deep within feeling different type of ways also a certain way you are thinking and feeling in some of type of negativity he is always wrong. Sometimes in your mind the problem is him or what he did, but he must always be wrong, and everything must be his fault and take the blame all the time? A woman at times can be thinking and know it is right but not necessarily true at every time it is her mind, her thoughts, her ways, her actions, judging the man when you are judging yourself because it is called being selfish and petty. Thinking at times looking at him he going to do something when he is just sitting there or just doing his own thing and your mind is what it is own falsely accusing him of something because he told you and lie that was false, so you must continue to keep falsely accusing him really, you are holding up the mirror to yourself 20 different reflections, persons, peoples, personalities, double visions all in one! Then you do not want to make love to him anymore or when you feel like it really that is not love that is pleasing your needs when you want some, he made you feel like that so get back tick for tac. It is times when you use love against and towards him out of context and insecurities have become your way of thinking of him constantly you do not give him or it a chance even yourself you may feel, think or even say but your actions show totally different signs sarcastically actions not to even say good job if you do how long do it last for that you cannot control your mind the way of thinking. It is yourself at times of not being happy with a peace of mind in your own world of mind set your way or the highway you set yourself up for failure and then jealousy because envy, the cheating be dead wrong walking away be wrong back and forth. A woman is not the only one or human being in life that gets knocked down and the only one that gets back up and keep moving. I did this myself when Cleopatra pushes me down and kept her foot on my neck and said I was going to lose everything and not accomplish anything in life. No relationship is perfect not even the hot sun that shines burning you up because you cannot take too much sun you will get burned up right? Women do not blame men for everything! From the heart Cleopatra is the heart my heart as well the angel's god has protecting her and her children good did happen at times, she is great news do you know there is nothing good said about me when you want to see get back on anyone that is evil and cold hearted cruel as well. Now look I am doing good now and who is wishing bad on me or try to do bad against me I hope the best for them. Where does God want us to pray over someone bad or wish speaking bad things over them and against them? Is this a clean heart, spirit, mind, soul or blessings let me no. I will not tell why everything you have going to fall and this what is going to happen to you is not that hurting God and speaking things over your own self that goes for me to. Now when you are a woman of God pray all the time keeping peace in your mind, body, soul, spirit, tongue God first everything stays because your heart is cleaned forgivable. After me and Cleopatra became partners she did not see my passion, sacrifice, love, strategy, focus, positivity, hard work, late nights with me working, and early mornings, feedback, perseverance, learning, blood sweat & tears, improvement, courage, sadness, injury, listening, hearing, loneliness, commitment, training, bravery, effort, pain, elevation, fear, rest, effort, sleeps, honesty, attention, team, work, support, goals, joy, time, most, test, 70 percent, 100 percent, guts, motivation, discipline, desire, business, plans, dreams, passion and God in me only thing she saw in me and said I was is a fuck up. I do not have nothing against woman/women or Cleopatra you do not put no one down when they are showing more than improvement will you say well I did it to her so it came back on me I can take that so does that mean it supposed to go on continually? Now this a man you do a woman wrong or anyone a man to anybody I agree it is a training process you go through a job a responsibility a workout replacing and putting back together what I or you broke apart it is a class; it is a process it is a while I agree depending on the parties that is involved everyone is not the same. Now when it does come together with both of your help then when the woman does not forgive truly, she tears the house down as well as the husband and herself. Is it up to the husband/man to fix everything? Now in this time it is that way with a lot of women now today some women feel like her actions and sins is the man brought out and made her that or this way yes to a certain point I agree not a permanent hold & grudge forever! Now it is some women do not agree with this on how much they been hurt or some that are just selfish as hell you have them ways and rights that is on you with your opinion's & facts even your feelings but do not use it as a tool and only for yourself especially when you do not want to receive. Everyone has their own journey but do not hurt one another back and forth. I have wanted Cleopatra to tell me and show me she did not have a problem every minute on me hurting and harming while I am doing a great job not supporting me or uplifting me as a loving husband should be. Already living in American is hard for myself as a black man having enemies dealing with police innocent so it was like she was doing and treating me like the world was I had to stay safe out here in this world. Being born as a black afro American is the first strike right there it is not easy, I know Cleopatra hold it down as a strong bold soft woman when I was incarcerated and by my side. Every marriage husband and wife there is good and bad in if anyone tell me their marriage was perfect and everything was the husband fault there lying, I have plenty family members who marriage that was worse than mines and they are still together I know it is people out there can take a lot of punishment, abuse, and go through too much. The woman, well some or most says and feels that they have the positive and love on lock down when you go through rough times you suppose to think and put in actions with the thoughts of the process taking your time. See they do not want to think about when they first fell in love all over again it be both or not at all and what they feel or thinking that makes them react. Women men is not the only ones with bad behavior women you do to we are humans like when you argue catch an attitude and say child please, whatever, anyway and then do not like him and say who you are you are not anybody, but you are with him your just mad at the time. It is times you make a small thing out of a huge, big thing then want the man to take the blame and make an excuse it is just her being a woman, right? Making that as an excuse to get away with certain things that line cannot be used all the time IT'S JUST ME BEING A WOMAN it is not used for every situation to get you out of because that man damn sure enough cannot use that towards you, how would you feel some will say I do not care. Now you can use the past to criticize, nag and bring her attitude rudely with demanding words that comes from cycles of behaviors learning from their moms, aunts, grandmothers, sisters, friends, cousins as well from what they have seen from growing up in hose holds of experiences. Now when they do get married some or most of them things put a reflection on their marriage been sitting down watching and learning now today children are learning faster, quicker, and smarter watching their parents. Some of these women are talking bad about their husbands looking in the mirror knowing they look pretty but the heart is ugly and say they do not have no cycles at all quick to tell the man about his and what he did need to stop and get right about his cycles. The woman does not even have to meet the father, uncle, or grandfather she can hear the stories from the man husband/man or when she does meets them it is a rap! Now when a woman is hurt, I agree she has pain of meanness, hateful, scornful, bitterness, sarcasm, silence, really a wall up but after she forgives it is over as she says but really, it is not over depending on the person and situation and the woman, but you know where I am coming from when she is dead wrong! Now when you come back to move forward and tell the man out of your mouth and from your heart what God told you then you mean it and you can change it when you get ready because what he did to you, so it continues this turns into so much unforgiveness as a well running dry. Silence can extremely be very nasty on how the woman uses it because she just knows what she does and being doing with her secret weapons that she does to her husband/man she does not want this done to her she knows out it feels vice versa. Please do not do something to someone that you do not want done to you it happens in life but do not constantly jug, provoke someone when there trying to honor you with respect for the wrong, they have done to you, and they have cleaned up themselves! You are treating as there still a smelling no good addiction and it will never go away so when you think, feel, say, and action it in your mind and come out your mouth with words you mean and do not mean apologizing then do not mean it because she is expressing her feelings her anger is taking over it is a get back!! You cannot control, rule, and run everything. The woman don't see at times the ways she be acting out towards her husband/man the role model she will set for her daughter watching her it would be good for the part when it's right and stand your ground, respect, don't be fooled, or used, lied to and played with and it also will bring spirits that the husband/

man will tell her what he sees and she will not listen to him because his word don't mean shit because what he has done. Most women feel like no matter what they do wrong the children still supposed to listen to them not saying she is wrong and be right. What I say right or man to a woman at times and it is the true and get mad at it because it is that and do not want to cooperate at times in her ways as a woman what do I mean by that mood swings change up? See then the woman those babies her son on mostly everything it turns into MY CHILD, MY BABY, MY KIDS, MY CHILDREN, ME ALL BY MYSELF and then the children be stuck in ways to follow that in ways it be bad spirits all the things the mother/woman been through she uses everything she has been through she can use those children raised up to hate they father a lot of women do this. I have seen women with sexual frustration never will I need a man or get a man ever again do not need things or ask for things and the daughter be looking mean and the son right along with her some cannot move on with their lives because what the mom has been through, and they stay there. Some love the mom no matter what it is and be hurting and just do not want to tell the mother or the mother does wrong, and the children ignores her at times because of her attitude and ways. The fathers see how the mother communicates as well to. Like Cleopatra she repeated a lot of her mother's bad habits with hers as well and only looked at mines and I was the only one had some in her eyes I did that to her at times as well I'm not perfect others in life had did this at times in their lives repeating some of the tings of communication, as we all in some way observed as a child whatever way it was some kind of wrong we all have done and watch and learned from someone or something. I can admit I was verbal, abusive, aggressive, controlling, jealous, and wrong I got my shit together though because I wanted it to work with Cleopatra, I just did not walk away just like that. It just was not enough for Cleopatra she did not say it is too late she lied to God, herself, me, the children and our because I did this before and begged me were in a deep relationship not to bring it in, someone then say it was too late because you messed up too much this is what a lot of women do. That's like playing the card game spades that's reneging to go back on a promise or commitment, yes I got cut, I got held up and criticized by my fellow lover as well as my partner, friend, woman, and soulmate I put my security in just like the woman with God especially when I was in a relationship with Cleopatra because I got saved and was changed into a clean creature I felt good and happy I knew cleopatra was happy to had to think and be positive but was she? Until this day Cleopatra is the most gorgeous, stunning, beautiful woman in the world on this planet the love of my life and I will take her any day, time but we all no she will not take me back? No, and people will say why would want someone that does not want to come back to you or want you any more or wants to be accepted because investing 15 years of a relationship is not that easy 1. Then 2. It is not that easy to let something go you love to walk away from your heart loves. 3. I still love her and is in love with her. 4. God knows this! Cannot never play with God or lie on him. A learned to let go still of Cleopatra because she would have control and power over me as a woman!! See what Cleopatra problem was when she stops putting her all in God and doing it her woman way, she started worrying about me and every move I was making and what people was telling her and listening to them because if it were fully on God, she would have not even let what people say or what I did in the past bother her. Look at me when I am on a pleasant humble day and scream and yell at me then say to me aggressively (WHO THE FUCK YOU BEEN LISTENING TO)? The good thing is that I have not gone anywhere. Then see did not understand by damaging our marriage by not making love to me and with holding it. If I was all about Cleopatra needs, she was selfish and stubborn not our needs because it all about the way God wants us to meet our needs for each other as one not what people say or want what we should do with our relationship. If God created this world by speaking to it into existence so why Cleopatra did not speak to it to existence when she took me back and married because she lied, she did not trust herself to trust me over again. She had to forgive herself then forgive me, but she lied because her thoughts in her mind you are not being fair or right. You do not deceive God is not mocked for whatever a man sows that he will also reap. Yes, I reaped what I sow in my home. What I did and this goes for the woman God watches all. Everyone sin towards one another is friends and confessing towards the devil not God because God nowhere in that, the devil is in the middle camouflaging as if he is a friend. He is laughing while you both are angry with one another. No sin iso greater or different then no other so how can you forgive this but not that, so you have appointments, dates, times, schedules, days when you feel like it. When have you got time and ready to forgive? Therefore, a lot of us where we at because we cannot forgive ourselves and others. Sin for sin back and forth to anyone towards you or others is rebellion against Adam and Eve was tempted in the garden of Eden. Now Cleopatra felt it is she so nasty, rude, disrespectful words and putting me down and disrespecting me. Her words anger, being mean, hateful and bitter was not sin and I was not God I was just a man, and she could get back at me. She said off her tongue, but you are not God, but you heard Gods word you sin against one another you sin towards God only me the man the head! See at times when Cleopatra said that is okay, she was thinking a long time that I will pay for her mistakes and mines. Then just always she loved to say whatever that mean forget you then. When she walked up on me after forgiveness provoking me saying go ahead go ahead do it, I dare you. What are you going to do this was the double dare you starting trouble setting me up for trouble she was starting because she was so angry and bitter not permission do not do it or what? Nothing means to her something and I always to be worried about when she said fine. This is the word in her way used to end an argument when she knew she was always right, and I needed to always shut up. I was not a puppy to play with to agree with everything she is right because she is the woman everything I dealt with her and her family and children I cried up and myself to sleep and as to her if it was fake and bullshit then came to apologize, the go back on her word confused and blame the Christian on me a person will blame you when they are confused because they do not know what the hell is they doing they cannot think straight or be focused so I was not broke down or picked on or got stronger it was all and only the woman. Cleopatra was compassionate and nurturing mom bonding. My compassion was expressing towards her and her children. Women say they are compassionate than men. That not true because when that woman is with that man she sees and shows everything to that, and she shows back. It is comfortable that he can trust someone finally with his secrets, hurt and pain, He been through to sit down of what he been through in life with work, consequences, battles, broken promises by family members, being let sown by mother, father, foster homes, not been given chances, showed his improvements and been let down hardly deep, facing his circumstances in life. It is the person everyone is different, but we all hurt and go through some type of problems, pains, hurts in life. I have nothing against women or men do not give one more than another God does not do this. See Cleopatra felt and knew she was on a higher holy higher level of God than me. She said it with hate and anger. Every time I said it with love baby God do not say that and we suppose to forgive more on be as one God comes first then us and our children and forgive. She will scream yes but you not God yes but I am your husband so what are you telling God then woman? See it is measured in the law in marriage. What have you sow? What have you reaped? Because Cleopatra knew and felt I am the only one sinned, reap, sow and deserved everything back done to me and pay for every bit Sleeping on the bus stops and away from her when she argues brought the past falsely accuse me curse me out this was not a sin this was a get back right women? I am still looking in my bible to this day and reading where wives can do this to husbands, and it is not coming up! No give and it will be given to you: good measure, pressed down, shaken together, and running over will be put in your bosom. For with the same measure that you use, it will be measured back to your husband over and repeatedly. Being bitter again when he has stopped it has come on him so God will handle it in his way not yours. God will have the mercy not you or the man the husband or wife. I wanted to have sex and make love all the time, but Cleopatra taught me how to be affectionate. I met Cleopatra needs I was just waiting on her 50%/50% 100% /100% but she made me overpay with her hot on my back with her whip in her hard or as if I were tied up to her tree and her slave. No one needs to say I am holding on to something no real prophets no where I am coming from and real lovers, from no communicators, human beings, people, adults, men, women I am being for real. A blind man can understand and feel where I am coming from no one deserve to go through this. Therefore, it is so many divorces. On women they get angry you tell the truth is truth God truth is the same for everyone. We all have the fair love that we owe to our spouses, so a woman does not get no better and even to a man. Both sides decide to do what they want to well I will wait on him no I will wait on her. No, he owes me no she owes no we owe God it is already his. We go to him he answers anytime said for where your treasure is there your heart will be also. Women when you are not bitter and give your husband the attention and care they deserve then you are sowing into marriage and your marriage will reap the benefits, just like you put everything into your all to your career, education, plans, money, house, credit, scores, children, future but do not get it twisted you cannot put the past on your husband and these things and expect your marriage to grow. Be in your marriage as your BUSINESS. Now if Cleopatra would have reaped love, forgiveness, trust, honest, forget as a testimony what she would got back. It is a two-way street all in one with God first. See I know a woman because she becomes strong of her strength, purpose, dignity, and love in herself. A virtuous godly woman always has her God given passion with an awesome bold spirit that has power or lots of compassion, a woman will fight against expectations and bounce right back always know she is and what direction she is going before she even gets there because she knows who she is. Now I hear all these women I am independent, I am independent but yes, they know when ask for help, she will follow her own path and a strong fighter. Every time she falls, she will get right back up like Cleopatra. She did not let me, or no one influence her decisions. It is times a woman can be balanced, and it is sometimes she cannot depend on the woman, the situation or problem she in even what she is going through good or bad! Now I said a woman cannot be satisfied even to a certain level. It is something wrong, she wants, says, it is something! Now a virtuous woman is all about her faith she believes in whatever she does she lets the faith guide her steps. It never ends with a woman she even helps with the cause. I spoke with a lady named Melba one day she was with 3 other women. She said that she does not want to sorry to her man or apologize because she stiff neck. She said that is going to be a down fall in a relationship. The 3 other women that was that was with her said the same thing. Women I know these kinds of women because every woman is not the same another reason a woman is never satisfied because she wants the man to do something better the next day after and after. You have a lot of women once they find out their man loves them the woman takes control. Some men want them to. They like that one that do I liked that in Cleopatra. She was to blind to see it at times. We were just a like. It is just that she was perfect in everything and her kotex smelled good. A woman also loves a man that has much respect for his mother and knows when to stand up to his mother in a respectful way. If she is going overboard with disrespecting his wife. He will take care of his wife. You have a lot of women hold on to their sons the most daughters to even far hers and feel like they going to get taken away and they are grownups living their lives. Women also change with age they change in there 30's, 40's, 50's, 60's, 70's their bodies also go through a change especially their mind set but other people will look at them and say girl or woman you are still the same you are not going to change for nothing or you have not changed one bit you still that same person but the person they tell know they have change themselves because no one knows you more than you than your own self. Cleopatra was very baffle when I carried all the groceries in the house at times, baby you do not have to do it all then not me "she" would change up on a different day when I am carrying some of the groceries angry and aggravated. She will say help me then I will say I am not at all women say just shut up be quiet and help. It would be better much better this way and vice versa that is not happening with disrespect towards the woman I do not think so! She felt that I can turn mostly anything into a sexual thing but if I said something to her about not wanting to have sex, I am having sex with someone else or going to right now as we speak lying next to one another. How crazy, yes so stupid or dumb. She will think when I am leaving because I am walking out yes. You are cheating because you are damn sure not sleeping with me. No not arguing I want to be happy, romantic, loved and humble like the woman you are pushing me away. Now to her talking about anything or any problem. It is important she a woman but when I want to talk, I talk to much I am less of a man I am not shit when she is talking to much do not tell to be quiet. She is a grown ass woman do not control her. Who you think you talking to watch out? If you not listening! I knew at times when Cleopatra would scream at times and every time it was my fault, she always had a lot on her mind, Now Cleopatra always had to get on me for washing my hands. I admit I only washed it for special occasions. Now see when Cleopatra asked me questions, she can run her mouth and there is no stopping her. I always tell her the truth. A lie is a lie we are all done lying about something. It done been a lot of times after she said she forgave me and went to counselling more after the forgiveness. She will still see me sitting down there thinking about good things it does not be the answer I gave her, or she want to hear because really you tell the truth. It is a problem because the woman cannot handle the truth, or it is something you done to make you a liar forever and the woman right and perfect. See now it will never be the top perfect answer for her because when I did what I did that I should have never done. She would not of be this way, she is now so it is all my fault. I can imagine how many women are like this then come back apologizing knowing they wrong and they over doing it. These women need to stop having the ability with the power to hold grudges and always right all the time as a mind reader and remember everything you said but wrong about what you said remembering what they said and did because they do not add up to what you did to her so she can cover up all her wrongs, sins, shit, dirty laundry under the rug. I like and love the obsession Cleopatra had with those shoes. Women think too hard, plan to hard and love hard to put everything into the way they think and plan before it happens. Now when it does not come out the way the woman plans it. They have a way to lash out if its mentally, physically they are lashing out and when we are with a man, he is the backbone as well as the protector and provider. When the woman looked up to him, she really loves him she be so much in love with the man she be out of space not bad, good! When that woman realizes on that man, they look for everything good in him to be right not perfect. They know as well as much as the woman knows vice versa. When hearts are broken a man gets broken down to the woman can break a man down. It is not always women he had to always do something wrong always only him. I know myself when I broke Cleopatra feelings her heart in so many ways actions were coming at me in talking, verbal, attitude, anger even movement brought me down. Facial expressions she had so many, and the change of the mind came more and more bitter and bitter it came in her mind with an attitude that danger could not face. She had he way to break her man her husband down even with the things. She said things she knew that would get to me and hurt me. She knows I love her and still will do and say these things and turn everything around on me and blame me for everything. It did not have to be true. She knew it was not true and it would turn the situation on me all on me in our relationship. She knows it broke me down bad. Get back yes this made it better right women? Every woman is not like this woman, but it is a lot them are. She knew she ruined my life. She was hurting bad and continually constantly getting me back. It is like a record playing over and repeatedly. They do not mean to do this they be angry but do not stop. At first, I thought that Cleopatra did not mean this she just angry. She does not want to break up and she want me to feel it that it but no she showed me wrong. Cleopatra thoughts were deep when the pain was involved nobody around her is or was going to be happy not even herself and swear up and down with Jesus Christ and the bishop telling her she was happy. He was telling God was telling him she was happy that is a lie because I was the one living with her not him. She was my wife just you women will say vice versa my husband. No one can tell you about women not only for you but for your husband as well. If you love him help him build together his thoughts is yours as well, you are not the 60/40 smarter one. A good family that man wants not only you he is the leader when he got it right do not keep him locked in the cage or up against the door with a gun up under his chin, yes you be that angry. I know I tried I even held her up. I was the one to make her feel strong. When I tried even more and harder there was more hell raising. She did not want to hear this or that in her mind the plan has already been made so when this man put it in motion and became a man of God, he wanted me to be for Cleopatra. She was blind with apologies back and forth and for being hard on me so damn much I even put my motion in action. A woman that Cleopatra is still is. She had so much expectation and belief especially being in love with me. I even put more time for this woman. It would have felt better to get the encouragement from her than the bishops back and forth other people vice versa. It was supposed to come from like she wanted from me but the most important aspect when I considered in Cleopatra is where is when restoring her back on course, but she would not let me especially with her woman hood is love, trust, respect, understanding, honesty. The considerably basic thing was God therefore I got saved and repented that was not to enough that is only for her, her family as Christian because to her I am not a Christian, she got a real man because she prayed and ask God to give me back to her after I messed up. Watch what you ask God for, and she lied to herself and God because her heart was not ready, so the bishop ask her this what you wanted. She said yes, I prayed and asked God to give him back to me. Now do women know what they want every woman is not like that so is not every man we all are equal in God eyes when I looked at her. I did not see no sexual needs I saw that God; love her children I was a man I slept on the floor because she lived with her mother. I even double check myself I even was feeling what she was doing, going, wanting, needing, asking, and saying. Even when she was not talking or saying nothing at all. When she was so angry so how much I was supposed to take? I valued Cleopatra when I got married. I treated her with kindness and respect. My quality time was myself, my wife and the children. I was too tough on her children as she says at least some man was, thank you Jesus because he blessed me, she ignored me on that. What I do not understand is that she can be tough on her children and tell me to stay out of it. When she is hard on the children after all she is the mother. She is the parent. She is the woman she is perfect. Like Cleopatra mother she is perfect. You cannot tell her nothing and this cycle is in Cleopatra. See when we were relationship, she said it right in front of children in our home disrespecting our relationship and did not care bringing up some other woman and did not care bringing up some other woman children from past that almost killed me in front of her children. When I was not cheating, lying, or doing nothing so she is right for doing this as a woman I will forgive her for myself, her and God says so will women use this towards men forever? I know I was a father I had the love, the wallet, took my son to sports games stood there with him. While mostly his mother was out there with their sons. I was the coach coaching my son even when the next year came and my son said dad, I do not want to do football so I asked him Trevor what would you like to do? He said Taekwondo Karate. I said OK where was the blood father? Just like you women say! I am saying it and I am saying it for my responsibility and being a stepping up to do another man stepping up to another man's job you right and the protector for my stepdaughter letting her know what bull crap was, what was games, set ups, where to go. I was there. I gave both gave good advice, it was encouraging that I do not make me nothing because I messed up. It does not make no mother than when she sins and mess up! I was a superhero I saved her children she did not do it by herself. I took them school shopping. I even put them to sleep. I did nurture and the reason why I am expressing it because I was appreciated. I tell you one thing R.I.P. to my father and mother I miss them both. The man is the head this the truth over the household. Head of the wife and marriage. There is not one marriage that is perfect. I heard this pastor say one time he said when something happens in the house it all falls on the husband. It is all on him and everything is his fault what are they teaching today. See number one you are not going to find a soulmate just like you who act, like, thinks and does the same thing you do, so remember there is going to be dislikes and likes, yes and nos. See a lot of times we want to say and do what we want to and leave God left out then when we do one another wrong try to blame God for everything or other person responsible or number one person our self this goes for me to. I had to learn something that is right women. Learn something to men you to! See me and Cleopatra was blaming one another but I stop I said you know what this is not my battle to fight. Then I step back I started ignoring her. I would just leave and talk to God. Then when I did that, she brought something else up bitter and angry because everything and sins I was held accountable for. She was acting like she was Jezebel, Debra, Spirits, Bathsheba, all in one but I could not do it by myself. She was speaking it, talking, claiming it, negativity putting no positivity in. Let me ask you a question? If you put in positive what you get back? Now I have done my research on women my homework and most of them have said that is just a woman, but every woman is not the same on certain days you catch her on she can be that woman, so I say that so say so every man is the same no good and all of them are alike! Right women? I am just asking a question? A couple of women told me you hurt. A man in his wallet, heart, and feelings good or bad right or wrong please do not take up for a woman on every occasion or situation not saying back them up when they are right, but you do feel sometimes or a lot of times you can go overboard all have been there still until this day, but we are talking about the woman. We are or I am not getting on them. What are your rights and wrongs that you cannot admit right up front at the time then debate and want to always be right all the time? Everyone is entitling to their own opinion especially a woman/woman I respect that, but you are not always right on everything you love to say I did not I was not wrong but when it is time to say your wrong when you have done wrong that is the time that is different everything changes. This is not saying women are bad and not good we cannot live with or without you. Behind a man or on the side is a good woman it is a good man to woman. A woman also has sexual secrets also as well secrets from her past that she will never reveal to know accept only God. She can be a good liar for a good reason to make you convince that is she telling the truth but all along she is lying she not perfect. What the circumstances is she will smile in your face and smile behind your back. See I know about the women she must be your priority she is right at times but never ever wants to be wrong unless she says it herself that she is wrong but coming from the other part her husband/man that is a different woman see things that a man cannot see. See like Cleopatra I admit as a strong woman that she is black and beautiful. She told me things that I did not listen to a lot of times that she saw that is did not like safety, trouble, health reason. It is general terms and specific things important and caring some women do not have advice to give at all. When I first met Cleopatra, it was not her butt, her size, her body, or about anything negative. When I first met her and saw this woman the value was the beauty, the spirit, the heart you cannot buy that not even loyalty. I was the right man to know just as much as she was the woman to know it is all right women. See I was not perfect I just wanted her to still give her man this man credit for trying! Still, right now this woman Cleopatra she is cold and angry. I disrespected, mistreated her and took her for granted at times. She did me the same way. Women when your man is incarcerated still love him even though it be a struggle. I know because when I got locked up, I got fussed and cursed out so pray and continue the journey. I was a man/husband that did household chores. I did things helpful and cheerful. It was unto the Lord. She was with the Lord

I was to. When she married me, I was the protector and provider? I married her because I was deeply in love with her. She was supposed to be a great help mate towards me not worse and say you forgive me but then throw me down not make it worse. What we came out of and put more burdens on my shoulders more and more that I was already carrying and providing for my family that she felt like that was not enough to her standards or needs and was not good enough. She played more mind games than professor in college that was teachers. She wonders why I am her ex-husband, and she is my ex. I thought that if my actions would do and speak everything will fall in place. When Cleopatra cried, I wipe her tears even when it was me that started them and at the time it was not me. I loved, kissed, and hold her when she was involved with herself or me in everything. I was not perfect. I did not have it all together you know a lot of women even Cleopatra said when they get cheated on, they feel nasty, and they are a treasure. Their treasure has been taking away but then they all forgive the treasure be separated the husband the wife and marriage even God. Do you know why God does not go nowhere it be us that leave God. See the woman and man accepts each other back and there and cried. We were supposed to keep giving our best to one another. She stops putting, giving, seeing, the treasures in our relationship. Some women invest in their jobs more than marriage stop even if you are making more than your husband or not. No, it is not about the money because when I was relationship Cleopatra, and I was making the money I am going to show you all a fact with an example. When I was making the most money back-to-back taking her children shopping, she said baby I need your time. Now stay home with me, I guess when all the businesses close things changed, Well I am sorry to tell you women are you putting all your all into your job and children instead of your marriage? Well, you are wrong God is first then your marriage. It is never that the love was gone you just transferred it elsewhere. It could be work, the children, family members, listen to mom or dad even gossipers yes setting yourself up while them hyping you up destroys your life while they are living fame of laughter in fame getting off on yours. The number #1 investment is God then your marriage. We know marriage is not perfect I even looked at Cleopatra and said remember when we first met. How we talked she got angry, bitter and madder. These days a lot of women are clueless about men these days "Not All Men"! That is not fair women sit back and do their homework. I have sat back and saw mines to on women from going to the streets, prostitution, years of drugs, drinking, having sex continually then going through it all must transition and transform back to a Godly woman and that is not easy that is extremely hard I know and understand, and women do not think one second or a minute that I have not been through it to a lot of men. Women can also be hot or cold the mood she is in what is she going through and all kinds of ways a woman can lock in and lock out she can switch up in so many ways you cannot even imagine. Just her being hot and cold knows that she is a hand full only the men right women? Only you can say that someone one you are telling you and you accepting is different. See I learned that when women are hot and cold, or it can just be either one it is a behavior of mixed different signals. How they handle it and for how the man to deal with it. This has men confused she will change up anytime and women do not say and so does a man just listen! You show your interest most of the time then you change up. Then you have the woman testing the man. She always doing homework at times a woman sends mixed signals then at times the man will respond that is okay. She will say at times then sometimes she will say even though I said no you should of did it anyway you should of knew the answer anyway. Your crazy, stupid, dumb, or just aggravating. It could be in a fun way, mean, angry, upset, or happy way! She will find something of it is good she still finds something. I know I increase Cleopatra attraction towards me. it was about her, and her ass was blind. See the part where she does not call back do not text back and ignore is not always on the man/men. She wants her way and can have it. This is when she sucks the teeth, I know I been there it means I do not care this does not mean every woman is the same or my putting Cleopatra in the same category with everyone in the entire world. No such thing the woman can be happy. She can be good and okay. She just cannot be satisfied. She wants more or something is not right, or it is something. Now women I know how you feel and understand when your hot and cold when your treated wrong by your husband/man. We know that I am talking about when you this way and the backup is dead ass wrong and an excuse on every

situation, I am just a woman being a woman "that is a woman". She can be suffering, painful and a punishment for nothing something from the past or having your own fit with your rude nasty attitude or your sweet charm! Do not forget the tease cannot leave that left out, I agree you can turn a woman button off even attraction one what about the man/ men? Then you have women buy clothes, shoes, purses and so many things they buy for themselves, or their husbands buy them, and they do not even wear yes women/ladies you thought I did not know this. I learned a lot of things myself off God, myself, others, my two marriages, I was in divorce two times form bad, good spirits, jobs, knowledge, wisdom, other relationships, fools, other marriages, women, men, my ex-wives, so the credit just do not go to me because I have learned from others to when I was in the world and out. I had to go through the storm to get to the sunshine. See women you are not alone. When I say alone, I mean going through things like used, abused, life, cheated on, pushed around, push down everyone goes through these things in life. It just in different ways, times, days, everyone has a story to tell. Women do you know when I was raised up you did not have a lot of people to talk to men like therapist, psychologist, groups, time no one was there to talk with these men in school then you have women say the father was not there to throw in his face put him down instead of encouraging him. Then when the man says to the woman well your father was not there or mother or both was not there that is not good man. What kind of a man would you talk like that to any woman he had a mother he should know better? I agree let that woman know the same thing! See I realize learning the woman is important so is a man they both are human, and they are God's children. When a woman first meets a man, she knows within the first 15 minutes if she will sleep with him. Cleopatra was on point with this. The women know their secrets I have told them a lot even though they know all already. See when women have sinned most have cheated with their minds a few have cheated and use their bodies, but a lot of men have cheated with what is between their legs their dick. It is still good men out there women there that listen to somethings that they do not even really know and do not benefit them at times. You have women today in these times have serious cycles and treasures of Eve. See silent woman is the loudest woman cry and every woman is not the same some handle themselves differently the silent can be in so many ways. How the woman is strong or weak with in herself. She is still holding up strong it can be different limit. The woman can be in an open environment and sitting there to herself and you would not know what is wrong with her or what she is going through. The woman can be at home and to herself the mood she is in she knows she can be in silent planning to when she does cry at times tears. Sometimes it does not always come out it depends on what the problem she is going through. You have women like to read people and use their eyes. What I like about Cleopatra as being a special woman every time she broke not of me breaking her only at times, she hurt me and did wrong to me or others. She will put herself using God and nothing but love the children times even using me. See it times it was wrong or right the silent woman is the loudest woman cry! A lot of women feel like they hurt is better, different and painful than men hurt. We do not know everything our soulmates are going through. We are not perfect. When a woman is fed up, she air's her dirty laundry because I know this woman name Ms. Shelly Davis and she told me her ex-husband was always cheating on her repeatedly, so she went to go cheat on him. Let me show you how a woman is prepared and cover her track. She went to get the man she was cheating with and brought him in front of her husband and said ask him. He asks the man and the man said no she said tell him the truth and the man told the truth and said yes, I slept with your wife. See women mess up to because when this woman broke up with her husband and divorced him, she was hurt from that relationship and jumped right into another to use it as a rebound because she was hurt and thinking it was the right choice and move to make men do this to jump into another relationship. I blame them for this both man and woman because when they do this, they do not even love themselves or respect themselves they supposed to love God and themselves. Men do not know how to cover their tracks a lot when they cheat like women do. A woman always keeps evidence on her man when he does wrong even when the man tries to hide himself or what he is doing the woman knows, find out. She finds away do not underestimate she finds out secrets, texts, lies, phone calls, conversations, how he smells, photos, etc. Every woman is not the same they are to be treated different because see my situation Cleopatra knew she had the upper hand on me. I would come right back and put up with her shit, but she only looked at was my shit, mess, flaws, sins, wrong doings everything about her was right, clean and perfect. She is a woman only her and only women been hurt and been through pain. She forgot the best thing in me. My heart was so good and still is that I help many is could I gave too much and much as I could even after the divorce. When the children's fathers still did not give anything. I love too much to because God gave me a heart to but what she does not understand she was not the only one went through this and fought all by herself and hurt. I did to then what her apologies was for back and forth and bringing the past. It really hurt me when she moved out and told me to my face that I did not think she could move out all by herself. Right to my face cutting my face when I knew she was that strong independent woman. When I first met her going to college and having her own money, but she came right back to me saying baby I am sorry for telling you that then the next day or later being angry and bitter for something from the past or disagreement. She will bring it right back up throwing it in this right woman. I am not angry or upset at Cleopatra or at all women it all me. What I did to this woman? She broke me down plenty of times as the man that I am and still is and I used nothing but God, love, me, and some of her I will never ever say I do not need her. Now today and from history women have cycles and curses of Eve and Cleopatra. Today they say it is different from when a woman gets hurt than a man shows me and explain to me and others that understand where me and the others that understand the facts, rights, truth, fair, God, and no favoritism let me know and others that know it is not right what being said and taught wrong. When a woman is hurt with a word or words verbal and actions. How is it different from a man I know it is a relationship together, Hello! Now if a man takes the woman talking to him any kind of way putting him down and unforgiveness does the woman ever think about this is enough I have gone overboard it is time for me to stop talking and show some action towards my husband. He needs some affection, romance, listening, hearing, love and act of good behavior towards him. I need to change a lot of my ways right here and now. I need to get on me. Do you women ever think or notice your men feelings get bottle and fed up. Cleopatra rejected me when she was with me and told me she forgave me and did not love me because of too much bitterness. She was blind. She rejected me by turning her heart away and she will say no because I cheated first before we got into a deep relationship! Okay that was the past did not we get over that with God and forgiveness, No! I did by myself she just said it not meant it from her heart like I wrote from mines. Writing this book right now from every blood that runs through my veins and every breath that I take and every move that I make. I agree with Cleopatra or any woman making a man pay back for what he has done to her even myself but there is a line of enough because she will be killing herself and the other person. She does not want to do it with God because she be angry that she does not see God she wants to. Do it like this the same way that husband sinned with God and their own way, but it cannot go like that for the husband. It cannot go like that for the wife, but she does not see or want it like that because she thinks and feels. It did not see me like that so I got to get him back it will not be for cheating on him most of the time, but it will be something worse because I am a real strong woman and it get angry that a woman does not want to use prayer, righteous, good Godly humble behàvior. She does not want to redeem and restore everything to its creative purpose, no she says and continue the wrong thing because he is the man/husband head he screwed up, so I am going to keep going until I get tired. I just want to ask women and men this, can you sin even if you have been sinned against you only be fighting fire with fire the devil with the devil. I told Cleopatra this she, rolled he eyes at me and cursed me out! Cleopatra did not know her mouth, putting me down, unforgiving, falsely accusing me, destroyed me, sometimes that is petty to women that is nothing big it got to be a huge sin a worse bigger sin. No sin is sin they will tell you humble no we or I know no sin is greater than the other but when it time for church as they say when the devil comes to break up your home/marriage what is to do go to God. Especially for men to but not just for men, women! Like Cleopatra she wanted to rely on words that she knows would hurt me. She was getting me back of course that seek revenge that feels good with the devil and yourself but kills the soul and marriage. I was struggling help me wife. She was struggling I help her. She wanted to get the hell from by her and not touch her until she felt like loving and touching me. See she did not understand that she had to be willing to do right for something who is doing wrong even though we were meeting each other wants and needs at times but I was meeting her 70% percent because I messed up even after forgiveness because a woman needs extra time even being selfish right women? Does not thew bible say bless those who curse you that was not hear it was he messed up that is it. It is over the cycle from her mother. She did not rely on God to change her heart, bitterness, hate, envy, unforgiveness, provoking, falsely accusing, bringing up the past that is seeing the person the same old person that same old man that is nasty in your mind there is no God, love in your heart because she kept looking at me saying shouting saying you are not God. I went through the abuse and suffering for what I took Cleopatra through. I was getting us back to God. She said you cannot make me pray with you to her own husband. I do not want to read the bible with you. Nothing supposed to stop us from praying nothing because I know you know God's word says both husband and wife separate themselves only fasting and prayer then come back together. Where will you be tempted by the devil so there it goes right there. I was not a Godly man to her or a child of GOD. She was saved and I was the devil towards her. She had to stay from around her husband God did not tell her this or bring this spirit she made this choice on her own. We both was supposed to show the true love of Christ. Now if we prayed together our marriage would have been strong and still together and trust in God not the pastor. He told Cleopatra you cannot make her pray if she does not want to but told me to pray with your wife and family, you are the head see the confusion God will say pray together. Jesus says again I say to you that if two of you agree on earth concerning anything that they ask, it will be done for them by my father in Heaven for where two or three are gathered in my name. I am there during them. I told Cleopatra God do not want us to be alone. It is him, me and you as one not just you and him and leave me out no God would not say that for no one God wants us together as the couple I and a family not you by yourself only with your children and only you the devil wants that. I wanted to be joined together with God, but Cleopatra was angry and isolated and discouraged, and I was all negativity every time she looked at me. In her eyes I was not a believer she was only. Another reason we were supposed to pray together. I begged for this be anxious for nothing but in everything by prayer and supplication, with thanksgiving, let your requests be made known to God, and the peace of God, which surpasses all understanding, will guard your hearts and minds through Christ Jesus, now if Paul in the bible says praying have better emotional health because when you pray you do not worry, you do not have bitterness, anxiety, abuse, please pray. Unforgiveness, stress, emotionally and robs us of the energy to love each other. Then when there is no prayer there is no love fighting, disagreements, then there is ignoring and walking away. I see women be alone for an exceptionally long time being alone you do not see and know is something you cannot handle because how you start to react do not sit there 10,15, 20, 25, 30, 35, 40, years probably longer because my grandmother did argue every single day. Cleopatra's mother did to, and my other grandmother did. I know God must send the husband/man. Just do not ignore it or make an excuse or take it out on your life or anis other man that God send along! See God knew I would mess up. He still closes to me. He still thought I was worth it does not trash or a screw up. God did not check my bank account he checked my relationship and tested my faith. I also thank God for protecting me from what I thought I wanted and blessing me with what I did not know I needed. See I understand everyone gets hurt but what I do not understand is that women stop always to stay and think you are the victim always all the negativity only as to come from the man. See Cleopatra lied to herself and God because she did not forgive me. She was bitter and did not look at her actions she looked at only me, my sins, my actions. She damaged us and was to blind to see that I did the damaging first yes, I admit that, but this sorry sack of horse shit cleans up his tracks and became back a king and married his Queen. A lot of negativities came from her at times. I looked at her crying. We hurt not just only her women and men! She gave up on the man who step up that did not do a perfect job but did not do the job at all the biological fathers did not do period. Then she did not want to take accountability at her own actions of hurting me, putting me down with words and falsely accusing, also bring up everything I did wrong to put in front of what she did bitter towards me to try to get away. When I was honest, fair, right and loving. When I was fighting for our relationship, she stops women will say and she will say because it is something you did, and she was fed up. I was to but we were supposed to fight together. Then tell me while I am doing good, she does not need my ass at all the same thinking, saying, cycle just from her mother's home with her getting out of the car cursing me out one minute, putting me down saying I had it before I met you then come right back ask and do not ask and say baby give me this. I will say at times crying why would ask me for something and you told me back and forth you do not need me wait a minute. Now I thought women or women was confused so what am I sisters to you feel when I am coming from as a man. Then at times where she will look innocent, nice, sweet, and apologize without fixing the apology with actions turn around and do the same thing so you did not mean shit and got the nerve to say what I got to only work on and not her and us or as one selfish at being all about herself. Then the way she disrespected me, her mom disrespected me her daughter internalized it and all of it was my fault from my actions with all their wrongs and actions as well. Then the son is watching how angry she was so leaving me would rescue your son your daughter yourself and everything and out me in a box that I was nothing but called me after we divorced arguing and apologizing again. Then saying I got to leave you alone period because I do not need your no-good ass. I am not a heathen I am not a savage I am not a punk I am a black man; your brother is not these things your father is not these things. You are a beautiful queen like you as a woman I will not call you these things with your rights, wrongs, sins, good or bad. Now when I was down lost everything was, she was supposed to kick me when I was down? Yes, she said the only thing it will be is that all the shit I have done to her that is it. How could she win for punishing me for my last past sins, how was she going to win in a relationship well our relationship. Now with my actions that I was showing by God and not my own I was being ignored. I showed her it was all about her00. A real woman needs and wants these things. Then a lot says it is to late or it was too late now you gave up. Every time a woman is acting crazy or doing wrong always have to do with a man done everything wrong to her to make her that way and do not care can be angry making excuse after excuse thinking this gets her somewhere. I admit a lot of sisters came to me with it I did not let go of what I held on to I could not move on to. I could not move on with my life so practice what you preach there is no different no excuse. We let each other down if women did not let anyone down, they will be perfect men to vice versa we even let ourselves down. I will tell you my sisters all color all races I make no excuses of my wrongs. I keep no record to put on anyone even myself only to give testimony and help others of what they are going through. I had to ask several women that came up talking with me and having conversations, what is up? Heaven what is down? Hell, so which one you choose to make a choice on. I also told them another thing I had to get over Cleopatra hurting me, I said when you are driving, and you are looking in your rearview mirror what will happen they said you will get into an accident and that is what happening to me with my life. I was told I was not keeping my hand on the steering wheel and looking forward. I was always looking in my rearview mirrors and looking backwards. A lot of us do this in life not just women! See out of sight out of mine of the planetary system. The spirit is vast and beyond this that plain earth to do with and the deep level of her soul is forever bonding with pure intention to make every move and movement matter to her first commandment is loving God then herself and her man and her children therefore I fell in love with Cleopatra. Cleopatra made love to me with her mind and soul her everything. I made love to her with my mind to I made her cum without my penis inside her. You know I took a lot of things out on Cleopatra, my stepdaughter Anita, my stepson Trevor. I did things to Cleopatra's mother Pamela as well because hurting her daughter was hurting her as well and the children, but I cannot take the blame for everything and other adults' action and sins, wrongs, with negativity that there all so good looking down on you. I took it out on the wrong woman a human being a good woman a good person for what I have been through in life just like women, is not the only ones go through things and take it out on other men that do not have nothing to do with the last man they broke up with not only the man they take it out on themselves other people as well for what happen to me. I did it to innocent people no one perfect but I am a man to admit that I was wrong I saw the people who loved me as wrong because how I was treated so wrong and raped, abused as a child to a teenager until an adult, so women, ladies, sisters do you feel my pain where I am coming from. What I have been through and experience in life? Some of you the same, different, worser but everyone goes through something! It is nasty for to say Oh you want someone to feel sorry for you because you keep doing the same shit repeatedly to people well a woman will say to women or to me. Now just think about all my wrongs, whoever we have made bad decisions, mistakes, repeated the same sins repeatedly. We all are different, but I will put no one down to tell them or make them or make them feel that I am doing something better than them what I will do is help not criticize them or put them repeatedly for something I cannot get over that's long-gone years and years ago like I said it was not right for me to do to people who did me right getting does not fix the problem. It makes it worse like when I slept with all them women in the past I thought it made me feel good especially in my mind, flesh, lust, spirit, and body but it did not I was addicted to the addiction that I was using my own body towards other women that was done to me I was used, abused, raped, mind played, abandon, misuse, mistreated, neglected, beat, whipped, and let me tell you something real women this why some women become prostitutes as wellbeing lied to so when I had sex with different women I thought the problem will go away but when the hours of pleasure became right back to misery, pain, hurt, worrying, memories, bad dreams, hallucinations. It is just like an alcoholic going in and out of a drug program or someone on crack using different types of drugs an addiction it is not only you that is the victim or going through something and I understand my mother Daisy with through it. My two aunties Wendy and Patrice as well as my ten uncles that was men that pass away David, Paul, Dale, Gary, Antwan, Joseph, Carl, William, Stanley and Thomas been through things that you cannot even imagine raising their children and women putting them down not all women! This is not about who gets the most points or who gets the right or wrong and gets the most credit this is about everyone goes through something, back to my testimony and story. When I had sex with them women all I thought about was how I was treated so I did most of it back in different ways feelings and thinking I was getting over when I was only hurting myself more, I did not love myself more I was killing myself for a thrill that lost for a couple of hours that did not do anything but drained me. I felt good with the devil but after the sex I was crying all alone to myself hurting going alone through that for so many years being raised up that is all I knew, and women mostly say they feel this and only go through this! Like one day I was talking to my cousin Sarah sitting in a Sub Mini Restaurant one day and she said to me I am glad my father raised 3 beautiful daughters to be strong to be strong and beautiful and go to college to get an education and open their own businesses. Be good women of God and respect themselves and a lady jump into the conversation and said that is one black man we need more men out here to be good supportive good fathers to their children. Now my cousin was and still is a good woman because she ignored that lady. Now was that right for that lady to say to her. She does not know her or her father or me to be talking like that to be disrespectful and rude in that manner and my cousin daughter Kathy was sitting down not only was they humble they was the better women. Now tell me what excuse that lady must come out her mouth like that to us? See what I am talking about. Like I said a woman makes love with her mind you can touch her in certain ways. It has her mind gone once you get her mind it is a done deal. A lot of women like to hang around men or themselves because this keeps down the drama and confusion and problems like I was saying about the woman mind. You do not have to allow a woman to think she knows it all to find out a woman period and all her secrets you will learn. Something every day therefore a woman is so complex. Every woman is not the same that is what makes it educated, deep, fascinating and most of all it takes time unconditional, love understanding, patience, wisdom, incredible, mesmerizing, and all they above God. The woman seduces the man to get what she wants. In times a woman in her life she does make love with her mind and in her life at times she needed a fuck as she says get laid be held been there done that she is lying. There are exceptions to the rule not everyone has done it like that but on their way. No, their own way no one is perfect. See I knew how to get Cleopatra the strong woman. You want to know what it was not for games I got in her mind! I did not rush her for no sex or getting between her legs ask her because I would not have waited 3 months until she made the move first. I respected her making love was not on my mind or her body, No! I watched her actions what was the little things that count that was God then her children then her. It becomes bigger than the mountain, sky, sun, moon, stars, and with the ocean and sky upon heaven. I am telling you how I feel. I build up an attraction when I told her the favorite song, she like making her smile by the group surface get closer than just friends. I knew how to talk with her like a woman should be treated. I never tease her to much this was her area and cycle from her mother watching her mother Pamela. I know what type of woman she was more than devastating it was a dream come true it was our own soap opera. I was the director saying action now cut. Action in any and every way she wanted to. See I had the drama going of fun therefore she always said, you a trip, what I am going to do with you, I do not know how I deal with you, you make me sick, you a hand full she never was bored. Let me tell you men something does not do this in a nasty way towards the woman because then she becomes emotionally damage and hurt the end. You want like the bitter bitch that comes out, beware I mean this as the angry woman vice versa in they for men same thing go for you women that treat men wrong with mind games, falsely accusing, provoking, cheating, schemes, scams, games, I hear women say any woman do that that is a little girl and that is a lie just like every man has done wrong and sin every woman has no one here is to say who is better than who but only! The woman mind changes especially affected by their cycles every month. They hormones change in the mind and body words to, even her looks emotional and sensitive. I tried to tell Cleopatra this. I got you do not know what you are talking about you act liked you got me all figured out and all put together I know you not trying to tell no body about themself you need to check you first it can be anything that trigger depending what mood she is in so watch what you say but not what she says! Before the period comes on or off and after it goes off its time, it is fertile! A woman avoids aggression depending on what mood she is in because she is not always right but wants to be. The woman also has the image of manipulating the man with her charm. Some women use they children as a survival win on certain things. A woman is aggressive in different ways responds to pain in different ways as well. See women love to do the thing called ignore lack of response you cannot do this to her you have to be the better man always no it is 50/50. I do not know where that comes from. The reason why the woman makes love with her mind because certain and a lot of areas of her brain half to shut down to be focus on you and her and her and you. One thing I can say about Cleopatra is that she is a strong beautiful black woman. She had to deal with me, her children, her job, being a wife, a mother, and most of all her family.

Chapter 15

Now what I will say is that when I lost my businesses my car, my money, my house, I mean everything God was teaching me a lesson. I am teaching me a lesson. I was reaping what I sow. Cleopatra said what goes around comes around she even said karma is a bitch this what you get everyone back her up women, pastor, bishop, children, her family accept her brother and grandmother her father came back to apologize to Jeffrey for everything he said credit is due to God and man or woman when they come to apologize with forgiveness, but when we divorced God was not showing her no signs that still was my fault right women and men? This is not something against women this is asking a question. Now when she lost her driver's license and needed 1,200 dollars to fix them and called me, I am just showing nothing we all go through something at times. When we are blind, and I need help with this and that I did not say one-time God making this say one-time God making this come back on you. I never say this or wish that on no body because Jeffrey will need Cleopatra one day again, she special people walking around here saying they do not need no body and do not ask no body for nothing see that is the wrong. Nothing see that is the wrong attitude and bad negative vibe with the Lord because God still people to us even. If you a woman living alone or a man, I will not say I do not need a sinner, a liar, a back slider, we all have been here I check myself check yourself because your no different neither am I. I had a service one day and a man who robbed me saved my life in jail with me, so this is love! Forgive that person for yourself and God not self for selfishness your way far away get away stay away get away because if you think you will along with a relationship with God that is a lie. See Cleopatra did not understand when she hurt Jeffrey her complaining at times was not all his fault. When I was, I felt her why I that is why I wanted to stay with God and prayer you cannot no one prayer with God if they choose not to. Even for me because I have been in that time when I felt God gave up on me but what she did not see me complaining was her fear and faith with God and fear, anger, bitterness, unforgiveness do not match together with your husband you be against him and still telling him you love him and then it is going to work out. Complaining draws fear and darkness it suffocates one another with no air of a peace of mind all these things cannot go together with God, now what does go is believing, doing, actions, God, light, faith, holy spirit. Forgiveness, passion see then negativity is not there it goes away immediately. This is not for anyone to tell me I need to let couples, relationships, marriages, let them deal with their own situations and problems. Do not do what the world say, or you do what you want to because then it becomes a tic for tac then gets worse attacking one another you be so caught up you help one another, and other people break you up even more. Then you be killing each other spirits then comes suffering of death making love and having sex do not feel right it do not be 100 percent for you both. See when Cleopatra became weak in her times of bitterness blaming Jeffrey for everything it was the silent woman cry of pain, hurt, get back, envy, bitter and anger he did not make her the woman to become this way forever and everything to be on him he will take it in for his wrong and actions but not hers to he can't be blamed the guilty man on stand in the house hold for word that comes out and every move that's being made! See lots of women do this and be capable of doing so and it be petty a lot of times and it do not even be necessary it has to be her point mood swings will catch you off guard sometimes. Now if you know your woman yes but not every time it will go like that. Every woman is not the same in a woman's eyes at times what's going on the role, part, and time in her eyes and mind she's right and can be wrong at times seriously knows that she's correct and don't want to admit to her wrong and action then come back with a charm to get what she wants and get off with her apology every woman bribe is different and the excuse to get off for certain things and certain times is let her calm down and she comes back to admit give her time and to calm down she's a woman that's fair and good but sometimes be careful of that! See the reason why I done caught up to woman/women is because I left one simple thing out, I never stayed quiet and paid attention! Cleopatra had the cycle from her mother see when the man falls sometimes in some areas the wife/woman was taught right in those areas being raised up Jeffrey will not say all he will say some areas it does not be no direction or guidance to help pick husband/man back up being weak this how Cleopatra was. Women can be weak in this area at times in their marriages we all make mistakes. You sit down with Cleopatra today or even lots of women and they will say it was all the man/men fault Jeffrey sat down with thousands of women and they told him this and he ask you did not do one thing? They all have said, NO! See this also be a secret on a lot of women holding things inside Cleopatra hold things inside of false pretense lies as well. Woman/women will hold so many things inside emotionally she is different in so many ways to explain and imagine can be on record and off, out of space in space, insane out of sane, drove and driving crazy. We all are crazy but not like women especially their crazy love including EVERYTHING! A woman will use certain things to get out of what their actions causes. See as Jeffrey and Cleopatra were getting older not getting no younger in our relationship living together things was not the same anymore. We were not agreeing on the same things I asked and begged her not to put up boundaries and keeps walls up this man is going to her me again and again because when you think, say, feel on this always each day what is going to be the outcome with no prayer keeping it in your mind in your heart, soul not moving on with your soulmate no love & peace what she going to do is move on for herself by herself! Just because you are a woman that cannot let the past go but you are telling the husband/man about his sins letting go of sins that people have done to him including yours and his own towards you God and himself. A SIN IS SIN there is no difference it is on people's feelings, opinions, facts, life and what happens in God sayings sin is sin man and woman can try to add or change but that do not count! Cleopatra was demanding with her force of getting back at Jeffrey much as she could in every way, she was not wrong at first because he had to earn her trust back and honestly, he did not because she lied when she told me he earned it back she was telling him what she wanted him to hear just like he did to her so let us continue the war right ladies? Now after a while went by then it got way out of hand, and I know to a lot of women in their eyes I am still wrong with my goods because they been through the same shit with men and they all the same and no good. Cleopatra was a seasonally woman as well a woman that was taught well, she knows a lot she has been through a lot and still standing strong but do not know everything and swear up and down she does Jeffrey cannot tell her nothing how he fucked up he got some nerve, but she can because her mess ups are different from mines, she is a woman. Cleopatra was brave, bad and bold and women there is not one minute where you talk bad about a woman, and she stands there and tolerate it same as a man. Peoples will read this book and learn something, some may like it some may not, some will experience new things some may not, some may take it for a joke, laugh, fun, knowledge and wisdom, opinions, facts, love, jealousy, debates, there points, different strokes for different folks everyone is not the same. You will learn about the man & woman even more God made man first then woman as well love this poetry and this writing straight from my heart hold on and grab on to the truth of yourself it is deeply still in love with God. Do what bring you happiness keep your marriages happy I share this with other people the book is a huge testimony I did it not I can and will continue. I will save other people marriages with my gift women & men it is what God put in me and I have his confidence in me because a lot of us not just men, we have no idea of what we have until the day we lose it. When Cleopatra forgave Jeffrey and told him she went to the Lord in his face, and he ask her is she going to bring this back up ever again she said no. What was left out was her heart was not fully cleaned as well as her mind with peace and very agitated rudely more cautious. There was no spirit of love the body gestures and signs were different I have feelings that I felt that was not right her mind was not renewed!! She hurt God, herself, and me heal all together from the past things. She was judging me so much from the past sins no matter what I did she saw only adultery, nasty, evil, abusive, control, and a no-good dog that is not going to ever change. There was no more love with God and us no more now for any woman she has God in her and loves her with her sins, love and all everything she is but tell the man quick he is not a man of God because a man of God would love his wife like Christ love the church and not do his wife like that. Now when the husband is getting his life right and together it is too late, he should have thought about that before he did what he did now in God eyes the man is still a child of God put not in that woman eyes. The love with God and our marriage was gone with Cleopatra it can't be God and the devil back and forth with arguing then back romantic, then be envy, pride, unforgiveness then forgiveness this is games right women? We know it is not that easy and simple true and sitting there letting all that time go by to save your marriage it is also being afraid, feared it is the man that only destroyed you so he will be that in your eyes for ever so you cannot let that go with so much hurt and pain you let it take over everything! See I had to lift her spirit with when it was down with my spirit when it was up because God says when your husband or wife is not a believer you do not walk away you stay there and pray. I stayed lifted to remind her of her beauty that is all around her and me and everything she did for me and stayed by my side she is still by myside until this day I can feel her. I made her laugh so much when she did not even want to smile this what she will say, YOU MAKE ME SICK I CAN'T STAND YOU and still smile. I told her the truth when she was in pain it matters sometimes and in the end it did not because she will come right back after cursing me out telling my ass off about the past apologizing to me after kissing me in the mouth. I thought something was wrong with her. Still not forgiving being scornful, bitter, angry, mean and selfish so I guess what women are going to say is do you blame her? She supposes to say what she is saying and do it and continue to do this woman to you that still do this please stop if you cannot control it or get help just like you tell yourself when you are ready and you tell your husband/man! Do not say he did it to me so I will stop when I get ready, I am telling you this you will beating your soul and spirit up because women if you do not heal from what hurt someone hurt you on your going to hurt people. You are going to have open wounds and continue to bleed, spoiled, be sour, cruel and rubbing that blood off your hands back on the person you say you forgave and others really yourself first God not left out he is already there we must ask for his forgiveness to. When I grew up and got older, I realized that one woman was enough and I was older to get more knowledge and wisdom to learn from God, myself and the woman. This man is still interested in Cleopatra this woman is the world life of AMAZING she is a jungle and a zoo all by herself she is a Leo a Queen lion I will bow down to her when she says so and not. I have so many reasons why I still will give anything to see and be with her life is to short she is a magic star good or bad. I admit I was a boy and a child playing around and confused playing her feelings and mines not knowing what I wanted but I came out of that with the grace and glory of God, and he is a witness to that. I was a man to take so much pressure and problems off Cleopatra she was not the only one that went through problems with Jeffrey. I cause some or most for the woman but not everyone, I could not do everything all by myself I would be in a mental hospital going crazy packed up with medication. Women today are saying all the shit men have took them through it is they fault so women out here that took men through shit it is all women faults? Is Every officer that shoots someone is wrong? Is every white man and black racist? Do all black men rob? So, the husband/man is continue paying for debts just like the system makes him pay even when he is innocent, he is just dead to the wrong, so when he lays down next to his wife, he is guilty until proven innocent. It is just like Adam and Eve in the Garden sinned eating the apple off the tree and then Adam blamed it on the woman God gave him knowing he was dead wrong. Now today still they are blaming one another instead of walking with God to fix it together. Do you see God made them both pay the pain and suffering was the man was to work and labor and the pain and curse was place on the woman child of labor during birth so there is just not only the man/husband in the marriage one was not by their self it was two! So, when the husband/man cheats, lies, abusing, lying, arguing, secrets, using the wife, ignoring her God sees it all now the big thing is how to deal with it I did not say brush it up under the rug. Do you really leave it in God hands after you forgive? Or do you bring it back up? God sees that to, or do you stir it up more being bold, smart, brave, hard core, have your knife out and he bet not say nothing you want to handle it all by yourself then go back crying to God because deeply you not your wrong. See you know God was not the one that hurt you so you are going to tell God everything you are not going to tell your husband fully the truth because he was the one hurts you several of times but how long will you keep that up? See a woman fantasizes a lot how they want their man to treat them even when are still getting treated good at times. Women the man thinks hard about his woman/wife when he is just sitting down by himself or in front of her and can even be out. He can be to a bar sitting down having a drink by himself walking down the street he thinks hard. I know I am a man just like the woman/women has the studies and teachings on other women because they are women men have the same thing as well as men it is not only sex. Jeffrey taught his stepdaughter Anita a lot of great things on how to be a lady and his stepson Trevor how to be a man. Do not have time for women constantly saying your just like every other man you all the same. A man gets affectionate and is emotional some men are emotional than women not just only women are emotional it is not a competition God love is all the same for one another. A man wants his woman to be content when a woman/woman sins it is not always because the man had to do something and that is all and making her sin always where does this comes from so, he is just making the wife/woman sin constantly? Not every situation and until she feels like it is ready to take her hand from around his neck like a storm with thunder lighting with hell coming down as rain over him dark clouds everyday even over him sleep with his eyes close. Do not falsely accuse your husband/man do not provoke him, insult him, offend him, not forgive him, bring things up from the past you will get what you are looking for. How can you want a change when there is no positivity in your change? Some women say his ass just need to stop acting like a baby when he is telling you to stop certain things that is hurting him. You both supposed to be on the same team together. Every time you are not going to win but damn do not lose more than winning your helping the devil win. A woman or wife that talk too much let other family members or friends put things in her ear is not a smart woman, because a real woman will listen to God, mind, soul, body, spirit and her husband not what another woman has to say about her husband. Women that do these foolish petty things are foolish and swear they know it all and got it together. Women that do this should have a nick name it should be head player and follower meaning they are playing games in so many ways especially with it mentally, physically, verbally, spiritually tearing their men down character down so bad! What is wrong with submission the excuse forever and always they cheat on us on everything. She wants the man to be careful with his tongue, but she can say anything out her mouth she did not mean that she is a woman she is sorry what did you do to her to make her that way? All women do not see themselves as whores, some women have said they are honest whores, depending on that woman her life experiences. Just like a man being a dog in life you have women that have been whores in life. Cheating women or not cheating can be toxic as well at times with their wrong doings. I said men to now do not take this the wrong way and try to change my words everyone is entitle to their own opinion which they are but what I am saying is by women I have seen whore's, they talk to me, growing up in their lives and doing their own thing. I have seen women friends call each other bitch but a man cannot call them that playing or joking for some or most women that is their fun of expression depending on them women. A nasty bitch that's disrespectful, slut, whore, manipulating, vindictive, devious, drama and petty that do not have nothing in common with a good Godly respectful beautiful woman of God especially one that is married. See I am a man that is applying my knowledge and wisdom now the married woman was once single first once upon a time or a couple depending on the woman and her life. So, she can get along with good, positive, God, encouraging other women. Not a woman that causes confusion and now today it is a lot of women out there like that a lot of women do not hang together because like I said women know how women can be but the ones that do hang together look at this, they just keep up fights, drama, manipulating, conflict, gossip, confusion, being bossy & bitchy the spawn of Satan with Jezebel spirits and other spirits in different fields. When that women character is professional, she does not hang with all kinds of women period like I said every woman is not the same. It can be woman of jealousy that is backstabbing or dramatic and toxic together and they dumb because they going to cross one another. Some daughters and mothers are like that they go back and forth saying it is a love family thing live away from one another or stay in the same house and be mad at one another. Every woman is not like that, but you have the woman/women say quick if the shoe fits to the one that is doing it or acting in the way or just minding their own business. A lot of women today cannot get along with their mothers. Some will say you talking bad about their mother when they can only talk bad about them why they are talking about everyone already so that daughter learned some of that from the mother. A lot of acts just like their mothers that is another reason they cannot get along and bump heads. They have each other ways apple not falling to far from the tree and blood lines selfish ways stubborn telling men off about they fathers and cycles and families and have ways of evil spirits. Now you let most women know about the cycle it is not over man watch out it is just getting started. Sometimes it will turn into an argument or debate when you're letting your wife/ woman know about her cycles and ways every woman is not the same. Everyone is title to their own opinion. See a lot of women feel like when they go through something repetitive that they forgive for it is ok to keep bringing up because it will heal her to get back at you but only makes the situation worse. It is ok to bring up the past if it is a testimony and to help someone else or if it keeps happening that is right and fair, and you cannot forget how is you doing and using the forget? That can be deadly or Alive how you use the word forget are you going to use it in God's way or the devil. No if you say there is no such thing you made up your mind already planned out on plat form how it is going to go your way you got it all figured out on a set up to set you off and the person with you. Do not take this in the wrong way, (IS IT ONLY AND ALL ABOUT WHAT MEN DO TO WOMEN ONLY)? After forgiveness and as you say we moving on it do not have to be cheating it can be something else another sin, so you do not think that hurts and gets aggravated or your only thinking of your thoughts only? So, when you're arguing about the same thing it doesn't get to a point of time of overboard, selfish, over again, boring, suffering, frustrated, envy or saying the same thing bringing the same topic up after you done figure out a solution to fix the problem then you came back and change it again and again. Is this not a long last memory of torture? It is like a woman putting make up on her face repeatedly she is rubbing every back on her husband/man in his face but everything on him repeatedly he is getting treated like a puppet really a voodoo doll she feels like it is good, but she knows it hurt and wrong, but I must get him back for what he has done to me and took me through. What does this do after so many years to her, him and the marriage? Did God say it was only about her hurt and pain and his sins some women will say why I got to put God in it? God was not it in it when he cheated or whatever he did wrong. If someone tell me God was not in their marriage at times, I will tell them they are lying because that wife prayed to get him back because she loves her husband dearly and he repented so God would not get him oh yes, he was feared of God. God law as one they are still together as I break this down this is not only about how the woman cannot be satisfied it is her ways, her rights, wrongs, herself, being strong. Being understood, being strange, good, stubborn, selfish, honest, faithful, prayed up, being in her ways you still cannot understand, and cannot live with her and cannot live without her SHE'S A WOMAN! She can and will always be a life saver and a wonderful caretaker, sweetheart, she can be a bitch when she is bitter and bring it out of her, she brings it out herself at times on her actions alone to as well! I am explaining to the women is it is not all the husband/men/man fault and being so hard on them. I know I feel your pain on the part to being abused, lied to, cheated on, constantly over again all the time, taking him back, children, all by yourself, neglected, misused, mistreated it's not right and dead ass wrong and a price is to be paid it just don't go away like that but not forever nothing last forever to hold on to someone that you forgave and you still see them as that same old shit and they cleaned it off of them and you. I agree you can still feel the shit inside so then do not take that person back because you are hurting yourself and that person if you are not going for another chance do not take it back because if you going to keep a reflection in the back of your mind it is going to eventually come out! You can be all good the first couple of years then when the thought comes up you cannot control it is going to control you and you are not going to have no control over it. A lot of women done told me it is going to last for how long as they want it to especially with your mood swings, they can be happy and angry you do not even know how you be acting your own self at times. See when a woman does her wrong of repetitive actions towards her husband/man see it becomes a bad behavior it involves unnecessary actions and words with body gestures or elements that are repeated many times then the woman says well you repeatedly did things over again to me. The woman that she is bringing up be long gone not in every woman/women situation I am talking about the ones that have gone on married with a husband while your miserable all these years still arguing with your husband. Then you be miserable not loving yourself, your husband/ man, and say he deserve everything that is coming to him and now and you laying right next to him, looking at him every day, do not mean it at times and come back to apologize because you know you're wrong. Then say you're going overboard when he is telling you no way you do not want to hear that then start all over again when he is not even doing that anymore you are just assuming and mad still. He is putting everything into himself, you, the family with God first and still it is not good enough for you or it is and your just afraid to give another chance to get hurt again. It is not good to forgive on that as a Christian what your husband has done but if it is anything else it is different, how so? In your way this is how you are handling things in the way how you want it no it doesn't work like that and I learned that from a woman (MY MOTHER) off mistakes she made and said she was wrong after it was over and my mother told the truth she said sometimes I was wrong and a lot of times your father was wrong I wanted things to go my way and I was afraid I was going to be hurt again and on that I was not right all the time I let my emotions over take the problem, myself, and the situation over board the way I was feeling was not always right. She let me know she had her wall up for things that was right and messed it up for her and blamed my father for everything at times. She told how no good he was and the good things about him she said the things about her to that she was nasty as hell with her mouth! My mother said no one's perfect and she said son I did a lot of wrong things to peoples and when I was in relationships I slept with married women husbands, different women, did my lying and cheating to. See Cleopatra will look at Jeffrey at times she will think on how to get him back because he knew the look, she will give to him see the sexual frustration adds on wanting to make love when she gets ready to and when she is means then change to being happy that do not last long. No husband/ man wants to make love with an angry, arguing, mad, bitter, wife/ woman bringing up the past in your face every day now while I'm focusing on humbling myself Cleopatra is mad that Jeffrey don't want to make love or have sex he like to put to in one so then he get cursed out now she's really think I'm sleeping with someone for the past and he been by her all these weeks, months, years, now she's pissed off that she can't get no love then calms down a couple of days later to get some then when he do think positive it's over it starts right back up that her vagina is hurting and sore then calm down and say bay I love you on top of him. She was already claiming things and speaking on things when nothing happens when she was supposed to be calling out to God praying with me, she was telling me what I was doing what I still was and what I already have did or done when I was laying right next to her. Now times when I ask to make love because I am on punishment and parole with a curfew, I cannot leave out the house I am on house arrest she was my parole, probation and prison officer all in one!! While I laid there at nights talking to God asking him is it over for you making him pay for what Jeffrey did to Cleopatra I am fearing God and still having faith in God and in my partner listening to her say she have God and tell him he do not have God and I am not God being very loud with hate and not submissive one time. Should I say no matter how long it can take let the woman do that to you for how long as you want it. God does not tell you or me this to tell your husband we all going to get him back together no that is you thinking, saying, and wanting that to happen bitterness comes back with wanting bad things to happen to your husband. No God says vengeance is mines that is how he says it goes and the spirit be God spirit to lead us not our says and ways. It is not a get back of power of control to destroy of get back and explosion no this is man and woman way. Therefore, your husband/man pulls away you push him away you done ruin your man attraction turned him off and way with hurting him. The woman brain is made to think 20 thoughts or more in one second. It is always a sorry from Cleopatra and every time she is right and never wrong until she says so with her charm her sorry means something Jeffrey do not do, he is talking to some or most women out there that do not like to be wrong his sorry is bullshit it does not mean nothing at all. She's in the light with the Lord with the Holy Spirit when she's sorry but when I'm sorry it goes like this she's telling me how she feel right or wrong it means a very important thing, but she ask me to tell her the truth on how I really feel and then she's sorry then she comes back with a different oppression I don't say nothing I walk away I know with God that's peace but with her that's eating her up no I did not just walk away from her. Is not that being the bigger and better man of God this is not a soap opera or the Opal Winder show this is a relationship our relationship and it supposed to be 50/50. I believe and know fairly on the 60/40 or 70/30 when you have hurt the woman/wife or husband/man yes but then not to drag no one until you want to let go because then it be to let go, and you be saying I should have been let go a long time ago. Then when you take your husband/man back going to bed with him mad with evil spirits in you rubbing them off back on him after you said you forgave when more skeleton bones have come out more than you can even imagine thinking that the husband/man was the only one brought the spirits. Nothing you did not forgive honestly from your heart. She is worth far above rubies who can find a virtuous wife. They are some out there. Life and death really woke me up I have learned a lot of things that how women at times put a mental defense up its psychology wired in them because she sits back and analyzes every detail of a man's actions, how he looks, what he wears, smells like, taste, and everything he is doing she knows her man. This why she knows her man so well she is looking and seeing perfection. Now this is a sense of Jeffrey power of his writing from his heart and passion that Cleopatra loved this power and loved to be safe. You cannot put anything together that is fake where two loving hearts are included nothing like that is fake can be together you both will do things you cannot even imagine she never forgave Jeffrey, Cleopatra also said if he did it one time, he will keep continually to do it and fuck up even more and over again she kept adding on words this what came out her mouth. In your soul, mind, brain, heart and spirit through the vessels, skin most of all there was bitterness. Then you have some women thinking things like money in their pocket or around them will bring they spirit back up feeling good. Tell you one thing it is people that have millions and billions of dollars in there, still get divorces and in the end they still not happy because it is not the money that makes everything happy. See the thing with Cleopatra she said she forgave Jeffrey but did not get over it with herself, God, and him she tried to do it all herself and he did not get her a simple sorry he worked his ass off. I use every damn energy I had I made it happen with God help she wanted to be left out then changed her mind to get in when she wanted to and when she knew she was wrong and still she did not accept me or anything I did. So, women do her and you that do this do not have to deal with this with God just like this goes for me and men vice versa. Cleopatra stayed so pissed off at Jeffrey and herself for a while the next minute let us make love, then the next minute do not touch me. Is that love or just being a woman? Now when we get married, she brings the past up now women will you say I am wrong from bringing the past up on what Cleopatra did to Jeffrey and her always, or we both are wrong or just say Cleopatra is wrong, but he must understand where she is going from as a woman to back it up to make it even with her? Will you do those ladies? Now if you bring past hurts into a new current marriage, you are not entering nothing new you may think you are, but you are not because you bring in all old dirty baggage even old spirits!! You have so many evil spirits unforgiven different confused connections before they even have a chance to grow for a chance to bloom and a lot of you do not give your husband/man air to bloom then you look at the man and say it is his fault and he made you this way, no that is on you now of your sins and actions. You said you forgave him, but you are holding on to a grudge in your mind, heart, eyes, it be all in you and the outside and including him because you are one these are so many things you must talk with the Lord about blaming the man for that to at times you cannot go to God because of him. Do not you admit that your wrong and say you're sorry come back and first thing gets you angry and it do not be another woman it can be a different situation you just bring the other woman or women in from the past that is still inside of you it can be about a conversation or topic. It is you thinking and wondering about that woman is not going to come back ever again but she is still there mentally in the back of your mind now you cannot even open because fear and faith does not work together with evil in your marriage only with God. There is mostly negativity I understand you do not want to get hurt again or even trust him again you even feel that God let you down. The spirits come worse and constantly there is no trust in yourself. Women you just do not have trust issues with only with the man/men in this world, or in relationships it be other insecurities with your life as well. Everyone one has issues with insecurity's it can be someone making them feel ugly it can be the church you go to around a certain person/people that hurt you man or woman, family members, friends and strangers to, but it is how you handle it are you going to hold on or let go some people like to hold on to certain things and want it to work thinking there doing the best job and not. Is it helping you and others as testimony's, messages, helping others how to deal with this matter you must first help yourself first before you help someone else with God first? Or you can do it your way by putting a hold on your marriage and your lives together. NO STOP goes and get your husband/man run him down when your wrong who told do not run behind no man because he the man and you are the woman or from what he did in the past to you or for all what he has done see that is using tools as a get back and getting used it is all about the wife or you both that is being selfish if your only thinking of you. See a woman that cannot forgive is a tape recorder it is in her mind to replay everything the husband/man did from the past she never forgets she see herself as a victim all the time I do blame her when she goes overboard, and she is wrong. She records even new things that she makes up and brings up that is not true what she feels like is because it already has been done to her every time she records and then she recalls on record when he makes one mistake. He can be cheating on you, your dog and a liar. How can you rebuild something that you continue to tear down your own self only way it is hard to build up on the way you see things, and feel after all those years you said let us move on? You made the choice to plan it that way or the highway, right? Even when you forgive you bite your teeth saying I cannot forget what you did to me bringing it out with hate not working it out. It can be times in church smiling holding hands then walk out the church cursing him out later I done seen it done in the church with relationships. Do not even show or know what sorry means just using the word, an apology or no action. It is stubborn, selfish because in your unforgiveness way not Gods way you will not bring it up no more as sin it will be for prayer something good or need help on not only negative. A real woman will put meaning and action in stop means stop. If you are saying you're wrong and your hard on your husband/man, then why your attitude is so mean, stank, funky and if you are screwing up with your own apology? Then just Cleopatra she knows she was not perfect, but her acting was different she wanted Jeffrey to be on point about everything. He owed her that for everything right or wrong? No. No sin is greater or better than the other. She never thought it was good in me. I was always shit and a fuck up can a wife/woman put her husband/man down not today if a man gets hurt take it like a man, suck it up and keep moving. These days in times you cannot damage your husband/man heart a quick apology will make it go away depending on what he did only or mostly. Will this not be damaging to a lot of marriages out there? Then when the man sees you have not forgiven him for years for what you have action towards him and keep showing now, he has put all his heart in. He cannot tell the truth or say anything because he is afraid that you are going to jump down in throat about the past not showing no love even times to make love it is a curse out comes with it, is that love or a curse? Yes, men feel and look at things maybe not in a lot of ways like you women we see things to not only you. Men are emotional in a lot of ways it can be weak and strong at times you are the woman you just do not soften him up he does it on his own at times. He also shows his expressions of how he cares and loves you and understands you and the same way you feel for him back. He cannot never tell you the truth about how your mind is set to think and stuck it has made up already that he is a liar everyday 24/7 sometimes when he is sleeps because soon as he wakes up you argue with even go to bed that way at times. Every woman in the world is not like this. Then it comes times where the husband chooses not to tell the wife certain things because she is going to argue or find something, he just wants to keep peace and she is calm at that time. Then she finds out something he did not tell her, and it was not anything about him cheating it can be something else. She will make a big thing out of that and then throw in his face we married now see she makes the changes see when he was telling the truth you called him a liar so he kept quiet because the things from the past will be brought up and throwed in his face. Then she does not ever think she is the liar then on telling you she is sorry for not forgiving you and bringing the past back up again and she will not do it no more she is honest and her and that is a lie. Then the husband saves his energy and brain not to argue, fuss, fight or debate so go drink or get on drugs because of the pain and pressure and no respect and love is nowhere there. The wife is still watching the husband behavior knowing she is I am going to catch him in something there is no prayer there is he is going to do it again! Claiming, speaking to it to existence and will not pray with him. Also saying why should I pray with him he is a dog and cheater. He is the evil one and as you say these things you speak to them in the name of the devil not Jesus the devil love divorces. Just like peoples who do voodoo and witchcraft they speak these things to existence and what makes it true and come to light is they believe in it just like you do with your marriages. You have some women follow their zodiac sign like I said every woman is not the same. You have the Leo woman she is warm and full of life she is self-involved. She represents her man once she leaves there is no coming back and she gives everything to her husband/man. Cleopatra is a Leo a Queen lion bold, bad, brave an aggressive woman a fighter. She gave her all and everything even her heart, soul tide together, body as well without exception. Her love is warm and passionate now Cleopatra the queen Leo was the fighter to go up against anything make up love. When she was bitter, she did not like to share but when her personal interest was endangered it was all she wrote Jeffrey loved her potential now my Leo and Queen loved the way she moved and walked he liked it to. He like the way when she will get ready for work looking beautiful still a great woman. When it was time to make love, she would not mine showing off and showing out to enjoy it more because he had her mind because being in love was the truth when we first met once you get a woman mind that is an awesome thing. You will do and say crazy things when you are in love with a woman, she had him gone to. Cleopatra felt like she could not be the source of certain problems when it was debate, she would not say Jeffrey was wrong it will have to be over and she come back on her selfishness to say ok baby I am sorry and she love him, especially when she punched him in his eye like a man one time and his eyeball was red inside yes crazy Leo Queen love. His Leo was really committed she was focused on herself and her children career as well other things in life that was important to her, Jeffrey knew Cleopatra. Even though we are not together anymore there is no way he can change his Leo Queen mind. When she was deeply in love with him, she was so mellow warm lioness providing all the time for him to a set up for us to go out and eat. She is stubborn and strong wild and crazy insane yes Cleopatra the WOMAN! This book is from my heart passion, poetry, truth most of all love please feel this and understand this where I am coming from, THANK YOU! Sometimes Cleopatra will let Jeffrey down and at times she will not he will do the same all the time was because he made her that way. She beat up the man for past things who she cared for and loved but he agrees with her to do things to him that he needed because the way he treated her that was wrong not when he did good no one allows that or to be treated in that way. There are reasons to do things and reasons not to we just find our own reasons to get back at peoples it is called a grudge. Cleopatra my Lion Leo Queen came with the truth for her King Lion, but it just had to be her jungle first as sometimes coming naturally then at times coming feisty. Jeffrey did treat her well and he admitted it he fucked up to. Now how she was raised she do not fuck up and he do not say that to say I am being or acting jealous of her family I am saying on the cycle on how she was raised in that area being high maintenance. Her background things coming from her mother things must go their way. Yes, she showed me off and herself with everybody. Being in love with my Leo Queen was serious and challenging just like a chest game to win but not every game. She is a woman of her own special way every time she made a move, she had a pawn to back her up always had a plan. Very outspoken sometimes was too outspoken then it became disrespectful and rude. Now another Jeffrey can say about Cleopatra the Queen Leo he had to show her things needed and had to be changed because if he did not, she did not want to be with him. It was too late not the Leo Queen woman lied to me telling me let us give it another chance love but listening to her mother. Then come back and say fuck you are a fuck up then say I am sorry for saying that she did not mean it she faked it. Jeffrey loved Cleopatra smile holding up her class drinking her wine and the woman she was to make something happen in the twinkle of an eye when she did it in the right way. Not when she was wrong and selfish, she needed time to herself he saw that or when someone did her wrong or himself, he left her alone. Then Cleopatra my Leo Queen was ignoring Jeffrey feelings thinking only about hers if she did know how, when she was wrong and feel the pain of him hurting by her hurting him, she did not care. It was just only getting backs not let us make this work together she was afraid to give me her all over again she was aware of my feelings, and she was ready to burn everything and everyone around her including me down. She was incredibly angry, bitter, aggressive, very destructive that she was making opinions and facts with decisions a lot of times that was not hers to make but, in her eyes, actions, ways, thoughts, mind it was just if you cannot deal with her ok bye. My Leo Queen Cleopatra never dyed her hair a natural beautiful woman. She loved to wear nice things and accessories, especially purses. She was the center of my world still is I am writing about her and to her in my eyes, soul, spirit, heart, mind with all satisfaction it is still not enough because she will add something on or in that is a woman. A woman must put her say so there is nothing wrong with that. My Leo Queen Cleopatra loved to go to the movies, and she just loved my surprises they blew her mind. I put her on any carpet to walk down on even glass as well when I took her to my brother's wedding, she looked her better than Jeffrey or any woman ever she was more than revolving world herself on the floor it is all about her and still is. Now you have some women will say that is how that woman is I am different. He agrees because like he said every woman is not the same and Jeffrey cannot put Cleopatra in another woman's shoes or in the same category he can only speak up and talk up for her. Then you have the Sagittarius woman she loves hard she stands for the truth she is silent when she needs to be, but she is strong and do not take no mess and if taken for granted she wants to be left alone. She is honest and love to travel she is the woman that need for adventure she does not like to be bored falls in love with passion fast and quick. Her mind stays in love at times she can be tricked on contact with a man that makes her happy. She is clumsy when it comes to sex sometimes not saying she is not good at it. Whatever it takes she will do everything in her power to have a great time. She wants a husband/man to laugh with her catch if she falls and be patience with her to give her enough time to find to share feelings, emotions, time and be more for real. Her relationship she takes profoundly serious and love people. Do not let her know all the time she needs to change because this will not make her happy, she is on her mission to bring out the best first in herself the husband/man she loves and everyone else she loves to be respected for her personality unconditional. This is a woman that cannot lie even when she wants to bid. When she decides to be entirely honest her life will get much easier, and even when she does not it will be easy for her partner to sense her dishonesty and decipher her behavior. She has no problem remaining active. When she settles down this is the woman cooking for her man washing dishes, she will never get bored with herself always find a reason to smile. This is a woman on a mission to make her life better. She is positive optimistic and strong. She can bring out the best those around her, especially her partner. Her mission is to make the world a better place and her beliefs should not be crushed or changed. She will make you laugh and bring new meaning to your life and teach you how to be happier. Sometimes she can lose sight on what she knows and become pushy in opinions that have nothing to do with you. She is kind, fun and adventurous but at the same time unreliable. Naïve and somewhat uncoordinated it does not matter what you buy her if it puts a smile on her face. She does not care much if things are practical or not, wearable or not, for as long as all attention is given, and her character well assessed. Take her some place she loves to go. Show her you understand her passions and strengths this is the Sagittarius woman. The next woman is the Pisces woman her attention will be turned exclusively toward the subject of her desire and enjoy every single moment of the rush of feelings that flood her heart. When she knows she is loved she starts acting like a child. Her laughter attractiveness come naturally when she is in love, and she will again powerful incredible strength from her feelings as if the world finally makes sense. It is the rational moments in life that drain her energy out of her batteries no matter for how long the relationship lasts. Someone might say she is a bit childish when it comes to sex. Shy and sensitive, she will usually pretend that she is a free-spirited seductress, while in fact she will feel bare naked on the inside every time, as if someone looks inside her soul. To genuinely enjoy sex, she needs a real intimacy with. When she finds someone, who makes her feel safe she will become creative and Godly experiment and try new things. This is a woman that will hold on to a relationship for as long as it inspires her and makes her wonder about it has outcome. She can often hold on to ideas of platonic love. She will change her mind quickly as soon as she feels pressured or disrespected or her love simply dies down. It is not possible to rely on her love, and she is always open for the possibility that there might be someone out there who can love her in a better way. If her partner wants to hold her it is best to simply let her be who she is and hope for the best. It is sometimes for her to tell the truth. The uncertainty of reactions of some people can be very disturbing to her and being introverted fragile nature gives her this inner feeling that she will not be able to protect herself from someone's anger or sadness, because of this she will often feel the need to be dishonest, especially when she has been burned by aggressive outbursts a couple of times. The main problem here is that she does not trust anyone. So, she cannot be trusted. To gain her trust and help her open, she needs to feel supported to say anything or do anything as if it was the most natural thing in the world. She needs someone who will not judge her, yell at her or have dramatic reactions to things she has to say. If she does not find such a partner, she will have to build an inner sense of security and be expectant of anything from other people without fear. When you date a Pisces woman, she will be exciting and unpredictable, with lot of creative and new activities along the way. It is important that she does not feel like she is the only one who gives vigor to the relationship, and she needs someone who can follow and make their time spent together even more satisfying. She will be a fool for romance, even when she acts like she is not, and she will love first dates, anniversaries and all sorts of special occasions. She needs to be free to act as she feels, and her partner should not be rigid and demand that their plans realize when the situation might have changed for her. This Pisces woman wants you to understand her the biggest problem this woman must deal with is the feeling that she does not belong anywhere, because of the position of the sun in the sign the image of the father is almost off. Either he was not present in her life, or he is wildly idealized, and she has difficulty finding a partner to achieve this image of an almighty man. Whatever the situation she can be lost and the only way she can compensate for her differences is to follow her mission, whatever she feels it is. Her partner must never obstruct her on this path, or their relationship will be no more now the Pisces woman has her likes and dislikes she is gentle, compassionate, and exciting, and she will do anything for her partner while she is in love. She will inspire and lift, fly above the clouds and take her loved ones with the smallest negative circumstances and she could end a relationship at any moment if she finds it lost its purpose. How to choose a gift for a Pisces woman be as creative as possible. Write her a poem, sing her a song, learn how to play the flute and surprise her by singing her favorite song or tune. Paint her a picture of the two of you in a place she wishes to see. Make a collage of your pictures together and frame it so she can hang it on a wall. She will enjoy a beautiful perfume, but when you choose one, take her sensitivity to smell into consideration. Every gift choose for your Pisces woman should be creative and romantic, and you should always spend sometimes thinking about the ideas she might cherish most. It is not that hard to buy her something she will like. Just let it be colorful or magical, and put some of your energy into it. This is the Pisces woman. Now you have the Libra woman when she falls in love, she starts questioning her decision to be in love, as if it were possible to control. For she will do anything in her power to fall out of love if a person she has feelings for is socially unacceptable for her standards. In general, this is a sign that lacks initiative, and due to the position of her sun, this woman can see men in her life as weak and passive. This will make her show initiative when in love even when it is not the time, nor the place to do so. It is almost as if she wants to show how liberal she is, but she suffers the exaltation of Saturn and is, in fact, quite turned to traditional values and appropriate behavior. Then the Libra woman has her sexual sex love making and ways she will go into extremes, on one hand showing her sexuality as if it were a given for everyone to see, and on the other being quite insecure in actual sexual encounters. Her problem with self-esteem will become on unbearable issue with a partner that disrespects her in anyway, and she might feel obligated to remain in this type of a relationship because of unconscious feelings of guilt. When she is with the right partner, she will want to experiment, try out everything that pops into her mind and communicate freely about her desires and preferences. Her relationship you can expect anything for as long as it is well packed. She will be caring and deep, but also be prepared to show her selfish, manipulative side, wrapped in candy paper. It can be hard to understand her position because she will rarely show her uncontrolled emotions and passions, so the right partner needs to know her deeply and intimately, including the things she does not want to show. In general, when she decides to be with someone, she will be committed and loyal. Even though she can often be too worried about other people's opinions, she will stick to her choices even if they are not good for her. You can trust the Libra woman in general she is faithful, but she does not always say what she means. Her emotions are often hidden because she feels they are unproductive or shameful, and she will not have a real outburst of emotions even when she would gladly explode. She cares more about the way she acts than about the way she feels, and this can leave her in a bad place for a long time. If you understand her deeply enough you will be able to trust her, but only if you feel her emotions. When you date the Libra woman, she will do dating for pleasure only for as long as she is not ready for marriage. As soon as she becomes ready, she will only look for serious relationships and will not take much of uncertainty and unclear emotions from her partner. Her need to be with someone for better or for worse is extremely strong, and dating her will never be casual, even if she says it is. She can be quite needy, seem incapable of doing anything alone, and her dates cannot seem to avoid the closeness and the road to marriage unless she is not interested to stay with her partner at all. The interesting thing about a Libra woman is that there is no middle ground with her. If she to date you she will probably want to marry you in the long run. You must understand the Libra woman this is a woman that must have unresolved issues with her father, and she is not easy to understand. She can be wonderful, caring, give you her undivided attention and be just and responsible more than any other sign. Her low self-esteem makes her dependent on opinions of others or too quick to show she does not care about anyone's opinion. She does not understand why other people do not act in the way she would, and this makes her question her every move. We can say that every Libra woman is indecisive, but the truth is, this woman cares too much about the future to let things slide and takes on too much guilt and responsibility. This inevitably leads to a state of self-pity and taking the role victim. Her likes and dislikes she is loyal committed and tactful. She will be prepared to give her life for the partner chooses. However, she can be too focused on other people and forget who she is in the process. This makes her control, inflexible and disrespectful, losing her ability to approach other people's characters and motives without judgment. She loves nice surprises do not miss her birthday or anniversary, but it would be much worse to give her presents only on those occasions surprise your Libra woman. Buy her flowers or some perfume that is well-balanced. She will value a piece of jewelry, a feminine watch or anything artistic and beautiful. She needs balance in her life, and she will like her presents to be moderate not too colorful or pap. She will always be happy to get an unexpected box of chocolate followed by a red rose even if she feels guilty about her weight and the chocolate she will eat. This is the Libra woman. Then you have the Virgo woman she falls in love she will probably get scared at first. If this happens outside of a relationship, she will probably be so shy that it will probably be so shy that it will become impossible for her to start a relationship at all. She likes to be swept of her feet by a partner who makes the first move. This allows her to feel attractive and feminine. Some of Virgo women can rationalize things to the point where they can approach anyone or at least flirt, but they will often not end up in a long-term relationship with a partner she was direct with. She must fall in love with someone stronger, more confident and more protective than she is. The Virgo woman sexuality this woman is not aware of her-sensual nature and her sexuality. This is the exact thing that can be attractive to some of her partners but anyone who wants to be in a sexual relationship with this woman, needs to understand that she needs a lot of time to relax and become intimate to relax and become intimate with her partner. She will never discuss her sex life with other people, and she will slowly get into the game of sex, only though emotional contact or by a clear decision of rational mind never on an impulse. In her relationship she will clean your house, cook your lunch, take care of your children, carry your suitcases and fix everything in your life with ease unless you stop her. Please stop her. She does not have to do everything on her own, all the time but she does not seem to understand this. Out of her need to help, she might make her partner feel incompetent or even stupid and she really needs to be careful not to cross the line in criticizing or contempt she needs to accept that perfectionism is not her best trait and that it keeps her from being happy about imperfect things in her life which are well all of them. Virgo woman can be trusted one hundred percent she is too smart and too loyal to give in to adultery and her morality and shy nature probably will not allow it to begin with. The only thing you cannot trust is her silence for when she will often compromise and sacrifice in order to hold on to the partner she loves. This can trick any one's sense of gratitude for this is the easiest of all zodiac signs to take for granted. When going out with this woman she will l want you to ask her calmy out at the begging of the relationship she will mostly enjoy the usual going out routine. Her partner is supposed to take her to a fine restaurant for a walk in the park and out dancing. She will not tolerate any sort of aggression or pushiness, at least until she develops deeper feelings and gets tied to her partner by things, she thinks she can fix. She wants to go out to clean places, and you will rarely want to take a Virgo woman to an underground club where she will drink beer out of plastic cups. Although she will understand the inexpensive and the relaxed nature of this type of place, she will rarely feel good in an environment in which everything smells of stale beer. Understanding the Virgo woman there is a reason why Virgo is a sign often described as a manic cleaner. This obsession with cleaning can be projected to all activities of a Virgo woman. She wants to clean the world of evil as much as she wants to clean her teeth or the bathtub. The most important thing this woman must face is the search for faith belief that she is better than she thinks she is. In most cases she is raised to not be fully aware of her beauty, goodness or value. Still, the faith in the beauty of the world and in her own fairytale will pull her with a strange gravity until she finds them. The worst thing a Virgo woman can do is settle for her rational choices, for she has the capacity for perfection in all areas of her life. The Virgo woman dislikes and likes she is caring, modest and loyal, able to fix anything that is broken, including a broken heart. This is a woman that wants to help and get involved in her partners life and be happier together. Unfortunately, she can get carried away and imagine that she knows best what is good for other people. Her kindness and support can reach the point of insult where het partners might ask themselves if she thinks they are incompetent to do anything on their own. Now the way how to get your Virgo woman a gift when it comes to birthdays and anniversaries do not ever forget them. Buy a gift that is practical and can be used. Whether it is a piece of clothing with the appropriate message written on it or some kitchenware, her present needs to be in sync with her tidy personality. If you want to surprise her, write her a poem. She will enjoy some verses dedicated to her melt her heart. Do not forget to check it for grammatical errors though. In most Virgo women, there is a hidden love for all sorts of art and might truly treasure a fine, discreet painting, or a sculpture that represents a certain message. This is the Virgo woman. Now Taurus woman falls in love she knows exactly how to behave. You can almost envy her spontaneous glow; the look she has in her eyes and all the things she is prepared to give up in order to satisfy the person she fell in love with. In the beginning of the relationship, she will carefully examine her partner to see if they are worthy of her feelings. Gradually she will build the trust up to the point in which she is ready to share her thoughts, her emotions, and her past if necessary. A Taurus woman yearns to be loved, passionately and tenderly, but has a deeply rooted fear of getting hurt. An analogy with a tender flower would be in order, for she needs a lot of care and attention in order to blossom. A Taurus woman is serious about her sexuality ways. This woman will want to be caressed, by herself as much as her partner. She wants to be kissed and love in every possible way. Orgasm is the last on her list priorities. She does not even care that much about sex her connection with a partner in it. She considers sex to be a particularly important part of an especially important part of a relationship because it represents an intimate bond where she can feel exactly how much she is loved. If she is not satisfied by her sex life. She will become cold and distant, although often prone to sticking to the same relationship even if does not feel loved, due to her resistance to change. A Taurus woman in a relationship is your mother, your cook and your lover all at comfortable, tender of the Zodiac. There is nothing mysterious about her once you get to know her. Although she will keep her distance for a long time, once she decides to open, she will become someone clear, stable, sweet and compassionate your lifelong friend and a partner in crime. It is often said that Taurus like things nice and boring, but in fact they are ready to deal with anything ugly, for as long as it is shared with, they love and are constant need for excitement as Venus must be.

Trust is something to be earned with a Taurus woman. She is careful about it probably more than any other sign, because there is a lot at stake when she decides to open. If she senses any dishonesty, she will lie without a blink if she feels she need to. Her senses for other people are like a fine antenna, linked to her emotional body and you can almost see her shiver when she feels betrayed. If her partner does not disappoint her and stay true, she will never let them down. When you date a Taurus woman, she does not need special locations or well thought out plans, for as long as she is valued. You can always take her to a nice romantic restaurant with fine cuisine and her favorite one is probably some small Italian place close to her home or whatever she likes. Buy flowers, show her how beautiful she is to you and lend her your jacket when she is cold. She will be satisfied with smallest signs of affection, for as long as you are not cheap or careless about things she feels strongly about. You must understand the Taurus woman. Understanding her might not be easy. It is almost impossible for some men not to take her for granted. Her compassionate nature and the feel she have for others is something. She expects from her partner and rarely gets. You need to feel her feelings this is what she wants her desires and needs. Be gentle, protect her even if she acts like she hates being protected and dial down the expectations. She is who she is either you love her, or you do not. There is nothing more careless than a partner feeding off her beautiful soul, while considering her boring and needy. Her dislikes and likes Taurus woman are strong, practical and reliable. When she falls in love, she is loyal and ready to settle down, have a bunch of children and take care of her partner in a way no other sign would return, she needs to be loved and cared about. On the other hand, she can be closed, difficult to reach, distant and untrue if she fears emotional pain. Her weakest point is the feeling of guilt that can take away most of her wonderful character and make her a deeply unsatisfied woman. How to choose a gift for your Taurus woman choose something expensive or practical. It is wrong to think that Taurus woman care much about money. They understand its value and recognize expensive things. Taurus woman can understand the link of material value with quantity of love when needed. Still, she will be swept off her feet by a creative, practical gift that she will be able to use. There is always a soft side to her when it comes to soaps filled with flowers, perfumes with natural scents and anything that will make her laugh. Buy her comfortable pair of fluffy slippers or anything that matters. She needs things in her life cozy, useful and colorful. This is the Taurus woman. Then you have the Scorpio woman Cleopatra, my stepdaughter our daughter is a Scorpio. This is the woman intentions and inner state are often misunderstood. She belongs to the unfortunate sign of dismissed emotions that people judge and run away from, way too often. When she falls in love, she jumps into the deepest pool of emotion ever known of all water signs, she is the one represents the depth of female emotions, sexual, protective, to and founded in the core of the earth. She will show her love through actions that cannot be misleading, and you will never see a Scorpio woman tease if she does not want to get involved. Her intentions are clear, her love even clearer, up to the point in which she gets hurt. When this happens due to the depth of her pain, she can become your worst enemy. A Scorpio woman sexuality, everyone can learn about sexuality from this woman. If she has not been hurt too bad in previous relationships. She will merge emotions with sex in a perfect balance. Her sexuality is something that defines her, and it needs to go as deep as her heart is prepared to go. There is nothing easy or light here and her sexual experiences need to be passionate and spontaneous, yet thoughtful, interesting and yet an important part of her routine, satisfying and yet giving. Even though this might seem like a true challenge for any partner, she is very easily pleased and simply needs someone to love her and respect her desires, for she has no problem with having initiative to create whatever she needs herself. A Scorpio woman relationship is always going to the extremes at least inside her mind and her heart. Even if she is well taught to hide how she feels, she will accumulate every emotion she ever had and end. Relationships for reasons that cannot seem to be explained. The main goal for any partner of hers should be able to find a way to communicate without words. She needs to be felt instead of heard and listening to her should not be an issue with words as sharp as knives most of the time. She can be possessive, but she will never ask for things she is not prepared to give back. If you want someone to remain faithful to you until death, you will have to fulfill her needs and show her you belong to her as much as you want her to belong to you. Can you trust your Scorpio woman yes, unless she is hurt? When her feelings are hurt, she does not really know how to act, and has trouble finding forgiveness inside her heart until her sense of Karmic Justice is obtained. This can turn her into that vindictive ex everyone easily identifies her with, but this is not a rule. In many situations this is a woman that simply knows what goes around, comes around. She understands that the universe always takes care of any deed, and even when hurt, many Scorpio women will remain true to themselves, with no intention to taint their honesty or their vocabulary. When you date a Scorpio woman just know she is rollercoaster. She wants excitement, change and cannot give in to the stale environment and do the usual routine every day. She wants to learn new things, experiment and have a lot of physical encounters and sexual tension. Still, however she might seem, most of all she wants tenderness and care. Her biggest dream is to find someone who will treat her right, and even though she might not like going to the restaurants which all couples visit or going to the movies for some romance, she will always be in the mood for a walk by the river or a long vacation out of town. When she is given what she needs, she will follow her partner anywhere understanding her is to know that she is not a typical woman, but more like a Goddess of female initiative, practicality and strength. Her body is her temple, and she wants to feel physical love more than anything else in her life. However, it is not easy for her to accept the personality she was born with, and she often allows her son to become the sleepy mass of energy that is not focused into things she loves. Her career needs to understand what she wants out of life. If she does not want her frustration and feeling she does not fit into the anyone's expectations or needs might make her a bit too hard to handle. Her likes and dislikes she is deep, smart and has strong boundaries. When she loves, she loves with her entire heart and is prepared to die for that real emotion. This makes her deeply sensitive, scared of betrayal, and often hurt and angry. How you chose a gift for a Scorpio woman. She is a challenging woman at times. When it comes to presents. She loves surprises, and she will cherish any good deed and a thought pointed in her direction. However, when a demanding situation arises, such as her birthday or an anniversary, most Scorpio women partners fall in desperation for nothing can be bought that will satisfy her. This is simply not true. She gives the impression of someone self-sufficient, some who has no needs, but if you listen carefully, you might discover she finds joy in the smallest of things. She will not care for jewelry, unless it fits her character, but she can fall to pieces over fluorescent stars for her bedroom. Her present needs to have real emotions hidden behind it, and you cannot miss if you just look inside your heart. This is the Scorpio woman. The Cancer woman now when she falls in love, she can have trouble controlling her motherly instincts. Although she can be perfectly capable to make a distinction between sexual and motherly caring relationships, true feelings can male her confused. If she runs into a partner that does not feel the way she does, she could easily get hurt because of her need to give everything she can to the person she loves, with no regard of her vulnerable to all sort of emotional vultures, so she needs to be careful to keep her boundaries safe and be rational enough to understand all the possible sides of a certain relationship a Cancer woman. Sexuality can be a weird territory for a Cancer woman, due to the fact in a way this takes away her instinctive sexual desire and makes her dependent on sensual, tender and emotional lovemaking, because of this she can have difficulty expressing her sexuality and she needs the right partner to recognize this and help her feel confident enough to develop this side of her personality. This is a woman that can be extremely passionate when she is in love and finds her love returned. She will be one of the least likely women of the zodiac to ever decide to leave a partner she finds true sexual intimacy with. In a Cancer woman relationship, she has this incredible gift of compassion that allows her to understand what her partners going through. This can make her an exceptionally good listener because she is able to put herself in other people shoes. She has the need to protect people she loves, and this can be a bit overexaggerated and strange when you look at her as a gentle being. This happens because she carries that motherly instinct inside every inch of her body and wants to protect her "child" from anything evil that may come. Just in case as if maybe their partner cannot protect themselves. When emotional stability is established and she finds herself in a loving relationship that is to last, she will want to do what is normal, get married and have children. A Cancer woman is trustworthy until scared or deeply hurt. She will not betray her partner in a typical way and will do anything to hold on to her family and her peace at home. If she does something to endanger it, she will probably lie. Basically, if her partner wants a stable home, one will be provided, but no one is knowing the sacrifices needed to get there or the possible obstacles this woman has overcome in order to find peace in this union. The Cancer woman is easy to date she would like to go to places that are intimate and romantic, with no loud noises or food that is too spicy. She likes the crowd but will like it more if the crowd is made from people she knows. Although she is not social in a typical way and eloquent as some other signs, she will have a couple of his friends and be quite popular among the emotional people in her life. It is best for her partner to surprise her with commonsense, wideness of views and education. What we rarely read in different astrological approaches to a Cancer and is Important to keep on mind is that she will really want to travel, maybe more than anything else. Understanding a Cancer woman, she is a woman has a mission to make a huge change in her life. She is strong and as all mothers ready to give her life for the ones she loves. Although she might seem too mellow and soft, she is a true fighter when motivated and needs her partner to understand this. If she is underestimated, she will probably swallow her pride and move on, but she will remain hurt for a long time. There is a deep understanding to her that all things are balanced in nature, and that everything we give comes back to us. You would not want to be her enemy, for she can use her incredible moral value and goodness to beat you in less than a minute. A Cancer woman likes and dislikes she is caring, loving and kind. She will be faithful and true for as long as she feels safe and satisfied. She is not a good pick for signs that seek extremes excitement and constant change, because she likes to hold on to things that make her happy and wont easily change her house, partner or a circle of friends. She can be irrational, over sensitive and too quiet, and the best way to approach her is to see her emotional side as her biggest virtue. How to choose a gift for a Cancer woman. She likes a gift with a sentimental value. It is best to choose it by listening to her words and sensing her reactions to things. If you see that she has got excited about something she saw in the window of a shop, go in and buy that exact thing. She will not care about specific occasion if you show understanding for her emotional reactions and needs that form along the way. Still, it is best to show respect for tradition and if she always got flowers for her birthday, it is a good thing to buy flowers each day, each year. However, her need to value tradition is not something she will hold on to over emotion, so try to choose some practical, not too expensive and most importantly something that feels like her. This the Cancer woman. We come to the Gemini woman. When she falls in love, she develops a sudden flare for sweet talk and cuddling. As fast as she fell in love, she can find herself out of it and there no guarantee that her loyalty or her emotions will last. Although Gemini is not such an emotional sign, she is a woman first, and she will have deep emotions in one partner for long enough, deep emotions although she might approach them superficially. Almost as if she does not really understand how she feels. It is a rule that a Gemini woman will fall in love with a well read, intelligent man, and she will never say that love is blind. She knows what she is looking for and if she cannot find the source of her satisfaction and emotions in one partner for long enough, she easily trades him for a different one. The Gemini woman sexuality is an incredibly special thing she representatives love to be naked in general but is not quite the same when a naked Gemini man walks around the house, and when it is a naked Gemini lady. She is not a typical woman when it comes to sex. When she feels right. She will simply make the first move. As opposed to a Gemini man, she will enjoy discovering emotions within her sex life and will be surprised by their intensity and intimacy she is capable of. She loves to experiment, change things and spice up her sex life in many ways, and always needs new excitements. A Gemini woman wants to stay in her relationship does not make her happy. She will not stay long. It is impossible to tie her down and protect her from the world, because this is the last thing. She wants from a relationship. She is an air goddess and needs her wings for flying. She wants to travel, move from city to city and meet new people all the time. If her partner is insecure in anyway, it will be hard to tame her. Gemini is a mutable sign, and she can be adaptable when she wants to be, but she also needs enough room to be herself. When she is tied down, she becomes deeply unhappy and can seem as if she is going to wither with a possessive partner. You can trust your Gemini woman, if she is free to speak her mind, she will usually have no reason not to tell the truth. The ruler if Gemini is Mercury and it has occasional need to lie about a thing or two, but this will mostly be in the scope of everyday activities and funny to talk about. In the case she feels in anyway restrained, she will most certainly start lying. This is her first line of defense so she can stay true to herself and keep her own little word safe. However, she is unpredictable and although it is the most wonderful thing about her, she cannot be trusted to be in same relationship tomorrow, however intimate she might get. Dating a Gemini woman is easy. She will want to see a new play or go to a concert. Her partner can really take her anywhere new. She will be thrilled to have an experience she never had before. It is important not to keep a routine because this is not what she wants. It might make her feel safe for a while, but in due time she will feel like going crazy if the dating scenario keeps repeating. Things need to stay interesting and fun, whatever they might be. Understanding your Gemini woman. She wants her words to mean something and if she does talk excessively, it usually reflects her need to be heard. She yearns for tenderness given in a strangely distant manner and needs to sense things deeply beyond her mind. Change comes easy to her, but she will not make it without reason, even if it seems like she did. She wants someone to move with her and not hold her back, gentle enough and rational enough, tall enough and enough. She needs a true human to love her. Gemini woman likes and dislikes her company is enjoyable. She will laugh and chat, have a lot of friends and probably fit in at any social event you can think of. When she is love, a Gemini woman becomes strongly outspoken, caring and open hearted. Unfortunately, there is no way to predict how long this will last. She is unpredictable and changes all the time, never too feminine, and rarely want to be taken care of and protected in a typical sense. How to choose a gift for your Gemini woman. Choosing a gift for her is easy. She loves presents in general and will be happy if you surprise her although it is not her birthday or Christmas. She could always use a new phone or a pretty case for it and would not be a mistake to make her something childish and thoughtful. Write her a letter. Think of her when you go to the supermarket as much as you would in a gift shop buy her newspaper she likes to read, or a muffin with a cup of coffee. Even if she does not work, you can always buy her a plane ticket or take her on a weekend away to walk through nature and feed the birds. This is the Gemini woman. I am now to the Aries woman when she falls in love, she will seem to be the most attractive woman. However insensitive this sign can sometimes be, she is primarily a woman. She will show her emotions through a typical flirting game and not be patient for an exceptionally long while expecting from loved one to have initiative and answer her obvious affection, she can show her direct, sexual nature with a lot of taste. This is her greatest trick she can show her body parts, put on red lipstick, wear a mini skirt or an exceptionally low cleavage and still not look indecent. The Aries woman sexuality she has a big sexual appetite is big but will in most cases show only when appropriate.

Chapter 16

Although it is often understandable how attractive she feels from her attitude, she prefers her sex life to stay as intimate as possible. Aries woman are not typical women when it comes to sex. They are much more aware of their sexual instinct and can quite emotional when they are physically intimate. It is unacceptable from her perspective for any woman to stay in an intimate relationship, let alone intimate relationship, let alone get married and have children, with a man that doesn't meet her sexual needs. When an Aries woman is in love in her relationship, she will be faithful and always in the mood to support her partner in all his endeavors. In most cases, arises woman has enough energy for two. This can easily be her problem. Even when she knows it would be best to let the person learn their lesson and find their own way out, she doesn't understand why she wouldn't take over the role of savior when she has enough energy and practical sense to do so. If she is not in love, the relationship can be a rollercoaster ride, from a sexual one to a non-existing one in a matter of minutes. She needs her freedom and as soon as she feels someone shows too many emotions, she is not able to answer to, she will easily end the relationship. You can trust your Aries woman she can be one of the most trustworthy in the entire zodiac. Still, the sign of Aries relies on the sign of Pisces, their predecessor and any unsolved issues from the past can lead into a deep circle of lies. Her biggest problem would be admitting to her new partner that her Ex tries to contact her. Not because she feels like cheating on him, but because she can't recognize her own connection to the past. Aries is a sign that always wants to move forward, and when the past catches up with them, they are not sure how to handle it. Dating an Aries woman this is a woman that would gladly visit a sports game or go to the gym with her partner. It is easy for her to blend into masculine activities, but this doesn't mean she doesn't have a need to be respected and treated like a woman. A fine balance is needed in her dating experiences, between activities that show her female worth, and those that can be shared in childish, Aries kind of way. Understanding your Aries woman when she seems to aggressive and loud try to remember that this is just the way she talks. She expresses herself a bit different that your regular woman. This is not such a bad thing because you will always know what's on her mind. It is sometimes hard for her to recognize her emotions and she can be easily losing patience for herself and others, but if you give her space to solve her issues on her own, and conflict will be avoided. There is so deep, warm emotional nature to her and a lot of energy she likes to give way to people she loves. It is important not to take her for granted and understand her efforts to make your life better. An Aries woman like and dislikes she is a warm, passionate person with a healthy sexual appetite and strong opinions. Still, she can be stubborn and inpatient. Her biggest flaw is the lack of understanding for the need of others to do the things themselves. This can lead to ger imposing opinions and solutions to problem of those around her when she really shouldn't be involved. How to chase a gift for your Aries woman she likes practical gifts with clear colors and simple cut. Everything she wears needs to show her sexuality in a clear and non-offensive way. Jewelry is a tricky territory since she will either not like it at all or wear a lot of it. However, make it expensive and discreet, she will treasure it a s a sign of your affection. You can always buy her a single red rose, or a hundred of them, but any flowers with a strong scent and a lot of character will do. When she accepts her gift, there is a tiny possibility she will not know how to react. Don't misunderstand this for a lack of gratitude. Instead, surprise her often. Be it her favorite lipstick, skis, rollerblades or a massage that is paid for, stay focused on her physical needs and never forget her birthday this is the Aries woman. This is about the Capricorn woman when she falls in love, she will have to decide to face her own feelings before she gives in to them and starts enjoying the relationship. In most cases, she will choose her partner wisely, with a lot of thought, and she will not make the wrong decision. Her sense of responsibility can be such a strong priority, that won't allow herself to take any risks, always choosing the safe thing to do and the safe partner to be with. This can make her deeply unsatisfied, but she won't be able to understand that there is no room for national decisions when love is in question, no more than there is room for brain in matters of the heart. The Capricorn woman sexuality she is much more open for sexual experiences than one might think. A Capricorn woman is showing her feminine ways and comes out to understand her own instincts. Her emotions are a different story though, and she might lack true intimacy and joy in her sexuality, As a result of too many rational choices and unconscious fears of emotional pain. In general, she wants her sexual routine to be regular and physically satisfying, unless she gives into some guilt trip and enters a masochistic mode in which her sexual satisfaction needs to be sacrificed. A Capricorn woman in her relationship when she chooses a partner, this is a woman that has the need to stay loyal, and often doesn't understand why anyone wouldn't be. The equation in her head is quite simple, and for as long as her relationships make any sense, she will stay in with them with no intention to disappoint or leave. When she feels the time has come for things to end, all her boundaries have probably been crossed and there's a slim chance there will be turning back at her decision. She is serious and strict, but her love goes very deep, and unless she is dissatisfied with her own life, she will support her partner and make them incredibly happy. Can you trust your Capricorn woman she is a woman that has no reason to lie, unless if fear overflows her common sense? The only thing that can make her act on instinct is panic fear, and if she doesn't feel any, she will have no reason to be dishonest. In general, she lives by the principle an eye for an eye and although she knows that all debts get settled by nature, when she is angry enough, she might take justice into her own hands. This is the only situation in which she might decide to lie, out of spite and the need to return the favor to an unfaithful partner. However, this will make her feel that guilt we mentioned before, and she will probably avoid situations of this kind. When you are dating a Capricorn woman if you are looking for a woman who Is low maintenance, this is unfortunately a Capricorn woman. She is most often undervalued, shoulder to shoulder with a Virgo woman, capable to take care of herself and not afraid to be alone. Her dates should be better than she thinks she deserves, to show her that nothing bad will come out of something good. She needs a lot of love to blossom, and this should be shown from the beginning of the relationship. She will not care much for extreme, exotic activities and she will settle for a dinner and a movie, every time, perfectly capable of doing everything else she wants to do alone. The thing she will love most is the tradition she will have with her partner after the relationship has already lasted for a long time. She should be given the opportunity to enjoy the repeated enjoyable experiences to build this tradition that will make her feel safe secure. To understand your Capricorn woman, you need to find a way to respect her but not take her seriously. This is an exceedingly difficult task, for she will give it her best shot to convince you that she is tough, strong, and that there is nothing she cannot handle in life. In fact, she is extremely sensitive, always shying away from her own heart, taking everything as a personal issue and sacrificing her own benefit for other people. If she doesn't end up in a role of a victim, there is a great chance she will take on the responsibility for everyone else's lives, and this is something you shouldn't allow to happen. Capricorn woman likes and dislikes she is an incredible rock to lean on at any time, even when she lacks compassion and an understanding for the usual, everyday problems of mankind. She is reliable and strong, ready to share and take responsibility, while focused on her focused on her goals, determined and able to endure. On the other hand, she is strict, always expecting her partner to be even better than she is, and this is not easily accomplished. She mis prone to a feeling of guilt and often slaves away to come to a certain point that she might not even need. How to choose a gift for her, a Capricorn woman is often too practical for a typical feminine gift, but also likes to smell good and feel good and cozy in her own skin. It is not easy to choose a gift for her, for she exalts mars as much as her ruler is exalted in libra, the sign ruled by Venus. Therefore, she seems to be torn up between the things she needs and the things she loves. The best choice here is to find a gift she will use but is also beautiful and chosen by her. When she sees something hanging in the window and reacts to it pick up this signal return there to buy it when you are alone and wait for her birthday New Year's Eve or your anniversary to surprise her with it. The surprise would be even better if this is something she thinks too expensive or makes a rational choice not to have it as if she set up for loving it from a distance. This is the Capricorn woman. here we have the Aquarius woman when she falls in love, she will follow her buildings for as long as she is unrestricted and free to be herself. The unconscious fear of losing her personality to other people of the makes her vulnerable to any sort of expectations and try to turn her into something she is not. Still in almost every Aquarius woman's life comes a time to grow up and realize that a certain amount of love should be enough for her to have a family raise child and take care of her husband. This is probably the hardest thing for her to do an A decision like this should be respected and understood as the ultimate act of love even when it seems entirely rational. her sexuality she needs a partner who was interesting enough and doesn't care much about the taboos of modern society. if she wants to show her sexuality in a certain way, she will probably do that despite everyone's opinion and not at all subtly. Her rational mind will in most cases keep her from making scenes, but she is extremely interested in all sorts of sexual experiments, and this includes outdoors sex and sometimes a display of intimacy in the strangest places you can imagine. She shouldn't be with a narrow-minded man or anyone who perceives her as unladylike. Aquarius Woman is a wonderful woman in her relationship she is exciting unpredictable and not someone to choose to be with if you are searching for a stable secure relationship without waves and emotional challenges. She doesn't like to be tied down although she would do anything for the right partner and unless she feels her biological Clock ticking, she will not give in to the formal expectations of a relationship. The most important thing one should keep in mind when she is starting in relationship with this woman is that she could be swept off her feet only by respect and they surprise her too in return. Trusting their query is if the relationship makes her feel secure enough to open and deep into her emotional pool, she will most certainly be someone you can trust without a doubt. however as soon as her personality is the thing threatened in any way, she will either break up or not only lie but also be fully aware of it take responsibility and still feel particularly good about it. Dating an Aquarius woman her need to break the rules can sometimes be uncontrollable not because she is out of control but because she doesn't want to be in it. If her upbringing was tender enough and her needs met when she was a child her rebellious nature won't be that difficult to deal with, but the fact is her inner opposition will push her in the direction of the most unusual activities you can think of. Therefore, she doesn't want to go on three same dates in a row especially not to a romantic family place when she would eat spaghetti. Instead, she wants spicy food something on foot she wants to go to a club to dance to live she wants dates that surprise her and last through the night. she needs new experiences every time changes excitement and she will never settle for less nor should she. Understand your Aquarius woman respect needs to be earned with this woman. She might never realize that respect is her given right and that she doesn't need to fight for it all the time. Her biggest challenge is finding inner emotional peace and when she gets hurt too many times, she easily closes her heart and move on with her life from a strictly rational point. Aquarius woman likes and dislikes her beauty of being in a company of her herself Unpredictable exciting nature her Humane outlook on the world and her understanding for things other people would run from. a not-so-great side of dating her is in her unpredictable and not so reliable side not only because she might be late every time you are supposed to meet but because it is sometimes impossible to know how she will react to anything other people do. How do to choose a gift for your Aquarius woman buy her something you would it buy for any other woman. it is important to understand that Under her detached exterior hides a real woman that likes to be surprised by something romantic and beautiful. this does it mean that she will be crazy about it doesn't red roses or a candlelight dinner and although she might be satisfied enough by something similar it is best to go with presents that are a little more unusual. If you want to pick out a gift, she will use look for technical things she might need in a purple or a silver tone. Pick out a good astrology reading or prepare some fireworks as an anniversary surprise. discover that it is incredibly easy to give her something she will treasure if only you rely on your creativity and your inner feeling of excitement. This is the Aquarius woman like I said every woman is not the same you have a woman like there zodiac signs follow them worship and believe in them and you have some woman don't I had to put the woman in here that do because every woman is not the same you will have some woman read this and say I like it some say I'm crazy they will say what they want to everyone is entitled to their own opinion. now I'm a Pisces a fish I'm putting my sign in there myself the man because too I Cleopatra sign in here the Leo so starting with my sign the Pisces the fish I don't go by this it's just what it says on my sign but certain things I agree with and you will have friends ex-girlfriends enemies associate's family members will say good things and bad things get it out it's OK Cleopatra would say that's him on a lot of it she will smile laugh be angry giggle cry scream whatever good or bad right or wrong it goes like this the Pisces man every time this man falls in love he will think he found the love of his life. With a certain relative view this might be true for each one of his loves. every relationship in his life is quite different from the previous one in each one presents an important lesson in love. his spontaneous changeable nature will make him fly high and live out a romance until there is nothing more in it to be happy about. he would love with a full heart never holding back and approaches loved one with care and respect. Unfortunately, you can never know how much time will pass before he realizes that he is looking for someone different and better suited for his character. a Pisces man will use his flexibility an adaptive nature to plan in acting in a way he is supposed to a lot of times he be himself. at times when he is hurt Unfortunately this can make him feel lost as he plays a role until he doesn't know what the truth is anymore. he also shows love through sex, and he will choose to do everything for his woman desires. he is in a chase for satisfaction not only woman or woman look for this hello you don't get the most of it this man needs attention and satisfaction, but it rarely has any value if there is no emotion to follow. Still as a man he might find emotion in each one of his sexual relationships identifying romantic love with the love for women in general. this confusion can lead to infidelity dishonesty and the constant search for his identity. Pisces man in a relationship he will be devoted for as long there is strong excitement over emotions he feels. his relationships don't last exceptionally long unless his partner accepts his romantic impulse and finds a way to create a stable foundation for their relationship to last. he will not be exceptionally reliable an agreement with him could change on an hourly basis. This can be annoying or exciting but the only possible way to deal with it is to be spontaneous and let him choose the direction however chaotic it might seem. can you trust your Pisces man? This man keeps his feelings balled up when you keep bringing up the same topic of the same passed over and over again then the feelings he lets out to someone else if you're not caring for him or listening some women will. his approach to truth can be quite challenging for his partner especially if he is dating a fire sign proactive and straight forward. in general, he not always wrongs on everything sometimes he will be careful not to be dishonest about important thing's and when he finds himself in a Truly intimate relationship he will have no reason to fear his partner and it will be easy for him to be honest. dating a Pisces man, it is very romantic unplanned and magical. He will treat his partner with tenderness and respect ready to jump into any new adventure for as long as he can be what he is. if he starts feeling pressured when he's doing the right thing, he will feel the need to run off and create the incredible date with someone else because he was forced into it and put down. Experiences shared with him should be treasured when he is given a second chance and you allow it when he has changes for real because no one or nobody knows when the time will come when he won't feel like being a part of them anymore. please understand your Pisces man is important just as much as you. however social he might seem a Pisces man is a loner. he needs to spend some time with his thoughts and experiences and if he doesn't have a chance to do so You will be driving him crazy. although he will be ready to take on any possible adventure, he would also like to spend some time at home doing something creative that reminds him who he is. He has a great need to express his creativity. every Pisces man is a man on a mission, and he must know that when he is gone, he will leave something behind. there are often too many expectations he sets for himself, and he can have trouble meeting any of them getting lost in irrelevant things to avoid dealing with his own inner disappointment. Pisces man likes and dislikes he is caring tender and sensitive a kind of man who notice his feminine side and because of this he can listen compassionately approach his partner and understand the feelings of everyone around him. his biggest minus is his inconsistency and his unpredictable character. no one knows where he will feel tomorrow, and his relationships can fall apart in the day without any obvious reason. he is sneaky as a good heart will give his last. how to choose a gift for your Pisces man his number one gift is attention don't start then stop the needs and wants to feel loved and cherished and this can be done by creating anything to express how you feel. he is not someone who wants to get a book for his birthday or a technical gadget he will not be able to use. he wants something more personal something that doesn't require analysis and something he can feel. you can always go with soft materials things he can touch and smell for his senses to awaken. this is a man who will appreciate a drawing as much as a soft piece of clothing or a pair of socks for as long as attention is being given and he feels appreciated. do not want this man to be someone else or try to change him let him be himself this is a Pisces man. now you have Cleopatra will she use this or look at this is bad? now you have the Leo man this man falls in love in incredibly warm and cuddly way. just think of a tank lion peering a making room to sit in somebody's lap. love will only strengthen his ego and he will genuinely enjoy the chase of his prey since he belongs to fixed signs of the Zodiac, He might have trouble letting go of relationships that are outdated holding onto the shreds of emotion instead of searching for a new partner. this can take away a lot of his energy and he should always be free to feel the same warm and cuddly sensation that makes his heart jump. he is the King after all, and the true King has the biggest heart. the Leo man sexuality he enjoys the creative and inspiring act of sex. he doesn't need a partner to share the same sexual relations with every day but someone who will allow experiments and be secure enough to show their sexuality as openly as he would. although he sticks to some traditional values, he still likes his partners strong and willfully fiery enough for the passion to flow. he would never settle down for a woman with low self-esteem who thinks of sex as a routine or an obligation. he needs to be surprised seduced and he wants someone to speak of his abilities strengths and enjoy sexy communication as much as he does. alien man in a relationship when he finds himself in a relationship, he would do anything to show how gallant confident and powerful he is. This is not something that he does out of insecurity but something that he finds Necessary to seduce the subject of his desire. He will Show off make you laugh and be the biggest hero you could have ever hoped for. If anyone is waiting for Prince Charming, he might be found in Leo for he feels acts like royalty. unfortunately, this can sometimes be taken quite literally, and he can act as if he is a spoiled Prince lazy bossy and thinking that he is the center of the universe. however, he might still win you over by pointing out his incredible attributes but turn out to be quite a disappointment if you hope he will become less selfish. trusting your Leo man, a Leo man can't be trusted except when he simply doesn't care about you. this is not the man that will spend his time in guilt does not secure about his decisions and choices of partners. he will lie if he doesn't want to deal with the boring consequences of his words never out of fear.in general this is not the man who is afraid, and this is what can make him such a faithful and trustful partner. still there are times when he doesn't see the point of honesty because he doesn't really want to get too attached or close to anyone. if you want to see if he should be trusted don't obsess. Instead, simply ask yourself do you feel loved? dating a Leo man being with him is being with a King he is classy sparkly and pompous. If you are a shy Tinder soul you will probably not enjoy the gestures of love that sometimes seem like he only wants to look good not even to other people but to himself only if it's for a Queen to marry. it is especially important for his partner to build the intimacy during his outer performance, and this can be quite a challenge. the best thing to do is finish each day with a quiet conversation about him. don't put him down and think only of yourself you will push the Leo man away. the more you are interested in him the more he will be interested in you, and this will end up in the actual sharing. understanding your Leo man to understand him you would need to know his weaknesses but don't use them against him because you're the woman or something he did from the past. his weaknesses are sometimes hard to come by. he is not the secretive he just doesn't want to talk about things that are emotionally difficult, and he would rather spend time in his pool of personal satisfaction then swim in negative emotions. the most important thing to remember about Leo is that his seemingly superficial nature is not superficial at all. the depth of Leo reaches to a point in which no compromise must be made for everyone around him to be happy. he has a difficult task as a leader and a ruler, and he should be respected because of the responsibility that follows no matter if he is aware of it or not. the Leo man likes and dislikes he is open hearted grand in his gestures and easy to talk to. he is comfortable to be with for he will enjoy a relationship full of respect and warmth. he has this beautiful hug warmth. he has this beautiful hug that no other sign has. on the other hand, sometimes, he can be bossy pretentious and self-involved to the point in which it is impossible to be with his partner. how to choose a gift for your Leo man choose something that will accent his manly physique or character. She wants to show his big shoulders or his great hair. Pack your gift in warmth in orange yellow or red colors. stick to things with value that show how much you respect and cherish him. buy him some nice clothes or a pen or pencil. he will like thoughtful gifts just as much but only if you utterly understand his core and are able to pick out something he always dreamed of or always like using. play with his inner child and buy him a present that can bring him back to childhood or something that Sparks his creativity. this is the Leo man. now you have the Sagittarius man in love when this man falls in love it is nothing new. he falls in love quickly he must win the hearts of many. in general, it is good to keep this man on a distance for a while until his emotions stable. even though he will enjoy spontaneity and romances that start on a whim he will have the chance to deep in his feelings only when he has something to fight for. He belongs to the fire element after all, and it is always important for him to be active and challenged in his passion on his way to win someone's heart. the Sagittarius mean sexuality having sex with this man is fun. he doesn't suffer from the typical lack of confidence and as in everything in life he wants to have a good time in his sexual relationship. He can be quite promiscuous and change a lot of sexual partners, but this can make Him an excellent lover who understands how to satisfy his partner. he likes everything in abundance sex too. still this nature ruled highly of a man that's a strong believer on what he puts his mind to. if he puts his faith in one true love chances are, he will last in his relationships sometimes only out of conviction. if he does this will give him enough emotional depth to be someone's true love. when this Sagittarius man is in a relationship, he is sometimes simply not stable. it might be offensive to say that a Sagittarius man is unreliable, but this is the closet to the truth when it comes to his relationships. he might be perfectly reliable daily but who's to say how his feelings will develop tomorrow or in just a couple of hours the element of fire gives this man enough speed in his changes that he seems hard to contain. still when he finds himself in a relationship with a partner who can follow his pace there is a great chance, he will become committed faithful an unusually stable. the most important thing he needs to find in his relationship is purpose in a sense of a meaningful future. when you're trusting your Sagittarius man in general this is a man who doesn't lie very well. Therefore, he will rarely choose to do so even when he is unfaithful or falls in love with someone else. we can say that he can be trusted when it comes to things, he says but he cannot really be trusted when it comes to the stability of his emotional affection. He is also a man who will easily give in to all sorts of delusions and idealism and this can make him untrustworthy not because he lies to you but because he lies to himself and sees the world through. dating a Sagittarius man can be incredibly fun his big smile will make it impossible for you to say no to any of his new ideas and activities he suggests. his sometimes-ridiculous faith in lucky outcomes might make him choose extreme or even dangerous activities and he needs a partner crazy enough to follow but still smart enough to stop him when needed. this doesn't mean he means control but more of a rational mind to help him make the right choices. dates with him would never be boring and although he wants to go to the movies and have a nice dinner simple thing like bees won't satisfy his need for adventure. if his finances allow it is very probable that already on your second day you might end up with him in a jet plane to a distant destination. understanding Sagittarius men at times he is often misconstrued to be superficial and childish whoever wishes to form a quality relationship with this man needs to understand that the sign of a Sagittarius is a continuance of Scorpio while preceding Capricorn so there can really be nothing superficial about it. this is the man in search for truth and he won't rest until he finds it. this doesn't just mean he seeks honesty in his partners but his own honest feelings. most often he doesn't even know why he doesn't want to remain in the same relationship or why he needs that much change and adventure. this doesn't stop anyone around him to understand that this is because of his search for that one true direction. He wants to find the place of absolute synthesis and truth and only when he finds it with one person, Will he remain faithful and committed to them. Sagittarius man likes and dislikes he is unreliable childish easy loses focus and he can sometimes be pushy with the need to impose his opinions and convictions on others. on the other hand, he is optimistic full of faith in a better future and filled with energy to create anything he thinks or help those around him when in need. How to choose a gift for your Sagittarius man there is nothing easier than buying a plane ticket for your Sagittarius man to any destination. he will be satisfied with the bus ticket too but if he gets a chance to fly his gratitude will multiply greatly. He likes things big and colorful even when you see him only in black beige or Gray. You can always choose a book of jokes funny things children say philosophy and the search for truth. he will value a useless present if it is absurd enough So go with a traffic sign for his apartment or something similar, he thinks he'd never get. This is the Sagittarius man. then you have the Libra man. When a Libra man falls in love he will see the subject of his affection as a person he is going to marry he can be quite Dependent one feeling attractive and loved but you will know he loves you when he starts talking about marriage. this can happen at the beginning of a relationship and a Libra man can move too fast scaring his partner away with expectations then seen unreal. This is a consequence of the air element of Libra that gives this man speed and intent, with a need to follow his ideas through. the incredible thing about him is his ability to rush into love in marriage even though his sign exhausts Saturn and he would expect him to slow down and wait for the right moment. someone would say that he wouldn't take things that lightly, but the fact is he can't waste time or relationships with no future or depth. he simply thinks it is best to know where he stands right away. Libra man sexuality he can be one of the best lovers. he cares about his partner's pleasure and absolutely loves the creative satisfaction behind the act. in case a Libra man has a truly damaged sun he can be incredibly selfish and incapable of forming an intimate relationship. the biggest problem arises when he relies too hard on Saturn being too formal strict cold or staff. This can even lead to impotent in other problems with expressing his sexuality in a healthy way. the Libra man in his relationship he takes a lot of effort in his family. whatever the situation in the insult Department this is a man who will stay in a relationship for a long time if he decides to be with someone. he would not give up at the first sight of difficulty and he would trust his feelings without a doubt. in most situations he will remain calm and trying to show a chest wait to resolve any issue in his partner's life or their relationship. when he obsessively gives in thinking he found the love of his life there is a great chance he will put too much focus on his partner lacking the ability to turn to himself and build his own life. can you trust your labor man? this is a man who can be trusted. sometimes he is not a regular unmovable character that would never cheat. in his search for one nice he can change quite a few partners some of them coinciding in time. The additional problem to trust for a Libra man is his low self-esteem making him question every decision he must make. he was sometimes giving up on his principles chest to get confirmation of his attractiveness and his ability to win someone's heart. however, if he truly decides he wants to be with you exclusively he would never break his promise of Fidelity for as long as he is given the image of a perfect love he signed up for. when you date a Libra man is gallant, tactful well dressed and even better behaved and of course in most cases he chooses a partner that is the exact opposite. This can be a problem if he starts telling you how to dress or behave because this only speaks of his way to feed his bruised ego. no partner wants to be in this position with a Libra man. with clearly set boundaries and enough respect he will take you to fancy places art gallery's theater and occasions where you need to dress up. he likes to create a certain image and the best way to date him is to show an understanding for his need to show your love to the rest of the world. he will want to be looked at cherished caressed and touched in public even though he might have a problem showing his own affection among other people. understanding the Libra man, he is not easy to understand. his role in the world is to find general balance and you must see how tough an assignment this is. he must judge show us the weight of our souls and give in to absolute justice. too much responsibility makes him incredibly indecisive for he understands what many of us don't place this possibility for each decision he makes and a set of consequences that might follow. his ego is bruised, and his party seemed to be shuffled while he might be lost on his own character and wishes just out of a need to please others. in order to find peace this means needs to break all his dependencies be able to be alone and leave any image or opinion people might have about him without fear. he needs to become aware of who he is without the influence of others. Libra man likes and dislikes he may seem like an insulted child unaware of anyone else's feelings on one hand and fully aware of the world and the way to reach balance in another. He can be disrespectful in the most ridiculous passive way sometimes unrecognizable to the person he dates but he can also show an incredible understanding for his loved ones if he forms a strong emotional bond. how to choose a gift for your Libra man he probably wants something expensive., even if he doesn't seem like a material type a set of fancy headphones an expensive professional camera or shoes that you're never buy at that price will make him feel valued and proud. he always wants something that looked fancy with simple lines in, and even boringly moderate shape is set of colors. so, go for page Gray well black and white if you aren't certain of his preferences. some moderate green might come in handy too. the perfect gift for him needs to fit his size and his mind. in need to stimulate his intellect or be uniquely beautiful and tasteful. it doesn't have to be practical at all for its long as he expires him through beauty or real creativity. this is the liberal man. now you have the Virgo man when this man falls in love, he will ask himself if he is in love for all the time. SA mutable sign he might claim love and discover that it was it really the feeling of love in just a couple of weeks. he can be exceedingly difficult to be with for his emotions are as insecure as in any mutable Zodiac sign but with the element of earth that his sign belongs to, he is somehow strict in his expectations. even though he is quite loyal to his friends when it comes to searching for the love of his life he rarely lasts in a loving relationship until he meets someone who can always give him the perfection he seeks or until he gives up on that one perfect love. the Virgo man sexuality his sexuality depends greatly on other personal traits such as one's ascendant and positions of different planets in the Natal chart. in general, the sign of Virgo is everything but sexual and this man can be a truly uninspiring lover. his partner might have to force some creativity. the good thing is in the fact that each Virgo likes to serve and in search for perfection most men born in this sign would do their best to understand the anatomy of their partner and be able to truly satisfy them. still their insecurities are often disguised by simple boredom, and they can be quite critical toward their lovers. it is often not easy to be with a Virgo man if you don't obsess about every hair on your body and every scent you might emit all the time. The Virgo man in relationships depending on what he is looking for Berger can be a very satisfying man to be with or a very annoying one. he is dedicated to his partner, but he is ruled by Mercury, and this leads to a sort of double personality that cannot always be trusted. he can be quite superficial when it comes to emotional closeness and intimacy, but he is intelligent enough not to let go of the partner he is in love with. He likes his routine and needs some healthy choices in his life whether he is aware of this or not and it can make him demand in a relationship. he does live dependent on traditional values, and he will really like if someone will take care of him while he takes care of the world. trusting the Virgo man, he needs to have a strict and strong moral compass in order to be valued. he cares for justice deeply and he will act accordingly as an earth sign, he is always in search for physical pleasure or goes to other extremes denying himself of any Hedonism because of his religion or a system of beliefs. if he finds too many flaws in his partner, he will without a doubt search for another one. even the most loyal Virgos have this need, and they have trust issues themselves as a reflection of their own behavior. if he stops trusting you even though you gave him no reason to pay attention for, he might be dishonest himself. dating the Virgo man, the mutable quality of the sign gives him enough sense to make changes that are necessary to always keep their relationship fresh. he will want to take you to a place where the plates are always clean, and tablecloths white an iron so you can spill your tomato soup on them and feel guilty is here he will go with you to any place that doesn't contradict his convictions but in time he might get bored of your choices always in need for a change even though he belongs to the element of earth. he is often too practical but when he is swept off his feet, he will be surprisingly romantic and tender. he needs someone he can genuinely care about and dating him becomes at least until he finds your first flaw. understanding your Virgo man. This is a man that has one mission in life to fix something. until he does it will not be easy for him to relax smile dance and be as happy as you might want him to be. he is serious because he has some serious details to commit to an unless he finds a way to make constructive use of his mind at his work he might drive you mad analyzing your every word. Let him have those already used things and fix everything around the house. his hands need to be put to good use or he will tell you all about the bad use of yours. burger is a sign meant to fix all that was broken and why you get annoyed by him think if you were made and chosen to be fixed yourself. the Virgo man likes and dislikes he is dedicated intelligent and capable always ready to make the necessary moves to make more money or a better environment for those around him. who would gladly sacrifice himself for the happiness of those he loves? however, his love for his partner will often last much shorter than you would anticipate, and he is not that reliable or trustworthy as earth signs usually are. how to choose a Virgo man, this is not a man that needs that many surprises. everyone likes a nice surprise here in beer the most important thing for him is to honor traditions birthdays anniversaries and successes. he will treasure a pen a notebook a laptop or anything he can write on even if he claims he is not into writing. buy him a transparent mainly watch with all the gear wheels shown or any book on how stuff works. he will want to see how things are made or fixed and he will be thankful for all sorts of fine tools that allow him to do something practical that needs to be done now. if nothing else makes him happy you can always buy him an enormous puzzle of 5000 little pieces. this should keep him occupied for a while. this is the Virgo man. Now that the Aries man, the Aries man sexuality he is very sure of. he is not afraid to show initiative and is immensely proud of his body, even when his belly spills a little over his belt. it is easy to feel attractive in his arms since he is always interested in sex however messy you might look. Aries man appreciates when his sexual partner shows interest in his body and feels confident and secure enough to show their own. he has little patience for insecurity shame and overall lack of confidence so breathe in deeply and openly show how beautiful you are. an Aries man in relationship, relationships are not easy to Aries in general, but Aries men have special trouble when needed to connect to their partner feel compassion and think for two. he finds it much easier to do everything alone and finds it rare in a partner to have enough energy to follow his lead. Aries me is prone to his partner to stay independent financially and socially if a relationship with this man is to succeed. Aries man in love, when this man falls in love one way or another you will know. there are two extremes of his behavior in this situation. as a conqueror and a warrior, he will feel the need to fight for love, for the heart of the one he desires and will stop at nothing for this cause. this means he will be persistent and repetitive in his attempts to win the attention of the subject of his affection. the other extreme would be a lost Aries's man, Incapable of understanding his own emotions. this could make him distinct like he has lost the ability to speak or even angry because of the inability to show how he feels. either way his behavior will be obvious, and you will not miss the signals even if you didn't know him that well. can you trust your Aries' man? if you are just one of his conquests, he won't feel obligated to stay true. Aries men can be a sexual predator when he won prize offer the other Conquering his partners one by one. He enjoys the thrill of the game it needs to feel deep emotions in order to stop. in case you are a Princess he won over by pure chivalry, you can trust him. the only way for him to keep the knight image of himself is to be just sincere and brave. Dating an Aries man, he is not much of a romantic and will probably do things by the book. he will bring you red roses take you to a fine restaurant in might put you in a limousine if he really wants to seduce you. when you go to the movies, he will buy tickets for the new action thriller, even though you would like to see a romantic steak in the restaurant even if you are a vegetarian. he will expect to have sex on your first date and will go on expecting it every time you see each other. your phone conversations will be short message is rare except if you create a hotline you will use for sexual interactions when you are not unable to see each other. understanding an Aries man, he may seem like a brute following his instincts in rarely using his brain however smart he might be. still there is a soft side to him. if his loved one needs his help and support, he will show exactly how much he cares. when he feels respected and loved he will let his down and seemed like a cuddly bear at times. an Ares might be ashamed thought but when he feels trust he can't help it. there is a warm behind the act nature to this man something that needs to be discovered in time and is reachable by approaching him with a lot of tenderness however he might act. Aries man likes and dislikes an Aries man is attractive strong and confident always ready for something new and exciting. he doesn't lack initiative or character and it is a fun competition to win his heart. however, he doesn't have much sense for anyone but himself he can be rough selfish and impulsive while approaching every relationship he has as a fighting arena where he needs to show his supremacy. how to choose a gift for your Aries' man. everything sharp red colored and hot will be a good fit. if he doesn't already have a collection you can always buy him a Swiss knife a set of tools a hat or a pair of shoes or boats or some clothes and give him something practical to use. don't upset S about his presence if you would have any resulting expectations, he will never obsess about yours. this is the Aries' man. now you have the Taurus man because the sign of Taurus normally lacks initiative, Taurus men can easily get a panic attack when it is time to conquer the subject of their desire. there is a collision between their traditional values and their gentle nature. any situation in which they are not sure about their assessment of someone's emotions is an emotional slippery slope. when they decide to make the first move this will usually be a product of a long analysis of the way the other person was acting even though they might not even be aware of it. if a Taurus man is secure about the way he feels and understands emotions of his partner he will be a gentle lover who takes care of his loved one for an exceptionally long time. Taurus man sexuality, this man is not very creature when it comes to sex. he is also not your typical man even though he might seem like one because of his traditional views. while tender and aware of his partner he is a passionate sensual lover who likes foreplay as much as he likes to be kissed and caressed. he understands the importance of emotions and sex and can be one of the best lovers in the Zodiac, but only if he relaxes and put some energy into the creativity for enrichment of his sexual life. with proper motivation he is to discover and share the real joy of sex with the right partner. Taurus men in relationships, it is imperative for a Taurus man to move. he has a strange mean to lie around all day long and eat with someone else is prepared for him with a strong tendency to become his partners "spoiled son" instead of a lover. This is not a rule but there is a phrase in every Taurus life when they'd rather do nothing. The most important thing for them is to get out of the house every day. this is easy when the relationship is new for it will give him enough energy and motivation to be creative and interesting as

Venus should be. However, when a Taurus man starts living with someone he must stay on the move. if not, he can become so static that even he would be bored by himself. trusting your Taurus man, most of the time he won't say a word. if he does it will be something superficial or opinionated in a way that no true emotion is shown. although he is clearly emotional, he has real trouble showing it. his sexual desire that follows emotion is something that scares him for he doesn't know how to connect these two. it is not easy for him to relax enough to open and share his emotional and sexual world with you. this can lead to mistrust by his partner because there is no real clarity on his inner self. when he does open his heart to some way, he gives away the gift of ultimate trust that should be treasured. this is when you know he would never let you down. dating a Taurus man, if he doesn't take you to the same restaurant all the time dating him can be quite beautiful. he has a flair for romance and attractive he would do anything to win the heart of his loved one. the most wonderful side of dating a Taurus man is the relaxed state with no stress at all. he can stay at home and laugh at you while eating whip cream off your shoulder or take you to watch a sunset in another country. it will all be the same to him four he feels no pressure to do any of these things and can be spontaneous. However, don't expect him to go bungee jumping this is just not his style. understanding Taurus men, he a complicated me with a strong emotional side that is to be incorporated in a masculine world around him. he can often feel inadequate because of this tenderness he is aware of and sometimes tries extremely hard to get rid of his soft side although it is one of his biggest qualities. when he is sad, he will hide his feelings from the rest of the world and maybe even from people closest to him. he needs a lot of tenderness and patient to become someone's perfect man a Taurus man likes and dislikes this man is generous, tender and devoted but can sometimes be too stiff and unmovable. If he is aware of his weaknesses he can turn to sports or any sort of physical activity in order to feel more grounded and ready for action. If he falls into his inner state, there is a great chance he will be born to himself let alone his partner. how to choose a gift for your taurus man, if you want an easy solution buy him something practical like a T shirt., the tourist man is connected to food and the sense of taste, so many Taurus representatives like to spend some time in the kitchen. Therefore, any interesting kitchenware can be a good bit in case he already discovered how much he likes to cook. if you really want to make your tourist man happy put on a sexy bra and panties prepare a romantic dinner and bake a chocolate cake with his name written in colorful letters. this is the taurus man. now here comes the Gemini man, when this man falls in love it is hard to say how long it will last. he needs change in response to the excitement and the surprising nature of their loved one. why he feels emotion he thinks that it goes the eerie rarely asks himself it is just something that will pass tomorrow. enjoying the moment, he could truly get on their partners nerves if they constantly tried to make plans for their future together. this doesn't mean Gemini partner doesn't care but he needs spontaneously in his life because everything else makes him feel tied down. he is gentle exciting changeable detached it can certainly make a woman laugh. she is all those things in one person all in one day every day. the Gemini men sexuality, this is a man who gives little meaning to the act of sex. he has a youthful glow around him and will usually be potent for many years, but he doesn't care about sex as much as he cares about the excitement that goes with it. he wants someone to challenge him but not dig into his insecurities. he needs someone smart enough who says the right things at the right time. he likes sex outdoors and can be quite a lover. if he is in a long-term relationship, he will expect change in their sexual activities all the time almost as if he is frightened of the routine and what it represents. Gemini means to be on the move always changing partners positions or locations. Gemini men in relationships you can't say that a Gemini man is dependable or reliable. he has no intention of letting their partner down, but he is not aware of the speed of changes in his field of reality. when he is in love for real, he will have seasons in his feelings no matter the love. from spring and blossoming desire to winter and unbearable distance he is a difficult man to be with if you expect consistency. the only way he can remain in a functional relationship is if he finds a partner who is self-sufficient and fully independent. if he finds a partner who catches a glimpse of his winter and leaves him tube or waiting someone to love him in the exact same way as he loves but with a little more patience. trusting your Gemini man, this is not because he's not a liar he's not lying but there is no way to predict what tomorrow will bring to his mind or his heart. There are many things he can say in the heat of the moment, and these are all complex mathematical equations that you must decipher if you want to know if he meant to say what he said I understand what he wanted to say. However, if he shares his life with a partner with real emotional death able to feel his inner personality that doesn't change overnight, he is a lucky man who would never betray his partners' trust. dating a Gemini man, there is no way of knowing where he will want to take you out he is not one of those traditional men who has the need to make the first step and will gladly accept someone's invitation to any place that sounds interesting. if he develops feelings, he will surprise his partner with different places presents an all sorts of creative spices to their dating life. it is impossible to get bored with Gemini, unless they talk too much, and this is also something that can be changed with one conversation. the best way to describe the dating life of a Gemini is anywhere in anyhow for as long as it is spontaneous and carefree. understanding a Gemini man, the truth is his nature is not at all light and superficial but overly complex and hard to reach. if you are superficial yourself you will never get beyond Gemini's surface that everyone can see. this is a man distant from his own emotions and needs to get to the burning core of his heart but doesn't know how to do that. if he's been hurt by his family there is a great chance, he would never go deep enough to understand himself and being it is even more difficult for others to see him. if someone recognizes the core of a Gemini men, they will find that there is a root to all that childish charm and an incredible inner beauty. Gemini men likes and dislikes he is positive adventurous and surprising always on the move in ready to meet any life challenge. when he is truly in love, he shows his childlike heart pure and untouched. However, there is a lot not to like when he gets distant and simply doesn't care anymore. he can be unreliable acting like a spoiled child and scared of his emotions. how to choose a gift for your Gemini man, take him somewhere he hasn't been buying him a book with practical instructions give him anything that has letters on it or can be used to write chat or take pictures. he likes different electric gadgets strange small things that can be used for his phone or by his finger. he wants freedom to use his present once and then throw it away.

whatever you decide to give to a Gemini man top it out with a smile. that might be the only thing you both needs. this is the German man. now the cancer man when this man falls in love all his insecurities but instantly surface. cancer men tend to stick to certain rules of behavior in courtship because it makes them feel a bit safer and more secure. what this mean often fails to realize is the fact that what he must show counts for a lot in A world of relationships even though society seems to favor something else in a man. He is compassionate and sweet and should show his emotional side. the right partner will understand this immediately. the cancer man sexuality although he would very much like to be the best lover on the planet a probably senses he would have a shot he seems to have trouble showing his talents in the real world. The most important thing to remember here is that there is no real sexual satisfaction for this man without emotion to follow. Although he will rarely admit to this, the fact is he is incapable of being a sexual brute, even if he is all muscles and only speaks of porn. he means to feel love have eye contact and a partner who challenges his emotional side. Cancer men in relationships. A cancer man is sensitive to his partner's emotions and has the need to connect on a deep level. if he was badly hurt by his family situation there is a chance, he will be too afraid to open even with the seemingly perfect partner. he doesn't like conflict and will in most crazy situations stay calm. when he is irritating by something, he will probably say nothing but swallowing negative emotions might make him sick so it is important for a cancer to find a partner who will support his expression. he is tender and caring will probably never forget his partner's birthday and could bore some of the Zodiac signs crazy. if one is for an adventure without emotional base or purpose, they shouldn't choose a cancer partner. trusting your cancer man, the simple answer is yes. you can trust your cancer man. he does confuse privacy with dishonesty from time-to-time Anne has the excessive need to protect himself from the outer world by keeping secrets but when he decides to let someone into his world he will share almost everything with that person. if he does tell a lie it will usually be about a small thing that could benefit them both. A typical cancer lie usually involves a secret savings account other than that he is not prone to adultery the chase of young new partners or in a desperate need for a constant change of scenery. dating a cancer man, he will take you to a fine family restaurant where the food is wonderful. he doesn't need decorations or a fancy image too sweet his partner off their feet. depending on the situation he will be perfectly fine with a romantic walk a cozy restaurant or a dinner at home. this is a man that usually likes to cook and even if he doesn't have the habit to do so with the right partner, he might enjoy a romantic date in the kitchen. dating him is really nothing like being in an earthquake, but it can be wonderful romantic and flattering. understanding cancer men, this is a man with the sun in a sign of the heart love from our mother our family and our inner feeling of gratitude. because of this he may seem weak or something like a forced opposite of weak and it is important to realize how hard it can be to be with a man with an accented sensitive side. Although civilization is on its way to accept all sorts of human natures especially the emotional one it always seems judged by potential partners or wildly misread in general. a cancer man helps his family issues to resolve and accept positive or negative and it is always best to have a peek into his relationship with his mother in order to understand him better. when he is well raised with a stable sense of security this is a man anyone who is after a quiet family life would want. A cancer man likes and dislikes, he is tender sweet and doesn't talk too much. although his sensitivity can stays hitting but most of the time, he will show it when it matters and this guarantees relationships that last, if he doesn't underestimate himself and choose wrong partners. he is genuinely interested in his partners life rarely says things just to get someone to bed and is usually a safe choice to start a peaceful family with. on the other hand, he can be meaty and insecure, and some more energized signs could see him as weak and boring. how to choose a gift for your cancer man, he will like things with traditional or emotional value. don't choose anything too expensive or impractical for he has the tendency to pile things in the basement closet under a bed and in his partner's purse. a cancer man wants to receive a present that shows love, and the best choice is something that has a personal touch to it. if not, you can always go with regular presence such as close ties wallets or a perfume with a fine scent that he will like on you. Anything that concerns his tradition and family is probably a good choice for as long as If it's tasteful and symbolic. he is a Patriot and usually loved his country, especially the locations he is bound to by beautiful memories. if you are looking for something to really surprise your cancer partner buy him a plane ticket to a place he always wanted to visit. he will hardly ever expect that but most dream of some distant destinations. this is the cancer man. now this is the Scorpio man, when this man is in love, he gets really attached a can often come too close to his partner. to the best of his knowledge a relationship with someone is either a relationship with "the one" or not and he will never settle for less than what he knows is right for him. His emotions are deep and extremely hard to change once they are there, so if his partner Sparks his heart there is a bigger chance that his love will turn to hate ban for it to fade or disappear. he will be intense in his approach and often dismissed the tender side of his emotions, as if it were expected of him to not show how weak he can be. with deep feelings involved Scorpio man is capable of incredible compassion and emotional understanding. A Scorpio man sexuality a Scorpio is a feminine sign turn to the emotional sexual connection rather than anything else. This man can be anything from a soft hearted wonderful and tender lover to a sexual deviant a pervert that will scare his partners away. this depends on his level of restriction and inhibition emotional or sexual and it is sometimes hard to understand. Scorpion men in relationships, it is often that a Scorpio man can be obsessive, possessive and protective there, but the truth is he can also be loyal, supportive, compassionate and incredible in bed. This man must deal with unusual emotional death leading to his extreme sensitivity and his need to close his heart in order not to get hurt. The only reason he becomes vindictive is in his deeply emotional nature and is incapability so forgive the depth of his injuries. He may seem fatalistic as if everything were too big to handle for, he is intense and observes his life as a series of small depths unworthy of living unless it is lived. Trusting your Scorpio man, as everything else that is black and white in his world so is trust. he can either be unconditionally trustee in relied on or entirely detached and painfully distant making choices with no regard to anyone else's feelings. he has the need to always speak his mind and in general he will speak the truth. we might even say that his biggest joy lies in giving his observations of the hard truth then nobody wants to deal with. however, if he is angry enough at his partner his mother or the entire world, he could be back quiet man that you can look at all day long and still not recognize his intentions or his thoughts. dating Scorpio men, when on a date this man will care for his partner as if they were royalty. he wants to see a tender soul in his partner someone who needs his protection and holds on to values and convictions without a doubt. he will borrow his sweater when it is chilly outside but there is no guarantee he won't take it back and become unpleasant as you say something that hurts him for unknown reasons. there is a great chance he won't speak much slow in his decisions movements in change he will take you to places that he finds romantic, and this could be anything from his basement or a dark hole of a club to a vampire gathering in his front yard. depending on his previous relationships he can be quite open on the first day and show his true self immediately or be hard to crack always on the watch of getting hurt again. understanding Scorpio men, to understand a Scorpio you need to understand just how emotional he is. often sensitivity asks for a partner that is slow and tender enough. Therefore, this man will often end up with other water element representatives or even better earth signs. he is on the hunt for the love of his life someone to die with or die for and if this is not you, he will probably end your relationship before it even started. there is a feel to him that comes out of his connection to Pluto the ruler of the underworld and even the most positive optimistic Scorpios have this tendency to observe things from their ending point. this gives them the opportunity to use the most out of life and understand the practical value of their experiences. a Scorpio man likes and dislikes, He is deep emotional loyal Thanksgiving right to the point when he gets hurt by the smallest thing. he can be painfully honest liberating and obvious in his character and intentions, but he can also be mistrustful possessive and jealous and even aggressive when looking for vengeance. How to choose a gift for your Scorpio man. A perfect present for your scorpion man is something that he has talked about a long time ago and being forgot. he loves to be reminded of things that awakened beautiful emotions inside him, and the best thing to choose is the one he chose himself. Saints this sign exalts you raining he will be interested in technology and computers but usually his focus is turn to the discovery up his own depth. you can't

miss with a proper psychology book or anything that will help him understand the flow of life. Choose something that can teach him about alchemy. alternative methods of healing or an honest way to understand God. that is a much better choice than that long wanted encyclopedia on world wars. this is Scorpio man. now we have the Capricorn man, when a Capricorn man falls in love, the first thing he would do is start acting strange. he is not familiar with emotion in general and he will look at the subject of his desire as in extraterrestrial That came down to earth only to confuse him. this will pass with the first love maybe with the 2nd but there are all ways that probability then he would look at his loving partner as someone from another world or time. he will have to learn slowly how to act in order to win someone's heart. if he is lucky enough for his first stroke of love to be returned there is a chance he will remain in the same relationship for an exceptionally long time maybe even for as long as they both shall live. he is one of the most stable stubborn deeply emotional signs in the Zodiac. he never takes anything lightly and he refuses to be superficial which makes his emotions profound and real when they finally surface. a Capricorn man sexuality he has enough sexuality and stamina to endure in incredibly satisfying sexual relations for an exceptionally long time. on the other Capricorn in is ruler Saturn inhibit every action that has no depth, and he will not be much of a lover unless he builds a true emotional bond first. when he does that's a different story, but he needs time to understand that what is needed for a great sex life is emotion. a Capricorn man in relationships. if you are looking for a man at which you can point your finger and say "He is difficult" that would be a Capricorn man. He is not easy to be with as an earth sign nor as someone who sun is ruled by Saturn. he can be two straight in his expectations might be impossible to meet. if he doesn't find the true magic of love, he will be possessive but stubborn without any compromises made or any flexibility. this is exactly why it is so profound and inspiring to win his heart and see him melt change and open for things he would never consider before he meets you. when he loves someone there is rarely anything, he wouldn't do for his loved one and it is safe to say that he is prepared to stay with the right partner forever and never doubt his decision or his emotions. trusting your Capricorn man. without a doubt but only if he has decided to be faithful. honest and Monogamous. In any other scenario everything can be expected, and he will act in the way he thinks appropriate. in general, he fears the feeling of guilt and as far as his awareness goes, he will not hurt like or cheat on anyone intentionally. still, it is a sign ruled by Saturn the planet of our unconscious and he sometimes loses control over his choices not even aware of it. this is the reason why he likes to control every little thing thinking he can avoid his own irresponsible actions. dating a Capricorn man. a Capricorn man will do everything right he will take you to the right places respect you take you home pay for your cab and hold your door. The ruler of his sign is exalted in Libra, and he knows that his biggest asset is his ability to be tactful well behaved and gallant. he will seem like this strong incredibly mature man who knows exactly what he wants and is afraid to get it. he will love being a date with someone who admires him but also keeps a rational distance an remains secretive. Understanding a Capricorn man. it is not easy to understand a Capricorn man. he seems to be cold and distant way too rational a critic, but we rarely stop to realize that he is afraid of failure strict toward himself and always trying to remain in control. He doesn't want to make a mistake for he understands the consequences of any action better than anyone else. this makes him cautious careful not to challenge karma Ann focused on himself and his practical goals they give him the idea he has life under control. he builds walls in order to stay protected sabotaged. scolded or even left by his father or other influential role models. when you get to know him and see his soft side behind these walls you will never want to be without him again. a Capricorn man likes and dislikes. he is strong reliable confidence in sure of his choices while at the same time practical and focused on his goals with a perfect plan. on the downside he can be demanding cold and distant UN compassionate and strict whip expectations that make everyone around him feel guilty or inadequate. how to choose a gift for your Capricorn men always respect special occasions and be as practical as you can. he can surprise by his openness for all sorts of weird things but before you get to know him it is best to stick to the traditional historical educational useful gifts that can last for an exceptionally long time. he has an understanding for an art with a lot of detail small but expensive signs of affection and likes things neat and to the point. choose a present that make sense that's probably the best way to put it. this is the Capricorn man. when this man falls in love, he will not exactly know how to show it. on one hand he will want to show exactly how exciting and incredible he is but on the other he will have trouble communicating how he feels. traditionally this is a sign rude by Saturn and it is clear how detached and unemotional this planet can be. in order to find ways to express his love an Aquarius man needs to build a sense of inner security and confidence, and this is sometimes hard for him to do. if he is to trust his own feelings they need to go deep, and this can provoke an unnecessary negative and a bit dark approach to true love. Aquarius man sexuality, he can have sex anywhere anytime and he needs a partner who can follow. his sexual appetite is big, but he can strangely go without sex for months. behind this behavior that many might find confusing hides the strength of his convictions and the entire belief system that most people don't even connect to sexual experiences. if he believes for some reason it is best to be alone for a while anyone around him might claim he is insane because the perfect woman is standing in front of him, and he was still stay alone passionately believing that this woman will wait if she is perfect. however, in most cases he will want to have sex often and if he is not in a serious relationship, he would like to change partners and not exactly be shy about expressing his sexuality. the Aquarius man in relationships an Aquarius man can be difficult to be with. his sun is in detriment, and this makes him vulnerable to all sorts of issues whip respect and sometimes makes him take everything that is said way too personally. he will not be hurt that easily because of his extraordinarily strong mind but the field of constant disrespect might make him distant and detached as if the person he is with doesn't deserve to understand his personality. this can be challenging even for a partner with an extraordinarily strong personality and the most important thing here is to set clear agreements on the way both partners will approach each other as soon as the relationship starts. trusting your Aquarius man most cases this is a man that can be trusted unconditionally but he will often be unreachable in a way that frustrates many signs of the Zodiac and awakens their own general lack of trust in relationships. he will never lie on a whim even when he seems like he would and if he decides to do so it shows a much deeper problem in his relationship than a simple unconscious need to cheat or let someone down. dating an Aquarius man, he will probably be late on your first date maybe on the 2nd and most certainly on the third one. his reservations will get cancelled in the meantime and the waiter will look at you as if he is sorry you ended up with this guy who didn't get a haircut for weeks. being you will have no choice but to go para gliding because what else could be more interesting than that? by the end of the date you will ask yourself if you were on a date at all or doing something you would do with an artistic weirdo friend. Although this will most certainly recognize you are Aquarius man in this paragraph. understanding an Aquarius man. he is talented Idealistic and Humane sticking strongly to his beliefs and guarding his ideals with his life. his mission is not to irritate everyone around him but to set them free of their prejudice and superficial rules of behavior. It is not easy to understand him because he doesn't use the usual forms of communication to show his inner self. most of the time he will simply hold on to the strength of his mind in have a distant dignified attitude that leaves no room for a closeness. if you manage to reach his core you might find that his image needs some true fireworks in his heart. Aquarius man likes and dislikes. he is exciting to be with intelligent free of prejudiced and fast. he will have no problem with his partner's history and will rarely be jealous. When we consider things, we wouldn't like in an Aquarius man you would see someone nervous edgy, strict in his convictions an Interestingly inflexible. How to choose a gift for your Aquarius man any modern shiny technical gadget will do. He will act like a little child if he gets a new laptop or a telephone with an instruction manual longer than your average encyclopedia. he wants to read anything from labels on a detergent bottle two science fiction novels. this is a man who doesn't care much about his birthday or Holidays but would love to be surprised buy something he really needs or a work of modern art that caught his eye it's any possible moment. This is the Aquarius man. now like I said about women also goals for men as human beings every man is not the same some follow Zodiac signs some don't. some men might say that that man not me that's not my sign some may agree some may not everyone is title to their own opinion. I don't worship this with Zodiac signs or judge anyone I put this in here because I respect other people's opinions facts thoughts feelings and what they think. so, to continue Cleopatra (THE WOMAN) that's a Leo the Queen wants to be the ruler of If R even the last word and me the Pisces in my ways of messing up that I have still growing up and still must learn. I'm not perfect I have a long ways lots of us do but back to what I was saying about me myself the Pisces man when I was with Cleopatra (THE WOMAN) it's so incredible how we represented love on our times can be wrong at times for each other swear up and down One no more than other the Leo women Cleopatra was caring selfishly about her own needs Been she will say that's not true you know I love you on everything and she will say she wrong in her time. She was incapable of forming an intimate relationship with me let alone Pisces. although it might be the obvious reality two Pisces when they are in a relationship with the Leo partner. in return the Leo women will think of Pisces man as weak an unrealistic completely separating from their own desires and the strength of their body or emotions. the truth is that the Leo and Pisces can both be incredible Lovers, but they will rarely discover this together. their roles and characters scene to be too different for them to find a way to coexist in a satisfying sexual relationship. another problem is the Leo wants to be the ruler over the Pisces this means in ways in a practical sense this means that Leo will burst the bubble of Pisces and endanger their sensitivity. idealism and go against their beliefs. this will ruin the romance between them and make it impossible for them to find any magic while they are together. Leo's openness and directive miss will make Pisces feel ashamed and rushed and their sex life could be delayed indefinitely until Pisces partner feels secure enough to get naked. because of differences in their approach to sex Leo will in most cases seemed like an insensitive brute unless Pisces start understanding their emotional depth even though it is so different from theirs. the best way for these partners to find a language that can sustain their sex life is by building emotional trust first and worrying about sexual satisfaction later. Sometimes they will seem dishonest to one another not because they lie but because their characters seem unreal. The Leo will think the Pisces is crazy or on drugs and the Pisces will feel sorry for the Leo and their lack of faith. The Pisces and Leo communication and intellect ideals Pisces have could be shattered by the approach of Leo if they get too close to one another. they could share many interests due to the creative power of both signs. Pisces will easily give inspiration to Leo, but the problem is in the way Leo might use it. The best way for them to create a safe surrounding for both partners is to stick to the subject they are individually interested in. a Leo is a warm sign deeply passionate about their doings and their desires. Pisces will rarely show the same initiative to realize any of their dreams and this their greatest difference. since Leo always shines a light on our virtues and shortcomings, they will not miss a chance to show their Pisces partner how unrealistic they are. this could help Pisces build a more realistic approach, but it could also affect their confidence and hurt them through a difficult perception of the world. the Leo and Pisces emotions both individuals are extremely emotional each extremely high in their own way. the fire elements women Leo belongs 2 makes them passionate and gives them the need to fight for their loved one and their emotions. Pisces is a water sign in much more passive showing their passion through the flow for anything convinced that perfection doesn't need fighting for and that real treasures are spontaneous and free of conflict. the middle point for these partners is in realization that not everything needs to be one as much as not everything should be uninfluenced. although true emotions are supposed to develop without difficulty sometimes life is still this is not something that happens all the time and sometimes things need to be let's go because they don't belong to us, and we don't belong to them. the Pisces and Leo values. it is interesting how much both partners will value clarity and honesty. Pisces understands the necessity of lies, but still lives for clarity of the mind and the realization up their true inner self. a great link between their worlds of values is in Leo's heroic nature they seem to have roots in a fairy tale of Pisces. as much as they will both values their individual set of beliefs, they will be able to find middle ground in the grandiose Character of Leo and the idealizing Nature of Pisces. Pisces and Leo shared activities and as a fixed mutable sign, they will have trouble synchronizing their need for changes in new activities. although the Leo woman is a fire sign always ready to start something new, they would like to stick to their routine and showed themselves in all the usual places every day. the Pisces man at times wants to be invisible and they will change the scenery often for people not to recognize them. Although they could share some interest and have activities, they would like to share they were rarely stick to the same place in same actions together for exceptionally long. Leo and a Pisces together spread entirely different kinds of love. the problem isn't in their element or dear connection through the fall of Neptune the ruler of Pisces. when they get attracted to each other they will be subject to the risk of great damage to their beliefs at times their inner faith and usually succumb to mutual disrespect because of a simple lack of understanding. The beauty of their relationship could be developed through the fairy tale approach of Pisces if they build the heroic image of their Leo partner to the point in which other differences between them fade. this is the Leo women and the Pisces man together Cleopatra and me. see Cleopatra was selfish and didn't understand that when she prayed and asked God to answer her prayer and God did she was not thankful for what God did because if she was she should would of changed herself as a good man of me changing I was pulled in different directions I was calm cool honest with a good heart informal and caring but I was not cheerfully giving all the freedom I need it fairly I was a faithful husband lover and loyal husband but when I was put down ★★★★ on a foot on my neck and my freedom was smothered an not respected I felt nervous an nasty really restless and slip and slide away to stick Anne stay around. she did not have a most reliable way to ensure loyalty is to have complete Faith in God in my integrity to let me know my love and his support is needed and appreciated. I know Cleopatra was warm hearty what can I messed up plenty of times and she's a real strong good woman turned into a bitter evil woman but after she said she forgave me in church in the circle of partner counseling in front of God myself and other witnesses and the bishop. with my charm and kindness, I calmed Cleopatra down. I listen to her with a close ear an open heart. Cleopatra also taught me how to assert myself and fight back in to stand tall. Her emotions where 100% mines were not in her eye's thoughts mind and actions towards me. it does not feel right when someone falsely accuses you it makes them feel like they're doing it because you're bringing it up the Same topic over and over again how would you feel? Like I stated before the silent woman is the latest woman's cry she don't want no one to read or lead her mind she knows love there for she gives love a man cheats with ★★★ ★★★★ a woman cheats with her minds her mind never stops going even when she sleep she's thinking when the man is sleeping the woman is up thinking please don't say a real woman won't do that I won't do that because I already know every woman is not the same but still she has good and bad in her and have done right and wrong no one is perfect then when you have women say I don't do that nasty stuff yeah really you let the Right man touch them. If it's too hot gotten out of her kitchen, she got to have the last word you can't win a debate with her it's either her way or the highway. A whole bunch of women can't stay together in one house 2 Queens can't be in one Castle 2 bulls can't be in one thing together and roar. only one lion can be King and one Queen. a woman has more game than a man. Some women take it's slow especially on certain times and days depending on what type of mood she's in every woman not the same you have some women or a lot been through of things of past with men can have curse other men out for nothing because in the mind men are not no good in all of them are not the same but if a man or men Are acting this way then you need to forgive them for themselves and for the next woman that comes along so they won't hurt that next woman that comes along because how he been hurt because the woman is different from the man And they feel in their own way that all women have been taking through more than men so they get treated different. Practice what you preach women when you tell someone to forgive and move on when they can't do something you have a hard time doing whip in yourself it's not easy for no one but don't make it as a weapon because you a woman or are you a man or what someone did to you and they done moved on with dear life and you still holding on defense with your hand in your wondering why you can't get to the other side. I believed in myself Cleopatra her children and I shouldn't got treated like I did, and I love them all.

Chapter 17

A woman just doesn't need love and satisfaction so does the man to understand what goes on in each other mind is knowing the soul of the body humble and reaching out to please one another. Another reason why a lot of women can't be satisfied because of things from the past before she has any hope of moving on from her present or future. Then Being so angry and bitter being dismissive two you're a partner emotion if can be meaningful and powerful things what we don't realize is that sometimes-verbal abuse can be worse than physical abuse sometimes both are wrong a lot of peoples ignore verbal abuse and physical abuse it can hurt in all kinds of ways. You know how Cleopatra hurt Jeffrey so bad I was pushed into going my way feel my pain woman and men. I had to go get help for myself I was about to kill myself I was going crazy and insane she did not understand I put myself in the hospital locked up from doing something else see men do hurt and go through pain see the women don't know by being blind her guilt or innocence in the past that will hurt and bother her partner. I know when you give your man your all and your trust you're afraid I understand that you just don't give trust back just like that and if you act out in a way that you can't control or handle that you have for giving where you think you will lead back to with common sense and common courtesy and you be so smart to be in what situation? bringing up the past is not healthy when you do this you don't want to be happy or other peoples or your partner to be happy or the people around you. It is and seem an awfully bad limited and miserable way to live. When Jeffrey told Cleopatra sitting down being humble not controlling I'm dealing with things too in our partnership not you alone he doesn't know no partnership that is perfect since everything gets to be his fault and on him he told her I'm dealing with you in your vengeance everyday bitterness anger hate and envy with pride being very moody. This behavior happens all the time she doesn't see that was a red flag on our relationship no she saw that's a red flag in my stop sign to hold up and take down with I say so when I get ready. When I felt like it was a threat to our relationship I put in for the help the 60% being the better man and what she said I am meant it I'm hard on him a lot of times just apologize but show no actions. For a relationship and a marriage to work you both need to be honest and open trusting and patient. It is drama down the road because it be no forgiveness with a forgiving heart with God's love. It be our way our feelings without God we just be saying a lot of time I have got you're not God saying all kinds of crazy things we say things that we mean that we don't mean and don't put action into stop and how to deal with it handling it in a right way not a perfect way. Now it does not have to be in cheating or lying no trust financially no love, it can also be told how God in flicks the inequality of the fathers alone the children and their children's children to the 3rd and the 4th generation. Through God proclaims his mercy earlier in these verses, he also revealed the long reaching impact of iniquity from parents to children. We go in certain direction due to the things raised up by parents even family members we do what they do or see and what they do if we don't do that the SIM and curses that be placed upon them come upon us in different ways on other things it can be the same in some different it comes and shows in different forms. We learn what we are shown and taught. It is positive to break the cycle with God and our actions but then other times it may be iniquity a generational sin. It can be to anger and substance abuse racism no love attitude unforgiveness physical or sexual abuse profane language drugs adultery lust pornification drama fights gossip any type of things that does not have to do with God then it comes back and forth where the couple marriages relationships point the finger at one another but but but. You then tell each other where your cycle is this from your family then tell the partner tell the same thing back maybe like a car race driving against one another in different cars not together pushing on their own gas paddles to win and what wind up happening? They get into a car accident they get hurt some die some be unconscious some be blind and can't still let go of the wheel and take over the wheel and still be driving with the car smoking and on fire they don't care some can be in a coma come out the in star right back driving and what happened to Jeffrey and Cleopatra. I never met one person or a relationship that didn't have iniquities and cycles until Jeffrey met Cleopatra it was all his fault he did her wrong he sent and I'm the one with cycles and family problems spirits curses and that's good what happened to him, and he deserve what happened to him. You know Cleopatra didn't sit down with Jeffrey she always screamed yell didn't recognize how to help the problem he was the problem he created the problem. The problem was on me all on me everything in our relationship of years being together you know that's like a pastor Bishop or anyone getting saved and when they get saved they say since they been saved for 10 years 20 years or how long short time or long time they never ever seen no more after that isn't that a lie? Correct me if I'm wrong. God knows that's the truth what I'm saying God will not go against what I'm saying is the truth. Instead, all Cleopatra did was get defensive with Jeffrey about his. Her love her husband her family her soul mate we both was in and out of sin he took responsibility for his behavior. When she took him back being forgave him while he was doing good being married being said while he was doing good she wished she wouldn't of never would of took you back make up a lie that he did a sin with a woman or other women when it was not that it was her sent action in mine coming back to apologize to me for messing up telling me I was cheating again with someone when I wasn't. A lot of women will say so if you know you wasn't being why you listen to her and let that bother you and didn't just keep praying and do you and keep doing what was right? Because I couldn't do it all by myself it takes 2 and she was pushing me away I want to and needed my wife love I needed my help mate!! Hug forgiving me was the biggest issue to straightening out the places she was bent in our partnership. See then when this unforgiving sin and these cycles was passed on the inner vows are self-directed. These are the things that Cleopatra said I'll never treat my children or my partner like my mother did with me and the way she did her husband my stepfather talking to him any kind of way and me telling her mom you can't just talk to him like that but then laughing at it later saying you all can't handle a strong black woman but said it was wrong and I knew it was wrong but can't change your actions and got the nerve to tell someone else about theirs they got some nerve I know I do. I was hardheaded a lot of times then say I'll never be poor again my man or anyone got me this way and forgot about richer or poorer. Being it be let another man or woman talk to me that way. At least put last, he or she will never hurt me like that again they better watch God got something for them speaking and claiming things. See I was trying to teach Cleopatra about inner fouls but a man that's a fuck up and like do shit she said can't teach her anything she's the instructor that's the instructor for school the Christian instructor the woman the mother the right path not getting into trouble or starting trouble alright telling me let it go but not doing the same in her mind I'm not trying is not enough is the same thing she's angry. See the problem with inner self and inner vows is that it assumes personal control over your life. When she made God, a promise being herself being me did she have personal control humble with God and her for real with that life first like I learned kidding yourself right with me and God when you make yourself a promise you make yourself Lord over that area. It was said instead of you ought to say if the Lord wills, we shall live and do this or that but now you boost in your arrogance. All such boosting is evil. Every woman has a different life lives a different life go through an experience different things same thing for men. Inner vows can kill us and our soulmate each other keeps Jesus away from us or you as well at the same time of growing and protection it doesn't do nothing but separate us the woman swear she knows it's all because of the man/ husband mistakes when her sins are cleaned, and she becomes teachable, and the man is unteachable in her eyes. The woman will look at the husband and say you need to pray and repent and pray for that curse your family has on you but then she has one until she says she does because you can tell her something and it's over just like that when you telling her to pray it's oh ok yeah alright this is not over or just not saying nothing or how that woman is or how she hanging herself and that situation at that time because every woman is not the same. See when a woman cheats, she cheats with her mind her emotions her heart is doctoring it can be for all types of reasons every woman not the same. A woman is a God since human being in a God's gift to man a lady. What I'm explaining to women is that you will never be free from the mistakes you made blaming others and mistakes others did to you until you repent be free but give yourself ask God forgiveness to leave that issue with Jesus and move on from harmful iniquities and inner vows not take them back to yourself your husband friends coworkers family members etc. This only makes your problems worse bring more darkness towards you and in you. See the woman will look at the man at how he lives what he is saying his actions must be on point there's no such thing as just leave the woman alone walk away all the time let her have her way that's a puppy playing with you. For both parties it's not only what you say is how you both live. See now today you have women and men putting their parent's 1st and children before their marriage therefore a man shall leave his father and mother and shall cleave to his wife, and they shall be one flesh. Women this don't mean or is not saying what you saying I need to stop talking to my mother or father I must cut them off when debates come with disrespect no we or I or no one is saying that only for the disrespect respect is due to a dog! it's the principle because if the wife is dis respected what happens? What out now!! Now today with bad times and good times in marriages it's not the same they don't know a lot of them they just go by what they have been taught from their parents or whoever taught them and brought them up that we have a good education and respect in God but in this area we are not good in how to talk to someone or be married because we saw our father and mother do it we knew it was right some no it's not but when they get into their relationship they still do it why? Because the curse the action the thought the soul the mind the teacher taught it like when I was raised to see my family I saw them do drugs fight women fight men kill peoples go to school not go to school go to church pray not prey argue fight no they're right love not love and look when I got married I didn't have a father role model at all on how to treat a woman but when they get married today these relationships change because in order for the marriage to work you have to prioritize. Instead of your father, children, mother coming first God and then your spouse must now come first. The marriage comes first not anything else it works in the 1st place for better or worse richer or poorer sickness and health death do us apart. Anyone anybody can see anything about your wife or husband that's your spouse not theirs. People can say anything go around telling everyone but only person back your marriage up is God and yourselves with action not only no man. The reason why Jeffrey and Cleopatra partnership stop was not all only him but because the man no good with his sin she has well stop listening to him and start listening to other people's come back and tell me what her mother said about him, her and everyone else and cry on her feelings being hurt see when you be around misery hurt peoples this what you become bitter angry and hurts depressed coming back to your husband or white when you tell her you not listening to me and you telling her you not listening to me so if you are not listening to one another how it's one partner fault women? Come on now is that smart vice versa on men to Cleopatra stop having time for our partnership our relationship us one soul there was no improvement. You a human being I'm not going to say man or woman wife or husband or both I'm just going to say person when a person have improvement in themselves and have proven themselves to God themselves and they saw me and the person is blind and can't see it and they still taking out one that person what they have whip themselves clean and the person says I don't care I need more than that that's not enough but you don't know they are being selfish and can't see what's good and it hurts more when they say you can't make me when you love them because they knew they felt they love and trust was taken for granted now it's an ongoing continue get back until it's a breakup or divorce because they said to you right back at you. At them first when they say I shouldn't have never taken you back they don't love God them self or you with chest then words itself and being in front of you right now they will mean it but go in a room by themselves to the Lord asking forgiveness and repenting it was wrong but telling you straight back in your face it wasn't. A woman does seek security and leadership with God first wife the husband over the wife as the head not the controller with Christ spirit of love and sacrifice. A man just doesn't be dominant at times a woman does too. She can be on a bad day from work in a bad mood someone pissed her off the children her boss in the moon she's in. You know Jeffrey was waiting for Cleopatra to change that mean he stopped waiting for her he changed by getting himself together and started standing up he thought that it would change the entire equilibrium of our partnership she fooled him because he couldn't do it by himself because no matter how he changed she saw him as the same person it was after he change all that time every single day. You know Jeffrey thought of himself when he hurt Cleopatra feelings and broke her heart because he was thinking of only himself because if he was thinking of her he wouldn't have did what he did to her that takes a lot of him to say and he mean that with everything in him to give action meaning and passion but her hurting him what does she feel because it's not no funny way a woman shows she has hurt someone or man/husband she will not let him know at times in certain ways putting up walls and boundaries not caring because she's afraid she will be hurt again being selfish tired and fed up but it can be too late for her as well of her selfishness of feelings going overboard but don't think with in herself she's wrong not one moment. You know in times in life someone needs guidance I seen this man named Leroy that knew my father he had an Expedition truck and was a drug addict and a dope dealer but then he gave his life to the Lord he stayed out drugs for 30 years and stop selling drugs and he used his testimony as helping people and made him stronger and a changed man so he pick people off corners sleep on drugs alcoholics teenagers relationships marriage couples anyone homeless all kinds of people he took them to programs he did not to worry or care about what would happen to him. He went to go just do it you have peoples in this world need that type of help I have that kind of heart whatever it is I can help within reason people I do my best from my heart. See in a relationship with each other there's no 60% for the woman wife and 40% from men/husband the health love support God first that the both of you are willing to receive influence from each other meaning controlling yourselves that your marriage is shared one with God you both. The women now today look at only the man who dominates a relationship or marriage the dominance is what creates the damage. The children also see examples of the mother that's the white putting down the father that's the husband of pastings and not treating him equal and not sharing input on decisions and doing it with the children and not doing it with the husband making him pay even more. I started to make decisions with clear patches at vice sit down hold my hand close a humble myself even when she rushed me, and I raise my hands up in the air with her provoking me saying you're going to hit me like you used to and a lot of times I will walk away and go for a long walk. I learned how to control myself and still get cursed out when she will call my phone from me walking away. Jeffrey was a man of value because he shared his thoughts with Cleopatra, he shared his facts, opinions without fear she didn't value his thoughts his action and attitude were go towards her to earn everything from her back. My thoughts were not important to her Because with a Peace of Mind when I sat on the bed to talk with her she would say loud to me who the hell you talking to about that? who the hell you been listening to or telling me stuff I gave God my energy first then he hurt I knew it had to take work and I knew just like that she was not going to just start trusting me just like that. Jeffrey stopped putting things in the way he wanted them to be he put in effort to understand Cleopatra and his actions showed it because she kept apologizing for wrongs with she saw him showing his actions she didn't just mean them he worked hard to listen to her and understand her as well. If you were to bring her face to face sit her down on a TV show or just in front of me or a witness in with her when you took your husband back and you forgave him did you not argue with him falsely accused him? Put him down call him a fuck up and he asks you not to bring this in to the relationship because if you do you will bring spirits worse than him in skeleton bones out your closet or demons and did he not also say when you forgave him did you mean it from your heart don't just say it with your mouth and he asks as a man if you need more time I'll give you that is this a man of God that he knew God gave him another chance and not to play with it. She will say I gave him another chance and he was cheating back with the same woman again I did yes why? She pushed me because when Cleopatra was my girlfriend I cheated on her then I didn't come right back to her I went to my godmother house to get me right as a man after I broke up with the other woman I cheated with on Cleopatra. I stayed with my godmother and then for a while I went back to Cleopatra she went to counseling with me it was not easy it was pain in hell but when she sat me down and said she forgave me being kept me all that time she did not know she broke a promise with God when she said I'm taking you back really we took one another back and tell the man you love you forgive him and get on your knees bow down to the Lord and ask him to answer your prayer be careful what you asked for because we asked for things really ask God for things and don't keep our promise watch what you ask I for because God gave me back to Cleopatra and if it was not God it was her speaking it's in claiming it's on me after I changed. How she was treating me and her actions on how she was doing me so what did she think she was getting out of that. If my son was to get out of a drug program and he was seven years clean no matter how many years and then stole everything at my house and I forgave him when he moves back in and I bring up what he did, argue with him every day, bring the past back up, he's not going out there getting on drugs and I'm falsely accusing him day by day saying you stole my money you have a lot of people say ignore that that's easy but they don't feel until it's done to them like I couldn't take a woman cheating on me what man will? We are humans but if I can't do this to my son or anyone what will happen? You know I seen people pick at people with these problems they know they stop getting on drugs and they go to pick them pick on them and take drugs to them and people be hurt by this they have feelings man they say Bay be weak baby a punk baby soft what does God say. Like some peoples use to say to me you that same person you still robbing you still selling drugs. It can be anything like my brother in Christ we were in a restaurant one day and his ex-wife Kathy saw him, and she said you still ★★★★★★★ everything you see loud to him in front of his kids off her being bitter 10 years saying she forgave him she started laughing and walked away with a lot of friends start laughing he started crying. I said it's alright brother the tongue is a double edge sword watch what you say. Now would that be alright for that brother to call his self a Christian and walk up to that sister if she were on the street homeless and say your ass always asking for food and money get your ★★★ up and find a job? No, it wouldn't so be careful what you say to people how you treat them this and on everyone. Women you don't roll your eyes when your spouse has a different opinion you don't judge one another and don't ignore one another you put all an energy into God in your loved one. See I let the control thing go I thought what it was to make me a man and how to have sex and the way that made a coward I made sacrifices I let the need to always be right allowed it's called give and take Jeffrey told Cleopatra she was right all the time to keep us happy he had to always be right, but he changed that. Cleopatra came with her attitude I'm a strong black woman and you can't deal with or handle me you think I'm one of them hoes in the streets what she will say towards Jeffrey and make sure he knew it. He would let it go for her to win mostly every argument to earn her back but when he started getting taking advantage of that was enough. It made it worse when I gave my opinion or freedom of speech

when it was fair I talk too much shut up I can only talk when she spoke
to me or ask a question because it only made it worse to say anything to
a bitter woman that blames someone for everything I did it even with
the Bishop in church to communicate from God to communicate with
Cleopatra because it was important to stand for what I believe in not for
her ways but in minor things keeping your mouth shut is a necessary
compromise. when God does send me a woman of God a submissive
wife it will be trust because we will be going to only God. See today
they are important needs that a husband and wife need to meet for each
other not mostly a wife or woman. See a woman will ask questions at
times she will ask, and this don't have nothing to do with cheating or
can't ask question at all. Where did you go sweetheart? Where you been
at? What did they say? How was your day? You alright? It is different
questions like how you feel about this or that it could be anything she
be trying to enter your world your mind it can be good or bad right or
wrong, but we don't want the bad is how you handle it and control
yourselves you both must understand each other woman and man with
patience loving communication with one another sitting down watching
listening hearing praying sharing each other's feelings you both can
improve not just only the husband. Jeffrey tried to tell Cleopatra every
time she said I don't care you made me this way so what. How can you
communicate with a person, or anyone even mean as well not to leave
me left out see I'm judging myself as well with a person who doesn't care
says this over again it shows it with no action? If a woman is bitter and
relies on forgiveness and not interested in listening then you might as
well be talking to a brick wall because just like that woman has said she
has put her wall up its ok to do that when you're going through it with
someone or anyone who have took you through pain but then you
forgiving someone and didn't mean it that wall goes against yourself
because you have not fixed your heart with God or you so how can you
do it with anyone if you can't get yourself right? See when your husband
is talking to you please stop what you are doing and listen to him turn
humble towards him out and in love to him showing action show him
attentive body language. When can into God's gates with Thanksgiving
and his courts with praise the thing about it is that is the idea that God
won't let a negative unforgiving adultery or any sane person into his

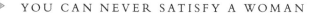

presence. We all I made in God's image. Negativity in bad words encouragement lies hurts our communication too as well so this goes God's way for women and men. The woman would say he didn't think about God when he send in cheated lied and used me yes he didn't he must get his life together repent then God will forgive him so when he does this God answers him what is the your child to start singing and don't forgive him and get him back is easy to tell him to forgive his father for leaving him or mother family brothers sisters or anyone and if he don't he would not be able to move on right? To forgive all those people that hurt him for what they did so as a woman you're different in God's eyes I'm asking it's different? You're just angry and mad as hell!! You want him to be focused on what he did and to keep getting wiped in your mind and eyes not the Lord or coming in and out. We are speaking the truth in love. Both men and women husband wife as one if God is not present being there is no teen or no marriage at all. Is also meaningless. Is just being angry see faith is important to have for communication don't only have faith in God but not in one another as well you want your husband to have it's in you no matter what you do because you're a good woman and a woman of God right or wrong seeming or not you're a child of God so why you can't see him in the same way? You have the right to speak a freedom of speech but watch what you say but rely on God to be the enforcer. That's faith it means trusting God to bring about change rather than your own nagging or beating or remembering what someone did behind your back but not knowing you did something behind theirs as well and you both did also in front of God's eyes. By mentioning a person's past mistakes when they are trying to change that's throwing stones at them while they are struggling to climb a mountain that's like my situation with Cleopatra every time Jeffrey got to the top she would kick him back down to the bottom how can you surrender to God when you're angry it happens fear in God's eyes when you both surrender both of your eyes will be open surrendering your hearts your minds bodies souls spirit says. This way everything will be used for good. Unforgiveness will destroy any relationship any marriage. You know some women shave their vaginas some women don't is what that woman wants for herself and that man because Cleopatra shaved herself, kept herself clean and open her legs to meet of the vagina sitting there as if it's his rose every single color in the world in the garden looking at her heart. She is looking at mines with her sitting with me on the beach that time when I laid the blanket out for her and me to sit down while the wind was blowing, and I passed her the glass with small teddy bear in it!! A lot of women shave just talking about women ordinary some don't because the air that blows down there when the man goes down there on the woman he does not want to smell a stank women's vagina. A woman does not want and when I have her own self smelling bad for her own self because she respects herself enough to know she is a woman some woman older let it stay growing because they say it does not only do nothing but grow extra and more some say they trim I'm a professional. I know I've seen it I even have help some women shave that I've been with some shave it all off especially my baby Cleopatra the real strong black Leo Queen woman yes I added it on with some nerve. Did I get it right women? Women hitting won't take place until you forgive see women are very curious to know what a man is always thinking with means of things already going on in her mind already like when I told men and women I was ready to write this book on you can never satisfy a woman guess what? Women first said and a lot are still seeing that's a whole world and book as well as we can't wait until this come out men what thing you not lying see is not always about sex with every man in the world on certain times and days weeks months years because he's human too it's not a sex thing with him when he's emotional feeling you they don't have to physically have sex with a woman to leave her mind booked or have it fuck or be ★★★★★★ her mind A man have the ability to maneuver himself to her deepest and most intimate desires. Men know what women like and, but they want beer is well whether he's going to deliver or not so he's able to use his masculine makeup in knowledge of woman to seduce her mentally. I was talking to a woman one day and I asked why you slept with that woman man she said and so those pitches slept with my men a point of time, so she didn't care but now she does. A lot of women are deceitful and devious creatures they are the seat boom in many ways even when they say how could you say that about every woman and having sometime or day of your life in it living. The woman captures the man and controls the man the woman allows the two think she's under control, but she wants to control the situation everything really and a lot of times the man don't even know about it. All women are deceitful and mindful don't sit there and say I'm not the type of women I'm a godly woman not saying you're not even they have had times in not perfect where I'm coming from and what I'm talking about a woman thinks about sex more than a man because they are high natured creatures. a real woman is competent strong seriously empowered long and high to the top this is Cleopatra. some women walked away with this book when I told them they told you something else you just too much I asked them things about women all kinds of things they didn't want to tell me because of what I was telling them already they were saying you know already you got it down packed you got everything, but I knew what it was already I was trying to make them reveal all the resources and they was like Oh no. I'm finding out anyway. Now I have spoken to women, and I have asked them where they from the hood or projects going to school or not different ladies or only regular places and neighborhoods and they have said that a man can a blow mind and don't be having sex with her mentally she didn't get with that man and blow her mind off that man. Real woman has a beautiful mind Cleopatra was beautiful and loved extraordinarily strong. I've seen a learn on my own is that most women have a lot of secrets they are very secretive every woman is not the same, but I learn if they let women know everything or certain woman or anyone then it would not be a secret. a woman will tell you a million things to make you believe her love is for you yes she has hidden secrets say one thing but in their mind is something different women keep secrets about their weight about how many men they have slept with the sexuality how much money they have or saved or even spent. Even looking at them then ask them what you're thinking about? They will lie at times with a straight lie looking you straight in your eyes!! I'm telling women and men don't show they real true colors at times, and they be mad. Women just stop repainting your man repeatedly and don't only let your significant other share and keep the family house, but he can't because you keep repainting him protecting your marriage is more than a skill. When Jeffrey and Cleopatra were making love, God was there we was a blessing to one another then when Cleopatra said Jeffrey sent her curses, and she was bitter he was unhappy. Did we love ourselves? Did she love me? Did I love her? All this is important. Unforgiveness hurting one another getting back at one another waiting on someone to pay you back for what wrong they did to you, or you did to them is like you owe them something. No one owes nobody nothing but love. See all these things be nasty, filthy, vengeance, energy, thoughts, emotions in spirits during sex it's not love no more there it's I got mines you got yours. Then you be training each other so spirits with lots of energy, with no life with force. Those demons exist not only exist with the man it also exists with the woman these spirits will suck your soul out of you literally and the women will mostly say no it's him, him, him!! He started it he's the man he's the head everything is on him. Women you are not the only ones that breaks down your man breaks down to just because he breaks down that don't make him no weak man he has feelings too you're not the only one that's always right. Jeffrey tried satisfying Cleopatra with all his heart because he started with God then himself. Jeffrey paused, back up, and went for walks and talk to God and took deep, deep breaths. Jeffrey did it with practice listening with his heart. It was in his heart but don't tell anyone that change they life, ways for you that they are doing good then come right back because you're angry and say you're sorry and they he walks out of the house. I talked to God because I told God what I was feeling thank God told me it was ok thank God told me to let Cleopatra know she's my one, my other half being God knew I was ok and God told me to listen to him and feel his spirit I notice the sensations I was having not even paid attention to myself talking with the Lord it was supportive and understanding but when I went to Cleopatra she was angry and rude I was being a friend towards her as well as a partner I got cursed out because it was all my fault and I made it all her like that. Jeffrey knew he can treat Cleopatra with kindness and understanding because he cares for her, and you know why? Because I was doing self-compassion I had to ask for forgiveness forgive myself I forgive her, but the thing is she said it but didn't do it. I said things and didn't do it as well no one is perfect we all do wrong and right. see a woman is never satisfied she's so many things in one is hard to explain she's a world all by herself she can be free a loss both at the same time sometimes just one the woman is victorious and an ass kicker she has a lot of confident in herself Jeffrey love Cleopatra sassiness, smartness and virtuous it was hot and ready. Always brave she was humble at times then unique. Cleopatra was sexy, determined and motivated when Jeffrey knew and wasn't. My Cleopatra states stylish even lying next to me capable and focused now let me tell you about a woman that's inspiring and creative God loves us Sky reveals the nature of his love for us and forgiveness, discipline, protection, provision, grace, mercy and liberation. God will never leave us he always comes through in love. Now today people take forgiveness and starting over for the advantage, the action of forgiveness kids watered down, abused, cheated on with words and promise physical abuse is not the only abuse. A woman is not the human being that wants to fall asleep next to someone she loves she feels good reduces depression and lives longer, healthy and once a good husband, a friend and protector so what does your husband want to do. You know it can be things your husband wants, needs and you don't know because you don't ask. Women mental verbal emotional face expressions are sometimes worse than physical abuse. My heart got so right it was better than poetry then Blues and soul music man I was out of space emotionally spiritually it felt like I was getting saved. Good relationships don't happen overnight this true love also requires effort. It requires a lot of sacrifices. Jeffrey loved Cleopatra because he bought with all he had in him it was everything Jeffrey put up with things he shouldn't have too like she did with him these women would be around here only what men took them through. What you did wrong? Nothing yeah right. Jeffrey put up with things to show Cleopatra he felt what he did wrong, and she did wrong to put up with things as well that he didn't personally find enjoying. Jeffrey accepts promises for the sake of us. Jeffrey embraces changes even though he took the go as a man for protection for the woman because it was the only way to go forward he didn't just leave right away he went to God, Bishop, pastor her children himself, her father, her mother, her brothers, her stepfather Jeffrey couldn't do it all and he only did it by himself. Jeffrey couldn't just leave and walk out just like that no he had to man up but women your time runs out just like men. Not being there through thick and thin walking through the hailstorm it will not be perfect my people there will be at times pain, sorrow, arguments, fights, anger, tears, drama it will not only be God love warm hugs caring only no marriage is perfect don't blame it all on your man. Don't be so smart to where you be blind don't see, don't hear, don't listen, don't respond, don't want no answer back, don't want a response, because what are you doing then woman? You both saying you don't understand but, but it is a stupid petty disagreement. It is times you fight; scream, yell and men cry too not just the woman. You give a chance for each other to explain one at a time. Share your facts and opinions. When you put someone pass on them every time they talk or explain when you called them out what are you for calling them something that comes out your mouth towards them and they haven't done anything but try to explain and they walk away from you? You be so angry too when they walk away maybe something else after that. Even more because they were not into you then you were so used to the old way you stay stuck that is not them. He does not be with them it be you. See when a lot of women get hurt and years go by and you say you forgive but you don't show love, I will tell you women when you show up sometimes and it feels convenient for you. Hold your man, hand when you're happy being with him. When you in your mood you abandoned him when you are at your most miserable life and self even if he gets one if when making love with him. He was cheater years ago then tell him sorry that's you feel like what mood you're in because you a woman as you say that in a wrong way to get your sex or love from him now and when you're ready. You don't disappear when they need you and reappear when you need them then say I don't need no man nobody right Cleopatra? or woman? When you love your husband, he did wrong you do too don't let him go through life alone. Don't let your husband keep suffering then when the divorce comes. Women say I was better without him, God and you sit there and you to yourself not only what he has done stop fooling yourself you too. Cleopatra didn't open her heart back open to Jeffrey because she was afraid that he will hurt her again she heard him at times because she came to apologize back and forth you know apologies can be just a tape player or old dusty record player and a roller coaster if you don't mean it. You can apologize but when you abuse him how does that make you? A lot of women say that's good it's worse some women hurt him bad but for them is different. Some sayings don't bring God in its conversation now you didn't think about God then so that tells you right there. It is times when men don't have time to think about sex women yes it's true. It's time like when he's looking for a job when his son or daughter gets locked up and he's trying to get a lawyer for him or her or both or whatever situation it is it don't have to be about him not thinking about sex it can be other serious situations the man is God's child God created man in his own image I wrote this book on women, so I know feel and understand so do the same for your husband/man. You also have women with life experience what they have been through and taught a woman experienced life with opinions and facts, cultures sex really lots of things. The older she gets the more she has experienced especially herself some things that's a few things because she learns more, she hoped to see everything and much more come to pass. The first thing on her list is God the next thing is herself then her children the reason why love is there because it is a breathtaking moment an amazing one where she knows she's deeply in love with her husband/man. She also learns that down in life everyone she has fallen in love with is not able to stay married. She also has had experience on true love is incredible and serious alone. Her next thing will be traveling but every woman is not the same, which every woman has experience being in love and falling in love. Please don't come with not me because I would still be with him and experience love after what we went through in life! Another thing every woman has experience is the wall bitterness, gossip, drama and more to come of their secrets not to tell. Another experience having a baby being a mother in marrying a man that's the father of the children or a stepfather that provides for them children being a mother may not be every woman's desire in this world we live in but having a baby is a life changing experience if she keeps her baby as she become an awesome mother well already is because she will die for her child or children therefore Jeffrey loves Cleopatra so much. Now back to what I was saying even if that woman decides to give the baby up to another family to have a better life because she can't provide for that child or children this is an experience that a woman or women is involved but never forget the experience. Yes I figured it out I'm a real man not only did I learn and find out about the woman I learn her experiences. I learned the woman she has multiple personalities and bipolar please have Cleopatra is claim quickly I am mentally crazy, and she got it all together is there something wrong with me but not her at all. A woman will keep giving childbirth and her children or child close to her heart. That's why when the child is born what does the woman first do she grabs her child, cries out of love and hold her child close to her heart with love embracing. Jeffrey looked at Cleopatra how she pampers herself no matter of her age she gets older, or we don't get back together her walk on life. Some women turn down the chance some won't with getting their hair done Cleopatra love her manicures, pedicures and her hair curl in front of her face of her making her beauty even coming out more. Cleopatra love to go out It was relaxing and fun for her Jeffrey went with her sometimes how many men did this. Jeffrey knew when Cleopatra became passionate about something. In her life it was a drive for something that meant a lot to her that really spark ambition and character she was not perfect on everything as just being bold to stand up for what she believes in and becoming involved in anything that had an impact on her life. He's helped her as a woman to take her mind off a lot of things. When she became passion about things, about herself experience for every woman is shopping buying her bra, panties, lotions, fragrances, body oils other etc. She will save up receipts just in case she changed her mind. Her mind goes back and forth at times because she's going to have fun and do it. Every woman has experienced confidence and self-acceptance for many women it's a struggle, but the goal is to focus on doing it every day. What Jeffrey liked about Cleopatra is that once she was happy and comfortable, she shined with more beauty he saw her for who she was. Like I said every woman is not the same and have a different opinion. See what I'm trying to teach some women and ones that be selfish because they are bipolar maybe just like their partner and their partner be just like them the woman be saying I'm not nothing like the man he makes me sick but still love his crazy but ass you are not crazy you cool, calm, humble and collect and you a woman. Then at times the women who wants a man how she wants him to be at times. See a woman will be at times I am different depending how she feels and what she's going through watch out now is not only the man with conflict it's both of you your soul mates. You have good problems and bad problems because Cleopatra always used to tell Jeffrey whether she was angry was pissed off herself or Jeffrey pissed her off she said you're not always going to stay and do the right things and that's ok we are not here to be perfect but to be fair.

I hope I could have said that she would have let me get away one time. A woman supposed to meet her mate needs as she wants her needs met. Jeffrey didn't just put himself in Cleopatra shoes he was sitting down waiting for her to walk in his shoes 50/50 right? It was empty understanding and entering her feelings and she will say hell no you didn't at all be angry we broke up we divorce only you, you, you. Your no good but she kept coming back saying I'm sorry that I'm not giving you a chance I've been upset with you I'm going to stop apologizing and bringing up the past so we can move on and me as well I'm tired of arguing life too short and I say you're going to say that and come right back and treat me the same with action like I'm she you calling me fuck up I'm doing the same shit I am not worth a damn. So, a lot of people even women will say well you know you do not shit right. So, don't listen to her that's not easy when you married to someone you love, and you see them and lay beside them every night. I became more sensitive she was too blind to see that's an everyday excuse was you don't know what a woman feels and what she goes through and how much pain she holds in and out and breathe why I don't know we were one she can't hear me, but I can't feel her no she did not want to she was selfish. Jeffrey invested his kindness, attention, communication into Cleopatra. See today you have women don't see or know that after God comes their marriage not your children, church, work etc. Hobbies, money, careers, only your relationship with God rank above your marriage in priority. Don't fall for other things people are saying and teaching today right now open your soul to God and your marriage the soul will come together as one. Jeffrey admits he had a bad communication with Cleopatra, but he got it right it wasn't about him it was about God, and it was about including us like God does and says God is a doer we must be doers one can't do and the other can't know it doesn't work like that. Jeffrey learned how to communicate because he got himself right to get a good communication with God then go to Cleopatra or she kept saying back and forth was I shouldn't, or I never took you back I should have never taken you back you not right there being in relationship to me women you will provoke and push your man away like this your man wants to be appreciated too. It will never be too late for a woman right because her sins are different only thing she don't do as much as a man is a cheat she's different right she special and great on all things. Everyone has good and bad in them look in the mirror. See the woman when Jeffrey wanted to talk Cleopatra didn't want to talk when she wanted to talk, Jeffrey talks too damn much baby where did you go? Who did you see? What has she said? I know where you were and who you were with swearing on her life and so calling mix it is putting me down like nothing when she knows she is the one in some more with all the nerve. When I answered I was a hoe and a dog and no good. When I refused to answer and was humble quiet, I got cursed out because I didn't be into mess. She always tried to enter my mind in my world the woman when I was patient loving and communicating and shut up on the woman's mind eventually the woman will come and apologize for her mistakes but how long will that last? Then you have all these women asking what you did wrong for her to act this way? What did you do? Is not one time or one thing really one question what this woman does to her man? So, all men are fuck ups? You cannot communicate with a woman who says I don't care; I don't care being cursed out!! I don't give a damn; I don't give a damn! You can't make her listen but only when the woman comes in and she's interested in listening then you might as well be talking and listening to a brick wall woman feel men see what we go through? You want the man to stop what he's doing, turn to you with love, listen, show your body affection actions, language and movement. Your man wants this too it's not a one-way streak give or take, take or give. Women are amazing because they regenerate and produce they get tired at times and don't go back in forth it's in there. You have old school women that's older don't tell secrets a lot or at all most women I had to find that out on my own, but I have seen some drama Queens tell all they business like I used to see some sisters of minds. I used to hear them say I know because I'm a woman. Being the part where they say they get aggravated and at times aggravate themselves I then heard a lot say I'm aggravating ass other women will say that's that woman not to me, but you have been that woman a time or day living in your life being aggravated or going through some problems feelings attitudes ways these other women have on your own life day living in time. I would like to ask a lot of women this why you can't leave the past in the past? Don't say we do but you men go back and do the same thing.

Most of you don't give the man time to change when he does fully change, and I asked a whole bunch of older women this and they said you know what baby as a son to me you know what sweetheart that be true. They said they'd be angry and bitter that's why so I said if you don't leave the past in the past something or a lot of things don't come back up damn they say yes maybe the same thing even more things because that's a typical woman nowadays she wants to do it herself each way and keep him on a straight narrow role that's what she want the man to think that she forgave him that's why she comes back and forth with I'm sorry then they debate an argument an apology a sorry being vengeance. Now you are the woman you love unconditionally right? I know no relationship or marriage is perfect you won't always be happy. You can't become your husband man best friend if you can truly forgive him from your heart in your heart like you would want anyone to forgive you you would never appreciate the flaws or one another. See women when he lies about cheating he's wrong he has sinned there is no trust if you are going to let him go right then I can understand that God can too you can too but if you say forgive to God yourself and him and take him back and don't be honest there was no communicating faithful which bringing up the past this what you asked for you asked to be taken through this because you didn't honestly truly did it forgive with God's love you just said it that's why love did come out only words came out. No action came because she was hurt, and it takes time until she says it takes. You can't read or lead a woman's mind it doesn't only have to be with someone always and only bed to her to make her become the way she is that happens too every woman or person in life every woman or person is not the same she can be selfish or in what type of mood she's in by herself moody, cranky, happy or not to herself. Now these are some examples of mind games that you woman be playing one day I was out and about and taking care of my business when my girlfriend at the time calls me and told me that my ex-girlfriend Shay called her and text her to tell me to call her on my girlfriend Leanne. Because it was important. Not understand the mind game she Shay my ex-girlfriend is telling my girlfriend at the time Leanne to tell me to use her phone to call her because it was important.

Chapter 18

When I call her from my phone and ask her why you text Leanne on her phone saying that you needed her to call you on her phone and what was so important? Is Shay my ex-girlfriend said I just needed someone to talk to then I said what was so important and an emergency to talk about Sheila? She said you know I needed someone to talk to and I don't want you to be throwing it in my face I told you, but you didn't listen to me then she said the man Felix that I got with I had to let go because he was on drugs bad very bad and you was right baby I miss you can you come over and spend some time with me? I said no that is not my problem and that's not an emergency that's your problem and then she said he was using me for sex but paying my bills so he felt like he can get on drugs and use me, but I need you back because she said I did it right, so I hung up in her face. Then guess who called me back and forth because I was out handling important business that day it was Leanne calling, she asked me what did Shay want what was the emergency? I said let me call you back I'm in the police station handling important business. I will look what happened another five hours later Lisa called back again and asked me what did Shay need and wanted? I said I'm eating I'm on my way home I didn't even get in the room all the way she asked me so what did she wanted? When I let her know what she looks like I said I put it all together. Shay was playing mind games and listen was curious and wondering the mind game she loses trying to play one with me, but I saw it all you see both women was trying to find out the what the man does not mean they the same perhaps some things to find out to have I was already taken but I was just looking, seen, watching, observing and paying attention. Now look at these women now and after that day it kept going for a quiet moment I'm listening to Lisa did she call you today? No! Back and forth she kept asking I did not do this woman who say dog man or man dog!!! No Lisa asks this in her Sherlock way called an act can you come over to fuck me and I said no, and you say men are dogs? I don't know some or most women will say what you did that's just women or two women all

women are not like that you got something against women so what are you saying? No this is a true story and Leanne argued at me about it because it was because of a woman named Shay that's an ex-girlfriend they got something started but got Leanne thinking it was me. Women do this at times it can be a man where he does not have no wrong in the situation and knowing her being a woman knowing how a woman thinks, act, talks, ways moves because like I have heard and seen every woman say I know because I'm a woman or that's why I don't have a lot of women friends. The last woman friends I have the better it is for me feeding them with a long-handled spoon. do you know I asked Leanne why was she thinking so much and she said I'm just thinking a little to see a lie right there just like with men as your woman say a lie is a lie because that was from her mouth and mind but deep inside at the same time she knew where she stood with security and having confidence in herself and the relationship she had with me but she still a woman being on point boundaries curious watching out being careful being a woman and most of all it's not saying I have to fight or argue over a man that's mines a woman is jealous!!! Not in a bad way. See when I say you can't satisfy a woman and you can't in the end because, so you do satisfy her then it's a problem with her with something else when it's a problem with doing it wrong is right then when is right is wrong then it's just not right at all leave it alone her alone go somewhere then come back leave stay gone come back I miss you! Go left go right go right go left at times a woman is confused she thinks a lot this will make her complicated in unpredictable a lot of times. A woman is a painkiller and a muscle relaxer all in one. Then she can be predictable at times. A lot of women can't get along with one another battling against each other as woman drama mothers', daughters', aunties, sisters', grandmothers even as women working together in restaurants together too much drama, she said this or that. The mother not getting along with the daughter the grandmother not getting along with the mother the sister not getting along with her sister you have had a lot of women saying it was all because of only a man they are this way they are today!! You know Jeffrey promised Cleopatra the world she looked around and apologize and he fulfilled hi part of the bargain not only have he shown her the world I've given her the world she said thank you baby then curse me out before he started back!! I was under so much pressure that I felt like I was shitted on she ignored me and talked to me in treated me wrong. I changed for the change of heart that I gave heart to her for giving pure and clean from honesty from that he did know was not a lie. I can't put or blame anything on God. Cleopatra was the best woman in the world for Jeffrey because she still is and will always be the only most precious jewel that walks by his side. She is more precious than rubies nothing you desire can compare with her. See that's what I was saying about the woman she's the headache the love the wrong the right the gone the frown there up the down the sound the drown the happiness the sadness then nothing that everything she comes into your life and become it. See I learned not only women come into relationships or marriages with children of their own and as well with their own challenges going through it hard with life even raised up hard with a struggle even men come with this and go through this too ladies!! Because at times you have the woman enter the relationship downing the other spouse some of it or a lot of times it is due to past experiences right women? The woman will see the man was innocent thing and guilty she was guilty on some things but not like him tell me how please in what kind of way cheating, lying. using. So, what the woman comes with. Because that woman can have things in her to break that man's heart trust violate his heart then he gets falsely accused for something then things change. This woman can have an education in seeing she's doing good, and the man can do better with education but is how you help him on that and guide him and lead him. Everyone needs this guidance and help down the path in life. See what I've seen and have experience how a woman or women have higher or sad, bitter, anger, selfish or for self-hire expectations expecting old everything to them because of what they've been through before in the past half are giving four but not have forgotten and have set they goes up as a short leash around their men necks not to be hurt again. Right woman? This don't only put pressure on your husband/man this puts pressure on yourself woman wife and children with your family. How can the head be the head when you won't give him a chance? You're really shooting the gun at his head at the start line not in the air!! I'm not making it seem that it's all on a woman and every woman is the same or bad it's just not all

on a man as of today in this world how things are. Every woman has the potential. This woman loves shoes this woman loves purses this woman loves hats like Cleopatra, but they are different in their own way but still on different days go through things in life different shaped same shit different days someday it changes. For example this woman I went to the store with one day she's my friend her name is Rosie she was going to a lady store for her girlfriend well her wife she's a Butch so we walked in the store she had her own FaceTime so she brought her an outfit with the shoes to match it so when she got home she was complaining about some things about the dress so she said God dam you said you liked it can I at least get a thank you? She rolled her eyes at her and said thank you, now is that a sense loving apology? Is that from the heart? Since someone is saying when a woman rolled her eyes if is right or wrong that's a woman being a woman. So now she goes back to complaining and debating about the dress sing its excuses for women to get away, but they said worse for only men. I'm just going by experience not bashing woman, so she went to go take a bath and when she was done, she put the clothes on her girlfriend plot for her and the shoes with the hat. Then we all left when we got to the restaurant we were smiling laughing and having fun when we all sat down being the girlfriend said girl that look good on you where you got that from? And guess what she said my baby brought it for me, so she got up put her hand on her hip because they took out their phones to take pictures then while she was posing and smiling she was showing off and showing out bragging about the same dress she was arguing about 30 minutes ago yes a woman changes up and then her girlfriend looked at her out the corner of her eyes and said know your ass something else rolling her eyes so they both something else. Well one is a trip and the other one is a trip and a half. Because I learned to the quiet woman that sign is the worst out of them all. See what a lot of women don't look at in their wrongs is that what break them up from their men is selfishness the only thing today is the man is a dog, a liar, a cheater is not only that!! Some women will say and feel they forgave their husband/ man but he's doing the same thing over and over again and he may be or not but at times it be you thinking in your mind the same old thing everyone else is precious in God's eyes sight but when you say things he did he that he's going to always be that way what do you expect? Do you know I understand woman or man when someone hurts you so bad you want to die you want that person to die as well because of that anger that depression it will wear your body out!! It affects you and the people around you. Pray, love that person like you would for yourself. Do you know a lot of women Amen go to marriage counseling today and they listen to the bishops, pastors and people not the love they worship of God they be worshipping to benefit themselves going to listen to the world but not knowing when they leave their circle to do it for God's sake and the marriage as one? I went to bed in anger plenty nights but then I went to God and changed my thoughts my heart, my doings, my soul, my spirit everything I changed. See when you don't forgive, and you are angry you see your soul mate is not true you even convince other peoples that they are not true. I repented for the dog I was I'm the problem after that I still was that person I was standing there and under Cleopatra influence of her ways thought opinions really her greediness her cutthroat times and sneakiness. I see women that wear their natural hair I like that that's their natural beauty I seen women that wear their hairdos and wraps a lot of women wear weave to look good for a new look to go with themselves and the way they dress some women don't wear weave at all. I see a lot of them wear weave so they here can grow even more to a protective style, so you have women get extensions to help her look good. See there's all kinds of things, spray, glue etc. with gel and more. See Jeffrey even tried to win a smart debate with Cleopatra Jeffrey said to himself let me sit back and let her come to me and when she spoke Jeffrey said in his mind it must be a valid fear point but not perfect and he had to disagree to agree she wasn't there fair with him as one together to put herself in his shoes like Jeffrey put himself in hers to feel an understand and feeling where she was coming from. She did not hold on or fill me you know we can be swearing that we know and feel we are doing something when we are not. You know I created the damage but I had to fix the damage that I created then when I got right and Cleopatra told Jeffrey ok baby it's fixed a lot of women you was probably doing the same thing over and over again that's why she didn't change because I didn't so why did she kept coming back and forth saying I'm sorry I'm ready to forgive you I need to stop

I'm not forgiving you right I'm sorry no it was her mind and heart that didn't change if you are forced in a corner and you can't get no air, no prep and you're getting pushback every time you're backing out pushing forward and the person pushed you real hard that's not helping is it? See really Cleopatra felt Jeffrey told her everything but the thing about it was influencing from each other not only from the woman or from the men only I couldn't never stand up because I was a fuck up and couldn't do anything right. Now women will say don't talk to a woman wife like that she deserves respect I agree just like that man does. See when you be wounding one another and hurting one another instead of blessing one another healing one another we are so angry and upset we don't understand what's going on when we don't know anything because we are upset and confused really aggravated at one another. m Cleopatra had a timer on Jeffrey really her own clock running the relationship on her time or it heavy police, a parole officer, Captain, Lt., Sergeant and Corporal I left out the major. So how is she seeking improvement? See Cleopatra only looked at Jeffrey getting right and his cycles only her family and it all together. See every marriage or relationship has a certain direction or path going down the wrong path I know mine did especially from my parents I did see a lot of things they did I learned from what I saw and still have good in me positive sometimes it was evil spirits and very bad inequity a huge generational sin but Cleopatra had some but she said when I told her she thought she was better Annie has some let's talk about it the false prophets told her don't care about what he or no one say. I had all kinds of things in my family cycle cancer quickness to anger substance abuse mental and physical abuse rape but guess what I never met a person who didn't have inequities from following the unbiblical example of previous generations until Jeffrey met Cleopatra she was saying it, but you couldn't tell her you will get curse or bust out and talked about and apologized to then get cursed right back out after the apology. At least I apologize but no form of action. Like it will be times we will break up and she will come get me or call and say I'm sorry and start right back up with the same old things now if I say you bringing the same old stuff and you not keeping your word or bond it will turn back on me that I made her this way so I'm the one to blame for everything. Now while her mother and family members passed things down to her she could not see it was self-directed see making peace promises to we and others it causes stress and pain. Everyone has made this or these at some point in their life or lives. See, Cleopatra didn't know when she made Jeffrey a promise to take him back, she made it to God. A lot of women will say when they break up with their soulmate, husband, lover, boyfriend, fiancé or whatever they want to call it they say they are not thinking about him anymore and he's not on their mind and saying I'm not thinking about him or even worried or concerned about him that's a lie because like I said a woman is just like an elephant she forgives but she does not forget well someone will forgive so she put up the wall and boundaries with words but still in her mind she thinks her mind never stops. Then some woman will say this does not mean she loves him or once you get back with him anymore or someone will say she not thinking about his shit at all some would say some go right back to ask it won't be over, but I think to some women do they know what they really want? See a real man will open communication to a woman especially when it's God loving and security for Cleopatra it was too late like she said. We are there talk to her she ignored me see love is not based on the woman first or men not even emotions the love is God action choice based on agape love. Don't God have this kind of love for us don't look down on your man saying going motions is on top because you know you have ways as well just as much as he do and we are not perfect to be in control about will all the time Jeffrey made the decision to fall in love with Cleopatra all over again that was his will he went to the Lord in like she kept saying after Jeffrey got it right I don't care I shouldn't have never taken you back in our home in front of our children you know if my stepdaughter Anita is right there telling her you're putting him down just like Cleopatra told Jeffrey her mother Pam put her stepfather down talking to him any kind of way that's not a cycle? No that's all on me making her that way and all my fault she wouldn't have been this way if it weren't for me, or her wrong doings actions and things and my sins was because of the man sorry man we are no good!! I made the choice to love her the best way and try hard to give her the world and be faithful to her as the same way Jesus would. That didn't have nothing to do with money, job the cause had to be hired to have her or emotions or circumstances finances. Women I would like to tell you something when men live with you is not only them you see their wrongs they see your issues too as well and you both change at times in your relationships. You know I sat down with a woman named Miss Lynn one day that brought purses from my lady business I had open up so I was talking to her she asked me how was Cleopatra was doing and I said we are broke-up but she is ok being Miss Lynn said you took care of those children real good I used to see you with them all the time so she started talking about my business and asks me what I still selling ladies purses accessories shoes clothes and other things I said no. Ms. Linda and I was by myself and not with Cleopatra anymore I said I don't want to talk about that so I brought up to her that a beach hour or slid don't have nothing in common with a married woman she said that's not true she said every woman is not the same she said because I slept with the woman husband before and they have six kids together the wife name is Joyce Cotton and the husband Miss Lynn slept with is Joe Tyson so Melba was sitting down and I asked her how did you do that? She said in a sneaky way with her charm and she said I took her damn husband because she was pushing him away and I had six kids from him and she said she was a bitch, whore, slut and sweet and nice so I call it like I saw it As well as she did I had to put this in there up under her belt she was a natural woman that has all them titles and that what makes her the best Queen and the best diva she is. Now Lynn and Janet are the best of friends until this day, and they talk to one another and have each other numbers. Now miss Linda said every woman has done this I said correct with a married man or not even if it was the intentions in her mind. Miss Lynn also said Jeffrey the ex-wife and the ex-husband Joe has accepted together as a family with the children and guess what? Miss Lynn called Janet on her phone then asked her and she said you're not lying or telling the truth and then Jeffrey card the ex-husband Joe and they was all on the line together and it was true Miss Lynn hung up but before she did she said Janet and Joe I will talk to you all later ok, they both said bye. Then Miss Lynn looked me straight in my eyes and said baby we want a big happy family now!! I see you even have pastors, bishops, prophets they don't have to even be pastors it could be any woman that been through it is their intentions in their mind once they get in the bedroom she fucked like she never in her life fucked before them be the worst ones. I've seen in the church not judging just experiencing seeing in life. A woman knows how to lie and analyze those men. Men are sloppy that's how they get caught women be wrong too they are not perfect they just do the opposite of how men do a lot of things men get caught most of the time. Another reason why some women are not satisfied on this level one sex because some or she thinks that a man enjoys an orgasm better than her. You know when I used to go to clubs when I was younger the woman in the club was looking for the same thing, I was looking for you know what I mean. The reason why I said the woman is bipolar because in her nature how she changes up at any given time, mood swing disorders, distinct periods, sadness, happiness, aggravation even hope, hopelessness, depression or depressive she changes up so much don't try to figure herself out or to keep up or understand her a woman can be more emotional than a man it's some men out here that are emotional than women but most women are more emotional than men but there are differences between the women with their experience of being bipolar. And I know it and complain about it any argument or debate. A woman hormone also has a thing to do with a strong development and severity of her bipolar disorder. Her mood swing does something to do with her period or cramping and PMS as well. Especially her cycle. you have a lot of women keep secrets away like telling the truth about their past or not discussing certain things a lot lie about the baby father's not letting people know they are bisexual or have HIV or aids. Keep secrets on that she used to be a stripper the past can be a big secret to her it is important to a woman but forgiving her man or husband is not easy to do I feel that intense a different secret even though secrets are secrets it can be evil wicked or good love and see the secret of unforgiveness will blow a man husband's mind she will not see nothing good. Really no one can see good that can't forgive. A woman is a strong beautiful secret a real woman that respects herself. Jeffrey asked Cleopatra how many men she slept with she just said not a lot see women are smart they tell you what they want you to know and not their business it don't even to only have to be their business when Cleopatra told Jeffrey she was not a whore or never was Jeffrey said but you told me you were an honest whore right? She said now I was joking and you trying to be funny right? Then she said while you had to bring that up? I can't tell you anything!!! Being she told you something else and I was a trip then I said you slept with me when I was with my woman right? Then she said you already was breaking up. See a woman thinks fast her thoughts anyways change up quick now you let that would have been me I will be on the stand for trial. See I even did it the right way loving Cleopatra I did my part by God satisfying her as the woman she was then and now today if I was in front of her face-to-face closeup no sex no making love or touching she is hard to heart eye contact and the way I did satisfy her Is that I understood the exchange of power. It was not no total dominance it was only balance and harmony sometimes people can't handle the truth sometimes men can't handle the truth women too. Sometimes men cannot handle the truth because of their preconceived notions that women are naturally better at lying. See a woman emotion change out multiple times thoughts stain come go Even in between. I did my research on a lot of women and one of the things that was said is what he did to me or that men or men do the same shit. They even said to me what did you do to that woman is something you did to her to make her that way. I said OK so what do women do to men to make them in their ways to do what they do? they said nothing this does not mean every woman is the same she wants more says more an even be unable to give constructive self-extreme at times. I'm writing this book to let women know to look at yourself your ways how you react on things don't let a friendship with your husband man for years and years holding things against him. don't be conflicting on goals and values. A lot of women and this world put up with my ass but the woman who I was in love with didn't truly forgive me from her heart. women don't change your man husband love his flowers be with him when his wounds are open and hurting times when it's rough spoil him because I'm not bashing women I'm telling them when times you listen to what family saying sister say mother say he say she say you would never be able to hear what God or your husband is saying but you want that's for yourself from your husband no matter what mood spirit billings emotions you're in. See women look at is this many men have hurt women us!! It goes both ways in many women have hurt men stop comparing who hurt whole the most

is start only helping!! When Jeffrey come with this to Cleopatra it wasn't
enough how can someone say you achieved something did your best
thing come back being not only down the person who they are in love
with but it coming from the self-did they not down themselves? Yes.
Day was hurt as they say. women when you heard that is a thing
everyone goes through and not do you only know this and go through
these men do too even a lot of animals in the wild in life. And you can
take that pain and hurt on for so long that you be feeling in saying you
he them she doesn't understand no you don't understand yourself
because years done went by and you don't say your movie on from this
is still be stuck so that's not one that person that's on you that do that
women like you tell your husbands baby you have to forgive your father
you have to forgive your mother, sisters, brothers being a victim of
being abused, raped, molest your baby mother, yourself what happened
to you as a child what happened to you growing up in the ghetto in the
projects and when the men or men tells the wives or women the same
thing as the women and women says for their sins forgive because if you
don't you won't move on with your life. I done heard women say now
you want to put guy in it now that you done fucked up when she says
God she's God's gift, but you are some of everything and she does not
mean that you know she didn't mean that because she was angry upset
bitter and hurt. You can't use God words you can try we all been their
men and woman. Women we know what hurt your feelings do you
know what hurt man feelings because you will blame everything on
the man we did not say we don't lie or have not cheated and have tried
to make in excuse an find a way out like I said we as men are sloppy
with our lies you do it quiet everyone has lied. see one of the ways a
woman can push her man to cheat is put him down after he done clean
himself up after doing wrong but women will say you don't know what
she's been through and how she feel to make her react the way she's
acting well she lying to herself God in him and the marriage she knew
the changed she just wasn't ready to herself to accept change on her
heart sell fair respect so be up front it was no excuse for her as well and
then she keeps putting him down emotionally mental and which will
affect him physically to the point that he will go to someone else and
seek encouragement confidence intelligence and positive it even to

another woman now a woman or most are some will say he's a dog no good he's married he's dead wrong and send he was married he was supposed to go to only God now when these things happen to a woman all hell breaks loose the man or men have hurt them so much they moved by themselves to be bitter angry have got to be envy, a grudge and you can't have God like that men or women no one but they just put in their way but not every woman. Every woman is not the same. Another way that a woman can push a man to cheat is not having confidence in herself. Because rather women know whether confident do make them look sexy, beautiful an amazing in some men's eyes. The woman meet and pick at every little thing that the man does in her way everything he do is wrong he don't have no air to breathe to do good she see them as dirty dog I don't see any good of what he's doing or what he's trying to do that can push him to cheating then it will be said no that's no strong men he weak well damn like the woman say how much can he take? This is fair women put up with men shit and we also put up with women shit!! How can you say you forgive for sin and negative behavior then bring it up back in the person face that you keep apologizing to or what you are falsely accusing men for what they are not doing to you you're just afraid to trust love and give them another chance again because you know with negativity they are going to hurt you again so there's no he did it again see I caught him no it be already in your mind with arguments, debates, business, madness, confusion you know why I know this because when people's hurt me do you know I made them pay and got back at them more than what they did to me was it right? No! The more I waited the longer I sat back that I was feeling good, angry in smiling, crying, grinning, cheerful down depressed all at the same time I was sending towards God myself and not only one person lots of people so learn something from my testimony. I hear women say men are more controlling I hear men say women are controlling I hear women say men are more controlling than men whip and in every which way I hear men say women are controlling with my games mental their mouth some women would say it's not my mouth is she if you can't handle a strong black woman or a woman. So why you came back to apologize for that mouth? You knew it was wrong the point I'm trying to make is they both knew it was wrong they both was wrong, but everybody wants to be right no one wants to die but everybody wants to go to heaven. It can be pried the wife may feel and know she's better than the husband because he has messed up the household and she going to make him pay real good well she gets so aggressive where she turns into a God of range for her own self being the devil like he was acting this was before he got saved treating his wife any kind of way his father not teaching him not how to treat a woman or wife because he didn't have a father figure there has a role model or guidance and the same as the wife no father dear with her mother or whatever she grows up and see her mother actions in ways reactions speech language because profane language can bring witchcraft and curses. Really, we all are equal no one gets treated or gets more than no way married as God says. Now today everywhere marriages go they don't teach they are equals they be too busy you you you and me me me no it's us we as one so if it was you then no it was you back and forth being someone can't take no more pinkies push down or both push each other down then it doesn't be a team anymore help each other up or take time like teams do. When I got saved for real I did it for God and myself it was witnesses there. Amen! I was head of my home but was not treated respected I loved at all because if I were I wouldn't got it treated as I was that same person that I was not after I got saved so I did what God said and he said go my son and do the position to serve me and do your duty and love your wife as Christ loved the church. I was going to church running to it. it was so much fun I was happy I was excited I even sat down humble with God praying on my knees. I trusted God with my life the problems and good and bad with the issues I did not take charge I let God do it it was one problem Cleopatra was left out she didn't want to be in now correct me if I'm wrong bishops, pastors preachers said you can't make your wife pray or come to God if she don't want to so be honest you all so how would your relationship my relationship be if God the man and woman is not involved? Every marriage is not the same but if God the husband and wife is not involved what will it be? A disaster! Just like if their husband is not there with God and his wife and family. It does say in the word if your wife is not a believer do not leave pray for her and if your husband is not a believer pray and don't leave but this may not remain an stay the same way because the longer it stays the more the devil will destroy and kill the marriage and he loves to do these too marriages being you have a lot of marriages divorce it don't only before cheating it be all kinds of things many of things God don't be involved then I hear finances did you marry for money? Women your hearts in feelings are not the only ones be dominating and let down. Control and cheated is not the only curse in a marriage only way multiple curses can be broken is that the husband and wife come back under the authority from which they first rebelled and that's God. Not married or listening to other people's who's married them with you or just you too. Do you know a lot of women be married to them passed an pastors and friends fami ly members to men to? Do you know it was times Cleopatra told Jeffrey things and Jeffrey didn't want to listen emotional with my health and he would only say he know that already he the one told you that? I would tell her calm down your diabetes baby your sugar she would be angry and say verbal evil things off her tongue like "well you the one brought it on for the shit you took me through I wouldn't be sick. Or have health problems if I was with your ass", I don't know why I got back with her ass. Now see when she told me about my ass good or bad right or wrong always listen to the woman she's right where they say this at? Now if you are telling or saying something forever you made it this way. when we say words and things we speak it and claim it into existence especially how our heart is like I'm going to use me for example one of relatives raped, abused and molested me and took me a long time to get over it and when I told them I forgave I didn't do it from my heart I just said while they on with their life I made money living hell going to jail going to prison drinking or drugs hurting depressed homeless living in the state of mind the world everyone is nasty I want love where's the love afraid of it afraid to give it so women can't sit there alone saying they go through it the most in men or a lot of people don't understand it just that peoples handle their situations different in life. What a woman really wants is a man to listen to her and be honest with her and love her the way the man starts when he first meet her like when Jeffrey first met Cleopatra it started out with the nice sweet things I said and did but the woman does not want this to stop stay on your job men didn't say we was perfect because I know as a real man a woman do not want or have time for foolishness because she has other important things to do herself time life moving forward and living this while Jeffrey loved Cleopatra she's a Leo and she's very aggressive in love very hard. I don't know how they do it but some married couples argue a lot because it's the make-up love or sex that be good when it's time to do it they get along better this way some women argue about their men not having a job then when he get one all the time she was arguing with him she wants to continue it because she was arguing for so long that she wants to be in control every woman is not like this but there are women who is another woman will say that's those kind of women or every woman not the same or what woman I've been dealing with. A woman at times would say whatever her men or a man wants to hear it does not have to be wrong at times, but her actions are her true attentions. A woman also makes decisions based on her emotions not logic. See a lot of women in their mind be bear smoothing out a rough situation in the relationship however in logical thought she 's lying deceiving and manipulating her mate she knows and aware of what she's doing but her underlying intent would not allow her to confess her actions which jeopardizes her relationship is still say it's all his fault he made me this way. Staying quiet has her thinking when she's dreaming she's fantasizing a woman is in her own mind frame mostly all the time she has her own ideology really saying she got her on ideas already you can't impregnate her mentally. I know as a man I did have my goals together when I got right with God when I was in a relationship to Cleopatra as you mean out there have your goals in your act together. I didn't do this for show off and attention I did this from the heart. Now see when men do wrong now watch this woman leave they ass right there and let them wipe their own ass clean they own shit and let them sit there and sometimes it be her shit that she can't let go and blame it on the man. Now when she does this don't run behind her let her clean and wipe the **** up that she messed up leave her alone let her be because you can't change her she has to change on her own. A lot of women don't mean from their heart they truly honestly forgive she thing was she saying without a conscious being aware but honestly, it's not what she means it's the opposite. Then it goes like this when you tell her she wrong she lied she plays the victim quick she comes with a cry anger bitter even smooth to get what she wants all over again. Someone needs to get on the media because the media television show reality shows talk shows give women a false sense of reality. Not all but most because I worked in the field of TV shows going to school for acting and commercial shows and my teacher Anna Gonzalez on the beach taught me the scripts and most of them was lies or selling products an even line for shows and movies. See I also write this book on the pain not only what women go through or what I went through men as well including all his human beings because someone or anyone has been through something I want to write to show you how to deal with your pain and not only understand it and feel you and understand where you are coming from as well as me with the journey it's not easy is life because someone out there has been through what I've been through and I'm not afraid to voice my opinions or fax the truth and not a lie I can be right or wrong in someone else eyes by not agreeing with me because everyone is entitled to their own opinion I'm not embarrassed or ashamed to speak out say what I feel it mean what I say because it's a lot of people out there understand me because they've been down the same road I have been down some even worse well a lot this a big huge world we live in. No matter who does not believe in me it's one thing I know they can't take away from me and that's me believing in myself and no it's people out there that will still judge you by your past and what you done to them and your cover and book I know I've been there down that road plenty of times where I have made the same mistake over and over again so I didn't mind the consequences that came with my punishment because the pain I caused not only on myself as well as other people's women family members and Cleopatra but Jeffrey do say this when Jeffrey pay for it some people felt like it wasn't enough out of the anger and vengeance and madness they feel like they are Gods because they make their choice, their way of choice in mind, actions to get and do pay back in the way. I say to women that been hurt by different men and then every time they get in another relationship it's not well at times. Well first they were supposed to get themselves right with God first, moved by themselves and with children if they have children or not then when they get themselves right with God then they life is right don't just jump because of feelings last or got to get some need a man only in God's way not your way. I blame women in that way on action when they just jump in relationships and don't fix themselves just like I got on these men like you get on them and tell them to love themselves and stop doing drugs stop cheating stop using stop cursing go to church pray yes I'm talking to you women how you going to get on someone after you don't separate it then got back together saying you was right but didn't come back with action with what you were saying so you didn't mean what you said just like you tell men like they can be hard headed you can be selfish this is not only in cheating for other things too as well that's important!! I see a lot of women that come in contact either the man who has hurt them or other men so then feel like when any man or that man comes in contact she will always have the same pain holding onto it always take out one others in on history don't do this until you die every dead gone please take this to your grave because women I feel you and understand you I have not been there to witness but men go through things too in this world we live in is life we all are individuals with God love. Sing with Cleopatra and Jeffrey stopped showing her the same thing I started showing her something different she even said it I did act and acknowledge the pain she went through. It comes times when it be so much pain it's too much on a woman I agree well like she tell that man he lied so he has to earn her trust back and everything that comes with it because once the trust is gone everything else is thrown out the window then it goes like this the women don't be sure being do be hard cold confused tired she used this weapon for good and as well in her mind to blow herself up and relationship as well. A woman intuition is so incredible it's all kinds of feelings as well she can feel it until before it even happens Jeffrey know being in love with Cleopatra is Just one of the most powerful force on earth. It's one of her higher powers she's connected with her spirit. A woman's intuition is stronger than a man. A woman knows when something is wrong even though at times a woman is better at expressing emotions in all kinds of ways deeply facial tone voice body and action she observed these powers quietly not when to bring them out at times when needed even mentally.

Chapter 19

When I write to you women mostly is to let you know respect this passion it is not a woman this passionate. It is not a woman thing a man thing meaning gender it is an individual thing we all get lonely at times. Where it is loneliness or in companionship in the season, in the minute, hour, day, week, month, year, you can always go back to God. This is what I write to you is mostly for the women especially for today typical women especially on how they react carry themselves and act out not all women. I am not putting no one down I am just letting women know men go through what they go through as much. All I am saying women do not nag your man/husband to death. He does something right sometimes compliment him on something when he walks in the house. You can say baby you look handsome you been doing a great job. Sometimes you got to learn how to call those things as not as they were call your husband/man a good man. When he is struggling with his issues, sins, wrongs, or rights you want him to do the same to you 50/50 tell him you see him trying I know what is in him. Do not curse him out, criticize, falsely accuse him then come back and say I love you off and on. How do you expect for him to believe in you like or you believe in him? When you got ways, he cannot even understand that has him confused. Do not be a woman like CSI and still talking about baby we still in love I love you and say a strong woman out here quick. Saying that is not no damn love, I am just being fair because at time it is different you cannot be married acting single a man/husband desire's love, respect, and affection. Women love respect, security, protection, safe, comfortable and patience. God first! Abuse come on in a lot of ways authority to Jeffrey worked on himself as a man better submission for him and became a better provider just not in Cleopatra way. It is natural for a man to seek woman and woman to seek man. I killed what I use to be because it was in order and obedience what God said become. Jeffrey also as well chose to be for my family and Cleopatra. See Jeffrey knew Cleopatra laughed if at times when she was sad and crying inside and outside. She was loving and giving even when she was worn out and exhausted even when I got so upset that when she felt like things hurt her so bad that it was killing her inside. She felt like I did not care then why did I change if I did not? She still was a strong woman she never gave up but only on one person me and I just hope she would have felt this same way for selfishness in her of it was too late my time ran out. Cleopatra was a woman with different types of shoes walking down different paths, sidewalks, rivers, really love and with a huge purse with everything in it good or bad. When she opened it, the lion will come out and attack that is why I see at times just as woman say I need to clean out my purse I got too many things in it just like her car. It can be times that she be driving around in it say she is going to clean it damn this car need cleaning. She is still driving around it and have not cleaned it up just life still carrying around walking around with them. Same excuses and problems not letting them go just only saying the man was the problem. His way what he did not looking at herself. I am waiting for love, attention, affection, caring, understanding and loyalty and am I wrong, I am a man I am not a human being as well I deserve a fair chance just not a fake or phony chance. I watched over Cleopatra family with great love. I am an awesome person. For any woman to be interrupted by greatness in her life is wrong I can be a man and say that or a man but when man or woman change make themselves better in life for the other person as well it is not right politely to encourage them. I ask a woman once to tell me a woman secret. She said now if I tell you then it would not be a secret now will it? Now see a woman is curious a clever I like the word smart! Too damn smart for their own good well Jeffrey knew if he asked Cleopatra what are her secrets? In so many ways she was telling me now that I did know I have to kill you in so many ways. You women know what I mean and where I am coming from. Another word of saying is intellectual in thousands of ways. Many of ways see a woman can have loneliness in her life as well and not let a soul know and sometimes a little out there and have a straight face like nothing is going on. Like focusing on one thing but thinking about another I would say a woman do not even have one mind in my opinion. What I have been in observing, learning, studying, listening to, seeing actions, and my God their mood swings I do not mean that in a bad way. The woman has her means and needs even critical thinking. It can be invisible with her to she can see things that a man cannot. An intellectual woman or a woman period any woman has major turn off buttons as well. A man has his to as well. When this man has a job and not a millionaire or billionaire or has a big-time job it quickly turns you off. A real woman would not settle for being fooled, used, abused, tricked, lied to mislead and cheated in so step back. See listen, hear, watch what your man/husband do not like t do not allow and you know yourself if it cannot be done to you, wait hold up as you say why should he allow it. Women look at one or two or three mistakes probably more than that yes that it because she can take but so much if she is like this and making an agreement to take a man/husband back. It is already a lie because she must work on her of getting herself right of the pain he has taking through. Now if she cannot do that then there is no love or relationship. Do you know people laugh at that it was not funny at all period to do a woman wrong or man wrong or each other but when you come back to one another and make each other pay off and on you feel like it is fun in eyesight saying yeah, yeah they did it to me I am getting them back that is fair but when you over do it? It is not funny women to say and feel that for as long as I want to for all this time I can do it because that time you could have been wasting on the Lord God your husband and you. You will not say right now he or I was thinking about the lord of course because he dogged me. She did not forgive me so she will say it was a waste of time anyway. She will say I did give you a chance but she just being a woman yes let me teach you something like you want to teach your men what kind of woman of God o the woman you choose to be because a woman of God would not be like that or act like that act out in that way. Just like you tell your husband/man in a Godly way correcting him that is not a man of God. Now it be times when you do not want to receive woman/wife the word of God or receive the message from your husband/man I understand it either what he has done even when he has not because a marriage is not perfect or any relationship but you as a wife/woman. Now today a woman wants to be received in a respectful way if your right or wrong. Now when your husband/man is not wrong and is in the holy spirit is it right to provoke him, falsely accuse, him put him down then have the nerve to tell him about the word of God then look at him while his spirit is good and tell him with rolling your eyes. I know you not telling me about the word of God you got a lot of nerve, child please, MMMMM, whatever, get out my face, then come back talking about some I love you. Now your man/husband does not hurt you do not think about both of you because you're not thinking about God first and you and what you have said and done to him with the actions of your sins your just thinking about his all the time even if when you do think, feel and pray on your wrong towards God with you on your knees towards the wrong you and to the same way when you get off your knees back to him it do not mean nothing at all. It is society it is the mindset. Now today I have seen a lot of women wanting and getting their man to read and getting on them plenty of women. Then when your man tells you to stop watching so much television it is a problem. He is refusing to pick up a book and you are refusing to put more time into him or whatever it is you have a problem. Women love to talk so do men so how you going to tell your man to shut up. No! if it takes 3 hours listen to ONE ANOTHER! See Jeffrey stop being ignorant towards Cleopatra he informed her opinion and facts on her feminism and how she felt about everything Jeffrey loved it because he was proud that he changed that Jeffrey did a good thing in change for God and himself and family but still being called and treated like a fuck up and he was not like shit. How do that feel just because you do not smell like shit does not mean you do not feel like it. She never saw that if it was all my fault and everything was on me. I backed up my claims. Jeffrey also paid attention to Cleopatra's words, her actions and feelings because when she said can I ask you something and you promise you will not get mad baby, Jeffrey would say no I will not after she forgave me laying down in our bed she will ask me why you cheated on me, and Jeffrey will say you forgave me for that. Why is you bringing that up? Then she will argue, get loud then curse me out. Women will say not all but mostly would say what did you expect her to do you made her this way then, what did you do to her to make her act this way. Please do not drag someone back and forth vice versa man you will kill yourself with hurt and pain that you cannot let go. A woman can be thinking of plenty of things she can be looking at a man or woman and can have her mind on multiple of things especially about her own life. She wants to be satisfied in so many ways you can't even imagine and when you do she wants more and more, needs, wants, say so's and demands it can be good or bad this is about a woman/women I'm just letting my passion out and experience what I've seen and learned about women in life and the ones I have been with cheated on been used by and the one who did treated me good that I messed up on, as well as my 4 sisters, aunties, mother, grandmother's thousands of women teaching me as well because I learned not only did a woman/women teach me. Now I can have my opinions facts or agree or not agree that does not mean I am right on everything I have lied I have done women wrong a man can say that tell and admit to his flaws and wrong doings and learn from his mistakes correcting by changing to be better. Now it's true I done sat down with plenty of women and saw it from my own eyes and heard it see the actions and reactions of them and hear them saying everything is a man fault now women and I mean plenty who have sat down in a relationship not every woman because every woman is not the same and I have seen how the man tell the woman I like you but I'm not in love with you or I just want to be friends then the woman and man agree to have sex with one another then that woman to have feelings for him see don't say that's not a woman some or most will say that's lust, flesh and the wrong thing to every woman have been here I know about the part and understand about at times men lying to you to fuck and have sex to use you to tell you anything, and vice versa of you letting things at times when at times blaming the men for al wrongs. When I know I sat down with this woman name Michelle. She said its time I sat down with girlfriends and sisters, and they must explain to Jeffrey that they did tell the truth of them still being in love with Cleopatra and we broke-up. I have not gotten over her. I told the truth straight forward and was not lying at all. The woman and him made the choice to be friends. They would have sex together and goes to another level with the woman. She can start saying I love you or it can be both telling each other they love one another. The women say it is on the man even when he tells her the truth. Like I met a woman named Makasy she saw me living on the streets she helped me and gave me some where to live. When I did not have nothing or nowhere to go looking and finding another I moved in her house. Really her parents' house with the father, mother that was married now make it 36 years, so I was sleeping on the couch at first. When I first moved in the brother and grandfather-n-law was the mother, father so she told me come sleep in the room with her because she knew I was uncomfortable on the couch the I was sleeping on so when I start sleeping in the room she was talking to me more and more. I was listening and hearing Makasy said I have been a virgin for 33 years, so I said that is a blessing she was listening when I told her I was divorced 2 years from Cleopatra and she ask me, are you still in love with her and have feelings for her? I said yes I do, she said why? I said because someone you been with so long and for years really a long time together being married to you just can't get over someone just like that that overnight just like a woman/wives/women saying or any human being in life how they feel pain, hurt, weeping but we as peoples sometimes do go overboard, anyway I let her know all the wrongs I did then I let her know all the wrongs Cleopatra did she said you are special and you have a great heart and then she said I wouldn't tell you everything is all on you and your fault and I said what woman/women/wife Cleopatra or other mothers have been teaching me. I said she's not hear to speak for herself and you don't know what everything she felt been through and experience because she's a woman just like you now I learned that from a woman and Makasy said I understand that but everything is still not your fault and only you did wrong that's selfish so myself and her started sleeping together and I let her know still that I still have feelings for Cleopatra she said I know I respect that at least you was honest with me and told me the truth. Now see not meaning this was not right in God eyes I am letting women know where you are getting your feelings and make wrong decisions as well and bad choices just as men because I know I can be a person judging myself. Everyone wants a love that lasts a lifetime but at times it be disappointment on heartache and wrong doings not just only cheating, using, lying and abusing women or your opinion or fact only be just because the husband the woman can have the wrong mentality at times her thinking I do not have nothing against women I am just telling the truth their thousands of thoughts, thinking, fantasizes, body gestures and personalities with memory. At times a woman can set a period of time during which specific work has to be completed she can be rushing, slowing down, patience, controlling, mixed up, a career, at charge, calm, collect, in a hurry or rush, speed, it's just 1`more and more and this is all in what's going on what's coming in going out what mind set she's already in or out she's a woman she can change up at any time and she's much different than a man it can be mood swings of hell of scornful bitterness or it can be good ways as well she's a woman and especially what mood she's in. Now I have walked up to plenty of men, and I have asked them what can you tell me about a woman? Most of them said I do not know a lot, but they speak about some things experiencing from women in the past, or the woman they are with some have said you have to ask a woman that because they are not a woman. Do that mean you suppose to down men and say everything is their fault believe me it does not go like that for women as being human beings, so the same thing vice versa. Then some will say in the profession that all women not the same or that is women you dealt with or saw like that. Now you can ask woman/wife is she married to Jesus Christ depending on what mood she is in with a good spirit. She will answer then when she is in a bad spirit she will tell you up and down thinking about something that she should have gotten over years and years ago and multiple thoughts in her mind, memories of confusion and women will say do you blame her! Now you have many women say what you, you must do something but that is not always true because it is a woman way in her nature to do her wrongs and a woman is past her time at times you can give her 10,000 dollars, 20,000, 30,000, 40,000, 50,000 and up. It is not about the money she would say not meaning that she must be angry because when she is watch out what do you mean? I was doing for myself before you came in the damn picture, you are throwing that in my face, what had I before you came in the picture. See at times seriously it does not be a throw up in a woman face as she uses against him at times. It is she is not forgiving him and guilty for her wrong doings would not admit it, blame and accuse him for everything. The number 1 the husband/man is trying to say is baby from the heart you are not appreciating me or loving ma and not seeing my responsibility as a man with trust, God first, faith, understanding and communication. Like the woman gets hurt in this way it is a different story because a woman is different than a man. Well, I am sorry to tell you people that feel in this way to put their opinion and take and put it how they want to just to make someone feel good or being selfish in their own way. It will be all kinds of ways with people following them making them angry. More bitter, unforgiving, scornful, having a hurtful soul more it is just like false bishops, prophets, pastors, evangelist leading people. They are not leaders because if they were they will be doing the same job Moses did and a lot of women today typically wanting their husband/man. What poetries men, movie stars, T.V. show actors, bishop, pastors and other men out there to be! A lot of women cannot get along together how you going to out slick a slicker it is not a game. When a woman knows you finding her out on certain things. She changes it do not have to be anything bad really depending on the situation. A lot of women feel like men let them down this is true please do not leave left out women hurt men than women say not how they hurt us. It just like us as sinners. It is in different ways, but it is still the same thing a sin. Some women will say men bring God in as an excuse to try to get away for what he done wrong how so you not going to let that side especially not God. See Cleopatra is a sophisticated woman. She is greatly confident. She was so deep of her own intelligence to ask questions that a person might feel reveal on his or her my or anyone ignorance, but one of the things where she thought she was so smart at was telling me and saying everything was my fault this is for women who say and feel in that way just because someone is wrong for everything that does not mean it is true. They will swear up and down with selfishness that it is true. Every woman is not the same day but on a different second minutes, hours, days, months, years, time after time that either have been through what that woman/wife. Women have been through did, tried, felt reacted you know what I am to say women I have seen plenty of women out of my family in my family and stayed quiet and observed and learn and watched the ways of a woman I said that is the same way my sisters and mom, aunties, cousins as women, grandmothers, reacted as women! A woman some or most will. Ask meaning in what way what I am trying to say coming at me in all kinds of ways. Cleopatra always had eyes contact with Jeffrey not only just being attracted but in love as well. She is a strong woman. She would not let anything, anyone or anybody mess up her reputation not even me. She loves to be appreciated about her man and give her the attention, pamper her, shower her with gifts. See I would like to say the same thing for me that in this world there is a lot of faulty, nasty, negative, thinking about forgiveness and the actions gets water down and ignored, advised and cheated on. I think that mostly women need to learn about what the bible says about forgiveness and how I applied it for myself. I even learned from people who done me wrong. See there is thousands of ways to be abused not being selfish in our own way because, because m but, but you, you, me, me we want God to please us all the time. We need to please one another and God. When Jeffrey got saved and gave my life to God at the same time when Jeffrey grabbed Cleopatra and he hugged her. I turned off my brain and let my heart do the talking ever since I loved God, myself, our children and changed. God made my life different I was excited. How can I not be real on something that I put my time, want, God, my all, responsibility, God whipping on me and his wrath, my repentance, my forgiveness, honesty, encouragement, I put love in it because I came back dirty, and God cleaned me up. I was healed from the inside. See now when a woman gets hurt it is wrong but most of them say it is because it is how men or y'all men or you men treated us because it will get out of hand sometimes. Women will hurt men sometimes and then act like you hurt them for all kinds of reasons and be selfish. See a man needs mental and emotional support too. It does not be times he does not think about making love Jeffrey knew he did not with Cleopatra that is why when she told him she prayed and ask God to give me back. I prayed for the same thing as well and having faith God gave us what we asked for. Then her asking me while I took you back. When I was saved hearing, saying you doing the same thing. I should not never take you back telling her man that is the same as telling God I do not believe in relationship, love, caring, and this is not my man. You do not build your relationship back to someone you forgiven, marriage, wife, husband or anyone. How do you expect to forgive you? You know a lot of women say since I let that mango my life has been blessed, good and a lot do be real and tell their sins of what they done they go through. It secretly says everything all the time was all the flaws on that man. Did you go back to that husband/man tell him you were sorry and ask for forgiveness? No, because the bitterness and scornful women. Women now today it is all the man fault everything. How can a woman be at peace because I hear and see them say that, but a man cannot? Women or men even a relationship is not perfect at all just do not give up despite any hurt or pain Cleopatra gave up on Jeffrey. When her mind was negative already to tell me, I wish I would not ever take you back. I asked her when we were home in the bed before she put on heels getting ready to make love dead serious I asked her baby I am giving you all the love you deserve right? Cleopatra said now why you ask me that with an attitude and still make love to Jeffrey. Then after the making love she was back see a woman becomes ten times the woman was before when she was given the love she deserves. It was not me it was that when I gave the love she was not ready to receive it because she was bitter. She was just like a cactus plant only thing I could do was water her and look at her but if I touch her it would not be in the wrong way. It will be the way she feels and say it is no matter it is me. I was bleeding every time I touch her the best part is that when the needles of the plant will fall off because at times she wanted to be left alone and not be touched at all and to herself. I could tell you everything or feel because at times when I walk in and talk to her and hold he she be angry, bitter with vengeance and push me away and say do not touch me. She will make the needles come out again out of the plant. She was to hurt my feelings put me in pain of the pain she was still holding on to. Jeffrey loved Cleopatra when she cheated, lying when she said baby I know you a good man. I have been too hard on you I am sorry; you are fucking that woman again. I am sorry you were at her house. I am sorry you hard on the children letting do certain things then come back and say she sorry for getting them right there of the principle that I am the husband/parent/man. Just like she is the parent/wife/woman. See there is many ways to cheat. I became a man that wanted and chose to be kept. I started thinking with my first head not second one. Now do you women appreciate your man/husband after he has hurt you? Do go tell him baby I deserve a good special man like you are giving him credit after he and you know he done made up for what he has done. Jeffrey showed it with action not with just saying I am sorry Cleopatra. Jeffrey knew he hurt Cleopatra bad she was not supposed to be so bitter that she could not love Jeffrey all over again and not love herself first. I was not only on God I was looking for other ways to make it work because I loved her still do! She did not even show me action with love while I was fixing myself. When I let her know she will scream at me and say I am. I know you not talking, or she has been hurt so what she does not care she was telling me leave me alone get from around me. Them when I do she will tell me you do not fucking love me because if you did you would not have left. She just told me to leave. Then it is you double and triple because you gone now and from women. She did not mean that she just hurt from what I did to her. I could not have ignored her because I came right back after she cursed me out. Jeffrey was not afraid to love again but at first he was but when Jeffrey got saved he left it in God hands, but Jeffrey knew Cleopatra was afraid to show it because she might get hurt again by Jeffrey. I did not blame her for that, but we need to stick it out with God. I could not keep taking the blame and being blamed for everything. Women will feel her and say we know where she is coming from. We have been through what she went through. Can you understand me and feel me or am I being a woman right now with feelings? Jeffrey could not fall asleep fast next to Cleopatra because the past separated her from Jeffrey and unforgiveness and depression that was the burning bed. Jeffrey will admit he was a boy, a child at that but then Jeffrey did become a man but had picked God heart up fixed mines and my queen Cleopatra. I cannot even say my Ex because I love her the Lord knows that these false prophets, teachers, evangelists, bishops, stop telling things in our relationship to husband/man, wives/women that. When your wife hurts you that is love but then say when he hurts his wife it is that man you got to pay 60/40 happy wife is happy life. No do not mislead God sheep like that because do not say that feel that, like that or does not agree with. We can be selfish to agree what we feel that is right. Jeffrey fought for Cleopatra to get her back because he knew what he would have felt like and been like of losing her and ever hear me or her say and feel you do not when you got a good thing until it is gone. See you here matters now today on cycle teach their daughters this when they are miserable and said you do not mix those men look at what he did to you be in their business. Now I did not say do not be there I said be in their business because they be miserable and do not want to see them happy because when you see them happy then change she is not happy! A woman cries in secrets. It can be times for battles many hurts and laugh at times it can be so joyful like Cleopatra. When she first met me, it was more than just making her laugh. Why she picks me back up just that fast in her Sentra. I like the names she called it her hooptie and poup it was other secrets. She just did not let me know everything right there and then that is a woman she did not give up easily. What I liked was that she was stronger than people thought. Now even when Cleopatra thought Jeffrey was a bad story all by himself and made her life miserable and burn in hell there still was times a lot that Jeffrey was good to her. She will never tell that part to me or no one. I still talk good and positive about the glass small teddy bear. I love pushing the surprise to herself and heart. See Jeffrey was real with himself Jeffrey prayed from his heart Jeffrey stop worrying about Cleopatra and focused on his behavior, his ways, what he needed to get into order to become. Yes the reflects did come back on me I was looking at myself in the mirror. See a woman has certain secrets. Anything that she feels embarrassed about she is going to keep undercover or in secret she will fall always feel highly about herself. She still is the jewels in Jeffrey life that is Cleopatra! A woman is not satisfied for long she says, feels and know when she leaves her husband/man to leave the one she was with yes that is the truth but do not be bitter for years, years, and years. I so not need a man. I do not want a man at all. I need my children and myself for years God will send you a good man. Do not be mad at the world and yourself. Even if a lot of different me cheated on you, abused and used you. You must let that go to move forward with your life not just jumping in another relationship right away no, because I did not just jump in one and I am a man. It is at times when women work or a woman she thinks hard of letting her job take away most of her children time. A woman loves a big house that is secure and well maintained, a beautiful garden a beautiful marriage and she still not satisfied. A woman will still complain even with sex it does not have to be bad. I heard a lot of women talk and they done said all kind of things about having sex shit he be killing me girl, but it be good still complaining about it, but it is still good that is just a woman. Then I heard another woman his beard be killing me, but it be good when the licks, sucks and eats this vagina good. Then it be he be ripping me open, and I can feel him going in my stomach complaining then saying it is good! Some women will say that is no women talking like that or putting they business all women done have talked no one is perfect. Long story short women learn from other women for being around one another. Therefore, they cannot stay around each other. She will tell another woman what she wants her to hear so once that man leaves so she can come into get what that other woman has not knowing it was her blessing. Now just her thrill with a woman with her etiquette goes with her reaction of her behavior, manners, good form, philosophy, culture, social, interaction, business, nice, best behavior, rules of conduct, proper, conduct, class, effort, polite, protocol, personal, genuine, game, code, standard, finishing school, good and sophisticated. A woman can lead a man on a man can also lead a woman on but the woman on, but the woman has the reverse psychology down pack. The woman disgrace herself or themselves in many ways throughout the years. She will determine a lifetime with you. She also can play with you she has so many things on her silent it does not have to be games not saying it is not at times because then she will be perfect. See Cleopatra will look at Jeffrey while we are having a conversation. Then I say something be right and honest. Then she says nothing see with a woman at times that can be your thinking because of how she said, and the conversation was not even over but the other way around. When she wants to be heard you are going to hear her loud and clear. Then when Cleopatra uses to say go good or bad. This was a silent watch good or bad the woman it was permission to go and to a lot of other women you know. She means this or that so why did you do it anyway? See women I know! Then whatever this is the eye rolling, sucking the teeth I do not care, or he should not have done what he did. He is going to pay for it depending on what he did. How long she says it last for. Then Cleopatra would tell Jeffrey if it were ok sit there and be thinking quiet on when and how to make he pay for a little mistake. I would make and big she will make putting everything on me and it will be for a long, long time for one day feeling like 5 years for one day. Cleopatra also I am okay, I am alright, it is okay, I am fine, it is dropped that really does not mean that every time. She just used that to the end the argument or disagreement when she knows she is right anyway, and I just need to shut the hell or shut the fuck up or I just talk to fucking much. Men I feel your pain of what you are going through. I just cannot feel only women pain focusing on one thing only men cheat not all men. Every woman is not the same so is every man is not! Jeffrey got his mind right so Jeffrey can respect Cleopatra beautiful body, mind, face opinion, fact and most of all listening. Now the right woman will have you backing you up saving money God first praying, eating better, health, strength, motivated, laughing constantly, making good moves. Now you have women say the man already supposed to be doing this that is bullshit because in a relationship they build up one another. If one is not good with doing something the other comes in vice versa. If you are going to tell or teach something do not do it with your opinion. Run with it then change it your own way. See this thing has people mislead, confused and brain washed! You are never too good to be nice to people and teach them good and learn tell them what you have been through. How to handle it in a right fair way not your way for fame, publicity. That is just like a lot of democrats and republicans they have debates. A lot of people feel and say they know that most republicans are nasty that do not mean you do not have some nice one's. It is nice democrats, and you have some of them that are mean and nasty. The republicans will sometimes agree with the democrats this called a debate. A fact people are entitled to them are own opinion and facts but right is right and wrong is wrong. Some people change up in office everyone really. You have independence as well the point I am trying to make is to women is men. You as women change up in marriages, relationship and it be just like the white and this world at times. See women how hard your man/men/ husband tries to satisfy you on any or try every level there is you must know what loves feel like all over again. If you truly forgive him and this is not only coming with forgiveness this coming all in so many ways, actions! Your emotional right? You know your man is doing the right thing and all the time while you saying you do not know what he done. He did why I am this way you made me this way your spending 90% of your time on that ignoring how you done lost interest in him going back to God holding God's hand with one and holding your husband hand with the other. A lot of you women say you do not know how long this take so you want to ignore. How long you will sit there lonely, miserable, provoking, not happy and pushing him away. So, all that you have done thrown back up in his face after he has done good you do not think his heart closes? Oh, you do not care! This man or men wants your time by him shoulder to shoulder you holding him not just him holding you they want you to do something with them. You do not feel like your man want you to watch or play a game with him doing almost anything. Especially the things he enjoys makes him feel loved all over again fresh and new. Now this is his time women! We know about yours it deep! Well, I would not say everyone because everyone does not walk in the same shoes, but I know to understand. What someone else been through at times they been through it already like me. Women I have been raped several times, so I know what you been through. I been abused so I feel you and I abused women and took it out on myself and them for what I been through. Women you do the same of cycles off your mothers, grandmothers, aunties, sisters, cousins, and other experience. It does not all be on men like the system treats black men something 10 years ago they will bring back up and throw in your face that you did time for. I have seen and learned how a woman sits down in a chair, couch in a restaurant and look out her window or a window from anywhere, place, time, moment and think, wonder, stare of her life. God or multiple things. It can be crying out secretly when it comes to truth a woman is quiet. Her bank accounts are separate from her husband. Her plans a lot of you do not need a man's companionship, traveling, protection for her. Caress towards for her security coming from a man. She loves to sit there with her legs crossed over depending on the woman and do her thing classy. A woman can have a one-track mind and multiple tracks at times. She can be talking about a lot of issues at the same time. She also multitasks cook, clean, wash dishes, take care of her children love and take care of her husband, wash, baby sit there is so many things the woman take charge on! She also is interesting and a mystery mysterious all by herself. She will be open with certain people for respect within herself not only do a man have to face the truth about himself so does a woman. At times, the woman can be in a way sometimes where she can be difficult sometimes and look at the man and say he got her aggravated when she is in her own ways. I know we have our own ways she is just being her mood at the time even impossible to understand. When she explains something or identify it is right 99% of the time. See this is one reason why the woman is strange, weird, curious, always observing. She is mysterious about herself but say a lot about her husband/man/men even her. This is about women/woman. She can be satisfied to a certain extent. Cleopatra knew I loved her. I knew she loved me. She was just afraid to do it all over again. God knew I loved her with every fiber in my being. Women have you went to your man/husband that you have and let him know how bad you have treated him with your own actions and sins without throwing the past back in his face or bringing back up to get away with your wrongs and let him know how he has been mistreated. A lot of things coming towards him. See a woman know how to accept a compliment depending on what type of mood she is in. It has been lots of women walked out of a bad relationship that is true and did they ever sit down themselves and thought what they did on somethings to mess up the relationship. As well as some will get mad at this some will say you got something against woman. Some will say what woman hurt you and every woman is not the same and most of all finally when she come to her time. She will admit in her time it is like saying or telling you not going to tell her what she is thinking what she is going to say. What to say or when she gets ready to quote girlfriends, I know that is right girl! A woman knows how to take a compliment of when you tell her, you did particularly good today, your beautiful, I know you prayed today. Sometimes a woman can put her own self down and not point out her wrong doings and weaknesses at times. Jeffrey was in a relationship to Cleopatra. How to say no sometimes I was saying yes to everything then it went overboard only person supposed to get spoiled I know is God. A lot of people that have children their parent's friend's relationship etc. This can be a good thing not all the time to a certain extent because everyone that is human beings will take this overboard. Especially if your raised up with it then you get everything. Then when you get said no it will be times you want to blame the other person and yourself. Then say I should not have never gotten into this mess. What mess? Don't you love that person? Now some women will say he did this. He did that okay. Get him I agree but when you do, when are going to stop? Then when he does it is a problem because he started it. Now you going to finish it and it be no finish most of the time it be a divorce, a breakup, a separation, a move up, a move down and still be married to one another still and be out there doing your thing women men just do not do this. You do to!! See a real woman knows how to stand her ground and say her peace and at times she gets out of control and out of hand and it is not this woman for mostly everything sometimes I can agree it is SOMETHING YOU DID; THE MAN DID TO MAKE HER THAT WAY!! Yes HIM/MEN/MAN. Your man/husband wants and deserve to feel good, and he has the right to ask. He knows what makes you feel good, now when Jeffrey laid down in bed with Cleopatra when he saw and knew what she wanted without her even telling me Jeffrey gave it and she wanted it when she got ready and we was in a relationship look at that then when she ask for it and he gave it guess what it still wasn't good enough are women or woman or some going to say because it's all what you done. See I was looking for spirit of love from her of relaxation being more confident this world has been good for both of us. Can you keep positive words women I am not saying women are bad we as men can live without you just slow down the negative words at times like when your husband/man talks to you do not come with negativity like stop with the attitude, gone now, leave me alone, shouting, gone. Whatever I did not say if he is dead wrong, I said when times when he is showing love and he wants that give in common courtesy, love encouragement just like you do when you in your mood swings and ways. You can love your soul mate but if one is loving and the other one is not, and this goes on for years and years what will happen? But, because, you just don't know, or understand, you, me, excuses run out so much, see when Jeffrey got saved I knew love, I went to God tired on my knees with the lust, flesh, lying, cheating, manipulating, worried, stress, foolishness, the curses, excuses, sorrow, abuse towards God by hurting him with my sin and my sin towards myself, Cleopatra, my family even other peoples I hurt family members, provoking, and accusing everyone else for their wrongs but me. When I repented the love was there when God forgave me then when I loved God then myself then I did right by God to give it to Cleopatra, but the most important thing Jeffrey learned was not only how to treat Cleopatra how to love her as a strong woman she is. My woman only her how God says love her not only how she wants to be love God as well first as Christ love the church then myself was humble walking away listening, hearing, I did not get the submissive wife it took time, so I backed up and let the Wife/Woman be I took my time, so I did not rush pain takes time I did not rush pain takes time to get over women I know. It does not happen overnight, and we cannot ever be God, stop saying do not put God in it. Then God is in it. Then we go to church we hear the Bishop, Pastors, and in the house of God say the most divorces and marriages is because GOD is not involved 3x then when we leave the church what happens? I am not saying women or men I am saying WE! Women and men to I am going to tell you when Jeffrey came with love to Cleopatra. Even with her being bitter off and on. When you can love a bitter woman that is a strong man like women love a dog. Some men or most men or thugs, abusive men, raped men, jailed men from jail and prison from broken down homes teaching them love in ways they do not know how to like a woman do not in certain ways. We are not perfect, so these men love to it is not. Every man in the world that is bad and no good has it been times in the life women where you have been told you no good, your nasty, your slimy, how you talk, how you treat someone or your man/husband and get away with it with baby I am sorry forgive me, ok! I get it is that's just men cheat more than women do so that is the only thing make it worse. Now it was taught then I can agree but back to Jeffrey loving Cleopatra only my woman #1 her (IN LOVE AS WELL) even seeing her love for me providing, protection, leadership, respect, my paycheck that is right I said it. She cannot say but because I did it. She came back to apologize can't say but because I did it and she came back to apologize back and forth yes I know from her and women because how I treated her back in forth but I got it right though didn't I? with myself and God & God & myself one relationship I made her feel secure she just didn't want to receive if at time and after she forgave me and on and on, being kind to her. As Cleopatra as a strong black woman, she was not going to fall in love with just any kind of man it must be the right one and praying to God asking God to give Jeffrey back to her he could not be too much of a fuck or shit as she says she did see good in Jeffrey because she would not have taking him back she got what she wanted and showed out child I got this from the woman, Her. Like she use to tell me everyone see you even home sit down somewhere. You know I saw the respect of the foundation that was necessary in order for herself to grow and love herself back as well because she was too angry she looked at only how Jeffrey was raised not her as well see this what I'm teaching women the way we also fall in love is off attachments to as how Cleopatra was raised as well so we fell in love both with cycle's stop saying the man has the worse cycles, woman/women was you there at the time he was raised? Men stop saying the same thing. What to do is encourage to break it and leave it in God hands in life we know it is not easy days every day but let us do whatever it is with the love of God to save our souls and the love of our lives. Woman/Women you are not the only one been through somethings I say this to men to. Jeffrey loved Cleopatra from the bottom of his heart, his mind, soul, spirit with every fiber in his being even with all the helping, understanding, communicating, responsible for her because if something would of happen to her Jeffrey couldn't live himself that's hard for her to believe but the things she did and said of hatred she will die for Jeffrey anyway so with her sins madness, angry, happy she did and Jeffrey didn't just because she said I didn't do nothing at all that does not mean that is true. See when a woman/woman is raised as child in the household with a single mother or father even both. Especially when it is extremely strict with a mom fighting, talking, shouting, screaming, cursing, control attitude this is mental abuse towards the daughter and physical and can damage the heart and brain with the soul and always told what to do. She will get men like this because that she saw me grow up around that. This is somewhat of love is the way to be transformed and expressed not saying she will as well have her awesome love there is light in her. See Cleopatra was comfortable with this in ways acting out and actions like her mom. Just like my household of being raised. It was abuse, drugs, alcohol, so what was so different? What will God say we will come our own opinions, God do not come with that he comes with the truth, light and facts always. We will not be right always but learn and stay getting back on-board holding hands together. When we fall we can get back on? Cleopatra could not be in love with Jeffrey ever again when she started saying I should not of never took your ass back. I was around her all the time. She did not show me no action of transformation for the transition for love for me again. She took me back loved me the stopped loving me. Then stop because just like Eve with Satan in the garden every time I had done right the devil tempted her and she grabbed his hand married to him ok get him again, there he goes he is doing it a woman's intuition's. So, the way Cleopatra saw Jeffrey is the way she saw that all the time that did not mean it was that, because if she started loving herself as well as our relationship then she would of saw, felt, action the fact she did not do it by herself not even me we did it. To her it was only about her children because I hurt her and did all the wrong, I am a man God still said we was in partnership. She said out her mouth off the tongue, feelings, actions, that this relationship was already separated so she relationship under false pretense thinking everything was going to be ok loving me so much a woman does love hard, but her heart was right, and her bitterness was scorned out even more. Cleopatra stated as well identifying in Jeffrey face that she does not want his ass and she do not need his ass. How can she still be in love when she shows and states that the love is no longer there and see me failing on everything there is on her and life as nothing where she sees me and herself as blaming me for everything as a separate entity from her husband/man and marriage and relationship is not nothing anymore. Still until this day I will take the 60% being wrong but I will not take everything blamed on me!! I showed her I appreciated her when she was blind to see it was not on me and my fault that was on her dealing with God like my own actions and sins towards her. I showed her I kept it there as a man of God I remained it there I even sing songs to her. I was all about action showing God myself and her I had to get me right ready in order before I started this was high level for me because I did not want to mess up something that I got back again and loose it was not easy to get back the first time so why mess up again. Did she see me as a person? A human being am I really shit we know how it looks and smells I did not even say her baby fathers was not shit I told them to always pray for them and love them with the wrongs, sins good or bad. With Cleopatra flaws, ways, attitude, bitching, complaining, getting curse out good Jeffrey still loved her just the way she was letting her know she was all that and a hand full. I even sacrifice who I was. I was afraid to say things because I was afraid she would keep blaming me from the past. How can I increase something from someone that does not want to give it to me? I was being more than a husband. I can, you can increase with and for yourself because the other person is putting you down and do not love them self or you. At times, a woman can be petty in many ways she does this also to see how he reacts pushing all kinds of buttons of his. Not does the woman/women can be petty she also can be competitive she can be comfortable with herself. Cleopatra would be very petty at times her tone will be outrageous say what she means and mean what she says with her madness into it and if I did not like it oh well the hell with it. She will know she is fine she is good she will know for sure say no quickly, I do not care, bye, so what, and let it be. Let me know without a doubt I am acting like a child and know every time she is right for everything!! Most women do not like other women see this the part where it comes in where a woman will say (child please) or (whatever) (stay quiet) or have her own opinion, statement or facts. See another woman cannot out slick another woman we will that depends on what they are doing, and that woman pertaining to that situation or problem, they do not have to be talking to one another at times they can just feel certain body gestures, signs, looks, fragrance, actions it can be I know her who do she think she is? It can be a false sense of who they want to protect they role and this is a woman insecurity as well in ways times in moments. Another thing I would like to say is women it is not about how much family members or friends matter it is about how much your man matters. Now black women talk about how men knock one another over. Do they see how they knock one another? Cleopatra was in deep politics with another woman being belittled and being angry as a straight threat towards her and it was not nothing at first it was her with her intuitions herself what she thought it was and not. Cleopatra would take a small subject and just blow it out of proportion and let Jeffrey know quick he has no reason never at all to tell her that she right for everything! She even enjoyed when I fall instead of helping me up. She was petty at times she was not afraid to call me out she was so narrow minded at times because her last word was not even last it was a paragraph she knows she was right even when she knew she was wrong, and she knew that I knew but like she said she did not care. When you say you do not care there is no love, no emotions, no feelings or nothing with love involved anymore. She didn't mind blocking me out at all times and ignoring me we are married because I cheated when I want to make love I'm a cheater, a liar, no good, slimy, all about sex, all about fucking but it's still good you love it and curse me out the same time telling me that's all I want to do and I see you as but when you want to make love you're the good woman and the saint. Just because Cleopatra is not the one that cheated her mouth and self is clean to make love to Jeffrey he does not understand why are you making love to the person who you treat, say put down as the enemy? Taking note of everything off me then it is not fair pain or equal it is overboard Cleopatra acted like she did not care but deep down inside she did at times. I could feel the balls beating up against me as she will say see the bitterness to control over her being afraid to be hurt again is important but when you start over do not bring that back up if we are starting a fresh start all over again. How do you women get angry at something your husband/man did but it is ok if you do it but not him? Women are better liars than men and very persuasive know how to get what she wants they are revengeful some women also have secrets like torn between two lovers or more secret lovers this man for this and that man for that. Cleopatra was persuasive and particularly good at it. She will learn things watching her mother and listening to her when Jeffrey got Cleopatra a car then Cleopatra's mom said to her husband being jealous snuggles I want a Mercedes Benz pouting whining like a baby at the same time now watch this I am up on the game just like the woman Cleopatra never did this when Jeffrey got with her she starts asking me for things pushing her lips out like her mom. You might as well say doing it in her way learning game from the mom. I have learned another thing with woman/women at times they or she can be petty she can be this way in multiple ways being spoiled and be a particular woman that like certain things and does not accept any and everything. I just learned so many things about the woman/women I can't stop writing I don't even know if I would end it, hopefully I do because the woman is encyclopedia, math, science, arts, dictionary, calculator, a brain and mind of the whole world by herself woman/women please stop the past hurts you will bring pain on your husband/man that's on you already I know he caused it so what do you do? Continue to do will fix it or make it worse? All that is weakness and not being strong. Do not just be a strong woman as on competing, competition, attitude of control no there's other ways to in your beauty and natural inner self as God made you!! See women that are hurt when you admit your wrongs the marriage/relationship will improve you know everything is not your husbands/man fault he did not get married by himself or to himself only. Talk to him do not ignore him because when you hide and put the mask on your face you close your heart, soul, love and everything else with it even God. See when Jeffrey got saved he took responsibility for his actions fairly as the man of God so it could result from the pain, but Cleopatra did not let the pain go Jeffrey could not do it all by himself. I did not be around no negativity or bad men people who will say or bring curses or spirits on me to take home to my family. Cleopatra pushed Jeffrey to go to church Jeffrey pushed her she pushed him to pray he pushed her she pushed him to read the Bible he pushed her but in the end of it all the woman is always right and never wrong!! I was defensive abusive, controlling, loud, angry and then I changed, and this goes for me, you are including everyone that been here and treat the person in the same way it is not them it is yourself with in things that you could not let go still blaming the person who has stopped completely from hurting you. This when you come in as a woman/women very bitter and it just don't have to be off of almost everything taken away it could be things that it's been time to let go and you are so defensive you don't want to hear nothing he don't have a right to nothing your treating him like the system he gets into trouble he violates his rights then does his time with God punishing him paying his debt off to society and still gets treated wrong he can be driving one day get pulled over he's at the wrong place at the wrong time, either way it go's everything comes back on him he does not have to be in trouble or a problem. See women are incredible but when it comes in when she can't forgive her behavior be very defensive there will be no honesty locks everything but and blocks out love as well in her relationship/marriage in her mind it's just accumulating more and more then it never goes away because then you have the mother's, sister's, girlfriends, coworkers, friends, associates even women in church women she don't know as well because of talks, dysfunctional silence, secrets, gossips, drama, and tell your husband/man you're not talking to anyone focusing on him more what he's doing wrong. He is just period!! Women change for God's sake and yours getting yourself right then your husband/man past hurts family members will damage your relationship especially when they home and relationship is already damaged like Cleopatra's mother Pam and her will say why we will be on great terms stating out her mouth to her mom you are trying to break up my relationship because your miserable and your marriage is not going right, or anywhere. Then my man is doing right and treating me good, and you do not like him Cleopatra is telling her mom this and told Jeffrey as well that her mom does not like no one Cleopatra gets with at all and do not like Jeffrey for what he did in the past and did not like him when she first met him. I have been with and around a lot of mother's/women/woman be protective of their children that's good tough love and unconditionally but at times they can be over protective and go overboard especially when they are grown and have moved out on their owned respect they parents feel that they still talk to them any kind of way treat them wrong and this is called being naïve now leave them in God hands it's times to stand up because when you don't then that will damage you even more and every time you get married or be to yourself this cycle will remain the same and be hard to break!! Jeffrey knows he had a bad defensive cycle and was very destructive, but Cleopatra had a great family as well as her that did no wrong until it was time for her mom and her to say it so where did she get those ways from? Her mom, you cannot change no one especially elders they be stuck in there ways even if they were raised one certain way even my ways at times but use that to hurt people repeatedly that is not right because you will not want it done to you especially when it hits you off guard. Jeffrey knows because people have done it to him, and Jeffrey did it to someone special that loved him with there all and everything Cleopatra. We did it to one another even before we got married and when we got married. See a woman wants you to love her without sex she wants is you to love her for who she is. I am not going to lie when Jeffrey met Cleopatra he was a child thinking and acting with his second head instead of my head, brain, smart and intelligent respectfully Jeffrey thought with the head between his legs. Then when I got saved and gave my life to God it was not about sex in the bedroom or sex period. Cleopatra will get on top of Jeffrey choking him being mean mad and bitter saying you are going to give me some dick today, then I want some love. Now is this not the woman being bitter in her way acting out thinking with what is between her legs and what she can get out of the deal and what she can get and want she is not thinking with love she is thinking I just want some dick he lost those privileges I forgave him, but I did not forget so I can use this at any time I can. It will always a weapon he did it first and what he took me through is that not acting or being selfish and foolish? Please do not come back with you have to continue to get him back constantly because this comes where it goes back and forth maybe the woman feels like the husband/man has not hurt enough of what he has taken her through and her hurt of his past doings is too much on her. I know for sure going on continually after you say you have forgiving and truly not you are the one that need help more the other person. We all have done some wrong throwing something up in each other face or someone's face. A woman has her ways, nature, mood swings, good, bad, wrong, right, control, power, charm, slick and most of all demands in ways a man can even imagine. Jeffrey hugged Cleopatra, he kissed her, he touched her, romanced her, sing to her, talk to her, tickled her, prayed with her and for her, wrote poems for her in church and got up in front of a group of people an audience and spoke it out from my heart now from my heart, soul, spirit, love, gut all I had in me that's a real man of God and I'm not going to speak or say negative now how many men do that in this world I'm going to say job well done because I know if I done it other men have. So, I am not so much a fuck up after all or shit. Other things I did without sex or not thinking about sex was help a lot, even when she was frustrated and not and me hearing women say that's a woman being a woman even with a bitter stank funky attitude is that a fuck up woman/women out there or Cleopatra no you don't suppose to treat or do a real woman/women like this at all even if she is in sin we all are God's children and he loves us all same for men/man /husbands. Jeffrey learned how to be affectionate and soft with Cleopatra he was hard, rough, mean and boastful controlling man. God showed Jeffrey how to treat Cleopatra and be gentle and walk away see but when Jeffrey changed then God was in him she did not change she got worse he was prepared for was that she was continuing to throw garbage on him as he never cleaned his ways, himself, all around Jeffrey up!! There is no credit there is no feeling sorry, there is no self-pity. There is God, love, respect and treating someone as a human being everyone as dogged someone in way tell me one that has not? There is only one and that's God!! Jeffrey learned how to do right by himself God and Cleopatra to show her affection without sex period or even expecting it to lead somewhere to get something credit for because I am the head and the man. Jeffrey even open up Cleopatra with humble honest loving sweet communications how was her day all the time helping her through she brought home a lot of times when she will come to be after times apologizing saying baby I'm sorry for what I've been taking you through and you was right when you told Jeffrey he was selfish and the reason why I'm going through what I'm going through is Jeffrey won't listen to you baby and I keep putting you down and bringing up the past and I'm sorry your right I'm going through it with these kids on my job and our children as well because I'm not listening to you. Cleopatra did not know it would have made us or Jeffrey even her feel much better if she would have listened for real and seriously right their close-up face to face and we will not be in this situation we were in the first place. I wanted her to feel me that same way she wanted to be felt there is no woman no man different. There is a commitment as one! It is right, life is not perfect. I start seeing it was not only about a man as well. A man needs good information, feelings, hugs, and connecting to him with attention he wants to be feel like he is the world and everything to. A man wants his woman to talk patiently with him it's not 60% percent woman needs and man 40% percent no it's 50%/50% equal woman and man treated fairly by God and he knows we both do and treat each other wrong at times and point fingers making up what's the punishment for the person who did wrong like they are both the real God with so much anger, hate, vengeance, unforgiveness, bitterness, no trust, no hope depression inside that you give up. When Jeffrey got saved he step up naturally nature, decisions, consulting with Cleopatra being passionate more Jeffrey started having conversations with her about the children but unforgiveness brought up the other women children Jeffrey was within the past before the relationship got deep and then say well you did not do this to her children and say things to her children in front of Jeffrey putting him down being her partner doing it towards God as well. It is being taught by many false prophets sayings and ways with actions damaged words that when the husband/man sins the wife supposed to keep reacting the way she's is because she been hurt too much because she's a woman and she's different after she forgives you and you made her this way so sit back and let and allow the same thing to go on no matter how long it takes let her continue to do this so you can be held accountable for everything you did until she's gotten over the hurt and pain when she's ready. A husband/man cannot lead an equal loving partner if the wife does not let him. Jeffrey looks at himself to see the things that was more important for Cleopatra the woman and our children Jeffrey put it all to the side for them. I sacrifice my own needs, wants, desires, things, comfort to love her more because she said it herself. Jeffrey just wanted Cleopatra to love him for him and respect him like the Lord says love and he love her as Christ loved the church. Jeffrey learned as well that Cleopatra was not my mother, she was my woman. Cleopatra knows when she said she forgave Jeffrey and did not say it from her heart she did not allow Jeffrey to fail meaning that I am imperfect God know this, Jeffrey know this, but Cleopatra just knew, thought shit, know God, fuck up, I should not never get into relationship with him I do not care and why you gave him to me. See a lot of you women mess up your marriages/relationship because they correct they husband/man all the time almost 24/7 even sleep waking up and tell them what to do when to do it. Coming with the wrong approach telling him you do not treat know lady like that, see your father was not there to teach you how to treat a woman when she does not use this for herself a lot. Jeffrey wishes Cleopatra would have let God be the controller after forgiveness because if she did it would have been left with God because she would not have talk to him in any kind of way and meaning she can say anything she want he took her through. I would love her to confront me and talk with me but not as or I were a filthy pig woman do not see that as a physically, mentally, wicked, abusive damaging break up or dogging out cheat on a marriage it is a happy, sad, miserable, bitter get back even and more to come it is not over just getting started you have not seen nothing yet & more to start over come over again thing. I know you might say that has just too much now come on that is how your mind is it goes on and on like a fuse. Cleopatra took Jeffrey for granted when he was doing good he was not perfect Jeffrey did wrongs just because Jeffrey did wrongs does not mean he was wrong all the time for everything. She took my good things for granted and only focused on my bad things she mostly wanted to pay attention to my faults, past tense, all negativity she saw in me bad behavior was my name. God wants us to think of one another in the best way of Love. All Jeffrey need from Cleopatra was respect, encouragement, love, a shot back at it in God's way of a partnership a man that wanted a shot of greatness looking for relevance and be challenged in a great way be given a great, great shot not being shot as a target. See women I am here to tell you when you pray love and forgive you remember and realize that good you do with God and yourself and what your husband/man does outweighs the bad. Jeffrey stops bumping heads with Cleopatra he started walking away he back up because he was not the boss or her, God was the boss. See it was about admitting to one another then together admitting to God, but Cleopatra told Jeffrey you hurt me to bad and too much, I am scared and afraid I am a woman you do not understand, and God can fix anything and that, so she kept bringing the past back up. Then it will hurt Jeffrey because we will not come to a understand or an agreement Cleopatra was bitter and put in her way. If we both had God we would not have lost, and they are teaching the women and women are saying it is the only thing they been showing us that the man is the head, so it is his fault!! I have been watching when a woman where I see that she can be self-centered only think of herself at times and never let the right hand know what the left hand up too. Her mind never stops she thinks outside the box and inside a lot at times be smooth at times and will not tell a soul at times stare down her victim. A lot of women say that they do not rely on a man for nothing, so it is some let it go to their heads some facts, opinions of what they experience or what they have been through or how they have been raised in homes with cycles. Every woman is not the same I heard a lot of women tell me I am hard to be

pleased then other women have walked up and said that is them women every woman not the same those men been dealing with the wrong type or kind of women I am, or we are not like that. Every woman has an ambitious inside of them Jeffrey like the way Cleopatra was an ambitious woman at times and nontolerance, precious, my baby, my sweetheart. Cleopatra was bossy her success was extremely magnificent her ambitious in her was not always right all the time she also was on a level rude at times. I thought I could play her mind and her intelligence now it takes a real man to be real and up front with this topic and admit his wrongs apologize fix it change become better do more for his self and woman but as her knowledge wisdom and mind it was not good enough it was her say, way or no way at all!! I saw the cycle of good in her which, she deserves everything because she worked hard to get it and I messed it all up broke her down and the blame of everything is because of me she never felt anything of off living from and off the past. Cleopatra did not even think about or put in action fairly that Jeffrey got back what he asks God for so let me reward my husband with his sweet pleasing behavior and great job well done. You can tell someone there doing good and still judge them and still see in your mind in the back of your head that the things are still happening so what you say that person does not mean a thing because your heart is saying one thing your mind is doing another and your thoughts and spirit is lost so is you on one accord? Your mind is made up already it be false, but you feel that it is true. You know I learned another thing to as well women/ woman/wives can take, learned, watch and accept ambitions from false leaders, teachers, prophets, mothers, fathers, family members, bosses, jobs and children that are teenagers and because when it's wrong this bring more hell and rage in her to beware so don't say so what you saying, let men do us any kind of way and fall for it and you got something against women? Or you said that we or I did not say anything you are doing all the saying. Women/woman/wives you do not only have hangover of life of being treated wrong men do to see husband/ man/men be hurt put down, and this puts a pain in him where he cannot move forward, and it is not all bad news on husband/man/men we also have paths where it is hard for us in life as well so much we can take and put up with life hearing us out. We cannot fix everything and take in everything and man up to our wrongs and yours as well we cannot do it all by ourselves. Even Jesus needed God. Now if a woman/women/wife speak about her mother good or bad problems what do you think the men do? So, when the man fails he is a failure forever because he is a no-good dog how long though. I know men/women/family members that done cheated on me by doing me wrong. I cannot hold that in forever I will be worse than them. What they did to me I cannot get away from my actions and wrongs so do not feel like because you are a bishop, pastor, woman, man, teenager, stars, or anyone you get better different or much more than someone else. Women write in their diaries and do not tell anyone. Some keep it in their minds. She has goals and men have courage to do it they like more action. See a woman can be hit hard with ambition I agree but do not use it towards someone as a tool get back out of control too much and overboard unnecessary and wives/women will say look what he did, so I am not ready to give in I need more time. Then when he asks how much it is let her woman/women be ok understandable. Then she will come on her own today and now as the black woman being the victim forgiving but not forgetting. How does it come out in the long run when nothing is happening and she wondering, fantasizing, speaking to existence? Where there is death and lies are in the power of the tongue and they that love it shall eat the front there of. Whoever desires to love life and see good days, let him keep his tongue from evil and his lips from speaking deceit. You brood of Vipers! How can you speak good when you are evil? Out of the abundance of the heart the mouth speaks. The good person out of his good treasure brings forth good evil. I tell you, on the day of judgment people will give account for every careless word they speak. Not only is she looking for something. She is hoping and praying over it to happen. What he is doing something he is over there. He is with her, he is not where he supposed to be, he is there but he is with her, he is doing right but it is too soon to rate, too much, not enough on time. It is good for right now, but she is changing. It is not about another woman it is you; it is me; it is everything, it is nothing at all, I am thinking about something, I am praying, let me be, I love you, you do not love me, I am sorry, I am wrong, your wrong, we both are wrong it is both of our fault. It is over I want to divorce you; I did not mean that I want to make love, that is all, that is it. It is too much, it is not enough, you are going overboard, time out, keep going, I said stop, really, do not go there, I need time to myself. We do not spend time together like we use too, you need to change. She satisfied to a certain extent or not at all or not enough just wants more. Wait until it comes out it is so much in me, I do not even want to know, I got to know. I got so much to say do not underestimate on her secrets! A woman is a challenged creature very content and genuine. Jeffrey knows Cleopatra gave it to me! All things, whatsoever, you shall receive. When you women/wives ask God for and to fix something and it is wonderfully replaced. How is your hometown and broken back down with you not forgiving your husband/man that is your actions and sins not his because he is the head and half to suffer long suffering under your watch and your command only Gods on. God is not telling you bad things to do on him before him against him that is your control of power of get back of force and pain. She is argumentative, up and down, nice, mood swings, stable, movable, and unstable, A woman changes up. She does not have to be this way on a bad thing or a bad note. See a woman can be laid back at times that do not want to have an opinion. Sometimes just staying silent about things and submissive and changing unto being assertive meaning she would step up when there is a problem and let her opinion be known do not take no bull crap. You will be able to catch a woman and sometimes not of her ways will never be known very strange. I said before a woman do not like to speak on or ask about her weight well now I am going to talk about the big women. They are not secure if they chose not to because they are aware of the satisfaction that they give. They are secure if they choose not to because they are aware of the satisfaction that they give. They love God themselves and love and care for the man that is in their life. The passion they give to their men. The support is amazing, wonderful, holding and soft big women are real women in the streets and a wife/woman/woman all in one as home. A real freak for her man at home will do anything by any means necessary to please and satisfy her man and knows her role. How to play it out good in a marvelous way and stays in her place. A man and woman together are like in chains they unite. I understand the power of a good woman and the touch. Women same way for your Husband/man/men!

This is what I write too you nothing to do with men against women or women against men it is real. Sometimes a woman knows what her man is talking about. She just wants to know. See it he is going to tell the truth. Men are in that way sometimes with their woman the most times are the woman with the mind and thinking all the time. She is the outgoing one! Now what I would like to ask most women is that can she forgive without punishing and trust without wavering really speak to her husband/man without accusing these are ways to love. You want your man to deal with you while your stubborn in your mood with your ways so do you agree to give him wins sometimes? Women let me tell you something the energy, motivation, focus, determination, drive, passion, inspiration, loyalty, commitment, devotion, dedication, all these things that you use to wake up to go to places, stores, nail, shops, malls, clothing stores, with friends, mothers, getting your hairdo, fried, colored, braided, laid to the side, getting a perm, a purse all these things you put all this into meaning yourself your energy time. Please black woman/wives/women, white even. Women who do not want to receive I know every woman is not the some empower. Your man with the same energy you got this is your purpose as a woman help meet, help mate, soulmate do not let it be from the pass because all you would be doing is putting weed down kill fresh grass that God done have blessed not only do husbands/men bring curses woman/wives do too as well. How can something stay fresh or have a good smell to it when you look at it and treat it the same old way. The dreams in his life, his goals are just as important as your vision and visions please use your energy wisely it is not all on him because he is the head. I like to tell women do not use abuse as a license towards your husband/man/men. When it is come to making love having sex in your secret way as one. He/ we know about the cheating but when you communicate with God yourself and him to each other needs do not open the garbage can back up with the lid open with the flies and maggots coming out then when he want to talk about it first thing comes out is that is all you like to do or want to do but when it is called I will give to him when I get ready, now what happens is the past enters her mind or she remembers things that she chooses to let the devil uses her.

Chapter 20

See after counseling you encourage your man not tell him he's shit or a fuck up, or even to continuing a thing that's an ongoing thing because you're not satisfied of what's happen to him or he has not suffered enough. Jeffrey asked Cleopatra and told her nicely let's pray can we pray replacing good Godly thoughts to remove the bad and what he was told was I don't care you can't make pray with you Jeffrey. See this brought failure, stress, mental abuse, nasty attitude with actions of rude conflicts and this was right down her alley it was her get back towards me!! Certain qualities Jeffrey couldn't handle from Cleopatra so he went to God then and kept going then he felt like she didn't love him anymore and did not care and she said that off her tongue out her mouth being in a relationship with him that she did not care, and she wish she wouldn't never ever taken you back. Then it was I don't need you to take care of me or my children I'm an independent woman I was doing this before I met you, so it was not partnership or one any right thing ever again in her eyes. Then when she first started telling Jeffrey and he was called to the house back and forth I'm sorry constantly blame is not all on the woman. Jeffrey love Cleopatra she did not take no blame or action at all!! At any means necessary at all. As well to say a woman can be silent quiet have a lot on her mind and can be thinking about so many things you can imagine. Another thing Jeffrey like about Cleopatra is that when she always said you make me sick you get on my nerves, do you know what that was most of the time? Love especially when she said I'm so aggravating yes women we know depending on what it is, but you all know where I'm coming from. Men are emotional to you have some men that are emotional than women. You must learn, study, and listen to the woman. Women holding a grudge or unforgiveness does not make you strong as you think in the kind of way highway be God's way. See why I wouldn't want to be the better person to apologize, forgive, happy, strong with an attitude towards my woman with now a woman loves and likes revenge more than a man most of the time there's no getting over it, because she thinks before giving a chance he's going to do the same thing over again. It is so bad it be a negativity in their mind it just doesn't be unforgiveness in the heart it be in the mind, mood swings of bad spirits darkness soul, tongue, body, home, bedroom in the church and coming out. Women you suffered long enough we have to MEN!! Didn't Jesus suffer. Cleopatra did not love Jeffrey or herself because she could not forgive him. See men go through things with raising other men children and it don't have anything to do with him then he is a cry baby, grow up be a man then things being throwed back up in his face or what women you been with or I been with no one, this life what goes on every day not perfect good times, bad times, struggles, rights, wrongs, a woman/women/wives might see something wrong the husband/man is doing wrong with her child or children and feel, see, think that this man or men come with a bad experience from his side of his family and can be right or wrong for what she has been taking through from her, family, her mom a lot of bad experience and let the man know quick you don't have nothing up on her back quick. Now everyone is not the same therefore it be so many divorces to I tried to tell a lot of women this like they tried to tell me. Yes, I told on myself. See uncomfortable is not good or right because then this go's on without the woman listening to the man you have men tell women the truth about the children and it won't be the truth because what lie he told years ago, that be a hangover what happens after you drink then go to sleep you wake up with a hangover being drunk from last night and women do this, and it be toxic and different types of alcohols. Now that is really an addiction of an addict. She won't even notice it. She will swear up and down she is doing the right thing. Now these be feelings of love they think yeah right that be their own feelings. Thinking about the past in your relationship. Deep feelings of bitterness, resentment, anger, hate, double and triple thoughts thinking and worrying herself and this that she will say I am not going to let you worry me to death. When she is doing it to herself at times know it and do not know it. Call herself bring a strong woman confusing herself she sorry she not sorry then when she says both what is that until she changed it. I heard a lot of men say at times I just tell her she right man. Well, it is something you men did wrong to her to make her become this way so one can get you mad and hurt yes that is true. It does mean something in there to for how long but get back overboard is enough can you respect this passion ladies, women, wives, from this book opinions, facts, yeas, no's, yes, maybe, I do not think so. I agree on this but not that. Women an unwillingness to let go of past hurts. How can you move on with your husband/man/men and you have not forgiven or forgave him he hurt you? Yes have you hurt him yes. So, what kind of sin is he committed adultery, he cheated, he lied, he started it I am going to finish it. So then when you listen to the devil, yourself, false anyone how will you ever give attention to God, yourself, and back to your husband. He should be a positive focus. Sin is a sin no man no woman no one can make excuse of getting out of sin or hiding it so it so if we know this we need to stop acting like we are Gods over the high mighty God in with us ourselves and marriages. When you leave left over food in your refrigerator to long what happen? It spoils! So, when you bring up old things what happen to your relationship? Someone gets tired or they both give up. See when a woman gets hurt it takes time for her to heal so does a man. A man just does not show it much as a woman do at times, but he does have feelings! See when You do not have no trust only does not break with adultery, lack of communication, no attention, no sharing not being able to express how someone feels, no love making, the first thing in should have put was God, prayer not in, letting the past sins reflect the new refreshing spirit God put in. Now I have seen wives tell their husbands what you trying to say I got spirits looking at them eating they food rolling they eyes turning their head and neck away. It is because they are thinking of what that husband done did to them in the past and he had some nerve to tell her to follow God and she can tell him quick fast in a hurry that she is holy than thou. What they call spirit is really flesh because a spirit makes you be quiet until God wants you to speak. Women you can put pressure scars, wounds, cuts, sores, blisters, and curses on your husband their will not be a future there will not be a present or a new beginning over old past things some women say they let their husband go because all he took her through. She did wrong and it be her at times not changing her ways that is not no past. It is reflecting off and on off what the husband did in the past. Then when it be divorced and over I cut him off. I am free Jesus thank you Lord and still do not be free because she has not truly fully forgiven him. What it really be you push him out your life. Can I get a yes on this? I see some men now today tell their wives that you never forgave me. They say now you got to bring that up, but she will tell you quick to forgive let go and let God on everything else. Are you thinking! You are woman you have a lot on your mind. You cannot forgive and mistrust or mistreat your spouse because when you do that you're torturing yourself and the sword be in your hand towards your husband neck of slavery he is in he feels this way because he is being whipped with all that unforgiveness you know because you go back to and apologize for your actions! They come back again. See I'm running about the problems, passion, living we live in out and go through from my heart. If you can't trust your husband/man Then don't go back to him because you're setting up yourself for failure for yourself and him, you spoke It you claim it some will say no I didn't, I repented but, can you see, but, you see, this what happen right, you men, all of you men are all the same we are not like that. Jeffrey put Cleopatra on a pedestal because he loved her so damn much and the wrong that Jeffrey did. I was being a man cherishing her it's a limit on everything because we will get big headed on things towards our spouses and use things towards one another and it don't be right. A wrong can't be right just because we say it is that don't mean it is. It's women and men that will read this book and don't like me to see what I'm saying especially women that got to find out. The true love life of story in themselves, something, surprise, curious, researching, finding out more, educational, educated, or they must for their reasons really observing more!! No One is perfect I was set up for failure because I was told and treated that I was only a fuck up and shit. She didn't give her feelings and emotions to God she gave them back to the past with the devil spirit using her like Adam and Eve like when I sinned like Adam. A Woman is also complicated because who she is and what she has to deal with in her wrongs and rights in her life as well as life period she does towards peoples meaning she's not perfect as she already know this some women and now they're perfect and you can't tell them nothing but some will think this because what they have been through and how they've been treated and cycles and because they think they can teach everybody especially men how to live their lives where their life is not perfect themselves and their own self. The Bible says a wise man is a man that admits he's not wise or smart when he fails and admits it and get back up repents and ask for forgiveness. Now with Cleopatra when Jeffrey used to sleep at night by her side and his penis be sticking up on hard because she used to brag saying you got a fat head but anyway when he would wake up she would say what you were dreaming about ask her what was you dreaming about? Then she would not say anything and then I will say why? Then she will say because your penis is on hard and sticking straight up, sometimes she will get on top of it when I was sleep but back to what I was saying I will let her know it was my heart because she's my wife she was the one lying beside me sleeping at night and I felt warm and good and cozy what does she believe that no because the things that she was remembering back from the past in the back of her mind in head. Cleopatra was being a woman her own self being curious she will ask was Jeffrey dreaming about her. And I will let her know about the dreams about me being raped from family members every dream was not the same, foster homes and in the streets I was dreaming about some of the dreams was about her and she will say what you really were dreaming about everything in life all over again? At that time it was not no lie or you know how a man is it was not that's a man for you it was the woman being curious you cannot tell a woman everything because she will tell you it's over and still be thinking in her mind what you both talked about sometimes it won't be over she always will be ahead so she will lay in the bed with her hand holding her head up looking at me sometimes on top of me asking questions and answering them before I could say anything. The woman is to and so good for her own good as something else and a trip. Now it's time to change up mood swings like crazy out of this world. Certain women don't have a lot of women friends you can't out slick a slicker at a lot of women don't hang together every woman is not the same. When the false accusing came the debates, arguing, false statements mental, physical, verbal abuse, criticizing, putting down, talking down on Jeffrey and he came to sit down to talk with her the talks was not working with Cleopatra. Then when I cheated she stop asking me why my penis was getting hard in good ways it changed she start telling me I was lying I'm dreaming about that bitch, whore, slut that I fucked on her while I was with her and it was not true at first with the arguing, debating and me walking away like a man and going to a bar sitting down to have a drink she didn't even know I walked on parks by myself. I pulled up in the parking lot in areas you couldn't even imagine with God to myself by myself crying at times there was no woman involved my penis was not hard. My heart was hurting my penis would not even get hard thinking about sex period I could not make love to an angry bitter woman. That's my fault to I know just because I say it is that don't mean it is so women will say in a good way then why you say it if you already know because this how it goes of the system everything is the black man's fault. He can have a business has been doing girl is something wrong. Innocent or guilty they just got to look something find out something on him or say have fun or something woman it's times you feel alone then you have God you're a human so does a man. A woman likes what she likes and more she knows what's good for her and what's not depending on that kind of woman her day, time, month, memory, fantasizes and all kind of things every woman is not the same. It can be at times of being immature because at times the brain be computerized some homes got broke up if the system gave these black women food stamps, checks, housing, section 8 this was saying I don't need a man period at all. How society done messed up their brains and allowed it. Some women need government assistance and help but not to use good father's and put the children through that as well!! I have seen some women get with no good men with the pants falling down thugs, gangsters or rather than being with a good man or hanging around ratchet women as all birds of a feather flopping together. On a woman she is always thinking more and more wanting more. See you have women listen to the mother's there's no problem listening if it's God and inspiration but when it be nasty, rude, disrespectful, gossip downright dirty to the gut that's uncalled for. Then after the mother talks to the daughter now then she comes home to her husband/man who she done fussed out or falsely accuse him from something in the past and run home and his arms be open and he's quiet holding her saying it's ok I understand, and they forget that she was a young woman once upon a time she doesn't have no man so her daughter can't have one. Now a man or men can be talking, and woman or women can say shut up, be quiet or calm down, but when we say it it's (WHO IS YOU TALKING TO)? Cleopatra knew her worth and value and very vulnerable. A woman also can be a terrible and treacherous creature she can get you and do so many things because you love her it doesn't have to be bad it can be good to things they do and want. See Jeffrey studied Cleopatra, but he had to love Jeffrey first and get himself together. You cannot love if you were never given it or taught or not raised up with no love period also not given to you but thank God I finally loved myself. See another thing about women is a bunch of queens cannot be in one house or one kingdom like Cleopatra (THE WOMAN) and her mother Pam they were to Boss Queens with many clashes of personalities not trying but doing it telling one another what's real and what to do how it goes her point, my point. My point her point and how it supposed to be laid down trying to tell each other who has the real source, deal, point, got it going on the right way straight to the god damn point. Women have been hurt yes but it is not ok to stay hurt because then you be in a trap of unforgiveness, and it be just like drinking poison and wanting the other husband/man to die you be so angry and bitter with hate. You want to be free or marriage or relationship you be saying and doing actions. I forgive you but I forgave him but men, they, you just do not know and most of the time you did not forgive you be thinking of things and holding on to things and beat someone getting mad especially the husband/man because he do not have known the reason talking at all he is not shit, he know better, he shouldn't be talking period, he do not have no feelings, he do not hurt or feel because how has hurt me and he has to understand how I feel after I forgave him and accepted him back and feel my pain where I am coming from. See men do not understand women. They must understand after they have hurt a woman. It is hard to earn her trust back after she forgives you. Then she can keep bringing it back up what you have done to her because she just means that but foe awhile you got to understand she loves that man/husband. She just needs more time to get back at the husband/man/men for what he did or done years ago, right? Now a woman is not perfect Jeffrey know when he was with Cleopatra she always kept her hair up. She also was at times clumsy and crazy telling Jeffrey in a minute I am crazy as well, but it takes crazy then be tired of Jeffrey he would make her sick then tell him baby I love you. That's my woman I am her sweet Jeffrey, Cleopatra heart was broken at times, but Jeffrey fixed it first with God, myself and her. We fought at times. I fought more than she did. It was days things did not go right. Cleopatra gave up on Jeffrey to see the amazing, good things he did only the bad things giving up on Jeffrey and telling him. It was already over coming from the store debating with Jeffrey looking at him bitter just saying I should not have never took you back. Now through all the imperfections she is God's gift and God still love her but in her eyes I am a fuck up and shit. Now if the shoe were on the other foot how would that feel towards Cleopatra/ wives/woman/women? I am still interested in Cleopatra she is a real good woman. It is not because she is gone. I lost something good no it is we both lost something good with hearts and gifts it is because Jeffrey loved her. Jeffrey did not sex her. Jeffrey did not sit back and let Cleopatra do all the work. Cleopatra even came with instructions she was not playing games. She is a strong-minded woman but did not like her when she was angry. Being strong minded and bitter yes. Jeffrey made her that way he could not change her. She had to change herself. She said the change told it spoke on it but did not show it with action so, what she did was an eye for an eye saying you did me wrong. She treated Jeffrey like shit dogged him out Jeffrey did it right back. Now this how you know Jeffrey was a real man because when Cleopatra wanted to make love, get freaky, have sex or do whatever to for fill Jeffrey being angry and her bossy way I will not do it with her I turn it down even her pray, God, love to read the bible, study the word and give God that time now that made Jeffrey feel good. Within Jeffrey only thing was missing is that a woman can be blind just as much as a man saying she see everything her vision is clear when it is blurry! I was with the love of my life, and I was devoted to her. I start waking up with God and a commitment with myself. I was this and that and not even around woman. See at times a woman can just be saying I am in this situation with this man, dog, shit, fuck up or just breath, think, do not speak, hold a lot in, be like I am not appreciated and can be breaking her own heart because she has not clean it up and the man will not be anything you can causing things on yourself/yourselves by you hurt me, you dogged me and women will say that is them or those kind of women.

Every woman/woman is not like that and most of the relationship she says she forgives do not forget she do not use it as moving on as positive as a testimony she moves on with her takes over the brain it be a bad spirit just like any other spirit that is not of God. I did not even keep my distance away from Cleopatra when she admitted everything was Jeffrey fault and it wasn't. See when a person blames you for everything it does not mean that they side it can mean they are being selfish and do not want to see their wrongs and failure that you owe them. If God put a time limit on sins man we all be in trouble, and I am not saying that to get out of my wrongs because when someone has done you wrong how long are you going to hold it against him or her or anyone. Now opinions, facts, statements will probably be like I am the person or you're the person you, they, we, seem like to me that you have a problem with letting things go so if we all have been here then we know who have messed up all of us no one is perfect. I am a good man and a great choice. I am valuable. I am smart. I am lovable. I am happy. I did wrongs bad, but I am proud of who I am today. See with a woman you never go after the sex you go after the mind. I would not say fuck her mind that is not respectful, loving, professional way to pronounce it is the best way will be silent! You can come in ways towards a woman that may not notice. Women I know a lot of you will say well that is a weak woman or blind or just sleep and not up on her game or alert on all things. No, I am talking about just in the same way a man cannot see certain things that the woman can. She gets his mind. It does not have to be always negative on something slick, players, games or jokes. A woman cycle changes every day sometimes all day long even when she is sleeping her mood swings, attitudes, personality, actions, looks a woman has a mind gone. Jeffrey had Cleopatra mind gone as well. See Cleopatra played roles like I did not have her mind. This is the part where she was better at. See then have the woman judge the man/husband/men differently because they see that it was different, and I would not do to him what he did to me. I sat down with a woman name Velma, and she told me that she cheated on her husband with a woman name Kisha. She said the reason why she cheated because her husband Marvin was always falsely accusing her of cheating and sleeping with other men, so then the trust was gone. She said arguments, started fights, unforgiveness, bitterness, being mistreated, misused, pointing fingers at one another. Velma said she set-up counseling coming from counseling at home in public and all kind of places Morris would argue with her. Marvin would bring up her sins that was nasty and he felt inside that the things Velma did was worse than what did. Velma said it will go back and forth the arguing. You were both Velma and Marvin are today they are divorce just like Velma said sitting down talking about it. It was all Velma or Marvin fault it was both of their faults what happen to them. Velma and Marvin judge one another what God say not to do because thinking the sins we be different when all sins are the same. Jeffrey had to wake up myself with the joy and come out the darkness to receive and manifest the light for him and Cleopatra. Women feel and will say that they are the strongest that love beyond anything or everything and fight the battles no one know about and cry behind doors and that is a lie because when I got save God Glorified me with the gift to put in my heart, soul, mind, body, head, feet to be a man of God to take care of my wife and feel and do this duty. It just that it was ignored! A lot of women will say they have been ignored so take and receive back what you dish out until I am, or we are satisfied enough be a man and accept it. See I can say that I stand up fighting and I did not go out with a fight for my relationship I did not have enough help. Help is especially important capture these words I am not a millionaire or billionaire, but I am a man that is rich in a lot of things. Yes! I am living, love, kind, joy, smart, God, prayer, plans, goals, God ministering to my spirit, and me with myself, moved myself, away from negativity, I am rich in helping others and others helping me as well. Jeffrey felt rich when he met Cleopatra and she met him. Jeffrey was rich when he got with Cleopatra. Jeffrey was rich when he fell in love with Cleopatra and her children. This how Jeffrey knew love was real because it did not cost a thing. Jeffrey is rich because he is happy when Cleopatra to him back all this love was deposit in us both in a life savings because I still can feel it my heart is beating, crying, smiling, laughing, burning, light with passion everyday even when I lay my head down to rest. See I learned many of the great achievements of the world were accomplished, by tired and discouraged people, who kept on working. Then I see people too weak to follow their own dreams, so they find a way to try to discourage mind. What I did was try my best to be strong and never give up. See I know that consistence and dedication is key to success. Now I would like to talk to the women about is help it is especially important. You never know when you're going to need it good or bad. One lady told me she is different from other women. She said she do not get angry easily. Every woman is not the same their different breeds of woman. A woman always feels like she is right even when she is wrong that do not make her right in the situation. A woman is a creature of brightness. You can see the darkness in her at times. You know I sat down with and elder woman one day and she said that if her husband is happy she is happy. She said she do not know what is wrong with the young generation of little girls today. Her name was Ms. Parks. The woman is the one so is the man the woman alone by herself mostly 60/40 or 70/30. Jeffrey loved Cleopatra when he cared for himself He had to love himself first. He understood the pain Cleopatra was going through and what family, jobs, school, life tool her through but how weird it did not come back, and she said she forgave me. Now let's move forward I did not make her repeat it repeatedly. She made me repeat, repeat, repeat. A lot of women will say well we need to hear her side, listen and hear her out. Now if she was writing from the heart it will be different will it not? I have said everything, I have done wrong. I love her through bad days because if I did not she would not call me back home and say I am sorry. Sometimes I did not go back because I felt and was taken through as I was not wanted there or a friend nor a husband or lover o felt like shit!! Why will I go somewhere or be around someone who does not want anything to do with me? I knew her heart could not be brought but my richness of love tried hard and the best. Another thing I would have like to talk to women about is the words that comes out of their mouth. Sometime this is especially important to understand what is going on. It says 21 death and life are in the bower of the tongue. A woman can use her words as a weapon and renege by saying something that she promises that she will stop and do it again and be at times dominating her man! Husband accusing him can be at times destroying their relationship. Words can hurt and bring love and life. When Jeffrey and Cleopatra met we fell in love saying good things to one another all the time then when the bad times came it was only

Jeffrey, all of him and his fault I am the man!! Cleopatra will tell Jeffrey baby I am sorry love for what I said how I talk to you, been putting you down lately and treating you. Then she will say you got a heart love. See when she was not bitter her heart was good and her words, tongue, with the mind but when she was mean so was her mind, soul, tongue, spirit, looks and love!! See when you ask for forgiveness for your sins you do and God cover and erase the sins, just remember women when you take those words to God and then you bring it to your husband/man then you say I am sorry please forgive me. That is, it right there this how God says it goes but times women change it then change and say but you're not God and you hurt me, and did you have God or think about God when you were dogging and cheating on me with another woman that bitch, that whore, that slut. See the woman is not looking at the impact that brings to the marriage after the fact that she went to the Lord and ask for forgiveness then she went to the husband and did the same and all she was talking not leaving everything right there with the Lord. See she is not noticing her tone, attitude, ways, revenge not paying attention to her love. Cleopatra will lift Jeffrey up then tear him down she only felt that God will make Jeffrey pay for everything and soon one day he will have to be held accountable for them by God not her at all only Jeffrey I am a mess up and trash. She still smells better than any garden all put together in this world. See I helped my help was not good enough. See when I did tell my stepdaughter Anita that still is a beautiful lady and always will be my baby girl I did tell her to get a man that believe in God had his life right, a good head on his shoulders. He had several plans, a job and education. He meets me first going to college, trying his best, have his pants up respectful and a gentleman. Now when I was with Cleopatra and things got rough and bad Jeffrey sinned she sinned struggle can she throw up in my face yelling and screaming remember what the fuck you told our daughter? You told her do not get to know a sorry man or no broke man and your ass is sorry what do you have and got to go to work to do something. What she did not realize she was sinning and bringing back spirits worse and skeletons that was dried up, stank bones from under the graveyard and watch this as us being married it is for better or worse, richer or poorer, in sickness and health until death do us apart. So, when I was trying to find a job it wasn't enough money when I did get one. It was not enough, and false prophets came in teaching the sheep that if the man/husband is not making more than you he is sorry do not marry him he is lazy. Now what God is saying about that man not your friend, mother, job co-workers, etc. but you're not being a wife or a woman then you're being a selfish, stubborn brat that cannot do and what she wants to see and know a woman has a guilty conscious it can be several different things. It will give herself away. Some women want depending on that woman what she is doing her ways herself when she has cheated they also is doing things you cannot see. It is like getting away with murder right women. When a man is not pleasing his woman/wife sexually, emotionally, time, physically, communication, listening, hearing God or not praying or doing nothing at all. She goes to another man and will make love with the other man that is pleasing her sexually and every other way. She still thinks about the husband/man who is at home who she is in love was with thinking hard and fantasizes. It is killing her softly this what Cleopatra was doing on Jeffrey when we broke up and Jeffrey was staying on the streets and went to God to stay with my Godmother that raised him. She pulled up on the driveway with a friend that she had sex with talking to my sister in the driveway. She said to my sister your brother does not have nowhere to live and stay and help him. Then Cleopatra said that is your brother and my sister said what brother I do not have no brother. See it was a lot of things Jeffrey told Cleopatra that she did not want to believe because of my ways, sins, and wrongs but she did sure make up her mind to accept and choose to listen to other people. People and my other family members but not me. See she was a great Christian that on a different level than me how was I treated and respected. Now you have a lot of women when they see their man/husband get mad most of the time he is guilty, wrong, sinning, it is something he did or up to something or something just is not right because a woman knows but when most of the time or sometimes when men or man see that a woman is giving herself away and guilty. It is reverse psychology back om him of his past things that he done to the woman or women that he does not just got no reason to talk at all he should not even open his month because everything comes out is lies, bullshit and wrongs. Even things he done that's new he cannot never read her mind not meaning at times that he still knows certain things and feels that she is not right on everything and for everything just remember she is a woman. So, what that supposed to mean what women will say just like Jeffrey learned from women and Cleopatra that is just men being men that's how they are then it will be but y'all are different then us. We go through we all go through it all. It is true when a man has a guilty conscious yes he gets caught so does a woman cheating or not and when she does it is like talking to a wall because the man is the ball. She is going to bounce the ball all around like giving her some money. When she been complaining in a good way and want it and you give it to her then it is how much of it can I spend. Baby well you say you needed some money some women would say she crazy I would not do that I will take the money. Yeah! Then when the women cycles will change up to. Anyone can have a guilty conscious but not a professional and smooth like a woman!! A woman is something else to much and a trip in a half. Now watch this I went to Miami-Dade college one day to visit Sgt. Mrs. Lang and she was on her lunch break, so officer Lang was sitting right there and she looked at me which I was tired she said I want some cookies buy me some cookies I said that is what you have a man for and yourself then she curse me out about my money and her wanting some cookies beat me getting angry, so she said Subs Mini Mart across the street go get me some cookies I said I will buy you some cookies but you have to get up off butt and come across the street to get them because I am going over there to eat and buy me a sandwich I am hungry Ms. Lang say you going over there you can bring them back when you finish eating I said know you're going to walk over there just like I did and come and get them you want the cookies right? So, she fussed me out some more so left Miami-Dade College walked across the street to Subs Mini Mart then got me a sandwich and I brought 3 different cookies. I got peanut butter, chocolate chip and raspberry cheesecake, so I sat down with my sandwich and cookies that I brought I started eating my sandwich, so Officer Long walked in I said here I got the cookies for you they right here guess what she said? You did not ask what kind I wanted then she I don't eat this kind. A thank you and being thankful would have been appreciated like my mother and father said and elders when someone buy you something. Now is a lot of women going to speak on this and say well she did not eat that kind or something or different it is more a little or ways of woman will never be known so she said get up so we can change them I do not eat these kinds then she walked out fast, and quick/ I said I thought you was tired and could not move she move for the cookies right? Now when she left the lady that was working behind the counter said to me and you still brought them for her. She told me I was crazy and let her buy her damn cookies. Every woman is not the same. A woman name Stacey let me know she says when I man cheats he forget about home and have more feelings for the other woman and look at her more and forget all about everything they have going on together, but she said a woman knows how to cheat. She will do her thing and come back home like everything is ok and still cook, clean, make love and take care of her man I said Well everyone is not the same and no one is perfect. We all have done wrong. Jeffrey had to help himself before he helped Cleopatra because He had to get a lot of things within him what he been through in life how I was treated so what Jeffrey felt he was inside, and Jeffrey was outside he took her through. It was mental, physical, stress, depression, psychological, abuse, hurtful and painful within myself and when I saw hurt, pain these that was said and did. I did not know how to handle it and react to it, I got help, God and spiritual, prayer, therapy and hospitals. Women, men need this help from the things they been through as well. Remember they cannot just brush it off and expect it to go away just like that, it does not make it right for men to take things out on women, people period they need help to ask your man did you ever had love or be loved. These men be messed up already going through living life not all but most. Like I had a friend name Josh he did 18 years in prison and his wife Pam stood by his side when he was in prison. When he got out she went to visit him. I told her when she went to visit him let him know to pray and go to church in prison. I told Pam when he gets out to get him counseling and go with him because he has not been around a woman for 18 years. When he got home he still slept with other women, but she was a strong woman to put up with him and that situation because God is good because that was a woman who understood what he been all through in life. Some women will say that's no excuse and his father did a life sentence in prison and left his mother so, what do they say to women that go through this with a mother or father because I know women that did Fed time, jail time and prison. One lady I know her name was Diana the same situation around women for 10 years. Now some women will say a woman is different she can hold out with sex and other things. Man, I done seen people go through worse things than me. As a man that been through hell high water and back I have been through some things. This book that I written to is about women mostly so as I continue this lady that I met her is Nickie name Vernise, but her biological name was Marah she sat down with me. She let me know that all men are no good period, so I asked her why you just came out of nowhere and brought that up. She said because my husband Randy just piss me the fuck off I just got off the phone with him we was arguing so I said I do not want to talk about it then she said he cheated on me with another woman name Sylvia and we are still married so she said she was divorcing him I said when she said I feel the time is right now so I said you still have feelings for him and then I said the man who your sleeping with when you first started sleeping with him you was thinking of your husband and going back home to him she said you right but it is starting to fade away everything the feelings, love, everything Marah looked at me and said how do you know all this I said I did my homework on women and observed them and studied them. They are not perfect she said you are something else, a trip, too much and a hand full. I said you a whole world by yourself, so she said she was sleeping with a man name Benny that's her slider and he takes good care of her, but she said she do not want to marry Benny because she already going to get a divorce from her husband, but she does not know I asked why she did this. She said Well he fucked on me with another woman, so I got me a man. What I was looking at and telling Marah was you do not have to get another man to try to satisfy you. She is saying she is happy when she not now her husband and her is separated. I told her straight up okay your husband cheated on you, and she said yes, and I got a slick nasty mouth I talk to him any kind of way a lot of times. I want what I want when I want it if I do not get it it's my way or no way. Now I want black women to look at this picture right here the one's that do this if your conscious is guilty and your

down with this. You will be by yourself so back to what I was saying. So, I said by your husband cheating on you and you fussing with him all the time before he cheated well you were shit then he became worse shit cheating then you went to cheat as well. Becoming flies together hopping together so you both were flies just hopping from shit-to-shit lets be real. So, then she caught an attitude, so I said OKAY how do feel right now? She looked me and rolled her eyes and sucked her teeth. I told her I know how your husband feel and the man who you're sleeping with on your husband and the women that's sleeping your husband on you. So, all stank and funky, so she said it's all the man fault. I said you did no wrong she said no I am wrong. See I learned that you must reach a woman mentally to make a connection. You must make it last but with her mind it worse than encyclopedia. A lot of women have told me the reason why a lot of women cannot be satisfied because it is she never know what she is want its more, more, more!! See when the woman cycle changes all day she changes as well. Her mouth will say one thing or thousands of things but her mind, emotions, body movement thought process action will be every which way. It does not have to be bad, watch out when it is bad. A woman will be having in ways she does not know or understand and tell you it's right and be a debate she wins no matter what the case is.

Chapter 21

Now one of the good things I can say about a woman & wives is that she knows how to satisfy her own self better than anybody. Now it depends on the woman. Now not all women are the same and they do not understand themselves. Some are not fully skilled. I've met some women to teach them some things to understand somethings. There are different types of jealousies. A woman's tongue can be her problem with her flipping of her lips can sink her ships. A woman can be all full of smiles and nice to get what she wants. She will use her psychology. A woman does not like another woman giving her man/husband/friend suggestions. She feels, sees, and knows when another woman is talking to her man/husband/friend and the a don't have to be sleeping with that woman at all. A woman can be pissed off, silent and do not even show it. Women these days are hard to find and to be in a relationship with her. It is not only based on men making them the way some or most of them are just their ways, actions and how they handle things not they as all women. Some women are secure, and some are insecure with themselves. Women that are secure they are strong willed and determined, however they still push a man out their life at times. Women that are insecure they are afraid of they may say something wrong or behavior manner that push a man away. A woman can be happy and content with life right now. Every man does not know how to get into a woman mind. Some men can be considerably basic. See a woman can't be satisfied because it comes from changing of the mind. A lot of women today share men and most of the time the woman/women know they have a woman or wife. A good woman will always be a good woman. Women don't play they have a secret of alliances that depends on the woman, because certain women can be caddy as hell. Women also have alliances with each other, because they have been though the same thing that, just some things. See Cleopatra (THE WOMAN) was woman with a strong presence she thought Jeffrey did not know. It just things I know to myself showing with action, love and appreciation. See a woman over thinks. Do you know women catch headaches more than men? Women fantasize, so much of dreams and certain ways with her wants and needs. She thinks and do not know how to relax. Sometimes she stays going. In Today's time you have women feel and say they do not have a man, want, need or can't find a good one. Are they in the way of God or in their own way of saying knowing thinking it's something he did to make her like the way she is this what they tell men? See a woman wants to be loved, helped, connected, appreciated, heard and valued. It is not all about the woman/ wife it's about the man/husband as well the man wants to be respected, helped, not controlled, pressured, put down or feel like a failure. See it's like when you give your women/wife a certain time you're going to be home or you're taking her out to dinner. If stops to do something else she gets worried, concerned, feared. The man word is broken, and he is okay. Now husband/man he will ask the woman/wife not to do something she knows will get to him and she does it anyway. See both parties mess up not all, just a man/man! A man feels at times he's disrespected and not encouraged. There are plenty of reasons you can feel cheated in a relationship or marriage. It is not only sex/adultery/ fornication with another woman/wife or man/husband. It can be feelings, things, actions, problems, thoughts, words, broken promises. It's just like playing games. It's not fair to cheat cheaters never win and we sit there. We all in life have different feelings as a woman. Every woman is not the same, she may feel this way one second then another way a few minutes, hours, days, weeks, months and years. She does not feel the same feelings as her husband/man vice versa for the man/ husband. It can be days they be feeling the same thing, and both be upset, hurt, aggravated, selfish and don't want to listen to one another, because they both feel the same way. They feel like no you did it like this, but guess what? They not getting nowhere! Now a woman that has been cheated on and done wrong do not want to share opinions or facts with her husband/man. Cleopatra (THE WOMAN) did not want to share nothing with Jeffrey at all. Most of the time there was no trust even after forgiveness, being incredibly supportive and sacrificing. When Cleopatra (THE WOMAN) would say baby I'm sorry I know you changed, I'm sorry you changed, but it was I'm getting you back, just like you did me. You know I'm learning and saying to myself more.

When you see a wife and husband is going through negative issues constantly with positiveness there is no trying to make it. What are you going to get out of the negativity? You have women who feel that when they put down their husband in front of the children, mother, family and friends. It is a payback whereas he lost that respect and not when she messes up. I see episodes that be different and vice versa. Women are very intricate and delicate individuals that can also be a quiet storm. A real woman brings great action of different important roles like when Jeffrey first met Cleopatra (THE WOMAN) she came with tough love, a great mother, help mate, a protector, nurturer the most thing Jeffrey like about her was his rose, just by herself being special general crucial to the world all in one. A powerful woman, but like I said every woman is not the same. A woman thinks 10 steps ahead she builds that way her secrets are very smart. A woman has 6 senses instead 5 senses whereas woman reads body language, tone of voice and really observing her surroundings. A woman does not like to be distracted. It is fun ad a joke when Jeffrey and Cleopatra (THE WOMAN) first years we met fell in love. I myself she was herself and it was the best relationship, she loved me for me. She loved me for me, and I loved her for her even the funny, joking part is when she will fart on me and around me and I will do it mostly to her this was love. Cleopatra (THE WOMAN) knew that when we first met that Jeffrey was a dedicated lover and did not realize a lot of times she offended Jeffrey it was like to her shit what Jeffrey did to her don't mean nothing to what she does to and more. Sometimes Jeffrey holds in a lot of feelings inside, because Jeffrey knew how bad he hurt Cleopatra (THE WOMAN), but I have feelings to you know Jeffrey observed things a lot of things about women he seen plenty of women just sitting there watching them talk. How other women are and their ways, but not tell you they own ways and say I know; we know because we are women too. We know how women are but want to tell their business and only let you know what they want you to know and tell you what they want you to hear on certain things how it goes the way it is because being smart too smart for they own good not letting the right hand know what the left hand is doing! A woman can be satisfied to a certain extent. When they have communicated their wants and needs. At least their needs are met. It is not always that man/men/

husband/friend made them that way all the time every woman not the same, but they know what I'm talking about in their ways. Now a woman will do you mean. What are you trying to say I don't have to be opening a bag of worms? See I love a woman intuition. Her intuition can be right or wrong her intuition is her insight as well as her healing. It's a strong power this what a part Jeffrey liked about Cleopatra (THE WOMAN) and a woman's instinct. A woman can't be satisfied, because her mind and brain want to over think, pick things apart, opinion, facts, which they think is true. This is based on over thinking and want to be right most of the time that do not mean that they are right, watch out! Its lie going through maze or puzzle. Her serious internal feelings a woman's intuition and instinct has all types of forces. Men at times can't catch it, but I have learned, because I have observed, listen, watch, received, heard shut-up and gave eye contact. A woman's intuition is also a myth really reality. Then you have other women behind other women intuitions. The woman knows how to hide her face, emotions, evidence and other things and throw up things that's a professional. A woman's instinct is her reactions and don't tell her she wrong when she doesn't feel like she not aware at times. See you must know with the woman/women the hands the rock the cradle rules the world the ways of a woman are never known. A woman trust is powerful and can turn into a weapon. A woman is Cleopatra (THE WOMAN). A woman can be as soft as a flower, but hard as a rock. A woman/woman don't know their own strength as a serious emotional creature. A woman needs and wants are consistent. See I must tell the women it's not all about you. See a husband/man/man needs effort, encouragement, respect, understanding from his wife/woman. We know you gave it to him. He messed up we pass that, because you said you forgave him, but not mean it from your heart. Your actions need to show more than talking. Don't roll your eyes, suck your teeth, be rude, angry, nasty, say whatever and don't judge your husband/man/men when he's in front of you. Don't look for things on him you're being a detective then looking for things when there's nothing. Then keeping it going by not picking. What do you get from that? I don't know where it comes from now and today where it states that when a husband messes up under sin the family the wife children home everything falls and is only on him. When the wife does it first or next it's still all and up only to the husband to fix everything by himself! That's nonsense. I know the honest right way by God is when the husband threats his wife not equal and does not lead and do his role. The everything falls apart. When he admits get back right with the Lord. He asks for forgiveness and forgives his self and ask his wife for forgiveness and she says yes, and times has gone by for years and starts over fresh and then the wife does not back him up then her part as a wife break up the home, because God says a wife supposed to be submissive to her husband and his rib and by his side encourage him love him. When a wife curses her husband out put him down falsely accuse him. She is doing the same thing to God, but these false teachers, preachers, leaders have misled the sheep and they will be judge first double as God, but word says. See it's about the husband and wife treating one another great not about the wife or about the husband No one! See the husband is the Leader on certain issues and the wife is the leader. On certain issues we, me you, us don't use these issues against one another in our way what we want when want it. It's always him. It's always her. No, it does not go like that we are not perfect. Then when it's a divorce. I was wrong woman and man some feel and say they did not do anything at all! See a husband must be honest with his self. Before he can be with his wife or anyone, so does her being honest with herself and everyone else not say she honest then come back and say but you but this happens from the past. That's not honesty that opening doors that you thought the husband/man open and all along it was you the thought still was in your mind them negative memories, see actions go both ways not your way. What you think forever they do because he hurt me. Now remember when God ask you. When you told him, you forgave him and took him back. Then soon as you got angry about something and he is standing right there in front of you and was not cheating you, just wanted to pick a fight, because you were angry and couldn't let goof something you said. You will then tell him I wish I wouldn't of never took you back bringing fights and argument back-to-back. Now when you get to heaven what will you tell God about these cycle that your mothers, family members pass down and men move to answer this same question this is no judge this is the truth. If you getting angry then what you think you towards God? See Jeffrey did not wait for Cleopatra (THE WOMAN) to change that would not fair to God with my spirit and God's spirit. I could have left with God taking me anytime, so I got myself right. I initiated the change in my life by standing up for me. Cleopatra (THE WOMAN) was like no you didn't you lying, you a dog, your no good. Then come back apologize to me. Women would say she was hurt, and she is a woman and look. What you took her though. She would come back and say she sorry. I know I was wrong, so does that it right? Right is right and wrong is wrong. Now every woman is different and when they do have a husband/man at times another woman will say girl, how you deal with him? Cleopatra uses to be with Jeffrey all the time. I would make her smile, laugh and blush. She didn't stay angry with me for a long time. See fairly its certain things men don't understand about women. Women don't understand certain things about men not all. Only about woman/women. There are strong women and there's weak women as well as strong men and weak men. You can have strong headed woman and it's what the man put on the table, and she expect as well equal footing in other words the agreements you made between each other. Now its areas that woman/women can be weak, and the man/men can pick up and help, educate, school, teach to help her in it's about a balance vice versa. See arguments, unforgiveness, anger be the culprit it then shuts down everything. See you have women that's enablers and don't have satisfaction there for the man then he must go get satisfaction there for the man then he must go satisfaction from someone else. As they say and do as a fact that another man got that woman, because he did not treat that woman right, so it become another man treasure! See a woman can blame a man for everything, so can a man blame a woman. The cycle repeats itself where both parties be used to it and notice a fact it becomes dangerous then that be the husband fault to, because he is the head of household and the man/leader. I don't agree with every woman does this I'm saying on facts today the systems, women, men, how things are going in today time and now! This is a dangerous way to live. Jeffrey told Cleopatra (THE WOMAN) she did not have to be angry, bitter, envious, hateful, because being that way all the time brings on bad health and sick problems. She then had diabetes and told me I made her catch it. I made her catch it. I brought the spirit on her.

You have women and men that's walking around here that say they are getting along good in their marriage, but fussing, fighting and arguing. See this is there way there say God is nowhere in that with He say she say that's drama, because God is not the author of confusion even debates! You can be angry, and sin not let the sun go down on your wrath, nor give place to the devil, so why bring old things back-up that is the devil right there waiting. Then they be right as a couple saying more negative things. Now you want to talk about God. You did not think about God when you did what you did. No one thinks about God in sin, wife /woman/women, husband/man/men then through up in each other face there's no make back-up in the mind, feelings, actions, but the sex, mouth, brings flesh, lust like a dungeon of dead lost souls being blind a woman fears a man anger, so does a man then the husband and wife be burning they house down it don't only be man's approach. He is a woman to. See when women be in their emotions, feelings, hurt, bitter, happy, talkative, in a mood you can't possibly explain they will hide certain things inside to not talk to deal with it alone by themselves. Everyone gets angry, envy, it its physically, mentally, emotionally, soul, spirit, mind, body, it can be a lot on a person's mind. See anger can be humble and not sinning or out in the open. A woman can bring confessions about themselves, but she will never tell you everything I don't have to look for the root of a woman's being. I just sat back observed and learned not every woman, because every woman is not the same, I got enough and some. I'm teaching women that this book that I write is understanding of holding on to anger and using it for the present that correct. I can understand her. Then she is holding on to it and using it from the past. Then most women feel that's not force get back, revenge, toxic or bitter. They feel like he/men/husband hurt me and that's it. God understands me. Most of the time there's no resolving the matter or removing anger and hate of thoughts. See a woman can let anger and bitterness go with pride as well as selfishness sit inside of her. Then she won't realize there's no future with us, what men did these women wrong or what women did wrong and that's it, because its, so many of men its them. Now is it a vice versa with men/ man getting treated this way and push away. I still say I love a woman in God's way. What she been through, so the same love for men as God

says of what they been through. See I'm teaching women unforgiveness turns your heart against your husband/man. You already been thinking lies about your husband and he's doing something negative and wrong off his past things that hurt you, so bad there's no wearing off or love. It's just words going back and forth with no action. A woman is physic, biology and science broken down in, so many ways that you, we, me or anyone can imagine. Her nature conversation the woman is inspiring and sensitive. The in-depth secret of a woman in other words a woman mental, physical, spiritual, emotional everything within themselves in and out by age group of life its everything from old school, generation "X", and the millennial perspective of each woman. Some women are insecure, and some are not. Some women like to share their secrets and don't depend on what it is. A woman is a woman no matter what. A woman can go through a hard ache and a headache. A woman also can yes a man to death. See a woman told me once the way I made love to her I have shown her the deep new height of fantasy that gives the creative flow. How I really showed compassion to that woman. I have learned that not only a woman/woman wants to be defended in public and corrected private, so do the man/men as well. I have set down with different women who like to judge, but you know where I'm coming from. It's so deep to where that you have some women to ask a man emotional thing or talk to him about sex, love, or did he cum or anything. It can be loving. See the spirit, mind and the moment soul. It's like whispering in that woman ears to get things flowing and what I mean by that in reality know how to love that woman be relaxed. If you ever think about it when you are lying beside that woman you can have a deep love where she wants to be touch felt and be in deep passionate love with her. See I have learned that when I met Cleopatra (THE WOMAN) before we already moved in together I was on her mind, soul, spirit mentality and physically making love and being in love including more also I was looking at her from the inside. What I was attracted to and what she wanted and learning more things outside of her more being together, separated a divorce. At times I learned as well when a woman keeps talking, so much being foolish you want to make love to her, but she does not want to at this time, because she is hurting from has been done to her, but then when she has time for needs and wants she want to get some love. It's different because she didn't cheat or lie etc. Not saying this is to get out of excuses. There nothing like a woman's storm there is multiple reasons, there's different woman ways to skin a cat. A woman will come in all kinds of ways that you can even imagine. You want to even see her coming. A woman is good playing the victim at times and based on the perception. See a woman can be dead wrong at times and be the bad ass, argue, fuss, debate then come back like nothing never happen and say baby I'm sorry lay on her husband/man/men/friend caress him. There are times he would look at her crazy like baby I told you this or don't say anything or certain things don't let it be her bringing up the past to get away for her apology meaning she just said it but did not mean it. You can get in a woman's mind that only if she allows you to. She can also let you think that you're in her head and certain things she will play right along with it. See for a marriage and/or a relationship to work it must be met 50/50. Every woman has a different story, but what about the man/men/husband? See what women don't realize is that when she makes a commitment to take her husband/man back to go through the past together, so they both can heal one another. After she forgives as God s way as a testimony, love, strength like when you first got married, I knew and seen women say I took him back. He did the same thing over again that can be true to a certain point woman/women/wife, husband/man/men, because every relationship and marriage is not the same and women you feel like you didn't do something to stir things back-up like false accusing, pressuring, putting your man/men/husband down not encouraging him or just saying he don't need none of this at all the weak man period? See I'm deep into a woman's inter being. A woman can put a man in a vicarious position even though a lot of women say men are no good. A man back can be pushed up against the wall. Then a woman come back with 60 percent of the issues as to what did the man do wrong or it's something we did to her to make her be in her feelings that are used, abused and left out. See a woman be in direct experienced in imagination through the feelings or actions of another person like Cleopatra she was a vicarious woman based on only from her state of mind, feelings, attitude, angry looks sarcastically sometimes, facts, opinions and unforgiving. I admit and took the whippings, slashes from God, her and family as well with their actions towards me after saying I forgive you in the church holding my hands kissing me, hugging me passionately then after she performed and suffered by one person as substitute for another or benefit advantage of another what value did she in her husband, because I gave everything to her I valued her she was my all and everything. When I mean everything, I mean everything men have flash backs to not only women, because if you have love for someone how can you love another woman like saying fairly and not using, feel where I'm coming from how people say they love someone let's make it work, let go and let's start over. Start fresh new and what happens. Well sometimes you must do this and that do not do what God says. I am looking for something in another woman Cleopatra (THE WOMAN) has or did or didn't have no God will send it time patient. See when a woman/women/wife read this book. Some are going to ask why you can't satisfy a woman, because a woman always wants more beyond the simple things. I have heard women talk and tell their story about their sex with different men. Then other women will say that not a respectable woman. As we know every woman is not the same about their sex life, which is true. Do you see how some women that their man has another woman, shows the bold and bad quickly? Keeping in mind she wants to get her sexual demand before the other woman does, because men do give themselves away quickly. The woman can tell by the smells, feelings, looks, touch, blow, wind, breeze, communication and time frames, at times a must entice her man to meet at home for some special treatment, Meaning showing the art of seduction and knowing what she is going to do and for him. In a woman world if she is sharing her man, who is going to get first. The power a woman has I'm telling you and please don't judge. There is no perfect woman, because most of you been there done that or some will say that's not a man or either one of theirs, because they wouldn't want to be sharing him right woman? Let me tell you something I rather be whip and beat by a man than by a woman. When a woman gets into a disagreement and it's their fault. Woman needs to learn how to clean it up or they screw their own selves with the man by pushing him out or away for good. A man can be completely innocent and truthful, but the woman doesn't see the truth in him, because of no trust or loyalty. Yes, ladies I know your feelings is serious he did something to make you like that or the way you are, but must you blame him for all the mistakes. You must not stay this way and blame him for all the mistakes. You must not stay way and blame him as the burning bed, your world, life, marriage will be a sin itself as you tell him. A good man like me with my flaws and all, I chose this topic of this book with women flaws as well and women have flaws sometimes it's out of security out of insecurity I like this one a balancing act and stability and beauty and most of all being loved. A woman doesn't like to go backwards can be strange or unique situation whereas a woman can look within or out of shell of a man looking backwards in relationship has you wondering if she wants to give that man another chance. I say to say we as a woman do not grow up to be a best friend with a man. A woman with low self-esteem can't tell when a man is cheating. The woman accepts whatever he says, but a strong woman that has experience will pick up on a man patterns of cheating. He leaves clues, mannerism and personality change little by little. You know false prophets tell married people (husband and wife) when they are doing each other wrong, sinning towards each other that still love one another, just because they are married. When the husband is getting pressured, cursed out, blamed from past issues, being ignored and the wife tells him she loves him that is not love. The mental abuse is not acceptable vice versa. The false prophet will reverse the issues and tell the wife the same thing these false bishops, prophets, evangelist, deacons, who they like to hear themselves talk. There are certain women that don't have an organism when they make love depending on that woman, you're with. Every woman is not the same. It's a different organism each time with a woman making love to her man. Some men see that as sex women do to some men. Women see it and know its love not only just that only. Some women get their freak on differently to they have a different erogenous zone on many levels. Some woman pleasures themselves and tell the man what they are seeking. You can never satisfy a woman. You have different facets of women rather it be the personality, their lifestyle, color of their skin that see a man different of wanting satisfaction from them. When I talk about you can never satisfy a woman it depends on if it is about the sex, lifestyle, personality, of who they are and what she needs and wants. Some women when they look for sex they pick and choose what man is going to fulfill their sexual desires, which could be a woman just wanting sex for satisfaction of the day or seeking more than that. She wants it and don't have to be the sex. It can change to something else, or she change up anytime! I said with a woman's lifestyle how can a man a accept it. A woman lifestyle rather they straight, lesbian or bi-sexual and provide with satisfaction. Now with this she's satisfied just like I said to a certain extent, she still not satisfied, because a woman craves more to meet the woman satisfaction. See the woman understand the woman, because they are too emotional creatures knowing and understanding what they both have been through. Every woman has her own mind set. It's like a straw that bends, but never breaks some women are self-taught some are not. A woman of action speaks louder than words, but her words are like sand between their toes they tend to slip out. A woman can be observing two men in a conversation and their body language to know that he is gay and making a pass at her man. Another way a woman know that a man is gay is when she is trying to get satisfaction when lying beside in the bed she touches between his anus and testicles how their accepting pleasure and the way their reacting! Some women test this on a man satisfaction and to see if she is going to get hers as well. A woman is checking things out. It is called experimenting. It is not only when she thinks if her husband is cheating. It is other things to she's a woman that is testing the waters. When a real man is looking into a woman eyes do you know he can fall in love with her. It's her attraction and don't be about no sex, now if he's child he thinks with his dick vice versa with a woman, when a woman is looking into a man eyes what attracts her to him. I 'm going to tell you, he is feeling in his heart. She is feeling that he is the one for her. Showing a sense of security, she knows that the man is interesting. Now when the woman is childish, she is being selfish, very petty attending to do things to annoy the man or people. Women look for more and more the woman want more of you. When she gets more of you, she going to want beyond the circumstances. Today she can want all of you and tomorrow she will want half of you. A woman mood is different from a man's mood. Men are emotional, but a woman is hotter inside and out! See a woman has different spiritual auras all colors on any given day then another changing sunny all kinds of reflections like I say she is sunshine on herself things in life. Her man/husband that lights up her life. Blue is trust, powerful, the ocean and sky. Their strengths from the ocean standing or walking slowly as the sun rise while the birds fly in the sky or when they are running in water. Purple is royalty and luxurious, she the queen in the man/husband world. Red is love and action. Green is her balance, natural or could be envy and jealousy. Orange is health, stand-up, happiness, thirst and wealth. Pink is for tenderness, caring, sympathetic, and charming, Black is God, rich, amazing strong, kind Queen bold, power, independent, class, mystery, elegance, and strange. Woman knows when to love deep with a new man that comes in their life. The woman must have a feeling of a dream come true. A woman is looking for manage things in a smooth manner with ease. A woman has mindset to think about what she needs to empower themselves when living alone. She fights to stay current today. Her inner beauty comes out more once she feels satisfied in the love making department and other things as well. Women wish to be empowered by success. Meaning that in all aspects of their life they want to be successful in a relationship in business in everything. The reason why they're not satisfied is they want more out of life than what their getting today that I can't even imagine. She's not fully fulfilled. It is like a moving ocean what does it do? Connects to the next ocean she's hail, storm, rain, thunder, lightning, the wave she wants more period. The woman/women are never satisfied because she is not pleasing herself. She does not want to be like anyone else this goes to fact when she felt like she fails in any little or big thing in life. She is not satisfied with her financial stability, and personal appearance. A woman is not satisfied sexual even when she is getting some sex and say it's good, because she says it, feel I, but her hormones rise to the occasion looking for more and more, because a woman/woman has an extremely high erogenous zone. Even when you're in her mind she is still not satisfied, because she does not want anyone to know too much depending on the situation. You can't find out her next plot, plan or moves. A woman mind is like a door with no knob. It shut and close whenever please. The knob is on her side. It's like a revolving door! A lot of women will say what about a man/man or what have you done to make her that way. It is something you did. This fact it's about woman/women. See when a woman is in her highest peak, she's alone and no satisfaction she uses something to pleasure her or to calm her down. She either can go through the motions or take a cold shower to cool her off, pray, relax and even more to come than you can't even imagine. Now a woman that's a virgin she tends to have a hard-warm feeling inside and it is taking her through an exotic feeling. When a woman is lying with a pillow between her legs alone it is a hot feeling inside of wanting a man to pleasure her. A woman needs the satisfaction of a man to be inside of her making love or sex a pleasure is fulfilled by the man the woman looks for more and more. When this is the man that is the one for her. It is everything she want in life. The woman is still not satisfied. A woman wants a man undivided attention love and happiness you can't satisfy a woman. Even giving her everything she wants, wants and wants more. You as you love this woman, and she is the one for you women vice versa know this for your man/men. A lot of women are not satisfied, because they don't know woman that act like both man and woman. Do you think their satisfied when acting like both people? They are self-empowered, and they don't think a man could fulfill their satisfaction. I don't need a man. I can do it all by myself. A lot of times it be the parent that teach them this. It is plenty of ways women can't be satisfied. It will be for a certain time then what happens? She will be with numerus people at one time and be in between, I got mines. What do you have? Now a woman can be pleased, but not satisfied. You some women can be indecisive. Meaning that they just don't know what it is they really want. Like I said every woman is not the same. What kind of woman are you? A woman those fights for what they want in life is strong woman. A bitter woman holding on to old news and won't let go is hurting themselves. Godly Woman a godly woman forgives from the heart and mentally, but do not forget, so basically that's a lesson learned. If she does bring it up it's only a testimony as opposed to an unforgiving woman. Who holds everything inside of her mind that connects to the body? A manipulating woman know she can reel a person into her plan to do what she wants and have it going the way she wants it. A curious woman wants to be in the know as hearing more of what's going on like people talking or something going on then you come back, and she wants to find out what happen what was said and she's anxious. A seductive woman one who seduce a man to come into her lair she also dresses sexy. Focus eye contact to him. It can be thousands of things knowing what a man like. Sometimes the woman doesn't even talk. No what type of room she's in lights low, music playing or off depending on the woman her style and mood she in! A seductive woman can give a man the best time of his life. God and the bible say going by God commandments. She is celibate until God brings her the man that is right for her. She is a praying woman patiently waiting for God to answer her prayer and keeping the faith. You have other Godly women that have gave their life to God living a Christian life. The woman has repented for their sins starting over again and asking for another chance from the Lord. Then you have the woman that provokes and falsely accuse her husband/man. She provokes him, so much that she pushes him to the edge. She pushes him out the door, which he had enough and too blind to see it, because she is focus on what's negative past things. She remembers in her mind of falsely accusing him, because she believes what she wants to believe, or someone told her or putting a word in her ear. She feels he is lying to her on matters that I important only to her. She looks at him as if he could guilty or not guilty until proven innocence, not only a woman, but a man as well as woman can't take, but so much. You have a shy and timid woman one who is very introverted. Meaning staying to herself a woman who don't like to be around a lot of people. Now you have the sassy woman their like fashionistas. Meaning bold like to stick out and being feisty also quick and clever. We have now been you the woman with the bad attitude. Its always negativity involve she always do not care about anything. I have seen a lot say it to with a nasty, rude attitude. I don't care very harsh the words she uses towards people she just doesn't want to be bothered. Personally, don't give a damn what people think about her even on helping her and can be a bitch! Then you have the woman that uses her husband/man with sex and uses it as a reward, because of something from the past or it be something else she can be keeping it inside and don't want to share the conversation. It keeps be several of things. See every woman is not the same, but its somethings every woman have in common. A class all by herself she is loving, warm, caring, alert, happy, independent, she yearns for that special someone. She is a human being she was created by the heavenly father, which was part from Adam and try sometimes to understand themselves. A woman always tries to figure out what they want to do and want they want to be you also have the woman/women that's straight. You have some women that say what they can't do. Then you have the woman/women know exactly what they want to do and work towards that goal to be successful not letting no one get in their way to stop them. In today's time you have women/woman. You got some women out here that are ruthless have no respect for the other women or themselves. With a ruthless woman they spare no expense in hurting someone for their own satisfaction and blame their actions on the people that their hurting that's how their getting their satisfaction. They don't spare any expense on getting revenge on a person. Some women have book sense, but no common sense and think they know it all. Never did nothing wrong at all telling someone off but can't get told off. Getting on them about what they did wrong, and they can't be wrong, so they are perfect. Yes no one is perfect. We know at times you can't tell or make them feel that their wrong. Now that's why you can't satisfy no woman. She is everything in the world you can't even imagine that's special and happy, but she is not satisfied. The woman that beat her husband/man mentally with words abusing him with her mouth being slick and rude. The classy woman is a woman that has it all going on and finesse she in a class all by herself she has a personality and a style to impress herself on anyone. When she steps into a room or anywhere, she is a center of attention all eyes are on her. The ambitious woman she the achiever. She is determined to achieve more and be successful. The silent woman tends to observe keeps things to herself to bring it out at the best time. Meaning words action and a bag of other things only what she wants to let out as a silent woman/woman their thinkers and observes more and more. She doesn't always want to think about things people underestimate on a silent woman/woman. The woman that's sexual she has wants and needs with desires being satisfied with their partner. Some women want it all the time. Some women want not as much. A sexual woman wants to be satisfied but the question is really. Can you really satisfy those woman/women? You have the high-end sexual woman who has a lot of class in finesse. She like it classy, tasteful and pleasing to mind, body and spirit. Now let me know if I'm lying. Now you have the low-end sexual woman who accepts anything that may come her way. Some women have their feelings and desires it can be high- or low-end sexual woman. Now the aggravated woman she is aggravated by any little thing or doing back to someone. She is miserable and irritated depending on that woman. She irritated on certain things in life. The spoiled woman she is used to getting any and everything she wants she can manipulate the mind. If she needs or wants, she knows how to talk her way int get it. The gold digger woman is a woman is always after a man/men and someone money. They know how to work their game on a man. Sometimes she doesn't have to do anything they will use what they must get what they want. The petty woman every little thing they nit-pick mostly about and worry about the smallest little thing can be jealous and an angry spirit. Especially things that's not important. The woman that has her blinders on, who's not aware of what's going on around her. She is always the last to know. There is so many different facts and meanings about a woman. Now the ghetto woman with no class. They don't care what they do. What they say and how they say things to anyone. Their personality is one sided and the attitude is not caring. The humorous woman that's full of laughter. They love to make people laugh. Keeping a smile on her face. The lazy woman is one who do want to do anything. They always tired. They do not feel like picking up and clean up behind themselves. The lazy woman only does what they want and necessary for themselves. The woman who self loves. She loves herself before she loves anyone else and stand her ground. A woman who doesn't love herself she can't be satisfied, because she will put anything else before herself. The dreamer a woman/woman that's dreams about her life. A woman that's has dreams that wants to come true. Looking for success in anything she does or have. Sometimes putting all things on hold to reach for the stars. Most men do not pick when a woman likes them and they are not seeing it, but other woman/women that observe. Can she tell when a woman/ women also has a crush for that multiple of things. When a man strikes up a conversation with a woman. A woman is trying to find out what his intentions are if its flirting, friendly conversation, business, games, because a woman look into a man eyes and misinterpret what a man is looking for from her. The woman can't be satisfied, because she can be looking, needing, asking, wanting more, because she wants everything. However, she gets and accept what she wants at that time. See it's like the time on the watch or clock it also changes the days, weeks, months, years and decades. She switches up, so quick you will notice it and wont it uncomfortable and comfortable the man is confused and acceptable that he's taking this from the woman. It's also her brain waves her nature and inner self. You have some women say I'm satisfied I don't know what kind of woman/women you been messing with or dealing with even that woman or whoever Woman says she can be satisfied that's a lie, because wants more and more like ocean changing up the beach. It's all the same It's the woman/women mind set every wave that comes towards you is not the same and when it comes to it can be soft or strong and jump up every time. When the wave comes, so it won't take you out them drown its wet already not only about sex or love other levels of the woman/women power. She will not have the last word see in the ocean she can take you out them to drown. She can take you out them to drown she can rescue you or she can be the saltwater woman/women where your eyes will be burning with tears, and it can be with good tears or and with the weather or regular water she's like soup if I could be cold or hot especially hot sauce bitter serious fire hot or regular. A woman is not to be estimated. Please don't underestimate her. The woman is like the sun she goes up and down get, so hot she about to bust and like the moon can be full of shit or bull shit. I like day and night she shines in the sun and in the dark, she glows with the stars sparkling. I know a woman is interchangeable as a man is to but not like a woman. The personality has a strong intention today and a beautiful personality as well but have a naughty personality tomorrow. Sometimes you can't know or feel how a woman is feeling inside. A woman technique is brilliant and crazy so many ways you can't even imagine. See a woman knows how to fake good and man does to, but not like a woman has common and educational sense whereas a man asks like he has nonsense, not every man. See when a man gets caught easily because his actions most of the time. A woman has thousands of techniques a woman/woman is mysterious, and a woman thinks before she speaks and smart. A woman/women is a crazy, smart minded, beautiful, weird individual that you can't never figure out or what she is ever thinking. Any point of time a woman/women as thinkers and are doers is why they are so independent and feel like two people. Especially being single having to enjoy our life woman/women as themselves open to fast. When getting to know a man and being with one. Now today a single woman dating is not easy especially when you do not have the class with style attracts a man to you. You can't satisfy a woman. Her personality, mindset, nature, ways that is how she will never be known of as a woman that she changes up at any time, because woman/women change their mind all the time. I'm coming in now with the black woman dating or married to a Caucasian man. She wants to test the waters, because she wants to see what it's like as well as the experience of being with Caucasian man. See you have many different black women that choose to be for various reasons. It could be love, money, a companion, sex or just a friend. It's an experience all by itself sometimes when a black woman meets a white man. Sometimes when black woman meets a Caucasian man, she is searching for the level of security such as a financial and protection. The woman looks for something new that will bring happiness to her life. Her color or his color don't mean a thing to each other or anyone at all. A black woman with a Caucasian man be together for love that shows he care understands and communicate, which is very important. When the black woman be with a Caucasian man for money it's like an agreement made to see each other. Usually, the woman is in the relationship for money is consider a mistress. When we talk about being a companion it's the black woman with an older Caucasian man who is looking for company. A black woman is looking for sex with a Caucasian man and wants the experience to know if he is satisfying her or not, she's still not satisfied. A black woman can meet a Caucasian man on friendship, business, communication etc. Now you have a black woman go to a Caucasian man for other reason's has been abused, used and mistreated. See then you have the black or white woman that has everything a great job, business, independent, car, money, own her house, personality, fashion style, travel, dreams, goals, future, plans, sex, love, classy, beauty and still can't get a man. Now I like this you cannot satisfy a woman opinion, fact and statement. See it's not a sentence it's a tutorial. It's like writing a report that never ever be finish typing on a laptop the fingers moving and don't stop. I learned something from women not all of them telling me things, just myself sitting back, staying quiet, observing, hearing, planning, and plotting. See a woman will be sitting or standing and a man can be present. When I am sitting down at times a woman would walk up. I would be quiet then another would walk over either sit down or stand next to me, because she knows me each woman would give eye contact to each other to feel the other one out. The emotions, ways, feelings, certain type of moods because a woman knows a woman. Then when the woman walks away. The woman that be sitting beside that woman will say she likes you and being so blind that woman sits quietly watching everything. I will say how, so I did nothing, or I did not say anything then some of those women I will see in public will say that. See in public will say that woman you were with she doesn't like me. See its deep a woman knows when other woman/women are nasty, a bitch, no good trying to get her husband/man everything about that woman. Why? Because she's a woman like a man knowing a man the opposite. Like I was saying the woman will hold a hold conversation with me not being the same way she was in from of the wife/woman/women, because she was smiling in her face and doing different behind her back, but the wife/woman/women already know, because the woman is a mind reader, the mind planner, the brain, pressure point ahead of it all. See you can't tell a woman/women/wife everything it's not a secret. Its certain things she should not know. She will say she can take everything, because it's the truth, but that's not true when she can take everything. Somethings are to be kept quiet even as a man doing the right thing I learned that hard, right, good, bad and smart ways, because you can be doing right and you can tell a woman the truth any woman now some women or most women will not agree, but when you tell the truth what comes after that what happen, did you, last time, yesterday, when, where, you telling the truth, I won't get mad, you serious, then another question, topic, charm, she will become and come physiological in way that's complicated where she is comfortable and not satisfied, but still happy, loving, caring and by your side. (To break these things down good or bad about the women) See a woman/women is a period, question mark, an exclamation mark, all internet, an equal sign, subtraction, addition, a comma, a money symbol, a picture, signature, parentheses, a sentence, a paragraph, a diary, a book, a shelter, a demand, a process, a calendar, year, decade, a business, a time, peace, numbers, words, a check mark, an email, a text, a woman is an answer, a phone call, tips, library, liability, health, jail, prison, files, a note, extras, short cuts, banks, malls, setting, support, a clock, games, advice, entertainment, music, sweets, a charger, flames, a director, interested, a woman is just like ingredients also seasons, balance, comfortable, efforts, a woman is a secret.

Chapter 22

1) A period- is her end point. The woman/women have stop completely she's done, tired, fed up no more it's over. It also can be walking away, and it also can be walking away. It isn't over with her purse in her hand or around her shoulder depending what mood she's in multiple ones or standing their looking you straight in your eyes not saying anything it's a stop right.

2) A question mark- Is asking yourself why things happen whether their good or bad asking the question or already know the answers finding out something without the man. Noticing anything or sometimes what she wants him to notice, just being clever or smart.

3) An exclamation point- Is seen as woman/women is full of excitement with the pep in her step. She screams and mean her say and be furious it's her aspiration.

4) Internet- She's finding out researching the good of life. Her mind it is our internet of the entire world. Good or bad in a relationship all things personal life within herself and others. Its different things she asks say do need and want she's a program.

5) Equal- Less than greater than 50/50, but she wants 60/40 or 70/30 it's not fair. It shows negative ways. This is not saying she can be perfect. She wants more and more be careful, I'm going to leave that up to the woman/women/wife/wives.

6) A subtraction- She is taking away the percentage of equal. She only wants to give a little in the relationship.

7) Addition- She's taking more than the equal part of life. Most of all the woman/women add more than she should. It's her actions, words, adding anything she just want to.

8) Comma- She love to separate things to be in place, prepared and making her next move without anyone noticing.

9) Money Symbol- She looks for the stability of saving money, however she can be at times an over spender.

10) A picture- Where she can be creative, and an antique treated very delicate. She's a work of art a painting all by herself theirs many things inside outside and around her. There are so many things you can see that she can't but within herself she sees the beauty in life as a woman. She is amazing she's all naturally of nature a beautiful woman.

11) Signature- The way she flows tell her story of signing her name.

12) Parentheses- She could be closing in on any giving thing at any giving time with her ending.

13) A sentence- Straight to the point, open, however she wants to put it at times she has a different say and way on things.

14) Paragraphs- She the beginning, middle and open ending.

15) A diary- She tells her story she vents her life talking about herself good or bad that day or anytime she is a daily person day by day the third person talk as she is.

16) A Book- The entire story of their life it can be a secret as well, look in my eyes where she's coming from.

17) A Shelter- Closed in she seeks the covering of a safe place, especially her heart. She is seeking that secure home blanket time of safety and secure.

18) A Demand- Something she wants going to get and find any way there is to get it coming in their way as a woman comes and blow the man/husband/men mind. I want it right now I want what I want. I want when I want it. It depends on what their approaching and who for what reason or reasons facts!!

19) A process- Step by step goes by managing herself into follow instructions to build it's like a plan she develops and execute.

20) A Calendar- She functions day to day, month to month, year to year even to a different life. She's have put things together that you can't even imagine.

21) Year- She three hundred and sixty-five days of different thoughts.

22) Decade- A work of work she is and what she has put together, meaning what she has done with ten years of her life as a woman with her goals and dreams.

23) Business- She knows and take care of her business, minding her own business what she has accomplished.

24) Time- You have women that's on time or not. Sometimes a woman dealing with time it runs out.

25) Peace- She wants to be at peace as woman she wants quietness it comes with happiness, humble and God.

26) Numbers- She's always calculating looking at the direction she moves makes and want to go, she is numbers.

27) Words- Where woman/women that words describe themselves.

28) Check Mark-She must be right on everything set-up as a list this what I'm coming to do and not going to this where I'm going and not going.

29) Multiplication- She/woman changes up multiple times of a person due their personalities all in one.

30) An Email- As a woman/woman she's a conversation piece full of information that's being sent out coming in deleted, inbox, archive, outbox, saved, flagged, all kinds of drafts, important, trash, junk, travel, work, sent, iCloud, VIP, also all mail there is.

31) A Text- She's a message and messenger.

32) Answer- She's the answer to your question, comment or gesture.

33) Phone Call- She's the number you dial and speak to she's interested in you with a conversation.

34) Tips- She's the woman that gives the information you want or need she's a tipper.

35) Library- She the woman that's a wealth of knowledge that gives history and all the information that's needed.

36) Liability- A woman that protects herself, husband and children staying focus also responsibilities, so things don't break the man/ husband does not do it all by himself she plays a part to as well.

37) Health- She thinks of the specific foods and drinks that's right for her body that's planned, fresh and checkups.

38) Jail- Unforgiveness that she can't forgive, or she has been betrayed. She is holding the man/husband in jail and his back is up against a wall and hers is to, because she can't let go of the pain. How the woman/women say nothing. She can be in jail as well of going back to the same shit until she's tired and if she's not then she's comfortable where she at same thing goes for the man.

39) Prison- A long term moment with no windows as saying I am the bars that hold you in my deep poetry understanding and putting myself knowing and feeling how woman/women/ wives is feeling. Bitter as well. Want to be the man as well as her aggressiveness. She's the woman/women is not Prison only by man well by and from the system as well. Going down destruction roads through life. Closed minded of always being right, No! You don't want to be a woman/ women/wife still in prison, so break the cycle, so find the road to freedom. I can't do that only yourself to free proving to yourself first before anyone else.

40) Files- A woman that's in order and in place where she can find everything and be on top.

41) A note- A woman emotional she can be the note that's written little with a big meaning.

42) Extra- She is something access that's additional.

43) Shortcuts- She takes the easy way out closely. She looks for the quickest direction or entrance to move.

674

Chapter 23

44) Banks- Sometimes she like to look at the dollar signs and a lot of times she likes to spend it.

45) Travel- She wish to travel and see the experience of other places such as countries, Islands, and States. She's considered of everything in the world. Knocking at the front door going on vacations. I say she is the jet or plane that flies high first class all by herself. I must hold her hand.

46) Malls- She a magnificent, wonderful, excited view of fun shopping.

47) What she set her mind to do. She will do with her all as well as she's in a specific setting that's comfortable to her. That is where her plan to be of progress a job well done.

48) Support- Having her back in whatever her goals and dreams are that theirs people their supporting her every step of the way giving the same back in return.

49) A Clock- She keeps ticking one day to the next twenty-four hours.

50) Games- It's how she plays. She can put it together and execute it and he won't know.

51) Advice- It is what woman give out information or accept.

52) Entertainment- She's the party all by herself with a class of red wine and roses with every special flower that will be added with the ones already there.

53) Music- Her loving of sensuous sounds and the lyrics that have them thinking about love in or out past or present whereas she reminisces about the past, present and future. Also gives that woman a fantasy to always think about when music is playing even when she is maintaining humbly.

54) Sweet- A taste of honey, sexual, nasty, thoughts are outrageous.

55) A Charger- A magnetic force in all kinds of ways. She's lightning power. She keeps going until she stops. She's the classy jumper cables and the battery all in one.

56) Flames- She can be high or low depending on what mood. She's in inside and out she can be cat woman or wonder woman.

57) A Director- She's a giver of direction of life. Also end it all telling things in her way.

58) Interesting- Her just being herself a woman!

59) Ingredients and Seasons- She's a recipe. She's sweet or tart on the meal. She's having the wine included. She's mixed all up-tasting right and good or not at times.

60) Balance- She can be even and uneven anytime.

61) Comfortable- Secure about herself. She is comfortable in her own skin meaning she not afraid of life.

62) Efforts- She achieve her goals and all her dreams putting in hard work. Striving to be the best she can be.

63) Secret- A woman is just like a cat when she poos, she cleans it up. If you know what I mean.

64) Offense & Defense- Offense is when she put her best foot forward and down, because she thinks of her game plan. Defense is when she is protecting herself from the unexpected. Women I know this could be for good or bad even towards yourself. It depends on the type of woman you are. She also can use this in a sneaky way as well and used towards others! She thinks she knows everything at times. She strategizes for good. She just knows how her game plan is going to work.

65) A Referee- She can be controversial or protective.

66) A Serious Pain – She's self-hurt. What mood she's in based seriously. What she has been hurt on.

67) A Serious Strength- It is how well she can accept what she is being told or not. Accepting the good with the bad in life.

68) A Pick-up & Down fall- Picking herself and husband/man it can be a job or anything moving forward. Also, a down fall as getting knock down then getting up dusting herself off and keep it moving. After going through, so much shit. Even a down falls herself for other wrongs and others that done treating her wrong done moved on truth their lives. She's still blaming them and not herself at all at times.

69) Eyeballs- She woman/women/wife/wives full dominate vision of seeing things that a man can't it don't even have to be just a man. She can see behind her eyes. She has eyes in the back of her head and around her body rotating watching.

70) Invisible- She's in the shadow not seen, but heard, its times where chooses not to be seen. See she can do things to a man that he can't see or imagine knowing. She knows she is wrong even when she doesn't know at times swear up and down. She is not wrong or getting back at something he did to her not letting the right hand know what the left hand is doing. I would feel the wrong and want because she has been through use. It is for good use or bad only no wrong is in her period and grab hold of her man and ask baby did I hurt you or I'm sorry and most time us man as men fall for it. She's the invisible challenge and challenger. The philosophy and philosopher the invisible visionary. She is the Scientist as well as good or bad chemical with great damn experiences. She's a zigzag. A woman is a million and one things a tip, tap, beginning and end, a bullet, a dashboard, a drive, a parkway, puzzle, because men try to figure them and give all. What they need say and want. She's an eagle and owl. You can try to figure she is a semicolon as well as a living will power. A woman is a diamond ring, which she is very value. A man is what he put himself to be.

Why does the black man go to the white woman? Some black men explore the other color because they feel that their own kind is not treating them way they wanted to be. They seek a white woman who gives him everything that he wants as to a white being submissive, caring and loving. Some black women feel and think that the reason why some black men go to white women because they will do anything they want and say!!

To be continued.............